Days of Love and Rage

Anand Gopal

SIMON & SCHUSTER

New York Amsterdam/Antwerp London
Toronto Sydney/Melbourne New Delhi

Simon & Schuster
1230 Avenue of the Americas
New York, NY 10020

For more than 100 years, Simon & Schuster has championed authors and the stories they create. By respecting the copyright of an author's intellectual property, you enable Simon & Schuster and the author to continue publishing exceptional books for years to come. We thank you for supporting the author's copyright by purchasing an authorized edition of this book.

No amount of this book may be reproduced or stored in any format, nor may it be uploaded to any website, database, language-learning model, or other repository, retrieval, or artificial intelligence system without express permission. All rights reserved. Inquiries may be directed to Simon & Schuster, 1230 Avenue of the Americas, New York, NY 10020 or permissions@simonandschuster.com.

Copyright © 2026 by Anand Gopal

Photo and illustration credits: page 22, Hussein Omar Samawi; page 41, Wasim al-Hamdo; page 48, Victor Blue; page 72, Abdul Qader Oseb; page 134, Anand Gopal; page 173, Wasim al-Hamdo; page 184, Yaqub Bayram; page 213, Victor Blue; page 267, Muhammad Abed; page 283, Wasim al-Hamdo; page 358, Mina Saba; page 394, Victor Blue; page 408, Muhammad Kullal.

All rights reserved, including the right to reproduce this book or portions thereof in any form whatsoever. For information, address Simon & Schuster Subsidiary Rights Department, 1230 Avenue of the Americas, New York, NY 10020.

First Simon & Schuster hardcover edition March 2026

SIMON & SCHUSTER and colophon are registered trademarks of Simon & Schuster, LLC

Simon & Schuster strongly believes in freedom of expression and stands against censorship in all its forms. For more information, visit BooksBelong.com.

For information about special discounts for bulk purchases, please contact Simon & Schuster Special Sales at 1-866-506-1949 or business@simonandschuster.com.

The Simon & Schuster Speakers Bureau can bring authors to your live event. For more information or to book an event, contact the Simon & Schuster Speakers Bureau at 1-866-248-3049 or visit our website at www.simonspeakers.com.

Interior design by Lewelin Polanco

Manufactured in the United States of America

1 3 5 7 9 10 8 6 4 2

Library of Congress Control Number has been applied for.

ISBN 978-1-6680-6217-3
ISBN 978-1-6680-6219-7 (ebook)

Let's stay in touch! Scan here to get book recommendations, exclusive offers, and more delivered to your inbox.

CONTENTS

Preface vii

BOOK ONE: LIVES—1

BOOK TWO: DREAMERS—73

BOOK THREE: THE REPUBLIC—167

BOOK FOUR: THE STATE—383

BOOK FIVE: BETWEEN THINGS ENDED AND THINGS BEGUN—455

On Methodology 497
Principal Sources 499
Datasets 501

Works Cited 511
Notes 525
Acknowledgments 565
Index 567

PREFACE

For many years, I have been reporting on wars around the world, and the story was always similar: despair, suffering, and tragedy. But one day, during these travels, I came across the story of a small group of men and women who, amid general devastation, managed to create something new. They lived in a northern Syrian city called Manbij, an out-of-the-way place I knew nothing about. Intrigued, I tracked them down. Over countless hours together, we pored over details and triangulated memories. I amassed thousands of newspapers and magazines, personal diaries, letters, and video clips depicting their efforts. But I soon realized that fully capturing their revolutionary experiment was beyond the reach of one person alone, so I recruited research assistants, who fanned out across countries and continents to collect memories from Manbij. What I found, eight years and two thousand interviews later, forced me to rethink my most cherished beliefs about freedom and democracy. These men and women briefly turned the world upside down, and this is their story.

BOOK ONE

Lives
1963–2010

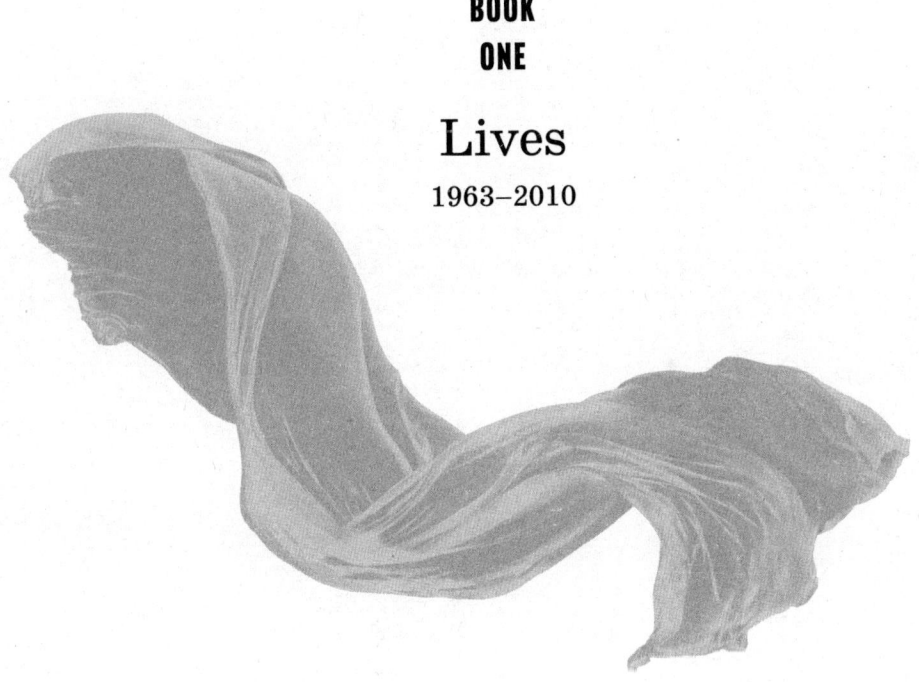

| ONE |

Little Hyena

I

Every afternoon, for as long as he could remember, Ibrahim Kasem would descend from his village of Little Hyena, wade into the Euphrates, wedge a line between boulders, and wait for a catch. Then he'd climb back up with muddied feet to the stone houses, where his mother would be grilling corn. Behind his house was a stubbled field where he and his friends would run races, and a bluff where he'd stretch out to sleep under the stars. Like most everyone he knew, he couldn't see any good reason to ever leave.

So when, in the winter of his seventeenth year, he was informed that the world as he knew it was about to end, he shrugged. He paid no mind when besuited men appeared at his door, displaying tables and charts, predicting that everything around him would soon vanish. When wandering mystics showed up in the village foretelling terrible squalls and violent gusts, he laughed. He had an openness to experience, even an insouciance, characteristic of the young. But he was no fool.

It was only later, when the end finally came, that Ibrahim realized how wrong he was.

Some days, Ibrahim stood on the highest hilltop in Little Hyena. It was an undulating country of scrub and bush, of rustling dry leaves. Below, he would have seen the river, as smooth as stone. On the far bank were low hills, blanketed by thickets of Aleppo pine, and on the hilltops were many mud hamlets. Just up the river, on an escarpment, stood the Star Castle, a fortress of ashlar masonry rumored to be of Roman provenance. As a child, Ibrahim had crept through its darkened passageways, under its vaulted ceilings. He and his friends had found strange writing on the walls. They had discovered doors to old passageways, which led underground, toward the river, but no one had the courage to enter.

All around the constellation of forty or so villages that hugged the banks of the Euphrates were caves, tunnels, even buried monasteries. Here and there one could see tells, mounds formed from thousands of years of compressed mud bricks, ceramics, bronze plows, smelted iron keys: the refuse of civilizations past. During sowing season, folks in Little Hyena would unearth indecipherable coins and shards of painted pottery.

The grave, distant memory of calamity was one of the threads linking these river cultures, scattered though they were across time. A trace of that memory is recorded some thousand years before the Old Testament, in the Babylonian epic of Atrahasis: In the beginning, it was the gods who farmed the banks of the Euphrates, but the "load was too great, the work too hard, the trouble too much." The younger gods rebelled, so the older ones invented a new creature to bear the labor: humans. The gods enjoyed their newfound leisure, but in time, the humans, multiplying fruitfully, grew too clamorous. The gods, annoyed, sent down a litany of plagues, but humans proved a stubborn lot. Finally, they decided to unleash a great flood. But Enki, the god of wisdom, took pity on a particularly righteous human named Atrahasis and advised him to construct an ark and load it with two of every animal. A violent storm engulfed the land, and the Euphrates swelled. Humans were lost. The gods, now repentant, wept and cursed their rashness. Fortunately, Atrahasis survived, and the gods struck a covenant: From now on, there would be women who could not conceive, and demons to snatch infants from the womb, so that the riverbanks would be overpopulated no more.

By the time Ibrahim encountered this tale in the Quran, Atrahasis had become Noah. Despite the covenant, though, the river flooded often after the great deluge of Noah. Each time, the survivors reassembled on the river's shores, as the region fell under the sway of the Romans, then the Byzantines, and, finally, the Arabs, who brought Islam. Under Arab rule, the Euphrates flourished. The Abbasid Caliphate presided over a golden age of scientific and literary splendor, even as Europe was mired in the Dark Ages. Abbasid thinkers invented the field of algebra, helped pioneer the scientific method, and introduced Aristotle to Christian philosophy. The great Jewish philosopher Maimonides wrote most of his treatises in Arabic. Like all empires, though, the grandeur of the Arabs eventually faded. The rivers fell under Ottoman dominion, and many hard, dry centuries followed. The desert swept over the old floodplain, and all traces of former life, save the tells, vanished. Bedouin tribes roamed these wastes, robbing travelers and warring with each other.

The tax-hungry Ottomans induced some of the tribes to settle on the shores of the river, where one could still coax the silted earth to bear fruit. Ibrahim's great-grandfather was one of these tribesmen. Villages mushroomed from this barren littoral: Big Sludge, Girls Hill, Red Hill, Red Cliff, Little Hyena.

Ibrahim was born in 1980 at home, with news of his birth traveling fast. Most of Little Hyena's two hundred households would have sent along sugar or sweets. As a child, Ibrahim played soccer with a ball of socks. Later, he graduated to *jakat ali*, in which twigs are hurled from a distance at a stick planted in the earth, and the first person to topple it wins.

The schoolhouse Ibrahim went to stood on a hill overlooking the barley fields of Mr. Weiss, whose return from the weekly wholesale market in Manbij, the nearest big city, a dozen miles away, was always an event. It consisted of three rooms of stone and mud that the villagers built with their own hands. Boys and girls of all six grades sat in a single classroom. While the sixth grade received their lesson, the first graders sat quietly in the back. Mr. Faraj, who lectured from the front, adhered to the belief that the rod was essential to a child's education. Ibrahim and the other boys lived in terror and awe of Mr. Faraj. One day, Mr. Faraj left Little Hyena on a trip and never returned. A new instructor, Mr. Jalal, took his place. Ibrahim was unsure if Mr. Jalal could read, but in any event, he was kinder to the students. Like other teachers, he took no salary, so the children took turns bringing him boiled chicken and freshly baked bread from home. On harvest days, he dismissed class and brought the boys and girls to pick cotton on his lands.

There were no high schools in Little Hyena, so when Ibrahim turned thirteen, he went to Manbij. He found it a dazzling, bewildering city of power lines and chimneys, billboards and marble statuary. He also found he had not been taught to properly read or write, so he dropped out and returned home to work the fields. He knew he belonged here, by the shores, where he could spend afternoons in the mini reservoir that Mr. Hasan, one of the few people in Little Hyena to own a water pump, had dug into the sand. On a warm day you could wade in the crisp water, and when you got cold, you could cover yourself in mud and then dip in again, until Mr. Hasan chased you out.

In the summers, Ibrahim's entire family, some thirty siblings and cousins and aunts and uncles, would gather at his grandfather's house. Under the light of an oil lantern, they discussed the planting schedule. The women knit patterned doormats and sanded down sheepskin into rugs. They doted on Adam, Ibrahim's youngest brother, who was top of his first-grade class. It was believed he might be the first in the family to graduate high school. Some of Ibrahim's cousins dreamed of moving to Manbij, earning hard cash on the pushcarts, but Ibrahim, who was now sixteen, knew the fields were his destiny. According to his father, a tiny section of the *hawijeh*, the sweet, fertile land along the shore, would one day be his. Ibrahim resolved to work that land, turning it into the pride of his parents, the talk of the village.

But then, in the spring of 1997, two months after he turned seventeen, Ibrahim's troubles began.

It was a fine May morning. He rose at dawn and tended the orchards and cleaned the irrigation gulch. In the afternoon, he headed down an old dirt path called the Crossing, which slopes gently onto a bank of shingle on the Euphrates. From there, he could see the reed canoes and homemade coracles navigating the shoals. But Ibrahim was fixated on a furrowed field neighboring his own, where a solitary figure was stooped over, working a scythe. He'd never paid much attention to the children who played there until recently, when one of them began to exchange flowered dresses for red jellabiyas. A few locks of brown hair would slip from her headscarf. Her name was Samira.

She sat on the dirt. Ibrahim had never seen her alone before. He walked over and stood before her for a few stupid moments, then retreated. Three days later, she was alone again. This time, he introduced himself. They spoke shyly of the barley harvest, which was one month away.

That night Ibrahim lay awake, his five brothers and sisters asleep beside him. In Little Hyena, approaching a girl was a delicate matter. The rules of courtship dictated subtlety, even an air of embarrassment.

A week passed. Every day, Ibrahim worked his field, then waited under a willow tree and surveilled the scene. The farm next door was hopelessly crowded. Samira was always surrounded by her mother and her brothers and sisters.

One morning he was busy in the gulch when he saw her sitting alone again, against an expansive sky. He went over and struck up a conversation. She was self-possessed, polite. Suddenly, he admitted that he could not stop thinking about her. Samira reacted with shock, then anger, as if betrayed by an old friend. In a sharp tone, she told him he was being inappropriate and asked him to leave.

Ibrahim returned home, determined to bury his thoughts.

A house was going up on an outcropping along Little Hyena's western edge, a task that belonged to the entire community. Under the *fazaa* system, neighbors would help each other clear weeds, dig wells, and erect dwellings, knowing that when they were in need, the favor would be returned. Money rarely changed hands.

Ibrahim decided it would do him well to volunteer. When he showed up, late one afternoon, the plot was already humming with neighbors. Villagers usually mixed sand, fodder, and river water, leaving the sludge to dry in the sun. They would lay these bricks on a bed of stone and fashion load-bearing beams out of cottonwood, which was Little Hyena's most precious resource. A plastic mat served as the roof.

The essential quarters in every home were the living room, where the family slept, and what was called in village dialect *al-nadad*, the pantry. Here, the women kept mattresses in duvet covers. They stored flour, and wheat to grind when the flour finished. They would keep yellowing jars of lentils; jams of pomegranate and fig; sun-dried aubergines; and salted ghee, wrapped in lambskin to last the winter. Behind the pantry stood the oven room, where women baked *saj* bread by slapping dough onto an earthenware stove using cottonwood sticks. Most oven rooms included *al-jeder*, a massive pot to boil water for bathing.

It took a week to raise the house. A few days later, Ibrahim was tending his ewes when he saw Samira approach his field. She spoke with his mother, asking for pepper. Toward the end of the week, he saw her again, playing with her younger brother by the sunk fence separating their lands. A thought began to churn within him: *She was interested. She was shy.* He boldly approached the field one afternoon while she was digging roots and said, "We have to meet." But she refused, and asked him to leave the property.

Ibrahim now understood. The next day, as he was weeding the gulch, she appeared nearby, in plain sight. He did not approach. Instead he looked down, digging in the gulch as if all Little Hyena depended on it.

Later, he was at the village grocery. His mother sometimes gave him an egg or two to trade for gumballs, or a bottle of Crush orange soda. He'd brought his government ration card, which he would use for cooking oil, ghee, and sugar. Samira approached with friends. Summoning forces deep within him, he ignored her.

Another week went by.

Then one afternoon, as he was digging near the gulch, she walked briskly along the perimeter of her land, and as she passed him said, "I'll meet you tomorrow, at the Crossing."

The Crossing had always belonged to teenagers. Wearing red-and-black jellabiyas, girls would fill a pair of steel drums with gallons of river water. The drums would be tied to iron chains, wrapped in a thick rope, and hoisted over the back of a donkey. Boys, in peach-colored jellabiyas, hair combed back, would hover nearby. The Crossing was notorious for its futilities, but the occasional success—the lingering eye contact, the exchange of a few words, the request for help lifting a drum—was enough to nourish hope.

Like most boys in Little Hyena, Ibrahim had tried his luck a few times, but was always met with stony silence. But that was before, in his breezy youth. On this spring afternoon, Ibrahim brought his friend Mousab, whose father owned the water pump. They sat on donkeys off the edge of the Crossing, in a copse of willow and alder. Under the brilliant noonday sun, a pair of riders appeared, their donkeys ambling down the slope. It was Samira and a friend. Samira pulled up, waiting for Ibrahim to speak. He stared at her in perfect silence. He lost his words. He was seized by a panic, he felt sick. Samira began to laugh, a shy and kind laugh. Ibrahim realized, in that moment, that she was not accustomed to thinking of herself as beautiful. He began to laugh too. She smiled and trotted off.

The next day, he found her and begged to meet again. He insisted that despite his seventeen years, he knew the weight of responsibility. That he was the oldest among his siblings, that he would take over the chores of Adam, his youngest brother, who had a fondness for books, so that the boy could study. And then he confessed the truth. This life, these fields, were not worth a single lira without her.

This time she did not react with anger, but with a soft resolve: She could not see him again. She asked him to forget her. She was not the kind of girl to meet boys at the Crossing. She belonged at home, where she was needed.

Ibrahim retreated.

—+-+—

At night, Ibrahim lay awake, listening to the cicadas. It was the season when families slept outdoors.

By afternoon, he was sluggish. Repairs on the barn went undone. He neglected to dig the seed line in the sesame field. He showed little interest in his mother's piping hot flatbread and salted butter. He steered clear of the eastern perimeter, which ran adjacent to Samira's property. The behavior began to attract the attention of his parents, so he avoided them by heading to the river. He cast a line, spending hours perched on the boulders near the *hawijeh*. He saw salmon, mullet, catfish. Once, he watched a group of fishermen from the far bank paddle over, light a stick of dynamite, and toss it into the water. The river grew silvery with dead carp. As they lowered the trawl, he decided there was no sport in this. He left his rod wedged between boulders and returned home.

Later that summer, when everyone was gearing up for the cotton harvest, news arrived that Ibrahim's cousin Sara was betrothed. Her mother delivered wool to Marwan, the tailor, whose own daughter had eloped with a boy from another village, a calamity from which he'd never recovered. Marwan stitched the bridal gown in cream lace. The women of the village gathered at Sara's mother's home, where they helped her sew duvet covers and embroider cushions for the wedding day.

The night before the wedding, the whole village assembled in the orchard behind Ibrahim's house. Illuminated by the pale glow of oil lanterns, they sang. A couple of Ibrahim's friends were sitting with girls they'd met at the Crossing.

Ibrahim went indoors.

The official festivities commenced the next morning. Ibrahim was miserable. The orchard was crowded with villagers from both sides of the river. A troupe of drummers took their places by the big well. A man was on the flute, and women began to ululate. The groom's father fired his pistol into the air. Men and women danced the *dabke*, and teenage boys swayed around the drummer, showering him with five- and ten-lira notes, shouting, "Shabash! Shabash!"

Ibrahim sized up the situation. After dinner, he disappeared behind the orchard with one of the drummers. When the music started up again, he found his cousin and whispered into her ear. She vanished and appeared sometime later, leading by the hand a girl in a stunning emerald green gown. Ibrahim froze. Months had passed since he'd laid eyes on Samira.

The drum resounded, and Ibrahim swung his feet in and out, tossing 100-lira notes at the drummer. These grand sums would expose the other boys as pathetic, childish. He felt the girls' eyes, every last one, on him. They lapped up his showboating, knowing nothing of his plots, of how he'd struck a deal with the drummer, who'd later return most of the notes after taking a cut for himself.

Ibrahim took hold of Samira's hands, and she did not pull back. A shadow of kohl ringed her eyes. They danced, the wedding spun around them. The darting children, the plump grandmothers, the towering alders, the rolling hills, the entire world spun around them. It was early evening, it was late night. It was the center of the universe.

In the days following, Ibrahim lingered on the edge of the cotton field, watching for a sign of Samira. She was nowhere to be seen. The cotton harvest was two weeks away. It was September, but the heat had not broken. Then one morning he spotted her passing behind the sheep stockade. He approached her in full view of her younger brother. "I need to see you tonight. It's important." Her eyes widened. She grabbed her brother by the hand and walked away.

Later that evening, a cousin of Samira's stopped by the house. On her way out, she took Ibrahim aside and whispered: She will see you tomorrow night, after dinner. Wait by the *taama*.

Ibrahim wasn't sure when Samira's family took their dinner, but to be safe, he skipped his entirely and headed for the *taama*, which stood at the end of a winding dirt path, half hidden among the trees. The *taama* was dialect for a type of communal pen, built of cottonwood, where villagers kept livestock. Depositing your sheep for the night would be as good as keeping them at home, because in Little Hyena theft was unknown.

When Ibrahim arrived, he changed into a cream-white jellabiya, which he'd hidden so his parents wouldn't notice. Long minutes passed.

The sky darkened. The *taama* was a ten-minute walk from the heart of the village. He stood studying the path winding up the hill, to Mr. Hasan's house, past which stood Samira's. The last lights on the hilltop were extinguished. He waited, standing alone as village life drained away.

The next morning, he found Samira's cousin near the grocer. "I didn't sleep last night," he said. "I'm being tortured." She told him what he already knew, that it was no simple matter for a girl to sneak out of the house. "But I have something important to tell her," he insisted. "It's a matter of life and death."

That evening, as the village settled in for dinner, he went for a walk. He wandered down the hill, lost in thought. He passed Mr. Hasan's house and came upon the outlying bosk and then the small clearing around the *taama*. At that moment he noticed a thin figure among the trees, and his heart stopped. Samira was looking up at him. Ibrahim was not prepared. He was wearing a mud-soiled jellabiya, like a fool.

"You have something to tell me?" she asked. She looked at him without fear. He knew in his seventeen-year-old bones this was his last chance.

"I want to kiss you."
She moved her head away, looked to the earth.
He kissed her anyway. She kissed him back.

II

Sometime in the 1920s, when Ibrahim's grandfather was a boy, a tall man from Manbij named Muhandas showed up in Little Hyena bearing a deed that claimed he was the rightful owner of the village, and many others besides. This was news to the people of Little Hyena, who had been working this land as far back as they could remember. Land was not like a shovel or a shirt, something to be owned; it was like air and water, belonging to the whole village. Yet Mr. Muhandas saw things differently. The French had acquired the country from the Ottomans and, in keeping with their faith in private enterprise, seized the rights to communal lands and gifted them to traders, men of learning and culture, who resided in the big cities. When the villagers protested, Mr. Muhandas threatened to deliver them to the colonial authorities.

And so overnight everyone in Little Hyena was working for the Muhandas family. They woke at dawn, toiling on land that was no longer theirs, laboring to deliver a fixed return every season to their lords. Leaf rust or a weak harvest or a freeze would plunge an unfortunate peasant into debt. Bankrupt farmers sold themselves into bondage. Overseers meted out beatings to slaves who failed to fulfill their quota. Up and down the river, the shores were now occupied by feudal plantations. Stories were passed down: the farmer who, having lost his crop to drought, tried to hang himself; the slave who'd lost his mind, saying *yes, sir* to children and sheep.

Syria won independence in the 1940s, and not long after held the first genuinely democratic elections in the Arab world. The feudal lords championed democracy in the big cities, so long as they were free to run their plantations out in the country. When peasants in Little Hyena requested a school for their children, the lords reacted angrily, threatening to lock up the petitioners. Schools were dangerous, the lords believed, because they allowed intellectuals to plant subversive ideas into the minds of these rustic folk. The intellectuals, on the other hand, were exercised by the undeniable fact that, democracy or not, Syria was a hopelessly backward country—and it was backward because people had forgotten their own past. It was the Arabs, after all, who'd presided over the region's golden age hundreds of years earlier. These intellectuals called for a renaissance—*baath*, in Arabic—to recover that lost splendor, and to catapult the Middle East into the twentieth century.

One day in the 1960s, a pair of men in blazers and ties appeared in Little Hyena and climbed the roof of the house of Mr. Zaki, known by everyone as the mayor for his courage in defending the peasants against the lord. They read aloud a proclamation, which included the line "Land for he who works it," and proceeded to deliver the astonishing news that the feudal system was hereby abolished. The state, which a group calling itself the Baath Party now controlled, was breaking up the great estates. Every peasant in Little Hyena would receive a share. The government nationalized the choice *hawijeh* plots right on the river. Ibrahim's family was given a ninety-nine-year lease of this fecund land at a nominal fee. It was as if someone had shown up at their doorstep with a humongous bag of cash. At first, Ibrahim's grandfather could not bring himself to believe it.

The government now provided seeds and fertilizer at rock-bottom rates. They extended low-interest loans for tractors and water pumps. They would tell you what to grow, but they would commit to buying your product—even in the event of a failed harvest. They distributed ration cards, which Ibrahim used at the grocer. The people in Manbij had it even better. The government established public bakeries there that offered bread at affordable prices. If you made it to university and got a degree in education, you were guaranteed a job in a public school. Get sick, and you were treated for free at the public hospital.

This strange new epoch was far from perfect. To get the best rate on a tractor loan, you'd need to offer a bribe. To jump your spot while waiting for a teaching assignment, you'd better have a wad of liras ready. Petrol pump owners would siphon subsidized gasoline and smuggle it across the border, selling it on the black market. Forget about running your own business or buying a second home. But if you were a villager in Little Hyena, one harsh winter away from slavery or suicide, the men standing atop Mayor Zaki's house—remarkable gods they must have seemed—were offering something people had forgotten was possible: a chance to build a future.

Some evenings, Ibrahim's father would paddle down the river, past the spits of land bearing a lone house or two, past the silent tells overlooking the water, until he came to a point where the banks pressed close—so close that, in the harshest winters, you could walk right across—and watched mechanical cranes carry blocks of cement. Workers completed the Euphrates Dam in 1973. It towered over the river hamlets, a Baathist covenant with the future. Before long, men in overalls appeared in Little Hyena, boring holes along the village edge. A truck arrived and filled the depressions with cement, erecting wooden pylons that brought the currents of the twentieth century to the homes and alleys of their hundred-year-old village.

—*—*—

Ibrahim's ritual began every day at dawn. He'd finish tying cotton bales and load them onto a pickup belonging to the Peasants Collective. (A state-run body, the collective promised cash—no matter the haul, so long as the land was worked—and the villagers of Little Hyena found themselves in the felicitous position of earning a guaranteed income.) He'd then pen the sheep, sweep the manger clean, unclog the gulch. Finally, he'd mount a donkey and clop over to the Crossing. He'd wait in the shadow of the trees until Samira appeared, and the two would ride their donkeys side by side. They'd keep a slight distance, in case chanced upon by villagers, and travel in silence. Down at the bank, they'd speak softly while washing their faces, filling their tanks. It was all over in an hour.

In the early evenings, they were back in the fields. A language developed—a tilt of the eyes, a wave of the hand—through which the lovers arranged nighttime rendezvous. Thursday was the night of promise: The villagers would gather in homes with television sets to watch *Al-Shanfara*, a soap about an outlaw poet. Samira would slip out to walk the darkened wood off the main road. She'd loop around the Luqman house, where people bought oil for their lanterns, and the Hasan house, whose eldest sons were working in Jordan. Ibrahim set off in the opposite direction, taking the long dirt path that followed the shoreline. He'd cut through fields to an old barn. It stood near a two-room concrete block that was built by the government, then abandoned, for reasons no one in Little Hyena could figure out. In the evenings, the building was taken over by village boys who played cards and smoked cigarettes. But the barn was always empty. There, Ibrahim and Samira lay next to each other on the matted hay, whispering in the darkness. Samira's family did not own an orchard, nor did they have many animals. But the land she knew; the land she loved. The stories she told him, the stories of her grandfather, of her childhood—all of it awakened a sense of possibility. Ibrahim understood now what it was to make a life for yourself, to have authority over your affairs. He spoke with a new confidence. For the first time, he imagined holding another human being in his care. She possessed a sense of what life should be; she was intelligent, a seer. He would kiss her brown neck. They would hold their breath, listen to the voices passing outside, smell the waft of cigarettes. She would gather herself, and the night would ebb before he knew it.

III

One day that winter, Abu Talib, who lived a few doors down, came for dinner and related a strange story. He'd been at home when a military jeep appeared. A pair of men who said they were engineers began taking measurements and speaking loudly into a walkie-talkie. They claimed they were surveying the land because a new dam was coming up, to bring electricity to more villages. It would be called the October Dam, in commemoration of Syria's 1973 war with Israel. As tradition called for, Abu Talib slaughtered two roosters, and his wife prepared a meal for their guests. He gave them two buckets of homemade yogurt for the road. Before they left, they pointed to the massif on the far bank. "Once the dam is built," one said, "everything from here to there will be submerged."

Nearly everyone who heard Abu Talib's tale was convinced that the old man had lost his mind. Little Hyena was perched on a hillside. It was a good ten-minute walk down a steep dirt path to reach the river. Most families rented a water pump to push water, against gravity, from the Euphrates to irrigate their crops. During heavy rains, the water sometimes overwhelmed the low-lying fields, but quickly receded. Ibrahim's grandfather told him about a terrible flood decades earlier, when the fields of the Abdullah family had been ruined. But the waters could not reach the village itself, of that everyone was certain.

Spring came early to Little Hyena. The humidity rose from the fields, the treetops grew dense and knotted. This year Ibrahim's family was expanding their orchard—fifteen plum saplings, six nut, four fig. Ibrahim was restless; he had not spent time with Samira all week: His friend Muaz's grandfather had passed, and, following tradition, the whole village switched off the television for seven days. Muaz spent most of his free time with his doves. Some days, Ibrahim sat with him as he dispatched the doves to Girls Hill or Little Sludge and watched triumphantly as they circled back to his farm an hour later.

One day, Mayor Rahman called a meeting in his courtyard. Night had fallen, and most of the village was present, sitting under old fluorescent lamps. Mayor Rahman spoke only for a few minutes. Authorities had informed him that upon erection of the October Dam, the river would indeed swallow the village whole. The crowd erupted with questions. A few men, led by Ibrahim's uncle, insisted that such a deluge was impossible against the hard facts of the terrain. Then someone floated a more sinister possibility: This was a ploy to scare folks off the land, perhaps so corrupt officials could scoop up the precious *hawijeh* soil for themselves.

Rumor took hold of Little Hyena. As Ibrahim and Samira lay together in the barn, they traded hearsay, wondering at the faraway forces conspiring for their homeland. Samira's home sat lower down the hillside than Ibrahim's, yet she spoke of the events with composure, even curiosity. As always, she was the wiser of the two. She'd never left the village in her short life, but she was skilled at standing back from the moment, applying reason where others succumbed to fervor.

Soon, a pair of villagers found work driving trucks bearing gravel and I-beams to the dam site, fourteen kilometers downstream. It was becoming more common for sons of the village to work elsewhere, since the pay was better. One of them told Ibrahim about the concrete structure growing by the day, the turbines, the rebar. A theory developed that it was the dam engineers themselves who were eyeing the lucrative riverside soil. Ibrahim promised Samira that he would never let anyone lay a finger on her family's land, or his own.

But around that time, just as Ibrahim's fields were bursting with golden stalks of wheat, two men from the Agricultural Projects Committee showed up, all the way from Aleppo. They established camp at Hajji Ahmed's house, the highest point in the village, and recorded the dimensions of the homes and fields of every resident, as if they were sizing up the properties for themselves. Folks urged Hajji Ahmed to kick them out, but the old man was afraid. Then one day they came to Ibrahim's door. They asked to see the family's ID booklet. One of the men flipped through the pages, which listed every member of the household for tax and conscription purposes, and stamped the front.

"You aren't married?"

"No," Ibrahim said.

"You know, a ton of iron and five tons cement is due every married couple." He spoke with the indifference of a bureaucrat.

"For what?"

"For when you people abandon this place."

That autumn, after the corn harvest, Ibrahim decided to get serious about providing for Samira. To start with, he'd need to learn how to read and write, so he enrolled in school in Manbij. He found a room in the city with two friends. He'd stay for the week, cooking for himself, then return to Little Hyena on Thursdays. Before leaving, he'd stop by the covered souk to pick up something for Samira: a compact, a barrette, a cassette. But in her even and knowing way, she encouraged him to stay put in Manbij, to save his money. The air of intrigue that hung over the village had everyone thinking about the future. Ibrahim began lodging in the city for two- or three-week stretches, saving on the taxi fare, which would one day go toward his wedding.

It was during one of these stretches that a friend appeared at his door. He had been dispatched by Samira, with an urgent message: Suitors were visiting her father. Talk of the flood was prompting proposals across the village, no doubt because of the compensation promised to married couples. Samira's parents decided it was time to give her away.

Ibrahim rushed back to Little Hyena. That evening, he and Samira plotted in the barn. She'd turned down four suitors already, including one from Little Rattle who had graduated from high school. "I want you more than this world," she whispered. But she could only fend off the advances for so long before her parents would settle the issue for her. Ibrahim sprang into action. He went to his mother and confessed everything: the hushed conversations by the gulch, the Crossing, the moonlight trysts. Life without Samira had no shape, no function. His mother took him by the hand and told him she had known all along. She kissed his cheek and urged him to do what he must.

He appeared before his father. His father had grown up in a time when his own father was a serf—when they lived and died by the whip of the feudal lord. He had come of age with a keen understanding of life: That which was given could be taken away, that which was won could be lost. He listened to his son, his semiliterate son, who'd flunked elementary school twice, who failed five times to pass the ninth grade, who had yet to see the right side of eighteen, speak of starting a family, and he exploded in anger. When Ibrahim should have been working the fields, when he should have been studying, he was running around with a girl.

"You want to take care of a woman? You can barely take care of yourself!"

Ibrahim pleaded.

His father pointed out the obvious: that Ibrahim would soon depart for military service, mandatory in Syria for all young men. For three long years, his bride would be living with them, another mouth to feed, while no one knew what fate held for the village.

Ibrahim swore he would work first, find a job in Manbij, send money home.

His father smirked. "And you'll become a millionaire in Manbij? Doing what? Loading oranges? While you're at it, could you see to it that you buy me a car?"

Ibrahim announced that he would take his own life. His father doubled over with laughter. A fantasy flashed across Ibrahim's mind in which he beat his father to a pulp.

The battle of wills raged for hours, Ibrahim shouting as if his life depended on it, his father smirking and shaking his head in pity, his mother nervously standing between them.

By evening, the matter was settled. The door to Ibrahim's future, to the mud-streaked children at his and Samira's feet, was shut.

Ibrahim dropped out of school again. He holed up in the barn for hours, smoking. The sight of food sickened him.

Samira was being kept under leash. He could not get anywhere near her.

Then one evening a boy from the Hamad household, whose family held wealth in the form of a recently acquired water pump, proposed. Samira's father, tired of her refusals, accepted on her behalf.

During the afternoons, Ibrahim wanted to sleep, to drift away, but his brothers, sisters, and cousins were everywhere. He went down to the river, sunk in his thoughts, and closed his eyes. He imagined he was floating somewhere far downstream, severed from the panic gripping his village. Citing the coming dam, the cooperative had stopped offering subsidized seeds, and the agricultural bank announced that they would no longer extend low-interest loans. The authorities did not want to encourage cultivation. Now, for the first time, families were facing hard choices. Ibrahim's father decided to try his luck in Jordan, where he'd heard work was available in construction. Seeing Ibrahim mired in gloom, refusing to eat, he decided to take him along and make an honest man of him.

Ibrahim was convinced that his father was stuck in the muck of old ways. The whole village was to blame, a village that hated the very idea of love, a miserable village in a miserable hillside in a miserable country. People here feared too much: gossip, omens, change. In truth, they feared themselves. If he could not be free to choose Samira, he decided he wanted nothing more to do with Little Hyena. He'd turn his back on these people forever. So when his father asked him to come to Jordan, he did not rebel.

Ibrahim arrived in Amman, in a neighborhood called the Valley of Blacksmithing, and was overwhelmed by concrete. Everywhere, he saw concrete houses, without ornamentation, without aspiration. Rows of identical gray concrete buildings with flat roofs and window grills, stacked on the hillside like boxes. It was as if color had been banned.

Ibrahim and his father took a room in a house with seven other laborers. The sons of Little Hyena and nearby villages were flocking to Amman for work between harvests. Ibrahim and his father helped construct houses, but now and then their pay was withheld. Once, Ibrahim's father was falsely accused of stealing bracelets by a woman who'd hired them. When Ibrahim tried to intervene, he was thrown to the ground by her teenage sons. Her daughter leaned over.

"You think you are a man?" she shouted, punching him until he was spitting up blood. The other workers stared at the floor.

At night, Ibrahim tossed and turned, pondering this alien land. Back home, people suffered, but they suffered together. Here, it was everyone for themselves, a survival of the fittest or most desperate. Despite forking over 25 Jordanian dinars a month for rent, the faucets sometimes ran dry, and the power would be out for weeks. Ibrahim could not stop his thoughts from straying to Little Hyena, to his mother's salted butter and flatbread. After three miserable months, he decided he could bear it no longer.

He told his father he would return to help with the wheat sowing, but in truth he had only a single ambition. When he arrived at Little Hyena, he saw fallow fields, pocked with wild grasses. Some houses were empty. The Hasans had decamped with their ton of iron and five tons of cement. His friend Muaz and his doves were gone too. But many families remained on the land, stubbornly growing sesame, cotton, and maize, even though it plunged them into debt.

He stood near the sunk fence on the edge of his family's fields, staring at the squat mud-and-stone building where Samira had grown up. He saw her brothers and sisters. They were older now, wearing jellabiyas and perhaps heading to the Crossing themselves. He called to her sister and told her that he had an urgent message for Samira.

The sun had set, the massifs looming on the far shore. He was waiting on the shingle far from the Crossing, near the scrubland bordering Little Hyena. The waters were quiet that night, free of boatmen. He saw her approach along the shoreline.

For a while, they did not speak.

"How is your new home?" he finally asked.

"They are good people."

Suddenly, she started crying. "What have you done with me?" She hugged him, pressed her wet cheek into his chest.

"I still love you," he said.

"My life was supposed to be with you," she sobbed.

Ibrahim wanted to take her by the hand, convince her to leave her new family behind. They'd escape to Damascus, to Jordan. They'd escape together, live on the run, live free. But even as he rehearsed these words, as he imagined their flight, their secret life in distant haunts, he knew he would never see her again.

Not long after, a flatbed truck crawled through the village. Work crews began removing the electricity pylons, the transformers, the cables. The truck drove off. At night, the only sounds in Little Hyena were the rustling tree branches, the leaves shaken by the wind.

—+ +—

Abu Talib had rigged his tractor to a water pump. He aimed the jets of river water into the irrigation channels, slowly unclogging Little Hyena's arteries one by one. The work would take three days.

His nephew appeared. He stood watching Abu Talib, and then told him, "They finished the dam."

Abu Talib looked up. "What did you say?"

"The dam, it's finished."

He left the water pump and headed down to the Crossing. On the shingle bank, a few villagers were gathered, staring at the river. Abu Talib took in a sight unknown to his seventy years: The Euphrates had stopped flowing.

—+ +—

Ibrahim was in the orchard that morning when he heard shouts. He went down to the bank, where he could see the dam in the distance. The river water, backing up, was climbing the hillside, pooling at his ankles. It was ice-cold.

A neighbor was pulling on his water pump, which was stuck in mud. Fishermen tied a rope around the machine, heaving.

Ibrahim rushed back to the orchard. As his legs carried him, he told himself, *This is not real, this is not real.* He found himself in his yard, shouting for his mother. Within minutes, his entire family was crowding the orchard. No one was sure what to do. Ibrahim wondered if he had imagined the scene at the Crossing, and raced back to check. When he returned, he was, for a few moments, speechless.

The water was rising.

The family now operated on pure instinct. His mother and sisters ran to the cotton fields, hoping to harvest what they could, as fast as they could. Ibrahim's uncle handed out saws to the men of the family to save the trees. Ibrahim and his brothers furiously worked the saw on the trunks of the apple trees, then the apricot.

It was dark when Ibrahim finally crumpled next to a tree, exhausted. They'd managed to rescue about seventy saplings, but hundreds remained.

No one slept that night. In the early-morning hours, water seeped into the Khalil house, which lay closest to the shore. The family rushed outdoors in a panic.

Now it was lapping at the walls of the Hussein house, now the Abdullah house.

At daybreak, Ibrahim summoned his courage and headed for the Crossing. He proceeded down the gently sloping dirt path toward the bank of shingle— but the shingle was gone. The bank, the abiding landmark of his years, had vanished. Frigid water was up to his calves. As he loped in the mud, eels darted. Clumps of hay floated past. He neared the Abdullah household, where women were shrieking. The river had loosened a water pump, their most valuable possession. It was the size of a motorcycle, and the waters carried it away.

At home, he found his mother sobbing because the cotton crop was ruined. He rushed indoors to help his brothers pack the clothes, the flour, the bulgur, and the tomato paste, wrapping everything in blankets. A third of the house was now sitting in water. A box of his keepsakes from Samira was submerged somewhere. Instead of fishing it out, Ibrahim waded over to the shelf and gathered, in a burlap sack, his brother Adam's second-grade books, his colored pens and notebooks.

Everywhere, villagers were escaping uphill. Women carried babies, men hauled large sacks of clothes. Wheelbarrows and carts were littered here and there. The water was rising with speed.

In the afternoon, serpents appeared. Fleeing the advancing water, they slithered up the Crossing, stretched out across the alleyways, coiled around the sacks of clothes, hung from trees. The men were clubbing the thick black invaders with shovels. The donkeys were braying wildly. An ox stood rooted in the mud, submissive to its fate.

Ibrahim and his brothers built a berm around the perimeter to keep out the rising waters. The family spent the evening on a makeshift raised platform in the front yard. The river inched up the berm. Ibrahim lay under the stars, trying to sleep.

The next morning, the water spilled over the berm.

"Everything is gone!" his mother wailed. Ibrahim furiously hacked down the cottonwood pillars of their own home, which he hoped could be sold or reused. He slogged through the water, carrying the beams, eventually reaching the main intersection outside the village. Up and down the road, men and women were shouting, cursing the authorities. Children were crying. A television crew from Aleppo arrived to document the calamity, but the authorities turned them away.

Ibrahim sold the cottonwood pillars to people in passing cars for a few hundred liras, enough to hire a taxi should the time come. When he returned to the village, the water was above his knees.

Some families were gathered at the graveyard, unearthing the bodies of their loved ones to inter farther up the hill.

Abdul Rauf, who lived near the grocer, was wrapping his water pump in plastic, layer after layer, obsessively. He was in tears.

"What are you doing?" Ibrahim asked.

"Keeping it safe," he said, "for when the water goes back."

By afternoon, the waters reached Ibrahim's waist. What remained of his mud house was melting. His friend Rami decided to swim to his own field, down on the *hawijeh*, which now lay in the deep. He swam past mattresses and old steel drums. When he reached the field, he submerged his head, and under the water he could see green stalks of sesame, swaying silently.

Rami came up for air. The new shore seemed impossibly distant. The sun was punishing, and his arms burned and his sides ached. Up ahead was the crown of a willow tree, bobbing on the water. He swam to a branch and pulled himself up to rest. The tree vines were thick, glistening. He held one and watched the shore, the sacks bouncing on the backs of old men, the women crowded together. Suddenly, the vine squirted away. Rami recoiled. *Snakes*. Seaweed green, stone black, hanging from the branches, coiled around the trunk. He shrieked and dove into the water.

That evening, the river devoured the schoolhouse. Ibrahim learned that some villagers, including Samira and her husband, had managed to hire a truck and flee that morning. The rest of the village gathered in tents on a hilltop. Many were unable to put up funds for a taxi. Their fields, their livelihoods, were now lying at a depth of some hundred feet. Others, like Ibrahim's family, had managed to pawn their cottonwood beams, but could not bring themselves to leave. Ibrahim sat with his mother in silence, while down below, the village was crackling in hundreds of tiny explosions as walls crumbled, beams snapped, and roofs collapsed.

Late that night, Ibrahim's house finally disappeared beneath the waters. The orchard was gone. So was the cotton field, the acre of sesame. The old barn, where he'd meet Samira. The copse of willows, where he'd changed into a white jellabiya for her. Ibrahim was thankful for only one thing: that his father, who had poured his life into these fields, whose own father had resisted feudal lords for the simple right to own what he grew, whose grandfather had survived blight and Bedouin raids to farm this land, was not here to see this.

In the morning, the water reached the asphalt. The main road was strewn with snakes, numb or dead. The mayor of a nearby town was running barefoot, flagging down passing cars, begging them to take families. Everyone did their share. Ibrahim tried to use the cottonwood money to hire vehicles, but the drivers waived the fare.

The authorities, who had been absent during this ordeal, now announced

they were offering land in the desert, almost two hours away. The people of Little Hyena were left with no choice. Soon the main road was thick with cars laboring under the weight of mattresses, irregularly shaped cloth sacks, even children. Women huddled on car roofs, clinging to chairs and tables. Their wailing could be heard from a great distance.

For ten days after Little Hyena vanished, a few families remained on the outcropping above the lake. Like survivors of an apocalypse, they lived among the alders and willows. Ibrahim's grandmother was one of them. She occupied a small tent and, though Ibrahim tried, she refused to quit the land of her birth. While the rest of the family sought refuge in the desert, Ibrahim sat with her and watched the waters. He could see donkeys orphaned on the hilltops, dogs cast into the backwoods. When his friend Muaz had taken his doves to the desert, he'd attempted to train them for their new home, but they'd flown off and did not return. Now, over the water, Ibrahim saw doves circling, and he was sure they had come home.

Some fifty villages now lay in the depths of the river. The tells had vanished, too. Officials arrived to celebrate the opening of the October Dam, but in all of Syria's newspapers and news programs there was not a word about the missing villages. The people of Little Hyena and its sister hamlets up and down the river moved to the desert, and then to shantytowns ringing the big cities. They were joined by tens of thousands of other families who were fleeing calamities of their own, from drought to joblessness.

Ibrahim's father returned from Jordan and found the family a small room in Manbij that was made of cinderblock and had a dirt floor. Ibrahim and his father rose at dawn, waited at a nearby roundabout with other day laborers, strangers from around the country, and occasionally got hired for construction jobs. They worked twelve, fourteen hours a day laying marble tiles and installing porcelain sinks, returning home covered in grime, shoulders aching. Before they sank into sleep, they made sure to lock their door.

All his life, Ibrahim had submitted himself to the dictates of fate. He'd dutifully done what soil demanded, what the elders said was necessary. By his father's writ, he'd abandoned his heart. By the authorities' orders, he'd surrendered his claim to a world in which many hands raised a home, waters were a common bounty, and trust was the coin of the land. To rail against these losses would be like shouting at the weather or cursing the stars. Only by submitting to fate would fate provide—this had been the credo of the river communities, and for a long time, Ibrahim had felt it in his bones. But now, in his exhaust-choked room, as pasty white fluorescent streetlights filtered through the window, he was surprised to discover arising within him a new sensation, directed against his father, his vanished village, the faraway forces he was only beginning to grasp, even against fate itself.

Ibrahim, at the age of eighteen, had discovered rage.

| TWO |

The Absolute Spirit

I

Hasan Nefi's greatest fear was to be forgotten. For many years, he relived old encounters, recalling the dung-tinged air of his parents' farm, his mother's charcoal grilled *kibbe*. It was only through his memories, in fact, that he could be sure he was still alive.

He was born in Manbij in 1963, in a one-story mud-and-stone house with a narrow courtyard and a gate that opened to the dust of Jamal Abdul Nasser Street. It was an hour's walk to the arid patch of land that sustained the family, where his father spent his days, year after year, for as long as Hasan could remember. He told Hasan of harsher times, when the Ottoman pashas came to Manbij and conscripted Arabs, marching them to their deaths in the trenches of the Great War. He spoke of the famine that struck the city, the bodies with distended bellies piled onto wheelbarrows, and of the French, who emplaced feudal lords and burned down houses at will. "You live in blessed times," he would say.

Hasan saw those blessings not in the soil, but in the written word. By day, his small hands tied flakes of hay and threaded the water pump hose, but at night, while his siblings were asleep, he sat reading in a room lit by a kerosene lamp. He asked his father questions like, "What do we mean when we say something is beautiful?" He read greedily anything put before him. He found his way to the Manbij Cultural Center, a two-story government-run facility downtown that housed the city's only library, and borrowed stacks of books he could hardly carry.

At school, he was given a homework assignment: *You are walking home one day when you meet a beggar. What do you say to him?*

The students were to write a paragraph. Hasan wrote three pages.

The next year, he was given a poem to analyze: *The poem discusses the idea of* will. *What does* conviction *mean to you?*

Hasan was asked to read his answer aloud in class.

His teachers found ways to encourage him, guiding him toward books outside the curriculum. He was gifted a volume by the poet Buhturi, born in Manbij in the ninth century, the court bard of the Abbasids in Baghdad. Buhturi was known for his rich, descriptive lyricism, which arched over the course of a poem from strife to solace, and always refused to bow to abuse:

> *If I'm ever mistreated, I'm apt*
> *Not to be seen at dawn where I was at dusk*

Hasan's father would come home at dark and collapse onto the floor cushion, holding a tumbler of tea in his callused hands. He couldn't understand what Hasan was writing, but the teachers were telling him that his son was a rare jewel. Hasan had identified in poetry the rhythm that marked his life, from his farmyard routine to the changing of the seasons that ruled the family's fortunes. He began collecting every poetry compilation and chapbook he could find, like those of the great Manbij bards Omar Abu Risha and Abu Firas al-Hamdani, as well as luminaries from around the Arab world. He learned that the rules of classical Arabic poetry were precise, set down centuries earlier. Whereas traditional English poetry usually employs five metrical patterns, most Arabic compositions consist of up to sixteen, known as "oceans." Each verse is called a "house." Hasan found that he was able to compose in these houses and oceans effortlessly.

Manbij was, in fact, known for its poets, and Hasan developed the theory that it was the artesian springs and majestic cedars that turned the city into a font of poetic possibility. At the Cultural Center, men in thick mustaches and caramel-colored suits read their poems, while Hasan and his friends listened. At home, Hasan and his friends gathered in his living room, glistening with sweat, fanning themselves, reciting creations of their own. They would read contemporary Arab poets, like the Iraqi communist Badr Shakir al-Sayyab, who dispensed with the strictures of classical meter to launch the free verse movement. In Sayyab's work, Hasan felt a bottomless melancholy, a yearning for a different world. But why Hasan felt so moved, or what sort of world he felt impelled to seek out, he was not yet sure.

One hot March morning in 1980, Hasan was walking on an empty road leading to his farmland when he saw plumes of dust approaching. A pair of camo-colored tanks lumbered up and blocked the road. A soldier waved him back; he was wearing an arm patch depicting a skull superimposed over a pair of crossed swords.

Hasan hurried home. Everyone was assembled. His father was silent and pacing, his mother shushing the children. When a knock came, Hasan opened the door to find five soldiers. They fired off questions: Do you have any weapons? Have you traveled recently? They searched the house and then proceeded next door.

A rumor circulated that the government was after terrorists, but facts were hard to come by. The main source of news was Radio Monte Carlo, which offered little detail: ten saboteurs arrested in the city of Homs; a criminal ring busted in Damascus. There were even whispers of arrests right here in Manbij—a teacher on the far side of town had supposedly been whisked away.

Some folks were saying the crackdown was necessary, because Syria had many enemies. When Hasan asked his father who these enemies were, though, he did not get a clear answer. At the Cultural Center, he looked for volumes that might explain the news, but found little. He settled for books on Freud, Skinner, and Jung, which led him to wonder about the nature of primal, irrational fear. He learned that against the salacious drives of the id, the superego is the seat of morals and values. Could it possibly be right that a teacher could get vanished without a trace, leaving a family devastated? Even if they were terrorists, they deserved their day in court. The question of right and wrong brought him to the philosopher Immanuel Kant; maybe, just by working it out logically, one could arrive at great moral truths, as the famed German thinker had said. Under a sun-blanched sky, as he watered the ruts of his fields, he leafed through an Arabic translation of Kant's *Critique of Practical Reason*. He would pause, dust himself off, move the hose to the next section, and continue. When he finished, he would climb onto a bale of hay, open his philosophy textbook, *The Problem of Work*, and prepare for his baccalaureate exams.

In February of 1982, news filtered from the city of Hama, a four-hour drive south. Radio Monte Carlo reported that terrorists had seized parts of the city, but reassured listeners that the government had quelled the insurrection. There were no further details, and the army started blocking the interstate highway, which ran through the heart of Hama. By now, Hasan had grown accustomed to passing an army checkpoint where Jamal Abdul Nasser Street blended into a dirt road.

One evening, Hasan was invited to a friend's house to play cards, but really, he knew, it was a chance to trade rumors in private. Once there, in a small guest room, he saw friends from school, and a few unfamiliar faces.

"Don't worry," he was told. "You can trust them."

The boys exchanged news and gossip. Their discussions soon turned to foreign events: That June, Israel had invaded Lebanon to attack Palestinian groups based there. As Israeli howitzers besieged Beirut, the Syrian government—which had thirty thousand troops on Lebanese soil—did nothing. The inaction came as a shock to Hasan and his friends. What Hasan had believed in his heart, what had been drummed into him by every textbook and every news program, was that the Syrian government was the staunch defender of the Palestinian cause—in fact, nothing was more important than Palestinian freedom. After all, the Baath Party believed that all Arabs, across all borders, belonged to a single culture and history.

That evening, Hasan and his friends spent hours discussing the scandal. He learned that while his government was officially allied with Palestinian resistance groups, in practice, the Syrian army had supported the right-wing Christian militias in Lebanon against the leftist Palestinian factions. He discovered that the army—Hasan's own army, in which his elder brothers and neighbors had served—had Palestinian blood on its hands, that it had played a key role in slaughtering more than a thousand people at the Palestinian refugee camp of Tel al-Zaatar in 1976. Meanwhile, his government was doing God knows what to its own people in Hama. At school, at home, in the market, people went about their day, grazing happily, while lies upon lies were smothering the Arab cause.

Soon the boys were meeting regularly. Once a location was settled upon, they would arrive alone or in pairs, carrying school texts in case they encountered a patrol. Each attendee had to be vouched for. No one, not even their parents, knew what they were doing. In candlelit barns, in tiny guest rooms, over cards and cigarettes and glasses of tea, a group took shape. They gave themselves no name, and beyond the dozen in their circle, hardly anyone knew they existed.

Then a man from out of town began showing up at the meetings. He was from the National Current Party, an outlawed leftist outfit, and Hasan listened carefully to his analysis. Nineteen years had passed since Baathists seized power—during which time they had ended feudalism, lifting millions out of poverty and giving birth to a new middle class. In exchange for this beneficence, however, people had to surrender all political rights, including freedom of speech and the vote. All government officials, including those belonging to the so-called parliament, were handpicked by the Baath Party. Photos of the great leader, Hafez al-Assad, were plastered everywhere. This trade-off—economic opportunity in exchange for political rights—was the grand social contract that underpinned not only Baathist Syria, but all Arab dictatorships, from Iraq to Tunisia.

This arrangement suited millions of Syrians well enough, but a minority was not pleased. Two opposition movements emerged. On the left wing was a small current of communists and Arab nationalists; the latter attacked the government's foreign policies, especially regarding Palestine. On the right were the great feudal lords, who'd been stripped of their wealth and privileges, making them implacably opposed to the government. They were joined by the merchants and souk traders, who lost profits when the state nationalized industries and monopolized foreign trade. These right-wing groups threw their support behind the Muslim Brotherhood, a banned organization that railed against the government's secular and anti-free-market policies. To make matters worse in the eyes of the Muslim Brotherhood, although much of the country was Sunni Muslim, Assad and many of his key lieutenants belonged to the Alawite religious sect. By the late 1970s, tensions between Muslim Brotherhood–aligned groups and the government had spilled into open war.

Hasan began to understand that his life had comprised a series of disparate facts, a swirl of impressions, without order, without purpose. Thanks to the guidance of the party, he realized he was, in fact, living in a realm of appearances—beyond which lay a hidden order, a true order: The imperialist powers were bent on destroying Arab unity, destroying democracy, and smothering the Palestinian resistance, and the Assad regime was their accomplice. With this stunning realization, the world suddenly made sense; Hasan began to understand that every pronouncement from the authorities, every headline from Lebanon, was a fiction. At the same time, he awoke to the terrible truth that those around him, his relatives and neighbors, were unwitting subjects of the kingdom of make-believe. Now, with the solidity of the real world in his grasp, he ventured into debates with family members. He read volumes in the library with new eyes. For every question life could toss up, there was a definite answer—and it could often be found in the pages of the party press, in its tracts and clandestine newspapers. In the face of this strange, muted war between the government and the "terrorists," his neighbors and relatives felt the kind of low-boil dread that crawls up one's chest. But Hasan would not succumb, because he stood on the hard ground of truth.

One day that spring, Hasan was on the farm when he learned he'd passed his baccalaureate exams. At home, his father slaughtered a pair of sheep. Hasan took a long shower, knowing he would never work in the fields again.

—⊹⊹—

On the grounds of the University of Aleppo, Hasan found willows and date palms, manicured lawns, shrubs sculptured to look like bishops and queens, and gushing fountains. A giant mural depicted a fierce battle under the words LONG LIVE SYRIA, FREE AND PROUD.

Hasan was assigned to Dormitory Unit 10, Room 419, with a friend from Manbij. It was a cramped cell in a colossal concrete block that was built, like all government buildings, in the prison aesthetic. Hasan, with his long hair and a perpetually faraway look that suggested deep wisdom, was quick to win admirers. Before long, he was secluding himself in stairwells, or in the dusky carrels of the library, to be alone with his books.

Though Hasan was away from Manbij, he felt at home in the Humanities Faculty's great lecture halls. He was steeped in the work of the poets who flourished during the so-called Age of Ignorance, before Islam. He puzzled over the mysterious Hanging Poems that, tradition maintained, were once suspended like jewelry in the Kaaba, the ancient building in Mecca. By his second year, he'd progressed to the literature of the eighth and ninth centuries, the age of Arab splendor.

Hasan soon fell for a quiet girl from Aleppo. They walked side by side in the moonlight and spent hours sitting in the garden, speaking softly. Hasan was shy around her, but not on the page. His poetry had matured, expanding beyond the bare outlines of his high school verses. He tore up those primitive compositions. His new work pulsed with the sense that beauty could be felt more than it could be spoken, and his readings began to attract fellow students. Soon, he was reciting in front of packed rooms.

A publishing house in Damascus took notice. They offered to put out a compilation of his poems if he could come up with 5,000 liras. This was an impossible sum for Hasan, but his friends took up a collection. When *Obsessions and Longings* was published, in the spring of 1984, Hasan was twenty-one, and he was a small sensation on campus. In his readings, he was too embarrassed to admit that the book's fluid rhyming couplets were an ode not to beauty itself, but to its instantiation in the person of his lover.

Hasan adapted to his celebrity with grace. He was a man to be seen with; his was a name to be dropped. Beneath this public persona, his secret life thrived, and he viewed it as inseparable from his art. An underground scene was bubbling on campus. There was a Muslim Brotherhood cell, even though membership was a capital offense. On the left, a communist cell was active, as well as Hasan's group, who styled themselves as the true leftists, the true nationalists. They believed that the regime had turned its back on the Palestinian cause and had to go, even if they couldn't articulate what should replace it.

He surrendered himself to party strictures; the Arab nation could only be awakened, he believed, through discipline—which meant being available at a moment's notice, even neglecting his studies if duty called. Late at night, he would slip off campus, walk the walled streets of the city, and paste flyers calling for the downfall of the regime. Once, he and his comrades posted the notices on university walls, prompting the administration to put the campus under lockdown. Hasan had a gift for this work, moving in these circles with ease. The party headquarters began tasking him with more challenging missions. From a farmhouse in the country, he would pick up copies of *The Vanguard*, the party monthly, and ferry them to Aleppo.

One night in 1986, he was entering Manbij on foot with the magazines under his shirt, taped to his belly. Suddenly, he felt the glare of a flashlight.

"Hands up!"

He raised both hands. In one of them, he held a volume of poetry.

"I'm from Aleppo University," he called out.

A soldier was standing close. He could smell his breath. The soldier's hands were patting down his arms, his legs. His back.

"What are these?"

He showed the poetry book. The soldier leafed through it.

"I'm a student," Hasan explained.

The flashlight's beam raked his chest, his belly, his legs.

"Get out of here."

Hasan walked on.

He decided to lie low and take a hiatus from party activity. Months went by and he did not visit his comrades. Instead, he tried to focus on his work. *Obsessions and Longings* could be found in bookshops around Aleppo and Manbij, and a life of furnished offices and oak tables awaited him. Word was he'd be hired immediately, upon graduation, as junior faculty. But for some reason, Hasan could not rouse himself to the prospect. A quiet life behind the lectern seemed insipid, aimless. He retreated into days and weeks with his girlfriend, wondering if it was time to raise her name with his parents. But then one evening his father went to sleep and never woke up.

For the first time in years, Hasan spent some weeks at home. Upon returning to Aleppo, he felt little desire to work. When he closed his eyes, he could see his father's sweat-glistened face, his thick hands running a hose along the earth. Hasan was lying on his cot one November afternoon, ruminating, when he suddenly sat up and left his room. The months away from political activity were eating at him. He exited the university gates and turned down Aleppo's winding side streets. The air was cool. He almost never took walks; he did his best thinking at the desk. But today he followed the streets until he came upon the house of a comrade he hadn't seen in a few months. Hasan felt a powerful urge to sit with him, to reminisce. He knocked on the door, but there was no answer.

He headed back to campus. In the gathering dark, he reached his dorm room. His roommate was buried in a book, and Hasan decided to do the same.

Some time later, there came a knock at the door.

Hasan looked at the clock. It was just past 11:00 p.m. His roommate answered. Before Hasan could register the scene, three men were in the room. He recognized one of them as the dormitory director, whom he'd met many times.

"That's him," the director said, pointing to Hasan.

"What is this?" Hasan asked.

An older man stepped forward and asked him to come with him. Hasan started to follow the men, but the older man told him to change out of his pajamas.

He put on trousers. Before he could slip his feet into shoes, the older man said, with some kindness, "Leave it. We just want to ask you a few questions. We'll have you back in fifteen minutes."

Hasan followed them, barefoot. When he stepped into the corridor, he saw it was crowded with men in military uniforms, wearing vests and holding rifles.

"What's going on here?" the dorm director asked.

"We have a complaint from a woman. Says he touched her inappropriately."

"What?" Hasan nearly shouted.

Outside, he saw multiple vehicles. Hundreds of students had come out to watch. His head was lowered into one of the vehicles. They departed down the city's boulevards. He was held by men on each side. The car turned into the Christian neighborhood of Sulaymaniyah. They entered a gated compound, ringed by barbed wire, and Hasan's heart sank. It was the political intelligence branch. His mind began to race. But how? He'd been away from the party for months. Someone must have concocted a false report against him. Yes, someone was jealous. A fellow student? Whatever it was, whatever would happen, Hasan decided then and there to say nothing.

They have nothing on me, he kept saying to himself.

They have nothing.

"Name."

"Hasan Nefi."

"Father's name."

Hasan answered.

"Mother's name."

He told him.

"Political affiliation."

"None."

There was silence. Hasan was in a blindfold. The room smelled damp.

"Political affiliation," the voice repeated.

"I don't belong to any party," Hasan said.

"Is that your final answer?"

"Yes."

The voice said politely, in a different direction, "You take him."

So there were others in the room.

Hasan felt hands moving him, pushing his back down onto wood. His arms were extended, tied down. His legs were bound together and to the wood. Suddenly, the top and bottom halves of the wood began to close in on each other, like the ends of a book. His toes were near his nose. He was screaming uncontrollably. He had the urge to vomit. Hands held him in this position. He felt the blows of a thick pipe—or was it bamboo?—on the soles of his bare feet.

When he awoke, he was lying on the floor. He could not feel his legs, and he wondered with a fright if they were gone. A sudden shock of cold November water hit his face. Soon, he was drowning. It was a waterfall; he fought to breathe. He could feel the force of a human foot, in a boot, landing on his sides, and it was only then that he knew he was still alive.

"Name."

"Hasan Nefi."

"Father's name."

Hasan answered.

"Mother's name."

He told him.

"Political affiliation." The voice was floating somewhere above him.

"None."

Hasan took a deep breath. A hand was grabbing his crotch.

"You're a young one," the voice said. "It's time to confess. Or we're cutting this fellow off."

Hasan mustered, "I don't belong to any party."

He was back on the wood. Toes to his nose, hoarse from screaming. The bamboo sticks were pounding his feet. He was on the floor, swallowing that November water, coughing, covered in snot. He felt himself being lifted.

When he was back on the ground, his blindfold was no longer there. He looked around. It was a cell, about six feet long and three feet wide. He looked at the black iron door. He had never felt so cold in his life. He took a thin blanket and tried to wrap himself, but he could hardly move. He fell into a long, deep sleep.

When he awoke, he could see daylight leaking in through the joints of the door. He was alone with his thoughts. Dread seized him. He found it difficult to breathe. He tried to stand but crumpled under the stabbing pain. It was freezing, but he was soaked in sweat.

Get a grip. He knew they had nothing on him. He had been careful. He would have to resist the interrogation, no matter what they tried. Without a confession, they would eventually have to stop. Either they would kill him, or they would let him go.

The door opened, and two jailers ordered him to follow. But he could not stand. One of them grabbed a clump of Hasan's long hair and began dragging. He yelped as the hair began snapping free of his scalp. He crawled as fast as he could, while they led him by the hair. Back in the interrogation room, he was asked the same questions. Another hour on the wooden board, which Hasan learned was called a Flying Carpet, and then waterboarding. The next day, the routine repeated itself. He kept his silence. Whenever he was returned to his cell, he saw guards dragging another prisoner away for questioning. It was like a factory, an assembly line of bodies.

Two days later, he was in the interrogation room when he heard a new voice.

"You want to continue lying to us?"

"I've told you everything."

He heard the flipping of pages.

"You are a member of the National Current Party. For the last two years, you have overseen distributing propaganda. You pick up your party magazine from the countryside, and you deliver to the city. You carry letters from the leadership in Damascus."

Hasan felt cold to his bones.

The voice continued with a litany of details. They had a comrade, Ziad, in custody. Hasan didn't even know he'd been taken. He must have spilled everything under torture.

Hasan felt an overpowering urge to sleep, to nestle in the corner and close his eyes and never wake. The image of his father flashed through his mind. Hasan found himself thanking God that the old man wasn't alive. He thought of his mother. All he wanted now was to see her, to hold her one last time.

Hasan began to talk. He recognized that his life was now sliding through a dark tunnel from which he could see no opening. He made sure to give his interrogators only information they already had. The torture lessened. Just fifteen minutes on the Flying Carpet, just one bucket of water. He was returned to his solitary cell. Beyond the iron door, the assembly line continued to churn, the corridors echoing with agony. After six days, he signed a confession.

II

Five years passed in a cell with ice-cold terrazzo floors, which always smelled of sweaty socks. His memory was stippled with gray, though sometimes a sensation would strike with crystalline clarity. He remembered the dung-tinged air of the farm. The chalky cast he limped around in during ninth grade, after breaking his leg on the soccer field. He wondered about his girlfriend, who was by now certainly someone's wife, someone's mother. He wondered about *Obsessions and Longings*, if it was now radioactive, erased from inventories.

Most of all, he thought about his mother. He'd left her behind, and the regret gnawed at him. Once, in 1989, he was brought into an interrogation room, and he saw her. He was taken aback. She'd aged considerably in three years. She looked at him with sad, rheumy eyes, and she seemed lost. The officer said they'd received information that Hasan was communicating with party members through his family, and demanded to know how. Hasan swore that he had not exchanged a word with her in three years. In fact, he would give anything just to talk to her, to hold her. For a moment, it seemed as if they were going to put her away, too. In the end, the officer seemed convinced, and she was released.

Hasan had no need to pass hidden messages, for he lived among his comrades. The cells were packed with prisoners from the three main leftist currents. There were communists, like Yassin al-Haj Saleh, a noted intellectual. There were old stalwarts of the late Egyptian leader Jamal Abdul Nasser. And there were plenty from Hasan's own party. He shared a cell with dozens of others, their mattresses demarcating the narrow footpaths through which he navigated his days.

The years stacked up, shuffled. It was 1988, and Hasan and a dozen others were in day seven of a hunger strike, demanding pencils. It was 1986, and the guards decreed that prisoners could leave their cells and wander the corridors until evening. Hasan roamed the three wings, which radiated like spokes from a hub. He was living, he understood, in a building shaped like a Mercedes-Benz logo.

It was winter 1989, and the men were wrapped in blankets. Hasan had procured a copy of Goethe's *The Sorrows of Young Werther*. He had outgrown his youthful foray into the stern rationality of Kant. Now he was exploring a different branch of eighteenth-century thought, the Sturm und Drang movement of early German Romanticism. Like those Romantics, Hasan was grasping at the heart of reality, what the German thinkers called Being, through that which the men in these confines understood best of all—longing. Hasan was deep in the study of Goethe's novel, which resulted in a treatise, "The Romantic Philosophy of Werther." In its pages, Hasan argued that in the novel's rejection of cold reason, which for Goethe was like an oppressive mechanical clock, one could detect Eastern influences. Hasan identified in Werther traces of pantheism, and inspiration from the great mystic poet Ibn Arabi. He hoped to find a way to smuggle his treatise to the outside world.

It was November 1991. Hasan had been inside for five years. There were no mirrors, and he wondered if he'd aged. Winter had come on early. A frigid draft flooded the cells. One afternoon, a group of officers entered the corridor. They called the prisoners in the three wings together and read out fifteen names, telling them to gather their belongings. The president, in an act of grace, had announced an amnesty for political prisoners. The men whose names were read jumped to their feet. They embraced and broke into tears. Some had been rotting away here since the early 1970s. Some had grandchildren waiting on the outside.

A few hours later, fifteen more names were read out, and then again that evening. Everyone had their belongings bundled, their mattress rolled up. Hasan kept his books and papers in order, waiting to hear his name. The cells were thinning.

On the second day, the head of the detachment peered through the bars at the remaining prisoners. There were eighteen left. "You all better unroll your mattresses," he said, with sympathy.

Hasan looked around his cell. No one could say anything. He lay on the mattress, trying to close his eyes. The frost was bitter. It had seeped into his bones.

He went to the corridor. The last of the amnestied prisoners were leaving, carrying in their bundles a full decade of life. He dug his toes into the grout between the stones in the wall, pulling himself up to a window grating. A crowd had gathered outside to welcome the releasees, emerging in the winter sunlight like stragglers from some lost tribe. There were screams of joy, sobbing. Amid the racket, Hasan heard a clear, shrill voice:

"Hasan!"

He scanned the crowd, and he heard it again.

"Hasan! Oh Hasan!"

He fastened his eyes on a shriveled old woman elbowing through the crowd. Hasan began banging on the grill. "Mama! I'm here, Mama!"

"Oh Hasan! Why aren't you free?"

"Mama!" was all he could reply.

"Hasan! What's happening to you?"

"Oh Mama!"

He climbed down.

Night fell, leaving each of the eighteen men alone in the shared cell.

"Why do you think ruling the country is so difficult?" Hafez al-Assad once said. "It's really very simple. Let's look at our people. He who has no car wants a car. He who has no house wants a house. A man with a salary wants it doubled or tripled. I can assure you we can satisfy all these demands. If we do, who will remain in opposition in Syria? One or two hundred individuals who take politics seriously. They will be against us whatever we do. Mezzeh Prison has been built for them."

Syria's prison archipelago got its start during the French colonial occupation with the construction of Mezzeh in an old Crusader fort on a hilltop overlooking the capital. A stay at the two-story fortress became a rite of passage for political activists, from anticolonial rebels to ousted presidents to Hafez al-Assad himself, who reportedly was briefly detained there before taking power. The Baathist government added more facilities to house enemies and miscreants: Sednaya prison, near a monastery town noted for an icon of the Virgin Mary, and from which some prisoners never returned; the so-called Palestine Branch, a dungeon in Damascus operated by the Military Intelligence's Branch 235 (to which, after September 11, 2001, the CIA shipped some detainees in order to outsource torture); Palmyra prison, set in the pink deserts not far from spectacular Roman ruins (in 1980, the president's brother led forces in a cell-to-cell rampage, killing as many as a thousand inmates); and the massive warehouse-looking structure in the Damascus suburbs called Adra.

In the spring of 1992, Hasan and his remaining cellmates—still eighteen leftists in all—were transferred to Adra. They were loaded into vans and driven into the city to stand before the Supreme State Security Court. It was Hasan's first court appearance since his arrest seven years earlier. He stood with eight others in a cage, facing three judges seated across from him. There were no observers and no lawyers.

The hearings continued for two years.

One afternoon, the head judge read out the charge against Hasan: "The criminal used weapons to overthrow the government."

"Your Honor! I've never touched a weapon in my life!" Hasan protested. "Sir, nowhere in my signed confession does it state that I was armed."

The judge appeared exasperated, as if Hasan failed to grasp the logic of the issue. "Did your group wish to change the government?"

"Yes, Your Honor."

"And how do you expect to change this government without resorting to arms?"

"Through our words, honorable judge. We were peaceful activists."

"Your words were a tool to overthrow the government?"

"Yes, Your Honor."

"A weapon is any tool used to overthrow the government."

When the judge read the sentence, Hasan struggled to breathe. Back in the cell, he kept repeating the number to himself, turning it over in his mind.

Fifteen years. He'd already served nine years, but the thought of six more left him listless in his corner of the cell. The charges were carefully calibrated to strike at the prisoners' political hearts. Nationalists like Hasan were convicted of "anti-nationalism," and communists were convicted of "anti-socialism."

Still, even as he could not envisage the long road ahead—the future, when he tried to imagine it, was black—his old life lay at an impossible distance. He took refuge instead in the one advantage Adra prison offered: books. The authorities here were less keen on examining incoming material for forbidden content, and through the volumes sent by his family, Hasan could read to his heart's content. He delved into Abdelrahman Munif's magisterial epic *Cities of Salt*. He was gripped by the intensity of Keats, the revolutionary fire of Shelley and Byron. Yet he began to question his earlier embrace of the passions, his complete rejection of reason. He found himself affected by Stendhal's *The Red and the Black*, in which the protagonist, a country boy, rises above his station, only to be undone by his own passions.

These imaginative wanderings landed him on the doorstep of Georg Wilhelm Friedrich Hegel. For the first time, he decided to undertake a systematic study of a single thinker, and over the months, buried himself in the great German philosopher's efforts to reconcile reason and the soul. Hegel proclaimed that all previous systems of thought, even if incomplete or mistaken, contained kernels of truth. Like a river gradually widening, fed by a tributary here, by headwaters there, human knowledge coursed toward perfect knowledge. For Hegel, history is not an arena of randomness. Instead, it operates with purpose, shepherding humans toward total understanding. Collectively, humans can grasp reality as it truly is through the infinite mind of the cosmos—what Hegel called the Absolute Spirit. Hasan pondered this idea. He wasn't sure Hegel was right—but he could not convince himself that he was wrong, either. He read and reread the *Phenomenology of Spirit*, until phrases from the text appeared at all hours, even in his dreams.

December 1995. Hasan was called into the adjutant's office. All day, prisoners had been filing in and out. A group of major generals and colonels were seated around the table. They pushed a paper toward him. He was being offered his freedom, on the following conditions:

1. Quit the party.

Hasan told them he didn't even need to be asked. He'd quit in a heartbeat.

2. Abandon political activism.

The pursuit of wisdom, the embrace of art—this was the world-historical mission. To revitalize the Arab nation, he would first need to revitalize his spirit. He promised them he was ready to walk away, now and forever, from politics.

3. Denounce your past activities.

How could he? As Hegel had shown him, the path determines the destination. He had arrived here only through the heartache and labor and wisdom of his years. He'd stood up to a tyrannical government, and for that he could never apologize. But were his *methods* the right ones? Perhaps there was another way to address the inequities of the regime. In the end, this realization is what led him to agree to the officers' demand.

4. Cooperate with the security services.

Hasan stopped cold. He would surrender everything, even denounce his past, but he could never, ever become a spy for the regime that stood not for nation, or class, or ideal, but only for itself.

He refused their offer.

Most of his cellmates agreed. The officers were furious. They said they'd offered benevolence, only to have the detainees spit in their faces. As they were leaving, one officer remarked to his colleague, "There's only one place for these pigs."

III

Hasan awoke to shouting. Someone was clanging on the bars. It was not yet dawn.

"Get up, dogs! Get up!"

A panic swept through the cell.

An adjutant appeared and read out thirty names. Twenty-two communists, eight nationalists. Hasan was one of them. They were ordered to leave their belongings.

The men whispered among themselves. No one knew if this meant release or if they were headed back to Aleppo, or perhaps something else.

They were handcuffed and shackled together, then herded onto a bus. Hasan's chest felt tight. The men around him were downcast. They sat for hours in silence, in the January air. The sun rose and warmed the metal bus, but Hasan was shivering.

The bus groaned to life, and by midmorning they were proceeding through the Damascus suburbs. Hasan watched the city rousing itself, oblivious to the ghosts passing in its midst. They merged onto the Damascus–Aleppo highway. But then they turned onto a second highway, heading into the desert, and his heart sank.

They pulled up to a pastel-colored gate. The pink desert stretched for miles behind them. On one wall was painted: THE LAW MUST BE RESPECTED TO PRESERVE THE DIGNITY OF THE CITIZEN.

A row of adjutants appeared. "You missed the Welcome Party," one said. It was already past 3:00 p.m., and most guards were done for the day. Tomorrow, he promised. Tomorrow.

For the first time since he entered the catacombs of the Syrian Arab

Republic all those years ago, Hasan and his fellow nationalists were separated from the communists. His group was led to a type of oubliette, with a small window high on the wall fitted with iron bars and a square grated opening on the roof. A pool of dark water had collected in the center of the room. The men huddled together in the deep cold, awaiting instructions. It was only when guards appeared with a thin blanket and a sheet of plastic that they understood that this was their new home.

The sun began to disappear. The men heard a pounding on the ceiling grate. They looked up.

A voice bellowed: "Sons of whores! Look down!"

The guard standing over the grate explained the rules here in Palmyra prison.

> **Never look a guard in the eye.**
>
> **Sleep at 6:00 p.m., wake at 6:00 a.m.**
>
> **No speaking or whispering after hours. No standing or using the bathroom after hours.**
>
> **Wear a blindfold or cover your face when sleeping.**
>
> **Sleeping on your back is forbidden.**
>
> **During waking hours, standing is forbidden unless called upon. Lying down is also forbidden.**

The next morning, around 9:00, Hasan heard sharp cries through the iron-grilled window. He did not dare move. The screams grew louder. He was able to pick out individual voices moaning in agony. They were his friends, the communists, separated from his group the day before.

There was a banging on the iron door. It swung open.

"Out, you shit-eaters!" a guard screamed. "Heads down! Don't look at us!"

They were corralled into the courtyard. Hasan and his fellow inmates stood with heads bowed and shoulders slumped. A group of guards stood nearby. The prisoners were ordered to squat and place their hands behind their heads. The Welcome Party.

A tire was produced. Hasan felt a dozen hands twisting and contorting his body, forcing his legs through the tire. Then his head was pushed through the same end of the tire, toward his legs. His spine felt as if it were about to snap, and a wave of nausea overtook him. His nose was buried between his knees. His dangling feet were tied to an iron rod to keep them from flailing. Guards then approached with metal cables as thick as garden hoses.

As the blows rained down on his feet, Hasan tried to keep count. The pain swallowed him like a deluge. He was hoarse from screaming. His legs were foreign objects that did not, could not, belong to him. Seventy, eighty blows, and still coming. He could not count anymore. He swayed in and out of consciousness.

When it was over, he was ordered back to the cell. He walked barefoot on the cold asphalt as if he were walking on shards of glass. In the cell, men were nursing their rotting feet. The smell of pus hung in the room. Hasan was shivering. He wanted nothing more than to lie down, but this was forbidden.

All night, Hasan could hear the footfall on the roof. When it approached, his muscles clenched. He lay on his side, perfectly still.

After some weeks, his body settled into a new rhythm. Everyone was up at 6:00, sitting on their rolled-up mattresses, fighting the urge to look at the ceiling. Breakfast was served between eight and ten. Obtaining these provisions was no easy matter. At the cell door, the guards delivered plastic containers of olives and tea to three cellmates, while the rest remained seated with their eyes averted. As the cellmates collected the allotments, they were whipped with the guards' metal cables. If anything was spilled, the guards descended on the transgressor with fury.

After breakfast came recess—what the guards called Breathing Time. The prisoners were led into the courtyard, where five or six were directed to clean the dried blood, the pieces of skin, and the vomit. They were also to tend to the wildflowers, which in the spring sprouted along the walls. Overnight, the guards roaming the roofs made note of infractions. Someone sleeping on his back, or whispering, or making stray eye contact, or dreaming. In the courtyard, the guards meted out collective punishment in proportion to the night's transgressions. They employed the tire, the bamboo stick, the lead water pipe, the studded metal belt used to fix tank wheels. On occasion, a prisoner was subjected to the German Chair, in which the body is looped through a chair's legs, allowing the operator to bend the subject backward, thereby straining, or breaking, the spine.

At lunch, the three volunteers retrieved plastic containers of bulgur and of cauliflower soup, though much was spilled over the course of the whippings. The containers consisted mostly of sand, and the cellmates spent lunchtime hunched over their meals, panning their bowls like prospectors for edible morsels.

At 2:00 p.m., the inmates gathered in the yard for inspection, during which they were not beaten. As they shuffled back to the cell, the day's torture was over. Hasan found that by 6:00 his eyes were heavy. He sank into his exhaustion. His days were spent in terror, and he realized that this terror was the real governor here, randomness its adjutant.

Eventually, Hasan and his fellow inmates decided that more effective organization was needed. They elected a cell leader, who was responsible for communicating with the guards. They settled on a system of rotating the food volunteers, so that the whippings were distributed evenly. Another prisoner was delegated to move through the cell, ensuring that voices were kept low. Most important, they erected a night-watch system: Each inmate took two-hour shifts to watch for the slipping of someone's blindfold or to stop a visit to the toilet. This was necessary because the number of possible violations multiplied at night. Since dreaming was banned, if the guards saw a prisoner tossing about, shouting from a night terror, or moaning in the ecstasy of old love, the entire cell would receive special treatment during the next day's Breathing Time. Snoring, too, was banned. For the unfortunate ones who could not help it, the inmates devised elaborate routines: The night watchman threw pebbles or, if he was nearby, shook the offender. All this took place in the fleeting moments when the guard was not overhead. The older men and the diabetics used the opportunity to urinate into bottles. It was then, too, that the inmates snuck in a quick shift of position, a yawn. These were moments of life, moments of victory.

Hasan took comfort in the laws of probability. During Breathing Time, he was beaten severely, on average, every third or fourth day. The other days, the worst blows fell, by chance alone, on other bodies.

One day, these laws intervened on his behalf once again, when he and his comrades were transferred to a cell packed with Muslim Brotherhood members. Now, instead of sharing the night watch, and the tire, with seven others, he could share these duties with fifty.

The demands of sheer survival forced the Brotherhood members to forget whatever prejudices they may have harbored against secular leftists. Here, there was no survival without cooperation.

Hasan's mattress was near the door. It was an ancient, rusted iron door, installed by the French during the colonial occupation. In two or three areas, cracks had spread, allowing him to peer out into the courtyard.

One day, some guards were huddled together. He heard ripples of laughter. Three volunteers were standing nearby, heads bowed, awaiting the containers of lunch. Suddenly, the sergeant turned to one of the adjutants and said, "No, really!" He had a huge grin on his face. He spread his legs, unzipped his pants, and began urinating into the soup container. It took ages for his bladder to empty. The adjutants were bursting into laughter. They ordered the volunteers to carry the meal to the cell.

Inside, only Hasan and the volunteers knew what had transpired. But they could not bring themselves to tell the others. If the soup was returned unfinished, it would bring a day's worth of brutality to the entire cell. The volunteers distributed lunch, which Hasan declined.

"Sir, oh sir!" The cell leader was banging on the door, calling for a guard. It was summer.

The guard appeared. "What is it, you dog?"

One of Hasan's cellmates had fallen ill, moaning day and night. The nightwatchman had been forced to muzzle him with a cloth. The doctors in the cell—the Brotherhood had many doctors—concluded he was suffering from kidney stones. But sickness was forbidden, so they had tried to avoid informing the guards until the cellmate's pain became unbearable.

"Sir, we have a sick man here."

The guard flashed fury. He ordered two volunteers to bring the patient into the courtyard. The ailing man was splayed out, moaning loudly. A group of guards descended on him and began kicking him violently. When they were finished, they ordered the volunteers to return him to the cell.

Within thirty minutes, the man yielded to his injuries. The cell leader was forced to bang on the door again.

"Oh sir! Please, oh sir!"

The guard returned.

"Sir, we have a deceased man in here."

"Who killed him?" The guard asked.

"We don't know, sir."

The body was removed that afternoon.

It was usually those over fifty, with various ailments like diabetes, who did not survive the daily beatings. But sometimes, younger inmates succumbed too, especially if they did not belong to political parties. It was as if strength of conviction conferred immunity from Breathing Time. For these people, the government periodically ordered their liquidation. Prison authorities erected nooses in one of the courtyards. As the condemned were strung up, they shouted out their names in the hopes that someone, somehow, would one day walk free and inform their family.

For some, the life "before," as they called it, was difficult to conjure. They struggled to visualize the faces of family members and old lovers. Once familiar city landmarks were lifted into abstraction, into a spare geometry of lines and curves and angles, without texture or depth. These inmates did not fare well.

For others, a girlfriend's clammy hand, the ripples of wrinkles on a mother's forehead, a father's baritone voice, were as vivid as the day they'd entered. Yet survival depended on learning how to manage these images, keeping them at bay when required. Most of the day was spent in a regimen of self-discipline, the inmates on guard for the slightest infraction—say, a stray glance to the ceiling—an incessant terror that did not permit the loss of focus, even for a moment.

Some inmates marshaled their energy to study the jailers. What was their motive in administering daily public torture? The inmates were already convicted, so there was no confession at stake. Some prisoners chalked it up to sheer unthinking brutality, but others were unconvinced. They wondered about a deeper purpose: If the regime is built on appearances, perhaps here, in the bodies and the cries of its victims, it becomes real. The word "real" can mean many things. In one sense, it is the opposite of imaginary, for we can touch, hold, and taste only that which is real. However, though Hasan could not hold in his hands the longing he felt for his mother, was it any less real? So there was a second sense of the word: When we say a dream is not real, we mean it does not exist independent of the mind of the dreamer—unlike, say, the Euphrates, which flows happily whether we're aware of it or not.

What can be more mind-dependent—and therefore more intimate—than physical pain? To expose that pain daily in the courtyard, to render it a spectacle, is to sever its intimate link with the sufferer. In this spectacle, every fold of the prisoner's soul—his hungers, his lusts, his agonies—attains an existence independent of him, and therefore becomes real, as real as the deserts of Palmyra, and therefore becomes, like everything else in this realm, the property of the regime. There was one order, one logic, whether it meant controlling the body politic, or controlling the soul.

"Cell leader! Cell leader!" The key was grating in the lock. Hasan stood. After the head of his cell had fallen ill from beatings, Hasan had been elected to the position. He stepped outside and presented himself.

The guards seemed excited. He was told to stand in the center of the courtyard and raise his head to the sky. He closed his eyes.

By the sound of it, the guards were having an argument. Suddenly, he felt an astonishing blow to the stomach. His air was gone, and he keeled over.

"No!" came the shouts. "That's pathetic!" someone cried. The guards were egging each other on.

"Stand up straight, you dog!" Hasan struggled to straighten his back. He kept his eyes shut. He felt another blow, near his sternum.

The guards had made a bet. Who was the most skilled in karate? To even the playing field, they restricted the competition to the flying knee kick. Highest kick wins. As the blows came, Hasan struggled to remain standing and keep his eyes closed.

He could not keep count. He found himself on the ground. He desperately tried to inhale, but his chest would not obey. A terrible fear overtook him. He had prepared himself for many things, but not to die like this, in the courtyard. The blows kept coming. But he could not stand. He tried to crawl toward the cell.

"Stand, you animal!"

He could not. In fury, or amusement, one of the guards landed a flying kick on Hasan's rear. He felt himself airborne, then tumbling.

He was without air, yet somehow panicking.

"Stand!"

If he did not stand, it would count as disobeying an order.

"Stand, you dog, or it's your last day!"

He summoned every ounce of strength, every spark of energy left in his failing tissues, and rose to his feet. He stumbled to the cell and collapsed.

Inside, he was aware of a cellmate's lips on his. The man was blowing, Hasan's chest slowly rising. Every movement, every breath, felt like a knife stab. Hands were lifting him, tying a bedsheet around his chest. He heard one of the doctors in the cell announce that his ribs were broken.

That night, in a silence disturbed only by the coming and going of boots on the roof, Hasan lay in excruciating pain. He again wondered if this was how he would die. The thought struck him as absurd, almost funny, that his years in the bowels of his country would end not with his execution, not with an act of heroic resistance, but as a human prop. He lay perfectly still, meditating on every muscle, every bone, until he drifted off.

The next morning, he could hardly move. Even attempting to speak brought agony. Producing himself for Breathing Time and the 2:00 p.m. inspection required the help of other inmates. He stood with head bowed, legs numb, chest throbbing. He was hardly aware of the adjutants, his energy instead concentrated on his feet. Every portion of his psyche was channeled into the project of remaining upright. Voices floated past him, screams. Sometimes his face felt the ground, and he could taste dust. Sometimes, the buildings around the courtyard careened to the right, to the left. He understood he was back in his cell, and he could feel hands on his face, grasping his shoulders, trying to keep his eyes from the roof, a thin plastic sheet for a blanket, the cold, the horrible cold, in this dead of summer.

For a long time, he did not speak. The enormity of the crime he'd committed against himself, against his family, by acting so foolishly as to believe in the political life, weighed terribly. The sensation of a wasted existence was impossible to keep down. Who was he to stand up to this system, when by doing so he'd condemned the only life he would ever live? With death here, waiting, stalking him on the rooftop, peering curiously through the skylight, how could regrets not surface, and with a mercilessness that could overpower even the most resolute mind?

For some years, Hasan felt he had not managed a single night's sleep. In the beginning, he was in the unrelenting grip of a terror that had monopolized the day's memories and all thoughts of tomorrow—a terror that had obliterated the present. Yet now, the injuries induced a strange effect. Unable to move, unable to speak, he sank into the netherworld even before six, even with the sun out, and slept more soundly than he had in a long time. By midnight or one, he was awake. At first, the prospect of lying perfectly still, listening only to the steps on the rooftop, generated despair. But as the days passed, he began to understand this nocturnal lapse, the long hours until sunrise, during which he heard only those footsteps and the desert winds against the walls, as hours existing outside the rhythm of torture.

He realized, for the first time, that he was prepared to die here. The sentences imposed by the court meant nothing. Many prisoners' release dates came and went, while they languished. He understood, more fully than before, that within these walls lay the world as it truly was. Everything beyond was grotesque fantasy.

The hours until sunrise therefore acquired a preciousness, even a sanctity. In these hours, in the darkness of his blindfold, he began to carry out long conversations with his mother. Now he was standing in the main lecture hall at the Humanities Faculty at Aleppo University, that great forum dug into the earth, the chairs in orbit around the stage. "The Use of Natural Imagery in Pre-Islamic Poetry." Now strolling through the chaos of the city center, under the canopy of the souk, past the minarets with their fluorescent tubes. Holding a hand, stealing a kiss. The warmth of sun on body. The cypress trees trembling in the wind.

Now, in the darkness, he began composing poetry, committing the verses to memory. As the months passed, he had conjured and revised an entire volume's worth—in the blackness of his blindfold, like Homer.

My features are the deserts of Manbij
My nature bears an Arab's sorrow
My heart sustains the love of Palmyra
In Muhammad's sacred course I follow

Quiet nights, perfect nights. Hasan wished they would never end. But end they did, and with the light came Breathing Time, for which he could still hardly stand, and by 6:00 p.m. he was again stiff as a log with fresh wounds. But it did not matter, because the dark came on once more, the winds buffeting the walls, the footsteps. He passed these evenings in intense meditation on the truth of this prison, which he realized was like a citadel against the raging fantasies of the world beyond, and one summer night, as Hasan was deep within himself, so deep he could not even hear an approaching footfall, he was shaken by a force greater than any physical blow: He was not here due to his errors and delusions. He recalled his Hegel: Caprice and untruth may be legion in history, but history is much greater than these defects. History in fact marches with a purpose—toward the Absolute Spirit. There were many routes to the Spirit, including art, religion, philosophy, and, yes, even politics. To his great surprise, Hasan suddenly saw his life's endeavors, the nights poring over philosophy texts, the months toiling on *Obsessions and Longings*, his pertinacious acts of resistance, in a new light. He understood himself as taking part in a journey grander and more vital than any he'd imagined. He realized that all his life, a life committed to the search for truth, he had been blinded by party ideology. To see the world as a party doctrine was to see nothing.

He suppressed with every ounce of strength the urge to shout, *I can see! I can see!* A flood of gratitude washed over him. He understood his imprisonment as, in some surprising way, necessary to liberate himself from rigid categories, from doctrines which could not speak to life, to the breathing, pulsing passion of the human soul. He was gripped by the idea of the Absolute Spirit, with the idea of an objective reality that is real, independent of our minds but somehow constituted by them, independent of our partisan whims, of the particular tyrannies we happen to live under. The Arab cause and the Palestinian struggle were still a part of him—no amount of suffering could eradicate that. But the old ideas of loyalty, the old ideas of what counted as truth—defined by political party—no longer meant anything to him. His new loyalty was to something greater, something unconquerable: to the march of reason itself. He knew then that his captors had failed, in some profound way, to conquer him. And Hasan wondered, for the first time, if this is what it meant to be free.

—✢ ✢—

By August 2001, Hasan had been in detention for fifteen years, five of them in Palmyra prison. During these years in the desert, prisoners had no contact with the outside world. Most families must have assumed their loved ones were lost forever.

That summer, he noticed some unusual activity: the sound of trucks, of gates opening and closing. Then one day the cell door opened, and instead of insults and curses, the inmates were told to assemble in the courtyard.

A voice commanded, "Raise your faces."

Hasan slowly raised his face.

"Open your eyes."

Chest pounding, he opened his eyes. An officer—a colonel—was standing before them, flanked by adjutants. Never in five years had he looked up to see the face of a jailer.

The colonel was perorating on loyalty and patriotism, on the vast international conspiracy arrayed against Syria. But Hasan was gaping at the prison, which he now saw whole for the first time. The courtyard, the cement walls, the rings of concertina wire, the Syrian flags, the posters of the Leader.

"We believe in fairness and justice," the officer concluded, "so I want to know, did anyone bother you during your stay? Did anyone trouble you?"

No one said a word.

The metal portcullis opened, and the inmates were herded into the cargo hold of a truck that looked like it was meant to ferry refrigerated meat. The truck began to move, and as they jounced along, Hasan allowed himself to feel a tinge of hope.

That evening, they found themselves in Sednaya prison, near Damascus. For a few months, they were penned together in a large cell—the conditions here felt like a luxury hotel compared to Palmyra—until one day Hasan was removed and placed in a small cell without windows or light. As his eyes grew accustomed to the dark, he could make out the contours of the room—the mattress, the toilet—and he realized he was alone. Hasan sank into a deep depression. After a few days, the door opened, and he was dragged into the hallway, in the blinding light, and led to an officer. A second prisoner was also there. The officer gave each of them 600 liras. The pair were then conducted through a labyrinth of hallways, up and down stairs, until they suddenly found themselves outside, in front of the main gate. Traffic was roaring.

Hasan and the other prisoner stared dumbly at the passing cars.

A guard yelled that no one was allowed to linger here.

"Brother," Hasan called, "we spent fifteen years in prison. I don't know where to go—I don't know where I am."

The guard, astonished, called his colleagues over. They stared at the two as if they had risen from the dead. In the frigid air, Hasan was wearing a torn shirt, faded sweats, and sandals. The guard, taking pity, called a taxi.

Hasan asked the driver to take them to the bus station. When they arrived, Hasan paid and received a 25-lira coin in change. He had never seen a coin of this denomination before, holding it up in wonder. "This is a 25-lira coin?"

"What are you, a caveman?" the driver asked.

We are cavemen, Hasan thought. *If you only knew.*

The bus to Aleppo was scheduled to depart at 11:00 p.m. He purchased a pack of cheap cigarettes, lit one, and inhaled deeply. It was his first cigarette in years, and he drank it in greedily.

On the bus, Hasan could hardly look out the window. He imagined himself knocking on the teal gate, a stranger opening, saying, *They moved out years ago*. No, his mother would open, clasping her mouth, shaking. She would look older, but not too old. He realized he was anxious, terribly anxious, more so than he'd ever been in Palmyra. He desperately needed another smoke, though it was forbidden onboard. They sailed down the highway, passing the dark shapes of villages and mountains.

They stopped at a rest area, under floodlights, and the other prisoner wanted to buy sandwiches, but Hasan was worried about running out of money, so they only drank tea. Then they were back on the highway. Billboards had sprung up like weeds. Hasan found he could not focus on this bizarre new mania for advertisement. He worried about running out of cigarettes.

It was 4:00 a.m. when they pulled into the Aleppo bus station. Another taxi, then another bus. Hasan sat in the cramped vehicle with his knees near his chest. He saw himself knocking on the teal gate, his mother opening the door, clasping her mouth, then turning away, furious. She'd say it was all his doing, his addiction to dogmas, his recklessness—it was he who had rejected her, rejected all of them.

He looked out the window at fifteen years of development, fifteen years of weddings and funerals—but were they real? No, the real world was behind him in the desert. This was the land of make-believe. He spotted the Book Roundabout, with its giant sculpture of an open hardback, marking the western verges of his home city. The sun had not yet risen over Manbij's minarets and concrete apartment blocks. The bus arrived downtown at Central Square. He was walking down Main Street, the shops still closed, only a few people milling about. There were new multistory buildings everywhere, new signage. But the streets themselves, thank God, were right where he remembered them. He was walking briskly in his sandals, almost running. He would have flown if he could. A faint pink dawn was bathing the concrete blocks. He turned right, then left. When he raised his hand to the teal gate, he was almost too weak to knock. When he did, there was no answer.

He knocked and knocked, and then, after some time, the door opened. It was his brother, who yawned and looked annoyed. Then he froze. His mouth was mouth agape.

"Well," Hasan said, "aren't you going to say something?"

His brother let out a cry, and they hugged and kissed. Hasan entered to find various family members emerging from their rooms, in pajamas. There were teenagers in the house—Hasan's nieces and nephews, whom he'd never met. His sister-in-law emerged. The cries and shouts of joy could be heard from the street. Hasan was laughing at the idea of this new family, these giants who were nearly adults. One of his nieces clasped his hand, grinning, and said, "I've heard so much about you." There were cousins visiting, relatives of his sister-in-law, and they filled the living room. Hasan looked right and left. He told his niece, "Wake up your grandmother." Her smile vanished, and her eyes reddened. At that moment, Hasan knew that his mother was gone.

In this working-class neighborhood densely packed with houses, the clamor attracted curious neighbors. Within fifteen minutes, the house was overflowing. People were shaking his hand, asking, "Do you remember me?" It was as if he'd awoken from a long slumber. He excused himself to shower. It was only in the bathroom, naked, pouring hot water over his head, that he began to weep, and he cried for himself, for his mother, for his country, for all those souls still entombed in those citadels, for everything lost, everything learned. For a long time, his tears would not stop.

Back in the living room, the neighbors told stories of their youth. They told Hasan that though they could not have asked after him, they in fact had never forgotten.

| THREE |

Oss!

I

One afternoon, when Abdul Qader Oseb was seven, his father stood him in front of a stall on a crowded street in Manbij. The size of a trash bin, the stall was jury-rigged with wood from old shipping crates. A set of planks formed the base and the shafts, atop which rested a small lipped platform. In another time and place, it could have functioned as a lectern. It was the family's most valuable possession.

"This will be yours one day," his father said.

The stall sold an assortment of whistles and various brands of bubble gum, mostly to children on their way to school. Sometimes, when the children didn't have cash, Abdul Qader's father would let them trade a hardboiled egg or a piece of pickled *makdous* for a stick of stone-hard gum.

Abdul Qader worked the shop every day after school. To him and his father, the stall was no mere wooden edifice; it was a philosophy. Abdul Qader was born in 1973 to a small Kurdish family that lived in Sarab, a hamlet lying just beyond the reaches of Manbij. Sarab was a patchwork of tiny plots, thatched-roof cottages, and barns built of rotting wood. Dirt paths wended around the cottages. But by the late 1970s, these dirt paths were paved with macadam, and Sarab became a proper city neighborhood. It was then that Abdul Qader's father gave up his plow and opened the roadside stall.

The philosophy of Sarab was *perpetual motion*. Life moves with a force of its own, like a self-propelling engine—to a more spacious shop, a larger family, a first car, a second floor of a house, a degree, grandchildren, and ultimately, in the smiles of those grandchildren, the possibility of eternity. You could see the principle of perpetual motion at work everywhere: The municipality opened Sarab Park, with stately cedars and winding trails, and then 16th of October High School, the neighborhood's first secondary school. Blocks of affordable housing went up, drawing families from the countryside. Abdul Qader's family built a home behind the shop: three narrow cinderblock rooms, the walls half painted, half coated in lime. It was the biggest house Abdul Qader had ever seen.

The summer of Abdul Qader's eighth year, he began showing up at the gates of a nearby ice factory. He collected slabs of ice and hauled them across town to the sheep bazaar on Jazeera Road. For two liras, he sold a cup of ice water to livestock traders. Authorities soon noticed the sinewy Kurdish boy who could carry his own weight in ice. He was offered a job at the government's cement factory, helping load bags of cement after school. He returned home after dusk, muscles burning, filmed in sweat, and gave the day's earnings to his father. Soon, three cinderblock walls replaced the wooden stall.

One day his father presented him with an old tin biscuit box. "Every day," he told the boy, "I want you to put a little away."

For years this little nest egg went untouched, while Abdul Qader grew into a hulking youth, the tallest boy in the neighborhood. Then, when he was thirteen, the Abu Naim Cinema opened its doors in a two-story pink building on Main Street. It was Manbij's first theater, and Abdul Qader had never seen a film before. After much handwringing, he dipped into his savings and purchased a ticket for *Enter the Dragon*. As Bruce Lee pirouetted on the big screen, soaring through the air, landing dropkicks, Abdul Qader was transfixed. His heart was awakened by how this slightest of men could flip adversaries twice his size and win the adoration of the entire planet. And was not this notion of human *will*, this sheer force of mind, at the heart of perpetual motion?

The trouble was, the art of karate was completely unknown in Manbij. When Abdul Qader tried to explain what he'd seen to his father, the old man couldn't stop laughing. Eventually, Abdul Qader located the only person in the city trained in the sport, a certain Mr. Fuaz, who took a liking to the boy and offered to instruct him for free. In the afternoons, the top floor of a Sarab cement warehouse became a dojo. In the evenings, Abdul Qader practiced in the alleyway next to his house, holding kata starting point, forming knife hand. Neighbors were mystified by Abdul Qader's grunts and stances. One frigid, rainy night, a neighbor awoke to shouts from the alley. He went outside to find Abdul Qader in a T-shirt, performing perplexing thrusts. "Don't you get cold?" he asked. Abdul Qader replied, "Someone like *you* gets cold. *My* mind is in control."

Down the street was the Coffeepot Roundabout, named for its sculpture of a tulip-shaped Arabic coffeepot. Most nights, boys crouched along the curb, hawking counterfeit cigarettes. Abdul Qader often joined them. Later, when they grew to become fathers, they would, in the Arab style, be addressed by the name of their first-born. The father of Issa would become Abu Issa; the father of Aisha, Abu Aisha. Abdul Qader was only thirteen, but he'd already birthed something new in the streets of Sarab. As news of his alleyway exploits spread—splitting wood with his bare hands, slicing and dicing invisible demons—he became known as the father of *Oss!*, that all-purpose karate interjection shouted when bowing, presenting oneself to a sensei, or flipping over an opponent. He was Abu al-Os or, in the local patois, Abel Os. After a while, people had difficulty recalling his real name.

That suited Abel Os just fine. He spent his days hauling 50-kilogram bags of cement, and his nights practicing *tai sabaki* in the dark. This left little time for books, so when he failed the ninth grade, he dropped out and worked full-time. Abel Os labored at the shop alongside his father, watching his old man put in fifteen-hour days, but the world was beginning to look different thanks to Bruce Lee's idea of *will*. He told his father, "We can do better than candy."

Abel Os imagined iron shutters, shelving, a glass-door refrigerator, and sections for produce, sweets, and stationery. He imagined a *minimarket*, a word he'd just learned from the radio. But Sarab had ceased expanding. There was no new construction, and wild grasses flourished on the neighborhood's outskirts. One day, working behind the counter, Abel Os suggested to his father that they take a loan to add a second room to the shop—which would require just two cinderblock walls and a bump in rent to the landowner. His father stopped what he was doing and gripped his son's shoulders. "Promise me," he said, "you will always be your own man." Abel Os wasn't sure what he meant, but he saw in his eyes a look that, many years later, he understood as fear. "I promise, Baba," he said.

Still, in the evenings, when Abel Os cleared the candy from the stall, packing it in a crate to carry home, he could not shake the vision of glass counters and shelves. But the cement factory hardly paid enough. His tin box hadn't grown much heavier. So, at age fifteen, Abel Os left home to wander the country, looking for work.

Abel Os drifted from muster zone to farmhouse to factory, from the industrial suburbs of Aleppo to the remote eastern scrublands. He learned to mix, mold, cure, and cube to make cinderblocks. He learned to thresh and winnow grain. He lived in shantytowns and farmhouses. Once, a group of workers were relaxing after a shift when the landlady rushed in: "Your friend Abel Os—he's lost his mind!"

The men looked at each other.

"He's in the backyard. He's screaming!" she cried.

They arrived to find Abel Os covered in sweat, with a look of intense focus, punching the wall. The men burst into laughter. "Ma'am, this is a sport," one said. "We call this, in the city, karate."

In Damascus, he lived in a workhouse, six narrow rooms surrounding a courtyard, five workers sleeping in each. All thirty men shared a hole-in-the-ground toilet, which had been clogged for months. No air-conditioning, no shower. The workers returned home bruised, beaten by overseers. Yet Abel Os was fixed on his vision. He visited the Workers Club, spending time not out front amid the clink of coffee cups but in the back, on a blue mat, at a punching bag. A television played Turkish soaps, and when he pictured his minimarket, he could see the name of one of the shows burnished in a sign across the entrance: Tear of Roses.

Eventually, Abel Os was called up to do military service. On the snowy heights of Mount Hermon, he volunteered to lead physical training of the 38th Brigade conscripts, jogging them through the winding trails alongside the karst cliffs. Men vomited and fainted. Abel Os would carry them on his back. They spent nights huddled around the propane heater, cut off from the villages below. It was springtime when he descended, returned to the barracks, and read the message awaiting him: His father was dead.

When Abel Os had left home seven years earlier, he'd been a taut, fibrous youth, possessing a body of fluid ease, without flaws. He returned nicked and scarred, his fingers misshapen by fractures. But now, at age twenty-two, he towered over his friends. His hands could swallow yours whole in a handshake, and his biceps, massive cylinders, could fell you in a single blow. Yet his deep brown eyes communicated warmth; they were eyes that abhorred violence, and saw in all things the glint of possibility. As he stood in front of his father's shop, which still consisted of three cinderblock walls and a wooden lectern, and into which a human life—his father's life—had been poured, he resolved to devote himself. He told his grieving mother, "We're going to turn this place into something."

He converted seven years' worth of savings into pull-down iron shutters, two additional cinderblock walls for a second room, a generator, and a wooden sign that read Tear of Roses. He installed a brand-new glass-door refrigerator. Every morning, before opening, he wiped the glass down. Some nights, he left the machine plugged in, and it could be seen down the block, a glowing testament to the principle of perpetual motion.

Tear of Roses was no mere stall now but a proper emporium. The shelves were crammed with bottles of Sinalco Cola, Crush Orange Soda, and Khazne Fruit drink, spiral-bound notebooks bearing images of unicorns and princesses, colored pens, and glossy photos of Syrian and Turkish actors. Abel Os sold cigarettes—not the knockoff Syrian brands available at the Coffeepot Roundabout, which tasted like sawdust, but knockoff Marlboro Reds, which tasted like foreign sawdust. The shop attracted a steady crowd. A pot of *juz muz* was usually simmering on the Primus, its eggs and tomatoes bubbling for visitors. Men played cards on an overturned carton out front.

Abel Os discovered he had a talent for solving problems. When a brawl broke out nearby, resulting in a smashed window and a torn poster of the president, and the perpetrators, all teenagers, were hauled to the police station, it was Abel Os who bore witness to the fact that the intent was merely to break the glass, not harm the poster. When city toughs catcalled women, he chased after them. Now, at the slightest neighborhood tension, people would say, "Let's see what Abel Os thinks." Anyone with a sad tale and an open palm could find succor at Tear of Roses, where a sympathetic Abel Os would extend credit. Sometimes it seemed half the neighborhood owed the shop money. But he never had the heart to call in the debts. If the people could've had their way, they would have named Abel Os mayor of Sarab. They began to call him "mukhtar," as in the old days, when village headmen solved community squabbles.

At night, he unrolled the shutters and walked around back, where his house, built by his father's hands, stood in the shadows. It was a home that smelled of lime and dust, a home where shampoo was diluted with water to make it last longer. The family—Abel Os, his mother, his two brothers and their wives and children—were confined to two rooms. They had a single bed, which they dragged into the courtyard on summer nights, taking turns drifting off under the stars. The family needed a second floor, but that meant turning more sales at Tear of Roses. To attract new customers, Abel Os envisioned adding an additional wing, with overhead lights reflecting off ceramic floors. The air would be cool and crisp, a cash register gracing the checkout. The supermarket would look out onto the tree-lined streets of Sarab, to its parks and mosques and schools. While Abel Os was working the punching bag in the afternoon, while he was lying in the courtyard at night, he conjured plans, calculating and recalculating costs. Yet what he did not know, what he could not have known, was that beneath Sarab's tableau lay a hidden realm, the true order of the land, and that no one—even someone as beloved as he—was exempt from its rules.

II

It was June 10, 2000. On television, the anchor struggled to compose himself. "Today, oh brothers! Today we lost a brother, comrade, friend, leader, teacher. Today is the day of sadness and resentment in every house, every school, every university, every factory, every farm and store, in each house and in each heart and in each man and woman and child. It was a piece of our heart that left us. His legacy and achievements, his thinking and behavior, will remain like a planet that will lighten not only the path of this generation but the generations to come."

Billboards were covered in black tarp. On the rooftops, women ululated and sobbed, holding each other and looking to the sky. Abel Os felt an ache in his chest, a loss so deep he could not find words. He closed Tear of Roses, and that night, for the first time in years, he did not hold kata starting point in the alleyway.

Thirty years was a lifetime—Hafez al-Assad was the only leader Abel Os had ever known. His death felt like the passing of a nation, a blow to the collective will that had lifted people from the baking dirt fields to the cool cement cubes of modern life. Under Assad's watch, Manbij had transformed from a cluster of mud houses to a full-blown metropolis, with gushing fountains and towering public schools and free clinics.

The basic theory of Assad's Syria was *shelter* from the terrible caprice of life—a sudden squall ruining a farm, a worrying mass appearing on an X-ray. These may be acts of providence, but the Baathists rejected the idea that the invisible hand of the market should determine whether a farm survived or a patient underwent an operation. So *shelter* was, to be precise, refuge from the vicissitudes of the free market. It was the government's job to protect people from the market, which meant that the government kept the lights on and mouths fed. And it could not be denied that what the Baathists had achieved—in an impoverished country emerging from decades of colonialism and centuries of feudalism—was nothing short of a miracle.

Millions of peasants became teachers and civil servants after the Baath Party broke up the great feudal estates and created a modern state bureaucracy—nearly a third of Syrians had public sector jobs. The government guaranteed employment to university graduates in the field of education. It provided free health care to the poor and cheap loans to farmers. Thousands of people lined up every morning at Manbij's bakeries for state-subsidized bread. Motorists filled their vehicles at the pump at state-subsidized prices. Housewives purchased cooking gas at low cost due to government price controls. Millions of people, like Abel Os's father, had been rescued from a hand-to-mouth existence. What he had, he owed to the Leader.

To be sure, life under the Baathists meant enduring the corruption that infected all echelons of government. Even the simplest tasks, like registering Tear of Roses, required a bribe. There was *wasta*, connections, that magic ingredient required to land the right job or rent the right apartment. But to Abel Os, these were not the fault of the Leader but of petty bureaucrats who, bereft of acumen or talent, lorded over their mini fiefdoms to exact misery on hard-working, honest people. Abel Os suffered indignities gladly because of the sheer power of perpetual motion that had ordered his life. After all, the opportunities were there for those who sought them. So as the crowd gathered around the shop each night, mourning their nation's orphanhood, they also discussed the possibility that life would march on, perhaps even hastening its step, through the beneficence of the new leader.

On referendum day, lines spilled out of 16th of October High School in Sarab. A man at the desk kept a bodkin, which he used to prick the finger of each voter, so that citizens could swear an oath to the new president—the son of the old president—in blood. Speaking to "parliament," the handpicked assembly of elites, Bashar al-Assad hinted at reform. Officials chanted, "With our blood, with our souls, we sacrifice for you, oh Bashar!"

There was talk of elections, of greater openness. Hafez al-Assad had grown up in a mountain hovel: "I am first and last a farmer, a son of a farmer," he had said. "The threshing floors of plantations are equal in my view to all the palaces of this land." Bashar, on the other hand, was an ophthalmologist—a specialty he was drawn to, he said, "because it's almost never an emergency, and there is very little blood." He'd trained at the Western Eye Hospital in London. His wife, Asma, grew up in West London, where she'd been known as Emma. She worked at an investment bank, though Abel Os wasn't sure what that was or what she did there.

Longtime dissidents circulated petitions hoping to crack open the door to political reform; coffeehouses attracted poets and artists. Abel Os was not part of this world, he hardly knew of it, but he could sense opportunity as well as anyone. When the government held a rally in Manbij to celebrate the new president, Abel Os was out front, waving the red-white-and-black Syrian standard, shouting Baath Party slogans.

A new mood gripped the streets of Manbij. The municipality was expanding 16th of October Street, where Tear of Roses was situated, adding a median—which meant more traffic, more sales. The government had previously restricted imports to cultivate local brands but now was flinging open the gates of international commerce. Abel Os replaced Khazne Fruit drink with foreign delicacies like Coca-Cola and Red Bull. He visited Aleppo just to get a feel for these fresh winds. On the freeway, he spotted a billboard that showed a smiling blond woman with a message: A NEW SYRIA IS COMING.

A new Syria. Abel Os liked the sound of that.

The truth was, New Syria could not be built in a day: Bashar al-Assad had inherited a dinosaur of an economy. To fund its social programs, his father's government had relied on aid from the Soviet Union. When the USSR collapsed, Damascus had instead pinned its hopes on oil and gas because the badlands out east, beyond the Euphrates, were shot through with untapped reserves. The derricks began working nonstop, and, for a fevered moment, officials nursed the dream of turning Syria into the next Saudi Arabia. But global oil prices were sluggish, and Syria soon found itself out of options at the worst possible moment. The population was multiplying, which meant more graduates expecting civil service jobs, more farmers expecting a guaranteed income. Bashar and his ministers had been saddled with a bloated bureaucracy responsible for subsidizing pretty much everything you'd need to stay alive—but with no palatable way to pay for it. The new authorities proposed only one solution: cut, cut, cut.

This was, of course, not only a Syrian story. In one country after the next, politicians embraced austerity. The wave of shrinking government crested in the West in the 1970s and 1980s, then crashed on the shores of the Middle East in the 1990s. Arab dictators dismantled social programs, hacked at entitlements, and privatized industries. In Syria, the most important subsidy to go was fuel, which pushed prices of consumer goods skyward. Cement—crucial for building homes for the poor—doubled in cost, as did animal feed, pesticides, and heating oil. Unemployment benefits vanished.

This new way of life—based on the credo of self-reliance—called for new rules. They came in the form of edicts promulgated in presidential speeches, or read by mannequin-like anchors on the evening news, or announced in tiny font in the back pages of the state-run dailies, *Al-Baath* and *October*:

> DECREE NO. 83, 2000: All state-owned farms are hereby privatized.
> LAW NO. 28, 2001: Private banks are now free to operate.
> DECREE NO. 36, 2001: For-profit universities are authorized to open.

DECREE NO. 48, 2004: Private insurance companies are now permitted.

DECREE NO. 55, 2006: The Damascus Stock Exchange is hereby established.

In all, the government issued some 1,000 new laws and decrees to liberalize the economy. It inked an agreement with neighbors to form the Greater Arab Free Trade Area and negotiated deals with the European Union and Turkey. In short order, supermarket shelves were choked with Chinese sneakers and Turkish sweatpants and Bangladeshi jerseys. For some, life was now Costa Coffee, art galleries, and English lessons at the British Council. Eager to attract foreign investment, the government hired American firms like the Massachusetts-based Monitor Group to burnish its image abroad. Asma al-Assad enlisted the services of Brown Lloyd James, a PR firm with an office in Washington, who placed a profile of the First Lady in *Vogue*:

> Asma al-Assad is glamorous, young, and very chic—the freshest and most magnetic of First Ladies. Her style is not the couture-and-bling dazzle of Middle Eastern power but a deliberate lack of adornment. She's a rare combination: a thin, long-limbed beauty with a trained analytic mind who dresses with cunning understatement.... No watch, no jewelry apart from Chanel agates around her neck, not even a wedding ring, but fingernails lacquered a dark blue-green.

The *Huffington Post* concurred:

> We couldn't help but notice the Syrian beauty either. In a region where the women love to cake on their make-up, it is very refreshing to see the wife of President Bashar al-Assad with very little on....
>
> We also noticed her love for Christian Louboutin platforms, sunglasses, and her signature wavy hair.

That unadorned face, that Diana of the Orient, was plastered on billboards outside Manbij, proclaiming the arrival of New Syria to motorists and shepherds alike.

The real mark of this New Syria was *opportunity*. The empty lot announcing the site of Manbij's first four-star hotel. The wedding halls sprouting on

Jazeera Road. The thicket of satellite dishes covering rooftops downtown. The apartment buildings going up on Rabta Street, with their cantilevered balconies and Western toilets, their ceramic floors. And if you were lying outdoors on a summer night on 16th of October Street, breathing in the dust kicked up by motorcycles, ingesting the fumes of the open gutter outside, perhaps you too would look to the high-rises on Rabta Street, their air conditioners hanging from the windows, and allow yourself to believe. You too might throw caution to the wind, maybe even break a few promises to yourself, or tell a white lie or two, because you believe, according to the principle of perpetual motion, that things have a way of working themselves out.

III

Abel Os went to three, four, five different wholesale suppliers, but the answer was always the same. Prices were jumping for onions, tomatoes, and cooking oil. Pretty much everything at Tear of Roses was marked up. The culprit was the vanished fuel subsidy. After it had been slashed as part of the reforms, filling the tank cost three times as much—which meant three times as much to ferry produce. Business was down. Many Sarab residents were in arrears on the shop's books—widows, university students, down-on-their-luck neighbors—and Abel Os could not bring himself to call in their debt.

One afternoon, he stood in front of a white stone building. He went in and approached the teller window. He explained his predicament.

"Who's your guarantor?" the teller asked.

Abel Os admitted he had none.

The teller wrote a figure on a scrap of paper and pressed it against the glass. It was the income he'd need to be eligible for a bank loan. Abel Os had never seen such a sum in his life. He apologized to the teller and left.

Whenever Abel Os wrote off his neighbors' debts, his brother Shukri shouted that Abel Os had no business sense, that in his hands the shop would fall to ruin. He made Abel Os swear he'd never extend credit to neighbors again. And for a few months, Tear of Roses again operated in the black. But prices kept creeping up. Traffic was sparser than ever. Sometimes it felt as if half of Sarab had abandoned Manbij for Lebanon or Jordan. One day, Abel Os was informed that the landlord was upping the rent. He proposed to Shukri that they borrow from private lenders if a bank loan was impossible. Shukri exploded.

"They are thieves! They will eat you alive," he bellowed.

Abel Os placed his brother at the till and took a job at Heroes Dojo, which had just opened. Under the pasty white lights, he dropped young bodies to the blue mat. He led them running barefoot through the streets of Sarab in the freezing rain. His co-trainer was a stout, open-faced ceramics trader with carefully parted hair named Anas Sheikh Weiss. He lived in a large house near Rabta Street, and people said his family could have bought half of Manbij if they desired. Where Abel Os relied on strength, Anas was a marvel of speed and agility. The pair became inseparable, wearing matching shirts, playing cards under the lamplight, falling asleep in each other's homes. Abel Os danced at Anas's wedding. There were professional singers, white tablecloths, Bird's Nest pastries, and cornucopias of banana, watermelon, and coconut for every guest. Abel Os put his thick arms around Anas and told a camcorder, "This man is my brother."

The wedding had awoken Abel Os. Some evenings, after practicing kata in the alley, he stared at the squat cinderblock structure that housed his family, and at the open air where there should have been a second floor. He was embarrassed to raise the subject with his mother.

Girls streamed past Tear of Roses every afternoon. When they stopped to buy a Coke or a notebook, Abel Os's muscles clenched and his throat dried up. Yet there was little he could do, because Tear of Roses was again in the red. And due to cuts in fuel subsidies, construction costs were spiraling. As the government privatized state-owned lands and invited foreign capital to invest, rents were soaring, rising some 300 percent in 2007 alone. What kind of life could he offer a woman?

The idea arose within him one day like a shameful urge. He continued his routine: a breakfast of tea and bread with his mother, a full day at Tear of Roses and Heroes Dojo, the kata in the alley, the quiet family dinners, day after day, all while the tin biscuit box's contents went unchanged.

He'd recently befriended a merchant from Aleppo who could arrange for Tear of Roses to offer Turkish wares at below-market prices. He'd be the first to bring this splash of modernity to the streets of Sarab. Tear of Roses then would attract folks not just from around Sarab but from all of Manbij. He carried out fevered debates with himself, studying the pros and cons, but as he did, he knew what he'd choose. After closing the shop one evening, he headed for the Cardamom Market.

On the northwest edge of town, the Cardamom Market, despite its name, was the city's principal wholesale bazaar. It was part warehouse, part agora. But nestled between the pyramids of cantaloupes, mounds of eggplants, and the Bedouin with their flocks of sheep was a new type of storefront. Abel Os entered.

He sat face-to-face with a man in a leather jacket. The city was now teeming with these moneymen, operating everywhere from the grimy backrooms of mechanic shops to air-conditioned top floors of strip malls. The man took Abel Os's signature and explained the system. Islam forbids interest-bearing loans, but the enterprising traders of Manbij had discovered a workaround. He'd sell Abel Os a "motorcycle" for 70,000 liras—a motorcycle that didn't actually exist. ("Imagine it's right there," he said, pointing to an empty corner.) Abel Os, of course, owned no such sum, so the seller wrote a promissory note for the amount. The seller would then buy back the "motorcycle" on the spot for, say, 30,000 liras. Cash in hand, Abel Os still owed the 70,000 liras, meaning he effectively owed thirty grand in principal and, with a wink and a nod, forty grand in interest.

Abel Os stood with Shukri, overlooking a weedy field at the end of 16th of October Street.

"This is yours," Abel Os told him.

Shukri asked again, "But how could you afford it?"

Six months later, Shukri and his wife and children moved into a squat one-story home that had been built on the lot. Abel Os still had not told them he'd used the loan from the motorcycle men to purchase the property. With Shukri gone, only his younger brother Muhammad's family and his mother lived in the house with Abel Os. He slept, for the first time in his life, in a room of his own.

Within weeks, Abel Os was back at the Cardamom Market. Another motorcycle was added to his name. Two more cinderblock walls went up at Tear of Roses. Crates of cabbages and sprouts materialized. Pepsi, Mars bars. It was a thing of beauty—three adjacent rooms with roll-up iron shutters. Tear of Roses, finally keeping pace with rising costs, was in the black again.

Now, at last, he was ready to raise the question of marriage with his mother. She found him a kind-eyed girl from the neighborhood. Mana was soft-spoken, and she teared up at any mention of savagery, at cruelty to animals. She was, Abel Os thought, a graceful being, almost too fragile to hold, so perfect he worried incessantly about failing her. His father would've been proud, so he decided the wedding should be grand enough to honor his memory. Three more motorcycles were added to his name. Paper cups were put out, along with bouquets of lilies and tulips. A disco ball hung overhead. Abel Os, in his ill-fitting dress shirt, swung his feet to a drum. Shukri and his karate friend Anas—in his checkered tie and polished shoes—clapped along. It felt as if all of Sarab were present, swaying and clapping, toasting their mukhtar and shouting Shabash! Abel Os wished his father could see him now, could see what he'd built with his own two hands.

But it was not long before the calls began.

"Abel Os, this is the third month in a row," said the voice.

"Sir, I know. I swear on my mother."

"Abel Os," said another caller. "Do you know the story of Fahim?" Fahim lived near Sarab Park, was in arrears, and had been put in prison.

At night, Abel Os lay in bed, ruminating. Mana asked, "Why won't you tell me what's wrong?"

Sometimes he would rise and retreat to the alley behind the house. *Jab* (ten to a side). *Jab and reverse* (ten to a side). *Punch, reverse punch, block.* He grunted. When nerves tightened, he was not one to examine his moods. Deliverance, he told himself, came only through sweat on the brow. He began keeping Tear of Roses open until midnight or later, catching whatever pedestrians he could. Long after 16th of October Street went dark, Tear of Roses glowed like an orb.

One afternoon a sedan with tinted windows rolled to a stop. The vehicle simply idled in front of the shop.

"What's going on?" a friend asked Abel Os.

"Nothing. Just ignore it."

That evening, Abel Os located a new moneylender at the Salal covered market. Two more "motorcycles" went under his name, the first of which he used to pay off the man in the sedan. The second, he reasoned, would finance Muhammad's wedding.

Abel Os unplugged the phone in his shop and placed it in a drawer at home. He found himself thinking of the factory floor in Damascus, the fluorescent lights, the rafters, the whistle of the steam pipes. His mind wandered to the fields, where he had loaded cotton under a blazing sun. Mana kept prodding him. "You know I can help. Just talk to me." But Abel Os kept quiet.

One afternoon, two men appeared at the shop with a bag. They began to help themselves to cigarettes and notebooks. They were walking out with hundreds of liras' worth of goods when Abel Os rushed over. But he recognized them. "It's okay," he said quietly to his brother. "I know them."

At night, Abel Os sat punching figures into his calculator, hoping a new arithmetic would reveal itself.

The home phone rang. "Just give me three days, chief. I swear," said Abel Os. "I'll have it on the fifth."

The voice responded, "I think it will be better if you send the money today."

"Please," he said weakly.

"Listen," the man growled. "Today, or we'll make you disappear behind the sun. We're from the Shiyuki family. If you don't know about us, ask around."

He hung up.

Mana asked, "Who was it?"

"Just my friend. It's nothing."

The dark had come on. Abel Os opened the tin box where he kept his life savings. He counted 1,000 Syrian liras, about $18. Five thousand short. He visited Gulay, a pushcart vendor, who was his oldest friend in the world. Gulay kept a wad of Syrian banknotes under the rug of his one-room house—his life earnings, which he hoped to augment with a loan of his own to trade his pushcart in for a larger model. But that day was far off, because Gulay was steeped in debt paying off his current cart. Still, he was not one to turn down a friend, so he unrolled the wad and placed 4,000 liras into Abel Os's giant hands.

The next day, Abel Os stood in downtown Manbij outside a pink building—which years earlier had housed the movie theater but now featured a huge sign over the second-floor veranda: SHIYUKI WHOLESALE. Inside, he found a teenage boy, the son of the owner. Abel Os stood quietly in the corner as the boy traced his finger down the ledger: "5,600 liras."

"My lord, the amount was 5,000 liras."

"There's the fee for our trouble."

"Sir," Abel Os said, "give me some time, please."

The boy said he was calling his boss. "Wait outside."

Abel Os stepped outside, blinking under the harsh sun. Instead of waiting, he crossed the street. Main Street would have been thronged with crowds, with fruit vendors and hummus carts, women holding up fabric at the haberdasheries, orphans knocking on passenger-side windows. Abel Os decided to slip in among the crowd, and did not dare look back. Now he was running, across the wadi, through the stands of pine in Sarab Park.

He slept at a friend's house that night, but the next evening, unable to contain himself, he stole back to Tear of Roses. The streetlights were out, the road deserted. Looking in the tin biscuit box, he counted only 200 liras, from the shop's earnings that day. His heart sank. He was rolling down the shutters, wondering where to spend the night, when he came face-to-face with four shadows that, after a moment, revealed themselves to be the police.

Manbij's sole police station lay in Security Square, a cluster of facilities that included the government-run Youth Center and the Cultural Center and a structure crowned in barbed-wire that housed the Directorate of Criminal Intelligence and law enforcement headquarters. Policemen were dozing in plastic chairs, while Abel Os stood in the corner. He understood not to speak unless spoken to, so he remained standing for hours. At some point an adjutant appeared, sized him up, and said, "You better hope Lieutenant Maymati is asleep." 1st Lt. Maymati was the chief of police.

"Why, sir?"

The adjutant began to laugh, stirring the other policemen.

Abel Os felt the powerful urge to sit, but he dared not move. He watched the policemen dozing blissfully in their chairs. They were transplants from small towns and villages. Manbij may have been the largest city they'd ever laid their young eyes on.

The night passed. Sometime after the dawn prayer, the door swung open and in walked an officer with broad shoulders, in puttees, two stars on his epaulets. He was flanked by a retinue of adjutants. He was mustacheless, unlike the police officers in Manbij, and this impressed Abel Os. He removed his aviators to reveal eyes the color of Arabic coffee. The sitting policemen jumped to their feet.

"I am Maymati," he said, announcing this fact as if he were a famed conqueror, standing before the city walls. He took a seat behind a desk and immersed himself in a stack of papers. An hour passed, as clerks and adjutants shuffled in and out, handing him documents to sign. When Abel Os could bear it no longer, he forced himself to speak. "My lord, may I use the bathroom?"

1st Lt. Maymati looked at the giant man standing in the corner, as if he had only now registered his presence. One of the clerks said, "He's the thief we caught last night, sir."

"If you'll allow me, sir," began Abel Os. "I'm not a thief. I fell into debt due to some bad decisions."

But 1st Lt. Maymati waved him off.

Abel Os was taken to a small room and made to lie down. Two policemen took turns inflicting *falaka*, whacking his bare feet with hard rubber tubing while Abel Os cried out.

After a while, he was again brought before 1st Lt. Maymati, who signed a document, stamped it, and ordered him imprisoned until the loan was repaid.

It was not until the next evening, under a darkening sky, that Abel Os was released. He hobbled down the streets alongside Shukri, who'd pawned his furniture to liberate his brother. Shukri refused to look Abel Os in the eye. When the pair finally made it to Sarab, Abel Os sighted Tear of Roses in the distance, its shutters down, its sign unlit, and vowed to never again take a loan.

Soon the wheat stalks out east started wilting and curling, and the land along the banks of the Euphrates shriveled and turned yellow. Scientists determined that the drought of 2006 was likely the region's worst in nine hundred years. The desiccated carcasses of livestock littered country roads. Many farms fell into foreclosure, and more than a million people fled for the cities. Ghost villages were swept through by dusty winds as thick as soup.

Abel Os hoped, with the country withering, that his dealings might be forgotten. He had told no one that he still owed payments on a half-dozen "motorcycles." And as the months passed, he did not have to, because no phone calls came. Meanwhile, Mana gave birth to a boy, followed quickly by a girl, and as Abel Os held these tiny creatures in his arms, he wished again that his father was there. His mother had become withdrawn, taking little interest in his growing family. Sometimes she came into his room, tugging at his shirt, to ask for help finding something. When she spoke, her eyes were distant, peering into some hidden realm. He took her to the doctor, who said it was what folks called the black water disease, and that it comes for the elderly. Due to budget cuts, though, Manbij's public hospital no longer had eye specialists. The ophthalmologists in Aleppo were too expensive and, unlike in the old days, unwilling to work for a public hospital. The closest affordable option was in Homs, a four-hour drive south, where an ophthalmologist was known to offer services for the poor.

Abel Os and his mother arrived by bus at Homs in the afternoon. New Syria was in bloom: Plans were underway to transform the old city's labyrinthine passageways and oriel windows, some of which dated to the Middle Ages, into Homs Dream, a luxury complex with tennis courts and five-star hotels. They found the eye specialist. He told them nothing could be done at his small clinic, and urged them to seek treatment elsewhere. "Once it's gone," he said, "it doesn't come back."

They found another option in Latakia, on the coast. They slept on benches, in the salty breeze of the Mediterranean. The next morning, Abel Os watched as a whirring machine pressed onto his mother's eyes. The doctor peered through the other end.

"Maybe we can try Damascus," Abel Os said after they left. His mother held his hand.

He was back at the Cardamom Market, but he was so behind in payments that his promissory notes were no longer any good. "My lord," he pleaded, "this is the last time. After I help my mother, I'll work for you. I'll do anything you ask." When they threatened to call the police, he left. After searching, he found a lender on the south side of town. This man had a long beard, like a religious scholar, and thumbed prayer beads. A contract was signed, two more motorcycles added to Abel Os's imaginary fleet. He put up Tear of Roses as collateral.

One afternoon, Abel Os walked into his mother's room. She looked up. "Who's there? Shukri?"

A few nights later, Abel Os led his mother to the central bus depot. They piled into a shared taxi, setting off in the darkness. He awoke to the saucer-shaped streetlights of Damascus. Since his previous visit, fifteen years prior, the city had sprouted luxury residences with names like Damascus Heights, the Eighth Gate, and Syrian Bonyan City. Billboards promised "The Life of Your Dreams," showing villas with country clubs and marinas. They approached the crowded Ibn Nafees Hospital. Above the entrance, giant letters assured, "IF YOU FALL ILL, HE WILL HEAL YOU." They sat in the bright waiting room for four hours. When the doctor finally appeared, he gave them only a few minutes. "It's a difficult case," he said. "Very difficult." She was conducted from room to room. The machines made a terrifying whine. The doctor returned, peering into her eyes, as if searching for something. He held up a bottle to the light and shook it. "Use these drops," he said.

He wrote the word in English: glaucoma. Treatment would cost tens of thousands of liras, but he suggested Turkey or Iraq might be cheaper.

The ride home was unbearably hot. Abel Os and his mother were stuffed alongside other sweating bodies, the sun baking the windshield. The rainless world outside seemed still, forgotten. Abel Os watched the passing scrubland and the abandoned sun-drenched villages. An endless world, rolling deeper and deeper into the gray horizon.

They buried her in the spring. After losing her vision, Abel Os's mother had been beset by a steady drip of ailments. There had been no money for a trip to Turkey.

Not long after, the police came to the shop. Abel Os was informed that 1st Lt. Maymati expected him the following morning.

Abel Os felt something clutching his stomach, but it was not the mildewy stench of a darkened cell, nor the blinding pain on his bare feet from *falaka*. He was seized by a more terrible fear: standing before his brothers, before his wife and friends and neighbors, and seeing the look in their eyes. His only relief was that his father had been spared the strictures of this new world, that he'd left his burdens behind long ago.

There was no recourse now but to confess, and when he did, Shukri exploded in anger and disbelief. Mana kept asking why he hadn't uttered a word and demanded to know what other secrets he'd been keeping.

That night he did not sleep but stood on the rooftop, watching the quiet city. For the first time, Abel Os began to ponder the question of fate. It was a special beast: It made its allotments, but through all of history, it never, ever allotted for people like him. That old generation, men of his father's age—those foolish, openhearted men who looked at rotting peasant cottages and saw sturdy cement homes, who approached life as if it were an itinerary, powered by perpetual motion—they would have no answer for this.

When the sun rose, he left the rooftop and went to see Anas, his friend from the dojo. As Abel Os unburdened himself, Anas kept asking, "Why didn't you tell me?" He produced a wad of cash, which Abel Os tried to refuse. But Anas insisted, and with great shame, Abel Os pocketed the money. It was enough to placate the most aggressive moneymen, who called off the police. But it was still nowhere near enough to save the shop.

The creditors arrived that afternoon, inspecting Tear of Roses, sifting through the produce, helping themselves to drinks. "Abel Os, this is like a hole," one said. "It's only good for storage." With proper supermarkets going up around town, Tear of Roses was marked down as almost worthless. Still, they collected the keys. Then they toured his house, which they decided would fetch a decent price on the market. Arrangements were made; he and his family would move in with Shukri. The creditors left.

Some days later, a few friends gathered in Abel Os's living room. Anas was there, and Gulay the pushcart vendor, too. A tray of bitter coffee and water was placed before them. It was only a matter of time before the next wave of creditors appeared—Abel Os was so indebted that he was now effectively working for the motorcycle men, perhaps for years to come. There was only one alternative: leave town. He'd done it before, but now he would be competing with boys half his age at the muster zones. Marriages were known to fray under the weight of separation. Everyone spoke increasingly in funereal tones, as if they, not he, were leaving friends and family to venture into the unknown. "You have to take the good with the bad," Abel Os consoled them.

He went to the next room to fetch more coffee. Shukri's children were down on the floor, playing with his own children. Only there, in front of the little ones, did he allow himself to cry. Then he returned to his friends and put on a smile. "You take the good with the bad," he repeated.

The state, that old god, was dead. It was a new god—the market—which had ushered them here. Between 2006 and 2008, global food prices skyrocketed. The cost of wheat and rice more than doubled. The drought withering much of eastern Syria prompted one of the largest peacetime migrations in the region's history. New shantytowns sprang up, ringing the great cities of Damascus and Aleppo. Yet many looked further afield, too, as the global financial crisis ground Syrian construction to a halt. Tens of thousands, maybe millions, crossed borders.

In the Sabra neighborhood of southern Beirut, Abel Os wondered if he'd arrived on a distant planet. There were alleys you passed through single file, forests of electric cables overhead, rainbow-colored puddles underfoot, drainage ruts and water heaters and thick pipes that branched up the walls. In this overcrowded, overwhelming city within a city, strangers lived on top of each other, beside each other, and with each other. Abel Os shared a room with twenty-two other men, a single window opening into the rear of another building.

The neighborhood shared a name with the nearby Sabra camp, which housed tens of thousands of Palestinian refugees and had gained notoriety as the site of a massacre committed by Israeli-backed Christian militias in the 1980s. Now, in addition to Palestinians, the neighborhood was a temporary home to thousands of Syrians searching for work. "In every construction zone and every hotel, the workers are Syrian," Abel Os exclaimed on the phone to his wife. Then, trying to bring a touch of lightness: "When the Americans sent a shuttle to the moon, they found a Syrian there, looking for a job!"

It felt to Abel Os as if half of Sarab was living here beside him. They were a lost generation, unmoored from their civil existence, rafted together in pursuit of their daily bread.

There was Khalil, who worked in a grocery. One day, he demanded his wages, which he hadn't received in six months, and was informed that the sum had been used for his uniform and his meals. Because his bosses kept his ID card, he could not report the issue to the authorities, so he continued to show up to work, day after day, hoping management would have a change of heart.

There was Ibrahim, who, after losing his home in Little Hyena, had eked out a living in Sarab moving bricks. Before long, he wound up in Beirut, building houses in an upscale neighborhood. He finished around four o'clock and would walk two hours back to Sabra. En route he would see women—"glamorous women," he told his friends, "beautiful women wearing tight clothes and heels." He was in shock, finding it difficult to even walk. Then he'd arrive home, to his house full of men where there was no sun, and the smell—he couldn't shake the smell. As everyone around him played cards and backgammon, he sank into despair, and then sleep. The next morning, he would wake and do it all over again. And wake he did, because the quickest route to disaster was to miss a day at the muster zone.

Only Fridays afforded the men any time for themselves. The ritual for newcomers from Manbij was to be taken by veterans to the beach, near the corniche, where all sorts of wonders were on display. "Women in their underwear," the workers were promised. "Women completely free." The migrants settled on an outcropping, bewitched. Ibrahim was more adventurous than the rest. He'd lead the group across the glass-strewn beach, throw himself into the water, and swim into the deep. A rope separated the public beach from the private resorts, so he'd swim past the final buoy and loop back to the private side, leading the expedition onto the white sands. The crew would order fruit drinks and sit in the embrace of the brilliant sun.

The women on show at the beach meant little to Abel Os, though. He went to bed thinking of Mana, and awoke with her image before him. Two years passed—desultory years, amid Beirut's gleaming high-rises, in which he did not once lay eyes on home. Here too he'd become something of a mukhtar to the Manbij migrant community, solving problems, lending his meager earnings to the less fortunate. But he held himself largely aloof from the rest, preferring to walk alone along the corniche, breathing in the fumes, glancing at the overstuffed taxis. He balanced along medians, shortcut under bridges. He lingered outside patisseries as couples sipped their coffees.

His hairline was receding. He hadn't been to the dojo in years, and it showed in his haunches. He sat alone on the bench, his attention fixed on the waves. The magic and wonder of perpetual motion, the stories his father's generation used to tell, had the feel of myth. He thought about Mr. Fuaz, his old karate instructor—long ago claimed by heaven, and for the better, as he was not fit for New Syria. It was Mr. Fuaz who taught him the power of *Oss*: not only an interjection but a focus of energy, a way of life. According to the Kyokushin school, *Oss* signals the power of perseverance. *Oss* demands, in karate as in life, the discipline to endure suffering on the road to self-mastery. *To persevere*—the more Abel Os thought about it, the more he understood the winding corniche and the sparkling glass towers as a trial. The motorcycle men, the men thumbing prayer beads and charging interest, the police—all a trial. Staring into the frothing sea, he decided that there was only one place on earth he belonged. It was teeming with his enemies, the men who sought his destruction. But in the spirit of *Oss*, he would face them, and whatever may come. He was going home.

BOOK TWO

Dreamers

December 2010–
December 2011

Prologue

By 2010, a decade of pro-market reforms, devastating drought, and the global financial crash of 2008 plunged the Middle East into an unprecedented crisis.

In Manbij, there were scenes reminiscent of the Great Depression: men pretending to be at the office while spending the day feeding pigeons in the park; long, agitated lines at public bakeries. Prostitution flourished, and drug use soared. For the first time, children roamed the sidewalks with outstretched hands. Suicide rates shot up. Reports of rapes and "honor killings" abounded. Tales of desperation were everywhere: murder-suicides, fathers drinking themselves to death.

In 2010, a debt-addled Manbij native named Zakaria took his four children, ranging from age two to ten, to the Euphrates. When he reached the bank, he asked the taxi driver to snap a photo: The two girls were wearing matching orange Minnie Mouse pajamas, the two boys squirming. Zakaria was standing behind his children, his hair wind-blown, the Euphrates lapping a few feet behind them.

When Zakaria returned to the taxi later, he was alone. The driver asked after the children, and Zakaria replied that he'd drowned them. The driver thought it was a perverse joke. Not long after, though, divers at the October Dam fished out four small bodies.

Zakaria turned himself in. At the station, looking utterly desperate, he burst into tears. "I walked around in shock," he said later, "and I saw my children everywhere."

Around the same time, a top Syrian official met with U.S. authorities, pleading for humanitarian funding, but the U.S. declined. The crisis was tearing the social fabric, potentially resulting in what the official called "social destruction," and threatening regional and even global stability.

The tempest was coming.

ONE

DECEMBER 2010

The education of Oday al-Hema began on a gray December day in 2010. That month, a Tunisian street vendor, under the boot of poverty, lit himself on fire. The act triggered mass protests and strikes, culminating in the overthrow of the country's dictator, who had been in power for twenty-four years.

But it was not this upheaval, unprecedented as it was, which awoke Oday from the slumber that had spanned the entirety of his nineteen years. Oday was never one to pay much mind to the news. The affairs of world leaders and the fluctuations of business cycles felt like a tax on his soul, draining whatever joy he might find in life. The grim propriety of the evening news, with its anchors in coats and ties and its formal Arabic, reminded him of his dreadful school days, or, worse, of his father's shop, where he suffered the daily indignity of hawking cell phones and mopping the floor.

Oday was a restless young man, a person of grand pronouncements and no follow-through. He fancied himself a poet but could not commit himself to the study of classical meter and verse. He was intrigued by Arab history but struggled to sit with books. It was only the hours after his shift, when he shed his officious regalia and met his friends, that held his attention. He and his friends scaled the rooftops and, looking out over the growths of satellite dishes and cables, smoked hash. Then they migrated to Abu Hajjal's Sports Cafe, where they played *FIFA 11* on the PlayStation for hours. When he finally emerged from that cavern, bleary-eyed, he smoked some more.

Amid this haze, the events of Tunisia hardly registered. Instead, it was through a series of chance encounters, woeful mishaps, and minor wonders that Oday discovered his calling — and it all began one frigid afternoon when he was walking home past an old alley built of Roman stone and heard a scream.

He peered into the alley. Between the stone walls, he saw two teenage boys trailing a girl with a backpack.

"Sweetie, you know it's okay," one was saying. The girl picked up her pace, but the boys closed in. One of them reached over and held her backpack. They were laughing.

"Let go!" the girl shrieked.

"Hey!" Oday shouted. "Leave her alone!" The boys turned and faced Oday. Before he knew it, they were on him, and he was swinging back. It was two against one, but Oday was quick-fisted and a few inches taller. When it was over, Oday was resting against the stone wall, blood running from his mouth. The assailants had fled. He looked up to see the girl with the backpack was not a girl at all but a young woman. Her brown hair was uncovered, cascading to her shoulders. As she leaned over with a Kleenex to stanch his bleeding, Oday realized he could not stop staring.

The next morning, Oday awoke early. In the vegetable market, situated in the plaza in front of his house, men and boys were setting up stands of dry beans and okra and lentils and tomatoes and onions. They unwrapped scales, and soon their battery-operated radios were squawking: *40 liras 40 liras 40 liras.* Oday studied the market because he knew that Hala—that was her name—would pass through on her way to Manbij Girls High School. He'd confided in Bushra, his sister, and the pair were watching from the balcony when she suddenly appeared, hair flowing amid a crowd of headscarves.

There was no science to his approach; Oday was in the realm of art. He knew that Hala's father was a decorated army officer; theirs was a family of means. The trouble was, he also knew Hala's brother, a hard-drinking, tempestuous young man named Abboud. He'd joined Oday and his friends many a night as they sat in the green haze of hash, ribbing each other, talking of women, dreaming of the beaches of Beirut. If Abboud knew what was budding in Oday's heart, he would tear him to pieces. In big cities like Damascus and Aleppo, teenagers went on dates, dancing in the sweaty confines of nightclubs and drinking arak on rooftops. But Manbij, despite its size, was like a village, where parents arranged their children's marriages as if they were joint farming ventures. No self-respecting family allowed their daughter to be seen with a boy, and there were perhaps no greater guardians of the family honor than a girl's brothers. Everyone knew tales of young women bruised, brutalized, or worse—in so-called honor killings—when their trysts were discovered. On Oday's own street, there was a girl who was discovered exchanging letters with a neighborhood boy. In a fit of rage, her brother suffocated her with a pillow.

Oday would need to plot his advance carefully. He recruited Bushra. They studied Hala's routine—crossing the plaza to school in the morning, returning in the afternoon. No deviation, no detours. They discovered that at some point she turned down a narrow lane, lined with Arabic-style houses. One block on, she passed an alleyway made of old Roman stone—this was where Oday had first seen her. Here she was completely alone for just moments—no windows, rarely any pedestrians. And so one afternoon, when Oday spotted her on her route, he raced down the stairs, around the plaza, into the narrow lane of Arabic houses. He turned and walked casually in her direction. They crossed paths precisely at the alley of Roman stone. She averted her eyes.

The next day Oday engineered another encounter, and he did the same the day after. A routine developed. Every afternoon, Hala walked across the alleyway of Roman stone, hardly a shift in her stride, while Oday approached. No words were exchanged. Oday would return home, flush with success, and pace on the balcony, smoking cigarettes. He'd visit Abu Hajjal's Sports Cafe and spend hours bathed in the glow of television screens. He drove out to the country to smoke hash under the stars and carried his secret within him, like knowledge of a buried treasure. Only Bushra had his confidence. Late one night, as the two sat on the balcony, looking out over the flowing traffic of Sundus Street, Oday confessed he was smitten.

Bushra took matters into her own hands. One morning, she approached Hala in the plaza amid a crowd of shoppers. They spoke for a few moments.

Hala explained to Bushra that she was studying for her baccalaureate, that her eyes were on her future, and that she'd heard about Oday and didn't want trouble—least of all from her brother.

"I'm not that kind of girl," she said.

Oday wanted to make a plea: *I'm not that kind of guy.* But to the world, to Aboud, and maybe even to Hala, he was—and there was no point in denying it. Certainly, his own parents would've concurred. His father had dropped out of the sixth grade, but afterward he wandered the Arab countries working construction sites from Libya to Saudi Arabia and amassed, by Manbij standards, a small fortune. He owed it all, he said, to God, who helped those who helped themselves, an idea he'd absorbed while building gleaming office towers and air-conditioned malls in Saudi Arabia. Within his own household, he imposed a strict theocracy.

The television was always tuned to a single channel, showing Quranic recitations. His eldest son, Oday's brother, got married a decade earlier, and even now Oday still hadn't seen his sister-in-law's face.

The rigid household regime fell hard on Oday: Jeans and hair gel were not allowed. Only traditional sandals were acceptable, as shoes were the devil's playthings. Poulaines, brogues, almond-toed, square-toed, any kind of closed toe—all were de rigueur among Manbij's youth but forbidden in the Hema household.

For Oday, this was all cant. He rebelled, as teenagers do, rolling cigarettes behind his father's back, slipping out the bedroom window late at night. With no mind for books, he'd barely finished high school. He was put to work in his father's shop, but his father often arrived to find that his son had abandoned the post to play soccer. The house shook with slammed doors, with the old man bellowing, "You come back here!" Oday would retreat with friends to a farmhouse in the country. They'd share swigs of Grant's whisky and sing old Arab songs. His older brother had a computer. A brisk trade in pornography developed among the friends.

But if the world saw him as *that kind of guy*, he decided, for Hala, that he would need to refashion himself and his universe—a universe that for the moment spanned only the few city blocks between his house and hers. He would leave his indolent friends behind, straighten up, apply himself. He would be steadfast in his loyalty to Hala, be her protective orbit. Like clockwork, he passed her every afternoon near the alley of Roman stone. He did not say a word or look her in the eye. He simply wished that she not forget him.

Bushra watched her brother metamorphose before her eyes. He quit the bottle and the aimless nights of hashish. He began to apply himself at the cell phone shop, keeping to his promised hours. Patience was not in his endowment, yet now he surprised his sister by declaring that, for Hala, he was willing to wait.

FEBRUARY 2011

The Egyptian masses, inspired by the Tunisians, overthrew their twenty-nine-year dictatorship.

For the first time, Oday paid attention to the evening news. As he watched the scenes of protest, he felt grateful to be Syrian. Here, unlike Egypt, people were taken care of. He knew President Bashar al-Assad to be a great man who'd stood chest to chest with world powers like America and Israel. The president had pledged to modernize the country. A billboard proclaiming New Syria formed part of the skyline visible from his balcony. Egyptians were scattered across the world, working as waiters and cab drivers and dishwashers. President Assad would not allow his people to suffer such indignities, and for this, Oday swelled with pride.

But he remained at an impasse with Hala. He did not know how to put her at ease, how to project responsibility. And to do all this while managing the threat of her brother felt like balancing the weight of the world. A friend in whom he'd confided suggested he write her a letter. That evening, Oday attempted to record his thoughts. But the words on the page were lifeless. He was no wordsmith. He tore it up, then began again.

The next day, he showed his friend the effort of his labors, a letter declaring his feelings. "Your message is very weak," his friend said. "The writing is awful, the handwriting is bad, the words and sentences have no flow." He took pity on Oday and wrote a long letter, borrowing sentiments he'd used for his own fiancée. He included lines from the bard Nizar Qabbani:

> *And I know I'm living in exile,*
> *And you're in exile,*
> *And between you and me*
> *There is wind*
> *Clouds*
> *Lighting and Thunder*
> *Snow and Fire*

The letter declared Oday was chaste in his intentions, that he desired marriage and family.

The next afternoon, Oday made his usual advance toward the alley of Roman stone. When Hala appeared, he dropped the letter at her feet and fled.

That week, Oday kept to his house. From his balcony, he watched the plaza for a sign of Abboud, Hala's brother. He awaited the knock at the door, Abboud charging in, his father's thundering voice, the hue and cry of the neighbors. He refused to report to duty at the shop. Relatives came to visit, friends called on him, but he would not budge from his bedroom. Around town, people tuned their satellite dishes to foreign channels, watching news from Egypt. But Oday kept his energies fixed on the plaza beneath his balcony.

A week passed. Finally, he dispatched Bushra, who intercepted Hala as she returned from school. Oday hid on the balcony, watching. The encounter only lasted a few moments, but Bushra managed to secure a meeting the next day.

That night, he burned through packs of cigarettes. He refused dinner

Afterward, jumpy from coffee, he walked circles around the plaza. When the next afternoon finally arrived, he stood, fidgeting, in the alleyway of Roman stone. He waited for the sound of footfalls.

None came.

Oday waited, and he must have cursed his boldness, his foolishness. He must have considered turning on his heels then and there, just as he'd quit soccer when he could not match his friends' quickness, just as he'd quit poetry. But then suddenly he found himself in that late afternoon staring at Hala, glowing in the sunlight.

It was she who spoke first. "Where have you been?"

Oday had rehearsed this moment for weeks, but now, in the terror of the encounter, he'd lost his words. So he held up the tissue she'd used to stanch his bleeding during their first encounter. He'd kept it this whole time.

"Don't ever stay away from me again," she said.

That evening, Oday stood on the balcony with his sister. The city was resplendent, its Ottoman minarets burning neon green, spires of concrete climbing to the heavens. Oday appeared rejuvenated, as if he'd emerged from some dungeon deep as the Roman cisterns that lay beneath their feet.

Here, in the pure air above Sundus Street, he knew no recriminations, no bitterness—his father and his iron cage no longer mattered. "This," Oday told Bushra, "is what freedom is."

MARCH

On March 18, 2011, state TV announced that armed gangs had staged a demonstration in Daraa, a town in southern Syria. In clashes, four young men were killed. At a funeral procession for those gunned down, there were again clashes, and more people fell. State TV aired images of seized weapons, which it claimed were of American and Israeli provenance.

Across Manbij, everyone was glued to their screens. No one had ever seen such images in Syria. Even Oday took an interest. He watched his friend's satellite TV, which showed a very different version of events: The protesters were unarmed, marching for political reform, and it was the security forces who had fired indiscriminately. These channels showed images of mobs setting ablaze the Baath Party headquarters in Daraa. Crowds torched the local branch of Syriatel, the telecom company owned by Rami Makhlouf, the president's cousin and one of the richest men in the country. Makhlouf, who was said to control around 60 percent of the national economy, was New Syria's capitalist par excellence.

People in Manbij felt as if they were watching scenes from Hollywood. The sight of a Baath Party office, even a regional one, going up in flames was simply impossible to believe.

Oday adopted a bearing of propriety in the face of such a shock. If people desired reform, arson and vandalism were not the answer. "We live in a civilized country," Oday said. "We can't be ruled by mobs."

He'd recently come to understand something essential about life that had been lost on the rioters but which he now grasped every time he watched Hala move through the market: We make our own future, not by pleading, not by protesting, but by taking charge of our lives. Late at night, while his father slept, he would steal out onto Sundus Street. The city was deserted. The turmoil down south had brought life to a standstill, as if people were bracing for a great storm. Policemen stood on street corners in twos and threes. Oday crossed the darkened plaza, working his way through the winding streets of the old city, until he looked up at Hala's window, a light burning. He threw pebbles, which rattled against the pane. If the light turned off, he knew to leave. If it flashed twice, he waited. And if it flashed three times, he raced to the nearby alleyway. Moments would pass in silence. The alley was unlit except, on clear nights, for a rectangle of stars above. Hala merged with the shadows. Oday held her face, which he could hardly see. Between the walls of Roman stone, they kissed.

There was much Oday wanted to say, but he was unable, so he asked his friend to compose more letters in his name. Notes were ferried. Under her pillow, Hala kept scraps of paper filled with Oday's scrawled messages.

Hala was younger by three years, but in wisdom she surpassed Oday by decades. Life for her was a long road, lit here and there by great way stations: university, a job at the municipality, a two-story house. Oday had not thought this way before. Hala would soon sit for her baccalaureate exam, and all were certain she was destined for Aleppo University. Everything in the coming months was to be subordinated to that cause—and Oday too was ready to submit. He disciplined himself to keep their rendezvous brief—five minutes, ten—so that she might not stray. In the meantime, he matched her energy, announcing to his father that he was ready to manage the family shop. The old man scoffed, suspicious of his son's sudden industriousness, but Oday appealed to his uncle, a teacher named Mustafa. He was perhaps the only adult who truly understood Oday, who saw his restlessness as an energy that, if directed properly, could allow him to prosper. Mustafa pressed Oday's father, and finally one morning Oday was presented with the keys to Mahci Communications.

The one-room shop was crammed with batteries and wires and car chargers and SIM cards. Oday kept a photograph of President Assad on one of the glass cases. The most important product—the Nokia phone—allowed Oday to solve his biggest challenge. He gifted Hala a phone, which she hid under her bed. He kept the shop open late and sat behind the glass counter, cigarette in one hand, Nokia in the other, in case Hala rang.

Cell phones were new to Manbij, and Oday found his forte as a salesman. He quit the whisky-pickled nights, the PlayStation sessions. While everyone else watched the news obsessively, Oday was working long hours at the shop. After hours, in the dark folds between the Roman walls, he would sit with Hala. She held his palm, tracing its grooves. He wanted to show her what he could accomplish. He imagined leading her by the hand through the narrow streets of the Great Souk, smoking a cigarette while she held gossamer-thin fabrics to the light. Sometimes he'd wonder why these dusty streets should have to contain them—he longed to bring Hala to the beaches of the Mediterranean. But where Oday dreamed, Hala planned, like a general. In fact, the image of her father, an officer—the epaulets, the brass—had seared itself into Oday's mind. He knew her father would not surrender his daughter to a mere cell phone salesman. So Oday forked over a month's savings to a tutor to help prepare him for the baccalaureate exam. He would become a lawyer, then enter the officer academy. Serve Syria, be a man of appointments, urgent missions. He would be chauffeured to Hala's house, garbed in martial raiment, and ask for her hand.

This vision depended on law and order, so Oday was drawn to the stern, paternal figure of President Assad, who, unlike the corrupt Egyptian and Tunisian dictators, was determined to shepherd his people through the present crisis. "Our president is a good man," he assured friends.

Twelve days had passed since the turmoil down south, and the news only grew more distressing. The rioting had not ceased, and more demonstrators were gunned down. The chaos produced wild rumors: The Israelis had invaded; terrorists had planted explosives in multiple cities; the U.S. was planning to bomb the country. In Manbij, prices at the market crept upward, as merchants feared instability. One day, to allay fears, a crowd gathered near the Book Roundabout. The local Baath Party branch had organized a rally there to show support for the government. The scene was joyous. The crowd chanted, "With our blood, with our souls, we sacrifice for you, oh Bashar!" Manbij's chief of police, 1st Lt. Maymati, sat astride a demonstrator's shoulders, holding placards bearing the images of the president and his late father. When Oday and Hala saw these scenes, they felt like a tremendous weight had lifted. Here was proof that the southern disturbances would not reach Manbij, that the city stood firmly behind their leader. Hala began carrying a postage-stamp-sized photo of the president to school.

Meanwhile, satellite channels were reporting that, in the twelve days since the start of the unrest, fifty-seven protesters had been killed. In the privacy of his rooftop, a friend asked Oday: By what right did the authorities kill unarmed protesters? But Oday shot back: What evidence existed that the protesters were unarmed? And by what right did they march in defiance of their president? Oday allowed that the rank-and-file soldiers were corrupt, and perhaps trigger-happy, but they were not trained to handle such a disturbance. Oday swore that the president would soon offer a path forward.

That evening, just as Oday had predicted, authorities announced that the president would deliver his first public remarks on the crisis. Life in Manbij came to a halt. For the first time in memory, the televisions in Abu Hajjal's Sports Cafe were tuned to something other than soccer. Even Oday's father switched the channel from Quranic recitation.

Oday and his sister watched from their living room. The president was standing behind a podium as a crowd waved flags and sang. They clapped and chanted in rhythm: *God, Syria, and Bashar only!* The president appeared sheepish at the outpouring of support. "It's hard for me to give an adequate response," he said. A man in a jellabiya and tribal headdress leapt to his feet and shouted, "Oh son of Assad! You are the one who has developed Syria! Oh hero of Syria and the Arab nation!" He was a tribal sheikh from Manbij.

As Assad began speaking, Oday told his sister, "Look how humble he is. He's actually embarrassed by all the attention."

For the next fifty minutes, the president expatiated on a range of topics. The protesters in Daraa expressed some genuine political and economic grievances, he allowed, but one could also detect the hidden hand of sedition, of agents provocateurs. "We have not yet discovered the whole structure of this conspiracy." The president acknowledged the problem of inequality. When the Tunisian revolution began, he said, "we realized that the causes lay in how wealth was distributed. . . . This is something we have tried to avoid, and we are calling for a fair distribution of development in Syria."

Oday was deeply impressed. Every day from his balcony, he watched the women begging on Sundus Street, the street children drifting like refugees. The president did not offer any concrete reforms, but the fact that the ruler was naming these injustices publicly was a rare thing.

In the afternoons, Oday liked to stand in front of his decal-covered storefront, smoking, watching the passing traffic. He recognized the desperation on people's faces, but he also couldn't ignore the allure of New Syria: the billboards promising whiter teeth, the cell phone tower on the Manbij Hotel, the terraced high-rises. Was there splendor like this in Egypt or Tunisia? He could feel New Syria in his bones, and Maher Communications was living proof.

APRIL

But Oday was in the minority. The president's speech failed to calm most nerves. An air of disquiet took hold of Manbij, as it dawned on the city that unprecedented and likely dangerous events were transpiring down south.

There was a pervasive sense too that something needed to give, especially after twenty years of economic transformation, in which much was promised and little delivered, forcing millions of people to abandon their homes and, in a great migration, settle in shantytowns and migrant colonies. But what precisely should happen, no one was sure. The older generation recalled the bleak days of the early 1980s, when neighbors were plucked from their homes and disappeared "behind the sun," as the saying went. This generation concluded that nothing was worse than the specter of chaos—*fawda*.

So people kept indoors. Traffic at the Great Souk was sparse, and soccer matches were canceled. Oday felt he alone was immune from such trepidation, so long as he had his nightly calls with Hala. He was to become a military lawyer and learn the intricacies of maritime law. His path would take him and Hala to foreign shores, to air-conditioned conference rooms. True, he struggled to sit still when a book lay open before him, but now Hala's voice was on the line, breaking down Punnett squares and balancing chemistry equations. They spoke for hours, and Oday could not deny that he was, for the first time in his life, genuinely learning.

And then he called one evening to find her line disconnected.

He rushed to her street. Hala's window was pitch-black. He tossed pebbles, but the light did not turn on.

The next morning, Hala did not appear in the vegetable market.

The day passed in a haze. Finally, Bushra went to investigate. She returned with news that the previous evening, Abboud had burst into Hala's bedroom, seized his sister by the neck, and threw her against the wall. He found the phone and smashed it. He told her he knew what Oday was truly about—he knew all too well—and that if she dared dishonor the family again, he'd kill her with his bare hands.

Oday shut himself in his bedroom and refused visitors. When he emerged, he'd lost weight and his eyes were sunken. He was gripped by a terrible fear that

Hala was in danger. He implored Bushra to check on her, so she visited daily. The news was both worse and better than he'd feared. Worse—Abboud knew that she and Oday had been speaking on the phone for a month; better—he seemed unaware of the midnight trysts. He had not told her parents. But he was stalking her every move, even walking her to school. Every evening, before she went to sleep, he entered the bedroom and threatened to kill her.

Oday returned to the shop. He sold more phones than ever. He was all smiles, greeting customers. It was only at home, in the evening, that Bushra realized he was in shock. He went to bed without dinner and did not emerge from his bedroom until the next morning. Then, after a while, he stopped turning up at the shop. He could not explain to his father that his life had just gone to pieces, and the old man, incensed that his son had slipped back into his old ways, threatened to repossess the store. Oday, face buried in his pillow, said, "Take it."

Oday dismissed his tutor and quit his studies and university preparations.

It had been an unusually long winter, the air still frigid, the clouds still low. Oday could not bring himself to step onto the balcony. It was over before it began, he kept telling Bushra. Just five weeks. For some days, Oday hardly spoke. Then, slowly, he began making inquiries. He dragged himself out of the house to visit friends. At some point he recalled he'd once bragged to an acquaintance, Yasser, about his romance with Hala. Mysteriously, Yasser had told him, "She's no good for you." But why? Oday decided that Yasser must have harbored affection of his own, and that it was he who spilled the truth to Abboud. Oday barged into the clinic where Yasser worked as a nurse. In a waiting room full of patients, he threw Yasser to the ground. Three men had to hold him back. In their arms, Oday allowed himself to be seen crying. "Why did you do this to me?" he asked Yasser.

The days blended. Late at night, on the balcony, wrapped in scarves, Oday stared out. Sometimes Bushra joined him, though they hardly spoke.

He finally reached Hala by landline one evening. Her voice sounded small. "If you love me," she said, "keep away."

Oday returned to the shop. He could not allow it to go to seed. Late into the night, the pendant lights burned, the smoke wafted. Oday played ringtones on the Nokia. Standing in front of the decal-covered storefront, smoking, he watched the traffic. New Syria had begun to lose its luster—Oday was soon sharing with Bushra his disgust at the blind optimism splashed on the billboards, on the radio. He saw the meanness of the human heart.

He was spending too many afternoons behind the window decals, watching young men in suits rush home. A friend prevailed on him to leave town, so he took a weekend junket to Aleppo. He rested in the shadow of the great castle, he wandered the labyrinths of the souk. In a department store in the gleaming Shahba Mall, he ran into a friend from Manbij, an artist named Sami Saba. He had long, lustrous hair—Oday called him Shampoo Sami. He lived in an apartment in downtown Manbij filled with half-finished busts and plaster statuary. Shampoo Sami drew him aside conspiratorially. The youths in Manbij were planning something to commemorate the fallen protesters—the martyrs—in Daraa. Would Oday be interested in joining? Oday declined the invitation, but that evening, back in Manbij, he was surprised to find that the idea had not angered him. He loved his president, but he could no longer see New Syria with anything but derision. Over the next days, as he disappeared into deeper and deeper gloom, there arose within him a kind of malice, a sick glee: He relished the chaos down south. If he was to suffer such torment, why should others be shielded from the naked despair of existence?

The rains came. The streets were slicked in mud, the leaves heavy on the boughs. The events down south had not slowed. More dead—more "terrorists plots," according to state television. But satellite television continued to tell of a different reality, as protesters smuggled clips out of the country. A new story was circulating: The protests in Daraa, now almost a month old, had begun when children spray-painted "It's your turn, oh doctor" on a school wall—a reference to the president's training in ophthalmology. The children were arrested and tortured. Some had had their fingernails removed. They were between twelve and fifteen years of age. When tribal sheikhs visited the authorities and pleaded for the children's release, Atef Najib, Daraa's director of political security and the president's cousin, reportedly told the men to forget their children and make new ones—and if they couldn't, send their wives and he'd do the job for them.

Oday was disgusted. But then again, everything in this society was beginning to disgust him—the blind deference to tradition, the domineering role of family, the impossibility of love. He appeared pained to be at the shop, and Mustafa, his uncle, took notice. He began dragging him along on errands. Mustafa had a dentist appointment in Abu Qalqal, a satellite town some thirty minutes from the city. On a cold afternoon, Oday clung to his uncle on a motorcycle. They passed the Coffeepot Roundabout and the grain silos, which towered over the suburbs. Mustafa mentioned the story of the boys from Daraa. Oday said that the president would take action and fire Najib.

Take action? Mustafa asked. Did Oday think that Atef Najib's behavior was an exception? Mustafa had worked in Daraa; he had friends there. He reeled off similar stories about other officials.

"The president is a good man," Oday shouted against the wind.

Mustafa spoke of the horrific abuses committed against people he knew personally. He mentioned names and detailed their injuries. "These are my friends. They are not terrorists."

Oday was quiet.

Mustafa was the most intelligent person Oday had ever met. He taught high school philosophy, with a specialty in the ancient Greeks. He could speak in syllogisms: Killing innocent people is wrong. Our government is killing innocent people. Therefore, our government is doing wrong.

Mustafa continued: The protesters were incredibly brave, because the last time Syrians had attempted such a thing, many years ago, the government flattened an entire city.

Oday had never heard of this.

Mustafa slowed. The highway stretched to the horizon, open country spreading all around. The land was spare and treeless. Mustafa recounted the events of Hama in 1982, the government soldiers going house to house, raping girls. He mentioned names—distant cousins and aunts he'd known growing up—who'd lost loved ones. There were bulldozers clearing mounds of bodies, he said. No one knew how many—fifty thousand, maybe sixty thousand people died. If you mentioned it, they would take you away. He spoke of an uncle—Oday's father's cousin—who, Oday had been led to understand, died of a heart attack before he was born. In truth, Mustafa said, he'd been disappeared for speaking about the Hama events. Oday said he could not believe it.

Mustafa pulled over, turned, and looked at his nephew. "Why would I lie to you?"

On the return trip, Oday did not talk much. He was prepared to concede that the security officials in charge of Daraa were out of control. The president should—and would—bring the hammer down on them. "Our president is a good man," he repeated. It was dark by the time the Manbij grain silos appeared, then the lit houses, the neon minarets. After bidding farewell to Mustafa, he found his way to Abu Bakir's Internet Cafe. His face lit by the pale glow of the computer screen, headphones in his ears, his eyes flickered over a series of YouTube clips of the Daraa events. And then he paced his dark balcony, dragging on a cigarette.

The next morning, sedans with tinted windows appeared on Sundus Street. Men in sunglasses and leather jackets were posted near the entrance to the Great Souk. The entire city appeared to wait with bated breath for a resolution to the events down south. But the morning brought fresh news of more massacres—and Oday was forced to admit that the protesters were unarmed.

The only hope, he believed, lay in the president. If he could assert his authority, the killings would be over in an instant.

Nearly two weeks had passed since Hala had been taken from him. He must have pictured her holed up in her bedroom like a prisoner, her bestial brother roving the hallway. He told Bushra he could not keep still, that his hollow daily performance at the cell phone shop was eating at him. How could he smile and hawk phones when Hala was entombed in her house? For that matter, how could he smile and hawk phones when people were being slaughtered in Daraa? Without having uttered a word to him, Abboud had managed to get a vice grip on his psyche. It was a new form of domination, a power even his father had failed to exercise over him. He felt as if he were locked in a closet, shouting, but no one could hear.

Bushra advised him to pour his energy into the shop, but he could not. A force of this magnitude, he came to realize, could not be contained. Something had to give.

Oday found Shampoo Sami. He told him, "The president is a good man. If we raise our voices, he'll listen."

Later, in Shampoo Sami's apartment, five young men spoke late into the night. None of them had ever contemplated anything like this before—to speak their anger violated every stricture that had governed their lives. It was like tossing a brick through a store window and going on a looting spree, or streaking naked through the crowded streets, or veering off the highway and plowing through fields and backyards.

According to Syria's so-called Emergency Law, on the books since 1963, unauthorized public gatherings—as few as five people—were effectively illegal. If you wished to hold a formal meeting with friends or colleagues about any subject at all—soccer, cinema, poetry—you were required to submit a written request to authorities fifteen days in advance. The meeting itself would be attended by the relevant officials and would often be crawling with secret police as well. Afterward, you were required to submit the minutes of the meeting to the authorities.

The five young men were university graduates from working-class homes. Their fathers had lived nearly identical lives: lifted from abject poverty during the Hafez al-Assad years, but halted in life's forward march under Bashar's New Syria. After hours of discussion, they concluded that due to the Emergency Law, the only safe place to congregate was a mosque.

That Friday, April 15, Oday told his father he was going to the mosque to pray. The old man must have raised an eyebrow, but he said nothing. Oday entered the Great Mosque in downtown Manbij. Two hundred worshippers were arranged in ranks in front of the imam. Sami stood near the entrance. Oday stood in the middle, among the worshippers. He had told no one of this plan except his sister. She'd worried that his anguish over Hala was pushing him to recklessness. But Oday and his friends had pledged to honor the martyrs, and they knew that the president would hear their voices. As the imam intoned, Oday must have shifted on his feet. The severe lighting, the imam's clipped speech, the pageantry of self-righteousness would have brought to mind his father's suffocating rule, part of why he hardly ever entered a house of worship. The congregation was reciting lines known to some one billion people:

I seek refuge from Satan in God. Bless Muhammad and Muhammad's family as you bless Abraham and Abraham's family. No one forgives my sins but You.

The men turned their heads to one side, then the other. "God is great," the imam called out, and the flock repeated the words and gathered their shoes.

As the young men filed out, no one was quite sure what to do. None of them had ever truly transgressed before—and Oday, from the earliest age, knew deep in his bones where the lines were drawn. Sure, he'd broken the law—smoked hashish, drank, visited brothels—but this felt different, a step into the unknown.

The congregation thinned.

The friends milled about. Shampoo Sami paced restlessly. The others watched him, but he would not meet their eyes. Everyone in the group was ready for something to happen. As the last congregants shuffled toward the exit, Sami was carried with the crowd. Now he was outdoors, pushed out the western exit into a covered market. It was Friday, so most of the shops were closed. The congregation was dispersing through both ends of the market. Time was running out.

Oday was now in the covered market, waiting for Sami's signal. But Sami looked back at them, as if to say, *You start and I'll follow!* The market was lit by Christmas lights. A man in a pleather jacket was leaning against one of the storefronts. A shop selling backpacks was open. The generator was puttering. A second man in a pleather jacket was loitering nearby. Two men, identically dressed? Something seemed off. Oday and the others were looking to Shampoo Sami, but he stood still as a statue. There was, near him, a third pleather-jacketed man.

The market was crawling with them.

The crowd dwindled. Sami and Oday kept looking at each other, waiting for someone to take that final step across the invisible threshold. Two whole minutes elapsed. The crowd was almost gone. Another minute.

And then a pleather-jacket man walked up to Sami. "Don't even think about it," he said.

Oday and his friend slipped away. They were walking fast, not looking behind them. The whole episode lasted maybe ten minutes, after which the souk was left with a few Friday shoppers strolling here and there, unaware that a handful of kids had almost carried out sedition.

That evening, satellite TV showed the first evidence that events had spread beyond Daraa: There were reports of disturbances in Damascus and Syria's port cities. The next afternoon, the president addressed the nation for the second time since the events began. He acknowledged that "there is a gap which started to appear between state institutions and the Syrian citizens." But Syrians, he said, "love order and do not accept chaos and mob rule."

Oday spent much of that week in the internet cafe. The unrest had spread to Homs, known for its medieval souks and clock towers. When demonstrators chanted "Freedom!," plainclothes men machine-gunned the crowd, killing some twenty-five people. Thousands held a sit-in by the main clock tower, and the government opened fire again.

In Manbij, Peugeots and military jeeps began patrolling Sundus Street. The mood of crisis was undeniable: Some shops were closed, and even the Great Souk was sparsely populated. More men in pleather jackets took up residence outside the Great Mosque. Oday was convinced he carried a message of great importance that must be directed to the president himself. Only the president could put a stop to the growing mayhem; only he would understand. He knew that no matter the consequences, he and his friends would have to try again.

He met with Shampoo Sami and the others. They would need to be more careful this time. Each agreed to tell a friend, falsely, that the action would be at a mosque on the other side of town.

On Thursday, Sami was summoned to the police station for questioning. He was asked if he knew anything about the plan the previous week to launch a protest. He swore he'd never heard of such a thing—and, he said, there was no protest, so how could he be responsible for something that did not happen? "Just be aware," the officer said, "if there's any disturbance tomorrow and we see you, we'll send you straight to Damascus."

That evening, Sami told his friends he was dropping out. But Oday was convinced they should press ahead. After all, they were *not* planning a protest—they were merely marching in sympathy with the fallen of Daraa. It was like an open letter, composed with their bodies and voices, meant for the president. "The president is a good man," Oday reminded them once again.

The next afternoon, Friday, April 22, was overcast. The streets had never been so empty. It was as if everyone had decided to barricade themselves in until the disturbances down south subsided. Despite the somber mood, Oday was grateful—a new mission burned within him, allowing a reprieve from the torments of Hala and his own desire to barricade himself.

He found his friends in the prayer hall of the Great Mosque. They were spread among the congregation, standing nervously.

"God is great," the imam said, and the crowd made for the exit. Oday was rafted with them until he was outdoors in the covered market.

A minute passed.

He was in the souk, looking around. Most of the shops were shuttered. The crowd was thinning, drifting away. He looked for his friends. Suddenly, it became clear—*there were no pleather-jacket men*. They were alone, completely alone, among the congregants. The ruse to send them to the other side of town had worked. Yet like a child lost in a crowd, where once familiar storefronts and passersby assume a sinister cast, the friends now felt something akin to terror. They were exposed, without the armor of excuses. Something would have to happen—but no one dared make a sound.

The crowd continued to thin. A man emerged from a barbershop to see groups of young men here and there, looking nervously at each other. Everyone present was familiar with the contours of collective life: They had stood shoulder to shoulder at Friday prayers and murmured "God is great"; they had thronged to the Municipal Stadium and shouted "Freedom! Freedom!"—the name of the Aleppo soccer club. They had stood as children in the freezing rain, wearing khaki shorts, chanting, "With our blood, with our souls, we sacrifice for you, Bashar!" But now they waited for one among them—an individual— to take a step against that which was imprinted so deeply within, in the hope that the collective would follow. The metaphor these young men later reached for was "breaking the wall of silence," which, like all figures of speech, lost its shine over time and repetition, becoming an empty incantation of a certain type of belonging. But there was an instant—at this dusky covered market, in this provincial city—when the phrase carried the force of great truth, because what Oday and his friends indeed faced was a boundary, across which lay oblivion, even self-immolation. And it was the fear of such nothingness that kept them frozen in place, legs weak, mouths dry, as the remaining congregants swarmed around them.

According to the famous opposition between the individual and the collective, one either acts for himself and his convictions, or he is subsumed by the herd. But here, on this Friday, this opposition dissolved, because to act—to stand in conviction—was to sacrifice for countrymen in a city none had ever visited. To stand there, heart hammering against the rib cage, and to offer oneself up required a reimagining of self and other.

The worshippers continued to filter out. Oday stood frozen on the sidewalk. And then, while a hundred or so congregants remained, someone offered himself up. No one could later remember who it was, or relate precisely how it happened, but a voice ricocheted through the covered market.

"Hor-rey-ya! Hor-rey-ya!"

"Freedom! Freedom!"

Suddenly, everyone froze in place—the congregants, the shop owners, the passersby. No one could believe what they were hearing. A terrible silence followed. Then, after what must have felt like ages, a second voice boomed through the rafters:

"Hor-rey-ya! Hor-rey-ya!"

"Freedom! Freedom!"

The voice belonged to Oday. His friends joined in.

"Hor-rey-ya! Hor-rey-ya!"

"Freedom! Freedom!"

People wandered into the covered souk from Main Street, gawking at the protesters as if they were possessed: a dozen voices calling for freedom in the open, in broad daylight. As the enormity of what was unfolding registered, some congregants fled. But a few remained. Cautiously, quietly at first and then with greater confidence, they joined in the chanting.

The crowd was almost fifty strong, strangers all—fifty strangers in a city of 150,000. A minute passed and the chants continued, the voices growing stronger and louder. The mood was as if anything was possible, as if their voices could be heard through the rafters, through the Great Mosque's masonry, through the entire city.

Then there were shouts. The protesters turned to see four men in jellabiyas and tribal headdress approaching from the market entrance. They were shouting something. No—they were chanting. The men approached. Their chant was now unmistakable: "With our blood, with our souls, we sacrifice for you, oh Bashar!"

They pressed closer. Now they were standing face-to-face with the protesters, and it was only then that Oday realized that these men carried swords in their raised arms. They were pro-government civilians. Government forces were likely not far behind.

Among the protesters, the instinct to flee must have been powerful. Chaotic crowds, smoke-filled plazas, children missing fingernails—scenes like these would have flashed through the protesters' minds as they calculated their next move. They did not have long. The swordsmen stood near the entrance to the souk so that protesters walked in the opposite direction, down the length of the covered market. The swordsmen kept pace, chanting: "With our blood, with our souls, we sacrifice for you, oh Bashar!"

Possessed of sudden wit, the crowd responded: "With our blood, with our souls, we sacrifice for you, oh martyrs!"

One swordsman turned beet red, screaming back the mantra of his youth as if someone had insulted his mother. His group edged closer to the protesters. The threat of violence was in the air. The protesters picked up their pace. The voices of the swordsmen grew louder, and when the protesters turned, they saw that their pursuers had doubled in size. A fury in their eyes, the swordsmen shouted: "God, Syria, and Bashar only!"

The crowd responded: "There is no god but God!"

The riposte rippled through the covered market, an assertion that Bashar was not, in fact, greater than all things. A few people were holding up phones as they marched, recording a spectacle unknown in the history of their city. In one video, Oday appears near the front, directing the movement. He is cupping his hands over his mouth, shouting himself hoarse. More swordsmen appear at the rear, and the crowd gains speed. The camera is shaking.

The protesters emerged from the covered market into the gray afternoon light. The sky was the color of slate, the ground slick from a late morning rain. They marched down Saladin Street, passing closed shops and old Arabic-style houses. Residents peeked through their doors at the commotion.

The protesters moved briskly down the street with the swordsmen close behind. In another video, Oday is raising his hands, like a victorious runner. Then he steps to the side to look at the passing crowd and the trailing counter-protesters. It's only a moment—the camera pans quickly—but you can see his face. It shows terrified wonder, an expression that says: Are we really doing this?

They neared Central Square, a plaza surrounded by businesses, a courthouse, and the Manbij Hotel, the tallest building in the city. And then the protesters saw them—dozens of men in pleather jackets, carrying bamboo sticks. A government agent shouted into his phone, "They're here! The terrorists are here!"

The protesters were penned, swordsmen behind, government agents in front. It now dawned on the protesters that they had marched this far—five hundred feet, a little over a city block—without any plan, without a route of egress.

One of the pleather-jacket men gave vent to all manner of profanity. He was in a lather, pacing back and forth, face red, shouting, "Someone is going to die tonight! Someone is going to die!" His comrades stood beside him in a phalanx, all wearing a look that said: *There will be no prisoners*. The swordsmen pushed up on the protesters from the rear. The chants broke into a cacophony of voices. What was to be done? There were no leaders to this movement, which had sprung from the heart, without a thought of tomorrow. The protesters were suddenly in disarray, pushing against each other, desperate for a way out.

Oday moved to the front. "Keep walking!" he shouted. He urged the protesters forward—through the pleather-jacket men. There seemed to be no other option.

The protesters inched forward. A new chant: *"Sal-mi-ya, Sal-mi-ya!"*

Oday stood just feet from the agents, close enough that they could get a good look at his face. The air vibrated with the chants: "Peaceful! Peaceful!"

Then a low-pitched scream from the rear: Protesters were being attacked with swords. The crowd surged forward with all its might, through the phalanx. But now the pleather-jacket men were ready for the kill. They began swinging their bamboo sticks like they were swatting flies. Chaos. The street was filled with anguished shouts. Protesters were on the ground. One got surrounded by a group of agents and was being struck with force. His legs twitched with every blow. In the savage confusion, the agents even struck their own comrades.

Oday tried to squeeze through the melee and suddenly felt weightless; he was in the air. He landed with terrible force. Five men were standing over him. His legs were getting lashed, then his kidneys, then his head. They were swarming over his body: "God"—*whack*—"Syria"—*whack*—"and Bashar!" *Whack*.

The few protesters still standing looked across the square and saw guns. The military had arrived. They trained their rifles on the crowd. But it was a knotted mass of bodies, agents raining blows onto prone protesters. One of those thrashing Oday had a peculiar look, as if he was ready to cross a threshold of his own and beat his quarry to death. The look on his face said: My country, paralyzed for one month, has been beset by a wide, deep conspiracy—and here, at my feet, is one of the culprits, one of the terrorists.

Now soldiers inched forward, sparking confusion among the pleather-jacket men and swordsmen. In that moment, summoning his deepest will, Oday managed to get up. His face was streaked with blood, and he felt as if his stomach had been punctured. He stumbled toward an alley. Some of his friends were still lying in the square, motionless. His father, Hala, Abboud, the rooftops, the dimly lit cavern of Abu Hajjal's—none of it mattered. His only wish, his sole reason for being, was to reach the alley. Behind him, a cheer. It was the counterprotesters, basking in their victory. Someone held up a placard bearing a photo of Bashar al-Assad. The counterprotesters filmed themselves: "This is a spontaneous rally in support of our leader!" a man proclaimed to the camera.

Oday made it to the alley. He hobbled along a stone wall. Behind him, a chant resounded through the streets: "God, Syria, and Bashar only!"

—+ +—

Oday was seated in front of his father. He was covered in bruises. The old man was shaking. To defy the authorities was to be branded. It was a black mark and meant being squeezed out of jobs, loans, passports. No family would give their daughter to a condemned man. His father looked at his skinny boy and began to cry. "Is this a game to you?" he asked. "Do you have any idea what they'll do to us?" Oday had expected a beating, a shouting match—but not this. He'd never seen his father cry before.

Father and son understood that the rules had shifted, that Oday had crossed a threshold that would reconfigure his every relationship. That evening, for the first time in his life, Oday found himself not worrying about his father's reaction. Instead, he had all of Syria—maybe even the entire Middle East—in his vision. A fellow protester who'd also managed to escape came over that evening, and they spoke about the government supporters, calling them *shabiha*. It was a word that originally referred to smugglers in the coastal areas, men in Italian loafers and aviators who scored riches on the black market created by the government's import restrictions. Now, around the country, the word was gaining currency as a catch-all term for government supporters. They were often from the Alawite sect—but the *shabiha* who beat Oday and his friends were Sunnis, just like them.

Oday wanted to track these *shabiha* down and throw a brick through their window. His Uncle Mustafa had joined the discussions—he was stunned to learn that Oday had participated in the afternoon's events—and argued that bursts of anger were no road to victory.

"Our slogans were all wrong," Oday said. "We should have demanded the overthrow of the regime."

"And replace it with what?" his friend asked.

They debated reform and revolution and revenge late into the night. It was the first time in weeks that Bushra heard her brother string together complete sentences. She saw he was now alive with a fire that illuminated the whole world, allowing him to see what he'd so long ignored: the spirit of meanness in a society where trust had been abolished; the rot at the core of school, work, the future. His city was littered with monuments to greed and caprice. The Manbij

Hotel, which had no guests, towered over Central Square while women begged in its shadows. The bronze statues of the dictator loomed over roundabouts where children sold cigarettes and packs of gum. Oday's life had been stifled by everyone—his father, his teachers, Abboud—because they said he wasn't ready, that he was *that kind of guy*. But in a single afternoon, he told Bushra, he'd proved himself as ready as he'd ever be.

The darkness had come on, and the streets were deserted. Central Square had been cordoned off. People had retreated indoors in a sepulchral mood, uncertain of the response their government had in store. Oday went out, limping through the streets. Most lights were already out. He turned down a narrow dirt lane, proceeding slowly in the blackness. When Hala heard the stones rattling her window, it took her a while to realize that the skinny figure in the street below was her Oday.

| TWO |

May–June 2011

The men stood in rows, heads bowed. Waiting among them, watching the exit, was Oday.

It was Friday, April 29. A week had passed since the events of Central Square, a week in which Oday and his friends pored over the details: the astonished looks on people's faces, the outstretched arms holding cell phones, the crazed eyes of the *shabiha*, the savage single-mindedness with which the protesters were truncheoned. In another time and place, observers might have labeled their sense of terror and their powerlessness "trauma," but Oday and friends had no such vocabulary. In fact, they felt they had endured a great trial, and through their success forged a new understanding of the limits of fear.

The imam called out "God is great!" and his flock said the words back. They were now filing through the exit of the Great Mosque. Oday was carried along. His friends had debated whether they should try again this week. At first, Oday was among those who believed that repeating the protest would be suicidal. But he'd lived a thousand lives that week: there was the moment he was lying face down on the pavement, taking blows; then that evening, when he hobbled toward Hala's window; then the following day, when a young woman dropped a folded piece of paper on the glass counter of his shop. When he opened it, his heart stopped—it was a message from Hala: "We will find a way."

By Thursday, Oday knew they must try again. Last week had drawn fifty protesters. This week, he predicted, they would attract one hundred. Soon, the protesters would outnumber the security forces.

Oday entered the covered market. The crowd was even more anxious than last time, and people quickly headed for the exit. Oday cried out, "Freedom! Freedom!"

Again the onlookers froze. But now a look of terrible recognition filled their faces. A few of them dared to join Oday's chant. In an instant, the voices collapsed into confusion. It was difficult to see what was happening. There were shouts of "Get back, get back!" A deep moan of "Oh God!"

All hell had broken loose.

The *shabiha* had appeared without warning and were among the crowd, swinging machetes. Bodies were on the ground, writhing. Oday and a few others managed to reach Saladin Street. "Peaceful, peaceful!" they chanted. And that was when they saw the next wave.

Baath Party members wearing armbands and carrying flags charged at them. "Peaceful!" Oday screamed, when a friend pulled him onto the sidewalk. "You're going to get us killed!" he said. As they spoke, the Baathists rushed past them, driving headlong into the crowd. It was a lopsided thrashing—security forces and *shabiha* outnumbered the protesters three to one. Oday saw a knee pushing into the neck of a long-haired protester—Shampoo Sami. He was about to rush to his friend's defense when he noticed that the police had arrived and were training their rifles on the protesters. He ran.

He emerged from an alley and crossed Main Street. The fracas was now a block behind him. He proceeded down Qambur Street, trying to look casual. Normally, Qambur was crowded with pedestrians visiting Bakir Books, doctors' offices, and confectionary shops. Today the street was deserted.

Oday reached the intersection of Qambur and Sundus, his balcony in sight. When he turned the corner, he found himself face-to-face with men carrying assault rifles.

"I'd like this one," 1st Lt. Maymati said.

Four young men were strung up by their wrists like flanks of meat. He was pointing to Oday.

A baton slammed into Oday's ribs. 1st Lt. Maymati was pacing the cell, enraged, as if the captives had insulted his honor. He said that the protesters would bring chaos to their city and that he was punishing them for their own good, as he would his own children.

Two of the dangling young men were unconscious.

As Oday hung from the ceiling, he wept, enraging 1st Lt. Maymati further. He raised his cudgel. *Whack*. Oday screamed.

1st Lt. Maymati raised the cudgel again. *Whack*. Oday screamed louder. 1st Lt. Maymati raised it once again.

Some captive protesters report that, in such moments, the cell sorts itself into those who will survive and those who won't. Those who count the blows, hoping each is the last, rarely tend to make it. But there are a few who use the fraction of a second right before the cudgel makes contact with skin to lift themselves above the dungeon, above cold cement. In that moment, they are steeped in the warmth of cardamom tea. They taste the pine nuts in their mother's *sheikh al-mahshi*; they smell their girlfriend's *oud*. They do not count. And they usually survive.

Whack.

―‡‡―

The next morning, in the officers' lounge, 1st Lt. Maymati was sitting with Abu Roz, the head of military intelligence. Two consecutive Friday protests had thrust the security services into crisis mode, and 1st Lt. Maymati and Abu Roz were determined to keep a lid on things, before the city became the next Daraa.

The pair were unlikely colleagues. 1st Lt. Maymati, clean-shaven and well-built, with a Romanesque visage, made it a point to know almost everyone, from carpetbaggers and sex workers to Baathist politicians and tribal sheikhs. Roz was round-faced and dyspeptic-looking, never seen without his army-issue camo, even when off duty. He saw the protests as threats to national security, and after the second Friday, he roped in 1st Lt. Maymati, who normally dealt with noise complaints and petty thieves.

They discussed the state of affairs: In two weeks, only fifty or so individuals had taken part in protests, a sure sign the situation was nowhere near the catastrophes of Daraa and Homs. On the whole, Manbij was loyal to the government. As for the protesters, it was hard to say who the ringleaders were. The young men hanging bloodied in the cells behind them were not talking, nor was it clear they had anything to say. Abu Roz wondered about agents provocateurs from abroad, but 1st Lt. Maymati laughed—he knew these were amateurs whose sin was not so much treason as stupidity.

Abu Roz wanted to ship the prisoners to Aleppo— but such banishment was a type of death, as they could be lost for decades in desert prisons and suburban fortresses, like that former prisoner Hasan Nefi, whose story was well known in security circles. The protesters deserved such a fate, the two agreed, but they worried the move might backfire; Manbij was a tribal city, and every prisoner was embedded in a mesh of brothers and first cousins and second cousins. Would they remain loyal to the government if their loved ones disappeared? This had been the grave tactical error of the security services in Daraa, and 1st Lt. Maymati was determined not to repeat that same mistake here. He suggested an alternative course: keep the disturbances "in the family." Secure—or extract—a pledge from the prisoners to quit. Tell them that if they're ever seen at a protest again, they'd be saying goodbye to their loved ones forever.

MAY

"My God," Hala said, shining the light of her cell phone on Oday. They were huddled in the alley of Roman stone. She had not seen him in a month. Oday's eye sockets were purple, his lips engorged. "Oh my God."

After signing a pledge to never protest again, Oday had been released. He retreated to a friend's farmhouse. It felt as if years had passed since December, when he and his friends used to gather in the barn to sip Grant's and smoke hash. Now he spent his days alone. He returned to the city only at night, creeping along the Roman walls to see Hala. He'd come to possess the terrible yet liberating knowledge of the regime's monstrosity, which cast all the other little goblins that had once haunted his life in a new, almost comforting light. What was his father but a tired old man, clinging to insipid dogma? What was Abboud but a younger, and in that way more pathetic, version of the same thing? The regime had beaten the fear of those lesser devils out of him, and Oday knew that if Abboud ever laid a finger on Hala, he would burst through her doors and fight him off.

On May 5, the regime deployed tanks to Homs. Around the country, hundreds of demonstrators were rounded up. The next day marked two weeks since Manbij's inaugural protest. When afternoon services concluded at the Great Mosque, the congregants filed out. The covered market was teeming with soldiers and *shabiha*. On Saladin Street, they were posted every few meters, and there wasn't a protester in sight. A few people gathered at Central Square, aware of the previous weeks' disturbances, simply to gawk. The soldiers carried rifles, and they looked jumpy.

Minutes elapsed—still no protesters. The square was now filling with *shabiha* carrying Assad placards. More pedestrians stopped to watch. The *shabiha* arranged themselves in formation. Just then, a young man stepped into the square. No one moved. The man looked uncertain, walking gingerly. Clutching their placards, the *shabiha* watched.

The man turned and faced the crowd. "Why are you standing there?" he shouted.

The *shabiha* and the spectators were still.

The man shouted at the top of his voice, "God is great!"

No one stirred. The *shabiha* were stunned at this almost suicidal display. The police locked their rifles on the solitary man.

"Freedom!" he shouted.

Before he could shout again or the spectators could react, he was set upon by seven or eight *shabiha*. He was thrashed until he no longer moved. His name was Mustafa al-Loz, and he was dragged away.

A chant arose from the square: "God, Syria, and Bashar only!"

Standing in this crowd, listening to this chant, was Abel Os.

Later that evening, Abel Os was sitting behind the folding table that served as his desk. He now worked as an assistant in a one-room shop that smelled like a car engine. The glass storefront was mottled with decals, one of which read "Hajji Ibrahim Real Estate"; "Furnished apartments," another announced. Business had ground to a standstill due to the demonstrations, so Abel Os had plenty of time to think. That afternoon at Central Square, a man had been beaten—almost torn limb from limb—in front of his eyes, but he had not budged. What could he have done? The issue called for introspection.

Abel Os held no firm opinion on the protesters. Many years ago, he'd marched down Main Street waving a Syrian flag to celebrate the coronation of Bashar al-Assad. But politics did not captivate him, only people. He was a problem solver: When a neighborhood boy was hauled in front of 1st Lt. Maymati for hawking black-market cigarettes, it was Abel Os who went to the station and pledged to guarantee the boy's propriety. And what were the protests, after all, except a misunderstanding between two sides? He yearned to mediate, to lower the temperature. The old Abel Os would have pushed the protesters and the authorities to sit across the table and hear each other out, but his flight to Lebanon had done violence to his self-esteem. He'd returned to Manbij without a shop or a home—they'd been repossessed by creditors. He and his family squeezed into a single room above his brother's house. Who was he to get involved?

Still, his failure to prevent the beating ate away at him. At night he asked his wife if he should have intervened. She snapped, "Where do you get your ideas?"

May 11 was the fourth Friday since the inaugural protest. As prayer let out, Abel Os found himself at Central Square, possessed by a desire to show himself that he was not the type of person to stand idly by. He would bring the sides together, heal this terrible rift, and in that way prove that the motorcycle men, the muster-zone bosses—the lords and masters of New Syria—had not won.

But his services were not needed, it turned out. The congregants emerged from Saladin Street in their usual numbers, but mixed among them were pleather-jacket men and Baath Party factotums. A rank of uniformed soldiers stood watch. After five minutes, it was over—the congregants dispersed, and the soldiers trooped off. Not a single demonstrator had shown himself. Manbij's protest movement appeared finished.

JUNE

The weeks carried on in this fashion: Abel Os standing in the square on Friday afternoons, the congregants emptying out of the Great Mosque, the soldiers sweating under the sun, the *shabiha* standing arms akimbo. Abel Os was no longer certain what he was looking for, so he stopped visiting Central Square.

The city of Manbij was at peace. But at the shop, Abel Os listened to the radio describe the tempest engulfing other cities. In Daraa, protests continued, landing hundreds in prison. Among them was a thirteen-year-old boy, Hamza Ali al-Khateeb. When his family recovered his body, they found it marbled with bruises and bearing multiple gunshot wounds. In the groin, there was a gash where his penis should have been.

An image of the boy's body circulated on social media. On June 3, fifty thousand protesters gathered in Hama. In a remote northwest region called Jisr al-Shughur, the protests morphed into violence. Dozens of government personnel were killed. As the protests spread, the government responded with ferocity: Six protesters were gunned down in the eastern city of Deir al-Zour, another six in the town of Ariha. In Daraa, the population was under siege, with the food supply running low.

Every morning, Abel Os walked down Rabta Street. He'd never seen traffic so sparse. The wealthy had vanished behind lace curtains. Classes remained in session, but parents made sure to walk their children to school.

On June 20, for only the third time since the events began, President Assad addressed the nation. Now, however, there were no minute-long ovations or rhapsodies. The president stood behind the podium looking gaunt and uncertain. "In the past, there were two models: socialist and capitalist. Many people believe these models have fallen," he explained. "We need time to look for a model which suits Syria." The model he searched for, he said, was one that "achieves social equity between rich and poor, the country and the city." But he gave no hint of what it might be.

Abel Os listened on the radio as the president offered jumbled thoughts on the problem of corruption, the role of the security services—"the state is like father and mother that embraces all with tolerance and love"—and the need for reform. Regarding the protests, though, he spoke with clarity: "Conspiracies are like germs, after all, multiplying every moment everywhere." The protesters were "terrorists" who'd infected the body politic, requiring emergency inoculation. This called for prosecution to the fullest extent of the law.

That afternoon, Abel Os's neighbor visited the office. Inspired by the president's speech, he was convinced Tel Aviv and Washington had flooded Manbij with weapons, and that the protesters at the Great Mosque had been armed to the teeth.

But Abel Os had been present at the Great Mosque. He saw with his own eyes that the only weapons were those in the hands of the security forces. A man had stood before the square, before the entire city, and offered himself as a sacrifice. He may have been imprudent, even delusional—but a terrorist? Abel Os was now hardly listening to the neighbor, and finally he left the office.

A strange feeling had overcome him, though he couldn't put his finger on it. He placed a chair on the sidewalk, in front of the shop door—like in the old days, when he sat on an overturned tomato crate in front of Tear of Roses, listening to his neighbors' anxieties. This word "terrorist" bothered him. He realized, after a turn, that he was upset, actually angry, with his neighbor's blindness. He could not understand his anger—to get worked up by faraway events like this was itself a foreign sensation.

That evening, a friend who worked at the Cardamom Market stopped by. Abel Os could not help but bring up the president's remarks, and his friend's face darkened. Abel Os mustered the courage to ask him what he thought of the protests.

"Downtown," his friend cautiously replied, "is like a foreign occupation." He studied Abel Os's reaction and saw that a troubled look had washed over him. "The country is on fire and massacres are being committed, but we are sleeping," he continued, watching his eyes the whole time.

Abel Os said nothing but looked interested. So the man ventured, "Forget downtown—let's do something where they won't expect it."

Abel Os now seemed surprised. He was hesitant to offer his thoughts, looking around the office even though they were the only two there. His friend told him that he knew everyone; he was like a mukhtar. If Abel Os raised his voice, people would follow. "You have a special responsibility, because your neighborhood loves you, and you have done so much for them. You could do something in the darkness, far from the security forces—just something small and symbolic to wake people up. People would then know that Manbij also wants to be free."

Abel Os was quiet for a long while. "The Cardamom Market," he finally said, after great consideration.

"When?"

"Nine sharp tonight."

Under the floodlights, Abel Os and three friends circled the main lot of the market on motorcycles, shouting "Freedom!" Shoppers and merchants stopped what they were doing. In the near silence, the chants carried across the lot. One of the riders filmed the group on his phone. As Abel Os circled, he caught the look on the faces of the marketgoers: wonder, astonishment. Just then, the clutch of headlights appeared. The group fled. Abel Os raced down an alley. Soldiers descended on the market, but the protesters had vanished. The entire action lasted four minutes.

That night, Abel Os lay in his bed, unable to sleep. He replayed the scenes in his mind: the looks on the shopkeepers' faces, the protester filming the procession with his phone in one hand, the other hand steering his bike.

The phone. Abel Os nearly leapt from his bed, suddenly remembering that his face had been recorded.

He hurried outside and rushed through the streets on his motorbike. It was past midnight. New checkpoints had sprouted all over the place. He reached the home of the friend who'd helped organize the rally, who said he'd shared the clip with another friend. That friend directed him to a third house, whose inhabitants pointed him to a fourth. It was 2:00 a.m. by the time he knocked on a door to stand before a stout, unshaven man, who looked to be in his thirties, and who introduced himself as Abu Shakir.

The clip was in his possession, and he seemed sympathetic as Abel Os begged him to delete it. Abu Shakir's brother had been among the conspirators in the first protest, and on that day, his brother was beaten within inches of his life.

Abel Os watched as he erased the video.

Abu Shakir was impressed. "You brought three people to the protest?" He invited him inside for tea.

As police cruisers prowled the streets outside, the pair sat talking until the first strains of the muezzin could be heard. They were like old friends, throwing off hopeless ideas, trading rumors. They agreed they faced a singular challenge: They needed to find a way to revive the protest movement, to signal to authorities that Daraa would not be forgotten, and to awaken their friends and neighbors from slumber. But each of the forty or so mosques in the city, along with a dozen parks and, of course, Central Square, were under occupation by regime troops.

Abel Os didn't know a thing about politics, but he knew all about squaring off against an opponent, about kata, kihon, and kumite. He knew Bruce Lee's maxims like the back of his hand: *Do not be assertive, but adjust to the object, and you shall find a way around or through it. If nothing within you stays rigid, outward things will disclose themselves.*

He began to wonder.

Be like water making its way through the cracks.

Abel Os had an idea.

No one could remember a time when the Manbij wadi, which snakes through the eastern quarters, ever swelled with rainwater. Mostly, the man-made gully just seemed to collect trash. During the day, its noisome vapors mixed with motorcycle exhaust and desert dust and the scent of freshly cut oranges from the juice stands. By night, the area was vacant.

Late one night, Abel Os crossed a bridge over the wadi, heading for a wealthy neighborhood of aureate balconies and lit storefronts. A few police milled here and there. Standing on a street under an awning, Abel Os watched them. A pair of policemen strolled from one end of the street to the other and back, their course lit by streetlamps. Every time, they passed him without noticing.

Abel Os waited under the awning. When the police patrol was on the far end of one of its circuits, a figure materialized and motioned for Abel Os to follow. It was Abu Shakir. The two entered an office building and climbed the stairs to the second floor.

Inside, eight men were seated around an oak table. Leather couches were tucked into the corners, and the walls were lined with wood paneling. A computer screen glowed on a desktop. For Abel Os, who'd worked in a one-room shop for so many years and frequented a karate studio with walls of unfinished cement and a single overhead light bulb, walking into a room like this made him feel like a conscript sneaking into the officers' club.

The room belonged to a pair of civil engineers, Ahmed Rahmo and Muhammad Bisher. Abel Os had heard of Bisher's younger brother, a onetime soccer prodigy named Abdul Hadi. The elder Bisher had graduated from Aleppo University and teamed up with Rahmo, his classmate. Rahmo opened the meeting. He spoke with the self-possession of an operative, someone who'd spent a lifetime plotting to overthrow governments. In truth, though, political words had never left his lips until this past March. From the first gun smoke in Daraa, he was glued to the screen. When he learned of the Great Mosque demonstration, he committed himself to tracking down every like-minded person in Manbij. This was Rahmo's métier, knitting people together. His phone stored the number of every carpenter and architect and lawyer in the region. He knew all the city's blacksmiths and grocers by name. Rahmo believed what he was seeing around the country was no mere protest movement—it was a revolution. And there could be no revolution without revolutionaries, so it was his calling to find them. He did not want the tremulous sort who preferred the anonymity of the crowd—he wanted organizers.

Abel Os was deeply impressed. Rahmo spoke in complete sentences, with an engineer's precision and a lawyer's grasp of argument. He explained that everyone gathered here had attempted to organize a demonstration. Most had failed. The city had witnessed only two successful protests in three months: at the Great Mosque and the Cardamom Market. "There's only one answer for us," he said. "Organize."

The men in the room introduced themselves. There was Abu Salah, a schoolteacher who'd attended the first protest. Lean, with a salt-and-pepper mustache and a bird-like bearing, he sat quietly every afternoon in the teachers' lounge as his colleagues repeatedly denounced the terrorists. Once, he tried to organize a protest in his neighborhood, but the security grip was too tight.

There was Munzer Salal. He was a religious scholar, but he wore jeans and dress shirts and seemed to take an interest in mysticism. With delicate features and searching eyes, he had a glance that would quicken the heartbeats of many women. Abel Os had never laid eyes on the youngster, but his family name—Salal—needed no introduction. They were one of the richest families in the city, owners of a covered market and many other properties beside. They were the closest Manbij had to royalty.

And there were others, eight in total, from all corners of the city. Abel Os felt as if he'd wandered into a secret society. Unlike him, the others were all university graduates. Only Abu Salah was solidly proletarian—the rest were drawn from Manbij's velvet class, the city's elite. Most of them wore dark suits and dark jeans and collared shirts. Large smartphones filled their hands. At one time, he would have shrunk in the corner in such company. But he was leaving the old muck at the door. Here, there were no interlopers, only comrades.

That night, they spoke about the evaporating fear. Just by being here, Abu Salah said, we are expelling the terror in our souls. He argued that the world had changed. The horrors of the 1982 repression were unthinkable today. "The United States will never allow Bashar to kill his own people," he said.

With social media on their side, neutrality was impossible. "Everyone in the world knows what is happening in Syria. The regime cannot hide its crimes." Abu Shakir pontificated on the meaning of "civilization"—we live in a global village, he said, a village of human rights and dignity for every man, woman, and child. Every human was watched over by a community of guardians, by the United Nations, and they would not allow Bashar to act with impunity. Sovereignty lies with the people, he said, not with the gang occupying the palace in Damascus.

But before the international community could act, it was up to them to take the first step. Ahmed Rahmo spoke of the challenge facing them: Demonstrations may represent the bottled energies of the repressed, the wild passions of the mob—but at their core, they are forms of communication. In fact, by conveying indignation, they are acts of *speech*, intended for two audiences: The protest speaks *against* some authority or policy, but it also speaks *to* the fence-sitters, the reserve army of discontented who are afraid to mobilize. This poses a chicken-and-egg problem: With security forces smothering the squares and mosques, gathering in numbers was impossible. But without gathering in numbers, the fence-sitters will not be moved to join the cause. The authorities had, in other words, severed the protesters' means of communication with the city.

Abel Os had never experienced a discussion like this. His head was swimming. He realized that the men were speaking, in a much more exalted fashion, of precisely the problem he and Abu Shakir had identified. Shyly, he floated the idea he'd been nursing since the Cardamom Market demonstration: a flash protest. Five minutes long, under the cover of darkness, on the outskirts of the city. These areas were unpatrolled—but there was no civilian traffic either. Instead, the protesters would communicate with the people of Manbij indirectly, by uploading videos of these demonstrations. If satellite channels aired footage of the action with the "Manbij" chyron splashed across the bottom, the people would understand a revolt was brewing in their city.

Ahmed Rahmo was besotted with the idea. Flash mobs, poster-making, chain of custody over footage—this called for organization. He proposed creating a body, called the Local Coordinating Committee: The city would be divided into eight wards, each under the responsibility of a man present here. Once this Local Coordinating Committee decided on a flash protest, the ward leaders would relay the time and place to their trusted contacts. The committee would assign videographers for each event. Operational efficiency would be of the essence: "If you come even a minute late," Rahmo said, "you can't participate."

The group elected Abu Salah as president of the Local Coordinating Committee, and two others, both artists, to oversee placard design. It was the first vote of their lives.

—⋅—⋅—

The video shows an empty street, the countryside dark on either side. The screen is lit only by a concrete sculpture of an umbrella, which occupies a roundabout on the city's edge. Pink and orange lights illuminate the canopy, giving the structure a glow like a jellyfish. A voice says, "Twenty-ninth of June, 2011," and the camera shakes as the desert wind whips the street.

The roundabout is now thronged with some two dozen people, their faces in balaclavas or wrapped in scarves. They are visible only for brief moments as they pass under the streetlamps. One large man appears to be playing the role of a coordinator—this is Abel Os. A few men on motorcycle circle the umbrella. The crowd chants, "The people want the downfall of the regime!" The cameraman's fear is palpable. He cannot focus for long, and the view keeps swinging down the road to look for police. Two protesters unfurl a banner: "The germs of Manbij will destroy the regime's immunity." And suddenly, there is the sound of whistles as lookouts spot approaching cars. People are now running. The video lasts 2 minutes and 35 seconds.

Abel Os lived close to the umbrella roundabout, and the location had been his suggestion. When he neared his house, he caught up with a protester he'd recruited from the karate studio. That protester brought friends, one of them a lanky boy who introduced himself as Oday.

Oday did not want to frighten Abel Os, so he did not mention his arrest. The group agreed to create a cell. Abel Os would relay the coordinates of future protests to Oday, who would pass the message to his friends over Skype. For his screen name, Oday chose CheGuevara00000.

The next morning, the clip aired on satellite stations, and before long, everyone in Manbij had seen it. Oday stopped by the real estate office and shook Abel Os's hand. "You just put our city on the map," he said.

Abel Os now saw Manbij's haggard statuettes, its waterless fountains, as his canvas. He realized he could turn the screw tighter by staging a flash mob on Rabta Street, one of the wealthiest arteries in town. The sentries changed shifts at 11:00 p.m., but the incoming guards were often late, leaving a brief window during which the street was unattended. He passed the message to the LCC, and plans were disseminated.

Two evenings later, at his real estate office, Abel Os fit panties over his face and stole onto Rabta Street. Hidden in the shadows was a group of protesters, including Oday and Shampoo Sami, also masked in panties. Down the street, a second group of protesters waited. Oday was listening for Abel Os's karate whistle, which signaled the shift change.

From a distance, Abel Os surveilled the sentries. But as the time slipped past eleven, they did not depart. Abel Os clutched his whistle. At length the two sentries, deep in conversation, disappeared into the night. Abel Os waited. The street was perfectly still. A minute passed. Then he put the whistle to his mouth and blew as hard as he could.

A couple of protesters broke into a run. Oday jumped into the street. "No, no—it's the signal!" he shouted. "That's Abel Os!" Pandemonium broke loose. All the protesters were running. Desperately, Abel Os blew his whistle again. He waved his hands and shouted. Lights were turning on in the balcony windows. Oday kept shouting, "It's Abel Os! Don't run!"

Abel Os could not believe it—the LCC had failed to inform one of the protest cells about the whistle. He caught up with Oday, who said that the other protesters had thought they'd heard him shout, "That's Abu Roz"—the head of military intelligence.

Within minutes, the police arrived. By then the protesters had disappeared, but dozens of residents had watched the confusion from their balconies. They saw young men running with signs, and spotted a large man in a mask who appeared to be their leader. When questioned by the police, they told them what they'd witnessed, and the name they'd heard shouted.

Back at the station, 1st Lt. Maymati recorded the identity of the alleged leader of Manbij's protest movement: Abel Os.

When Ahmed Rahmo and Abu Shakir found him, Abel Os was hunched behind his desk, the iron shutters drawn down over the storefront. He'd refused to go home. It was some time past 3:00 a.m. "Whose idea was it to use a whistle?" Rahmo laughed, wiping his eyes, but Abel Os was not amused.

The pair, undeterred by the aborted protest, labored to convince Abel Os to put the mishap behind him. Another scheme had already come into focus: A college professor had apparently assembled a network of nearly five hundred anti-regime engineers, doctors, and pharmacists from around the province. He had cobbled together this secret band over months and now proposed a procession in a Manbij suburb, far from security forces—in broad daylight.

"If you try this, it's the end of me," Abel Os said. "Everyone knows me now." Oday had shouted his name at the top of his lungs.

"If you are afraid, you can stay home."

Abel Os felt that his star, which had shone brilliantly in the revolutionary firmament for twelve glorious hours, was already fading. How stupid, how oxlike, he was! He reproached himself for failing to plan better, for landing himself in this position. All his life, from the acrid roundabouts of Damascus to the sun-blanched construction zones of Beirut, Abel Os had yearned to be understood and accepted. And why, when he already possessed all the riches a man could hope for? He had a loving wife, two children of boundless energy, and a healthy reputation. Perhaps it was the idea of sitting before his fellow men as equals, an image his younger self could never have conjured. The gift of respect was too great to squander. He blurted out, "No, I'll be there."

When Abel Os appeared at the village mosque the next afternoon, he was sore from having slept in the office chair. He saw Ahmed Rahmo and a few others—but the throngs of doctors and engineers they had promised were nowhere in sight. He counted only ten protesters.

"Where is everyone?" he asked.

Ahmed Rahmo looked embarrassed.

As the congregants dribbled out, a few launched into chants. Abel Os slipped on a mask and, with a heavy heart, joined in. Within a minute, the protesters dispersed. Abel Os climbed onto a motorcycle and left.

At home, his wife was beside herself. "Do you really think you are some great leader? Are you really this selfish? Do you think about me? About your son and daughter?"

Abel Os sat before her like a condemned man. He couldn't remember ever having felt so weary. His only wish was to bed down, wrap himself tight, and sleep for days. But as the afternoon passed, sleep proved elusive. He spent it as one does when sights and sounds take on new, sinister shades—when the squares of sunlight slide across the floor, when the opening and closing of car doors clutch at the heart. He acknowledged he had gone too far, that *this* was the wrong type of threshold to cross. Why not quit? Images of muster zones in Beirut came flooding back: the serenity, the sea breeze, the soft nights with fellow workers. He could return to Beirut to wait things out. He could master the real estate game, rent homes to migrant workers from Manbij. The thought lifted his spirits, and he was talking himself into leaving then and there when a knock came at the door.

He stepped outside to find eight or nine police vehicles and many, many muzzles.

Abel Os's blindfold was removed, revealing a dusky room. Every breath was a stab, the result of multiple fists and batons on his torso over the last dozen hours. His mouth tasted of metal.

"Do you know why you're here?" said a voice.

Abel Os shook his head. He felt the sudden blow to his jaw and keeled over. He had been identified at a protest that afternoon, the voice said. When Abel Os claimed he knew nothing, he felt a powerful burst of cold across his face—from an iron bar or perhaps a hose.

A few hours later, he was brought to a second room and shown a cell phone video. In the clip, taken from behind, a large man in a polo shirt and track pants, wearing a mask, is running toward a motorcycle. "I've never seen this person before in my life," Abel Os said. The voice laughed: "You are wearing the same clothes!" Abel Os looked down at his track pants and his blood-stained polo shirt. The owner of the voice stepped into the light and revealed himself as 1st Lt. Maymati.

"So, you are the mastermind, eh?" 1st Lt. Maymati asked.

The next morning his cell door was opened, and 1st Lt. Maymati and Abu Roz stood at the entrance. "Put your shirt on," Abu Roz said. "We're moving you." For a moment, Abel Os thought he was being transferred to another Manbij facility—but then it dawned on him that they meant something much worse. He lunged toward Abu Roz's feet, pleading for mercy. The security chief kicked him off.

He was loaded into the van, officially registered as "Prisoner Number 1," the first detainee from the city of Manbij to be banished to Syria's prison archipelago.

| THREE |

July–August 2011

JULY

Something in Mina Saba's life was communicating dread. Whenever things felt askew, she clung to that simple yet profound order: *Be honorable*. She would obey the command as if it had issued from the lips of the archangel Gabriel himself. This was the way of the *shawi*. The cosmopolites in Damascus and Aleppo deploy this term of abuse for the seemingly uncouth and unlettered tribal folk of eastern Syria, but the people of Manbij had made it their own. To be *shawi* was to uphold bygone values: loyalty, family, hospitality. And, maybe most important, to be *shawi* was to live with honor. That obligation fell on men and women alike, but for Mina, honor meant acting the way a good woman should. Sure, Manbij was brimming with sex work, adultery, elopements. But in this city, the patina of honor mattered more than anything else.

There was the story of Mariam, who worked as a waitress in a hookah bar. Her husband could not bear the thought of her leaning over to take orders, laughing with smoke-smelling men. The couple divorced, and Mariam was unable to remarry. There was Mina's neighbor, Mona, who'd been caught in flagrante with a boy in a farmhouse. Mona was dragged away screaming by her brothers. Her father interceded before she could be drowned in the Euphrates, but Mona was never the same. Twice, she made attempts on her life. Wearing a proverbial scarlet letter, she was cast into spinsterhood.

Honor was the reason why, when Mina's brother Sami gained admission to art school in Damascus, the family was dead set against it. The capital was a farrago of pulsing nightclubs and dimly lit alleys. Miraculously, Sami returned with his honor intact. He'd matured into a responsible young man, even if he'd picked up a few peccadilloes—chief among them his flowing mane. If he'd avoided trouble, it was because he had the privilege of ignoring much that Mina could not. No one had to spell this out; she'd gotten the message in spoonfuls hundreds of times a day in a hundred subtle ways: at six or seven, a scolding from her mother for sitting legs akimbo in front of company; at thirteen, hauled indoors by an aunt who hissed that girls of that age didn't play with boys. At seventeen, she stood before a mirror, adjusting her headscarf for the first time. This was, after all, a tribal city, and she was, before all else, a daughter, and would be someone's wife.

Manbij was quiet now, but elsewhere, protesters continued to fall. For Mina, who had just turned twenty-nine, these events were like a hard wind blowing steadily against her lowered head. She rose every morning at six, in the shadow of the Manbij Mills, where her husband worked, and which towered over the earth like giant AA batteries. The government-run mills provided grain to the city's bakeries and to hundreds of surrounding towns and villages. The structures, built from tens of thousands of tons of concrete and millions of bricks, were so enormous that even when Mina left home, walking her two sons to school, she felt she was never truly free of their presence.

Every morning, she made her way to Assadiya Primary, where she taught fourth and fifth graders. The school stood in front of a midden. There were rutted clearings through which skinny Kurdish boys led their goats. Small shacks had sprouted on the edge of the lot, their slate roofs and cinderblock frames containing countless lives. Some residents begged for handouts along the nearby highway; others had fallen to selling their bodies. Mina used to discuss this grim scene with other teachers, speaking as if this neighborhood on the south side was a symbol of all that Syria had left behind in its march into the twenty-first century. But now, with events such as they were, she kept quiet.

When the Daraa protests began, her husband called a former colleague who lived there. "It's all lies," said the man over the phone. "It's as peaceful as heaven." But when he visited Manbij, the colleague broke down in tears, confessing that the situation was beyond comprehension, that the government was slaughtering dozens of people a day. When her colleagues discussed the events in the teachers' lounge, Mina said nothing, thinking only of a fellow teacher, a Palestinian named Zahra. Many years earlier, Zahra's brother was secretly recorded criticizing Bashar al-Assad. He was sent, ironically enough, to the Palestine Branch, that notorious dungeon in Damascus, where his testicles were smashed.

Be honorable. But what was honor in such a system? Once, in the eighties, Mina's neighbor disappeared. When his sister went to the authorities, she too was taken. She returned home after a month. Her husband, unable to banish images of unknown hands and eyes on his wife, divorced her.

There was no television in the teachers' lounge, and Mina was glad of it. She longed for the serenity of the pre-Daraa times, when she could visit the souk and bask in the badinage, the encounters with forgotten friends from Manbij Girls High School, the haggling at the spice scales. There were moments when she could conjure that era—every afternoon from eight to twelve, facing a sea of small faces looking expectantly at her—but the second she stepped outside, the sensation vanished. Her husband tried to distract her by taking her to the mall in Aleppo, but she could not shake the feeling that tomorrow, or the next day, everything would be torn asunder. It was not her habit to be concerned with faraway tribulations. Rather, her sense of doom was concentrated on a nearby source: Sami.

The troubles had begun two weeks earlier when, without warning, he quit painting. Art had been his calling since high school, when he'd failed a vision test due to color blindness, which thwarted his attempt to enroll in the officers' academy. He poured his energies into the brush and, as if to rebel against his former aspirations, quit school, grew out his hair, and rented a tiny apartment that he turned into a studio. The Manbij art scene, such as it was, took notice when his black-and-white acrylics appeared in the Cultural Center, and it was agreed that the young man had promise. Earlier that year, he told Mina he planned to finally take up color. He envisioned a mural populated with the totems of human history: men on bay-colored horses, huts burning blood-red, amber shafts of light piercing the clouds to shine onto Creation. Sami claimed he could see it all, floating in front of his eyes.

Not long after quitting, he showed up at Mina's door. "Sis," he said—he never used her name, "I want you to have this."

He handed her a sealed letter, written on a torn piece of canvas. "Promise me," he said, "don't open this until I die."

"What's gotten into you?" Mina asked. But he did not reply, and Mina could gather from the wild, determined look in his eyes that he was about to do something reckless.

The letter sat on Mina's bureau for many days, and she had no desire to open it. She knew her little brother better than anyone: The signs were evident from the start. His apartment was increasingly frequented by young men she'd never seen before, and when she brought over lunch, they would stop their conversation. He went to sleep in his jeans, his shoes by his bedside. He was obsessed with the internet, spending hours on the computer.

Finally, one day in June, she asked him: "Have you been to a protest?"

Sami laughed and denied it, but she caught a gleam in his eyes. A few days later, she asked again, more forcefully.

"Sis, it's not for us, it's not for you and me," he said. "It's for Anwar"—Mina's son. Mina felt a flash of anger. She wanted to slap the boy—he was just a boy, a little child, without responsibilities of his own. At his age, twenty-six, men were supposed to be planning a future. *What utter stupidity*, she thought.

"What do you want?" she asked. "What's your goal?"

"Freedom, nothing else."

All week, Mina could not shake her mind free of Sami. She saw his life as a path through dense bosk, in one direction leading to a clearing, to a wife and children and an atelier in Aleppo, in the other, vanishing into the growths. She discussed the situation with her husband. One thought was to appeal to her father, a feared disciplinarian. Born in a mud house, he'd worked for decades in the post office, retiring with a pension and a healthy gratitude for his station in life. But he'd suffered health scares, and Mina was not sure his heart could handle the news.

That left few avenues. Mina visited Sami's apartment every day after work, but he was unmoved by her entreaties. He could be mulish about the simplest things, like quitting cigarettes. Nor was Mina the type to throw herself at someone's feet. So she tried the silent treatment, avoiding his apartment for several days. But Sami hardly noticed, absorbed as he was with his new friends. She sent her husband, who sat him down, man to man, and delivered a stern lecture that he was going to bring tragedy upon them all. Sami ignored him.

Images were now invading Mina's consciousness: Sami in cuffs, her father splayed out on the floor from a stroke, her mother standing over him, wailing. Mina was reprimanded for seeming distracted and aloof at work. Some nights, she awoke covered in sweat. She grew accustomed to lying awake, her husband snoring beside her. One early morning, long before the muezzin announced the dawn, the thought struck her: If she could not stop Sami, she would have to keep him safe, and that was only possible if she gained his trust—like someone charming her way into an enemy camp.

One evening she sat in front of him, his black-and-white acrylics adorning the wall behind him. He was getting ready to go out with friends—where, he did not say.

"I know what you are up to," she said. Sami smiled mischievously, and Mina couldn't believe it. Consumed by abstract ideas like *freedom*, he was ready to plunge the entire family into disaster. Mina hadn't thought much about freedom and wasn't even sure what it meant, but she certainly knew about loyalty—and, when it comes to those you love, loyalty can sometimes mean deception.

"Tell me," she said, "how can I help?"

At first, Sami was wary of Mina's sudden change of heart and kept her at a distance. But she was importunate, prepared to carry on for months, with plaintive pleas here, feigned enthusiasm there, until she got her way. Sami's defenses crumbled, and one evening he invited his sister to help design placards. As she daubed the word "Freedom" in black, red, and green, she wrested details from him. She learned that he had sunk far deeper in conspiracy than she'd feared. Two weeks had passed since the last protest, when someone named Abel Os was carried away. A story swept the city that he'd been banished to Palmyra and had possibly named his co-conspirators under torture. Local Coordinating Committee members were expecting the police to burst through their doors at any moment, so they stopped sleeping in their own beds. After heated discussion, they decided that the only way to save their comrade—and themselves—was to hold another protest, giving the authorities the impression that Abel Os was one of many, that the movement was much larger than it appeared.

The Local Coordinating Committee formulated a plan based on the observation that the rural hamlets ringing Manbij were free of security forces. "If the people out there won't join the revolution," Sami explained, "we'll bring the revolution to them."

It was late. The silo lights were burning outside. Mina watched her brother as he spoke, this child with his oceans of enthusiasm. With all her might, she urged her younger brother to step back, to see his parents' sacrifices, but Sami was unmovable. It was stitched into his very being: When he dropped out of school, he'd been impervious to his mother's tears and his father's rage. Only Mina had supported him then. Now she was cast in her mother's role. She pleaded. But Sami pulled up clip after clip on his phone, showing her scenes of crowds fired upon in Homs, funeral processions in Douma. There was a shine in his eyes.

At dawn he collected the placards and banners and flags. The Syrian flag features two stars superimposed on thick red-white-and-black stripes. The stripes represent the great Arab empires of the past, like the Abbasid Caliphate, while the stars symbolize Arab nationalism. But now, with Arab soldiers firing on defenseless Arab crowds, what could these ideas possibly mean? So a new flag spread among the protesters. It was in fact an old flag, a green-white-and-black standard with three stars used during Syria's brief democratic period in the 1950s. "This is the flag of freedom," Sami said.

Sami hid the flag in an alley near the mills. The next day, he pulled up on his motorcycle to gather the contraband. Mina watched from her window. The city had fallen into its Friday afternoon numbness, the desert wind beating the stone walls. Her brother raced off, hair flying behind him.

That evening, Sami was at his parents' house, pacing in his childhood bedroom. The sound of street traffic could be heard through the walls, which, Mina noticed, unsettled him. It was bedtime, but he was wearing his boots and jeans. In a low voice, he recounted to Mina the afternoon's events. About two dozen protesters, all on motorcycles, had gathered. Children emerged from mud houses. As soon as the protesters unfurled their signs, the children began throwing stones. Under the hailstorm, the protesters tried to raise a chant. But then adults joined their children. A man shouted, "We don't want terrorists here!"

The protesters scrambled, racing down dirt roads, cutting through wheat fields. Ahmed Rahmo of the LCC reached a nearby village, where farmers rushed him with sticks. He fled to the home of the village chief, begging protection. The chief promptly handed him over to the secret police. The story was the same for Abu Shakir and the others. In a single afternoon, the entire LCC leadership was thrown behind bars.

Sami had escaped by a hair, abandoning his motorcycle and hitchhiking back to the city. He cursed the city of his birth. "Manbij is a city of *shabiha*," he told Mina. "They deserve to live like this!" A city of sheep, docile and unthinking, without a filament of courage. They thought only of themselves, of their next promotion, their self-indulgent romances and mind-numbing television soaps. Mina was not so sure. She understood the power of fear, the way it could smother you, turn your every waking thought into a negotiation with a higher power.

It was late, and before she left, she embraced her brother. As Sami climbed into bed, she noticed he was still wearing his boots.

The phone rang just before 4:00 a.m. When Mina answered, she heard her mother sobbing.

She rushed to her parents' house. The lights were on, her mother and father and sisters gathered in the living room. Her father looked pale. An hour before, a dozen police had appeared at the front door. Sami escaped through the bedroom window but ran into a second contingent of police. Her mother's uncontrollable wailing had prompted an officer to threaten her father: If he did not shut the woman up, he'd be arrested as well. The old man insisted on going with them to the station but was told there was no point: Sami was being sent to Aleppo.

Over the next days, the family camped out at home. Mina took leave from school, and her husband from the mills. Her mother developed the theory that, just as Sami was taken in the early-morning hours, he would be returned then, so she kept a vigil through the night, sitting by the door. Her father visited a few Baath Party factotums he knew from his days in the post office, sometimes bursting into tears in front of them. One apparatchik promised to put in a word, but the answer came back: This was a matter of national security. Sami was already in Aleppo.

Through these Baathists, the old man learned the names of Manbij's organizers. Abel Os was believed to be the ringleader. No one knew where he was. Ahmed Rahmo, Abu Shakir, and the rest of the LCC were in Aleppo. Prisons were overflowing with protesters, and it was uncertain how authorities would keep them housed indefinitely. What was clear, though, was that the family should forget Sami. "I'm really sorry," one factotum told Mina's father. "He will be gone a long, long time."

AUGUST

When Mina was a child, she used to look at the world map and imagine that all the pastel-colored jigsaws belonged to her own Syria, to a political party called Baath, to a man named Hafez al-Assad. She owned a book that detailed the wonders of the world, and she pictured herself on the stone-tiled streets of Luxor, walking under the shade of porticos, as Hafez gazed down upon her from colossal posters. She loved the man like a father, confident that under his stewardship she could set foot anywhere in the world with pride and grace. When he died, she sobbed outside the gates of Manbij Girls High School.

The new leader brought a different kind of hope. Before, the nationalism textbook delineated the duties of a good woman: *My mother does the chores, she irons our clothes so that we can look smart.* Now, the text was altered to push against old tribal mores: *My father helps my mother do the chores. He helps her clean and iron.*

As soon as she graduated high school, Mina attended a leadership camp, an essential step for anyone hoping to join the Baath Party. She received instructions on the use of firearms, switchblades, and machetes. She was up at dawn, crawling through fields of artichoke, the callouses on her hands and knees marks of honor. But when she returned to the bunker at noon, she found Alawite girls, and others with *wasta*, connections, still in bed. In the evening, she and other recruits completed laps around the fields. But the *wasta* girls were nowhere in sight. They only returned to their bunker in the darkness, laughing and smelling of attar and alcohol. Mina achieved her certification in the use of the bayonet and graduated with high marks. But so too did the *wasta* girls. For the first time, Mina felt the sting of inequity. Despite encouragement from her instructors, she chose not to apply for party membership.

Life since then had been a steady slide into cynicism, fear, and now, with Sami's disappearance, terror. He appeared one night in a dream, his face gray, standing in a field with thousands of young men. When she ran to him, she could not find him amid the ashen faces. Weeks passed, and her husband would discover her in the living room in the early hours, eyes red. What had it all been for? Sami's future was finished. Either he would languish in prison for decades, or he would return blacklisted. The revolution in Manbij was over. And what had they accomplished?

In other cities, hundreds of people were being rounded up at every demonstration. Mina wondered where they would be sent. She imagined Sami packed in a cell with dozens of filthy young men, wiggling like worms. But she didn't share this image with her mother. Instead, marshaling her most authoritative tone, Mina promised her Sami could not be held much longer, that the prison system was already at capacity. It was during one of these conversations that the family received hopeful news: The revolutionary named Abel Os had been released.

A small crowd gathered at the real estate office in the Sarab neighborhood. Abel Os was celebrated as a returning warrior, and the young men, Oday among them, spoke to him with reverence.

One young man said he'd collected a group of youths to stage a protest and revive the movement. But Abel Os snapped: "Who are you? You are the son of whom?" When he introduced himself, Abel Os shot back, "Since when do you people think you can just go out and protest? This isn't your concern! This issue is much bigger than you." His voice was bitter. He pointed at the others. "This is bigger than all of you! Do you have any idea what they will do to you? You are young! For God's sake, think of your family, think of your future. Don't be so selfish!"

The young men were speechless.

"The revolution is over," Abel Os said. "It's over."

Still, the young men gathered at his shop every night. Finally, after much cajoling, Abel Os agreed to share his story.

Aleppo Central Prison was at its bursting point. The cells were standing room only. When one person felt the urge to turn, the others would have to adjust. On the third day, Abel Os was removed from his cell, blindfolded, and led down a corridor. He could hear wheezing, coughing, sobbing. Inside the interrogation room, he was pressed into the Flying Carpet. As he teetered on the edge of consciousness, he could smell his own unwashed feet. He was struck on his soles with what must have been three or four cables bundled together. It landed on his skin with every syllable from the adjutant: "Just . . . tell . . . us . . . the . . . names . . . of . . . one . . . or . . . two . . . peo . . . ple . . . in . . . your . . . group . . ."

A new voice promised, "One or two, and you'll be able to go home."

He then felt himself hanging from the ceiling, beaten like a piñata. He tried to count his way through it. By blow number fifty-three, he was numb. "Okay!" he shouted. "I'll tell you."

He was untied, and collapsed to the floor.

"There was one who was with me," he panted. The interrogators waited.

"His name," said Abel Os, "was God."

He couldn't remember much of what happened next, just that he'd unlocked a reservoir of fury in the assailants that he never knew existed in members of his own species. There were sticks, hands, boots, saliva—but these were no longer distinct sensations. He felt himself merge with the adjutants, with the stone floor, the air. He felt a remarkable oneness with nature, and warmth flooded over him. He was being kicked in the nose. The blindfold slipped, and fingers were digging into his eyes. He felt his pants being pulled off. A tingling spread over his body, elevating him to a state of euphoria, and he wondered if he'd passed into the next world.

He was roused by cold water. When he looked up, he saw the faces of his cellmates, who were tending to him with scraps of their shirts. Two days later, he again felt himself corralled through the corridor. He passed a din of voices that were now muffled, now rising again, and he understood he was passing cells. With hundreds of prisoners in each cell, the sheer number of detainees was beyond comprehension.

Inside the interrogation room, his blindfold was removed. The floors were streaked with blood. The room was thick with the smell of vomit. He was made to kneel, hands tied behind his back. An adjutant appeared. He held a rod up to the light. "This is pure silicone," he said admiringly. He screamed, "What did you chant?"

Abel Os replied weakly: "Freedom."

Whack. He felt the room spin.

"Say it again."

"Freedom."

Another blow.

"Again!"

Abel Os remained quiet. The adjutant seemed offended. "Are you refusing an order?" he screamed, and slammed the rod against Abel Os's face. He tasted blood.

"Again!"

"Freedom!" *Whack.*

"Do you support unity or freedom?" the adjutant demanded to know. Abel Os was having difficulty thinking straight.

"Answer me!" *Whack.* "Who is better?" *Whack.*

Abel Os couldn't understand. *Who?*

Whack.

Suddenly, as if the force of the latest blow brought him to his senses, he understood. The adjutant was referring to soccer teams—Aleppo Union or Aleppo Freedom. He was partial to Freedom, but thought it wise to say Union. This sent the adjutant into a paroxysm of rage. As the blows rained down, Abel Os learned that his interrogator loved—indeed was madly passionate about—Freedom.

For the next week, Abel Os was kept in a room fifteen feet to a side along with dozens of other battered men. It wasn't possible for everyone to sleep at the same time, so inmates took turns standing. His feet, the color of ink, were suppurating. His ankles had ballooned, making him feel as if he were standing in buckets. He wondered, for the first time, if death would be the better condition, and he pictured himself rising from a pit of fire, ascending through the hard cement ceiling and into the warm Aleppine night, cosseted by the breeze.

On the tenth day, Abel Os was taken for fingerprinting. He held up a numbered sign and faced the camera, then turned right and left. He was led to the courtroom, and when he entered, he gasped. The room was packed with men, at least five hundred—and every single one appeared to be a protester.

Abel Os waited his turn. He was called to the front and presented with a choice: sign a confession and walk free, or be transferred "elsewhere." He scribbled his name under a statement admitting he was 1) a protester, 2) an anti-government saboteur, 3) a sectarian, and 4) a motorcycle terrorist.

The Abel Os ordeal shook many in Manbij, but Mina was elated. His story had in fact corroborated snippets her father had gleaned from his Baathist acquaintances. The regime was simply overwhelmed. It seemed to face a choice: release the detainees after brutalizing them—or execute them. Holding them indefinitely was not an option. Execution may have been the preferred strategy, but that risked pushing the neutral side—in most cities, still the majority—into the revolutionary camp. Manbij, for instance, was firmly loyalist, but how would its tribes and clans react if one of their sons returned in a body bag? The regime therefore largely reserved executions for those from cities where the uprising had already spun out of control: Daraa and Homs.

So Mina was unsurprised when, one afternoon in mid-August, Sami showed up at his parents' home. When she arrived, the family was standing over him. His hands were stuffed in his pockets as he gazed at the floor.

"What have you done to us?" his father shouted. "Do you know how lucky you are?"

When Sami saw Mina, he ran to her. They hugged, and she kissed him again and again.

"You're on the blacklist," her father continued. "How are you going to feed yourself?"

Late that night, when they were alone in his bedroom, Mina held Sami's cheeks.

"What did they do?"

His face clouded over. He reached under the mattress and fished out a cigarette. They went to the rear balcony. Sami rolled up his sleeves, and she saw that his skin bore welts and lesions. "I didn't sleep for a month," he said. Then he fell silent. Mina did not press him.

"Well," he said after a while, "here I am. I signed a pledge never to protest again."

The rest of the Local Coordinating Committee was released that week and came home to a conquered city. Life was slowly returning to normal except for the groups of policemen and intelligence agents on nearly every street corner. The engineering office that had served as headquarters of the committee was under twenty-four-hour surveillance. Like Sami, everyone had signed pledges. 1st Lt. Maymati visited each man, informing them all that strings had been pulled, but their freedom rested on honoring the pledge. "The next time we send someone away," he warned, "they won't be coming back."

For four months, Sami and his friends had lived, breathed, and dreamed revolution. Life had become a sequence of steps in a conspiracy whose outcome, they were convinced, was preordained. But recent events were a rude reminder of designs much grander than theirs. Now, in the cold light of day, the thought that real estate agents and artists and schoolteachers could shift the course of their country seemed absurd. The thirty or so young men who'd formed the backbone of the protest movement had briefly felt comradeship and solidarity, but these pleasures had since been overwhelmed by greater forces that held their society together—the naked truths of order and power.

Sami tried sitting again in front of a canvas but found he had nothing to paint. Soon after, he was fired from the high school where he taught art. Yet he viewed the opprobrium as an opportunity. After all, he was gifted something rarely afforded in Syria, new or old: a reprieve. He would seize this moment to make friends abroad and quit Syria for good.

Sami's retreat from this doomed movement, from danger, should have been welcome news to Mina. As the eldest of the eight children and with three of her own, life was constant anxiety: when little Anwar tumbled from the heights of the jungle gym; when their brother Saladin enrolled in the officers' academy. Yet Mina was surprised to find her relief now tinged with a dull sensation that could only be described as melancholy. There persisted a festering sense of disgust at how Sami had been treated. She saw him every day that week, and her eyes kept being drawn to his covered sleeves. What had been his transgression? He'd never hurt a soul. He'd never even uttered a harsh word. Sure, he'd fallen in with a suspect crowd—she could only guess what he and Oday got up to in the farmhouse. But he was as softhearted as they came. He could pump iron and guzzle protein shakes by day, then tear up when they watched the soap *A Very Hard Birth* at night.

Only much later did she realize that she'd lacked the vocabulary to describe the confusion reigning within her. She was not accustomed to thinking of Sami's ordeal as *injustice*—for the very idea of something being unjust implies that there is an alternative. When a loved one dies of cancer, we mourn, but we do not find their fate unjust. We may rail against the seeming inequity of God's will, but we perceive in the loss the limits of human agency. Existence may be unfair, but it is unfair in the same way a roulette table is unfair. So we call such a death a *misfortune*, even a tragedy, but not an injustice. There is no escaping death, no alternative, only the vague, sometimes desperate hope to forestall it.

Misfortune was the entire framework through which Mina understood the strictures of her life. Misfortune does not inspire rage, only fear. But what Sami had endured, she began to realize, was no misfortune. Perhaps she'd been moved by the daily television images of panicked crowds fleeing bullets and tear gas; perhaps it was the scenes of packed plazas in Egypt, or the vision of Ben Ali, the Tunisian dictator, running up the stairs of a jet to flee his country. No, Sami had not suffered a misfortune, because there existed an alternate reality, one in which he could walk the streets of his city with pride, in which he did not have to quicken his pace at the sound of footfalls behind him. Nothing about this regime was preordained. He had suffered not misfortune, but injustice.

It took days for Mina, who for so long had lived according to the dictates of solicitude, to grasp this new sensation. She spoke to her husband about the rage she felt at the men who'd laid their hands on Sami. She could not picture their faces, but she could see their hands—pale hands, well-manicured hands, gripping cables, holding cigarettes. Gripping Sami's brown arm. She saw their hands in the teachers' lounge; they belonged to her boss, who had ordered the staff to warn students about "terrorism." She saw the hands of the military police who stood at the mouth of the Great Souk.

Her husband did not share her rage: He still believed this was the order of things. It was their lot, a fate that could not be meddled with. He despised the regime but was resigned to the iron necessity of power. He did not like his wife voicing her newfound rage—not because he denied her right to do so, but because he was afraid.

Mina turned to her sister Hanan. Six years younger, she was studying to be a teacher at Idlib University. Education was not her passion, but graduates were guaranteed a job at a public school, a policy of Hafez al-Assad that had not yet been scrapped in New Syria. When the Daraa events began, a few protests broke out on campus, but they were quickly snuffed out. She phoned home to see if things in Manbij were any different, but her father would only say, in his sonorous voice, "May God protect Bashar al-Assad!" Hanan lived in a slate-gray concrete building, sharing her dorm room with three women. One day, two students who lived across the hall were heard referring to the disturbances as "protests," not "terrorism." They were denounced by Hanan's roommates, leading to their eviction. Hanan and her friends rallied to their defense, holding a sit-in outside the office of the residence hall director. Relations between Hanan and her roommates immediately turned icy. She went into her room one day to find a photograph of Bashar al-Assad on her pillow. When she tossed it in the trash, her roommates informed the residence hall director. She and the other malcontents were made to parade a Syrian flag around campus, on threat of expulsion. Not long after, she discovered the wall near her room covered in graffiti: "Fuck your mother, you are destroying our country."

Soon, almost everyone around her changed their ringtones to the Hafez al-Assad paean, "Our Country Is Precious."

When Hanan came home for summer break, she told Mina she had no desire to return to Idlib in the fall. Her sister felt a flood of relief that quickly gave way to excitement. *Someone shares my rage*, she thought. Mina and Hanan went to an internet cafe, where they watched YouTube videos of suppressed protests. Their younger sister Maya stood guard nearby. At night, after putting the children to bed, Mina lay awake and sorted through the day's rough scenes and emotions. Slowly, she stripped away the confusion and held before her, for the first time, a clear vision. This rage, so pure, demanded a response.

Mina and Hanan conspired. Hanan knew two friends who'd suffered similar indignities at university, and one of them also had a brother who'd been detained. Mina visited the wife of her brother Saladin. He was an officer in the armed forces, away on deployment, and his wife spent nights anxiously scrolling through the news. After she saw what had happened to Sami, she no longer believed that her husband was off fighting terrorists—and she was sure he would agree, if he could speak freely. She would not rest easy until he was home by her side. Peace, for her, was more than a slogan. Mina also visited the Palestinian friend whose brother's testicles had been smashed and who now, as she watched news from Homs, also understood the sufferings of his inner sanctum not as misfortune but as injustice.

A couple of weeks after his return, Mina visited Sami in his garret. As she described her vision, Sami's eyes widened. He was shaking his head—but Mina had already made up her mind.

On a regular Thursday afternoon at the Coffeepot Roundabout, there were few men to be seen. But there were women everywhere—carrying loaves of bread, fanning themselves in wicker chairs. Mina was sweating profusely.

She counted ten women. They wore black abayas. Sweat was pouring down her back. Hanan swore that a couple of boys from university would come—but it was one o'clock, and they had not shown. The women stood at the foot of the tulip-shaped structure marking the roundabout. Mina looked to Hanan, who'd covered everything but her eyes. The previous day, the two of them had visited the Great Souk to purchase green fabric, and then a haberdasher on Rabta—the other side of town—to buy black-and-white cloth. They'd thought they were so clever.

Down the street stood the military recruitment center, where conscripts were inducted. Mina could see a pair of sentries standing by the gate. In the other direction loomed the Manbij grain silos.

By two o'clock Hanan's male friends were still nowhere in sight. Doubt stole into Mina's thoughts. The sentries stood still in the heat. Mina began to panic, convinced this was a rash, selfish stunt. But ten women were here. Ten women had placed their faith in *her*, of all people. She'd spent hours at each of their houses, talking through the steps, assuaging their concerns. How could she back out now? *I am so stupid*, she repeated to herself. She closed her eyes, willing herself to see Sami's exposed forearms. At that moment, she shouted, "God, Syria, and freedom only!"

The women stopped chatting among themselves. She shouted again, louder. "God, Syria, and freedom only!"

Hanan held the revolutionary flag. The women formed a line. They seemed unsure if they should follow Mina's lead, even after everything she'd told them.

"God, Syria, and freedom only!" Mina shouted again. She was watching the sentinels down the street. Could they hear? They were not budging.

"God, Syria, and freedom only!" Hanan joined in. The women circled the coffeepot sculpture like votaries to some graven image.

"God, Syria, and freedom only!" Now the other women were quietly joining in. People stepped out of nearby mechanic garages. A few cars slowed down.

"For the martyrs of Daraa and Homs!" the women cried.

Mina led the marchers away from the military recruitment center toward a high school. More people were stepping out of their homes to gawk. A man appeared and paced alongside the demonstration. His muscles were bulging from his shirt.

"Peaceful! Peaceful!" the group chanted.

They approached the high school. Suddenly, the burly man jumped in front of Mina, his eyes wild. He pulled a knife and lunged at her. She ducked.

"What's wrong with you?" someone shouted at the man.

"Terrorists!" he bellowed.

Some shopkeepers rushed to the scene. One said, "They are peaceful protesters! They are women! Are you crazy?" The burly man took a swing and was wrestled to the ground. Mina looked back to see the women frozen in place. No sign of police. She shouted, "Go, go!"

They marched back toward the roundabout. The show of support from the shopkeepers invigorated the women. Their cries could be heard down the street: "Peaceful, peaceful!"

At the roundabout, Mina stuffed the revolutionary flag into her purse. The procession had lasted only five minutes. The women dispersed. Mina fought every urge to glance back at the military recruitment center, but lingered for a moment at the roundabout. When the imperative *be honorable* was imprinted on your body and your stance and your gait, it no longer belonged to your waking, conscious self. It was like riding a bike, or swimming: a thousand intricate movements in symphony, conducted by some lower, deeper self. An untrained ear can rarely conjure the right note but can usually identify the wrong one. Standing there, Mina felt, for the first time in her life, a dissonance between what she knew in her heart and what had been stamped on her body.

She tried to walk calmly through the alleys, back to the mills. She could hear a vehicle approaching. *This is a revolution*, she kept telling herself. *Every revolution has victims*. A car pulled alongside her. She did not look over. *This is a revolution. Every revolution has victims*, she repeated, like an incantation. But she could not accept it. Life had much in store for her. She had brought children into this world. She desired nothing more, at this point, than to be in her husband's arms. The car was pacing alongside.

She wanted to turn and surrender, beg forgiveness. The absurd thought struck her that perhaps they would show mercy if she gave herself up now. That they, too, were bound by the imperative of honor.

But she did not turn.

She looked straight ahead and walked. The car sped up and drove away.

FOUR

September 2011

On a rooftop overlooking the Coffeepot Roundabout, watching these women stuff flags into their purses and then disappear into the alleys, was a lanky, gray-eyed twenty-three-year-old named Abdul Hadi Bisher. He could not believe what he'd just witnessed.

That evening, in an internet cafe, he chatted online with his best friend, Oday. The protest had been the city's first in nearly two months, but details about the identities of these mysterious women were scant. The more Abdul Hadi and Oday pondered the realities of the situation—on one hand the unremitting repression, on the other the women revolutionaries—the more befuddled they became. But soon their bewilderment turned to shame: What kind of men were they? These women were risking so much more—and yet they marched under the Friday sun, in the open, while the men hid indoors.

Oday was getting worked up. "What's our excuse?" he asked, over and over. He tossed off wild plans: revive the nighttime flash protests, spray-paint walls, set *shabiha* cars ablaze. All summer, fear had been their true master, but Oday could no longer contain his rage. He would proceed, with or without his friend. Abdul Hadi feared the wrath of the regime, sure, but now a deeper fear tugged at him, which lay behind every decision he'd ever made. Abdul Hadi could endure many trials, he could even be brave, but what he hated most was to feel left behind.

—✦ ✦—

One afternoon when Abdul Hadi was five years old, his older brother's friend said he wanted to show him something. Abdul Hadi wasn't supposed to leave home without permission, but he was a shy, solicitous boy, so he didn't say no. They walked down a broad avenue called Post Office Street, under a row of plane trees, and entered a square with big buildings, the walls crowned in barbed wire. There were many flags. Hafez al-Assad stared down from giant posters.

In the middle of this jumble stood a squat yellow building. Shouts and yelps could be heard from the courtyard. When Abdul Hadi entered, he saw teenagers running barefoot on the asphalt, kicking a ball. They pranced and tackled each other. One dove, trying to block a shot from hitting the net. The ball whipped around and rolled toward Abdul Hadi. "Go on!" the boys said. "Don't be afraid!"

That evening, Abdul Hadi begged his parents to allow him to return to the Youth Center the next day. "No boy of mine will play soccer!" his mother said. She knew all about the game's demands—the after-school practices, the road trips—because one of Abdul Hadi's older brothers had neglected his studies while attempting to pursue a career in professional soccer. He'd never made it to the big leagues, and the lost years could never be recovered. She understood what Abdul Hadi did not, and could not: that the family had moved to Manbij from the Euphrates region, where Abdul Hadi's father had been a peasant, and where his grandfather had been enslaved by a feudal lord. Organized soccer was an indulgence for boys with tutors, boys who could afford to skip their homework and ignore their baccalaureate exams and still land a job because of *wasta*. Soccer was not for boys like Abdul Hadi. The Bishers were new to this city, with hardly anything to their name and only themselves to rely on. For their family, life's path was well-trodden by the peasants of Hafez al-Assad's Syria. Study hard, avoid trouble, and make it to university.

One day, Abdul Hadi was led by his mother to a wooden cart loaded with onions and potatoes. She gave him very serious instructions: The next afternoon and every afternoon after, he was to come home from school, retrieve the cart, and push it through the streets of his neighborhood, calling out prices.

Abdul Hadi did as he was told. But he also wasn't so easily dissuaded.

On Fridays, he'd tell his parents he was visiting a friend, only to head for the Youth Center. At first, he simply watched. But, with increasing confidence, he asked to play, sometimes with boys three or four years older. He was lightning quick and nimble. He played barefoot—cleats were an impossible dream—and returned home with his feet swollen and bruised. When this was spotted by his father, he received a good thrashing, but still he kept sneaking back. Older players at the Youth Center noted that Abdul Hadi had remarkable endurance, playing in the summer heat and in sleet and mud. He received more thrashings at home. He was finally noticed by a coach in the youth league. When the coach visited Abdul Hadi's parents, encouraging them to send him for tryouts, his father related the tale of his son who'd squandered his school years chasing a silly dream. And if Abdul Hadi was always away at practice, who'd run the cart? Abdul Hadi tried out anyway—and won a starting position. The team raised money to purchase his uniform, including cleats. He'd pass the clothes to a friend though his bedroom window, then change under the bleachers. His name spread, and his father was beside himself—"Soccer isn't going to feed you," he insisted. But the old man could no longer stand in his way. Abdul Hadi was now fourteen, lean, taut, and celebrated as the most promising footballer in the city.

Abdul Hadi was playing in Aleppo under floodlights, two or three hundred people in the bleachers. The defense of Al-Jalaa, one of the top teams in the third rung of the Syrian Premier League's youth division, had been impregnable. The Manbij City Juniors had played a conservative, possession-style match, emphasizing ball control and short passes. In the fifty-eighth minute, they turned to a quick attack. The ball ricocheted off the goalkeeper's hands and into Abdul Hadi's orbit. He swerved around defenders, cutting toward the goal, and when he shot, the ball curved like a comet past the goalie's fingertips. He was mobbed by his teammates.

Opinion was near-unanimous: Abdul Hadi was destined for the adult clubs.

Like the Premier League in the UK, professional soccer in Syria is based on the relegation system. The top tier—the Syrian Premier League—contains such stalwarts as Aleppo Union and Aleppo Freedom and the powerful Army club. Every season, the worst teams are demoted to a lower league. Since the beginning, Manbij City has played in the third tier, the lowest league.

The abiding purpose in Abdul Hadi's young life was to make the Manbij City squad. Every morning before school, he'd climb the fence of Manbij Municipal Stadium, where the club plays, and train. He'd run thirty, forty laps, practice his footwork, and build his endurance. But then he'd have to go to school and, after that, help his parents. He was running a tiny stall next to his house, which sold biscuits and potato chips. It was this stall, not soccer, that consumed most of his hours—and with business floundering, it seemed he had to work twice as long. Days and weeks were organized in this fashion, tending to the cart, smuggling in a moment of soccer practice here and there. He couldn't afford to attend road games, because that meant a full day away from the stall. He found himself as a substitute on the youth team, the starting eleven reserved for those with more flexible schedules. Some of these starters were rising to stardom in their own right. They came from solidly middle-class families, and their parents drove them to away games and paid for time with personal trainers.

Getting benched was for Abdul Hadi a great calamity, but his father insisted it was a providential sign. His father wasn't a religious man, but he understood the deep truths of this realm. Beneath the niceties of neighborhood hookah bars and sports clubs was the true order, a hidden order, which dictated every breath and every step a human being might take. There were the haves and the have-nots. And nothing—neither sheer determination nor cunning—could upset this balance. Abdul Hadi's great sin, his father told him, was that he was trying to flout this order, to reach for what did not belong to people like him.

When tryouts for Manbij City's adult squad came, it was a foregone conclusion that Abdul Hadi's game was too raw for the big leagues. He hid himself from friends when the final cuts were announced. Oday visited his house multiple times, but he refused to come out. Weeks later, when he finally emerged, he appeared to be the same shy, solicitous boy as before—except now one could detect a distinct chip on his shoulder. He was quick to take offense, sensing the shadow of insult behind the mildest ribbing.

Yet he told friends he was glad of the outcome. His dream was not for himself, he said, but for the next generation. He began coaching in the youth league, and quickly earned a reputation as a brilliant tactician. He scoured the city for promising recruits. His father worried he still had not understood the rules of the hidden order, because he so badly wanted to win—and winning now meant besting not only the other team but those who insisted the world was not designed for people like him. Sometimes he bent the rules, enrolling children above the age limit. He drove his players hard—some said too hard—but in the end he was beloved. Unlike other coaches, he trained alongside his players, running laps with them, sweating as they did. He took an interest in their life off the pitch, and you could often find him in the courtyard of the Youth Center, advising the children.

Emboldened, he enrolled in the Sports Institute of Aleppo, where he earned a degree in personal fitness, which allowed him to obtain a job as a gym teacher in a Manbij Girls High School. Now, finally, he could tell his parents he'd arrived. Sure, it was a far cry from his brother Muhammad, the engineer, who was the pride of the family. But a steady income meant that his days at the cart were a thing of the past. What remained was soccer. He signed up for the *shaabi* league, made up of working-class teams that included the occasional professional. Abdul Hadi emerged a star forward for Dignity, scoring key goals for the team in a championship against Jazeera, from the city's east side.

Yet the success was a chimera. In truth, he felt the terrible grip of loneliness,

and neither Oday nor his other friends understood his isolation. Within this city of tribes, his tiny family was alone. He began to see why his parents were adamant he stick to his books—how his father was merely trying to protect him from the same hidden order that had beaten him down too.

All that changed, though, on April 22, 2011, when protesters at the Great Mosque overturned his world. He hadn't attended the protest, but that evening he watched the YouTube clip over and over. When Oday told him about the second protest, and described the violence at the hands of the police, he saw the category *people like us* anew, as a legion of those cast out by the hidden order. Oday introduced him to Abel Os, who'd run a grocery stand, just like him. When Abdul Hadi attended the nighttime flash protests, he understood, for the first time, that he was not alone.

SEPTEMBER

In August, the regime's forces laid siege to Hama. By the end of the month, clips were circulating in Manbij showing protesters on gurneys, spouting dark blood. They showed apartment buildings cratered by regime missiles. When the siege concluded, fire engines hosed down the blood-stained streets. The army had left graffiti on the walls: *There is no god but Bashar.*

Two weeks had passed since the women's protest near Abdul Hadi's house. Oday and his friends were still in the dark about who was behind it, but it didn't matter. Oday, charged with a fresh awareness of one's limited time on this earth, could no longer contain himself. The city's quiescence, he believed, was a moral failing, and it was up to them—on Oday and his friends—to do something.

It was late Thursday night and a light was burning on the top floor of Oday's house on Sundus Street. Inside, a group was seated on floor cushions, smoking cigarettes. There was Maraar, a pole-thin, pensive young man, the first in his family to attend university; Nidal, a thickset gold trader and amateur chef, a habitué of fine restaurants and wearer of fine suits; Oday, who'd called the meeting; and Abdul Hadi. It had taken Oday considerable effort to convince his friend to attend. Besides the women's protest, nearly two months had passed since a demonstration. In that time, Abdul Hadi followed the news of the entire Local Coordinating Committee getting thrown behind bars. He'd been present when Abel Os had shared his story—*Unity? Or Freedom?*—with the neighborhood youths in rapt attention. He'd heard about the gruesome torture inflicted on Ahmed Rahmo, the committee president. If he himself were taken, he would not be walking free like some other committee members—he did not have *wasta* and could not afford bribes. He'd just disappear, forever. But Oday begged his friend, delivered sermons about solidarity, and swore that he'd stumbled on the perfect plan.

Earlier that day, an activist from a town north of Manbij had visited the city, using an internet cafe to upload footage of a protest. He was reported to military intelligence, who arrested him on the spot. A convoy of family members were planning to come to Manbij to plead his release. What if, Oday proposed, Manbij activists accompanied them? They would not chant or march—they would not utter a word. They would simply sit in front of military intelligence headquarters, where the prisoner was being held, in absolute silence. No signs, no slogans—technically, it would not be a protest.

The four discussed Oday's idea for hours. A sit-in at the busiest intersection of the city could be seen as a significant escalation. Yet if they remained completely silent, what could the authorities say? Imagine the throngs, Oday said, piling out of the Friday sermons, confronted with the sight of young men sitting at the doorstep of the most feared institution in the city. They'd return to their comfortable living rooms unable to shake the image. They'd tell their friends, their spouses. They'd be forced to ask themselves, finally, which side they were on.

Nidal was enthusiastic. Maraar, a suggestible type, went along with the plan. But Abdul Hadi was unsure. Oday's father was a man of means, and Nidal had never wanted for anything. From the earliest moments of their smooth-nailed youth, they could afford to indulge in risk. And perhaps it's the certainty of a landing cushion, more than material possessions or haute tastes, that truly characterizes the wealthy: They live by the faith that everything will work out in the end.

"If we're going to do this," Abdul Hadi said, "we need to make a pact." He held out his hand. "If any of us are caught, we will never betray each other. No matter what they do to us."

Oday clasped his hand. "I don't care if they rip out my tonsils!" His eyes gleamed. "I will never betray you!"

Nidal and Maraar offered their hands.

All summer, Hala and Oday had continued to meet in the alley of Roman stone, hiding themselves in the shadows. They hardly spoke of her brother Abboud anymore, though they still proceeded with caution. Oday didn't tell his friends of the romance, not even Abdul Hadi. Hala had just begun her freshman year at university, which meant they could not meet as often. But Oday felt a powerful urge to see her before the sit-in.

The couple sat, holding hands, on a campus bench under the shade of tall cypresses. He told her about his group's plans, to which all she could utter was, "Be careful. Please, if you love me, be careful."

"Trust me," he said. "I know what I'm doing."

She placed her head on his shoulder.

Growing up, Abdul Hadi knew never to look at the gate of the military intelligence building. Everyone knew. Now, in the early-evening light, as he sat facing it, he could not peel his eyes away. Two guards were posted in front, with a row of Hesco barriers behind them. Oday's crowd numbered about two dozen.

After some time, a guard approached and asked the group to disperse. No one budged. No one even spoke.

On the second floor of the building behind the gate, lights were on. Abdul Hadi, who was wearing a mask, stared at the light, the light of a prison—a slaughterhouse, really. The family of the detained was among the protesters. They sat closest to the gate.

Another guard approached the group and demanded they disperse. Still no one stirred. A few passersby stopped to gawk—but Oday had miscalculated.

Once word spread of a disturbance downtown, people avoided the area entirely. Fear was still their master.

The gate opened. Out strode a short man with epaulets and brass buttons: Abu Roz, the head of military intelligence. He sized up the crowd. "I understand you are all frustrated," he said. "But this is a public area. You can't disturb others when you want something." His tone was surprisingly friendly. The family members asked after their missing relative. Abu Roz said he'd been transferred to Aleppo, and promised to inquire into his status. (What Abu Roz didn't know, and what the family wouldn't discover until much later, was that their relative, a young man named Muhammad al-Kinj, had already been tortured to death and dumped in a mass grave.) Abu Roz again appealed to the crowd. "This is bigger than all of you—it's even bigger than me," he said. "Please go home."

The energy in the crowd defused. Some were looking to the side streets. Others were standing up, apparently convinced by Abu Roz's message. Oday sensed the moment was about to pass. As if on instinct, he jumped to his feet and shouted, "The people want the downfall of the regime!"

Abdul Hadi couldn't believe it—this was supposed to be a silent sit-in. Oday shouted the slogan again. What was he doing? Abdul Hadi rose to his feet, preparing to bolt. There was a madness in Oday's eyes, a mania to his voice. Abdul Hadi would need to run. But he couldn't move. Oday shouted again. Abdul Hadi could not move. His life had been structured by fear of rejection—a fear greater than any physical privation. Yet who was he to demand loyalty from others? What he asks for he must give. He could not abandon his friend. He now had a decision to make, he understood, and in an instant, Abdul Hadi found himself shouting, "The people want the downfall of the regime!"

The mood transformed at once. A few others, and then a few more, added their voices. Now the entire crowd was chanting, their voices carrying down the empty streets, through the open windows, into living rooms and kitchens.

The group was swaying on their feet, chanting, "*Hor-reyy-a, Hor-reyy-a!*"— Freedom, freedom!

The sit-in transformed into a procession, circling in front of the gate. The guards appeared nervous. Oday's voice thundered, "Leave! Leave, Assad!" And the crowd chanted back. Oday had the look of a man possessed, as if by screaming he was unburdening himself of all the horrors of the past few months, the many massacres in faraway towns and cities.

The people in the crowd were no longer anxious, distrusting strangers. They were joined in a strange unity, emboldened, enraged. They marched to the gate and back, and then down a side street. Looping around, they reappeared at the main gate.

Suddenly, the lights went out. The protesters halted. The streetlamps, the house lights, and the storefronts were dark. Someone had cut the power.

A shout: "They're going to shoot us!"

The panicked protesters scrambled in different directions. Yet it felt as if somehow their numbers had doubled or tripled. Shadows multiplied.

Then there were screams. "Get off me!" and "Oh God!" It seemed that *shabiha* had been loosed on the crowd and were now swinging their swords. Abdul Hadi struggled to find his comrades. Soon he and others were running down a side street. The footfalls of pursuers sounded just behind. He spotted Oday across the street, running in the same direction. They reached a fork in the road. Abdul Hadi broke left, Oday right.

Abdul Hadi saw the municipal soccer stadium ahead. He slipped through the iron gate and sprinted across the field. Behind him was a riot of voices. Someone was being attacked, someone was screaming in pain. A whistle pierced the night. But Abdul Hadi kept running across the red clay dirt, just as he'd done many times before.

At home, panting, Abdul Hadi recounted the events to his brothers. They advised he skip town at once—if any of his comrades were caught, they likely wouldn't last under torture. But Abdul Hadi refused. They'd made a pact, and betrayal was inconceivable. As the night wore on and he sat on his rooftop in the cool September breeze, his nerves began to settle. He wondered if they should try again the next evening, but this time hold their silence longer. Downtown, the streetlights were back on, and a calm pervaded the sleeping city. Here and there, he could see headlights of a few vehicles. It must have been past 3:00 a.m. The headlights coalesced, forming a convoy, which turned onto Post Office Street, past the Conscription Center, and rounded the Coffeepot traffic circle. The lights were pulling up to his house.

Before he knew it, officers from the Directorate of Political Security were storming the house. They seized Abdul Hadi and marched him to a waiting jeep. His brothers threw themselves onto the hood of the truck, pleading, until the soldiers threatened to kill them. As he rode through the city streets, he tried to push through his shock, to collect his thoughts. How had he been discovered? He'd been masked, and it had been pitch-black. *They got nothing on me,* he told himself.

At the directorate he was conducted through a dark maze of hallways and thrown into a cell. He instantly spotted Oday, crumpled in the corner, with an eye swollen shut and a fat lip. His jellabiya was covered with blood. Glancing up at Abdul Hadi, Oday's other, unblemished eye started welling with tears. "I'm sorry," he said.

"*You* gave us up?" Abdul Hadi exploded in fury. "You're a liar!" he screamed. "The other day you were swearing on your life. And you couldn't even last a half hour?"

Oday said nothing. Under the dull yellow light of the cell, he looked like a ghoul.

Later that afternoon, the two other conspirators, Nidal and Maraar, were thrown into the cell. Abdul Hadi stood over Oday. "You're such a brave man, are you?" he shouted. "Selling out your own friends?"

Nidal and Maraar had to hold him back. They tried to explain that Oday had snapped under torture and that it wasn't his fault. But Abdul Hadi would hear none of it. That evening, Nidal and Maraar slept between Abdul Hadi and Oday.

The group was soon moved to the central police station. The transfer offered a glimmer of hope: They were no longer under the jurisdiction of Abu Roz and the intelligence agencies. This was 1st Lt. Maymati's territory—his cells were filled with pushers and prostitutes. Perhaps he would handle this as a criminal matter, not a national security case.

A guard pressed his face to the bars. The prisoners sat up. The guard passed around cigarettes.

By the next morning, Oday had not moved from his spot in the corner or uttered a word in twenty-four hours. In the afternoon, an old man appeared in front of the bars. He looked at Oday and gasped, "My son . . ." Oday saw his father and sobbed like a child.

That evening, Oday was led out of the cell for interrogation. "There he goes," said Abdul Hadi. "Our own secret agent. Who is he going to rat on next?"

Oday, in a blindfold, sat behind a desk. A voice asked, "Are you the leader of this movement?"

Oday replied, "There are no leaders."

The voice grew acidic. "How is that possible? Every movement has a leader. Where do you get your orders?"

"From my conscience."

Bang. The inquisitor slammed his fist on a desk. Oday nearly jumped.

"Do you think I'm a rich man?" the inquisitor asked angrily. "My family is poor. We've been working our whole lives. Your father owns shops, he even has a plot of land."

"My friends are poor. They have nothing."

"Forget your friends. Is this worth it? You're throwing your life away."

"Was Hamza al-Khateeb worth it?" Oday asked, referring to the child from Daraa whose penis had been severed by security forces.

The inquisitor wrote something down. "You've made your choice," he said.

The next day, an officer appeared in front of the bars. He was a large man, with epaulets and gaiters and steel boots. His face was red. "So you're the ones, eh?"

The group looked at him expectantly.

"The others protest at night on the outskirts and don't bother people. How do you have the balls to demonstrate right in front of our center?"

No one spoke.

He left, and a few hours later the guard appeared holding a paper. Abdul Hadi rose.

"I have orders," the guard said, "to ship you all to Aleppo."

Maraar began to weep. "It's over for me," he sobbed. "I've ruined my life."

Abdul Hadi put his arm around his friend. "Listen, you are going to be okay," he said. "We're going to be okay."

Maraar buried himself in Abdul Hadi's chest. "You've got to be strong," Abdul Hadi said softly. "You are a hero. You've done this for our city."

The next day they were loaded onto a bus. Oday's face was pressed against the window drapes. Maraar was quiet, but Nidal and Abul Hadi were worried about their friend. Abdul Hadi focused on the passing city, the stream of slate-gray buildings, and wondered if he'd ever see his hometown again. He wondered who would break the news to his parents. He'd participated in his first protest—with Abel Os—by sneaking out of his house late at night. His parents had no inkling he'd been involved until the moment the military jeeps surrounded his house. He wondered about his brother Muhammad, who was away on military service, and whether the news would reach him. He pictured his sister, a teacher, being told to clear out her desk.

The guard who'd given them cigarettes was accompanying them. He kept saying, "You guys are heroes. Just stay strong."

No one could muster a response.

"No matter what they do to you," he advised. "Don't give up any names."

The cell in Aleppo Central Prison had no windows. About a dozen people were packed inside. A bulb cast shadows on the cinderblock walls. On the afternoon of their arrival, for the first time in days, Oday spoke. "Maybe you all hate me, but I want to share something."

He began to recite a poem of his own composition. For many years, Oday had honed the art of the ghazal, rhyming couplets that expressed love and longing. Now, that longing was directed to freedom:

> *We raised our index fingers at him and his malice*
> *Just as we'll soon raise our flag above his palace*

Nidal and Maraar embraced their friend, praising the ghazal's beauty. Abdul Hadi did not speak.

The next morning, Abdul Hadi was taken for interrogation. He was blindfolded and forced into a tire, his rear sticking through one end, his head and feet through the other. He was struck on the feet with a thick cable, forty, fifty, sixty times.

When Abdul Hadi was released, he felt hands clawing at his body, and he felt a terrible cold. He recognized his own nakedness. A voice asked him about his past. It knew everything about him: his work at the grocery cart, his heroics on the soccer field. "Are you a hero now?" the voice bellowed as he was struck. The voice spoke of the time he'd gotten into a fight with a neighborhood bully. It petrified Abdul Hadi by bringing up his first love, from years ago—a neighborhood boy, the same age, with whom he was seen everywhere. It knew the name of his mother—it claimed to give details of a mole on her inner thigh, it spoke of fucking her.

As he was flayed again and again, the young man who'd become a beloved coach, a fearless forward in the *shaabi* league, and a daring activist, was stripped away. What remained was the shy, solicitous boy who only wanted to belong. The voice called him a faggot, and he felt the weight of many men pinning him down, pushing his face to the floor. He was told he would get what faggots deserve, and he felt the terrible cold on his bare skin, and then everything went black.

The next day, Abdul Hadi kept to himself in the corner of the cell, not wanting the others to see him cry. His feet were blistered and oozing pus. He wondered if he would ever see his family again. He thought of his house, which had been a single story when he was a child but to which his brother Muhammad, the engineer, had added a second floor. It was sky blue, the only house that color in the neighborhood.

That evening, Abdul Hadi signed a statement confessing he was a terrorist. The others followed in short order.

Back in the cell, he sat among the dozen other prisoners in silence. Around him were the sounds of hands scratching scabies, hands rummaging in tangled hair, digging for lice. The air was heavy with the smell of feet and sweat. There was no dinner. When the cell finally went dark, the four erstwhile comrades huddled together. Each stood waiting their turn for two yards of space because, without room for everyone to lie down, sleep could only come in shifts. Abdul Hadi decided to wait alone. He crab-walked around a few prisoners, groping the walls, until he found a spot farther off, as far as his swollen feet could carry him from his old friend Oday.

| FIVE |

October–November 2011

At the heart of every protest lies a paradox. What feels absurd or quixotic to a single person—rewriting a law, changing a regime—becomes thinkable only when tens or hundreds or thousands of people act in concert. The movement is like an organism, with a metabolism—it thrives by attracting bodies and energy—and a will of its own. In certain times, under certain conditions, the movement will succeed in winning popular approval, or prove too disruptive for the status quo to persist. The collective succeeds where the individual could not.

Shift the view, though, from the crowd to the individuals who comprise it, and we see another way to understand a protest: as a sacrifice. Protesters brave bullets; they steal time from work or school or family; they willingly give up comforts and expose themselves to the possibility of great suffering. But asking individuals to sacrifice is no easy task. When marchers get mowed down and neighbors are disappeared, most people will stay home and wait to see which way the wind blows—after all, what difference can a single person make? It would seem irrational to expect anyone to make great personal sacrifices, especially when the movement itself has no guarantee of winning. From the perspective of the individual, then, it's always safer to allow others to assume the risks. If the protesters win while you've sat on the sidelines, all the better: You've had a free ride.

Social scientists call this conundrum the *problem of collective action*. A protest's power lies, in part, in its size, but few people will join a social movement when the risks of participation are so high. In Manbij, revolutionaries were contending with this hard truth. In five months, only about three hundred people, in a city of 150,000, had participated in a protest. Just twenty or so were organizers, and even that highly committed group had failed to recruit their own friends and family members. These leaders paid a dear price, suffering torture and losing their jobs. Meanwhile, the public's silence was jarring. The masses were choosing not to risk life and limb, and who could blame them? In the south, the revolution had been raging for half a year with little to show except body bags and broken families.

In the ten days after the sit-in at military intelligence headquarters, Manbij police conducted dozens of raids across the city, seizing activists from their homes. 1st Lt. Maymati employed a tactic he called "selective terror," targeting and brutalizing the movement's leaders, while being careful to keep matters "within the family" by avoiding the involvement of higher authorities. None of the detainees were shipped off to Aleppo. Instead, after a few weeks of spine-bending torture, they were back in their own beds.

The strategy seemed to work: By the end of the month, the protest movement in Manbij looked to be dead and buried.

The authorities began to relax their grip. The checkpoints became sparser, the pleather-jacket men no longer present on every street corner. Only LCC leaders remained under surveillance. But slowly, in upholstered drawing rooms on Rabta Street, old-style Arabic houses on Jamal Abdul Nasser Street, and other private fortresses where free thought survived, something like a salon scene emerged. LCC members and fellow travelers gathered under cover of darkness to reminisce about the heady days of summer, to follow the news from revolutionary cities, and most of all to dissect old decisions.

Through these postmortems, two strands of thought developed. One school, which might be called the stonecutter approach, maintained that all was not lost: Despite their obvious failure, the protests had managed to deliver tiny blows to the regime's legitimacy. Every demonstration, no matter how fleeting, exposed fresh cracks in the facade. If the regime ever did collapse, it would not be solely because of the final blow but also because of the many blows that had come before. The population was ready to burst—they were simply waiting for the regime to buckle. The lesson, therefore, was to stay the course and keep holding nighttime protests until the multitude of fractures could not be ignored.

The competing view—call it *propaganda of the deed*—held that the population was in a stupor. They were uncertain, apathetic, perhaps even self-absorbed. Small nighttime protests would not sway anyone. Only grand, heroic gestures could shake the city out of its somnolence and incite the masses with revolutionary fervor. Activists following this school of thought began setting ablaze vehicles belonging to known government supporters, hoping this would terrify the regime. Once the masses saw the regime's weakness and the revolutionaries' heroism, they would awaken and take a stand themselves—so the thinking went. By late September, one or two cars were burning a week.

As the revolutionaries debated, there was one man—perhaps the only one in the entire city—who grasped that neither approach would work. Neither tiny blows against the regime's edifice nor brazen acts of sabotage truly reflected the real reason people were glued to their couches, keeping their mouths shut. Fear was the master here. He knew that people would not join the protests until it was safe to do so, but it would not be safe to do so unless everyone joined. For the past five months, he'd spent nearly every waking moment thinking about the impasse, and by autumn he believed he'd stumbled onto a solution.

OCTOBER

For many years, Hasan Nefi believed he inhabited a dream world. A decade earlier, when he'd emerged from fifteen years in prison, he could not escape the sensation that everyone around him was asleep. Sometimes, friends would ask him what life had been like in that desert dungeon, and Hasan would describe it, only to see their eyes cloud with distance. He wasn't sure what he loathed more, their pity or their skepticism. After a while, Hasan stopped speaking of his time there, resigning himself to the fact that the real world lay somewhere amid the glowing stones of Palmyra.

Upon his release, he was barred from government employment and deprived of a passport. Old friends drifted away, perhaps out of an abundance of caution. After much effort, and copious bribes, he enrolled in university to finish his degree. Without a job or the ability to travel, he turned to the written word. He was the first person to arrive at the Manbij Cultural Center's library in the morning and the last to leave. Drawing on verses he'd committed to memory during his incarceration, he published a poetry collection—though he struck any reference to the prison. Before long, he'd become one of the city's most respected poets.

When the events reached Manbij on April 22 at the Great Mosque, Hasan happened to be a block away. He was drawn, with every inch of his body, to the chants echoing down the covered market, but a friend pulled him away. Hasan should not be seen near a protest, his friend said. Given his past, authorities would immediately suspect him as the ringleader.

For a few weeks, Hasan was in a daze. The walls between his real and make-believe worlds had suddenly collapsed, and, for the first time in his life, he was at a loss for how to respond. Then he came to his senses and made contact with members of the LCC. Life transformed overnight. As Manbij's foremost political prisoner, his opinion was much sought after. He believed that the Syrian revolution should be viewed not in isolation but rather as part of a much greater upheaval that began in Tunisia and would eventually touch every corner of the Middle East. They were living through what he labeled a moment of "historical transformation" that would alter the fate of the entire planet. These revolutions were as seismic as the great upheavals of history, like the French Revolution of 1789 and the Russian Revolution of 1917. Those revolutions birthed not only new governments but new moral universes, new conceptions of right and wrong, of what we owe to each other. So too, he believed, would the great Arab revolutions usher in a new ethos—indeed a new type of human. The key task for revolutionaries, therefore, was not only to oppose dictatorship in the name of "freedom" but to conjure a different type of existence, where the values of solidarity and self-expression reigned. For forty years, such an ethos had been absent: Society was built on fear and small-minded jealousy, neighbor against neighbor, brother against brother. The challenge for revolutionaries was to animate the silent majority with a new vision of what it might mean to live together. Until now, the revolutionaries had only articulated what they were fighting against. But people also need to know what they are fighting *for*. Activists had to *show* the masses what they were fighting for. Indeed, as Hegel taught, the future was implicit in the present, just as a towering oak tree is implicit in the tiniest acorn.

One source of inspiration lay in Libya, a country undergoing a revolution of its own. Hasan met with an old communist friend, and the two discussed events there. What held their fascination was the creation, in the eastern city of Bayda, of a revolutionary government—in operation even before the regime had fully collapsed. Activists had seized a state building, hung a revolutionary flag outside, and declared themselves the new authority.

Protesters in Syria did not control an inch of soil, but Hasan wondered if territory, at this stage, was even necessary. What if revolutionaries simply announced a rebel government? This would provide the protest movement with the one ingredient it had been lacking: vision. It was *vision* that could break the paradox of collective action. Vision was what turned self-preservation into sacrifice, reason into imagination. No one wants to join a losing cause, but if a movement can stand for something greater, if it can transcend cold logic and commune with the profound, then people's hearts will be moved to risk everything. After all, humans engage in activities all the time that are, strictly speaking, irrational. They attend services at mosques, they enlist in the military, they risk voyages on the open sea in hope of a better life. They ignore prudence in the service of jealousy, ambition, and even love.

By autumn, Hasan was holding almost nightly gatherings with members of the now-defunct Local Coordinating Committee. His ability to pierce the fog of daily events, to approach politics like a military general, won him respect. This faculty was no accident of birth but rather had been learned through his decades in an underground party. Joining such an organization had been like earning an advanced degree in strategy and leadership. The Local Coordinating Committee, on the other hand, or what was left of it, had grown up in an era when political parties had been eradicated—a political "desertification," as Hasan put it. They lacked the experience of smuggling party literature or taking directives from leaders or debating strategy and tactics. They were political newborns, groping their way to maturity while trying to avoid arrest and torture. So when Hasan advanced his proposition, the demoralized men of the Local Coordinating Committee listened. His idea was simple: To project a hopeful vision to Manbij's silent majority, the revolutionaries should form a government-in-waiting.

NOVEMBER

They came in the dark, in batches. A solitary bulb burned in the farmhouse, casting a pale glow on the bare fruit trees. Abel Os was among the last to arrive. When he lay in bed at night, Mana by his side, he could still hear the adjutant shouting. *Unity? Or Freedom?* Members of the old LCC had called on him at all hours, beseeching him to attend, swearing on God that the grounds were secure, that every precaution had been taken. In the end, he was practically forced into one of their cars and driven here.

Inside, a woodstove struggled to warm the room. A large revolutionary flag hung on the wall. It was the first time Abel Os had seen one up close. A damp but not unpleasant odor rose from the cement floor. He imagined that the grounds were resplendent in summer, bursting with orchards and nurseries. Abel Os wondered again why he was here. Since his release, his store of bitterness ran deep. He tried to imagine the men here stuffed into tires, limbs flopping, screaming from the depths of their souls. How quickly they would give vent to secrets, how quickly his name—Abel Os—would be on their lips.

Hasan spoke first, explaining that the revolution in Manbij would not succeed without leadership. The protest movement needed to project authority to the street. They should no longer view themselves as supplicants, desperate to make their voices heard. No, they—as those who stood for dignity—were the people's true representatives. They were to see themselves as the future rulers of this city. They should convene what Hasan called a "revolutionary council," which would show the masses that hope lies on the other side of fear. This revolutionary council, elected by the protesters themselves, would guide the revolution in Manbij. Through circulars and communiqués, the council would offer a vision of a free and democratic society, the very inverse of Assad's Syria. It was only with such a lodestar that the masses would join the movement. Hasan hoped that the creation of a revolutionary council in Manbij would inspire similar councils around the country, forming a sea of participatory democracy.

Abel Os listened carefully to Hasan, moved by his eloquence. He'd never before laid eyes on him, but he knew Hasan had languished in prison for years. He was the very soul of resilience, and Abel Os couldn't help but admire him. Abel Os studied Munzer Salal, who was listening to Hasan eagerly. Munzer came from a wealthy merchant family and had never seen the inside of Assad's dungeons. If Munzer were caught, Abel Os knew, his father would move mountains to save his son—as only a man with his deep pockets and connections could. He'd seen it with his own eyes at Aleppo Central, where the tire and the electric cables were reserved for people like himself, people bereft of *wasta*. Within those walls, the only law and order was the lira. Abel Os decided to speak up. "If we do this, we are no longer protesters. This is a new line we are crossing," he argued. "If they arrest one of us, they'll come for all of us. They will execute us on the spot."

As he spoke, Abel Os kept glancing at the door, half expecting uniformed men to burst through.

Ahmed Rahmo replied by recounting his experience at the village protest in July. He'd been whipped with a pipe and stuffed in a tire, but still never spilled a single name. Ahmed Rahmo was a taciturn man, known for being scrupulous to a fault. Unlike other engineers, he never cut corners by using low-grade cement or wood. He examined every issue at length, from all angles, before he acted. He argued that whether the movement succeeded or not was up to the people in this room—after what they had endured, neutrality was no longer an option.

It was well past midnight. One man after the next was speaking about how he'd risked his life, time and again, and that it should not have been for nothing. Then Anas Sheikh Weiss spoke up, arguing in favor of the council. Abel Os had been surprised to see his old friend—his karate partner for many years. He had had no clue that Anas harbored revolutionary sympathies. With powerful arms and an even more powerful voice, Anas was expounding on the fence-sitters, which included many of his friends and neighbors. Their hearts lay with the movement, he claimed, but they were stricken by fear. If the revolutionaries don't offer hope, he said, the masses would stay on the sidelines forever.

With the meeting in full swing, the idea of a revolutionary council arose again and again. Abel Os was among the minority who remained fearful, but even he could grasp the logic. Someone moved to draw up a structure, and

Ahmed Rahmo's name was put forward as president. But Rahmo was uncomfortable. "Do you think I'm Bashar?" he said. "If we are going to do this, we need a real vote." He asked for a volunteer to run against him. No one stirred.

"Come on, people!" he urged.

Finally, with some embarrassment, two other men agreed to run. As each name was called out, the people shyly raised their hands, as they could hardly know by what measure they should decide—the three candidates were of similar qualifications: Abu Salah, the schoolteacher who had served as Local Coordinating Committee president, was beaten mercilessly during the first protest; Abu Shakir was hung from the ceiling and whipped. But it was not the difficulty in choosing that made the attendees self-conscious. No, it was the mere fact of raising their hands, thereby undoing an education that could be traced to their earliest days, when they were made to recite paeans to the Leader in the schoolyard, and when asking the wrong questions aloud earned a father's blow. It was against all sense of propriety that they raised their hands, and this felt both terrible and exhilarating all at once.

As the votes were counted, Abel Os noticed the peculiar alchemy of the process, in which many minds merged but somehow still retained their individual dignity. He felt, for the first time, an inkling of a different way of living alongside his friends and neighbors. The results were tallied, and Ahmed Rahmo won the presidency of the revolutionary council.

"This is what it means to be free," Ahmed Rahmo said. "You are flying, you are moving through the air. But I'll tell you, the real freedom began when we first went to the streets, and today is the culmination. We are free, my brothers, and now our job is to free our city."

He produced a list of "ministerial" positions drawn from his consultations with activists, and as the meeting progressed offices were quickly filled:

Office of Media—Charged with transmitting cell phone videos to the evening news, issuing communiqués, and supporting a new species of journalist, the "media activist," whose revolutionary participation consisted of getting word out to the international community. The office was to be headed by Aimad Henezel: veterinarian, heavyset, lover of rococo furniture and imported baklava. He hailed from a neighborhood in west Manbij that bore the name of his family, who were among the city's gilded set.

Office of Social Services—Ahmed Rahmo had intended that this important post be filled by Muhmmud Bisher, his partner at their engineering firm, but Bisher had refused to attend this meeting out of fear. So Rahmo assumed the role himself. In the event the regime collapsed, this office would keep the lights on and the streets clean. It would oversee the crucial issue of subsidies for bread and animal feed and fertilizers and fuel—matters of life and death for any ruling authority in Syria.

Office of Political Affairs—This was Hasan's baby, and everyone agreed he should be in charge. Hasan hoped to use the office as an incubator for political debate, an organ through which the group could refine such hazy concepts as *freedom* and *dignity* into a concrete platform.

Office of Humanitarian Aid—The crisis was growing by the day: families fleeing regime tanks in Homs, entire towns in Idlib Province evacuated. Manbij attracted a trickle of refugees. And then there was the decade-long crisis unfolding on the city's streets: old men sleeping on sidewalks, families escaping a drought-ruined country. Delivering aid to the needy wasn't merely about winning hearts and minds; it was also about righting the wrongs of the old order. Ahmed Rahmo proposed that Anas Sheikh Weiss, who'd been secretly fundraising to help the besieged cities of the south, helm this post.

They established a half-dozen others, including the Office of Legal Affairs, which would offer representation to anyone ensnared in Assad's courts; the Office of Education, tasked with compiling statistics on the number of schools and students for a revolutionary seizure of the public school system; the Office of Medicine, assigned to collect pharmaceuticals, recruit donors, plan makeshift hospitals, and study the health sector in preparation for its seizure; the Office of Religious Affairs, led by Munzer Salal, who was a Sufi scholar and whose mission would be to recruit imams to the revolutionary cause; and the Office of Military Affairs, charged with encouraging soldiers to defect.

The final post caught Abel Os by surprise. The Office of the Revolutionary Movement would be responsible for planning protests, making signs and banners, and liaising with activists around the city. This office was to be the tactical nerve center of the city's revolution. Ahmed Rahmo proposed that it be placed under the authority of Abel Os and Abu Salah—two working-class members with an ear to the street. Organizing protests was no simple task; the city had not witnessed a demonstration in nearly two months. In addition to reviving the movement, the office would attend to other details: ensuring protest attendance, drawing up contingency plans, recruiting those who lived near the security branches to act as sentries, and arranging for volunteers to film clips. A ten-minute protest could make for days of work.

There was a crescendo in Abel Os's chest. He felt the urge to be seen, at once, by the motorcycle lenders and the moneymen and their overseers, by his friends milling in muster zones in Damascus, by the workers in the shadows of the steel behemoths in Beirut. He felt that his life, until now, treaded on a kind of illusion, in which he held himself at a distance from things, from the people and places that could remind him of his smallness. In ordinary times, that illusion was necessary, even producing a reality of its own. He understood that the illusion reigned outside these farmhouse doors, but in here, in the soft light, he felt the force of shared destiny. The council posts were put to a vote and approved. And then, God help him, in those early-morning hours, Abel Os felt that he was transported from the muddy farm grounds to a new city, where people walked without fear and meetings like this were held in broad daylight, where the likes of Ahmed Rahmo and Munzer Salal were his brothers. He suddenly believed he could shed the weight of the past, make a new start, open a shop, a karate school. Revolution, he began to grasp, was the great equalizer.

The council members agreed to one rule above all else: secrecy. Each leader was to recruit others to staff their respective offices—but no recruit could know the identity of any other member. Like a cell, each recruit would answer only to his supervisor. After today, the entire council would never meet together in one place, and, most important, they agreed to never attend a protest. The revolutionary council would direct the movement from the shadows.

They drafted the council's first manifesto to upload onto Facebook and print on leaflets. What struck Abel Os most was the tenor of the debate: measured, thoughtful, respectful, and, strange as it seemed, conducted with solemnity, as if the city's fate hung on every decision. And maybe it did. Or maybe these were delusions of grandeur. Abel Os wasn't sure, but for the time being, he didn't care. The issue of regime supporters arose. Munzer Salal called on the council to threaten anyone linked to the government—including civil servants—and launch a campaign to set their cars ablaze. Hasan responded calmly, but his words were forceful. Some one-third of Syrians worked for the government, he said. Were they all counterrevolutionaries?

If they were with the revolutionaries, Munzer replied, why hadn't anyone seen them at protests?

Hasan retorted that people need to make a living. They are afraid, on the fence. If they haven't moved, he said, it's because *we* have not inspired them to risk their lives. *We* have to win them—that's what it means to be a revolutionary. We don't simply state the truth, like a prophet, and expect people to flock to us. Hasan argued that they should view every member of society—even Baath Party hacks, or neighbors blasting pro-Assad tunes—as a potential ally, unless they tried to harm a protester. We must meet people where they are, he explained, and bring them to us, through our actions, our vision. In the end, Hasan swayed the council, which voted against making threats in the manifesto.

The sun was rising. The attendees shuffled out in groups. In the northern horizon burned the scattered lights of the city. Abel Os climbed into Ahmed

Rahmo's car. The Manbij silos loomed ahead. As they drove home, the pair agreed that once the first flyers hit the streets, they would need to keep away from their homes, and Abel Os wondered if he'd sleep soundly, in his own bed, ever again.

—◆ ◆—

Plastered over storefronts, stenciled on Roman walls, printed on leaflets littering the flagstone walks was a message: *Change is coming*. The leaflets were signed "The Constituent Revolutionary Council of Manbij and Its Countryside." Some of the leaflets promised a government-in-waiting; others called on the people of Manbij—"a sleeping lion"—to rouse.

The reaction was immediate.

Checkpoints materialized around the city. People felt the pats of soldiers' hands. Trunks were searched. Activists began receiving late-night visits from agents. A young man in possession of a protest clip on his phone was briefly detained and brutalized. Intelligence agents were visiting Abel Os's office nightly, sipping tea.

And then people began to go missing. Parents visited 1st Lt. Maymati, but answers were not forthcoming.

Leaflets appeared accusing individuals by name of being regime agents, declaring them to be "legitimate targets." That night, the Revolutionary Council held an emergency meeting at the farmhouse. Everyone denied having a hand in the new leaflets and agreed to condemn them, publishing a statement promising that the council "won't take revenge on anyone, and our revolution is for all Syrians, so no one should fear it." Whether the offending literature had been published by an overeager activist or as a regime plot, no one could say.

What was certain, though, was that the mood heading into December was charged. The troubles in Homs and in the south had not been quelled. Reports of protesters abducted and shot came daily. A growing number of conscripts and officers were defecting. In the Idlib countryside, deserters ambushed and killed eight security personnel. Some protesters were taking up arms, forming small guerrilla bands. In early December, the United Nations, which estimated that more than four thousand people had died, characterized the events as "close to a civil war."

The regime drafted a law decreeing that "anyone providing weapons . . . intended for the carrying out of terrorist acts" would get the death penalty. Rumors began flying about the authorities clearing out cells, marching inmates into courtyards and vacant lots and open fields, and dumping bodies into pre-dug graves.

| SIX |

December 2011

Abdul Hadi froze, listening to the sound of boots marching down the corridor. The judas window opened, and a guard bellowed out a name. The summoned man gathered his belongings as another prisoner squeezed his hand. The other inmates recited prayers aloud. The door opened, allowing in a breath of cool air, revealing several uniformed men. The prisoner shuffled into their midst and the door slammed shut. The man never returned.

Every day, the cell thinned by two or three people. Abdul Hadi discussed the situation with Nidal, who was trying to put on a brave face. Whatever's going to happen will happen, Nidal said. Their time was going to come, and one needed to accept it, make amends with God. But Abdul Hadi had never been able to understand the Holy Book, or the metaphysical. As a child, he often stared at the moon, wondering how it could float in a sea of infinite blackness, a blackness that seemed the very essence of dread. He felt as if he were staring into existence itself, and he saw nothing at all, no angels, no jinns, and certainly no God. He hardly knew how to pray, and now, as his cellmates disappeared daily, he felt he was afloat somewhere in that dark sea.

With fewer men in the cell, they were no longer forced to sleep in shifts. Abdul Hadi settled himself in the corner farthest from Oday.

One morning, the sound of footsteps swelled again and the judas opened. A guard barked out, "Abdul Hadi Bisher. Nidal Kinjawi."

Abdul Hadi could hear his heart throbbing in his ears. He felt too weak to look at the other prisoners. Suddenly, he was reminded of his parents. In a panic, he realized they would receive no word of his fate, and the image of his mother roaming the streets of Aleppo flashed before him. He managed to turn and look at Oday and Maraar. Both were crying.

They were herded through a long corridor. They passed cell doors with spy holes, rooms seeping the fumes of raw sewage. They were shoved into a tiny cell with no windows, and the door was slammed shut behind them. It was endlessly dark, and Abdul Hadi suddenly felt a terror the likes of which he'd never known. He desperately tried to summon the image of his mother, her puffy hands, her stricken face—but there was nothing, just the dark sea. For the first time in his adult life, Abdul Hadi began to sob.

Nidal did his best to comfort his friend, arguing that there was a power greater than them, greater than the butchers that roamed the hallways, greater than the butcher-in-chief in Damascus, and it was to Him that their care was now entrusted. This only made Abdul Hadi sob harder.

They lost track of day and night. Abdul Hadi spent those hours in the darkness in fierce bargaining with his future self. He made resolutions, he swore on his parents, he even appealed to the black, formless void.

"If you ever get out of here," Nidal asked Abdul Hadi one day, "will you ever attend a protest again?"

"Never," he replied, without hesitation. "It was the biggest mistake of my life."

"Me too."

At random intervals, the door opened, the room filled with dim light, and a meal of stale bread, olives, and French fries appeared. A bitterness arose within Abdul Hadi: The ordering of his brief life had been based on a single principle, *wasta*, and it was through blind fate that he was born to a family without allies in the right places. His father had built with his own hands a single cinderblock room with dirt floors for his family. He'd slouched over a grocery cart from early morning until late night, so his children wouldn't have to. And what had Abdul Hadi done with such a gift?

One day, the door opened and they were dragged out by the guards, through the dark corridors. They found themselves outdoors, squinting under the brilliant sun. They were handcuffed and shoved into what appeared to be a cattle trailer. In the cargo hold were two emaciated men, skin clinging to their bones. Their heads listed to one side, then the other, as the vehicle jerked to a start.

When the truck finally stopped and the door opened, Nidal nearly collapsed with relief. Before them was no vacant lot, no ditch—it was another building. He allowed himself to feel the tiniest stirrings of hope. The skeletal figures in the cargo hold were hooded and marched around the corner, out of sight. Nidal and Abdul Hadi, on the other hand, were marched into the building.

They were conducted through a labyrinth of hallways and shoved through a pair of oak doors. The room was crowded with prisoners, divided at the center by an aisle. Nidal spotted Oday and Maraar and nearly shouted with joy. At the aisle's end stood a desk, behind which sat a man in judicial robes. Prisoners were being summoned. The judge read out charges. When they included weapons possession, the men were sent through a door on the left. When they did not, they were dispatched through a door on the right.

Abdul Hadi heard his name. "Did you participate in protests?"

"No."

"I have your signature."

"They tortured me, so I was forced to say that."

The judge studied the confession. "Have you ever handled a weapon?"

"No."

He stamped the document and called out, "Next!"

A few days later, under an overcast sky, Abdul Hadi sat in the back seat of a bus, watching stone villages and tawny brown soil sail past, then the squat apartment blocks and the giant book, held by outstretched bronze hands, announcing the western gate of Manbij. When his eyes fastened onto the gray high-rises and the shawarma shops, he suppressed the urge to cry. For a young man unable to find anything in the sea of infinite blackness, Abdul Hadi wondered, for the first time, if he owed his life to the providential. After all, had Abdul Hadi and his friends refused to sign the confession when they'd first arrived in Aleppo, the investigating officer might, in frustration, have appended further charges, including the possession of weapons. He'd heard that had happened in other cases, and such young men were never seen again.

But for the moment, Abdul Hadi was in no mood to interrogate grace—they had arrived at a roundabout near downtown Manbij, where four cars stood waiting. Abdul Hadi immediately spotted his father, standing in front of a taxi. He jumped out of the van and ran to him. His three friends bounded out after him, racing toward their waiting relatives. Oday reached his father, whose eyes were brimming.

Abdul Hadi embraced Nidal and Maraar. Then he climbed into the taxi, without so much as glancing at Oday, and buried himself in his father's arms.

That night, as his father and mother slept soundly for the first time in months, Oday slipped out of the house. Checkpoints had sprung up on Sundus Street, so he took the backstreets. When Hala saw him, standing by the old Roman walls, she nearly cried out. He looked like a sack of bones. She held his face. "What were they feeding you?"

Every night, while their families slept, the lovers met in the Roman alley. Hala had never doubted he'd be returned to her, yet she'd been forced to cage her torment. She'd turned to prayer, which she performed with ferocity, and

Oday swore he had felt her presence. Oday had been inducted into two secret worlds, mirror images of each other, a heaven and a hell. He confided to Hala about his hell, which was thick with the odors of the cell, odors he could smell even now on his clothes, his skin. He described the eyes of the interrogator—bloodshot, framed by dark circles. He recounted Abdul Hadi's cold stare boring into him from across the cell. In the other world, he was with Hala. There, he saw the city through the eyes of love. Every stone, every ogive window, sang to him.

But at home, his parents noticed that Oday had grown sullen, quick to anger. Whenever he left the house, his mother grabbed his arm. "Where are you going?" she asked. He shouted at her and broke his arm free. During his confinement, she'd often sat in front of the Directorate of Political Intelligence, begging to be told his whereabouts. But Oday wanted to hear none of it. When his father tried to broach the subject of his internment, Oday shouted him down, too. The balance of forces in the house had turned upside down. When the old man asked Oday to run an errand, he ignored it. His brothers and sisters spoke in whispers around him. He'd become impulsive, walking across town at odd hours for a shawarma, or demanding time alone to sit in the park, or listening to music on his headphones while guests were visiting. He was moving through his days with a barely concealed contempt. But Hala asked nothing of him save his presence. Sometimes they were together for minutes, sometimes until the first streaks of morning light. She stopped asking about the cell. Nor did she broach the issue of Abdul Hadi. Some nights, they did not speak at all. They held each other in silence, bundled in coats, the wind whipping the portieres, the stars burning above.

On December 18, the villages of Mount Zawiya, in Idlib Province, a hotbed of revolutionary activity, were stormed by regime tanks. Upward of a hundred people—civilian protesters and a few defected soldiers—attempted to flee through the valleys. But regime forces occupied the crests, firing down with anti-aircraft rounds and snipers. The defected soldiers shot back with rifles, exhausting their ammunition, before finally raising a white flag. The survivors, civilian and rebel alike, were then rounded up and marched to a field. Each one was shot in the head. The imam was bayoneted through his neck. Some seventy-five people were killed, including children as young as thirteen.

The next day, a clip was uploaded to YouTube showing rows of mutilated bodies. It was possibly the largest massacre since the protests had begun. The citizens of Manbij awoke to flyers, authored by the Revolutionary Council, denouncing the tragedy. In teachers' lounges and mechanic garages, people plucked up the courage to mention the atrocity. It was only after seeing the flyers, for instance, that Ibrahim Kasem dared to raise the subject with a friend who worked with him on construction sites. For years he'd nursed a rage he could not name, against which he held the memories of Little Hyena—the flutter of velvet butterflies, the sweet waters of the Euphrates. He still hadn't accustomed himself to the acrid vapors and merciless solitude of the city. When he'd moved here years ago, after the flood, he was astounded to see elderly women on the streets, hands outstretched. "That is someone's grandmother," he kept saying. Such calamities would have been unthinkable in Little Hyena, but that was a different country. In Manbij, he lived with his brothers, sisters, and parents in a one-room house that measured fifteen feet to a side. He'd often journey to Beirut to work, sometimes earning seventeen dollars a day at construction sites, though bosses typically stole what they could. One winter he'd returned home and, with little fanfare, wed a girl selected by his mother. He took his new bride down south, where he spent years hovering around muster zones. He returned to Manbij after thousands of hours of labor, not a lira richer than when he'd left.

In all these years, the rage never left him. And now, as he watched clips of the massacre on the tiny screen of a smartphone, it took shape into something tangible, something dangerous. He confided in his younger brother Adam, who shared his rage, and who understood from the first the regime's true nature. Adam had already achieved the unthinkable by earning admission to Aleppo University. This was a chance for the entire family to lift themselves out of the failure that was New Syria. Ibrahim never once doubted him—it was Ibrahim, after all, who'd trudged through the rising waters of Little Hyena to rescue Adam's schoolbooks. While Ibrahim wandered the Levant looking for work, Adam nestled into a corner of the house and studied with an intensity that mystified the family. Now the payoff was close at hand. Adam was finishing a degree in English literature at university—his thesis was on T. S. Eliot—and he was home for winter break.

Adam and his college friends were outraged by the massacre, as they had been by the many previous massacres, but they'd been careful not to utter a word, even within the confines of their dorm rooms. Now, though, with this mysterious Revolutionary Council supposedly directing a resistance, they felt they were no longer alone, and that there was someone in the shadows with an actual plan. The protests were not mere chaos; there was a logic undergirding it all. Manbij had not witnessed a demonstration since Oday and Abdul Hadi organized the failed sit-in three months earlier. Adam and his friends wondered if they—and they alone—could revive the movement. Unlike the residents of Manbij, they could stage an action to commemorate the fallen and then retreat to Aleppo—an hour away—and disappear into the metropolis.

On Friday, December 23, congregants spilled out into the street between the crumbling mud-brick Sheikh Aqeel mosque and an adjacent graveyard. Among them were several of Adam's fellow university students, including Mohsen, who was studying medicine, and whose father had vanished into regime custody years earlier; Rahim, who was studying English literature, and who had a passion for Joyce and Woolf; Tariq and Alaa, who were sons of the head of the state bakery, which provided subsidized grain to the city; and many other fresh faces, from nursing students to engineering majors.

The imam and the regular worshippers had surely noticed the crowd's nervous energy. Still, when it began, it took them by surprise. With a sudden cry, a chant erupted: "Freedom, freedom!" Some bystanders took courage and joined.

Like clockwork, patrol cars arrived on the scene.

Over the past eight months, Manbij had witnessed maybe a half-dozen protests. They usually went according to script: The congregation is abuzz, people wait uncomfortably, someone drums up the nerve to break the silence, his friends join in, tepidly at first, then with greater conviction, some passersby run, others throw caution to the wind and begin to chant, the authorities appear, and everyone flees.

But now, as the police approached, batons in hand, a strange mood overtook the crowd. It was as if, behind the phalanx of policemen, the protesters could sense thousands, or even tens of thousands, of their silent brethren, ready to rise. It was almost certainly folly, but such was the hope that the existence of the Revolutionary Council stirred, and when this mood overtook the demonstrators, they whipped themselves into a frenzy of chanting. The police appeared astonished: They had never seen the enemy hold its ground.

Meanwhile, a few blocks away, a second group of university students took to the alleyways, chanting, "Freedom! Freedom!" They were heading for Sheikh Aqeel mosque to join their comrades. When word reached the police, they abandoned their positions and ran to block the column—leaving the crowd at Sheikh Aqeel blissfully free. A wild cheer went up, as if the narrow street had become a small patch of liberated territory. The crowd grew mirthful and determined. They circled the street and sang revolutionary songs. Placing arms on shoulders, the men swayed like seagrass, shouting the word "freedom" over and over.

The police returned. The crowd was undaunted. The vehicles had sealed one of the street's entrances, but the other remained open—as did the cemetery, where protesters had hidden motorcycles. The crowd moved as one, inching closer, inching back, inching closer.

And then everyone stopped.

There was a shout, or a series of shouts. Some time passed before the situation became clear: Four protesters had been arrested at the other rally. At this point, a fever seized the protesters at Sheikh Aqeel. Perhaps the images from Idlib of rows and rows of corpses, heads gashed open, finally pushed them over the edge. Whatever the cause, something ineffable passed through the crowd, something which every man there had counted as among his deepest desires but which was, until now, the preserve of madness. For a brief moment, the protesters, maybe without even thinking, inverted the order of the only reality they'd ever known: They picked up stones. In their hands were pebbles, fist-sized rocks, shards of concrete as large as a human face—whatever they could get a hold of. They were no longer chanting. The policemen inched forward. The two sides were ready for war.

One of the patrol car doors swung open and 1st Lt. Maymati appeared. He pleaded with the protesters, promising he would release the detainees. No one was going to Aleppo, he insisted. This was a dispute among the city's sons, so there was no need to involve outsiders. Just back off, he urged, and he'd do his part.

A protester asked for a guarantee their comrades would be released. 1st Lt. Maymati promised that if they dropped their projectiles now, he would personally retrieve the detainees. The temperature lowered as the protesters put down their stones. It was at that moment—choreographed expertly by 1st Lt. Maymati—that a half-dozen vehicles arrived at the other end of the street. All hell broke loose. The vehicles plowed into the crowd. Forty or fifty people were crushed. On the other end, security personnel rushed headlong into the scrum, swinging batons. Protesters fell, and many were trampled.

A few protesters managed to slip into the graveyard, running to their bikes. But the police, loath to abandon their vehicles, zeroed in on their netted quarry. They threw the bloodied bodies onto their trucks and drove off.

Crouching among the gravestones, the remaining protesters quickly counted heads. They called friends. Around town, phones were lighting up with their desperate messages. All told, it seemed some thirty people were in custody—the largest haul in Manbij so far. If they were accused of holding stones—a weapon—the death penalty awaited. Their transfer to Aleppo had to be prevented by any means necessary.

Revolutionary Council members took to the phones, beseeching friends, relatives, anyone they could think of, to prevent the unfolding calamity. A plan came into focus: congregate at Central Square, in the large bus lot facing the Manbij Hotel. At this point, protest would be suicidal, so the call was simply to gather for evening prayers, which was, in theory, not illegal. If enough people turned out, and if they all sat together in peace, perhaps they could send a message to the authorities without uttering a single chant.

The sky was overcast, the air frigid. Most storefronts were closed. A Syrian flag flapped atop the hotel. The police were nowhere in sight. In the waning light, family members of the Revolutionary Council stood to pray. More worshippers arrived—friends, relatives, complete strangers. "Prayer is not illegal," the worshippers reassured each other. The father of one of the arrested students reached out to tribal sheikhs in the countryside, who brought vans full of supporters. People emerged from their houses to join. The crowd organized itself into serried ranks. The worshippers lolled their heads to one side, then the other, reciting the evening prayer. More people arrived. They sat on the asphalt, waiting their turn to pray. People talked among themselves, but not a single slogan or cry was raised. Ibrahim's brother Adam arrived with others who'd fled the earlier protest. Political intelligence headquarters loomed across the street, but Adam could not see its entrance: In front of him were rows of people. To his right and left were people. Behind him, more people.

Hala answered the phone to find Oday out of breath. He'd been on his balcony when he spotted patrol cars speeding toward Sheikh Aqeel mosque. Calling around, he'd learned of the protest, and thought with scorn of the young men risking their lives for nothing. But then, as the afternoon progressed, something strange took place. Messages poured into his phone about a sit-in at Central Square. He received notes from friends who'd never uttered a political word in their lives, from relatives who'd previously condemned the protests. Something was churning in his city.

Hala told him to be careful. As a former detainee, he would forever be under suspicion. "Keep indoors. Don't even go out for food," she advised.

Oday was quiet.

"Do you hear me?"

He told her, in a soft voice, that he wanted to see what the commotion was about.

Hala lost her wits. "What are you talking about?"

The argument lasted almost an hour. In deference to his demons, Hala had held back until now. When he'd described the steel baton across his beautiful face, the blood gushing from his mouth, her heart broke into a thousand pieces, but she'd bit her lip, resisting the urge to tell him the truth—that he'd brought this upon himself. Who'd asked him to engage in this death march? So that one day, after they get married, he could head for work in the morning and never return, leaving her with the children, in a third-floor home, his parents living below? As a former detainee, he was effectively unemployable, but she accepted this blow to their future with solemnity. Her relatives would someday snicker that she'd squandered her life, and her family's name, for an utter fool, and yet she had not once raised a protest. Such were the wages of love. But for Oday to err, be granted a reprieve from God himself, and then err again—that she could not stomach. She was ready for anything—she could stand before her brother Abboud and take his violence, she could consign herself to penury—but she could not deny providence.

But Oday was not hearing her reasoning. "Do you know," he asked, "what this regime has done? Do you know what happened in Idlib?"

She replied that she did not care about Idlib. She cared about him, about them as a couple, about standing up to Abboud, about planning their wedding.

And what, Oday asked, of all the weddings that would never happen? The families destroyed, the people disappeared, simply because they want to be free?

Hala replied that what was unfolding was a tragedy, but a tragedy bigger than the two of them. They lived in a *system*, with gears and levers, that had been in operation for forty years. In four decades, the world had witnessed wars and coups and the collapse of governments, yet Syria hummed along. Who was he to think he could change anything?

Oday countered that it was this mode of thinking that had allowed the regime to dominate their lives. She said his future—and therefore hers—would be ruined. He asked: What future is there with this regime in power? She asked if he planned to marry her and leave her a widow.

Oday shouted: Are you with the revolution, or with the tyrant?

She replied that she was with him—Oday—and no one else. She was not with the revolution, or the tyrant, or Israel, or America, or Russia, or this party or that party. She was with him alone. She asked if he had stopped to think, even once, about how she suffered while he was locked up.

Outside, the sky darkened. Oday insisted that he deserved an answer: Was she with the revolution or against it?

"No, I need an answer," she cried. "Do you want to marry me, or do you want to take part in all this?"

Oday replied that he wanted both. She said that was not an option.

"I want both!" he shouted.

The line was silent but for Hala's sobbing.

For a long time, Oday didn't speak. A year had passed since he'd first laid eyes on her, accosted by the bullies in the Roman alley. If love is an education, one might say that their year of secrets, moonlight trysts, and wrenching absences were enough tutelage for a lifetime. Perhaps that's what it took for him to become a man, to assume duties to family and future generations. Yet the past year offered a second education too, one of action, one in which the future generations in question were not his progeny but the people of his city. Perhaps, in his silence, he was confronted for the first time in his young life with the nature of tragedy, with the question of how a person should respond when faced with a truly impossible choice. The question before him was about modes of life—life in the world, in the story of his community and his country, or life in retreat, behind fortress walls, alone with the soul of another. Twelve months ago, that question would've had a simple answer, but whatever now lay ahead, that old world, and those old answers, were gone forever.

"Oday?" She was still crying. "Oday? Do you want to give up this love, after everything we've been through? These protests might end at any second. And then what will you have?"

He remained silent.

"Oday, please," she cried.

Moments passed.

"If you attend this protest, I can never speak to you again."

Oday did not utter a word.

"It's been really wonderful to know you," she cried.

They remained on the phone without speaking. For how long, she could not later recall, but at last, as the air filled with the gray light of dusk, she hung up.

— ✧ ✧ —

Abel Os ignored the first message, and the second. He received a phone call from a council member, and he ignored that too. But when he received a visit from a group of neighborhood youths, he could ignore it no longer. At the very least, he told himself, he wanted to see. And what he saw shocked him so thoroughly he was finally willing to reconsider everything he thought he'd understood about his sacrifice, every bitter thought that had wormed its way into his brain.

Central Square was packed. He wasn't sure he'd ever seen this many people in a single place, not when the authorities held pro-government rallies, maybe not even at the Municipal Stadium. There must have been a thousand people there—*one thousand people* in front of the Directorate of Political Security. He could see the outlines of people on the Manbij Hotel roof, filming the scene. He spotted other council members, though no one else knew about their membership. The atmosphere was charged, the crowd restless.

And then the square filled with a growl of vehicles. The police at last converged onto the square. Abel Os counted a dozen patrol trucks. The sidewalk in front of the Political Security Directorate filled with uniformed bodies. Fifty? One hundred? He couldn't get a good look—but it was clear that the city's entire security force was present.

The crowd was alert, looking in all directions. Rumors circulated. When news reached them that the regime was sending reinforcements from Aleppo, a council member blanketed the highway with nails.

No one raised a chant. But the crowd frothed at the edges, people spilling onto the sidewalk, and there was a loud hum.

The police were not trained to handle such a massive assembly. Now and then they forayed in, swinging batons, and the crowds fell back.

Still, no one chanted. People fidgeted, unsure of themselves. Many of those present had never allowed themselves to dwell on their relation to the events of the previous eight months. They'd lived on pure instinct, looking the other way, distancing themselves as best they could. But now, after the avalanche of messages on their phones from friends and relatives, after the Revolutionary Council's flyers, they'd ventured to the square—and they were astounded to see so many others, just like them. They must have thought, *Am I really here? Are we really doing this?* The effect was of a collective trance, a surreal spectacle of a thousand humans pressed together, boxed in, frustrated, anxious, struggling to keep their voices to a murmur.

In the crowd was Oday al-Homsi. He pushed his way through elbows and bellies, aiming for the front. He soon came face-to-face with Abdul Hadi.

The crowd was roiling, as if it were ready to explode. The sun was almost gone.

Abdul Hadi's eyes were wet. Oday approached his old friend, and they embraced.

Everything that happened next may have taken place in less than a minute. A disturbance rippled from the edges of the crowd, perhaps due to a jumpy policeman. The council members were trying to keep the peace without giving away their identities. Bodies were pushed to and fro, and the entire mass lurched.

Then, out of the thousand people, it was Oday who screamed, "This is Manbij, hey, hey!"

In an instant, in this corner of the square, the trance was broken, and the repressed energies of the nearby crowd were unleashed. The throngs swayed and clapped, "*Yed wah-deh, yed wah-deh*,"—One hand, one hand! The chanters were no more than a few dozen, and they encouraged the others to join. A ten-foot-wide ring of empty ground separated the chanters from those who could not bring themselves to utter a sound. But in the twos and threes, people approached the chanting mass and were absorbed, as if the chant had exerted some force of attraction.

The circle around Oday, now in the hundreds, chanted: "Now, now, now, the traitor out now!"

Something had shifted, perceptibly. Abel Os couldn't believe he was hearing the word "traitor"—referring to Bashar al-Assad—from the mouths of so many citizens.

The crowd shouted, "He who doesn't participate has no honor!"

With this final push of peer pressure, those who'd kept silent finally gave in. The entire square—all one thousand—was now chanting in unison.

A military jeep pulled up. In it was Ahmed al-Issa, the top religious official in Manbij. He implored the crowd to disperse, but the throngs chanted back, "We don't want you! We want the prisoners! The prisoners!"

Two soldiers accompanied Issa as he forced his way into the crowd. They found Abel Os—who, in the authorities' eyes, was the movement's puppet master—and asked to speak with him. The crowd surged to protect him, fearing he would be arrested. But Issa assured them he wanted someone to negotiate with on behalf of the protesters. Reluctantly, Abel Os followed him and disappeared behind the jeep. When they reemerged, Abel Os announced that the security forces promised to release the detainees if the protesters dispersed.

No one budged.

Trust was a debased currency. The chant rose again: "This is Manbij, hey, hey!"

A fire truck appeared.

"This is Manbij, hey, hey!"

The truck rolled toward the knotted masses. The protesters held their ground. Oday and Abdul Hadi were near the front. Firemen unspooled the hose and aimed it on the crowd.

"This is Manbij, hey, hey!"

Everyone knew what was about to happen. There wasn't a person in the square who did not expect it, and when water hit the bodies in the square like a beam of lumber, people tumbled onto each other. A new chant arose from the maelstrom: *"Shabiha, shabiha!"*

The crowd had splintered into several groups. The police moved in a blur, swinging at the soaked protesters with batons. Some demonstrators fled for the alleys. Some tried to escape to the covered market. Abel Os took shelter behind a bus. Oday and other young protesters ran to the park, returning with stones. Soon the police found themselves under a hailstorm of rocks. They seemed terrified—the city had crossed the Rubicon: It was fighting back. Stones smashed into windshields, denting the firetruck, the patrol cars. A dozen young men formed a front line, launching their stone missiles at the regime forces, while others worked the supply line. The security personnel retreated behind a row of parked cars. The air was filled with scattered chants, the shattering of glass, the thud of stone on chassis. And then a group of military intelligence soldiers behind the besieged police raised their rifles and aimed at the crowd.

The hailstones continued to land on the cars. The chants continued to echo.

A gunshot rang out.

Instantly, the chants stopped. More shots. The air was now filled with screams. The regime was shooting at the protesters.

Pandemonium. People tumbled over each other to flee. Some escaped down alleys, some took refuge in the park. The regime forces continued to fire.

Within minutes, the square was empty. Still the shots continued.

In the alleys, running through the streets, split into groups, were nearly a thousand people. They slowed to a trot, then they walked, even with regime forces not far behind. They did not halt. Instead, they did something that surprised everyone, including themselves: They chanted, "The people want the downfall of the regime!"

The sight of these people fleeing for their lives—people of all ages, men who were bricklayers and gym teachers and electricians and doctors and neighbors and friends—turned something in the hearts of all the residents of Manbij. For eight months, they'd been told their country was under siege from within, that they were facing an enemy who abhorred their nation, their way of life, their very being. They'd been told that terrorists were plotting to tear their homeland to shreds. But here were the authorities, here was the government, shooting at citizens. The veil withdrawn, people could see that there were no terrorists here, only their brothers, husbands, sons.

And so, impulsively, people stepped out. They emerged onto the street and joined the procession. Out came Ibrahim, who'd never given a thought to taking part but whose baby brother was somewhere in the swarm, among the marchers. Out came Mina and her husband, walking hand in hand, disappearing into the stream of bodies. Out came housewives and mothers who had never imagined themselves on this stage, or any stage. Out came so many more. And who were they? They were ordinary people, thrust into extraordinary circumstances. They might have watched grainy footage on television and shook their heads, they might have passed homeless hags with crenelated teeth and said, "there but for the grace of God," they might have lined up for work under the girders and cranes of dusty lots—they might have lived a thousand lives in anonymity, had the regime proved more powerful than the truth. But truth stands on its own, and only lies require scaffolding.

Now, in the darkness, under the pale fluorescent lights of balconies and minarets, the crowds marched and chanted. The regime forces kept pace, guns trained at the throngs. Their voices were heard from the balconies, and even more citizens came out. They came for love, they came for rage, they came because they believed it was the right thing to do. Out they came, and through the darkness they marched, even if they did not know, and could not imagine, where they were headed.

BOOK
THREE

The
Republic

January 2012–
January 2014

Prologue

Every political system, whether one of popular consent or of tyranny, is built on innumerable acts of faith—the faith that traffic lights will work, prescribed medicines will heal, evening news tells the truth, enemies are who the authorities say they are. Revolution reflects, if anything, a profound crisis of faith. It ushers in a new mode of understanding, where old solidities crumble, the preordained is exposed as a contrivance, misfortune as injustice. The world, once unitary and complete, has splintered into distinct realms: the kingdom of make-believe and the kingdom of truth. Inhabitants of that second realm find themselves facing the tantalizing possibility that life isn't merely given, it is made.

And so, as people awoke, they streamed to squares and avenues. In forgotten hill stations and cinderblock shantytowns and dust-swept cities, crowds marched and chanted and raised the tri-star flag. As the calendar turned to 2012, the country was in full-scale rebellion. Soldiers were refusing orders to fire on their countrymen. Officers were defecting. The government no longer had the manpower to crush protests in every town and suburb. Emboldened, even more people came out. The word on their lips, printed across their banners, was "freedom." It was the rallying cry for a generation, prompting astonishing feats of sacrifice and solidarity. And as in the Western world, it was perhaps the supreme value of the Arab Spring, the scale on which all other convictions and principles were weighed. Yet to raise a slogan is one thing, and to construct a new order—the reign of freedom—on the ashes of the old is another thing entirely.

What does it mean to be free? No one chanting in the packed squares could yet say for sure. No one slipping through alleys, bullets whipping overhead, could yet offer a confident response. They were about to find out together and, in the process, confront their deepest beliefs about this human life.

ONE

January–March 2012

ODAY RECEIVES A VISITOR

In mourning, Oday avoided the northern sweep beyond Sundus Street, the alley of Roman walls, but he buried himself in his daytime work hawking cell phones, and his nighttime work plotting revolution. His efforts earned him enough to rent a two-room house on the outskirts of town. It was there that, one evening, he was sitting with a few protesters when one of them announced he'd invited a friend. A few minutes later, the door opened to reveal a tall, broad-shouldered man in an olive uniform with epaulets.

Oday sprang to his feet. "You!" He turned to his friend. "You invited *him*?"

Oday tried to flee, but his friends nearly tackled him. He was removed to the kitchen, where they assured him the visitor had come alone. Oday peered out the window and saw no vehicles. His fear turned to rage. "I do not want this *shabih* in my house!" he shouted.

At length the friends led Oday back to the living room, where he accosted his guest. "You didn't just assault me in prison, you insulted me!" he said.

"If it will make you feel better, you can insult me in return."

But Oday, still heaving, could find nothing to say to match the indignity he'd suffered.

"Then let's save our insults for Bashar al-Assad," the visitor replied. "That is, of course," he said with a smile, "granting you don't report me to the authorities."

Oday had difficulty believing what he was hearing. If the past eleven months had thrown the world upside down, this was the pinnacle of inversion. He and his friends sat down with 1st Lt. Maymati, Manbij chief of police, leader of the counterrevolution, and listened to his confession.

THE STRANGE, MARVELOUS CAREER OF 1ST LT. MAYMATI, PART 1

When Abdul Wahab Khalaf was a teenager growing up in the countryside of Raqqa, he had trouble being taken seriously. Perhaps it was his whip-thin frame, or his embarrassed look of shyness. He was the target of playground abuse, which may have attracted him to figures who rose above village anonymity. There was the cousin who'd joined the air force and returned home in a triumphal procession. There was the uncle who, by enlisting in the police academy, upset the natural taxonomy of village life by making tribal sheikhs travel hours to gain his audience.

Abdul Wahab threw himself into his books. He stunned his friends and parents by acing his baccalaureate exams and gaining admission to the law college at Damascus University. Law offered a fast track to the brass, so after graduation and two years at police academy, he emerged as first lieutenant and assumed his initial posting, in the city of Manbij.

It wasn't long before he became a household name. As one Manbij native later put it, recalling his first meeting with the city's new police chief, "I walked into his office, and he was sitting with his feet on the desk. There was a bouquet from the Manbij Girls High School, thanking him for his service. The interior minister was on the television, and he pointed to the screen and laughed: 'Look how this jackass lies to us.' This was before 2011—you wouldn't believe how shocked I was. This guy wasn't afraid of anyone."

1st Lt. Abdul Wahab was friendly and respectful in his dealings with law-abiding citizens but pitiless toward the pleas of the criminal. A colleague later recalled, "His favored method of punishment was the *falaka*." Striking detainees' bare feet was a practice that did not necessarily distinguish him from the rest of the corps: "It is known to us officers that a criminal only confesses to his crime if he is beaten and tortured," the colleague recalled. But unlike his comrades, he was also seen as incorruptible. In all his years in his post, there was not one person who would testify to having slipped him a bribe.

One summer, *Valley of the Wolves*, a Turkish soap, aired in Syria. The series follows a Jack Bauer–type intelligence agent who infiltrates the mafia-controlled deep state. One of the hero's sidekicks is a mafioso who renounces his ways to side with justice, a fearless and loyal auxiliary named Maymati. Merciless, and with sangfroid in his pursuit of terrorists and crony capitalists, Maymati was a man of action.

1st Lt. Abdul Wahab was transfixed by the serial, ordering work to halt whenever an episode aired. It was not lost on people in Manbij that their police chief not only bore a striking physical resemblance to the Turkish hero but was also a man of action—once, in a shootout with smugglers, he ran into a hail of bullets to rescue a colleague.

The name stuck, and after a while, some people could hardly recall the birth name of Manbij's chief of police, 1st Lt. Maymati.

Sitting in Oday's living room, 1st Lt. Maymati attempted to recast the story of the past few winter months. Did Oday ever notice that when the police emerged from the station to put down a protest, their sirens were on? This was to alert the protesters to flee. Did it ever occur to him why prisoners were always transferred from the intelligence services to the police? This was so that 1st Lt. Maymati could ensure that they were not sent to Aleppo. Or that not a single protester had been struck by bullets? This was because 1st Lt. Maymati ordered his men to fire over protesters' heads. The truth, 1st Lt. Maymati now claimed, was that he could see into the protesters' hearts, and he could understand their fury.

Oday wasn't sure what to say. It felt too convenient, too calculated. Eight months earlier, he'd been hanging from the ceiling like a shank of meat, tears streaming down his face, while 1st Lt. Maymati's baritone voice said, "I'd like this one." The man was a liar, a perfidious liar. Why was he here? Oday was not a leader of this movement. Why wasn't he visiting members of the Revolutionary Council?

"I have nothing to say to this man," Oday announced.

1st Lt. Maymati said, "I'm trying to meet with the revolutionaries I arrested. I want to make things right."

Oday could not stand to look at him.

"I want this man out of my house," he said.

In revolutionary circles, 1st Lt. Maymati's visits were all anyone could talk about. Some were willing to give the commander a chance, but others were convinced this was a regime plot; security forces were known to try to infiltrate opposition groups.

On March 15, the one-year anniversary of the uprising, thousands of demonstrators flooded the street in front of Sheikh Aqeel mosque. Their procession was soon attacked by security forces. Protesters were dragged across the pavement into waiting pickups. One of the detained was a friend of Abdul Hadi's, who sounded the alarm, bringing others to the scene. A standoff ensued—hundreds of police on one side, thousands of protesters on the other. On the government's side were 1st Lt. Maymati and his counterpart in the intelligence services, Abu Roz. 1st Lt. Maymati ordered his men to hold fire, but Abu Roz retorted, "What do you expect us to do? We're letting the city be run by a mob!"

1st Lt. Maymati insisted he could solve the problem himself. He walked toward the crowd, some of whom held large rocks. The crowd, enraged, chanted, "The people want the downfall of the regime!" 1st Lt. Maymati was undeterred. The chants died away, and people stared incredulously at the police chief walking directly toward them. He was now standing face-to-face with the demonstrators. He said, "Listen to me! I support your demands. You are on the side of history."

"God is great! God is great!" the crowd cried. "The defection of the lieutenant!" a man proclaimed wildly.

1st Lt. Maymati was buffeted by dozens of hands. He looked confused, desperate to shake free. Delirious, the crowd marched toward the soldiers, carrying 1st Lt. Maymati with them. Someone ducked beneath his legs, trying to lift him onto his shoulders. The crowd chanted: "May-mat-i! May-mat-i!"

The police, watching this melee, assumed their chief was under attack. They could not open fire without endangering him, so they rushed the crowd. Stones and batons flew. Dozens were thrown to the ground, lips and foreheads split open. And a dazed 1st Lt. Maymati was carried away by Abu Roz's men.

A week later, 1st Lt. Maymati was sitting somewhere in the bowels of the Political Security Directorate in Damascus. Someone had uploaded the clip onto YouTube, leading news anchors to proclaim that Manbij's chief of police had defected to the revolution. Now, in Damascus, he was asked to explain himself.

A few days later, 1st Lt. Maymati appeared on state TV looking worn and diminished. "I deny all accusations against me," he said. "I was merely trying to deescalate the situation. I am, I assure you, a loyal servant of the Syrian Arab Republic."

No one was sure what to believe.

| TWO |

April–June 2012

A REAL MAN IN THE FAMILY

In recent weeks, relations had soured between Saladin Saba, Mina's brother, who was a captain in the regime's army, and his commanding officer. Saladin, who was stationed near the eastern border, had a penchant for releasing captives, while finding ways to avoid assignments that would bring him face-to-face with protesters. Under growing pressure from his superiors, Saladin plotted an escape. It was his brother Shampoo Sami who connected him to the Manbij Revolutionary Council, which made a farmhouse in the suburbs available as a hideout. Saladin became one of the first military officers from Manbij to defect.

When Mina's father learned of the defection, he was overjoyed. "Thank God! Thank merciful god! I have a man, a real man, in my family!" he shouted. But then the reality sank in: "Saladin has destroyed us! They will fire Mina!" Meanwhile, Saladin kept to the farmhouse, hardly stepping outside for fear of being spotted. The Revolutionary Council arranged for food and drink to be delivered once daily. After a few weeks, he was joined by a second officer, and then a third. By April, a coterie of defected officers was housed at the farm, and the Revolutionary Council held a meeting to decide what to do with them.

They gathered in an old, weather-stained barn. The mood was tense. Around the country, regime tanks were wreaking havoc on farmland and in villages. Having reconquered most of Homs, the regime was intensifying its offensive in Idlib. Under the pale glow of fluorescent tubes, the council members discussed the question on everyone's minds: arms. An officer who had defected from Idlib relayed eyewitness reports of massacres. He argued that it was only a matter of time before the regime turned its sights on Manbij, and that the revolutionaries needed to prepare themselves. Protesting would only get you so far, he insisted. He knew dealers; he could procure weapons. Open a front against the regime here, he advised, to take pressure off the revolutionaries in Idlib.

But the thought of resorting to violence made most members uneasy. The protest movement, after all, *was* succeeding. Six months ago, they could hardly carry out a flash protest; now Friday demonstrations were drawing thousands. Hasan argued that they should meet people where they were, winning them *politically*, not through force of arms. Abel Os argued that the presence of weapons among the revolutionaries would give the regime a pretext to increase their repression. Besides, the current level of slaughter could not last, because the international community would soon support the peaceful protesters.

Yet the opposing view also had compelling points in its favor. Munzer Salal argued that the regime in Manbij would never budge without the revolutionaries injecting an element of fear. He and fellow council member Anas Sheikh Weiss belonged to families linked to the Muslim Brotherhood. They had grown up at the knees of their fathers, listening to tales of a regime that, when challenged, reacted like a cornered animal. Indeed, the Muslim Brotherhood had begun life in the 1950s as a peaceful organization dedicated to contesting parliamentary elections. But once the Baath regime consolidated power and outlawed opposition parties, the Brotherhood believed they had no choice but to resort to arms.

For Hasan, the repression of the 1980s was a bitter lesson that weapons can't substitute for mass action, but for Munzer, it was proof that the regime only understood one language. Back in 2005, Mustafa Tlass, the minister of defense, said, "We used weapons to assume power, and we wanted to hold onto it. Anyone who wants power will have to take it from us with weapons."

MEANS AND ENDS

All around the city, and in remote farmhouses and garrets nationwide, other activists were having the same debate. Those advocating the peaceful approach were convinced that the regime would use the excuse of an armed opponent to "destroy entire cities," as one activist put it. The opposing side believed that talk of a peaceful struggle was quixotic at best, irresponsible at worst. The revolutionaries had been peaceful for almost a year, but so far had nothing to show for it beyond being shot at, thrown in dungeons, and tortured. They hadn't won even a single meaningful reform—the regime had simply grown more rapacious.

The sky above the old farmhouse paled, and the men inside, huddled around a thermos of tea, were nearing a compromise. Mired between the poles of launching a guerrilla war and holding fast to peaceful demonstration, one attendee raised a third possibility: The council could create an armed wing to protect protesters. If the authorities fired on demonstrations, the rebels would shoot back, but they would not undertake offensive missions. The burden of restraint, he argued, would fall on the regime.

No one was quite satisfied with this compromise, but it was enough to garner a majority vote. Hasan and Abel Os were the dissenting voices. "You don't know," Abel Os warned, "what you are about to unleash."

But the others had already moved on to discussing logistics. The first question was where to source matériel. A Kalashnikov was running about $2,500—eight months' income for a typical Syrian. The weapons would have to be found on the black market. Yet no protester was willing to actually meet with a smuggler—until Oday volunteered. Traveling under the stars, he took the back roads through the Aleppo countryside into Idlib, which was now a war zone. He returned each time with a single rifle hidden in a gym bag.

In the end, the council bought about twenty-five rifles, most of which had seen better days, and cached them in the desert. Even with this paltry arsenal, though, the siren song of the red-hot barrel, its power and weight, was too much to keep at bay. One afternoon, a prominent civilian regime supporter named Riad al-Asleh was in his car at a crowded intersection on Jazeera Road. He operated a network of informers, feeding intelligence about protests to authorities. In his tire shop, he displayed a regime flag and a poster of Bashar al-Assad in sunglasses. At demonstrations, he carried a two-by-four, which he used to attack protesters. His greatest wish, he told customers, was to torture protesters himself—if only the authorities would allow it. That afternoon, traffic had slowed to a crawl. Young boys selling water worked their way through the congestion. Just then, a motorcycle puttered up to Asleh's car. A man aimed a weapon and shot him in the head. He'd used a silencer.

In an emergency council meeting afterward, everyone accused council member Munzer Salal, who had acquired a silencer for the cache. But he denied it, claiming the whole episode was a regime plot to sow division among the revolutionaries. The argument lasted hours. In the end, bereft of evidence, the council was unable to censure Munzer. Instead, they elected to keep stricter watch on their weapons, and buried the cache in a new, undisclosed location in the desert. They agreed to avoid meeting for the time being, or even sleeping in their own beds. And they waited for the regime's response. But none came. Perhaps it was the situation around the country—several towns had even slipped from government control. Or perhaps, with the mood of brio and defiance on the streets, the pleather-jacket men simply did not know how to respond.

⁕ ⁕

On Friday, May 25, Manbij witnessed the largest crowds yet. Around the country, the armed protesters had linked with defected soldiers to become guerrilla bands, sometimes on the offensive, sometimes the defensive. These bands were calling themselves, collectively, the Free Syrian Army—though this was no unified organization, only a branding. That Friday, for the first time, the crowd in Manbij raised chants for the FSA. The regime forces stalked the protests, perching on rooftops and blocking roads. But they did not discharge their weapons. Hundreds were detained, savaged, then released the same day.

That week, activists called for a nationwide work stoppage to protest the regime's intransigence. In Manbij, the council spread the word. Abel Os went to the Cardamom Market, where he'd once met the motorcycle men, and spoke to workers. At night, Oday and his friends littered the streets with flyers. They stole through the Great Souk and spray-painted *Strike!* on the shuttered storefronts. On the morning of May 30, the city was empty. Workers stayed home, and merchants kept their businesses locked. Suleiman's Fruits was closed for the first time in living memory. Palace of My Eyes Shawarma—where golden-brown rings of chicken spun twenty-four hours a day—was closed. No one had seen anything like it. Abu Roz had called for backup from Aleppo, only to find hardly anyone in the streets. It was no longer possible to know whom to arrest—the entire city, it seemed, was in rebellion.

The following week, as the throngs squeezed into Rabta Street in yet another demonstration, the roar of motorcycles suddenly drowned out the chants. Four masked men drove through the crowd, one waving a tricolor revolutionary flag. "Long live Free Syria!" they chanted, and then revealed Kalashnikovs. Aiming to the sky, they fired multiple rounds. The crowd was in a frenzy, and the security forces, who had been tailing the procession, backed away. They radioed their supervisor for orders, but received no reply.

What they didn't know was that one of the men, in a balaclava, firing his weapon to the heavens, was their very own 1st Lt. Maymati.

| THREE |

July 2012

THE STRANGE, MARVELOUS CAREER OF 1ST LT. MAYMATI, PART 2

Syria was no longer in rebellion—it was in the throes of civil war. On May 25, 2012, the regime fired on protesters in the Houla region, northwest of Homs. In response, Free Syrian Army rebels ambushed government positions. That evening, regime forces, including *shabiha*, entered a nearby village and went house to house to loot and kill. The United Nations confirmed 108 dead civilians, the majority by summary execution. As the thick Levantine heat took hold that summer, fresh massacres were reported weekly, prompting Free Syrian Army units to form around the country.

In Manbij, the Revolutionary Council managed to keep its gunmen disciplined, holding a defensive posture. Still, protesters struggled to resist the urge to take the fight to the enemy, even though arms were hard to source. Foreign countries were reluctant to send weapons to the Free Syrian Army, which in truth was no army, only a motley collection of militias. So the black market became a prized terrain, and those who knew their way around its shadowy corners soon proved their worth. For decades, a brisk arms trade had flourished on the eastern borderlands with Iraq. People used firearms, which were illegal, for hunting and to fire off rounds at weddings. In Manbij, the doyen of these dark arts was a man with thinning gray hair and a sly smile named Abu Habib. Impulsive and quick to anger, Abu Habib didn't participate in the protests, because he wasn't sure what he could offer, but now, with the country awash in blood, he'd found his niche. He scored a half dozen rifles on the black market, then approached friends in the revolutionary movement. Together they raided a string of small police stations deep in the country, on the banks of the Euphrates, and netted dozens of weapons and thousands of rounds of ammunition— all without harming a hair of a single policeman. The Revolutionary Council demanded that the group surrender the weapons to the general cache, but Abu

Habib, who despised the council's defense-first mindset, refused. Instead, he hoped to expand his outfit—which included seasoned protesters—into a formidable fighting force that could liberate Manbij. What he needed, though, was funds. He turned his eyes south, to the Kingdom of Saudi Arabia, which viewed the uprising with suspicion, fearing that the Syrian example would inspire its own subjects to press for democracy. But Abu Habib had dealt with Saudi smugglers before and knew that some of the country's private citizens had more money than they knew what to do with—and that they supported the cause.

On July 11, a video appeared on YouTube showing a dozen masked men wearing ill-fitting camo and holding government-issued rifles. A man spoke in stilted formal Arabic. Next to him was Abu Habib. They announced the formation of the Army of the Two Sacred Places, or Jund al-Haramain, referring to Mecca and Medina, as a new Free Syrian Army brigade based in the city of Manbij. Most of these men had little time for religion, but they hoped the branding would attract Saudi money. When the Revolutionary Council learned of the group's formation, they demanded that it be dissolved, but Abu Habib struck a compromise—they would keep themselves as a distinct unit but remain under the authority of the council. Manbij now had two armed factions, one headed by Saladin Saba, Mina's brother, consisting of defected officers, and the second under the command of Abu Habib, and comprising protesters and workers—most of whom had never handled a weapon.

A few days later, security forces opened fire on demonstrators near the town of Jarablus, eighteen miles north of Manbij. One protester was killed and many were injured. Jarablus hugs the Turkish border, which makes it the gateway through which goods and people reach Manbij. Abu Habib informed the Revolutionary Council that he planned to liberate Jarablus from regime control—and that there was little the Revolutionary Council could do to stop him. The town, a tenth the size of Manbij, had only a small security presence, and the regime forces were taken by surprise. The rebels quickly seized the court, the civil registry, and the police station. All that remained was the State Security Directorate, where besieged regime officers chose to fight until death.

The battle raged through the night. The sky flashed as the officers fired RPG rounds from the rooftop. By dawn, their ammo was spent. The rebels bulldozed through the wall, finding tattered and exhausted soldiers. Abu Habib told the captives to face the wall. One officer was weeping. A second officer, who was from Manbij, claimed his superiors forced him to fight. A third begged to join the rebels, insisting he was working for the revolution from the inside. Abu Habib placed his weapon on the back of the first captive's head.

"This is for Salim al-Hariri," he said, naming a protester-turned-rebel who had been killed the day before. He pressed the trigger and the body fell limp. The other captives did not move. The weeping officer fell silent. They continued to face the wall. Abu Habib proceeded down the row, naming fallen protesters, until the bodies of all the captives lay on the floor.

That afternoon, July 16, the tri-star flag of the Syrian revolution replaced that of the Syrian Arab Republic atop the international border crossing. Flying high above the squat houses, it was visible for miles around. Jarablus was the first town in northern Syria to fall under revolutionary control, though no one knew for how long—retaliation was sure to come.

The following day, Abu Habib's fighters surrounded the police station in Shuyukh—the largest town between Jarablus and Manbij. When the officers rejected his demands to surrender, rebels opened fire. They proceeded to fight with a professionalism that belied their backgrounds as farmers and laborers. They understood proper formation and attended to supply lines—because Abu Habib was on the phone taking instructions, though his men were unsure from whom. By evening, the regime managed to deliver reinforcements through the rear of the facility, and the besieged officers redoubled their defense. With the rebels now exhausted and running low on ammunition, Abu Habib made another phone call.

Not long after, as dusk fell, a police vehicle pulled up to the scene. The door opened to reveal a tall, broad-shouldered officer: 1st Lt. Maymati. He walked over and embraced Abu Habib. The rebels could not believe what they were witnessing. With Abu Habib by his side, 1st Lt. Maymati announced that he—and two commanding officers with him—had been behind Jund al-Haramain's creation and had been directing strategy from afar.

"There is no more Syrian Arab Republic," he proclaimed. "I will talk to them"—pointing to the station—"and give them the reality." The astonished fighters began to cheer, chant for freedom, and praise God. 1st Lt. Maymati disappeared into the police station. Hours passed.

It was close to dawn when he reemerged, his eyes bloodshot. The fighters assembled. He shook his head and said, "They are blind. We only have one option—let's turn them into ghosts." No sooner had he finished the sentence than gunfire rang out from the police station. The revolutionaries took cover behind a clutch of houses. 1st Lt. Maymati had left his truck near the station. He needed to return to Jarablus to raise backup. The windshield was blown out and the chassis shot through like a sieve. He looked to Abu Habib and said, "Wait here—don't shoot back until I give the order." He ran into the hail of gunfire. He reached the car, climbed aboard, pushed the seat flat, and drove off. The other rebels did not budge. 1st Lt. Maymati returned within the hour, with a fresh convoy of rebels, who poured their fire at the police station. The besieged men shot back wildly, then with less intensity, then finally went silent. An hour later, as the rebels remained crouched behind the houses, a helicopter landed on the roof, rescuing the policemen. 1st Lt. Maymati drove his bullet-riddled cruiser into the courtyard, scaled the building to the roof, and planted the flag of Free Syria.

THIS IS ALL OURS!

The next day, July 18, a bomb ripped through a highly fortified room of the National Security headquarters in Damascus, killing President Assad's brother-in-law and the minister of defense while wounding the president's brother and other top officials. To the functionaries and security officials in Manbij, it must have felt as if the world was collapsing. They pleaded for reinforcements. In the evening, a large convoy of armored personnel carriers entered the city and headed for Security Square, where most government officers were concentrated. As the city went to sleep, the government readied itself for war.

In the morning, residents discovered that checkpoints around town had been removed overnight. Government forces had retreated to Security Square, which was surrounded by blast walls. A pair of snipers sat on the roof of the Manbij Hotel. Rumors swirled. Abel Os feared blood on the streets. He organized a demonstration that marched from Sarab. The protesters chanted, "Sal-mi-ya, sal-mi-ya!"—Peaceful, peaceful!—and carried the tri-star revolutionary flag. Under a brilliant sun, he led the procession across the wadi. Cars honked and people waved from windows. The procession neared downtown. Abel Os eyed the alleys, trying to guess the regime's angle of attack.

But the real action was in a dusty police cruiser in Jarablus, where 1st Lt. Maymati was sitting with a few fighters. He called Manbij authorities—who still believed he was on their side—and proclaimed in a faux panic that rebels had amassed three thousand fighters to march on the city. Military Intelligence Chief Abu Roz and his comrades, barricaded in Security Square, now faced a moment of truth.

For fifteen months they'd been on a war footing, swearing to protect their president by any means necessary. At first, the protesters—the "terrorists"—were a tiny band of troublemakers, but slowly, inexorably, they'd won the allegiance of the street. Abu Roz must have wished that he'd heeded his instincts and gunned the protesters down on day one. Now it was too late. He called Aleppo for instructions, pacing in his office like a condemned man. He'd ruled like a deity over his adjutants and attendants but was now a mere mortal: weak, wanting, insecure.

In the police station, the city's men in uniform gathered around a walkie-talkie. Their leader, 1st Lt. Maymati, was nowhere to be found. A forty-year order was collapsing before their eyes. Ignoring Abu Roz's entreaties, they climbed into their vehicles.

Hasan Nefi was at the library when he heard the news. At once, he spread a message to the Revolutionary Council members: "Secure City Hall!"

Posters of Assad, the elder and the younger, adorned the face of City Hall, a four-story structure built in the Brutalist style. When Hasan approached the entrance, he saw a sight unimaginable in all his years: There were no police here. There were no police anywhere. Pedestrians stopped in their tracks, looking around as if they'd suddenly been transported to an alien city.

Council members, wearing ski masks and carrying hunting rifles, entered the facility. They found the governor, looking pale, fidgeting behind his desk. He said he wanted no trouble, that he had no interest in the dispute between the people and the authorities. "I only want to go home," he pleaded, "if you will allow me." Hasan promised no one would bother him. The governor did not know who the men in his office were, or whom they represented, but it did not matter. Strength, authority, power—which for decades had intangibly but so resolutely ruled over 150,000 lives—no longer inhabited this desk, this body. Where it lay now, no one was quite sure.

Hasan exited and walked toward Security Square. The Manbij Hotel roof was empty. He studied the blast walls enclosing the square—not a regime soldier in sight. Where were Abu Roz and his men? A group of locals gathered near the blast walls. They looked as people did during the very first protest—like children lost in a crowd, searching for their guardians.

No sound emerged from the square itself. Nothing stirred. Hasan and a group of pedestrians tried to peer through the slats of the blast walls. Then, carefully, they squeezed themselves through an embrasure. Now they were inside the square. No agents or pleather-jacket men in sight. The small crowd approached Baath Party headquarters. It was empty. The Directorate of Political Intelligence was empty. The Directorate of Military Intelligence—empty. Every bench, every parking lot, every guard hut, every building—blissfully, terrifyingly empty.

Then gunfire.

Several regime pickups were speeding through downtown, stuffed with fleeing soldiers and police and regime agents. When the convoy reached the Sailboat Roundabout, on the west side, they came upon a fleet of old jeeps and

station wagons and police cruisers—1st Lt. Maymati's convoy. He had around fifty fighters—not three thousand—but it equaled the size of the regime column. The two sides exchanged rounds. Windshields exploded. The rebels took aim at the drivers, but the regime troops shot wildly. Bullets hit parked vehicles and buildings. Muhammad Bayram, a fourteen-year-old on summer vacation, who loved soccer and watched the European teams whenever he could, was standing in front of the aluminum shop where he worked. A bullet struck him in the brain.

After a brief engagement, the regime convoy pushed onward. People emerged from their houses—women carrying babies on their hips, children clinging to their fathers' legs. The convoy sped past the Book Roundabout, onto Highway 4, which leads to Aleppo, and disappeared over the horizon.

Hundreds of intelligence soldiers, agents, party bosses, apparatchiks, functionaries, and factotums were gone.

—+—+—

At first, no one knew what to think about the suddenly orphaned city. Abel Os thought that the exit was an elaborate regime plot. He went to investigate and found locals at a military outpost kicking a fallen statue of Bashar al-Assad. He walked in a daze, walking and walking, until he understood he was no longer alone, and would never be again. He ran back to the protest he'd started, which had now swelled to three thousand people. Someone passed him a microphone. He turned to address the sweaty faces. "Brothers," he began. "Thank God—after forty years, our city is free."

In that moment, the distance between people vanished, and the private fortresses of fear and distrust crumbled. The crowd was frenzied, pushing to get a glimpse of Abel Os, as if sighting the speaker with their own eyes would give events the solidity of truth. Word spread so quickly that it seemed everyone learned of it at once. Women leaned over the balustrades, ululating. Car horns blared.

A procession of dirt-spattered pickups was spotted in the northern quarter. As the trucks wended their way through the streets, tri-star flags flying, a shout went up: "The Free Army! The Free Army!" The Free Syrian Army caravan approached downtown, and a roar was heard: "My country! My country!" The citizenry flooded the streets, swarming onto the cars stalled in the traffic.

Mina was at home, but she could hear the commotion. There was a knock on the door. She opened it to see, in government-issued fatigues, streaked with dirt, her younger brother Saladin. She shrieked and kissed him. In his months as a rebel, he'd gone bone-thin, his face burnt country red. Shampoo Sami fought back tears. Saladin invited his younger brother into his vehicle. They checked on an army post in the neighborhood, which was empty save for a lone recruit, an Alawite who'd been left behind by his comrades. He clasped Saladin's feet, begging for mercy. Saladin put his weapon down and said, "Don't worry, we're all in this together." The recruit burst into tears. Saladin gave him cigarettes and money and told him to take a taxi out of town.

Central Square was packed; cars could not move. Trays of sweets were passed to the rebels. Mina and her sisters worked their way through the throngs, shouldering coolers with two-liter coke bottles filled with ice-cold water. The revolutionaries grasped the bottles with their grimy hands. One rebel exclaimed, "You are the true sister of men!" The crowd grew. Abel Os attempted to speak, but his voice was submerged under the chanting, the shouting, the singing. And what songs! On one corner, people had broken into an impromptu rendition of "Our Homeland Is Paradise." Dancing on car tops, a second group was crooning "We Trample on the House of Assad." Singing men, ululating women, car horns, clapping, laughter, cries of joy, inarticulate shouting, screaming—yes, a single scream, unlike the rest, rising from the crush. A reveler was pointing to the roof of the Manbij Hotel. A cable—no, a muzzle—rested on the ledge, aimed down at the masses. People scrambled in terror, shouting, "Sniper! Sniper!"

Abel Os and a friend headed for the hotel. The facility, which had never hosted a guest because the revolution had canceled its opening, was unlocked. The reception desk stood vacant. He pressed the elevator button, but nothing stirred. They made for the stairs, panting up five flights. Abel Os was carrying a large pipe. On the sixth floor, they stopped to listen. Not a sound from the hollows of the stairwell. On the seventh floor, they pressed their ears to the roof access gate. Abel Os knew the sniper would fire as soon as they appeared. They waited a few moments—not a sound. He uttered a small prayer and cracked the door open. "We are friends," he called out. "I'll help you leave the city." The air was filled with distant shouts, honking. He inched the door open. The rooftop was a little city of boilers and cables. His eyes swept the premises—boiler, boiler, cable. Empty. Abel Os breathed deeply, and laughed. "It's empty!"

He gave an assignment to his friend, who raced down the stairs. He returned with two others, carrying a spool of fabric. From the rooftop, they unfurled the green-white-and-black cloth, which activists had woven and cached months earlier, and hung it from the summit, an enormous revolutionary flag that billowed against Manbij's tallest building like a sail.

From the street, Oday watched the flapping banner. He grabbed Abdul Hadi by the hand and said, "Come with me!" He snatched a revolutionary flag from an FSA vehicle and raced to the city's sole transmission pylon, which towered above the post office like Manbij's own Eiffel. The revolutionary standard clenched between his teeth, Oday scaled the tower, while Abdul Hadi shouted after him, laughing, "You're crazy! You've really lost your mind!" He gripped the rafters, balancing his feet, not looking down. At the summit, he planted the banner. One hundred feet above the trash-strewn street, this was the apex of the city. The roar of the crowd reached his ears, and he raised his fist. Looking out over the throngs, he must have found it difficult to believe what had come to pass. This cluster of cement blocks, with so much corrugated iron and so many Ottoman windows, with electric cables and stone minarets, this city, so ugly and so beautiful, was shedding its past. Oday could finally say: Here, too, there are heroes.

Down below, the crowds toppled the blast walls and surged through Security Square. They roamed the plaza with élan, their heads straight, hungrily staring at the edifices of their torment—the headquarters of military intelligence, political intelligence, and the Baath Party—as if someone might remove the buildings. When they'd had their fill, they surged toward the structures themselves.

The norms of society were, for the time being, suspended. In this great inversion, the people believed they had the right, even the duty, to take possession of whatever they pleased. The multitudes gathered outside political intelligence headquarters and, in a flash, burst through the door. In the bacchanalia, they set upon the posters of the Leader, tearing them to shreds. They smashed windows. They kicked walls. They even tried to uproot courtyard trees. Then a hush fell over the mob. Someone had broken down the door to the main compound. They entered the building the way a child steals into her parents' bedroom, rifling through drawers. They reappeared on the street with the appurtenances of Baathist rule: a Flying Carpet, a torture tire, an electric chair. The crowd pounced on these instruments of doom with a cathartic fury. Now the mob held in their hands documents in manila folders. They were tearing into their plunder when Hasan noticed and ran over. "No, no, no!" he shouted. He asked a few revolutionaries to guard the compound. "This is all ours!" he shouted. "We are against the regime, not the idea of *government*! This is our state now!"

Hasan and the other council members devised an emergency plan to guard government installations. Volunteers armed with hunting rifles took up watch in front of the intelligence directorates, the Youth Center, and the Cultural Center. They had no sooner assumed their posts when a roar went up again, now in front of the hotel.

Atop a knot of people, balancing on someone's shoulders, was 1st Lt. Maymati. The crowd was chanting, "Maymati, Maymati, forever kicking Assad's head!" Rebels were firing madly into the air. But the hero of the revolution was flailing his arms, trying desperately to be heard. He was shouting, "Go indoors! Don't gather! The regime may attack!" He was gesturing to the sky, but his cries were lost amid the jubilation.

The city was teetering on chaos. No one had expected the regime to simply quit. No one had been ready—except Hasan and his comrades. They'd been preparing for this moment for eight months. The time to act was now. Hasan called for a meeting of the council. As Hasan walked, the houses continued to empty, the streets filling with men and women. They greeted each other, friends and strangers alike, as if they were only now beginning to understand they belonged to one and the same city.

THE REVOLUTIONARY COUNCIL IS IN SESSION

When Abel Os showed up at the gate of R. H. High School, in the southern quarter, a gunman refused him entry. "You need someone inside to vouch for you." A second guard saw him and said, "Let him enter, man! He's a leader," and clasped Abel Os's hand. His whole life, Abel Os had clasped the hands of others, calling them "my lord"—and now, suddenly, it was his hand that was clasped. He looked around at hundreds of people in the playground. Men were embracing each other and weeping. Others were engaged in heated arguments. He spotted Oday and Abdul Hadi, who'd attended high school here, carrying a revolutionary flag. Hundreds of people gathered at the gates, and some snuck inside, all with the same question on their minds: Who was the new authority?

Inside, Hasan Nefi was composing a statement on his laptop. His message was read through loudspeakers in dozens of mosques around the city:

> The city of Manbij has been liberated! Authority has passed to the Revolutionary Council of Manbij and Its Countryside. People should continue their work as usual. No one should transgress against state institutions or employees, as they belong to all citizens. The Revolutionary Council is here to serve the people.

In a packed room, Ahmed Rahmo stood to speak. The diffident engineer, who'd used his office to organize the secret network of protesters, and so impressed Abel Os with his logical mind, quieted the crowd and called a meeting to order. First on the agenda was security. The challenges were many, from the possibility of regime retribution to looting. The council called for the formation of neighborhood militias to protect the streets at night. They distributed hunting rifles and pistols to volunteers to guard government installations. A vote was held to turn the Manbij Hotel into a temporary prison to house looters and other violators.

The attendees then debated the role of state institutions. There were lights to keep on, streets to sweep. Tens of thousands of residents relied on subsidized bread to survive. Schools would need to be reopened by autumn. Fortunately, it had been the role of the Office of Political Affairs—headed by Hasan—to examine these issues. Hasan presented his plan, based on months of study. The idea, he said, was that nothing should change. The city would continue as before: The council would send the regime in Aleppo all municipal fees collected from electricity and water bills, state bakeries, and agricultural banks. The regime, given its dire straits, would not turn down hard cash, even from a "terrorist"-controlled city. To keep the cash flowing, the regime would have to deliver grain, fuel, electricity, and water to Manbij. It would also have to send salaries for the five thousand or so municipal employees needed to keep the city running.

Next, the group mooted the question of military factions. The council agreed that only local FSA units could serve the city. And all local fighters should subordinate themselves to the Revolutionary Council. They knew that this last point would be a touchy issue. 1st Lt. Maymati was a hero on the streets. Abu Habib and his fighters had already defied the council once. The council agreed to hold a meeting of all gunmen the following day.

As the sky darkened, the celebratory fire outside died down. The meeting ended, but visitors continued to stream into R. H. High School. Most simply wanted to see their new leaders with their own eyes. Demand was such that Hasan and other council members spent the night at the school, which was turning into a headquarters. With the energy on the streets having dissipated, a new mood took hold. Neighborhood youths with clubs and batons and hunting rifles set up checkpoints. In nearly every living room, families gathered for dinner and discussed the new reality. The future had been blown wide-open, but now came the creeping fear that even in their liberation, they were not truly free.

As Abel Os lay in bed that night, he pondered the gulf that lay ahead. They had clasped his hand today—and tomorrow he did not know if his city would remain standing.

Mina, her husband, her sisters, and their children stuffed themselves into a pickup. The vehicle rolled through the darkened streets. With the windows up, the family sang a song written by a revolutionary from Homs:

> *Free, free, freedom, we want freedom*
> *Despite you, oh Bashar, we will gain freedom*
> *Oh Mama and Lala and Lala, oh Mama and Lala*
> *It's Homs, what's happening, Mama and Lala?*
> *A child was martyred, oh Mama, and what's the baby's fault?*
> *Stay away, oh soldiers, don't obey the oppressor*
> *Free, free, freedom, we want freedom*

They drove through the empty streets. Mina pressed her face to the glass, watching the mills pass, the silhouettes of apartment buildings, the roundabouts. She did not want to go home, but to keep driving, driving until tomorrow, when the sun would warm the city and the bustle returned to the crooked streets, when one hundred fifty thousand people would embark on the daring and potentially absurd project of governing themselves.

| FOUR |

August 2012

NEW EYES

For many hours, Oday stood on the balcony above Sundus Street. The city below appeared unchanged: The same carts overloaded with cantaloupe and watermelon, the same striated chicken turning slowly on axes, the girls in rainbow foulards walking in pairs and threes through the crowds, the dense heat, the smoke-stained walls, and the old cement spires. Yet beneath it all surged a new power. People walked differently, with confidence, as if they now truly knew the city's streets. From the balcony, Oday could see the entrance to Security Square, now stripped of its blast walls. Pedestrians ambled freely up to the Directorate of Political Security and the Directorate of Military Security, gazing up at the two-story structures like they were monuments of a vanquished civilization. The tri-star revolutionary flag hung from electric cables and awnings. In the evening, people did not go home when the market closed. Old men placed tables on the cobblestones near the market, playing cards. Voices floated up to the balconies. Everything felt new: There was a different sky and a different wind. It was as if new and unknown birds alighted on the branches.

As Oday beheld the city, his triumphant city, he pondered the caprices of fate. Had there been no sit-in, would the authorities have conducted arrest campaigns across the city? Would Hasan Nefi have realized that a revolutionary council was needed? Whatever he thought, Oday did not discuss the matter. But his friend Abdul Hadi did, and he was convinced that their months in the dungeon, along with the trials of so many others, were necessary steps to liberation.

These days, Abdul Hadi left his house in the morning, jogging under the plane trees of Post Office Street, through the crowds milling at Security Square, and walked up to the Youth Center, where, a year earlier during a soccer match, he had kicked the ball so high that it sailed over the barbed wire and landed squarely on a poster of the giant face of Bashar al-Assad. Enraged pleather-jacket men shot at the ball until it was a tattered hide. Now, finally, there was no image of the Leader staring down.

Abdul Hadi spent hours in the old government compounds, like Baath Party headquarters and the mayor's office, soaking up the cream-colored walls, the handsome couches, the official documents stacked on oak tables. He discovered a government phone book. He and his friends began making prank calls to government offices, a stunt that would once have sent them, in the old argot, to their "aunt's house"—that is, into the bowels of the prison system—but which now only produced laughter. They called intelligence branches in Damascus and issued bomb threats. They phoned army hospitals, posing as military officers and pleading for ambulances. In the evening, they toured the city on motorbikes, seeing the lanes and roundabouts of their youth with new eyes. Rolling brownouts left entire quarters shrouded in darkness. The great fountain near the Book Roundabout was dry. They passed through checkpoints manned by gunmen from the Free Syrian Army. Who were these scraggly, underfed men? No one had seen them at the protests. In fact, militias had mushroomed overnight, each carrying the flag of the FSA. After asking around, the friends learned that some rebel outfits—the Dignity Brigade, the Manbij Revolutionaries Brigade, and the Manbij Martyrs Brigade—operated under the authority of the Revolutionary Council. These factions protected key installations, such as the Municipal Bakery, which produced tens of thousands of loaves daily to feed the city. Other groups struck a more independent stance: the Free Men of Syria Brigade, a mostly Kurdish faction linked to a left-wing guerrilla group called the Kurdistan Workers Party; the Knights of the Euphrates, a motley collection of bricklayers and peasants; and Ammar bin Yasser, a faction drawn from one of Manbij's *shaabi* soccer clubs, Jazeera, and named after a companion to the Prophet Muhammad.

"What's with these Islamic names?" Abdul Hadi complained to a friend. "Ammar bin Yasser, Jund al-Haramain—what century is this?" He believed the factions should take names like Freedom or Unity—names all Syrians could support.

By whatever name, though, there were now eight factions operating checkpoints around the city, and the Revolutionary Council was determined to get a handle on the situation.

A QUESTION OF LEGITIMACY

In late July, Ahmed Rahmo, the president of the Revolutionary Council, set off to pay 1st Lt. Maymati a visit at the military recruitment center. He found him in uniform, combing through files for information on individuals serving in the regime's army. Rahmo demanded to know who had authorized Maymati to assume such a responsibility—and the first lieutenant shot back, asking Rahmo who had authorized him to run the city. More than anyone, the regime's withdrawal was due to Maymati, and his double-agent status had transformed him into something of a local celebrity. To Rahmo, though, Maymati was nothing more than a vigilante. The city needs the rule of law, Rahmo insisted, not the law of the jungle. The argument erupted into a shouting match. Maymati insisted that until an entity was strong enough to exert control, it was his job, as the guardian of law and order, to step in. The dispute ended without resolution, but that evening the council issued its first official statement as Manbij's governing body: "First Lieutenant Abdul Wahab Maymati has been informed that he is not wanted in any military capacity in Manbij, and that he will be punished for any military activity he undertakes."

The next day, Maymati folded up his uniform and vowed never to work in Manbij again. He was quitting the city altogether, promising to return only when all of Syria was free.

Not long after, the council convened a meeting with leaders of the new militias. Ahmed Rahmo introduced himself as the city's president and instructed armed groups to obtain licenses from the council to operate. Immediately a shout went up: Who gave the council legitimacy to issue such orders? Who bestowed Ahmed Rahmo with the office of president? Council members asked, in return, who gave the armed factions authority to establish checkpoints. What right did they have to search vehicles? There was such a thing as civil rights, Rahmo insisted, even if the regime had trampled them.

Abu Habib of Jund al-Haramain shouted that his men had sacrificed themselves on the front lines in Jarablus—and that this alone gave them the right. He looked like he had not slept in days. "If you don't like our behavior," he threatened, "we'll leave the city and head for the front lines."

One council member, a leftist, could barely contain his rage, responding, "May God accept you," implying a wish that Abu Habib die on the front lines.

Abu Habib pulled a grenade from his pocket, screaming, "May God accept us all!" Fighters rushed to his side, prying the weapon from his hands. His group stormed off, leaving a stunned room.

Over the next hours, the remaining factions hammered out an agreement, granting authority to the Revolutionary Council to direct security inside the city. Only Jund remained a rogue faction, a problem the council decided to postpone for another day.

THE REVOLUTIONARY YOUTH MOVEMENT

One evening, as the director of the Municipal Bakery was driving home, a pair of vehicles pulled up, forced him out at gunpoint, and carried him off. People whispered that it was Jund fighters, targeting the director because he was a former government employee. Only the Revolutionary Council's intervention yielded his release. A few days later, a doctor was kidnapped. Before long, there was news of home break-ins around the city, amounting to thousands of dollars in losses.

Abdul Hadi, Oday, and their friends were discussing the crime wave one afternoon as they walked through downtown. Before them stood City Hall, its entrance guarded by gunmen affiliated with the Revolutionary Council. "There," Abdul Hadi said. "Is that what a government should be doing?" City Hall held all Manbij's property deeds, tax records, and birth certificates. The building faced Main Street, and on any afternoon, thousands of pedestrians streamed past. If regime helicopters targeted the gunmen, they would cause a massacre—and the city's documents would go up in flames. Abdul Hadi believed something had to be done. An idea struck him—they should do what they did best. He stood with his friends in front of City Hall. The midday traffic was roaring down Main Street. There were six of them, with Abdul Hadi standing on the curb. He shouted, "Civilian buildings for civilians! Civilian buildings for civilians!" As his voice rang out, street life ground to a halt. His friends joined in. "Civilian buildings for civilians!" they chanted. More pedestrians stopped to watch. For forty years, there had not been a single protest in Manbij. Then, over fifteen months, the streets were roiling with discontent against the dictatorship. Now, there was a protest against the *new* authorities. Freedom, once uncorked, could not be put back in the bottle.

The Revolutionary Council's office was on the third floor. Surprised by the outburst, the council invited the group upstairs. Abdul Hadi, Oday, and friends were soon sitting face to face with Ahmed Rahmo. Council member Anas Sheikh Weiss was also present. Meeting officials of the previous regime had been impossible without *wasta*. Abdul Hadi had passed by City Hall nearly every day of his life, never daring to guess what transpired inside. And how often had he stood in the corner of some government office, or in line under a harsh sun, waiting meekly until his turn was called? Yet the months in the underground movement had been an education in equality. Abdul Hadi spoke to the council leaders with the cool assurance of someone advising a colleague. He demanded that the armed men be removed for the safety of the neighborhood and the documents. Anas Sheikh Weiss responded that the gunmen were necessary to protect the documents from looters. Abdul Hadi retorted that Anas Sheikh Weiss, who commanded the guards outside, was also head of the Office of Humanitarian Aid—a conflict of interest.

Anas looked taken aback that this man half his age was criticizing the council. "Don't stick your nose into complicated affairs," he responded.

Oday, who could not believe the tone, saw red. Oday's greatest strength—and weakness—was his unquenchable ardor, his aversion to disinterest, his ability to feel quickly and deeply. "Take your soldiers somewhere else!" he shouted, at a volume that startled the council members.

Ahmed Rahmo offered the group an office in City Hall, saying that they could monitor council activities. "We don't want an office," Abdul Hadi said. "We just want you to act like a proper government!"

The group left without success. Oday paced back and forth, eyes burning, as they stood outside discussing their next move. "We took down one dictator, we can do it again!" He suggested arming themselves with stones to attack the gunmen, until Abdul Hadi grabbed his shoulders and said, "Have you lost your mind?"

Meanwhile, Anas Sheikh Weiss phoned Abel Os. The pair had been inseparable years before, when they trained side by side in the dojo, and when Anas had rescued Abel Os from loan sharks. But when Abel Os answered the phone, he could hardly believe this was his old friend. "Get down here," Anas ordered. "These are your kids. Get them out of here." He spoke in the urban Aleppine dialect, with no trace of the *shawi* they'd grown up with, and his haughty tone came as a shock.

"They aren't my kids," Abel Os said, with effort. The shame of his years was welling up.

"They worship you."

When Abel Os arrived at City Hall, he found Abdul Hadi and friends near the entrance. He considered going upstairs to the office of the Revolutionary Council—of which he was a member. But then a young man in the crowd, who'd marched behind Abel Os in many protests, said to him, "You know, they'll always see you as a vegetable peddler. They'll never give you real responsibility." Abel Os refused to believe it—he'd risked his life alongside those men and knew them in a way Abdul Hadi and his friends did not. Still, Anas's tone, his touch of smugness, the *assuredness* without open impertinence, was something he'd endured his whole life. It was as if, from birth, the world presented itself differently to people like Anas. Dark alleys weren't potential traps, they were opportunities. People like Anas carried themselves knowing that the world's many rules, visible and invisible, were ordered for their benefit. They had never questioned whether it was *they* who should assume control over the city—Abel Os would have never dared imagine it himself—because it was they who'd rightfully controlled the city before the horrible Baathist interregnum. The Salal market, the Henezel neighborhood: These were the names of the city's landmarks, as well as the names of men on the council. In a very real sense, as confirmed by the property deeds stored on the floors above, the city belonged to them.

Abel Os decided not to see the council members. Instead, he told Abdul Hadi and his friends to regroup at his home in Sarab. He had an idea.

The gathering consisted of some twenty young men, most under the age of twenty-five, sitting in the twilight in Abel Os's front yard. The vapors from the nearby open sewer bothered some attendees, but Abel Os was accustomed to it. In front of the compound wall stood an empty space where Tear of Roses had been, before creditors tore it down. Abel Os could not afford to offer tea to this many guests, but no one seemed to mind. "Oh Abel Os," one of the attendees said, "in the Revolutionary Council I bet they serve dinner, eh?" and laughter rippled through the group.

Abel Os began the proceedings by summarizing recent events: the kidnappings, the proliferating armed factions, the council's aloofness. The protest that evening had been the first of its kind, as it did not target the regime but fellow revolutionaries. He asked the group: Is it right to protest against revolutionaries? There was a spirited discussion, with the majority agreeing that what mattered was fealty to principles—freedom and dignity—and not to people. If any entity strays from those principles, whether that entity be the previous overlords or the revolutionary government or the rebels, should it be afforded the privilege of power? Abdul Hadi said that this was the story of history: Yesterday's freedom fighters become today's dictators. *Someone* had to safeguard the principles.

Abel Os proposed that they launch a political party, to continue the peaceful struggle against the regime until all Syria was free, while also holding the revolutionary government to account. "This will be the party *of* the revolution," Abel Os exclaimed. "A true democracy has independent parties."

Abdul Hadi and others disagreed. They'd spent their lives in the shadow of the Baath Party, and from his experience, Abdul Hadi argued that parties were merely vehicles to hoard power. "We're here for the good of the city, not for personal ambition." As a child, on the way to the Youth Center, he and his friends would pass by Baath Party headquarters and wonder at the sorcery taking place within. The lives of thousands were summarily decided within those walls. No, parties were the road to corruption and tyranny. "We don't want to take power," Abdul Hadi said. We aren't even *against* the Revolutionary Council or the rebel factions. We just want to make sure they stay true to their principles.

If not a party, then what? As the discussion stretched into the night, a new notion emerged. They wished to plan protests, to monitor the work of the council and the factions. They needed a structure to formulate and propose policies to the public. A space in which they could educate themselves, and foster debate about the direction of their city and their country. They called this new body a *tajammo*, a gathering or assembly. Everyone in the city would be free to join. They tossed out various names—Movement for Democratic Syria, Youth of Democracy—until they settled on the Revolutionary Youth Movement.

That night, for the first time, they spoke about the political system they hoped to see. What did freedom and dignity mean when translated from protest slogans into the flesh and blood of a polity? Abdul Hadi and a few others argued for socialism, a name much tarnished under the regime's slogan "Unity, Freedom, Socialism." But if there was no genuine freedom under the Baathists (and little unity, either), there was also no genuine socialism. "I argued that the system of socialism is good, but it hasn't been put into place here on the ground," recalled one of the participants. "The people who control the country are actually capitalists, like Rami Makhlouf," the president's cousin, estimated to have a net worth in the billions. Unbridled *rasmaliye*, capitalism, posed as grave a danger to freedom and dignity as dictatorship, Abdul Hadi believed. The others knew little about such matters, but they listened to Abdul Hadi carefully, with the attention of children listening to parents spilling the secrets of adulthood.

The next day, the group claimed the abandoned Baath Party headquarters as their own. "Look at Abel Os, he's the secretary general of the revolution," Abdul Hadi quipped, sparking much laughter. They scrubbed the floors, arranged desks. They avoided the upper floors, for fear of air strikes. They drew up responsibilities: Oday would oversee organizing protests and fashioning a logo; Abdul Hadi would obtain supplies; Abel Os would coordinate with the Revolutionary Council and the factions. Residents soon began to show up to look around. In forty years, no unauthorized organization had ever dared operate in the open. Every group—from poetry salons to chess clubs—had required government imprimatur to operate. Yet here they were, establishing a new organization and asking no one for permission. They held public meetings, inviting debate and discussion. "We're going to change this city," Oday said. "We'll do it without using a single bullet." By week's end, almost seventy members had joined the Revolutionary Youth Movement.

A STATEMENT ISSUED BY THE REVOLUTIONARY COUNCIL OF MANBIJ AND ITS COUNTRYSIDE

Dear Fellow Citizens!

The Revolutionary Council is fully aware of the criticisms directed against us, which sometimes amount to defamation, and the council assures you that your criticisms, despite their exaggeration at times, are appreciated. The council is based on a vision of participatory democracy, a vision that recognizes *responsibility* as a duty, not merely a lofty title. We have high hopes for our fellow citizens, and we need well-intentioned guidance. We need concrete actions and initiatives. We welcome whoever has an idea or a comment—so long as it is an actual contribution. And so we welcome those whose actions are louder than their words. Time is passing and the enemy awaits.

—*August 5, 2012*

THE ASSEMBLIES

Word of an independent organization spread through the city. Some people walked up to RYM headquarters simply to gawk, and by nine in the morning, the space was already a hive of activity. Members discussed the previous day's events. Abdul Hadi scoured Facebook for news from around the country, reading aloud notices of rebel advances and regime air strikes. Each morning presented fresh challenges: On one occasion, someone reported that the Free Army had arrested—or kidnapped, depending on your point of view—a doctor for charging exorbitant fees. RYM activists visited the battalion headquarters and secured a promise from the physician to lower his rates in exchange for his release. "We felt responsible for the revolution," a member later recalled. "We felt guilty when there was insecurity or no rule of law, because if something was wrong, people would blame the revolution." The group mediated disputes between rebel factions. They demanded that armed groups keep clear of civilian institutions. When a Free Army faction refused to vacate a school, RYM held a protest in front of the facility, forcing the much-chagrined battalion commander to remove his troops.

The group devoted a good portion of each day to planning weekly protests against the regime. Abdul Hadi and Abel Os felt it was important to fill Central Square with bodies every Friday, to remind citizens that the regime was massacring their brothers and sisters elsewhere. On Thursdays, the group scrawled messages of solidarity for besieged areas on placards, making signs in red, green, and black. They prepared a list of speakers, disseminated news of the protest through the mosques, and set up audiovisual equipment. It was Abdul Hadi's job to test the amplifiers—which he sometimes did by playing the sound of approaching aircraft from his phone. As his friends scrambled in terror, he and Oday burst out laughing.

On Fridays, the square overflowed with people. Thousands of sweaty men and women jostled and craned their necks to listen to the speakers, which included RYM activists, Revolutionary Council members, and sometimes, visitors from other cities. Soon others sought to replicate RYM's success: August birthed a half-dozen new assemblies. The first of these was the Future Youth Assembly, which brought together about ninety people to provide services for the needy. Future Youth initiatives included "My City, My Home," a campaign to beautify Manbij's streets through trash collection and by planting seedlings, while recruiting artists to cover walls and building facades in revolutionary murals.

Not long after, Muhammad Bisher, Abdul Hadi's older brother, launched the Civil Tendency Assembly, envisioning it as a watchdog over the council. While the Civil Tendency claimed to be nonpartisan, the Change and Development Assembly was explicitly leftist and egalitarian, operating under the slogan "neither leaders nor subordinates" and espousing the radical principle that no member should outrank any other. The assembly launched a health insurance plan to provide free care to the poor, with the aim of eventually working with the council to create a universal insurance scheme for the entire city. The Free Patriots Assembly, also leftist, advocated for a strict, French-style secularism, demanded the creation of a court system based on secular law, and insisted that the Revolutionary Council diversify its membership to include women and minorities. Some assemblies were based on profession: The Liberal Teachers Assembly, for example, called on the Revolutionary Council to reopen schools and to apply the rule of law. It also pushed to expand private education and championed the free market. At the other end of the spectrum, the Peasants'

Collective Assembly sought to impose price controls and make cheap credit available to farmers. The Free Ladies Assembly became the first independent women's organization the city had ever known.

Some assemblies were allied to the Revolutionary Council; others, like Muhammad Bisher's Civil Tendency, took an oppositional stance; and the rest were neutral—but together they represented a counterweight to the ruling authority, like mini-parliaments of the people. The assemblies recast politics from an elite conspiracy transpiring behind closed doors into an everyday activity accessible to ordinary men and women. In a city where all political speech had been forbidden, the assemblies became vital venues of public opinion and civic action. They were debating clubs, mutual aid societies, and protest groups all in one. Some were effectively workers' unions, some were craft guilds, and others were artist collectives. Though this assembly movement was unprecedented in Syrian history, it nevertheless echoed revolutions past: During the French Revolution, for example, the Jacobin Club and the Girondins were important revolutionary associations.

Manbij was the first city in Syria to develop this form of participatory democracy, a flowering only possible because the regime was directing its fire elsewhere. As the largest liberated city in the country by population and acreage, Manbij may have been deliberately saved for later reconquest by Assad's forces. The regime was mired in a struggle for tiny towns and suburban enclaves in the outskirts of Aleppo and Damascus, subjecting these areas to a vicious onslaught from the sky. Manbij had, so far, escaped this fate.

It was the day before Eid. The city had enjoyed liberty for one month, which lent the Eid celebrations an especially festive air. Families crowded the Great Souk, and there was a new excitement in the faces, the voices, the hand gestures and greetings. Old men in *shemagh* scarves gathered around plastic tables to sip bitter coffee and trade news, while old women sat in wicker chairs fanning themselves. Downtown, people stood in lines outside the confectioner, swarming the *mushabbak* pastry stands. On the west side, near the Sailboat Roundabout, neighbors put out tables loaded with dates, cookies, and soft drinks to break the day's fast. Rebels with rifles slung over their shoulders flagged down cars, inviting motorists to help themselves to the spread.

The sun slipped behind the western flats, the sky was crystalline, without blemish, save for a faraway glint, like a shooting star, or a proud, majestic bird swooping toward this city of revelers, and it was only when it was almost overhead that people realized this was no avian visitor or a beast of any kind but a machine, with seams and rivets, and at once the world exploded into flames. All one could see was thick smoke and all one could hear were the most terrible screams.

Across town at Central Square, people rushed into the street. In the distance, a column of smoke rose to the sky. No one had seen an air strike before, and no one was sure what to do. More people filled the plaza, looking at one another, hoping someone would have answers. Sirens could be heard. Just then, the air filled with a horrible roar and before anyone knew what had happened, a fierce heat engulfed the square. The trees were on fire. The buildings were on fire. Everything was on fire.

Firas al-Ali, an activist, later recorded his memories of the day:

> Nothing could be heard but the voices of the rescuers and the clamor of the cars and ambulances. The people gathered around a destroyed building. Someone said: "there's another plane! It's going to target us!" . . .
> I was frozen in place. . . . After watching the sky for five minutes, people returned to the area and some began chanting against the government and denouncing its crimes. . . .
> Suddenly, the plane returned and fired brimstone at the crowds. Those who were able to escape survived, while dozens met their deaths. I was hiding behind one of the buildings and watching the sky. I did not dare photograph the scene. The crowd stirred fear inside you, a fear that did not leave. . . .
> I headed toward the other side of the square, near the park, and I saw more ruins. I saw my friend—he was stretched out on the ground and was bleeding heavily. I ran toward him . . . and carried him to the ambulance. I returned to the scene to count the injured and document the crimes of the regime. I saw that some people were gathered around the scene of the crime and they were shouting—because under a car door was the head of a woman, which had been severed from her body and was lying by her waist.

That evening, a new terror crept into the city as it dawned on people that their experiment in freedom could not possibly last. The regime would not—could not—countenance the existence of a free city of this size, this vitality. In that day's massacre, over forty people lost their lives. The warplanes had loosed ordnance on multiple targets, seemingly at random. The next day, the first of Eid, the city abandoned the traditional festivities—the billowing pavilions offering sweets, the throngs in the market—for the austerity of white funerary tents. The assemblies took up collections for the bereaved. Some survivors fled the city that very night, heading for Turkey. Others stayed put. Among the dead was Sabah al-Maamo, a mother of five. Her son Muhammad, only fourteen, spent days in a haze of grief and rage, then joined the Revolutionary Youth Movement.

As August closed, fear grew. The Revolutionary Council had planned to open schools in the fall, but parents were now afraid to send their children. Real estate prices crashed as investors looked to unload their holdings, which they worried would soon be turned to cinders. The late summer nights were quieter, more restrained, as if people understood that hope and fear, like an intoxicant and the morning after, always come together. People turned the lights off at night in the belief that regime aircraft could not target what the pilots could not see. Some comforted themselves with the knowledge that in two thousand years of history, Manbij had confronted many tragedies and survived. To them, the darkened city was teeming with ghosts—a Roman legionnaire stricken with dysentery, a mendicant who drew his last breath in a temple's cool shade, a child looking up at a tiny circle of sky from the bowels of a well, through the eons, down to the present, to the children drowned by their own father's desperate hand, the mother who died waiting for a son who never came home, the boy who loved soccer and was in the wrong place at the wrong time. These ghosts were impossible to contain, and as the skies thundered with jets, a grim traffic of greater and greater congestion, they haunted many hearts. The night sky often flashed, and ambulances arrived from other towns, rushing the dazed and the bloodied to Manbij's public hospital.

Like an awakened beast, the regime was coming.

| FIVE |

September 2012

A TIME TO LISTEN

According to *October*, one of the regime's dailies, the city of Manbij had fallen under the control of "terrorists," and its people thirsted for liberation. The periodical was no longer available in Manbij, but one could access its content online. Those who tired of *October*'s breathless coverage of the Syrian Arab Army's victories—real and imagined—could turn to (the now ironically titled) *Revolution*, another regime daily. Bashar al-Assad allowed private media, but it was controlled by his cronies and hewed to the regime's editorial line. Newspapers like *The Nation*, *Our Land*, and *The Baath* ran almost identical content, speckled with photographs of Bashar al-Assad attending a conference or shaking hands with delegations or simply looking at things.

Huzayfa Osman, a member of the Future Youth Assembly, had once dreamed of writing for these papers. Years prior, he'd struggled to place freelance articles, until one day he received his big break: *October* had accepted his poem, an ode to his unquenchable love of home. Yet when he flipped through the pages on publication day, finding his name in bold black ink, and proceeded to read the verses, he was stunned: The editors had replaced the word "home" with "Assad and his family."

He vowed never to write for or even read a newspaper again. The broadsheets with their bleeding ink and onionskin pages were only good for wrapping falafel balls and french fries. But the liberation had roused old dreams. Osman and a friend toyed with the idea of publishing pamphlets. When they brought the idea to the Future Youth Assembly, the plan morphed into something bolder: a newspaper. Future Youth members pooled donations and rented a small printer. One member spent a week fiddling with layout programs until he understood the basics of design. They elected an editorial board and solicited volunteer reporters. They called the new publication *The Sun of Freedom*. "We didn't have much money, we didn't have jobs," recalled one participant. "We tore up our university IDs, stating that we are leaving the university for the sake of the revolution, for the sake of this newspaper."

The first issue had the look of an old Xerox copy: colorless, with smudged ink. The lead editorial quoted Che Guevara: "We cannot be sure of having something to live for unless we are willing to die for it." It carried an article lambasting the Western powers for refusing to send weapons to the Free Army. "It is clear that the blood of Syrians, and their souls, mean nothing to the world."

The issues were available in stationery shops for a few Syrian liras, and sold out within a day. That week the *Sun* doubled in staff to six people, all volunteers, who collected donations to rent an office downtown. They decided to release the newspaper weekly, and eventually daily when revenue grew. The pages expanded in size, now with splashes of color. Each issue carried news from around town, updates on battlefield exploits, announcements from the council and the assemblies, and ruminations on political theory and history. Readers submitted their own reflections too. One individual wrote:

> I came across two editions of *The Sun of Freedom* . . . [and] I felt like I found a treasure. I started reading voraciously, like a famished person craving fresh bread, and the words on the page took me back, back to the time of fear, to the time of my generation. It was a time when we were terrified to say the truth, even to our wives in bed. We used to say things we did not really believe, things we did not accept. . . . We flattered those with ugly faces, despite how much we hated to look at them. . . . We lived under these conditions and our children inherited our fear. We told them, "Don't stray." We told them, "Kiss the hand of whomever you cannot overcome."

In a series of articles, Hasan Nefi articulated the vision of the Revolutionary Council's governing strategy. In the twentieth century, he wrote, the two dominant forms of politics were communism and nationalism. Communism exposed itself as a failed ideology after the collapse of the Soviet Union. As for nationalism, it had inspired millions during the postwar years—Hasan among them. But decades of sclerotic dictatorships in the name of Arab nationalism had "wreaked havoc and destruction to social structures, and politicized our country in a way that is extremely primitive and barbaric." Communism had failed and nationalism had failed. What was left? What should the people of Manbij aspire to?

Hasan answered that "we should start from the person himself, with what makes him human: his dignity, his freedom ... these are the core, the need of every living being. The *individual*, not the nation or class, is the starting point of all political analysis." The new, post-dictatorship society should be based on the individual, on their needs and wishes. All associations should be voluntary, a "civil society" of cooperation and mutual aid. A politics that placed the individual first and foremost, Hasan believed, was the essence of freedom.

It was not long before another group of activists launched a competing publication, *The Free Path*. Whereas the *Sun* struck a distinctively highbrow, literary tone, the *Path* adopted a proletarian approach, with tabloid-style headlines and muckraking investigations. "If the right to speak is now taking its first baby steps," the *Path*'s lead editorial declared, "it is now time to listen, for that's what makes speech worth it." For the *Path*, "listening" meant canvassing popular opinion, investigating allegations of impropriety by the factions or woes afflicting the streets. In an early issue, the *Path*'s investigative team managed to infiltrate the Manbij Hotel, which had been converted into a makeshift prison until a permanent solution could be sorted. The prison was operated by an FSA faction. It reported:

> The prisoners are kept in a room seven meters in length and three meters in width, and there were approximately fifteen prisoners in the room. There was no window. When the power goes, the place becomes pitch dark.... One of [the prisoners] showed us brutal signs of torture on his back, due to one of the FSA brigades.... The prison system, they say, is based on the principle of bribery—pay and you can leave.... We call on the security forces of the revolution to reform these conditions!

Increasingly, the *Path* directed its ire at the Revolutionary Council itself. The lead editorial on October 8 inveighed against the revolutionary authorities:

> It has been more than two months since Manbij has been living completely free and independent from the Assad regime, and for more than two months we are waiting for the Revolutionary Council to perform its duties.... The price of a loaf of bread has gone up at the bakeries due to the rising cost of fuel.

In the old days, such an editorial would have gotten you disappeared. Now, though, the council had instituted a strict regime of freedom of speech, so it fired back the only way it could—with the pen. In editorials, the council argued that it needed time to stand up a police force and proper court system. And the council opposed price controls on fuel, which they feared would turn traders against their rule—and more importantly, because they believed such restrictions were inimical to the spirit of freedom.

ON FREEDOM, PART 1

But what, after all, was freedom? The Revolutionary Council proclaimed its rule in the name of freedom—but its critics, like RYM, believed that they too were acting in the name of freedom. What both sides quickly realized, however, was that freedom was a devilishly imprecise concept. Freedom of speech, assembly, arms, religion, markets, travel, conscience—was there a term more protean, more elastic, or perhaps even more abused than "freedom"?

The *Path* carried a series of articles on the subject. One contributor wrote that freedom means that "the individual can freely exercise intellectual, political, partisan, and religious affiliations . . . without being restricted by authorities." At the same time, though, "I am not free to stand in the middle of the street and stop cars from passing, nor do I have the freedom to throw trash wherever I want." The writer was arguing that liberty means *freedom from interference*. We should not always be free to do what we please, but we should always be free from intrusion, whether from neighbors, our relatives, or the government. As another contributor argued, "Heed the saying 'Your freedom ends where the freedom of others begins.'"

The British philosopher Isaiah Berlin called the view of liberty as noninterference "negative freedom"—freedom *from* external forces. This is freedom of the "Don't tread on me" variety. Anyone who yearns to be left alone—anyone who says government shouldn't "stick its nose" in our business—wishes for this type of freedom.

Two weeks later, the *Path* published the work of a writer who argued that according to Islam, freedom was only worth having if people were allowed to blossom, to reach their true potential. Other articles expanded on this idea that freedom meant self-actualization—finding your true self, becoming the person you hope to be. That required breaking the shackles on your personal development—especially the shackles of poverty. Someone who is hungry cannot be said to be truly free. Berlin called this "positive freedom"—the freedom *to* live your best life. For those advocating this view, the Revolutionary Council should design policies that allowed citizens to achieve their potential. That might include, for example, taxing the wealthy to ensure that everyone had enough to eat and a roof over their head.

Negative and positive liberty—the freedom *from* and the freedom *to*—are often in tension. When you tax someone, you impinge on their negative freedom. But when you don't tax people enough, you inhibit positive freedom, especially for the poor. The Revolutionary Council rejected the concept of positive freedom, insisting that its role was simply to ensure freedom of the press and assembly. But with the first winds of autumn, people began to talk among themselves, in assembly meetings and in cafes. Something was amiss in the council's vision.

| SIX |

October 2012

NEWS

Many villages in the Manbij suburbs were bombed by aircraft last week.... The city of Manbij suffered an air raid at night when two military jets targeted the Aleppo highway and the funeral of Ziad al-Jamil, which led to three severe injuries. —*Path*

Last Thursday morning, the city of Manbij suffered a mysterious and unique air strike: The jets did not drop explosive bombs [but instead] dropped a type of chemical which appears as white spider-like threads ... which spread across the city causing panic. —*Path*

There was a low turnout of students to junior high school this week, because air strikes and shelling have destroyed our children's dreams of returning to school. —*Sun*

The city of Manbij witnessed a strike of doctors on Saturday. The strike was to protest the kidnapping of people in general and of doctors, pharmacists, and medical workers in particular. —*Sun*

The former deputy of military security in Manbij, Hadi Ali Ibrahim, who is known as Abu Roz, is based at the October Dam, where he is threatening all those who pass by on their way to Manbij. He swears he will come back to the city to enact revenge, and he has stolen cash from drivers. —*Sun*

> The free students of Manbij organized a strike against exams on Thursday, announcing that they are refusing to take them and calling them a farce. They pledged to march forward in the path of liberation. —*Path*

> We received many complaints from residents in the Jazeera Road area about the high bus fare, which is now 25 Syrian pounds [35 cents]. —*Path*

THE WILL TO LIVE

After an infernally humid summer, old men and women basked in the easy air of autumn, sitting around folding tables with playing cards, dragging on cigarettes. The sky was overcast and unflecked, but what God did not provide that autumn in the form of color, citizens contributed, in blood orange red and emerald green daubed onto walls and the blank faces of buildings. The streets trilled with this revolutionary art—murals depicting fluttering flags, silhouettes holding hands, the names of far-flung towns under siege, caricatures of Bashar al-Assad, and entreaties to the international community.

In late September, the Revolutionary Council expanded its cabinet to allow greater participation. The changes were in response to swelling criticism, especially from RYM. Indeed, RYM's ear to the street was turning it into a kingmaker, and council members often approached the group to solicit support. As RYM rejected overtures left and right, they raised independence to a virtue. Steeped in solidarity with one another, swearing allegiance to no flag but the three stars of revolution, they found little attraction in the wider world of political jockeying. It was Abdul Hadi who spearheaded this approach, consumed as he was with ferreting out the slightest improprieties of the revolutionary bodies. The school where he was employed as a gym teacher remained closed, so he spent his days roving the streets, checking on Free Army checkpoints, the bakeries, the municipal buildings. RYM finally accepted an office in City Hall. Abdul Hadi took note of the lines of supplicants and the comings and goings of revolutionary dignitaries from Aleppo and further afield. Once the dean of practical jokes, he'd shed those fatuous trappings for a dead-eyed seriousness. "You have one chance to build this country," he'd lecture the younger members of RYM, who were increasingly in his thrall. "If we fail, we have no one to blame but ourselves."

Some nights, RYM held parties at their headquarters. A surviving video shows a group of young men, some only teenagers, huddled together for warmth in a crudely lit basement, passing around a microphone as they sang:

> *Oh heaven, heaven*
> *Our country it is heaven*
> *Oh country with its dear soil*
> *Our country with its dear soil*
> *Even your fire is heaven.*

There is Abel Os, his eyes fixed somewhere in the distance, his baritone filling the room. Abdul Hadi is beside him, a slight smirk on his face. Oday is seated a few cushions down, not moving his lips, simply watching, with a look that says: *I can't believe I helped create this.*

Some nights, they debated. Though Abel Os felt marginalized on the council as the only Kurd and one of its few working-class members, he continued to defend the organization. But Abdul Hadi was increasingly defining himself as an oppositionist: "Democracy needs opposition," he'd say. What both sides could agree on, though, was that the absence of law and order might destroy the revolution. A Revolutionary Police force was needed. The council was offering salaries for police officers through the sales tax it levied on bread, but the funds were hardly enough to buy weapons, let alone vehicles. The old regime police cruisers were in the hands of the Free Army, so the only hope was to convince the rebel factions to surrender their spoils—and perhaps donate a few rifles too.

In late September, RYM called a meeting of assemblies to discuss the issue. The gathering, which took place in the Youth Center, was the first joint meeting of Manbij's dozen or so assemblies. It was thought that the meeting might last hours—as long as needed to convince the assemblies to form a united front and demand that the armed factions relinquish matériel for the police. Abdul Hadi was slated to speak. It had been here, in the empty lot outside, that he'd honed his legwork all those years ago. Standing near the lectern, he took in the crowd—three hundred people, perhaps the largest indoor gathering since liberation. The doors were shut to keep out the chill. The old squeaking chairs once held people listening to Baath Party presentations, interrupted by the stray shouts of soccer practice outside. Now there was only the groan of the generator. As Abdul Hadi stepped to the lectern, the groan seemed louder. Suddenly, the world went dark. Perfect silence. Then, slowly, the screams of men.

Abel Os could not see a thing, but he could feel the dust, taste it on his lips. Silhouettes appeared in the haze. Everyone was fleeing. They were scrambling over chairs, clambering up the auditorium steps, heading for the doors. Locked.

People threw their bodies against the door until it gave way and the pure nighttime air poured into the hall. They tumbled onto the street, dazed, coughing violently. When they looked at the hall, they saw it was still standing—and there in the night sky, like a wayward satellite, were the lights of aircraft careening toward them. The jet had missed the Youth Center, striking a neighboring facility, and now looked to be returning to finish the job. In the panic, people clawed their way past each other. But there were survivors still inside the hall. The force of the blast had exploded windows and collapsed beams. People were trapped under the joists, crying out in pain. The lights of the aircraft appeared larger in the night sky. Abel Os broke from the crowd and raced back—into the Youth Center—to rescue the wounded. Oday followed, and then Abdul Hadi.

As the aircraft loomed overhead, it changed course to release a warhead onto the fleeing crowd. It missed its mark but struck a house belonging to the Shami family, who'd had no part in the revolution. Abdul Baset Shami and his wife, along with three children and a nephew, were killed instantly.

As people fled through the unlit streets, the aircraft swooped around for a third volley, strafing shadows, storefronts, parked cars. A young man who'd joined RYM just days earlier was left paralyzed. Many were rushed to the hospital to be treated for smoke inhalation.

That evening, rescuers found amid the rubble the foot of Yamen Shami, age five. Scraps of flesh were hanging from boughs and branches. The Shami family's two-year-old daughter was wedged between fallen chunks of concrete. As people tried to dig her out with their hands, the *Sun* snapped a photo, showing a screaming child, caked in blood and ash, her hair singed. The caption read, "Her will to live is stronger than their missiles."

The city lay shrouded in darkness; the power did not return. The faucets were dry too, as fighting near the October Dam had disrupted pipes. Oday and the others went to bed with the dust in their hair, in their eyes.

| SEVEN |

November 2012

NEWS

The Free Syrian Lawyers Assembly was established, and it includes lawyers from Manbij and its countryside. —*Path*

Despite torrential rains and the bitter cold, several demonstrations took place in mosques on Friday. . . . The demonstrators called for the fall of the regime and the unification of the ranks of the Free Syrian Army, and they condemned the Israeli bombing of Gaza. —*Path*

In an operation carried out by the heroes of the Free Syrian Army from the city of Manbij, the October Dam was liberated from the gangs of Assad. —*Path*

The School of Agriculture was bombed at 2 o'clock on Wednesday, [resulting in] several civilian casualties. —*Sun*

The *Sun of Freedom* has learned that a female nurse has joined [an FSA] battalion, not only as a medic but also as a fighter on the front lines. —*Sun*

A STORY ABOUT THE DAYS OF EID

In early November, the rain came in sheets, leaving the streets slicked with mud, the gutters oozing raw sewage, the effluent sloshing onto the stone walkways and squelching underfoot. For the first time in years, the wadi was swollen with floodwater.

Once the skies cleared, the streets filled with thousands of sticky, earth-smeared people. Eid al-Adha, which commemorates Abraham's willingness to sacrifice his son at God's command, had turned the city inside out. Lights were hung from the rafters of the Great Souk. Oday visited the stockyard to select a fat-tailed Awassi, then tied the animal to the roof of his car. He took the direct route home, past the alley of Roman stone. It was nearly a year since he'd lost Hala, and only now did he feel free of her. When he wasn't at RYM headquarters, he was tending the cell phone shop, which assured his father that his son was ready for the full burdens and joys of life. Young women were produced at home, cousins of cousins, friends of neighbors. He kept cool but confided in his sister that the meetings, in full view of the elders, were a cruel and unusual punishment. Abdul Hadi was worried that his friend would succumb to the demands of marriage and abandon the movement. He preached the virtues of freedom and independence, a life without obligation. Wake when you wish, go home when you wish, answer to no one—a vision of permanent revolution, a life devoted to the barricades. Abdul Hadi himself had no plans to settle down, not while the city, this experiment, needed him.

RYM activists fixed their attention on the coming winter. Manbij's refugee population had surged; schools were overflowing with barefoot children. Meanwhile, the regime continued to unleash its fury. One afternoon a silvery aircraft appeared overhead and dropped its payload onto the Manbij Hotel. There were casualties, and one side of the building suffered extensive damage. The pilot crashed in a nearby town, where he was apprehended by rebels. A video shows him blinking under the harsh afternoon sun, bruised and bloodied. "Why did you drop barrel bombs on civilians?" a rebel demanded to know. "How could you kill defenseless children, women, and old people? What kind of orders did you receive?" The pilot answered weakly, "We are being told that there are armed groups and we should kill them."

Under such unrelenting attacks, the mood was grim. The *Sun* canvassed celebrants. "What Eid are you talking about?" asked one. "How are we supposed to celebrate while thousands of martyrs have been killed by the regime? . . . How are we going to face the mother who lost her children, the man who lost his entire family?" A woman offered, "Eid is for children, not for us." And it was the children who were out in numbers, despite the threat from above. Lines of boys and girls formed outside the *mushabbak* stalls and at Al-Dalati Sweets to buy shimmering rhombuses of baklava and thick wedges of chocolate cake. Boys carried the tricolor flag, girls painted their nails green, black, and red. They arrived home laden with delights, fingertips numb and lips chapped, and their

parents pretended, for the moment, that the universe conformed to their love, would protect and nurture it, no matter what the skies foretold.

GIVE US THIS DAY OUR DAILY BREAD

Abel Os always awoke at dawn, dipping coarse-grained pita bread into a cup of steaming black tea. From childhood, when he hauled ice blocks or wagonloads of cement, his day commenced with this spartan breakfast. Around the city, tens of thousands of people partook of the same ritual. Lunch and dinner, too, hinged on the fibrous brown pockets of wheat. *Khobez*, in the local argot, was no mere accompaniment; it was what transformed bare victuals into a proper meal. Bread was the barometer of well-being, an index of happiness. In some Arab countries, like Egypt, the words for life and bread are identical. Bread was life itself.

In the Arab world, he who controls bread controls hearts and minds. He who doesn't is not long for the throne. Attempts to raise the price of bread have incited protests, riots, even revolutions. Hafez al-Assad had carefully orchestrated bread distribution: the government purchased wheat from farmers and trucked it to state-owned mills around the country. In Manbij, this wheat was threshed, winnowed, and ground into flour at the gigantic mills where Mina's husband worked. The government delivered the flour to the city's dozen privately owned bakeries and its two public bakeries. The middle class and the wealthy purchased their bread from the private bakeries, which were conveniently located in their neighborhoods. The poor obtained bread from the public bakeries. The difference in price between private and public was only a few cents, but for families living hand to mouth, it made all the difference.

The entire system—from farm to mill to bakery—was government controlled. Farmers could not sell wheat on the market, as the state purchased all harvests at a fixed price. The government mills, in turn, set the price at which private and public bakeries could buy flour. All of this meant that for the consumer, bread was heavily subsidized—and therefore affordable. When Bashar al-Assad inherited power, a bundle of bread cost 6 Syrian pounds—about a dime. This was enough for a family of five for a day. By 2011, free-market reforms that affected fuel and other inputs had forced the government to raise the price of a bundle of bread to 15 Syrian liras, a 150 percent increase. For the first time, millions of families faced the question of how to afford their daily bread.

Upon liberation, the Revolutionary Council raised the price to 20 Syrian pounds, using the additional 5 pounds as a sales tax to fund its activities. Sales taxes are regressive—hitting the poorest families the hardest—but the reaction was muted at first: Perhaps it was believed that this was the cost of freedom. But then, one morning in late November, people lining up to buy bread discovered that the price had risen again, to 25 liras—a further 25 percent increase. An impromptu protest outside Municipal Bakery quickly mutated into a riot. Demonstrators burst through the bakery gate, assaulting the staff. Guards fired overhead to disperse the mobs. Several young men were arrested. (Later, the Revolutionary Council apologized to the protesters and encouraged them to file a civil suit in the newly established courthouse. Amid the world's deadliest civil war, a rebel body was not seeking retribution but advising its accusers to hire a lawyer.)

This latest price increase stemmed from the rising cost of fuel, which the Revolutionary Council, owing to its faith in free-market principles, refused to regulate. The shockingly high prices at the fuel pump spawned an informal market in petrol. Here and there at roadside stands children sold gasoline out of Pepsi bottles. Their hands and faces were smeared with fuel, itself laced with additives. The prices at even these fuel stands were exorbitant.

Private bakeries used the excuse of fuel costs to double or even triple their prices. A woman complained to the *Sun*, "Merchants have become like a blood-sucking leech on the people, or like a weevil that eats through wheat." The council formed a Consumer Protection Department to monitor the bakeries and penalize price gougers, but it lacked resources to do the job well. By November, even middle-class residents could not afford the private bakeries, and lines formed at the public bakery, where bread continued to sell at the subsidized rate. Calls for price controls multiplied: "Whoever raises prices more than necessary should be held accountable!" demanded the *Sun*. Perhaps the free market was fine when making widgets, but not for human necessities like bread and fuel. The *Path* went further, demanding widespread regulation of industry and commerce. The newspaper also proposed welfare programs targeting the poor. Yet there was a growing sense that the Revolutionary Council, as presently constituted, would never impose such measures. Some members were themselves merchants; the idea of levying progressive taxation, of asking the wealthy to contribute extra to support this fledgling democracy, was unthinkable.

The Revolutionary Youth Movement, whose members had long toiled on the edge of poverty, demanded that the council revamp its membership. The group, together with allied assemblies, unveiled a comprehensive program to revitalize the city, calling for term limits for the Revolutionary Council, a price-control committee, the establishment of labor unions, and municipal funding for assemblies.

As ever, it was Abdul Hadi who led the charge. "We're still waiting," he told friends, "to taste real freedom."

THE SENATE CONVENES

At an old municipal building on the edge of town, hundreds of people crowded into a lecture hall. The November night was unusually balmy; people sat sweating in plastic chairs. The lampposts outside were switched off and the lights inside kept dim. Air strikes were on everyone's minds. Nearly all who'd participated in the revolution—from the protest movement to the assemblies—were present. A member of the Revolutionary Council stepped to the lectern. He began his remarks by defending the institution: Fuel prices were climbing because of factors beyond the city's control; taxing merchants would spark capital flight or, worse, turn an important constituency against the revolution. The council had made progress on law and order: It had finally established the Revolutionary Police, a force of thirty-six men—hardly enough to keep the peace among hundreds of thousands of citizens, sure, but it was a start. The council had also inaugurated the Revolutionary Court of Manbij, comprised of seven judges and a public prosecutor.

But the deeper problem, the speaker explained, was legitimacy. The Revolutionary Council had been created in secrecy, during the protest movement phase. It had been impossible to build a broader constituency without risking arrest. Now the council could operate publicly, but the threat of air strikes made holding an open ballot impossible. Just imagine, he said, how the regime would feast on lines of voters. So the Revolutionary Council was proposing a workaround: the creation of a new body, called the Council of Revolutionary Trustees, that would act as the highest decision-making entity in the city. This new council would address the issue of legitimacy by opening membership to anyone who had contributed to the revolutionary movement before liberation, "whether their participation was in person, or with their money or their words." Because this new body was open to *anyone* linked to the revolution, there would be no question of its legitimacy among fellow activists, or so the council hoped.

The Council of Trustees was to function as a sort of senate, a legislative body that would write the city's rules, monitor bread distribution, and regulate trade policy with other cities and abroad. Its proposed bylaws called for a grievance office, through which a citizen could submit a complaint against any senator. The senate would also appoint a Military Council to control the city's Free Syrian Army factions. To oversee all this work, the senate would elect a president and a seven-member executive office to manage day-to-day tasks. This executive office, in turn, would select a new "revolutionary council" to serve as the city's executive branch. What the new rules amounted to, in fact, was placing the Revolutionary Council under the authority of the senate. All elected officials—from the senate president to the council members—were to serve four-month terms, with the senate maintaining the right to recall any officeholder through majority vote.

As a model of governance, this new system was without parallel in the region's history. Manbij would be ruled by a six-hundred-member senate, made up of individuals from all walks of life, who would write the city's laws. The notion that officeholders could be recalled by simple majority vote, or that citizens could register their grievances through a formal mechanism, was unheard-of anywhere in the Arab world, or indeed even in many established democracies. With an independent parliament, judiciary, and trade policy, Manbij would be operating as a de facto city-state—an extraordinary achievement during a terrible civil war.

Yet when the speaker finished his remarks, distributed the bylaws, and ceded the floor, not everyone was convinced. One person complained that the procedure for selecting the new revolutionary council was convoluted. Others took issue with a stipulation in the bylaws that explicitly barred price controls; the new body was merely supposed to "communicate with merchants to reduce prices and urge them to not monopolize." One speaker argued that merchants could not be so easily persuaded—RYM activists had tried—and that the senate should take decisive action to force down prices and punish violators.

The biggest dispute, though, concerned the question of senate membership. Abdul Hadi criticized the clause that forbade membership for anyone who participated in protests and then quit. He saw this as directed against his older brother Muhammad, who, after attending a few protests, ceased his involvement for fear of arrest. He also denounced the bylaw that called for each senator to contribute 100 Syrian liras monthly to support the institution's operating costs, which discriminated against poor and working-class candidates. Another speaker pounced on a key line in the bylaws: Senate membership was open to "real revolutionaries"—anyone who took part in protests *or* supported the movement "with money or words." How could they verify, during the period of secrecy, whether someone donated money to the movement? Oday stood to speak. "Am I a 'real' revolutionary? Who decides who is a 'true' revolutionary?" he asked. "Can I create an organization and hand out certificates of participation for 'real' revolutionaries?"

"The whole city knows you are a real revolutionary," the speaker responded. "We're talking about those who want to take advantage of the revolution."

Abel Os chimed in. "There are people in the room I've never seen at a single demonstration—but they have friends in the right places. They have money! That's why they are 'real' revolutionaries."

An argument erupted. The Revolutionary Council members who had drawn up the bylaws looked exasperated, as if children—RYM—were interrupting the work of adults. They rolled their eyes, they sighed loudly, they snapped at the speakers on the floor. At one point, a council member barked, "Is this a game to you?" But it was no game to Abel Os. As a child, working at his father's bubble gum stand, his dreams encompassed the paving, the dirt fields, the expansive sky, all of which had seemed his. In time, though, he'd come to understand that such features of the natural and human world were already claimed, that his family had arrived too late, and that he was meant to serve those for whom the city was a possession. And then, with the protests, all the edifices man had built to rule over his fellow man had crumbled; he was in the same farmhouse as the Salals and the Henezels, dreaming up the contours of a new society. But now, as the council members lectured RYM on responsibility and propriety, he saw in their impatient smirks the familiar supercilious looks of overseers and motorcycle men and apparatchiks, and he could no longer control himself. "The young men with me sacrificed everything to participate! Do you want to see the scars on their backs?" he thundered, referring to RYM. "I've never seen half the people in this room at a protest!" Other senators were trying to shout him down. Abel Os bellowed, "We don't acknowledge this body! Who is with me?" The auditorium fell silent. Abel Os had bowed before foremen, policemen, businessmen, but he would not bow before fellow revolutionaries. "Who is with me?" he asked again.

Abdul Hadi stood up.

"Who else?"

One by one, RYM members stood. Abel Os gestured for them to follow, and he led them out the door.

For a few moments, the hall was quiet. Then the speaker said, "We will continue." The Revolutionary Youth Movement was the only assembly to boycott the senate. The discussion proceeded, and the others in attendance cast votes for president and executive council. Manbij's government took shape. The event should have been occasion for celebration, but the mood was downcast. Senators had believed they enjoyed a popular mandate, but now, for the first time, they would have to contend with an organized opposition movement. Gone was the sweet unanimity of the barricades, because the revolution had just lost its innocence.

| EIGHT |

December 2012

NEWS

Last Wednesday, the city of Manbij suffered an aerial bombardment which targeted a residential building and some shops on Jarablus Street, leading to the martyrdom of nine people. —*Path*

The city's hospitals are suffering from a severe shortage . . . after the regime cut off the supply of medicines. —*Path*

Water was cut off from the city of Manbij for periods that lasted more than four consecutive days in some neighborhoods, forcing people to collect drinking water from rain. —*Sun*

When winter began our suffering began. . . . the electricity is cut off for days in some neighborhoods and is very weak in others . . . there are neighborhoods that only see the light of the sun. —*Path*

On Thursday, December 6, 2012, an exhibition of oil paintings by the artist Ahmed Humeidi opened. It was called *A Space for Forgetting.* — *Path*

THE ASSEMBLY REPUBLIC

In the bitter cold, the crowd began quietly, but soon their voices gained confidence. There were boys as young as ten holding handwritten signs. Workers on break from their shifts at the bakeries and the garages waved revolutionary flags. The crowd marched around Central Square, then down Main Street, and people came out to watch. A group of demonstrators raised a banner that read:

"The people want a new revolutionary council!" Leading the procession, his nasal voice cutting above the rest, was Abdul Hadi Bisher.

Only five months had passed since the first delirious days of liberation, but they were five months in which Abdul Hadi felt he'd come to understand the hidden order of things, down to the tiniest detail, and he believed that fate had placed onto his shoulders a tremendous responsibility. In those more innocent days, he and his friends had ransacked the old Baath Party offices and made prank calls to regime nurses. To be "free" had been to smoke and drink with abandon, to do what moved you, to sprint through the street simply because you could, to climb construction yard gantries and shout to the heavens. But those summer months were already a hazy memory, like the frolics of distant youth, and now, confronted with the questions of taxes and law and order, Abdul Hadi had come of age fast. His duties, he believed, were sacred. He was a guardian of the revolution, a keeper of its inner spirit, a defender of democracy. He watched the work of the assemblies like a hawk, often showing up unannounced at meetings simply to ensure that activists weren't bickering or succumbing to the temptations of power. The awkward goofiness of his youth had become a certain charm; he knew when to deploy the wisecrack, when to stare with steely resolve, when to admonish and when to praise. When he saw the senate hall filled with men he'd never seen at a single protest, he realized that if the Revolutionary Youth Movement did not take a stand, no one would.

Day after day, Abdul Hadi stood behind the lectern in the RYM basement headquarters, and as members huddled in their winter coats and blew on their hands, he expounded on the need for democracy—*true* democracy, not what passed for it in the Revolutionary Council's imagination. The council members insisted it was impossible to hold a plebiscite while warplanes roamed the sky. But where the council saw the impossible, the activists of RYM saw a hurdle to clear. The question was representation: how to ensure that the senate or the council truly represented the people. In RYM's discussions with other assemblies, a new possibility emerged. Manbij already had representative institutions—the assemblies. Nearly two dozen assemblies were in operation, traversing every neighborhood and every ethnic and occupational group in the city. There was the Muslim Youth, the Free Doctors of Manbij, the Free Lawyers of Manbij, and many more. Following days of meetings, Abdul Hadi and his comrades proposed using the assemblies to conduct a ballot, which would approximate citywide elections. The idea was for each assembly to elect five delegates to form a People's General Assembly—a counterweight to the elite-dominated senate. The People's Assembly would then elect a new revolutionary council. Members of the old council would be invited to stand in the elections, as would representatives of the armed factions.

In this proposed system, the senate would remain but would be paired with the People's Assembly—something like the House of Lords and the House of Commons in the British Parliament, or the U.S. Senate and House of Representatives. But the lower house, the People's Assembly, not the senate, would elect the new "revolutionary council." The basic unit of democratic participation would be not the individual voter but the assembly. A citizen was free to join an assembly and cast their vote through that body—or even run themselves. There would be no long lines at the ballot box—and no targets for warplanes—because voting for the lower house would take place within the headquarters of the assemblies. Since assemblies formed the building blocks, the new system effectively did away with the distinction between the governing and the governed—a radical experiment in self-rule.

The proposal captured the fancy of rebels, workers, and students—but not the Revolutionary Council. President Ahmed Rahmo argued that the city was not yet ready for such a vote. Forty years of dictatorship had stunted civic growth; how could they hold polls now, just six months after liberation? Hasan Nefi believed elections should wait for the war's end, and he penned a column in the *Sun* lambasting the assemblies. "Every day we hear about the emergence of new assemblies, but we know nothing about them except their names. As for their program, or their intellectual or social content, it is completely absent . . . its members do not even know what they want." The charge was not unfair; some assemblies were no more than political debating clubs, others mere charities. But supporters insisted they were a vital form of popular democracy, even if they were new and evolving. The council found itself in the minority, and the assemblies pushed ahead. In early December, the lower house met for the first time, to choose a new revolutionary council.

Election Day was unseasonably warm. RYM launched festivities with a procession through town, chanting, "How beautiful is freedom!" The People's Assembly convened in a sprawling high school campus, with tree-shaded walkways and cement benches. Inside, hundreds of people were milling about or seated in plastic chairs, smoking, chatting, drinking tea. At the front of the room sat the ballot box, swathed in gift wrap. RYM had hung revolutionary flags and posters on the walls. Over the preceding week, People's Assembly members had swapped pledges of support and cobbled together electoral lists. Attendees were to vote for council offices, including the presidency; the president would govern for a one-year term. The old Revolutionary Council was boycotting the vote, but some of its members stood for election anyway. Facing pressure from the old council, Abel Os had initially declined to run, but the night before, Oday and Abdul Hadi led a delegation of RYM members to his house, where they implored him to throw his hat in the ring—without Abel Os, the new council risked losing legitimacy. "If you don't stand with us," Oday threatened, "we'll abandon you." Abdul Hadi emphasized that the velvet class dominated the old council. To them, Abdul Hadi reminded Abel Os, he was forever a vegetable peddler. Abel Os put his name forward.

As voting was underway, the power went out. Ballots were tallied by candlelight and the glare of camera crews from national and international media, there to record the Syrian revolution's first genuine election. The results were announced, and a cheer went up. Muhammad Bisher, Abdul Hadi's older brother, won the presidency. Posts were filled for five offices: Services, Public Health, Finance, Justice, and Security. Abel Os was elected to head the Office of the Revolutionary Movement, tasked with keeping the street protests alive and liaising with the assemblies. He received the most votes of any candidate.

The new Revolutionary Council was more representative—and, because of the election, more legitimate—than the first body. All week, celebrations and rallies took place around the city. The *Path* crowed, "Freedom is a dream that's begun to bear fruit, as we've seen the remarkable success achieved by the first democratic elections. . . . This is reality and not imagination; we are in Manbij, not Switzerland, watching with our eyes and not on television screens." New president Muhammad Bisher pledged to his constituents: "If I do not carry out my duties, confront me by means of protest and through the press." Oday spoke at a gathering, declaring that the elections had birthed a new form of democracy. "Welcome," he told the RYM audience, "to the assembly republic."

ON FREEDOM, PART TWO

The members of the old council found little to celebrate. They believed that personal freedom, not democracy, was the ultimate value around which a society should be organized. At best, democracy was a means of securing freedom; at worst, it could be a tool of tyranny. Exhibit A was Manbij's economic crisis. The *Path* carried an essay about the man who'd drowned his children prior to the revolution, warning that "the Euphrates crime might be repeated on a larger scale if the crisis lasts much longer." A population struggling simply to survive was not ready for direct democracy, the council argued—hunger pangs do not lead to rational choices, let alone enlightened voting. History was littered with examples of desperate masses voting for demagogues or autocrats. The famed nineteenth-century French statesman François Guizot argued for the *juste milieu*, a government in which the property-owning middle class ruled through representative institutions. It was believed that the middle class voted with their heads, the working class with their stomachs. Means, discernment, and above all, education, were necessary to exercise the vote.

For the old council, education was the mark of the true democrat. The senate mooted changing its rules to require a university degree for membership—held by less than 3 percent of the population. They believed that the educated elite of Manbij should govern in the interests of the population. It was they, after all, who had steered the city into this unprecedented era of freedom. Their good intentions guaranteed good governance.

At RYM meetings, activists debated the old council's intentions. Yes, council members were true revolutionaries, and yes, they cared for the city—why else would they have risked their lives to protest the regime? But what kind of freedom depended, ultimately, on the goodwill of an unelected minority? The ideas of negative and positive liberty—the freedom *from* and the freedom *to*—didn't seem to shed much light on this problem. The experience of the assembly election showed that there was a third way of thinking about freedom.

Every word has a history, a story, that offers a record of our evolving beliefs and presuppositions. In 1798, French colonizers landed on the shores of Egypt in the name of *liberté*—a word that, in Arabic, had meant something very different from the Enlightenment term "freedom." Prior to the nineteenth century, to be "free" [*horr*] usually meant to not be a slave; until the colonial encounter, the word "freedom" was not applied to personal rights or types of governments. This might seem surprising, yet the Western genealogy of "freedom" follows a similar path: "Liberty" comes to us from the Latin *liber*, which has roots in a word that is the opposite of slavery.

In the first months after Manbij's liberation, activists conceived of freedom in terms of interference—to be free is to be left alone by the government. In the aftermath of the election, though, RYM activists began exploring the older, pre-colonial sense of the word "freedom." In downtown Manbij, a long avenue called Kawakibi Street runs through the city's working-class quarters. The street is named after Abd al-Rahman al-Kawakibi, a nineteenth-century writer hailing from Aleppo. A trenchant critic of Ottoman colonialism, Kawakibi launched what is thought to be Aleppo's first independent newspaper. Later, he fled to Egypt, where he was likely assassinated by Ottoman agents. Shortly before his death, he penned *The Nature of Tyranny and the Struggle of Enslavement*, which defined freedom in opposition to slavery. What does it mean to be enslaved? It means having a master, being subject to the arbitrary will of another person. The heart of the matter is not interference but unaccountable power, or what some thinkers call "domination."

Interference and domination are different—a rebel faction may leave you alone, but they could, if they wished, establish a checkpoint in your neighborhood without your consent; and in that sense they have unaccountable power over you. This casts a different light on Manbij's revolutionary experiment. Citizens were free to publish and assemble, but were still subject to the unaccountable power of the council, of merchants, of armed factions. In fact, once you looked, domination was everywhere: in the wholesalers who decided prices, the bosses who determined wages, the bank officers who provided loans, the husbands who headed households.

When you are under domination, there is no mechanism requiring the person holding power over you to act in your interests. There is no way to contest your master's decisions. The only way to safeguard against domination is to erect institutions that force those in power to act in your interests, and to create laws and organizations that can contest these decisions when necessary. A classic example is a labor union, which compels bosses to consider the interests of workers and gives workers the ability to resist company decisions. The Romans called a system of government based on these principles *res publica*, or the public interest, from which we get the word "republicanism." Arabs call this *jumhuriya*, from the word for "to assemble" or "to gather."

So against the council's idea of negative freedom, the right of citizens to be left alone, RYM activists were arguing for a type of republican freedom—which meant building institutions to hold power accountable. Manbij's burgeoning democratic system, with its senate and ruling council elected by the People's Assembly, evoked a long tradition of republican experimentation, dating back to the ancient world. Like the republics that came before, Manbij was following no blueprint. These systems had not sprung forth, fully formed, from the mind of some political genius. Hasan and other council intellectuals may have known their Plato and Machiavelli, but the ordinary men and women who forged this order did not have the foggiest idea of the tradition in which they stood. Instead, they built assemblies and councils because they faced the exigencies of collective life. Thousands of people, in hundreds of ways, asked: How do we live together? Some solutions were preposterous, others unworkable, and some flickered with potential.

Just as there was probably no single discovery of fire—one can imagine men and women experimenting in different times and places, a dazzling light throwing shadows against a cave here, illuminating a darkened savanna there—so too was democracy discovered anew, time and again. Democracy, like a

Promethean fire, could set loose the most fervent energies and tame the most rapacious giants. But like Prometheus, the activists of Manbij could not have guessed what they were about to unleash.

CONGRATULATIONS.... WE HAVE TWO COUNCILS!

After a few days conducting media interviews, the newly elected Revolutionary Council settled on its first order of business: stabilizing bread prices. They decided to reverse the recent price increase, a move that required them to give orders to the Municipal Bakery. However, the Free Army faction guarding the premises was loyal to the old council and refused access to the facility. He who controls bread controls the city—which meant that the old council was effectively refusing to relinquish power. The new council accused the old council of staging a coup. But the old council would not budge, insisting that the elections were illegitimate and the city was unready for a plebiscite. For RYM, this was a provocation against the revolution itself.

Friday, December 28, was christened the Day of Bloodied Bread at demonstrations around the country, in protest of the regime's practice of bombing breadlines. The next day, RYM activists gathered in front of the Municipal Bakery, occupying the courtyard and chanting, "The people want the handover of the bakery!" Another Free Army faction offered to take over the bakery by force and deliver it to the new council, but Abdul Hadi and Abel Os refused, insisting that their movement remain nonviolent. The sit-in lasted into the evening. The protesters were threatening to halt bread distribution altogether unless the old council relinquished control. In response, the old council pulled a trump card, refusing to surrender the facility while agreeing to lower the price of bread back to its November level.

It was a brilliant tactic; the new council's platform had been, above all, to lower the price of bread. By lowering it themselves, the old council was effectively saying, *We can run this city just as well.* RYM's ranks were thrown into confusion. Oday believed that the price decrease was a major concession, and that the old and new councils should strike an accord for joint rule. But Abdul Hadi insisted that the principle at stake was democracy itself: To allow the old council to worm its way into a power sharing deal would effectively overturn the elections. He was in the minority, the mood on the street swung to compromise. "Let the two councils unite!" shouted protesters at the sit-in. By early morning, the encampment's numbers had dwindled, and the RYM cadre quit the action.

The defeat of the sit-in emboldened the old council, who now refused to vacate their headquarters. The *Path* noted sardonically, "Congratulations.... We have two councils ... a premature, disabled child and an old cripple. Congratulations to us and our crippled democracy!"

One afternoon, Abdul Hadi and his brother Muhammad paid a visit to the headquarters to demand that the old council members leave. In the main office, they found Hasan Nefi.

"What are you doing here?" Muhammad asked. "You were not elected to this council."

Hasan replied that the new council members were usurpers. Muhammad demanded the keys to the facility, to which Hasan responded with derision. The two men were from the same humble origins, but in Muhammad's eyes, Hasan represented everything that was wrong with this city—the cliquishness, the elitism, the sense of entitlement. Perhaps the stories of his father, who'd bowed instinctively to superiors, whose own father was beaten by his master's hand, flashed through Muhammad's mind. He fired a volley of insults, in the midst of which the words "you're a whore for the regime" left his mouth. There were many things one could say to Hasan—he'd ventured to the limits of human endurance in prison and lived to tell about it. No insult was enough to pierce his armor of self-regard—except one. Call him anything, but do not say he worked for that monstrosity that had masqueraded as a government. Unable to control himself, Hasan lunged toward Muhammad. Before they knew it, they were trading blows. Abdul Hadi rushed to his brother's defense and swung for Hasan's face. Bystanders separated the two sides, dragging the Bisher brothers away as they cursed.

That evening, Muhammad Bisher met with the head of the Office of Military Affairs, which commanded most FSA factions in the city. The two discussed how to respond to the defiance of the old council, drawing up plans to appeal to revolutionary governments in other cities and rally protesters through RYM. Then, after ruminating, the head of the military office offered another approach: arrest the members of the old council.

Muhammad fell quiet, pondering the offer. The power had gone out, and they were sitting in the faint, dancing light of candles. Could they arrest fellow revolutionaries? Would it spark a civil war? The new council's inaugural statement, which Muhammad himself had penned, declared, "We pledge that we will respect all international conventions and human rights." Yet government was, in essence, an organ of force. Two governments could not exist simultaneously. An orderly transition of power was essential for democracy. The new council had done everything the right way. They campaigned, they stood for election, they offered multiple olive branches to the old council. And yet the old council members viewed *him* as the usurper. Not, he realized, for this or that proposed policy—no, for the simple fact that he and his fellow citizens had dared to run their own affairs. The velvet elites had always believed that the city was their rightful possession; the schools, markets, and entire neighborhoods bearing their surnames was evidence of this terrible fact. That was the real usurpation, and Muhammad realized, for the first time, that his revolution was not only against the Assad regime—it was against its mentality, its spirit of domination, which had infected so many quarters of society. He did not speak, but his anger was visible in the flickering light. He knew he would have to do something. But he must have imagined the scene: Rebels leading his old friend and business partner Ahmed Rahmo at gunpoint into a waiting cruiser. The press would be there. The picture of Hasan Nefi, the city's most renowned political prisoner, once again in cuffs—once again a political prisoner—how it would look! In the mouths of his enemies, how the scene would transform into a new, dangerous story.

Muhammad did not speak for a long while. "Let's wait," he finally said. "Let's strike when the time is right."

| NINE |

January 2013

NEWS

The [revolutionary authorities] arrested 35 young men for standing near Manbij Girls High School and harassing students. After their parents were summoned, they pledged not to repeat their actions. —*Sun*

The Free Path visited the Revolutionary Police station, where police are on strike . . . due to "the delay in paying our salaries . . . and the refusal of some officers to add new policemen." —*Path*

A number of people on 30th Street organized a sit-in that lasted four hours, protesting the continuous electricity outages over the past fifteen days. Protesters blocked the street by setting fire to tires. —*Path*

Qadri Jamil, deputy prime minister of the Syrian regime, said that the regime continues to receive Russian-made weapons. —*Path*

A WOMAN'S PLACE IS IN THE REVOLUTION

As winter mists settled over Manbij, and housewives draped wine-colored carpets over the balconies, the blackouts arrived. Apartment blocks lay in darkness, interrupted by a candle in a window here, a generator-powered bulb there. The shelves of Zara and Moda and Bata were mostly bare. The jewelers locked away the lapis lazuli bracelets and gold-plated earrings and stood at the shop entrances, sizing up passersby. In the evenings, Mina walked Post Office Street end to end, peering at the deserted boutiques, at the young men looking this way and that, the clutches of women hurrying home. She liked to visit the Coffeepot Roundabout, pause under the snout of the giant sculpture, and breathe. She wanted to fill her lungs, drink the air. This, she told herself, was the air of freedom.

For most of her life, she had lived in the shadow of two gods, honor and fear. The fear was a low-level dread, the kind that hums in the background as you fold laundry and chop onions. And honor, an equally powerful numen, presided over everything—from what she wore to how she sat. Then, on that sweltering August day fifteen months prior, the forces of fear and honor came into contact, they clashed, and Mina survived. That was a day she relived a thousand times in her memory: the procession around the sculpture, the bulging muscles of the *shabiha*, the women's voices in the Friday stillness. Yet it was a temporary victory. In subsequent months, as the protest movement engulfed the city, the old gods reared their heads once more. When the government began shooting at demonstrators, she was told the streets were too dangerous for a woman. When Central Square filled with thousands of men pressed together, chanting until hoarse, she was told such an environment was no place for a woman. It was only on July 19, liberation day, that, for the first time in her life, her chest felt truly light; now she could finally square off against the dictates of honor.

In the first few weeks after liberation, she roamed the streets, unable to believe what she was seeing. The cement walls, once bare and gray, were now covered in reds and greens and blacks. Fragments of verse graced the facades:

> *Were fate cradled in my palm*
> *I would wash my nation's eyes with lightning's spark*
> *And kindle revolution that would rouse even stone to arms*
> *While cleansing my lands of the shadows of chains*

Streets had become open-air art exhibits, with canvases resting along walls and tree trunks. Walls featured caricatures of Assad, showing an enormous proboscis, his head shaped like an Easter Island monolith. There was Assad dishabille, Assad steering donkeys, Assad with arms flailing and blood gushing. When Mina saw these sacrileges, she felt titillated, and she wanted this air, this mood, to suffuse her. She had a sudden thirst for knowledge, for history; she wanted to study revolutions past, examine previous exercises in democracy. She visited the Cultural Center, which housed the city's public library. She'd spent her youth here, poring over self-help guides and classical Arabic texts. But the Cultural Center was shuttered for fear of air strikes. Still, she showed up almost daily to see if, somehow, its doors would open. During one of these visits, she noticed a flyer pasted on the gate: "If you are a woman who wants to stand up for the revolution, join the Free Ladies Assembly."

Not long after, Mina was in a basement near Rabta Street. Two dozen women sat in a circle, passing around coffee and *fatayer* pastries. The leader of this all-female assembly was the sister of Munzer Salal, the soft-skinned activist from the Revolutionary Council whose properties were strung across the city. In fact, many of the women present were wives or sisters of council members. The organizers presented a vision: The women would aid the revolution through clothing drives for the needy, literacy campaigns, and blood donations. They spoke with an air of authority that surprised and confused Mina. As they elaborated on the plan, she felt increasingly restless, but could not name what troubled her.

A woman covered in a head-to-toe niqab, only her eyes visible, spoke up. She offered her services and declared that she was ready to do anything to support the revolution—as long as it wasn't mere talk.

"Are we only a charity," she asked, "or are we ready to do something more?"

Someone replied: What more was needed? Women carried a heavy burden in this revolution; in fact, their participation was essential. They were mothers, wives, sisters—they were nurturers. A second woman asked: Can any grand experiment survive without nurture? The men needed love and support, and this was something the Free Ladies Assembly could provide. The men had the onerous task of running the city, so it was up to the women to look after the city's children, to care for the wounded.

Mina watched the other women nod in agreement—except for the woman in the niqab, who was as still as a statue. Afterward, Mina approached her and said she appreciated her question. "You're right," Mina said. "We *should* be doing more." The woman was tall and broad-shouldered, and had dark brown eyes. She responded, "Are we just wives and sisters? Aren't we also revolutionaries?" She introduced herself as Israa. She was a cousin of Anas Sheikh Weiss, a member of the old Revolutionary Council. Mina pulled her aside and recounted the women's protest the previous August, and as she did so, the crux of the problem struck her with incredible force: This was not revolution. What is revolutionary about clothing drives? Sure, the city needed basic services, but why couldn't women have a say in how the city was run? "There isn't a single woman on the Revolutionary Council!" she exclaimed to Israa, as if this glaring fact were a revelation. "Why is that? Who does this revolution belong to?" They decided to raise the issue at the next meeting.

Mina felt ready to thrust herself into the city, into its crowded hospital wards and makeshift camps. By God, this was why she had been put on this earth—to act, to be one with the citizens of Manbij. She could hardly wait for the next meeting. She phoned one of the organizers to say she wished to put the question of political work—that is, that the Revolutionary Council was all men—on the agenda. But when the next meeting came, the agenda was much the same as the previous week: blood drives and crocheting scarves for the needy. When Israa demanded that a few minutes be set aside for the council question, the organizers looked at her and Mina as if they had lost their minds; in this deeply conservative, deeply tribal city, the overriding imperative—*be honorable*—was stamped on their psyches. An organizer responded tersely that they did not get involved in "men's affairs."

Afterward, Mina and Israa walked home together. Mina was patient, a virtue necessary to survive the steady dose of stubbornness and insecurity and jealousy one is afflicted with when living among men. But in those rare moments when her patience thinned, she could not hide it: restlessness overtook her. She and Israa had been flattened, tossed aside like peels—were they children among adults? Israa declared that she would let the others have it at the next meeting. Mina had never met a woman like Israa, traipsing around in a niqab, utterly fearless, a rebuke at the ready when crossed. "You aren't a woman," Mina joked. "You're half man, half woman!"

That week, they plunged themselves into assembly work. Mina had been fired because of her brothers' revolutionary activities, and now most schools were closed anyway, so the assembly became a full-time profession. The pair went everywhere together. They visited the public hospital, a cavernous structure in which patients were wrapped in blankets on hallway stretchers. Young children suffering from thalassemia were wired to bags, their yellow faces watching the guests warily. With parents reluctant to send children to school—a favored target of regime warplanes—Mina and Israa convinced mosques to open doors to students, and they recruited volunteer teachers. Religious leaders denounced the women for teaching secular subjects in a mosque, which moved Israa to pen an article for the *Sun*:

> He who doesn't have a grain of knowledge has come riding in on his horse of ignorance . . . under the pretext that the mosques of God should not teach mathematics or the Arabic language. Does he know about Ibn Sina and Ibn al-Nafis, who developed the science of medicine? Or al-Khawarizmi, who excelled in mathematics, and Ibn Hayyan, who shone in chemistry, all while the West lived in darkness?

At the next week's meeting, it was business as usual: discussions about blood drives and sewing winter clothing. Then Israa interrupted and demanded to know: What is liberation without women's liberation? Mina was emboldened to speak up: "We have to free our minds," she said. "We are as shackled as we were before." No one responded. Later in the discussion, when Mina raised her hand to speak again, she was not called on.

The following week, organizers named one of themselves president of the assembly. Mina spoke out: "There are no rules, no internal procedures, no voting!" The organizers demanded she wait her turn, to which Mina shot back that they had refused to call on her. Israa spoke, lambasting the organizers for their lack of transparency. Now people were shouting. Suddenly, Israa stood up and said, "I can't do this anymore!" and stormed out. Mina jumped to her feet and followed.

That evening, Israa and Mina decided there was no turning back: A new assembly, focused explicitly on women's rights, was needed. They scoured the internet for examples of organizational charters. Israa copied by hand the platform of a women's organization she found online and presented it to Mina. They christened the new body Women of Freedom.

A few weeks later, a dozen women sat in a circle in Mina's apartment, in the shadow of the mills. Some of the women had marched alongside Mina in that famed protest; others were university friends of her sister. A few were here in secret, without their husbands' and fathers' and brothers' knowledge. Mina outlined her vision: The dictates of honor loomed over every apartment complex and cupola in the city, but if women banded together, they could push back. Women, Mina said, should have a hand in running their own city. They discussed the situation in Manbij—not just the crime, the mounting economic crisis, and the regime jets, but the pitiful condition of women. Honor killings, underage marriages, jealous husbands: Women would need to fight two revolutions at once. After much discussion, the group composed a founding statement:

> For a long time, we have been screaming for equality, so will this call have an echo? Sometimes, this expression "equality" causes misunderstanding: equality with men does not mean that women take away men's rights or contest them. A woman is a different being and has different duties, so she has different rights. The equality we demand is to obtain our rights, just as men receive their rights—that is, the right to fully participate

in the revolution, without facing mockery or chauvinism from those with sick souls. Because men do not have the monopoly on our homeland or our revolution!

They held a vote, and Mina was elected president.

The group sent a delegation to the old Revolutionary Council. The council headquarters felt like the center of the universe. Men were running from one room to the next, carrying sheafs of paper; one member was speaking loudly into a landline. Mina had been waiting for this moment since liberation, or maybe since the first protest, eighteen months ago: to sit face-to-face with her comrades in struggle, to sculpt a future for Manbij's women. As the women waited for an audience, she felt they had gained admission into the revolution's inner sanctum.

But when Mina raised her proposal—that women have a seat on the council—the council members prevaricated. One explained the situation in the city—there were two competing councils, the street was divided, the revolutionary government precarious. One hundred fifty thousand people under revolutionary authority lived in the countryside—the sunburned, tribal, patriarchal countryside. "You know how it is," the council member said. He said he believed strongly in women's rights, but that the time was not right. A second council member lectured at length about "revolutionary responsibility"—to rush things, to upset the city's conservative ethos, would risk alienating the rural constituencies. Mina felt her chest grow hot. The women sat quietly, listening to this disquisition. The trouble, a third council member explained, was that council membership was a full-time job. The women had children and husbands to attend to. Mina found herself, to her surprise, without a response. Then Israa chimed in: "What about me? I'm single." The men looked over this tall woman, draped head to toe, only her deep brown eyes showing, and an awkward silence filled the room.

Only Hasan Nefi offered his support for a woman's seat. Mina knew of him but had never seen him before, and she was impressed with his equanimous demeanor, which she struggled to reconcile with that of a man fifteen years in Assad's dungeons. But Hasan was in the minority. The other council members were united in opposition. In the end, they offered a compromise: The woman could have an "honorary seat" on the council, without voting rights, until the situation in the city stabilized.

Mina refused.

If we can't be your equals, she said, we'll go our own way.

She gathered her comrades and strode out. When she left, she asked, "Was

I acting like a dictator? Should I have taken their offer?" But the women were unanimous. They could not belong to an organization that did not respect them.

The wind gone from their sails, the Women of Freedom did not meet for days. Then they tried to rouse the support of other assemblies. Israa visited the offices of the Future Youth Assembly, but they seemed uninterested in the women's cause. She met with the Free Students Union, whose members would hardly look her in the eye. The truth was, women's equality was low on the agenda of most revolutionary groups. Mina's father had warned her: "People are not angels like you think. They'll never take you seriously." Mina opened her diary, in which she'd recorded events momentous and trifling since the tenth grade—her first kiss, a catalogue of her son Anwar's earliest words—and wrote, "We belong to this city, but the city does not want us." She composed a poem, which the *Sun* published:

> *You gaze upon me, wonder in your eyes. Why?*
> *You wait for my words to falter and die. Why?*
> *I wept your tears, called your name to the sky, and still you ask: why?*
> *Free yourself from the prison of familiar chains,*
> *Stand tall with dignity, bow only to the poor in their pain.*
> *My father, my brother, my son—*
> *With you, we shall build our dwelling place,*
> *Together,*
> *fingers intertwined, Binding wounds . . .*
> *And then, the question will vanish from your lips: Why?*

Women of Freedom met again. They debated the idea of freedom. Before, some may have thought that to be free was to be left alone, to be exempt from the heavy hand of authority. In that sense, they were indeed free. But if, as RYM argued, freedom meant something deeper—to not suffer the domination of another, to have no master—had they ever truly tasted freedom? The trouble was, domination was everywhere: not just between ruler and ruled, but between husband and wife, mother-in-law and daughter-in-law. Mina said they were waging a two-front struggle, against the regime, on one hand, and against prevailing attitudes, on the other. "Now we have our freedom," the group wrote in the *Sun*, "but the bigger concern is our liberation from the remnants of tyranny that have dominated our minds for many years. . . . All this falls on the shoulders of women!"

BUT THERE IS A SECOND COUNCIL

Waking up under Manbij's gray skies that winter was unlike waking up anywhere else. The days began in silence, but by late morning, the air filled with clamoring, which coalesced into phrases, then complete sentences: "The people want democracy! The people want unity!" Protests were daily, sometimes hourly: vivacious processions of colorful bunting and streamers, marches through the city center, sit-ins that materialized without warning in the squares, impromptu lectures delivered under the conifers, artists who colonized the alleyways, displaying their canvases. The *Sun* and the *Path*, bundled in twine, were available at storefronts. The dispatches carried news from the front, analyses of national events, poetry, short fiction—but above all, pages devoted to the fact that Manbij had two feuding governing authorities.

The old council controlled the bread furnaces, but the new council enjoyed the democratic mandate. A Neutral Committee had formed, tasked with finding an acceptable merger between the two bodies, but talks were dragging. The situation vexed most activists, but Mina saw an opportunity. She took Israa to the new council's headquarters. When she asked to speak to the president, Muhammad Bisher, she was ushered in. Mr. Bisher was alone, seated behind a folding table, wearing a crisp gray suit. Not a sign of the august ceremony that marked the old council. He welcomed the women, and asked about their education. He appeared genuinely curious about the new group, offering advice on crafting bylaws and collecting members' dues. He issued a license; as a registered assembly, Women of Freedom were now entitled to nominate five members to the People's Assembly. When the council's term expired in ten months, they could stand candidates for the council. He encouraged Mina to run.

When he learned that they lacked a headquarters, he motioned them to follow. Soon Mina and Israa were sitting in the back seat of his vehicle, peering through tinted windows, as if they were visiting dignitaries. Mina whispered to Israa, "Is this real?" She no longer cared how long it would take for the men of the old council to come around. The new council was *her* council; she would defend it with all her might. Mr. Bisher found a small office beside a refugee-filled school. "If you ever need anything," he said, placing his hand over his heart, "the council is ready." The women spent the afternoon scrubbing the place clean, arranging chairs and desks. That week, Women of Freedom conducted first-aid trainings and workshops on mutual aid. The assembly worked with the new council to design a sanitation service, and soon dump trucks were rumbling down city lanes. It organized vaccination campaigns and established a watchdog committee to ensure that charities did not waste funds.

But it was the assembly's lectures on politics, religion, and women's rights that captured imaginations. Israa wondered if these ideas could be put on the page. Every Sunday, she passed boys in her neighborhood gathered around the latest issues of the *Sun* and the *Path*, their fingers smudged with ink. As far as she knew, nothing like what the Women of Freedom discussed appeared in the pages of these publications. There were four newspapers in the city, but none devoted to the concerns of half the population. She found herself gripped by the image of young men holding open the pages of *her* creation—and why not? It was true that she and her comrades had zero experience in publishing, but neither had their male counterparts. She visited the offices of the *Sun*, where editors were enthusiastic and gave her a crash course in design. She did not own a computer, so she borrowed a friend's laptop to assemble the first issue, for which she solicited columns and artwork from fellow assembly members.

When the inaugural issue of *Peace Be Upon You* hit the stands, it was the first broadsheet in the city's history devoted to art and politics made for and by women. Mina and Israa held the copies up to their noses, breathing in the sweet ink. The issue showcased the assembly's interest in promoting secular education, and featured a caricature of a stubborn imam, looking cross-eyed, his head trapped in a giant padlock. The first edition was just two pages, but before long the paper grew to a half-dozen sheets, and included denunciations of the old council and muckraking investigations. One feature uncovered the pitiful conditions at the public hospital, where children languished without enough blood, even though activists had conducted multiple blood drives on behalf of the Red Crescent. Another was an exposé of aid organizations that sold donated items. *Peace Be Upon You* also featured a health column (issue 6: "What Is Eczema?") and a recurring feature on Israa's greatest passion, theories of the occult. One piece speculated that the Egyptian pyramids were giant power plants.

Meanwhile, Mina, who developed an interest in civil disobedience and theories of nonviolence, lectured at assembly meetings on Martin Luther King Jr., Gandhi, and Nelson Mandela. Though her brother was a leading rebel, she believed that arming the revolution had been a grave strategic mistake: In the long run, ragtag revolutionaries would be no match for a heavily bankrolled state army. Israa wasn't sure what to make of Mina's arguments—her cousin Anas commanded one of the city's premier armed factions. Others balked at the idea of nonviolence under a regime that bombed breadlines and hospitals. The early revolutionary movement, with its chants of "Peaceful,

Peaceful!," had been comprised of thousands of anonymous Gandhis who paid for their bravery in blood.

GIRLS OF TOMORROW

The question of armed violence exposed a deeper division within the group. Some women adhered to the dictum "separate but equal"— women and men should enjoy equal political status, but they should play different roles in society. After all, women could not be expected to withstand the physical rigors of construction work any more than men could be expected to give birth. But other women rejected this idea, arguing that it was a slippery slope back into the clutches of honor. The leader of this wing was a soft-spoken dentist named Huda Muhammad. Not only did she disagree with Mina on the question of peaceful resistance—she believed women should join the Free Army on the front lines. She moved to Manbij after the liberation with her small daughter Rachel, named after Rachel Corrie, an American who'd been crushed by an Israeli bulldozer as she attempted to save a Palestinian home from destruction. "She was not the type of person who'd fear how the community looked at her," a fellow revolutionary recalled of Huda. "For example, the way she dressed— it was stylish, very form-fitting, unlike anyone else in Manbij. And she would smoke hookah in public, which women in Manbij never did."

Before long, Huda and her sister split with Women of Freedom and established a new assembly, Girls of Tomorrow. They were soon spotted on the front lines, at firing ranges, and at Revolutionary Youth Movement meetings. "The motto of our assembly is 'no leaders and no followers,'" Huda explained to the *Path*. "Do not think badly of us because we mix with armed rebel men . . . have you forgotten this is a revolution?"

The group's Knowledge for All campaign established a revolutionary library—the city's only active book repository, since the Cultural Center remained shuttered—featuring seven hundred titles in the fields of history, literature, science, and philosophy. Huda took part in revolutionary theater programs and penned a health advice column for the *Sun*. She was interviewed by various revolutionary outlets, and began to criticize Hasan Nefi's idea that the collapse of communism and nationalism left the individual as the only surviving political ideal. Individual rights were important, she argued, but so was the importance of belonging, of community. A politics that exalts the individual as the highest good, the greatest value, will inevitably lead to alienation. In fact, the very opposition of individual and community, of self and other, was a false dichotomy. "People are displaced from time, displaced from place, displaced from country—but there is a diaspora of another kind, which is to be a stranger in your own community," she wrote. "I don't blame you, you are a stranger to yourself, look for your lost self, try to summon it, and when you find yourself, you will find your country."

With these splits, Manbij, a historically conservative bastion, now had three women's assemblies. The *Sun* began running "I Am a Woman," a section written entirely by women, featuring poetry, political tracts, and philosophy. Mina told the press that the role of a woman revolutionary was to fight on two fronts—against the regime, and against the traditions keeping women bound. Her assembly and Girls of Tomorrow were denounced in some quarters, ridiculed in others, but the women pressed on. "Some predicted that we would not last a week," she told reporters. "But here we are."

| **TEN** |

January 2013

NEWS

RYM announced an open peaceful sit-in, beginning the morning of Tuesday and ending only when the two revolutionary councils reach an agreement. —***Path***

On January 15, 2013, the senate elected a new executive office. —***Sun***

A large number of Manbij's battalions, brigades, and divisions came together to elect a Military Council tasked with preventing uncontrolled military phenomena, such as carrying weapons on the streets, and with policing violations committed by the Free Army. —***Path***

There has been a slight improvement in the security situation . . . the percentages of thefts and kidnappings have decreased. —***Path***

Fuel prices decreased this week, as a result of regulations on oil refining. —***Sun***

A STORY ABOUT THE SWEETEST THING

Despite the dull skies of January, the mood on the streets grew lighter, more adventurous. The winter chill was not as harsh as had been feared. Rebel advances elsewhere preoccupied the regime; the city had not suffered an air strike in a month. As a result, more families were sending children to school, and in the afternoons, boys and girls, bundled in oversized fuchsia and lavender and tangerine coats, spilled onto the streets and squares, bringing much-needed color. People lingered outdoors; the Great Souk was thronged with shoppers in crowds of a size not seen since before the revolution.

Despite the internal strife, the city's republican institutions—the senate, the People's Assembly, the two councils—held strong. The city's leaders were accustomed to opening the pages of the press and reading denunciations of their work or explosive investigations against them. Once, they sued the editors of the *Path* for defamation regarding an article that alleged revolutionary leaders were pocketing profits from bread distribution. The defendants presented their case to the Revolutionary Court, which acquitted them of all charges. Activists celebrated this triumph of free speech by marching through the streets holding marionettes representing the defeated plaintiffs.

Even prices stabilized. Muhammad Bisher's council imposed a price control on fuel, warning that "all those who violate the new price will be sent to court." For the first time, the cost of staple goods was not the main topic of conversation in the market stalls and city squares. The new spirit conjured fresh energy, bold plans. Home, a revolutionary artists' assembly, proposed an arts festival, which they dubbed Syria Mosaic, for the rich tapestry that was Syria's many confessional communities and ethnicities. Women of Freedom threw themselves into preparations. Manbij had never held such a festival, so these groups were venturing into terra incognita. Through weeks of preparation, an agenda emerged: an exhibition of local artwork, a gallery of traditional handicrafts, a pop-up theater. Manbij had no theaters, so organizers secured a wedding hall in which they could stage productions. The band platform was converted into a proscenium, with thick silver curtains draped behind to form a gleaming, otherworldly backdrop. A documentary crew captured rehearsals for "Adam's Dream," a sketch performed by displaced children. Afterward, one of the children, a boy, crows to the camera, "In school, teachers are always telling me I am gifted in acting." A dramatic sketch performed by adults shows a man in tribal headdress bent over a fallen comrade. "Our history is one," he shouts to the dying man, "and so are the people!" The play is a commentary on the great powers circling Syria like vultures. The camera pans to the test audience and there, seated in the back row, are Israa and Mina. "The scene should be longer," Mina advises. "You get me? Not everyone has the same awareness level. So you have to explain the background and political orientation of each character. Because the audience will be average middle-class people."

One member of the Home assembly was Sami, Mina's younger brother. A film crew captures Sami, who has transformed from the shy young man of two years prior. A lifetime had passed: protests, prison, liberation. Now, he appears before the camera grinning with confidence, wearing aviators and a black baseball cap. He's shorn the locks that had given rise to Oday's nickname, Shampoo Sami. "Would you believe me if I told you I was happy in prison?" he says. "Kahlil Gibran comes to mind: 'If you're imprisoned in a meter-square cell underground, shackled and fettered, saying "no" to your jailor makes you freer than him.'" He is sitting in a park; behind him, an abandoned Chair-o-Planes ride is nestled among cedars and pines. What is freedom? "It's the morning breath when you wake up, and you look at the sun, and you inhale and exhale for the first time," he says. "You fill your chest—that's freedom to me. It's the sweetest thing. The sweetest thing, to live as a normal person, with rights."

Nervous excitement churned within the city's assemblies on the days leading to the festival. At the Women of Freedom headquarters, Israa stayed late every night, scrawling verses on placards. At the Home collective, activists trained street children, who normally sold tea and biscuits while breathing exhaust, in the performing arts. By the eve of the festival, they'd blossomed into a well-coordinated troupe, an assemblage of limbs and torsos that swayed in unison. On that last day of preparation, the clouds had finally cleared. The air was crisp and cool. Surprisingly, the power was steady. In the early evening, lights burned on Rabta Street and near Central Square and along the roundabouts of Sarab and Hazowno. In the boxlike apartments, windows came alive. The unseasonable weather drew crowds to the Great Souk and Central Square. The grocers and tea stands on Jarablus Street were doing a brisk business, as were the garages and workshops. Not everyone saw the sparkle in the indigo sky, certainly not Muhammad Ali Najjar, who worked at a mechanic shop. The jet swooped toward the street before most people could run. The ground rocked. Windshields exploded, people fell. There were unearthly screams. Muhammad was hit, as were several relatives, including his seventeen-year-old son. One victim was ten years old.

It took some time for people to realize that the regime had deployed cluster bombs, seemingly at random—there was no military target. Eight people were dead. Activists visited the hospital, where they filmed bodies lying on the blood-streaked floor. "This is a child!" a man screamed into the camera, pointing to a flayed corpse. "A child!"

Members of the Home assembly held an emergency meeting to discuss whether to postpone or cancel the festival. Some chided themselves: They had allowed themselves to be lulled into complacence. A few weeks of good security, clear skies, low prices—what did it matter? It was as if Assad had noticed the lightened mood, the crowds on the street, and reminded them: *You are never free of me.* By now, almost everyone knew someone who'd been killed or wounded in air strikes, and among those untouched, a terrible guilt took hold, as if fortune had selected them for no good reason, certainly not for their merits or virtues. The planners wondered if they were selfish; to push forward under these circumstances—to call for crowds to gather—risked catastrophe. But the alternative was a form of surrender. Bashar al-Assad had lost political control of this city, but he continued to exercise power—fear was, after all, still written into many hearts. To cancel or postpone the festival was, in essence, to propitiate Assad. It was to deny the transformation of the previous six months. As the night wore on, a sense of defiance rose among the organizers. One told a documentary crew, "We are all on the verge of death. Each and every Syrian can be killed at any moment. So tomorrow there will be a funeral. And tomorrow we will continue the festival. It's okay—so long as it is for the sake of the revolution."

ON NARRATIVE

The next morning, the doors of the Syria Mosaic festival opened. People filed through the pergola, entering the cavernous hall, its ceiling speckled with stars, the stage's fey backdrop shimmering. The exhibition hall displayed *A Space for Forgetting*, a gallery of oil on canvas: One piece portrayed a boy in a black baseball cap, holding in his hands a small jet, or possibly a paper airplane, overlooking dun-colored apartment blocks rising above a girdle of walls; another depicted a forest shrouded in mist, the trunks flickering like phantoms behind a bold, articulated cherry tree, its fronds the color of fire. Musicians performed a flute and percussion concert. Crowds gathered around a puppet show, which used a revolutionary flag as a curtain. Children, bundled in their coats, craned their necks to watch a long-nosed marionette, a bumbling Bashar al-Assad, as he flubbed his words and uttered gaffes that set loose roars of laughter.

But it was the main event, the theater performance, that drew the largest crowds. Several young actors, portraying protesters, marched with fists raised across the proscenium. A masked man appeared, pantomiming gunfire. The marchers fell like dominoes. What were they doing? The production, from script to rehearsals to performance, was conceived entirely by locals. There was not a professional actor among them. As the marchers lay prone, the audience was in complete silence, enthralled. The masked gunman roamed the stage. Not a word could be heard from the spectators. They were, each of them, transported into the performance itself, because each of them had lived this story.

They had marched down the avenues, they had stood body to body in Central Square. They had fled in terror as the authorities raised rifles, aimed, fired. This was their story.

The philosopher Alasdair MacIntyre argued that humans are, essentially, storytelling animals—we use stories to make sense of the world, the actions of others, and ourselves. Our lives therefore exhibit a narrative structure, with a beginning, middle, and end, with definite turning points, and with a clear purpose: to live as well as we can. In this view, life is not a series of disparate events, episodes without connective tissue; rather, life forms a cohesive whole, and our conscious mind cannot but help shape the ephemera of existence into meaning. The narrative structure of our lives is most apparent when something goes awry:

> When someone complains—as do some of those who attempt or commit suicide—that his or her life is meaningless, he or she is often and perhaps characteristically complaining that the narrative of their life has become unintelligible to them, that it lacks any point, any movement toward a climax. . . . Hence the point of doing any one thing rather than another at crucial junctures in their lives seems to such person to have been lost.

The laid-off worker, spending his day on the park bench, afraid to face his wife; the wife who discovers her husband's affair; the parent who outlives his child—these are people torn, often violently, from the narrative structure that had guided their lives. The story in which they were breadwinner, romantic partner, or caregiver has mutated into something unintelligible. To lose the plot in such ways is to suffer what is perhaps a uniquely human trauma. Healing—in effect, rewriting the story—is possible but often a collective task. And so, just hours after a warplane obliterated the lives of eight neighbors, with the auditorium at capacity, and as the amateur actors, playing deceased protesters, lay still on the proscenium, the music swelled and from stage right and left emerged several young girls in white leotards and red frocks. They pirouetted around the bodies, these tiny angels, until one by one the bodies rose—and turned on their attacker, the masked man, overpowering him, slaying him. They had, if temporarily, rewritten their story, reclaimed their role as protagonist. Past traumas were relived and confronted; they were—here, now, for a moment—vanquished.

The applause was thunderous.

A SPACE FOR FORGETTING

For days, the Syria Mosaic festival had the city buzzing. Mina's mind fixed on the exhibit of oil paintings. *A Space for Forgetting.* Did she want to forget? She wished, in fact, to commandeer her memory, to blot out the air strike but cling to the festival itself, to its colors, its energy. She wished she could bottle this fervor, deploy it as needed. Women of Freedom met in the days following the festival, feeling renewed. They issued a new call for recruits: "Anyone can join . . . you don't have to be a great poet, but you do have to be a great citizen."

On the first Friday after the festival, crowds once again filled the streets, basking in the strange January warmth, their mere presence a rebuke against the regime. RYM led a long procession through downtown, snaking around honking cars, chanting that they would not quit until Bashar did. One could always see Abdul Hadi near the front of such a demonstration, with Abel Os and Oday not far behind. Maybe the anger over the strike could not be contained, or maybe the festival had emboldened the street, because this parade of sign wavers and chanters was more alive than usual. Mina was with her two young sons, en route to the market, when the column of protesters marched past.

Mina took the boys to Al-Twal Clothing, and then treated them to shawarmas in the market. "I want you both to share," she instructed, "and not fill up. We're having fish for lunch." Her mother was cooking; Mina was bringing her family, and Sami, fresh off the success of Mosaic, would be there too. She was in line, amid the smell of sizzling fat and dust and exhaust, when she suddenly found she could no longer breathe. The shawarma stand, the traffic, Al-Twal Clothing vanished. Two seconds passed. Then she heard a thunderous sound, a nauseating sound, and the world exploded. She was groping the ground, the tiles. She found the small hand of one of her boys. It was moving. A second hand clutched at her wrist. In one direction, the sky was black; in the other, a gray haze. With all her might, she hoisted the boys in her arms, carrying them like footballs, and ran toward the haze. She came upon a man on a motorcycle. "Don't worry, sister," he was saying. "You are going to be okay. Don't worry." But Mina was not okay. She needed to leave, to be as far away from here as possible. She was crying. "Take me home," she sobbed.

As they drove through the streets of the Hazowno neighborhood, people emerged from their houses, lifting their heads to the noonday sky, looking to see if the jet would return. When she reached home, her father was at the door. Mina and the boys were caked in dirt. For a moment, her father's eyes watered, and then he gathered himself. "You dog!" he screamed. "Look at you! Goddamn your revolution, goddamn your assemblies!"

It was 4:00 p.m. when Mina and her family sat down for lunch. It had taken her a few hours to recover from the shock, and she now felt the sneaking, guilty sensation of being alive. She did not want to know the toll from the air strike. She was here, surrounded by the lights of her life, and that's all that mattered.

In the end, the strike had wiped out an entire city block. For days, survivors and bodies were pulled from the rubble. If the revolution had unleashed hidden energies—solidarity, charity, hope, it also laid bare reality's brutal caprice. You could have rerun that day a hundred times, conjuring a hundred different configurations of people, of chance encounters. There is perhaps a deep nihilism in the knowledge that these particular deaths were arbitrary, even as the act itself, the release of munitions from a flying machine tens of thousands of feet in the air onto a crowded quarter of a city of no particular strategic importance, was somehow necessary in the historical sense of the word, because the sheer fact of this war would soon have reverberations across the region and, ultimately, the globe. But then, those arbitrary lives were themselves the accretion of chance encounters: A man was fond of drink, of dancing. He enjoyed the syrupy smoke of narghile cafes. When his father finally convinced him of the value of a settled life, he chose the first bride on offer—but had he been in a sour mood, or hung over, perhaps he would have selected the second or third. They built a warm home, and sired sons and daughters, the third of whom was a long-limbed boy named Taha Radwan. Taha enjoyed soccer and setting off bottle rockets. He would tease, and sometimes bully, his younger brothers, but also assumed an air of propriety around them, even at age seven. He liked to visit the confectioner next door, but one day—the day he must have passed Mina as she visited Al-Twal Clothing—he chose instead to visit the candy stand across the street. Had he stuck to his routine, he would have been with his parents when the missiles struck, and ended the day buried under mounds of rubble. Instead, his day ended at Al-Hikma hospital, where doctors performed emergency surgery, removing his kidney. A *Path* reporter happened to be there when he woke. "Taha held his kidney in his hand," he wrote, "and with courage and despair considered what he had lost."

| ELEVEN |

February 2013

NEWS

Thirteen prisoners escaped from jail during the night through a window they broke open. Police were able to recapture some prisoners and continue to search for others. —*Path*

Approximately 2,000 new families were displaced to Manbij from Aleppo, Damascus, and the areas of Bab, Safira, and Tabqa. As a result, 23 schools opened their doors in the Manbij area to absorb the displaced. —*Path*

On Thursday evening around 8:00 p.m., a massive explosion shook the city of Manbij. It's believed to be a Scud missile. Additionally, explosions were heard near the city of Manbij throughout the day. —*Sun*

HOW IBRAHIM DECIDED ENOUGH WAS ENOUGH

In the early-morning glow, Ibrahim nursed a tumbler of coffee and studied the highway, its asphalt netted with hairline cracks, as it shrunk into the eastern horizon. It felt as if hours might pass before he sighted movement, but traffic was unpredictable: now a rush of logging trucks and shared taxis, now an hour of golden silence. It was only fifty miles to Manbij as the crow flies, but the space between contained worlds: vast mountain chains, the winding course of the Euphrates, and a patchwork of liberated mini republics and regime-controlled enclaves. These slices of regime territory harbored intelligence agencies that flew the two-star Syrian flag and dispatched agents provocateurs to liberated soil. The crucial job of guarding the approaches from such infiltrators fell on the rebels, on gaunt frontline volunteers like Ibrahim.

After Adam, his younger brother, joined the sit-in two Decembers earlier that marked the turning point in Manbij's protest movement, Ibrahim was himself drawn in. He marched down the city's thoroughfares, dodging police on Aleppo Street, hiding in the shadows of Rabta Street. At a demonstration at the Sailboat Roundabout, he took shelter as security personnel volleyed tear gas. He was chased through the alleys of Sarab as regime forces hurled gravel—not unlike the gravel on which he'd walked barefoot, near the Crossing, waiting for Samira, all those years before.

Sometimes his thoughts returned to Little Hyena, to its rock-studded hills, its Roman catacombs. He was now married, with two boys and two girls, and before the revolution, he would take his brood to visit the remains of that submerged realm. But it was the nights skirting his own government through the streets of his adopted city that led him to his calling. He attended every protest that reached his ears. He had not the slightest clue who the organizers were—though he recognized the giant frame of Abel Os from Lebanon—and he didn't care. He'd lose himself in the sea of bodies and, as the protests swelled in the summer of 2012, often found himself near the front, hoarse from chanting.

After demonstrations, he'd be at construction sites around the city, nailing skins of insulation onto cement skeletons. It was steady work, but did not provide enough to expand his house, which remained a hovel with dirt floors. For that, the family's hopes were pinned on his younger brother. Ibrahim told friends that the best decision he'd ever made was to wade through the floodwaters of his childhood home to retrieve Adam's schoolbooks. Adam majored in English literature at Aleppo University, where he was a star pupil. The young man had taken an interest in modernism after reading T. S. Eliot's *The Waste Land*; he liked to intone, to his perplexed brother, *Shantih shantih shantih*. But Ibrahim received the shock of his life when, on liberation day, a column of pickup trucks pulled up in front of his house and out stepped, from the lead cab, in a bandolier and camouflage jacket, his baby brother. Ibrahim could not believe it—Adam, who used to spend his time memorizing Shakespearean sonnets, was now a rebel. Ibrahim did not know what to say, so he burst into laughter, and they embraced.

Not many weeks after, the first air strikes pounded the city. The scrubland along Aleppo Road sprouted displacement camps, filled with people who'd lost their homes. Some were from Manbij, but many hailed from Homs and elsewhere. A friend visited Ibrahim one night, and the two stayed up late, drinking tea and discussing the situation. By morning, the pair decided to join the Free Syrian Army.

They received training from other young men who could hardly handle weapons themselves. Then they deployed to Aleppo, where rebels were advancing on regime positions in the crowded slums of the city's east side. Ibrahim belonged to the rear guard, which frequently came under fire, even as the front line faced assault from earth and sky. His unit occupied an abandoned house, which bore gaping holes from previous missiles. Across an expanse, which glittered under the sun from discarded energy drink cans, stood a cluster of unfinished buildings. Snipers nested on the roof. Ibrahim wedged his rifle through a crack in the wall. From first light until evening, he watched the building.

Fifteen days passed in this fashion. The rebels took losses at the front. Sometimes the wounded were brought back to Ibrahim's station. Finally, the rebels broke through the regime's cordon, seizing a stretch of neighborhoods. The snipers abandoned their position, and Ibrahim's unit decided to decamp.

The new objective lay on the far side of the Euphrates: a middling town of rundown houses and mud-spattered storefronts called Ain Issa—Spring of Jesus—which served as headquarters for the regime's 93rd Armored Brigade. Capturing the sprawling base would sever a major east-west highway. Ibrahim's unit found a cluster of houses near the outskirts, all abandoned, and decided to take shelter while waiting for resupply convoys. He was teamed with a shy young man named Ahmed, and the pair bivouacked in a ramshackle house that would have smelled of dust and stale tea, with a few children's toys scattered about. The family had left in a hurry. The power was out, and we can imagine the desert wind howled, spraying grains of sand onto the windowpanes. Ibrahim crawled next to Ahmed for warmth. Food was hard to come by, and most nights he lay awake thinking of fried chicken, called "Kentucky" in the local patois. No one slept much. Lying together, he and Ahmed discussed soccer and the countries they wanted to visit. Ahmed had never left Syria, so Ibrahim described the beaches of Lebanon, the women. They did not broach the war or the revolution. It was as if they had been conscripted into the cause, buffeted by forces greater than they cared to examine, and to lie here in the darkness, in this strange village, was something to be endured with pride. And they were, in a sense, conscripted—after witnessing their own government deploying machines paid for by their own taxes dropping their payload onto the homes of their neighbors, what choice did they truly have?

Early one morning they awoke to gunfire. The cement walls of their shelter were exploding in little puffs. When they ran outside, they found themselves under a hail of bullets. Their comrades took positions and fired back. Ibrahim crept toward the house to fetch more rounds when the earth shook and a cloud of dust burst before him. He watched Ahmed emerge from the dust, sailing into the air, tracing a perfect parabola, hovering at an apex higher than the tallest house, then plunging downward, accelerating, accelerating, accelerating. He hit the ground almost soundlessly. When Ibrahim found him, he looked like a crumpled shirt. Ibrahim carried him to the car, Ahmed's body feeling like a giant water balloon, and as he placed him in the back seat, he knew his friend was dead.

Only later, after the unit had made their getaway, regrouping in a field of wheat and barley, did Ibrahim realize he had not eaten in two days.

A PORTRAIT OF A REBEL AS A YOUNG MAN

Ibrahim rarely went home, spending every minute with fellow rebels. Most had joined the Free Army just as he'd done—with a friend, impulsively, after witnessing carnage. There were nearly a thousand FSA units around the country. They hardly differed in outlook, or even had much of an outlook, except for wanting some vague form of democracy. Which unit you joined depended entirely on your social world; everyone knew someone who knew someone who had a cousin in the Free Army, and in this way you were recruited. Ibrahim and his compatriots did not receive a salary. Bullets were so precious they had to keep count. Yet they did not dwell on what they lacked, because the reality was that they were, for the first time, taking part in something larger than themselves, something so grand, so cosmic, that it was hard to comprehend.

The front lines near Manbij attracted mechanics, bricklayers, and vegetable peddlers—young men who hailed from homes of naked concrete and breezeblock in the shabby, crowded suburbs encircling great cities. The front lines also attracted poets, dreamers, and brigands. There was, for example, Hasan Sex, a commander who oozed charisma, and perhaps a good deal more. Mr. Sex was renowned for his mettle; once, as battalions gathered to ambush a regime position, the mood in the rebel camp was grim. "Fear and tension hung over the place," recalled one of his comrades, "especially among people of the area, for the regime there had great strength, including heavy weapons and the support of aircraft. So Hasan Sex played some revolutionary songs, and he and many of the fighters danced into the night, not caring about the battle they were to fight, and the death that possibly awaited them." Then Mr. Sex led a charge under cover of darkness, surviving a barrage of bullets—and the rebels stormed the position.

But Hasan Sex was most known, as his name implies, for his interest in fornication of all styles and manners (and it was the word in English, not Arabic, that formed his nom de guerre). He belonged to a respected upper-middle-class Manbij family: father a customs inspector, mother a housewife.

After high school, he attended a vocational institute. As Mr. Sex himself recalled, "Because these teachers were from the coast, they were dressed in revealing clothing that was not typical for Manbij. We students were happy and we were tempted." Hasan was able to get close to the teachers because, in the words of an acquaintance, "he is very bold and funny and speaks in a bright tongue, so everyone wants to sit with him. Hasan started to get to know the teachers . . . staying up with them to play cards. He secured their request for gifts and food and spent money on them because his father was rich. . . . Here, the relationship between Hasan and these teachers developed until the point at which he was having sex with them in their apartment, which was attached to the school." Hasan's affairs were discovered by the principal, who threatened expulsion. "But Hasan managed to clear the air with the principal and arranged a night out with the teachers. He assured the principal that it would be worth it. Indeed, they wound up all having sex together, and since that day, Hasan was known as a teacher's pet."

It was perhaps then that Hasan earned his distinctive sobriquet, along with a reputation that was no doubt enhanced by a stint, after graduation, in Damascus, where he availed himself of the city's many brothels. He had hoped to invest in this industry in Manbij, but then the revolution broke out. Now Mr. Sex devoted his time to revolution, pledging to return to the garden of earthly delights only after "we are free."

Bilal Assaf, another rebel from Manbij, faced death in trenches and alleyways around the country. His unit was ambushed one day:

> We defended our positions. Abu Yahya and I were next to the Assil factory, which manufactured women's lingerie. A tank approached us. . . . Abu Yahya wanted to target the tank, but the tank opened fire first. Abu Yahya was hit on his hip and leg.
>
> We pulled his body out but his leg was stuck, eventually detaching from the rest of his body. We called for an ambulance, as he was about to die. I had to carry his leg separately, and we rushed to the field hospital.
>
> Abu Yahya was a soulmate of mine, my best friend in the world, and I wept bitterly.
>
> We arrived at the field hospital, where the doctor asked, "Why are you carrying his leg?"
>
> "Can't you just attach it back?"
>
> "No, just go bury it somewhere," the doctor replied.
>
> "Just try to fix it, please!" I begged.

"That's impossible. How can we fix this?" the doctor insisted.

I sat helplessly for fifteen minutes, then returned to the battlefield.

Abu Yahya woke up two days later. They had covered his lower half. I sat next to him on the bed.

He asked, "How could you leave me behind like that the other day?"

"Who left you behind! You went out to target the tank," I replied.

"Did I hit it?" he asked.

"Yes, you did, you turned it into a pile of scrap!" I lied.

"Are you serious?" he asked.

"You saved us," I said.

I just wanted to lift his spirits. He did not hit the tank—the tank targeted him first.

His uncle arrived at the hospital. He whispered to me, "Are you going to tell him about his leg?"

"Wait, he doesn't know?" I asked.

"No."

Abu Yahya was lying in bed. He said: "My leg is itchy—I can't reach it."

"Which leg?" I asked.

"My right leg," he answered.

I laughed and told him, "So what am I supposed to do?"

"Could you please scratch it for me?" he asked.

"Where?"

"The ankle," he said.

I pretended to scratch his leg, moving my hand around his bedsheet. He started to tell me, "No, not there, move up a little!"

"Stop messing with me, I can barely handle this!"

He replied innocently, "I am serious. It itches. Please scratch it for me."

My heart was aching in grief for him.

He asked me once again. "I know it's too much to ask, but could you please scratch my leg? I'd do it myself, but I really can't reach."

He lost consciousness shortly after.

I went on thinking of some way to inform him. I remembered an episode of *Spotlight*, where someone wanted to tell a woman that her husband had died, so he asked her, "What time does he usually come home?" And when she answered, he replied, "Well, this time he is never coming back again."

Bilal rehearsed his words. Sometimes he imagined giving him the news straight. Other times, he reached for metaphor. After a while, Abu Yahya awoke.

We helped him sit up. It was me, Abu Aido, Abu Nour, and his uncle—the people closest to him. We were standing around him. I thought that he would start to cry and scream the moment I told him.

"Abu Yahya, the doctors aren't here," I said. "We have something to tell you."

We closed the door and lit a cigarette for him. He took a puff, then I said, "Abu Yahya, thank God you're still alive. Now, your duty to our struggle is over." He was listening carefully. "The rest of us will go back to the battlefield, and maybe—probably—we will die. But you: You have done your duty. There are no more front lines or battles for you. You have lost your leg."

He stared at me. After a while, he asked me to remove the blanket, so I did. Abu Yahya was born in 1997, so he was still very young. I thought he was going to cry the moment he heard the news.

His first words were, "Well, thank God I'm alive. What else can I say?"

I looked at Abu Nour; he was crying. Abu Aido was crying as well. We all cried, except Abu Yahya—he refused our pity. But we knew that he was very young, and he had not seen anything of life yet.

After a while, he looked at me and asked, "Abu Assaf, I want to ask you, is my guy fine?"

It took me a moment to realize what he was talking about. "I don't know. I didn't see it," I answered.

"Can you check?" he asked.

So I peeked beneath the blanket, but it was wrapped in bandages. I told him, "I can't see a thing."

The doctor came in, so Abu Yahya asked him directly, "Is my penis fine?" He added, "God knows, that's the most important thing."

The doctor started to remove the bandage. The testicles were fine, the shell's fragment having missed them, but the tip was damaged.

"What a shame," Abu Yahya said, then he continued, asking the doctor: "Is it going to be good?"

The doctor replied: "Yeah, it will be fine."

"I mean, will it be functional?" Abu Yahya asked.

"We do not know yet," the doctor answered.

I told Abu Yahya, "Look, once we get the internet connection turned back on, I am going to bring you a phone, and you can figure that out yourself!" Everyone, including Abu Yahya, laughed.

Shortly after, Abu Yahya left the field hospital and went home a hero.

HOW FOREIGN POWERS WADED IN

Despite the steady stream of recruits, the Free Syrian Army was perpetually short matériel. Given the $2,500 price tag of a Kalashnikov, most volunteers made do with knockoff Chinese and Saudi models. But if you fired those long enough and then rested them against the wall, they would bend. There was also the problem of bullets, which were chronically in short supply. It was the heyday of unctuous weapons smugglers, who purchased arms from corrupt regime officials, pilfered them from military units, or, if they were enterprising, tapped the international black market.

The situation was aggravated by the Western powers' de facto arms embargo; in theory, this applied equally to the black market and to the Syrian regime, but Assad was able to obtain weapons from the Russians and the Iranians, which meant that, in practice, only the rebels suffered. "The only way to understand the embargo," the *Path* fumed, "is to see it as a green light for Assad to burn, destroy, and kill this revolution." In the face of Western indifference, revolutionaries clamored for relief from other powers. The *Path* pleaded, "We call on our Qatari and Gulf brothers and say to them: The West doesn't care about Syrian blood—but why don't you?"

The Gulf regimes, led by Saudi Arabia, were deeply suspicious of the wave of revolutions cresting across the Arab world. Riyadh's greatest fear was democracy spreading to its kingdom, which was, after all, itself a brutal dictatorship. But then, one year into the Syrian uprising, Hezbollah, a Lebanese Islamic militia allied with Assad, sent fighters across the border to help the regime suppress revolutionaries. Hezbollah is backed by Iran, the sworn enemy of Saudi Arabia—prompting Riyadh to reverse course and, cautiously, begin sending token support to select rebel factions. Meanwhile, Turkey and Jordan, which share borders with Syria, began to send a trickle of weapons to a smattering of rebel groups. Finally, Qatar, which had its own complex rivalry with Saudi Arabia, tiptoed into the conflict by backing a few rebel units.

Still, the first two years of the Syrian revolution were a one-sided affair, with the regime lavishly supported by its patrons and the revolutionaries left with crumbs from regional powers. Yet the rebels continued to make gains, liberating towns and villages across the country. In 2013, eager to back a winning horse, regional powers increased support. But this still did not even the playing field. Aid primarily landed in the coffers of a handful of rebel groups, meaning most factions continued to receive peanuts; Manbij now featured some eighty FSA units—of which only a dozen received any type of aid from abroad. Most munitions came in the form of small arms, with anti-tank and anti-aircraft weapons, which rebels so desperately needed to protect civilians, effectively barred by U.S. writ. So most rebel units made do with some combination of private donations and brigandage. Middlemen appeared; they had contacts with Turkish and Jordanian intelligence agencies, who allowed armaments to fall off the back of the truck, so to speak, while earning a handsome profit.

The United States was reluctant to intervene. The conflict had become a dense soup of acronyms, a battlefield too complex, too unpredictable for Washington's tastes. U.S. officials were primarily concerned with weapons "falling into the wrong hands." In 2012, the CIA launched a top-secret program to better control the flow of weapons, while avoiding lethal aid to the rebels. When news of Washington's "non-lethal" support became public, revolutionaries reacted bitterly. "If they really wanted Assad to step down from power, they would have allowed other countries to supply the armed opposition with quality weapons," asserted the *Path*. "Only Russia's position on Syria is worse in its inhumane attitude toward the Syrian people." Barack Obama's declaration that Assad's use of chemical weapons would cross a "red line" inspired further derision. The *Path*:

> Anyone who hears the West's proclamation regarding chemical weapons will be struck with admiration at the humanity,

compassion, and mercy that has suddenly landed on them, as if the slaughter in Syria has not been ongoing for two years, and as if death by missiles and bullets and barrel bombs is different than death by chemicals. They are not looking out for the Syrian people, only for their own interests, and are afraid of our countrymen taking power.

THE SORDID TALE OF THE MAN THEY CALL THE PRINCE, PART 1

Alone, forgotten, embittered—this was the mood in the shabby rooms, barely warmed by woodstoves, where the men in Ibrahim's unit and so many like it huddled. The rebels' only hope lay in the oil fields out east, the natural gas deposits in the Palmyra deserts, and the border crossings. The crossings were choice targets; with control over ports of entry came the power to levy duties on imports. Having seized Jarablus, one of the crossings into Turkey, rebels now turned their sights to a second, smaller crossing that lay sixty miles to the east: the town of Tel Abyad, or White Hill.

Ibrahim's unit and a dozen others were in an abandoned village on the town's fringes. Days passed. One afternoon Ibrahim spotted clouds of dust rising on the horizon. At first he worried the regime was massing, but as the vehicles drew closer, he saw a motorcade with revolutionary flags whipping in the wind. A cry went up from the fighters: The Prince!

Ibrahim had heard his name but had never laid eyes on him. The Prince—people used the English word—was a figure of legend. It was said that he was the greatest commander on the eastern fronts, that he'd often slipped behind enemy lines to launch ambushes, that he'd run into homes to save children. As he stepped out of the vehicle, the rebels clamored for a better look. He was a slight man, long-fingered, a head shorter than his lieutenant. A second convoy pulled up. Out came a bearded man in a jellabiya—Maymati. Another cry went up among the fighters. Since his expulsion from Manbij, Maymati had been roaming the wastes of eastern Syria, attacking regime positions and attracting followers. Despite his peasant garb, he still possessed an officer's bearing, standing straight, broad-shouldered, his voice the richest of baritones.

Over a meal, he and the Prince conferred. Their lieutenants were seated around them, listening as the men discussed enemy positions and logistics Then the Prince called for the rebels to assemble before him. Speaking in a raspy voice, he explained that the objective was the immigration and passport office abutting the border. The plan called for one unit to approach the city from the east, engaging police positions, and a Kurdish unit to attack regime checkpoints on the western side of the city. Meanwhile, Maymati was to cross into Turkey, then lead an attack across the border from the north. But the pièce de résistance in this elaborate pincer movement was a gambit the precise nature of which the Prince refused to disclose. The battle would commence only when he gave the word. Then, with an air of ceremony, he climbed into a pickup and drove off alone.

Overnight, Maymati's forces climbed the roofs of empty buildings on the Turkish side of the border. The passport building loomed ahead, across a narrow no-man's-land separating the two countries. At first light, his group opened fire. Other rebel units managed to pin down regime soldiers on the east and west sides of the city. Helicopters rushed overhead. Bullets were flying across the border. Turkish authorities canceled school that morning, warning residents to keep away. Regime elements pressed right up to the border, dangerously close to entering Turkish territory. Under heavy fire, Maymati's men regrouped at an evacuated school. Regime snipers were firing from the roof of the passport building. Windows burst. Multiple civilians—Turkish citizens—fell wounded.

Amid this tumult, the Prince slipped under the chain-link fence that served as the border wall. He trudged through fields of wheat that reached up to his belly. He passed grain silos, a large parking bay, and warehouses. He took cover behind a tree. Across the street stood the passport building; he'd approached it from behind. As shots rang out, he studied the structure. The roof was crowded with soldiers. On the ground floor were conscripts, tasked with guarding the entrance. The Prince used his phone to call one of the conscripts and gave an instruction—and all of the conscripts slipped out the front door, leaving behind their weapons.

The Prince had spent days arranging their defection. Now he stole around the front and entered the first floor. Empty. He waited. At length he was joined by three of Maymati's men, who'd snuck across the border. The Prince then pointed his rifle out the window and discharged rounds. A soldier on the roof, thinking that comrades below were fending off a rebel advance, raced down the stairs—and found four barrels within inches of his face. The rebels tied him up.

Minutes passed. Maymati and his charges had arrived. The rebels below now outnumbered the soldiers above. The Prince dispatched the prisoner as an emissary to the soldiers on the roof; he returned with their names and ranks. The soldiers must have realized the end was near.

A camera captured the final moments. Rebels are gathered at the foot of the stairs. There is no power. The sun is streaming through the stairwell; the fighters are like shadows against the powerful glare. They crane their necks as if peering up to heaven.

A fighter in a bandanna calls up, "Throw your rifle down this way. Come down in your underwear!" The Prince is standing near him, dragging on a cigarette. "Don't curse at them," he instructs coolly.

"Come down and you'll be safe!"

There is movement. Someone is descending. The rebels cock their rifles, inching into the stairwell's glare. Maymati climbs a step. He climbs another. There is a slight but visible stiffening of the rebels' bodies. The men above are cornered animals. What have they been told? They are mostly conscripts, far from home, on a rooftop overlooking the dusty warrens of a rundown town in one direction, the verdant hills and gleaming office towers of Turkey in the other. Down below, in the darkness, await terrorists, extremists, perhaps death. Could they be blamed if they elected to end this siege on their own terms, storming the interlopers below, taking to the next world whomever possible?

Maymati takes a third step. The Prince, still dragging on a cigarette, is watching. Maymati, on his tiptoes, reaches up—and returns with a rifle. A shout goes up among the rebels. A figure materializes from the glare, walking gingerly down the stairs. Maymati stands with open arms, as if to say, *It's only me*. The regime soldier embraces him. A rebel kisses him on the cheek. We can now glimpse the soldier's face: He is smiling. The Prince reaches over, cigarette dangling from his mouth, and embraces him. "Don't worry, you're safe," someone says.

The soldier is now surrounded by a dozen rebels. Maymati asks, "How many are left upstairs?"

"The lieutenant," he replies. "And there are a lot of guys with him." His voice wavers. "There are a lot of guys who want to defect but they aren't able to. I swear! I swear!" He is suddenly close to tears, grasping his head.

"Don't be afraid!" the Prince says.

He looks increasingly disconcerted as the rebels swarm around him. "I don't fear death," he insists. "That's why I'm still alive."

Maymati continued to coax people down, one by one. After an hour, only one soldier remained, a sniper. Maymati shouted at the top of his voice, pleading for his surrender. But the sniper, an officer, refused, replying with a barrage of invective. "Enough!" the Prince screamed, and produced a sticky bomb, old Syrian army-issue, and barked at a captive, "Where is he?" The captive pointed to a spot on the ceiling. The Prince slapped the bomb there, directly under the sniper. The blast blew out the windows and the front door.

Maymati and a comrade crept up the stairwell, pausing at each landing to listen for movement. The roof was four stories up. When they emerged into the blinding sun, they spotted the sniper, writhing. He appeared to be stunned.

"Do you know how to fly?" Maymati asked.

The officer looked at Maymati blankly.

"I said, do you know how to fly?"

The officer slowly shook his head.

"Well, let me teach you." He hoisted the wounded man up, carried him to the edge, and tossed him over. The officer did not scream as he fell.

Ibrahim's unit entered the town to find the streets deserted, the buildings pockmarked. Rebels tore down the Syrian regime's flag and the Assad posters. Ibrahim helped carry wounded regime soldiers to ambulances, which sped off into Turkey. People were now emerging from their homes, or coming from Turkey, crawling under the border fence. "I'm a free Syrian!" one man shouted, throwing his hands in the air.

The fighters gathered atop the entrance gate to Syria. Ibrahim looked up, where a few fighters stood against the cloudless azure sky. They were struggling to hoist the revolutionary flag, like at Iwo Jima. As the flag was righted, a cry went up from the gathering crowd: "Long live Syria, down with Bashar al-Assad!" Pride surged through Ibrahim; he and his friends, bricklayers and construction workers, had driven off an *army*. He looked back at the Turkish gate. The space between the two gates—to Turkey and Syria—was some thousand feet, a space that had once marked the divide between the grime of his life and all that had been denied to him—the glass office buildings, the leafy boulevards. Maybe—just maybe—this rundown gate would no longer be a threshold between worlds.

Above, a man stepped to the edge and raised his fist. It was the Prince. His hoarse voice carried down to the crowd, which chanted rhythmically after him: "The Free Army forever, trampling Assad's head!" At that moment, the town, and maybe all of eastern Syria, belonged to the Prince—his daring, his selflessness in seizing the crossing was already the stuff of legend. The men with Ibrahim, gazing up at their commander, were ready to follow him anywhere. A videographer on the roof was attempting to obtain a comment. "Prince! Oh Prince!" But the Prince was uninterested. Instead, he kept his eyes on the flag whipping in the wind, and—for the first time on camera—allowed himself to smile.

The Prince was born Nawras al-Jasim in Manbij in the early 1980s. As a youth he drifted to Lebanon, where he worked as a security guard, then reported for his mandatory military service, guarding the Lebanon-Syria border. Upon completion of his duty, he fell for a local girl, married, and moved to Greece. He'd settled into a life peddling trinkets and wandering the streets near the Acropolis when the Syrian revolution erupted. He returned to his homeland and joined the Free Army near the border, where he was drawn into battle with Hezbollah, the Lebanese militant group that was aiding the regime. It was here that his legend took life. He managed to kill a Hezbollah commander, stripping him of his weapons and walkie-talkie. Commanders of the Lebanese militia used code names on the radio network: the Scorpion, the Viper. As he carried the walkie-talkie, he continued to receive transmissions meant for the deceased commander, the Prince.

When the regime crushed the uprising near the border, Nawras—now known as the Prince—returned home. The Manbij he arrived at was a free city; he struggled to make sense of the dizzying array of assemblies and councils. So he approached a cousin in the movement—Oday al-Hema. Oday brought him to a Revolutionary Youth Movement meeting, where the Prince recounted how he'd killed Hezbollah members by his own hand. The group burst into laughter at this stranger spinning yarns.

That week, a spate of kidnappings shook the city. The Prince gathered a group of friends, tracked the kidnappers to a farmhouse in the country, and rescued the captives.

The activists of RYM were no longer laughing.

One day, the Prince appeared at a demonstration led by RYM in solidarity with the town of Safira, about an hour away, which was under regime siege. From the stage, Abdul Hadi shared news trickling out of Safira: air strikes on civilian homes, *shabiha* going house to house executing people. The Prince could not contain himself. He grabbed the microphone and declared, "I will go defend our brothers! Anyone who is willing to join me, I will provide the guns!" The audience cheered, and a few days later, people learned that he had kept his promise. By the time he returned to Manbij, his legend was growing.

But where did he obtain the weapons? As his forces liberated villages, he hunted for regime supporters. In one village, he nabbed a pro-regime tribal sheikh, tied him to a beam, and paraded his prey through the dirt lanes as the villagers watched in astonishment. The sheikh was released only when his family paid a huge ransom—which the Prince used to equip his forces. This proved a profitable venture. Before long, the Prince was in the kidnapping business—but his quarry was limited to individuals linked to the regime. He was collecting tens of thousands of dollars in ransoms, more than he could even use, so he distributed the surplus to the destitute, the displaced, the widowed, the families of martyrs—and so earned the adoration of the poor, who saw him as a Robin Hood in a Hi-Lux.

After securing the border in the battle of White Hill, the Prince turned his attentions to further border crossings, stretching all the way to Iraq. One post after the next fell, until the regime lost fully half its border. Between battles, the Prince's men replenished themselves by raiding the homes of regime figures.

As the Prince built this empire, other Free Army units jostled for a piece. One was Jund al-Haramain. Though its fighters had their indulgences, hashish chief among them, they had chosen the unit's name, with its implicit reference to Mecca and Medina, in an attempt to attract Saudi funding. When that failed, they turned their sights on the city's most vital resource. Despite the old Revolutionary Council monopoly over the flour supply, Jund seized one of the city's two public bakeries. Meanwhile, other factions inked deals with private bakeries, offering protection in return for a cut of sales. These "bread brigades," as residents called them, soon diversified into fuel and livestock. East of the city lay a stretch of scrubland where merchants peddled barrels of crude to buyers from around the country. Each oil well was under the control of a rebel faction—a de facto privatization of the country's hydrocarbons.

The revolutionary press was quick to condemn this smorgasbord of corruption. Said the *Path*:

> I was told by people close to me in the town of Ras al-Ayn about a battalion stationed outside their homes. The battalion raided their home after they sought refuge in Turkey. The battalion took everything: furniture, electric appliances, kitchen products. Even perfume bottles. In fact, even love letters, the one thing they had of their memories, were taken by the "liberators."

IBRAHIM HAS DOUBT

For long hours, on the outskirts of Ras al-Ayn, a border town that had been liberated by the Prince's forces, Ibrahim manned a checkpoint. The road in front of him ran straight as an arrow to the horizon. Most nights, he was with Ali, a rebel from Manbij who, like him, had joined the armed resistance after witnessing a regime air strike. They had followed their commander—who had pledged loyalty to the Prince—here to the edge of Syria. They spoke often about the Prince, a man they both admired and, increasingly, loathed. Where did rebellion end and brigandage begin? Ali swore that if he were asked to pilfer goods or shake down motorists, he'd quit on the spot. When Ali slept, Ibrahim was alone with his thoughts, and he must have pondered the mutations of a once-noble cause. For eight months, he had offered his body to that cause, and survived unscathed—so far. For the first time, he obsessed about death, about the mysteries of fortune, the thousands of imperceptible choices and accidents that had delivered him here. He counted his blessings for his own father's stern hand—what a beating he would have received had he ever been caught stealing as a child! He thought often of his children; his son was twelve, his daughter ten. When he went home on leave, his daughter would run into his arms, but his son would stand sullenly in a corner. It took a few days for the family to coax the boy into conversation—but by then, Ibrahim would be set to depart. In the end, the boy's eyes watered as Ibrahim climbed into the jeep, Kalashnikov slung across his back.

Ibrahim was fast asleep one night when he heard a scream. It was 2:00 a.m. He stepped outside the guard hut. Three white Hyundai H-100 pickups were parked nearby, shocks of wheat in the beds. Ibrahim approached a farmhouse, from which lights were flickering. Inside, he saw six men lying bloodied on the floor. Rebels were thrashing them with the butts of their rifles. Ibrahim and Ali tried to intervene. "These are dirty *shabiha*!" the rebels exclaimed. But the men crumpled on the floor were wearing jellabiyas, not military fatigues. That they were mere farmers seemed obvious, and Ibrahim confirmed his suspicions when he interrogated one of the captives. He realized that the rebels had seized them for their vehicles. As Ibrahim tried to help the men to their feet, Ali threw his weapon down. "If you don't release them," he shouted, "I'm quitting. I didn't sign up for this!"

The next day, the men were released, but the rebels kept one of the vehicles. For weeks, Ibrahim mulled over Ali's heroic stand. A feeling rose in the pit of his stomach, which he would later recognize as disgust. Only the existence of men like Ali, men unchanged even as the world around them collapsed, kept this feeling from snuffing out the flame of his rebellion. And each new disgrace seemed to push Ali into a rage that could only be sated through some bolder, more reckless feat of self-sacrifice. One night, he volunteered to target a nearby regime outpost. Ibrahim and his comrades insisted they should wait for backup, but Ali was anxious to do something, anything, except sit at the checkpoint and watch his superiors rob people. For an hour, Ibrahim beseeched him to hold back. But Ali laughed him off. Under a moonless sky, he and two others crawled through the wheat fields while Ibrahim waited back at the guard hut. Ibrahim lost phone contact within an hour. The sun rose over the fields. Ibrahim roved around the perimeter of the guard post, dialing his friend's number over and over. He never saw Ali again, and they never recovered his body.

Some weeks later, rebels caught a regime officer attempting to sneak past a checkpoint. Ibrahim delivered him to rebel headquarters, an old farmhouse not far from the highway. He presented the captive to his commander, who was hunched over some papers at a desk.

"This is a corporal we caught at one of the checkpoints," Ibrahim said.

The commander looked up. Without a word, he shot the captive in the leg. The man crumbled in a wail of agony. Ibrahim stood fixed to the spot. Blood as dark as Coca-Cola gushed from the corporal's thigh as he screamed and screamed. The commander said desultorily to Ibrahim, "Thank you, you can go now."

That night, when he closed his eyes, Ibrahim saw the dark blood gushing from the corporal's leg. The next morning, he said to a comrade: Take me back to Manbij.

At home, as his son and daughter watched, Ibrahim spoke bitterly to the comrade who had driven him back. "I'm not risking my life to fight alongside thieves." His wife served tea to the two men, but there was no sugar. Ibrahim went to the kitchen to find the shelves mostly bare. What had he accomplished in these eight months? He surrendered his pistol, his Kalashnikov, and his ammunition to his comrade. He kept a grenade. "You're welcome to visit me as a guest," he said with rage. "But if you ever ask me to fight again, I'll throw this at you."

Later that evening, his son asked, "Are you really staying?" And Ibrahim knew then, without a doubt, that he'd made the right decision.

The next day, his younger brother Adam paid a visit. He too had grown disgusted with the dissolution in the ranks. He had quit the Free Army that morning, but he was not ready to quit the armed struggle. "There's something new," he said, a gleam in his eyes. "Something new is coming."

| TWELVE |

March 2013

NEWS

Three consecutive air strikes hit the city of Manbij last week.... The regime planes struck several neighborhoods near the Prophet Jonah's cemetery, some of which fell on a funeral procession. Seven were killed and fifteen injured. The second air strike occurred on March 2, 2013, hitting Rabta Street. A young child, Hasan Hosni, was killed and ten others were injured. The last air strike occurred on Sunday, March 3, 2013, and hit an agricultural area east of the city. One person was killed and five were injured. —*Path*

RYM organized a sit-in ... with the goal of unifying the two councils. —*Path*

A considerable number of teachers have not received their salaries for some time, and the number is growing. The Social Solidarity Committee for Educators is providing funds where possible. —*Weekly Letters*

During the past few weeks multiple kidnapping gangs were caught in the city.... The news spread across the city like a sign of hope, and people expected harsh punishments to be enacted on the kidnappers ... but we were all surprised when after a few days several gangs were released from custody. Rumors spread that those individuals had paid sums of money in exchange for their freedom. —*Path*

> In a quick visit to the city of Manbij, the Free Army welcomed [opposition politician] Ahmed Moaz al-Khatib. In front of crowds, al-Khatib opened his speech by discussing Islam and Islamic civilization over the centuries, emphasizing the role that Islamic civilization played in modernization and development. —*Path*

YEAR THREE OF THE REVOLUTION

> Two whole years of pain and struggle. Two years of catastrophe and massacres. Two years of destruction and ruin. Despite this, the Syrian civilian holds on tighter to his desire for freedom and dignity. The increase in the regime's brutality has increased the people's faith in the possibility of change, no matter the sacrifice. A Syrian knows that the losses, no matter how great, will be fewer than the losses that will hang over him if the regime continues its reign. The revolution is entering its third year stronger. It's entering its third year with conviction. We don't say this just to raise our spirits and for the sake of being optimistic. We say these truths because we can feel them on the ground. . . . Victory is patience. Our fate as Syrians is a blood-stained path to our freedom and dignity.—*Path*

WHAT TO DO ABOUT CRIME?

Even as these sentiments appeared in *The Free Path*, most readers grasped a grimmer reality. The truth was, the Free Army's string of town liberations had ended. Russia and Iran had upped their support to Assad, halting rebel momentum. To break the stalemate, the Free Army required more weapons, more rounds, more fuel—which, without foreign support, meant more kidnapping. As spring arrived in Manbij, corruption was all anyone could talk about. Declared the *Sun*:

> Just as under the Assad regime, corruption in our city has appeared like a natural phenomenon, spreading through all institutions, assemblies, councils, battalions, and even among those who call themselves "real revolutionaries." I can quote the poet Nizar Qabbani, who said, "In our neighborhood a

rooster comes and a rooster goes, but tyranny remains." ... To cure the city would require a new organization that is stricter and bolder, and which can hold wrongdoers accountable.

"We might not fret every time the Free Army loses a military position," complained the *Path*, "but we mourn from the heart when some Free Army elements lose their ethical compass. This war has become a war of morals more so than a military war." The *Path*, though a secular publication, was introducing morals into the discourse, and by this they meant, increasingly, a sense of right and wrong in a cosmic sense—that which could transcend the particularities of time and place, that which *everyone* could agree on. They began to call for religion as an answer to the anomie. "The demand for the intervention of Islamic battalions grows louder, as they have made great strides in the hearts of revolutionaries with their deeds, morals, and honesty." Only a handful of the war's one thousand factions were religiously oriented. These Islamic battalions kept to the front lines—rarely interfering in the governance of liberated cities—and did not molest civilians. They took a harsh stance against crime, especially kidnapping.

The largest of these groups was Ahrar al-Sham, or the Free Men of the Levant. Unlike the Free Army, which carried the tri-star banner, the Levant Free Men preferred a white flag emblazoned with the words: "There is no god but God, and Muhammad is His Prophet." Against the FSA's vision of a secular democracy, the Levant Free Men championed a religious government with no barriers between mosque and state. And unlike the resource-starved Free Army, they were lavishly bankrolled by Qatar—with an armory so well-stocked, their fighters seemed impervious to temptation.

The Levant Free Men appeared first in western Syria, then gradually spread eastward. By the winter of 2012, they had opened up shop in Manbij, though with only a few dozen members, making it one of the city's smaller factions. Most of the fighters were not Manbij natives, and the presence of out-of-towners among the rebel ranks aroused suspicion in some quarters. Many activists worried that the group would push an anti-democratic, anti-secular agenda in city politics. The authorities, too, were divided. Ahmed Rahmo, from the old Revolutionary Council, told reporters, "We ought to live in an age of freedom, and so long as we have accepted that, we must welcome those of all ideological persuasions." But Muhammad Bisher's new council was more wary of the bearded men, arguing that groups should make a public pledge to democracy before being allowed to enter the city.

As the councils bickered, crime was growing worse. The Levant Free Men responded by conducting their own raids to arrest kidnappers, a job that by rights belonged to the Revolutionary Police. But the police themselves were mired in scandal, relating to a pair of women who, upon being falsely accused of passing intelligence to the regime, were tortured in custody. In the debate over how best to address crime, one man offered a fresh solution—the people should not vest their hopes in the inept police, or in the bearded men of the Book. In his eyes, there was only one man who could save the city—himself.

THE SORDID TALE OF THE MAN THEY CALL THE PRINCE, PART 2

One evening, representatives of the city's factions and councils gathered at the home of a local commander. On the agenda was the crime wave, in particular the need to establish more checkpoints around town. Partway through the discussion, the Prince and his entourage barged in. The Prince—by now perhaps the most powerful man in the city—declared that the root of the problem lay with the Revolutionary Police. "Who gave you the right," the Prince demanded of a police commander, "to torture women?" The police chief responded, "Who gave *you* the right to interfere in police business?" and then volleyed a curse at the Prince. Calmly, without a word, the Prince reached for his holster, pulled a pistol, and fired at the police chief's head. The man ducked just in time, the bullet missing him by inches.

Later that same night, the Prince and his charges surrounded police headquarters, firing rounds into the air. They burst through the doors, shooting an officer in the shoulder, and arrested an individual they believed to have had a hand in abusing the women. It took a week of meetings, and many pledges to hold the corrupt police accountable, for tensions to deescalate.

But the incident emboldened the Prince, who then erected checkpoints looking for thieves and kidnappers. Among the city's political bodies—the two revolutionary councils, the senate, and the assemblies—opinion was divided. The old council, which still controlled bread distribution and so was the de facto power in town, saw the Prince and his cronies as vigilantes, undermining the city's institutions. The new council, which enjoyed legitimacy due to the election but lacked revenue because it did not control bread, took a sympathetic stance: Poor, tribal, offering rough-and-ready justice, the Prince was cut from the same cloth as the new council's mostly working-class members. They saw the Prince as a champion of the people and a useful bulwark against the elitism of the old council and the ineptitude of the police.

In late March, the Prince's forces received a tip about a regime cell operating out of the municipal electricity works. Fighters raided its garage to find a trove of

pro-regime paraphernalia: flags, placards, and golden busts of the two Assads. The Prince invited the *Path* to report on the haul, which he took to be proof of pro-regime elements organizing a comeback in the city. The Prince posed for a photo, a foot on each bust, holding up a flag. He is staring past the photographer, looking triumphant, as if in balancing on the Assads' heads he is perched atop all of Syria. The old council saw the raid as yet another example of his vigilantism. The Prince's forces were arresting people left and right on charges of criminality or regime ties. He refused to turn these suspects over to the court, instead demanding a ransom. Freedom cannot survive, the council members argued, when someone takes the law into their own hands.

The old council took their worries public, waging a press campaign. The assemblies held debates. RYM pledged to remain independent, but most members, like Oday, had a soft spot for the Prince and his heroics. In interviews, the Prince fired back, declaring himself the city's only hope. Tensions reached a breaking point, and when a confrontation finally came, it was over something seemingly trivial. The Prince's forces arrested a pair of archaeologists for excavating sites without a permit; one of the detainees appealed to the Levant Free Men. The Islamist brigade stormed the Prince's compound, arresting several of his fighters. The Prince and his forces promptly headed for the Levant Free Men headquarters.

Abel Os was home when he received word that the Prince was about to attack another faction. He'd lived many lives in the past eight months: the first sweaty days of freedom as he climbed the stairs of the hotel and unfurled the giant flag; the suddenly haughty tones of his old friends; the thrill of the ballot box, the incredible sense that his city had spoken and chosen *him*. Through it all, with new friendships and new rivalries, he'd been sustained by a simple, unbreakable idea: *We're in this together.* Now a new threat—brother against brother—loomed over the city. If he did not act, the democratic experiment itself would be imperiled. He rushed to the Levant Free Men headquarters.

He found the Prince's fighters arrayed outside the compound, a wild-eyed Prince pacing back and forth. Abel Os pushed his way into the base and spoke with an LFM commander, then returned outside to confer with the Prince. For the next hour, Abel Os mediated, until finally, as darkness fell, both sides released their captives. Abel Os put his hands on the Prince's shoulders and said, "Remember, we have only one enemy."

But the Prince wasn't so sure. He said, "We revolutionaries don't want the bearded ones in our city." As they drove off, the Prince's fighters fired rounds in the sky.

The senate held an emergency meeting that evening. For the first time in months, RYM attended, along with many other assemblies. There was talk of calling in brigades from Aleppo to quell the tension, but RYM argued against outside intervention. Instead, Abel Os proposed to solve things the way he knew best—protest. A mass demonstration for unity would show both sides that the street wanted peace. He argued for a strictly nonpartisan protest: No one should be allowed to raise the name of any leader or battalion.

RYM won the vote. They led the senators, the assemblies, and the two councils through the darkened streets, heading for Security Square. It was a remarkable sight: The political factions, at odds for months, had finally joined hands for the common good. As the procession marched under the balconies, people emerged from their houses to join. The marchers waved the tri-star flag of the revolution, singing songs of unity and chanting for the downfall of the regime, as in the older, simpler days.

The crowd filled Security Square. The protesters placed their arms on each other's shoulders, rocking, chanting for the Free Army. Then, near the front, a few senators raised a hastily scrawled placard that read DEATH TO THE PRINCE! They managed to lead a section of the crowd into this chant. When the words hit Oday's ears, he could not believe it. He tried to push his way to the front, demanding that the protest remain nonpartisan. But the crowd was too dense, the mood too fervent. It was as if the senators had uncorked something deep and primal in their section of the square. The protesters, their faces sheened in sweat, were in a frenzy. "Death to the Prince! Death to the Prince!" They were mostly friends and relatives of the old council members, and their message spread outward in waves. The crowd was on the move again, emptying from the square. They marched—ran, really—through the streets, heading west. Past the soccer stadium, crossing the wadi. "The people want to execute the Prince! The people want to execute the Prince!"

The RYM members watched in horror. Would the Prince, drunk with power, open fire on the masses? Would the battle fever spread to the Levant Free Men? When the crowd reached the Sailboat Roundabout, it was clear that the march had a single target—LFM headquarters, to show their support to the Prince's enemy. The senators were at the front, triumphant; they had expertly manipulated events. RYM decided to quit the rally; they could not, in good conscience, take part in whatever was coming next.

Almost no one slept that night. News spread that the senators were conspiring with the Levant Free Men to call in powerful allies from Aleppo to save Manbij from "a pro-regime criminal known as the Prince."

The rumors reached the Prince. At 10:00 p.m., he positioned armed lookouts on the roof of his headquarters. Most of his faction was miles away on the front lines, leaving only eighteen fighters as his Praetorian Guard. Then came the news from lookouts: A column of 4×4s was approaching Manbij from Aleppo. There must have been at least a hundred vehicles—perhaps the largest military force the city had ever seen. When the Aleppo brigades neared the Prince's command center, they dispatched a messenger. The Prince was informed he was wanted by Aleppo's rebel court for "crimes against the revolution." The Prince said he recognized no authority save the court of public opinion. He told the emissary that he would appear in Central Square at 7:00 the next morning to submit himself to the judgment of the masses. The emissary agreed, and the appointment was set.

The Prince, Hasan Sex, and other commanders settled in to sleep. They awoke, the phones reading 4:00, to the terrible sound of gunfire.

The Prince's headquarters was surrounded. From his second-floor windows, he could see the Aleppo fighters on the street, on the rooftops.

The Manbij night cracked, whistled, and shook. The smell of smoke filled the air. The Prince was shouting into his walkie-talkie for reinforcements of allied units while men fired wildly from the windows. The Aleppo fighters were returning fire.

The battle woke the city. Families gathered in kitchens and living rooms, and the intrepid few ventured onto balconies and roofs. Manbij had never witnessed full-scale violence, not during the French occupation, not during the Second World War. RYM members were huddled around a walkie-talkie, straining to decipher the shouts and pleas coming through the airwaves. At some point they heard a familiar voice:

"Everyone come to Central Square! Everyone to Central Square!"

It was Abel Os calling for a mass protest to end the violence.

Over the next hour, as the sky paled, the square filled. Abel Os and Abdul Hadi led a procession west—toward the fighting. It may have been madness, leading a crowd of civilians into a raging firefight. But Abel Os believed, at the core of his being, that the sight of the masses, in whose name these rebels were fighting, would bring the two sides to their senses. The group marched slowly, without clamor, like a cortege. Then, as they neared the battle, Abel Os and Abdul Hadi led a chant: "The people want to stop the fighting!" The procession had grown to hundreds. Those living nearby had spilled onto the streets in their pajamas, some of the children holding plush toys.

The procession reached a checkpoint. It was manned by the Levant Free Men, who refused to allow the civilians to pass.

The crowd grew. An argument erupted between the protesters and the LFM guards. Who were they to halt the free movement of civilians? The guards' eyes darted nervously over the swelling crowd. The protesters pushed up to the checkpoint, threatening to burst through. Suddenly, a guard fired his weapon into the air.

Chaos. People tumbled over each other trying to flee. Abel Os ran toward the guard, pleading with him to stop firing. He realized that the guard was a youth from his neighborhood.

"Ali, what are you doing here?"

"We're going to get that asshole the Prince!"

"Didn't you join for the sake of God? And here you are, fighting someone from your own city?"

But it was hopeless. The fighters continued to fire rounds into the morning sky. "Get back," a young fighter screamed at the crowd, cocking his weapon. His eyes were bloodshot. "Get back!"

The Prince's fighters climbed the rooftops, firing down at the Aleppo rebels. Smoke rose from the streets. Now the earth shook. Chunks of concrete exploded in puffs—the Aleppo fighters were launching RPG rounds. The Prince's men were resisting valiantly, but they were outnumbered. As rounds landed, there was worry the Prince's compound would collapse. Finally, a few defenders stumbled onto the street, arms raised. The Prince was still holed up inside. The Aleppo fighters rushed in.

They found the Prince writhing on the floor. He had taken a bullet to the shoulder. Next to him, Hasan Sex was also wounded. The Aleppo fighters arrested them. Senators and members of the old Revolutionary Council accompanied the Aleppo fighters while they ransacked the Prince's compound. As the Prince was carried away on a stretcher, a senator leaned over and spat on his face. Another senator shouted, "This is what happens to anyone who dares fight us!"

The fighters set the Prince's headquarters ablaze, and his faction's documents went up in flames.

That afternoon, the senate announced that the Prince and his lieutenants had been sent to prison in Aleppo.

As the guns fell silent, a strange mood overtook the city. For the first time, revolutionaries had turned on each other. It was not until evening that anyone ventured out. Some came to gawk at the visitors, with their long beards and state-of-the-art weaponry. Some milled near the scene of the battle, collecting shell casings as mementos.

The next morning, the Aleppo fighters packed up their belongings. The procession of 4×4s, mounted with machine guns, and with six, seven, eight men packed onto the beds, advanced slowly through the streets. All told, some seven hundred fighters had descended upon this republic to capture a single man. Residents lined the street to watch the force depart. As the convoy disappeared, people returned to their lives. Shops and schools opened. The senate scheduled a meeting for that evening. The old council members warned other factions of what was in store should they, too, ignore the rule of law. For the first time since liberation, rebel groups dismantled their checkpoints. The Revolutionary Police now assumed these posts.

After a few hours, people learned that not all seven hundred Aleppo fighters had left their city. In fact, exactly six men stayed behind. None of them had ever been to Manbij before. None of them were even Syrian.

| THIRTEEN |

April 2013

NEWS

Mr. Zakaria al-Khalaf gave a lecture on the concept of freedom in Islam in the Manbij Al-Aqsa mosque, and it consisted of the definition of freedom and its types (freedom of religious beliefs, ideologies, speech, and criticism), and he offered a positive conception of freedom. —***Path***

A Revolutionary Police officer named Abdul Karim told us that most Revolutionary Police officers stopped working because the payment of salaries was stopped. —***Sun***

Two demonstrations took place after Friday prayers in different locations, although they shared the same goal. One could be described as Islamic, and the other as secular. . . . The question remains: why divide our demonstrations when we have a common enemy and shared goals? —***Weekly Letters***

ABDUL HADI SPURNED—AGAIN

The tension in the city, for months subdued, now rose. What the old council and senators had achieved—the removal of a vigilante—they paid for with trust, the revolution's true currency. There was a distance now in the faces of revolutionaries, an aloofness in their greetings. The sense at RYM headquarters, no doubt shared by the other assemblies, was that a line had been crossed. Innocent blood—revolutionary blood—had been shed. Abdul Hadi thought of his brother Muhammad, president of the new council: When he'd been advised to arrest members of the old council for refusing to relinquish power, he'd declined. And yet the old council did something much worse: They nearly sparked a civil war on the streets of Manbij.

For Abdul Hadi, this realization had been months in the making. In that sweaty schoolhouse on liberation day, the council had announced its membership without even gesturing toward inclusivity. Then the old guard blithely ignored the election that had so inspired the street and the assemblies. Even that heartbreak could have been forgiven; activists labored for months to force an agreement between the two councils. Yet these efforts, too, had failed. The old council jealously guarded their privileges, budging for no one. For months, Abdul Hadi had been sounding the alarm among his comrades, because he, more than anyone, understood what lay behind the cold handshakes and airy promises of the old guard. Years ago, his brother Muhammad and Ahmed Rahmo, now competing council heads, had been engineering firm partners—and on that first day, back in 2006, when Muhammad had come home nearly jumping with excitement about the new venture, his mother warned: Be careful with these people, they will never accept us.

Abdul Hadi did not mention that memory to friends, but it must have haunted him. He could not see himself in the faces of the old council. Take Munzer Salal, the suave businessman and religious scholar, one of the lights of the old council. The majority of Manbij's population consisted of people who'd emigrated, over the generations, from the countryside. Many, like Abdul Hadi's father, had grown up in the fields, pants rolled to their ankles. They read and wrote with difficulty. They moved to the city for their children, who found jobs in construction or transport or, if they were fortunate, earned degrees. Munzer and his ilk were cut from a different cloth. Their families had emigrated from other cities, their hands were delicate, they managed estates. They were captains of industry or titans of real estate. They even spoke a different tongue; whereas most Manbij dwellers spoke *shawi*, the guttural drawl of the hinterlands, those of the velvet class spoke *hadhrani*, with its clean tones and aspirated phonemes. So one way to tell the story of Manbij is to speak of the *hadhar* and the *shawaya*, the urban and rural, the "civilized" and the tribal—categories that overlap, though not perfectly, with those of rich and poor. This was the story Abdul Hadi told himself. It was also the subtext of divisions in the revolutionary ranks, which sowed rancor in debates about strategy and tactics. The question of who governed Manbij was not merely about who had the right to set tax policy or distribute bread—It was also a question of identity: To whom did the city truly belong?

Matters came to a head when revolutionary authorities in Aleppo announced elections for a Provincial Council. The body would govern all liberated territory in Aleppo Province, an area that included Manbij, among many other cities. Each city could nominate candidates, and the revolutionaries of Manbij agreed to put forth a unified list, comprised of members of both councils. To guard against air raids, the election would take place in Turkey. But when the delegation from Manbij arrived, members of the new council realized that their names had never been submitted—the old council members had only advanced their own candidates. In the ensuing uproar, Muhammad Bisher nearly came to blows with members of the old council. But nothing could be done, and they were expelled from the premises. In the end, Manbij elected a single delegate—Hasan Nefi—to represent the city to the national and international community.

Back in Manbij, Abdul Hadi exploded in fury. "This is a coup!" he shouted in an RYM meeting. He was ready to fight the old council members himself. His dire prophesies had come true: The old council believed the city was their rightful property.

The Turkey fiasco rang the death knell for the new council. Without control of the bakeries, the council had no means to tax the population, and without a seat on the Provincial Council, they had neither foreign aid nor nationwide legitimacy. The old council forced Muhammad Bisher and his colleagues to vacate their headquarters. The People's Assembly, the body that elected the new council, was declared defunct. The old council and the senate were now the sole rulers of the city.

RYM took to the streets. They held signs that read "Thieves!" and "The Aleppo Council does not represent Manbij!" The press lambasted what it saw as usurpation. "Where is our unified revolutionary council?" the *Path* raged. "What happened to our pain and worries?" The Free Students Union warned in a statement, "The people who have rebelled against a 40-year-old regime will not hesitate one moment to bring down this council!"

Abdul Hadi was stricken. He tried to imagine himself transported back to that warmer, more innocent era, when fellow revolutionaries marched arm in arm, and a thick wall separated the forces of hope and reaction. Try as he might, though, he could not unsee the hidden order of things, the gears and levers of greed and ambition that made this city run. But this gift of sight was also a curse. Abdul Hadi began to feel utterly foolish. His whole life had been an education in a basic truth: that the planet was already apportioned—every office, every building and plot of land belonged to someone. Even the smoggy air, the green waters of the Euphrates, the silvery carp had their rightful owners. That was the way it was, and that was the way it always would be. When hearing the news of the old council's "coup" in Turkey, he tried to convince himself that the city belonged to those wealthy men, that resisting their stake would be like resisting the weather. But he could not accept such a conclusion. The revolution had peeled his eyes open; even as he saw the hidden realm of power and greed, he realized that at the heart of the old council's putsch was not ambition but fear. They were terrified that the city's lower ranks would sit with them at the same table, shake their hands as if they were all men, as if there were no masters and no servants, as if the city was a common bounty. Abdul Hadi could draw only one conclusion: The senators and members of the old council were no different from the Baath Party—they were enemies of the revolution.

Abdul Hadi put pen to paper. He lacked the gift of language like the poets and scholars of the old council, but he believed he had more fire in his heart than the whole lot. For the *Sun*, he wrote:

> There are people who pretend to be revolutionaries who have slipped into this revolution, since they did not join the revolution for the sake of victory for the oppressed or for the sake of salvation for Syria. Instead, they joined for money and money only. This group of thugs has removed their masks and revealed their true face.... We refuse to let the blood of the martyrs and heroes be cheapened, so we the people will hold them accountable for their filthy deeds, just as we will for Bashar and his followers.
>
> In the end, only the truth will prevail.

Convinced that the Turkey elections were rigged, Abdul Hadi raised this point at RYM meetings, and the others were inclined to agree. Everyone knew *Valley of the Wolves*—the Turkish soap from which Maymati had borrowed his nom de guerre. The hero of the series is a state employee who secretly works for the so-called Council of Elders, who actually run everything. "This is the deep state," one of the new council members recalled. "The Aleppo council elections were the same—there were people behind the curtain, a deep state, who decided who will run and who will win. The rest was mere formality." Uday and Abdul Hadi were now arguing that the people had risen to overthrow Assad's deep state only to replace it with another. Abdul Hadi began to say at RYM meetings, "The Pharaoh is dead. Long live the Pharaoh!"

ABEL OS LOSES HIS REVOLUTION

When he considered the events, Abel Os felt as if he were again locked in that tiny room, cinderblock walls on all sides. Life had been simpler when he was kneeling on the tiled floor, the voice shouting "unity or freedom," his muscles tensing before the blow. Outside, his comrades were marching shoulder to shoulder, saints and martyrs all—and in there, in the vise of the death machine, he had survived on the strength of such knowledge.

Now he felt enclosed again, hemmed in on all sides—but who was out there? Looking back, those old strictures revealed themselves as fable. Good and evil, right and wrong, were supposed to keep to their respective sides. He'd marched hand in hand with men he'd once called "my lord." The revolution was supposed to be the great equalizer.

Yet if the Revolutionary Council and the senate were fanning the flames of division, how were his own comrades responding? He worried that Abdul Hadi was no longer concerned with merely acting as the revolution's watchdog. At RYM meetings, Abdul Hadi had begun calling the council and the senate members *shabiha*—which, as much as Abel Os agreed that the council had trampled on democratic principles, was a stone too far. He worried that Abdul Hadi's fixation on the council stemmed from the fact that his brother had been sidelined. And Abel Os couldn't help but sympathize. But he recognized that Abdul Hadi's envy and resentment were hardening, and he saw in his eyes something new, something worrying: a rage great and deep, as if a lifetime of psychic wounds had coalesced into pure hatred.

Abel Os tried to talk with him, but Abdul Hadi retorted, as if reading from a script, about the accumulating grievances of the past few months: the overturned election, the rising prices, the crime. He swore he harbored no envy, that his rage was not personal—it was for the city. Yet Abel Os could see that it was impossible to separate the personal and the political; not when Abdul Hadi nursed memories of being bullied in the schoolyard for his ramshackle house, not when he'd watched the wealthy boys be lavished with personal coaches and personal tutors, not when he was forced to relinquish his soccer dreams to become a gym teacher. Abdul Hadi saw, everywhere, the hidden hand of privilege keeping doors shut. *Of course* this was personal, he said, because the city belonged to him as much as it did the Revolutionary Council.

Abel Os grew despondent. He agreed with Abdul Hadi's diagnosis, but what was to be done? The regime was unleashing massacre upon massacre, while the revolution was devouring itself. After the Prince battle, Abel Os couldn't bring himself to leave his house. For the first time in years, his thoughts returned to

Tear of Roses. His old shop had been more than a business—it was a world. There, in the virtue of a hard day's work, far from squabbling and jealousy, he'd glimpsed salvation. Those old days with the radio blasting, the pot of *juz muz* on simmer, the neighbors beseeching him like supplicants—there, he had value. There, he meant something. Here, in this revolution, he could offer nothing.

A week passed, and Abel Os did not attend a Revolutionary Youth Movement meeting. The group felt his absence; Abdul Hadi, Oday, and the others visited his house, pleading for his return. But he was stubborn.

Without Abel Os, the RYM headquarters felt hollow. Still, its members carried on, planning protests, holding debates. The city was quieter than it had been in months. After the Prince's fall, many factions were cowed. Crime was down. And it was in this context, on a warm evening in April, nine months into the city's republican experiment, that the RYM headquarters received visitors.

A MEETING OF WORLDS ON A WARM APRIL EVENING

Abdul Hadi left home in the mornings, walking along the colonnade of pine trees on Post Office Street, past the two-story houses with their oriel windows, past the cement walls, which were decorated with fragments of verse, images of daffodils, crude drawings of missiles and barrel bombs, the shaded outlines of the Syrian map, the likeness of a child gazing up to the heavens. He entered Security Square, now free of blast walls or checkpoints. The square was really a wide avenue, crisscrossing Post Office Street, with buildings and landmarks crowding around. It was a vista rich with meaning: It was here that Oday had planted a flag on liberation day; RYM's headquarters stood on one side of the street, and on the other, the Revolutionary Council kept their office. Between them stood the Cultural Center, still closed. But it was the building standing exactly where Post Office Street ended that caught Abdul Hadi's attention. This was the Youth Center, where as a child he'd kicked around a soccer ball. Here, on a clear summer's day, he'd been able to peer down the length of Post Office Street to spot the sea blue facade of his home. Since liberation, the Youth Center had been abandoned, the soccer leagues canceled for fear of air strikes. But now, six visitors—who'd stayed behind when the Aleppo brigades left—had made it their new home.

They visited RYM headquarters one evening. The muezzins had finished their song, and the electric lights had come alive. Three guests were seated in the courtyard. As on most nights, one would have heard the susurrus of the mulberry trees, the faintest patter of gunfire. The guests were doing the rounds, as they wished to acquaint themselves with Manbij's democracy. The main speaker introduced himself as Abu Huzayfa the Egyptian. He was squat, with long hair and a long, tar-black beard. Clad in a bandolier and carrying a Kalashnikov, he appeared not a day over twenty-five. He introduced his "brothers": Abu Qatada the Tunisian, thick, long-haired, cross-eyed, and Abu Noah, tall, almost beardless. Neither said a word.

Abu Huzayfa the Egyptian explained that they journeyed to Syria to fight against the dictator, joining a tiny rebel outfit called the Emigrants and Partisans Battalion, and had waged many battles in the slums of Aleppo. He showed off his body, pocked and riven with wounds; he'd narrowly escaped death in an air strike and had taken a bullet to the leg. He and his "brothers" had once found themselves trapped in an alley, tanks closing in. They'd stared death in the face, readied themselves for it, when their comrades broke the siege. They'd rescued civilians from the rubble, carrying dazed children on their back, as bullets hailed above.

The RYM members were impressed.

Oday asked if they had run checkpoints in the slums. Abu Huzayfa laughed. "We're not here to interfere in people's lives, we're here to fight tyranny." He was a deeply pious man, he said, and had left friends and family to battle injustice in Syria.

The RYM members couldn't help but admire such selflessness. Abdul Hadi and his friends had also risked their lives and futures to stand against tyranny, and through the torture and humiliation they never lost faith that the world would take notice. And yet the so-called international community had abandoned them. Here, in the flesh, was actual international solidarity—and they were requesting nothing in return.

Abu Huzayfa asked RYM about their mission. Oday explained that they organized protests against the regime and acted as a watchdog, holding the revolutionary authorities' feet to the fire. Abu Huzayfa again laughed. "Protests? Do you think this regime will politely pack up and leave because a few groups are raising banners in Manbij?"

No one spoke.

"This regime understands only one language—force. That's why we are here, that's why we've risked our lives."

Abu Huzayfa asked the group who they expected to take Assad's place. The group offered various answers: revolutionary councils, a people's parliament. Abu Huzayfa shook his head. "From what you've described, your city is divided. You can hardly govern three hundred thousand people. And yet these councils and parliaments are going to govern thirty-five million people across Syria?"

The group went quiet again.

"What matters," he continued, "is the moral character of whoever replaces Assad. What if we overthrow Assad just to have a new Saddam Hussein take his place?"

"The Pharaoh is dead. Long live the Pharaoh," Abdul Hadi piped up.

"Exactly. What matters is justice. We need a government that will enforce justice." That word, *adalah*, had hardly left protesters' lips. Instead, they chanted one word, freedom, *horreya*, as if it were an incantation. Freedom of speech, freedom of thought, freedom, freedom, freedom. What about justice? Oday had to admit that nine months of *freedom* had brought division, acrimony, and poverty.

"I'm ready to die," Abu Huzayfa said, "for a *just* world. There's no other reason to be on this earth." The injustice began with Assad, but had spread, like a virus, to the entire body politic. How many people were defiled by living forty years under this regime? In fact, he said, the *Path* had carried an editorial on this theme not long before. He found the issue and read aloud:

> Assad corrupted the minds and souls and patriotism of the people. He turned them into programmed machines who praise and worship the Pharaoh. I will give you an example: During the period in which the Free Army was liberating areas held by security forces in al-Tabqa, they found written intelligence reports about children under the age of seven. My point is not about the corruption of the security forces but about the simple citizen who wrote these reports and sent them to the security forces. There are many like this citizen.

This was an uprising, then, to cleanse souls. When you snitch on neighbors to the secret police, or remain silent while your neighbor is being sent to a charnel house, you've abandoned all morality. And for what? For the sake of one man. "We've turned the dictator into God, and in the process, forgotten the real God, who is greater than all of us," Abu Huzayfa said. The chaos in the city, the competing councils, the power plays and rivalries—the so-called revolutionaries want to replace the old God with a new god, themselves. "But there is only one God, and if you believe in Him, you will be willing to die for your country, for your fellow humans."

It was an impressive performance. Abdul Hadi, above all, was moved by Abu Huzayfa's eloquence. Unlike the council members, unlike the so-called international community, here were men willing to live their ideals. Abdul Hadi did not have a religious bone in his body. He loved the pleasures of this world better than anything on offer in the next. But he could respect men who'd left the comforts of home to journey far, and risk much, to stand up for what was right, what was just.

Abu Huzayfa explained that the battles on the Aleppo front lines continued, but that he and his "brothers" had grown disgusted with the corruption in the ranks of the rebels. Three days earlier, they—the six men who had come from Aleppo and stayed—had quit their rebel group and declared allegiance to a new entity, which was calling itself the Islamic State of Iraq and Greater Syria. They were committed to fighting the tyrant, he said, but were equally engrossed in the question of what came next.

He said, as they took their leave: "If we don't think about the future now, the future will pass us by."

That evening, RYM members discussed the meeting. The visitors were unlike any they had encountered. They were gracious and eloquent, but there was an ethereal, mysterious quality to them. The men acted as if they possessed a knowledge of such secrecy and import that it concerned the fate of the entire city, maybe the entire world. Oday said he'd welcome anyone who opposed the regime, but wanted to learn more. Another RYM member observed that, as foreigners, they were refreshingly not linked to local politics. But others contended that their foreign status was precisely what was concerning. Manbij was already awash in rumor and innuendo. Could they trust newcomers who had no ties to any faction in the city? In the end, what everyone could agree on was that they knew too little about the visitors. It was decided that RYM should keep its distance.

But at home, Abdul Hadi's thoughts lingered on the Youth Center, on the visitors with bulging biceps and bandoliers, the steely-eyed look of Abu Huzayfa. Abdul Hadi wondered if they, as outsiders, might grasp the enormity of the violation the old Revolutionary Council had inflicted on the precepts of solidarity and brotherhood. The next day, against the advice of his comrades, he decided to pay a visit.

A black flag hung over the entrance to the Youth Center. Printed on it, in a strange font, were the words "There is no god but God" and "Muhammad is the apostle of God." Abdul Hadi was ushered into the courtyard. Two men, wearing what appeared to be military vests, stood by the door. Abdul Hadi realized with horror that they were strapped in dynamite. He began to feel he'd made a mistake. The air was thick, treacly. One of the dynamite-wearing guards brought glasses of tea and *lahmacun* pizza. It was hard to believe he'd grown up within these walls; the doors had been shut since the air strike a few months earlier, and the place had gone to seed. He sat in the shade of a mulberry tree. The tiling was speckled with the stains of fallen berries, like little gun wounds. The smell of rotten berries hung in the air. Swarms of flies were moving across the courtyard, as if they comprised a single organism racked by strange, convulsive spasms. The guards watched him eat without uttering a word. A strange noise issued from the building. He listened to what sounded like the groan of a distant lawnmower, or the plaintive gasps of a man moaning. Or was it a song? Someone was singing. In the quiet air, the voice carried. The flies were swarming Abdul Hadi's hands as he ate. Flies drowned in his tea.

When he was finally summoned to the rear courtyard to meet Abu Huzayfa, Abdul Hadi felt nauseous. Abu Huzayfa and Abu Qatada were seated on plastic lawn chairs. They were armed and wearing dynamite vests. Abdul Hadi said he was curious to know the group's opinion on the divides plaguing the city. He began to narrate the story from the beginning: the announcement of the Revolutionary Council, the election, the "coup." Suddenly, the earth rattled as a jet crossed the Manbij sky. The ISIS members seemed unconcerned. But visions of thick smoke, of hands reaching up from collapsed beams, must have flashed through Abdul Hadi's mind, for he immediately took his leave.

That evening, when RYM members learned that Abdul Hadi had visited ISIS headquarters, they warned him to stay away. When Abel Os heard about the visit, he tore into his younger comrade. "We've been praying for a long time," he said. "Who are these Islamic battalions to come and tell us how to pray?" In Abel Os's view, ISIS and other Islamic battalions had nothing to do with the revolution. After all, he didn't kneel before the adjutant in that dank room so that these interlopers could raise a black flag. The only flag he recognized, the only banner that transcended the acrimony and the jealousy, was the tri-star standard that hung outside RYM's headquarters. For those three stars, he would fight, he would die. Not for the black flag. Abdul Hadi thought that Abel Os was overreacting, and he tried again to convince him to participate in RYM meetings.

But Abel Os had seen enough and resigned that evening.

Without Abel Os, their founder, their north star, RYM members felt orphaned. A dark mood pervaded the meetings, which only lightened when someone brought up the old days: the whistle protest, when Abel Os was mistaken for the security chief Abu Roz, prompting activists to flee; the time Abel Os hung Assad in effigy; his triumphant return from the lockup. All only two years earlier, but it felt like decades had passed.

RYM elected as its new leader a young man named Nabeel. Shy, unlettered, a habitué of smoke cafes, known for his affairs with older men, Nabeel was a close friend of Abdul Hadi's. In fact, some might say he was in Abdul Hadi's thrall. The two were rarely seen apart. While some RYM members were on the fence about the Revolutionary Council, Nabeel understood Abdul Hadi's rage—and was ready to help.

A DEBATE ABOUT THE HIGHEST PRINCIPLES

In mid-April, much of the country's attention was on the Syria-Lebanon border, where rebel forces were dug in against regime soldiers and Hezbollah. Just four months prior, it had seemed as if Assad was teetering on the brink of collapse, but the injection of thousands of Hezbollah fighters had saved the regime. Now it was the rebels who were in retreat. In Manbij, activists were holding solidarity protests, blood drives, and fundraising campaigns to assist their beleaguered brothers on the front lines.

There was a newfound push for the revolutionary factions to put their differences aside. The efforts culminated in a citywide summit in the anteroom of an old house downtown. Abdul Hadi and Oday were there, as were Munzer Salal and other luminaries from the Revolutionary Council, along with leading senators. As soon as the meeting began, Abdul Hadi hurled accusations at the other parties. His words were bitter, his eyes red, his voice strained and tight. Munzer Salal explained the twists and turns of the previous months and Abdul Hadi must have thought: *lies, lies, lies!* He demanded an apology from the old Revolutionary Council. Surprisingly, the council members acknowledged they had been hasty both in dismissing the results of the election and in their Turkey machinations.

The mood softened. The council proposed a new election, open to everyone, that would settle the matter once and for all. Oday and most other RYM members were placated, and the meeting ended with an agreement to halt protests against fellow revolutionaries. The group—the senate, the council, and various assemblies—would henceforth hold joint rallies against the regime. Only the tri-star standard would be raised; the black flag was banned. A cheer went up among the participants, which morphed into a chant: "The people want the downfall of the regime!" That Friday, the city witnessed an energetic joint demonstration, and hope rose that unity was at hand.

A few days later, there were nationwide protests against Hezbollah and Iran. In Manbij, protesters thronged Central Square, where senators, council members, and RYM activists took turns on the megaphone. Abdul Hadi issued an address about unity, about burying the past—words he shouted even as his chest burned with the desire to hold that past to account.

He handed the megaphone to Munzer Salal, who spoke about Manbij. Theirs was a city of great heritage, he said. The Assyrians built a capital here, and the settlement subsequently passed into many hands—to Alexander the Great's progeny, and to the Romans, who dubbed it Hieropolis, and whose memory is preserved in the crumbling walls, the semi-buried stelae. In the Middle Ages, some of the greatest figures in classical Arab poetry lived here, their names gracing the city's schools and boulevards: Abu Firas al-Hamdani, al-Buhturi. Manbij birthed revered poets well into the twentieth century, including Omar Abu Risha, who became Syria's national bard. The city's treasures—original manuscripts, coins—were housed alongside thousands of volumes of literature, philosophy, and religion in the Cultural Center. Science and knowledge, verse and prose—these achievements were Manbij's gifts to the world.

And now, Munzer continued, these treasures were in danger. A battalion freshly arrived in the city—calling themselves the Islamic State of Iraq and Greater Syria—had just expanded from their headquarters in the Youth Center to occupy a second facility: the Cultural Center. Since liberation day, the council had resisted efforts by factions and assemblies to use the space; precious volumes and artifacts might go up in flames if the regime targeted whoever was inside. What's more, several valuable generators and refrigerators were stored

there. Now, ISIS had broken the locks and entered without permission. "The Cultural Center does not belong to any faction," Munzer shouted. "It belongs to the city!" People gathered around him, cheering his speech. "One city, one hand, one history!" voices shouted. The bodies swarmed, and soon a section of the crowd split off, Munzer at its head. They were marching to the Cultural Center.

Abdul Hadi could not believe it. "You are splitting the rally!" he shouted. It felt like the old story repeating itself: a pledge for unity evaporating at the council's behest. They had agreed to refrain from criticizing any faction in the city, but here again was Munzer, unilaterally changing course. It was as if he and his gilded friends could not help themselves.

RYM activists marched after the first contingent. Security Square filled with protesters. Munzer and his group were chanting, "Out, out, out!" Two ISIS guards, wearing dynamite vests, eyed the crowd. Abdul Hadi and RYM launched a counterprotest, shouting, "Unity, unity, unity!" But Abdul Hadi was losing control: Some counterprotesters began to wave black flags and denounce the council as thieves. The mad jumble of chants continued for minutes. The ISIS guards appeared nervous. "Get back!" one growled. "Back, back!" But the protesters, egged on by Munzer and allies, pushed ahead. The young men were in a fury, hurling insults at the ISIS guards. In truth, they knew little about these six newcomers; rather, their rage was directed at any faction that chose to occupy city property instead of battling on the front lines. The ISIS guards shouted back in their thick Egyptian and Tunisian accents. Finally a guard raised his Kalashnikov above the heads of the mob, aiming into the sky, and loosed rounds. As the shots rang out, people tumbled over each other in panic. Then protesters regained their composure and pressed forward again. Fearing a bloodbath, Abdul Hadi and Oday raced toward the guards. But it was too late, the mob was already at the gates. The guards aimed rifles at the sweaty protesters.

An ISIS commander emerged from the Cultural Center. He approached Munzer and invited him inside. "Let's understand each other," he said. "We're on the same side."

Munzer entered the Cultural Center and was escorted to an office, where the commander introduced himself as Abu Azzam the Egyptian. Munzer asked him what right his group had to occupy the Cultural Center, to which the Egyptian replied that the premises were vacant, and they were safeguarding its holdings. The conversation continued for some time, until Abu Azzam finally asked Munzer what he and his comrades hoped to achieve with their councils and senate. As Munzer began to reply, the Egyptian interrupted. "Tell me about democracy. What do you think about it?" Munzer knew he was speaking to a man seized with the convictions of faith, and being no stranger to religion himself—he was, after all, a sheikh with a degree in religious law—explained that democracy was not blasphemy. In fact, it was consistent with Islam, and perorated on the long history of elections in Islam. "Consultation is part of Islam," he said. "And Islam tells us nothing about *how* a state should be organized. Democracy does not violate Islamic law."

But Abu Azzam asked, "What are the principles of democracy?" The question, in essence, was: Is there any value more sacred than majority rule? Suppose, for example, that the majority votes to legalize rape. This was an old worry about democracy—the tyranny of the majority—to which its defender might retort that certain principles were inviolable, no matter what the majority chose. But that means democracy is *not* a foundational principle—there are higher, more sacred values that no election should trample. What are those principles?

Some protesters outside would have surely identified these highest principles as "human rights," but Abu Azzam could ask: Where do such rights come from? Who authorized them? Are they empirical facts, or something more mysterious, difficult to pin down?

Most people don't know why they support human rights—they just "know," on pure intuition. But intuition was not good enough for Abu Azzam. Intuitions can lead us astray—history strewn with values once thought to be common sense, only to be overturned by later generations. Abu Azzam wanted hard facts, something to point to when moral disputes arose, something that was true at all times and in all places. You think it is wrong to seize someone's property for the benefit of society, and I believe it is morally right. Who's to decide? Who arbitrates when values clash? Democracy had no answer for this. In fact, democracy operated on a profound falsehood, that ordinary people can solve such problems without guidance. Look around, he said, and see the choices people make when left to their own devices. Humans need a well-hacked path, they need guardrails, they need lampposts. "This city is in chaos," he observed. Look what democracy has wrought.

An hour passed, and the debate continued. Munzer insisted that such foundational questions were irrelevant. The highest principles were known to all; they were written in our hearts. But Abu Azzam pointed out that in Syria people had flouted such principles with abandon, for decades. A dictatorship depended on the moral rot of everyone, not just the tyrant. After all, the system only works if everyone keeps quiet. Assad's system, he said, was no different than democracy—Munzer was simply replacing one arbitrary god with another. Tyranny of the majority or tyranny of the minority is still tyranny. The real principles—the principles of justice—were inscribed in the Quran, and in the sayings of the Prophet. No one could dispute the power of these moral precepts, even fourteen hundred years later. A society based on Islam, Abu Azzam declared, does not collapse into anomie.

Munzer found himself in a difficult position. For months, he'd been warning against the excesses of democracy; he was certain that too much power for too many people would spell disaster. He opposed the populism of RYM, and believed that those who know best—the educated, the wealthy—should rule in the interests of the citizenry. Yet now he found himself defending democracy against a figure to his political right. Manbij's different factions disagreed on how best to implement democracy—rule of the wealthy, or of the masses?—but never before, in all his discussions with other forces, Islamic or otherwise, had someone attacked the idea of democracy itself.

The debate grew heated. A second ISIS member appeared. He was from Tunisia and, as Munzer later recalled, "as big as Hercules." Voices were raised, and suddenly Munzer felt himself lifted off the ground, Hercules's hands gripping his sweater. "You're an infidel! What is this democracy talk!" There could only ever be one sovereign: either the people, or God. Munzer freed himself. Eventually, the door swung open and the leader of the group appeared. Are you still jabbering, he asked, and thrust a finger into Munzer's chest. "Send your people home! You are trying to create a civil war in the city!" Munzer countered, "*We* started this revolution, *we* risked our lives to protest against the regime, *we* liberated the city"—he was shouting now—"and we'll never let *you* give orders!"

The leader was wearing a vest of dynamite. He carried a Kalashnikov in one hand, a dagger in the other. He moved so close Munzer could feel his breath. "If you don't stop creating discord," he hissed, "I will cut off your head myself and hang it in Central Square."

Outside, Munzer gathered his followers and instructed them to leave. The protest, having lost its vital force, was now listless, without purpose. A few people milled about, perhaps in sheer curiosity. As Munzer was leaving, Abdul Hadi asked what had transpired indoors, but Munzer looked at him coolly, as if to say, *Leave that to the adults.*

Those who were with Abdul Hadi that day record a strange look washing over his face. He watched Munzer, that diminutive, soft-skinned man, with those perfect hands, with his entourage, disappear down the street. We can only wonder at the wheels that may have turned in that moment as Abdul Hadi stood in icy silence. The image of the mighty senator slinking away at the rebuke of those strange visitors would have impressed him deeply. The visitors' gravitas, their irreverence for the city's encrusted hierarchies, would have exerted a magnetic pull. The fresh possibility of upending the hidden order, of commanding respect, would have forced him to rethink what he'd taken as given. His brother had not participated in the protests because he was undertaking mandatory military service; if he'd been arrested, the hammer would have come down on the whole family. They could not avail themselves of the connections that an operator like Munzer enjoyed. No *wasta*, no secret life of cigars and leather couches. In another possible world, Abdul Hadi was looking down from the third story of City Hall, as Munzer and his ilk waited in the brilliant sun, like humble supplicants. *Authority*—was this what Abdul Hadi truly wanted? *What matters is justice*. The words of Abu Huzayfa, that strange Egyptian, who'd left hearth and home to journey here, would have rung in Abdul Hadi's head. *Justice*. For so long, the word *freedom* had been on his lips; but there was no freedom without justice. But justice for whom? Through most of history, in fields and towns and cities, people struggled for their daily bread, without a shred of justice, without even the hope of it. They lived, even on this very land, as serfs and slaves and concubines, entombed in the citadels of princely terror, chained to the walls and whipped, stripped of property and dignity. Such horrors predated the current regime; it was in the soil of the earth, in every nation. But he understood that history allowed moments of respite, even flickers of hope, when the meek rose against the mighty, when men stood on a plain, hand in hand, equal in body and spirit. These moments were few and far between—the epochal revolutions of the Western world; the great Arab struggles against colonialism; the likes of Che Guevara and Omar al-Mukhtar, that famed Libyan independence leader; the words and deeds of the Prophet and his companions, who rose in the name of justice, against the iniquity of the *Jahiliyyah*, the Age of Ignorance, and offered a template on how to live, and how to live with others. No, Abdul Hadi was not a religious man, but for the first time, he could appreciate how the strictures outlined by the Prophet were not mere impositions, but a guide, maybe the truest guide of all, for how to live a just life.

But for now, as the square emptied, as the ISIS guards returned to their post, as Abdul Hadi walked home with Oday and friends, his talk was not of the next world but of this one. The senators and councilmen had violated an agreement, once again. Reneged agreements and rejected elections: It was as smooth a coup as possible, and now there was no turning back. For Abdul Hadi, there could be no more appeals to brotherhood or the common good. No, only one road remained.

Revenge.

FOURTEEN

June 2013

NEWS

Dr. Ahmed Taan gave a lecture titled "What is Secularism?" held by the Islamic Action assembly, which organizes lectures every three days. —*Path*

On Monday, more than ninety young people demonstrated at the Sailboat Roundabout in Manbij against the attacks carried out by our Israeli enemy on our homeland and our people in Damascus. —*Weekly Letters*

The Girls of Tomorrow assembly invites young woman to join, under the slogan "We can build the future hand in hand." The assembly launched a reading campaign, called "Knowledge for Everyone." —*Sun*

Guests from the Muslim Brotherhood met with more than 100 intellectuals on Tuesday. This interesting and serious meeting included a lecture, the recitation of two poems, and a question-and-answer session. —*Weekly Letters*

At approximately 11:10 p.m. on Tuesday, a plane was spotted flying over Manbij.... Before 2011, children would greet an airplane by waving their hands in the air, but today they laid their palms over their hearts out of dread ... and these airplanes are paid for with our money! —*Weekly Letters*

NEW BEGINNINGS

In May, regime forces launched an offensive to recapture Qusayr, a city on the Lebanese border. Assad's forces unleashed a barrage of artillery and helicopter fire. Rebels from Aleppo and Manbij rushed to support their brethren. In response, more Hezbollah fighters arrived. The regime had relied on the Lebanese Islamist group before, but in smaller numbers; now the border skirmishes had morphed into a full-blown war between Hezbollah and the Syrian rebels.

In Manbij, revolutionaries followed the Qusayr battle blow by blow. Theirs was no longer merely a struggle against a dictatorship, a purely internal matter. The conflict had become globalized. While the revolutionaries had been abandoned by the international community, which usually meant the West, another international community—Russia, Iran, Lebanese militias—was flooding their country with guns and men to crush the revolution. In the face of external enemies, the city's internal divisions seemed frivolous. After ten months of competing councils, squabbling rebel factions, protest and counterprotest, a new mood of unity took hold on the streets. The walls were adorned with graffiti extolling the martyrs of Qusayr and with aphorisms such as "Freedom is the force of the law, not the law of force."

Senators felt the shifting winds. They decided to dissolve the Revolutionary Council and call elections for a new "unity" government. They argued that it was time to reach out to the city's disaffected parties—RYM and the Bisher council—and encourage them to run.

When the nominees of this newest Revolutionary Council were announced, RYM was split. Abdul Hadi refused to participate. "These are the same names," he said of the candidates. "The same exact names." Oday, too, boycotted, believing the nominating process to be rigged. But some RYM members took part, finding Abdul Hadi's protestations increasingly tiresome. For them, he and his followers were a captious sort. Why not give the new council a chance? The war was bigger than their divisions.

So the majority of RYM showed up for election day, which took place within the crumbling vaulted archways of Sheikh Aqeel mosque. The new council president was Mustafa Hajj Abdullah, an affable lawyer who'd earned his wings in the secret protest phase, during which he'd suffered imprisonment. In his victory speech, he pledged to abandon the exclusionary attitude of his predecessors, build a big tent, and include the opposition. He promised to resign if "fifty people submit an objection against me."

Abdullah's first task was to form a cabinet, through which he saw a chance to bridge the city's divides. Over two weeks, he convened meetings of each of Manbij's occupational groups to hold elections for cabinet posts. So the city's teachers gathered in the senate headquarters and conducted a ballot for the Education Office head. The lawyers did the same for the Legal Affairs Office, the doctors for the Department of Health, the mosque imams for the Office of Religious Affairs, and municipal workers for the Public Services Office. The leadership of the Office of Military Affairs was decided by a vote among the city's eighty or so battalions. Journalists, including those from the *Path* and the *Sun,* voted on the head of the Media Office. The city's seventeen charities held a vote for the director of the Office of Humanitarian Relief. With mass voting impossible due to the threat of air strikes, such innovative electoral methods allowed the council to greatly expand its legitimacy. The vote echoed the "guild"-based republics of medieval Florence, where professional associations—textile manufacturers, cobblers, blacksmiths—were the basic political unit; guilds sent representatives to the executive body, which ran the city day-to-day.

The final cabinet list better represented groups on both sides of the city's political divide than the previous council; from the "opposition" came Abel Os, that gadfly of the revolutionary establishment, who was voted head of the Office of the Revolutionary Movement, which coordinated protests; a journalist known as "For Manbij," who'd previously belonged to the Bisher council, was elected head of the Media Office; and Mina's brother Sami Saba—Shampoo Sami—who had links to RYM, was selected head of the Office of the Secretariat. The new council included an independent "impeachment committee," which would investigate complaints against serving council members.

The priority of the new administration was bread. One of the council's first decrees read:

> To the esteemed owners of private bakeries in Manbij and the Manbij countryside! Please work to comply with the mandated price of bread at your shops.... Those who refuse to sell at the appropriate price will be penalized legally.

The decree marked the first attempt since liberation to combat inflation and price gouging by traders. This was just the beginning of the Abdullah administration's ambitious program. The council inked a deal with rebel factions guarding a huge quarry near the October Dam; by selling gravel, the council hoped to raise enough funds to purchase wheat from farmers directly, bypassing middlemen and lowering the price of bread. The council also unveiled plans to address overcrowding at the public bakeries, a situation that not only exposed people to air strikes but also forced them to turn to private bakeries. Under the new system, the council conducted the city's first census and deputized point people to distribute bread in each neighborhood. This approach saved 30 million Syrian pounds a month by cutting down on waste and corruption.

Even the harshest critics of the old council were impressed. The *Path* wrote, "We've seen that, from the beginning, [Abdullah] was different from the rest. The previous revolutionary councils operated behind closed doors . . . [but] Abdullah is open and reaches his hand to everyone, breaking the barrier between him and the street." The new council launched its own newspaper, *The Council and the People*, which carried updates on official activity. The council's military arm established a magazine, *The Free Syrian*, which carried war reportage from the front, fighters' diaries, profiles of martyrs, and fiction.

These publications were part of an explosion of new periodicals to hit the city: *The Declaration*, a weekly, focusing on political theory and literature; *Spaces*, a left-wing theoretical journal launched by Hasan Nefi; and *Weekly Letters*, which sought to portray Islam as a religion of peace and tolerance. RYM launched its own periodical, *Panorama*, with Abdul Hadi's penning many of the articles. And the tentacles of the internet had finally reached Manbij, as Facebook took off during this period. The forums—with names like "Exposing the Hidden Manbij" and "Manbij Eyewitness"—were bazaars of rumor, innuendo, and manifestos.

Young poets took up the pen, pitching to publishing houses, hawking chapbooks on the street. Novels, fragmentary and mimeographed, passed from hand to hand. As the city neared the one-year anniversary of liberation, people cast off the fear that defined the early days, when only the most committed revolutionaries founded assemblies and launched periodicals. Now everyone thought they could, or rather should, put thoughts to paper. They had once lived in a realm of playacting: raising a hand in salute, affixing portraits of the president to the wall, speaking with the most elliptical locutions. Now, though, due to the wild inversion of the last year, everything was laid bare: the prisons, the gears of power, the levers of wealth and prestige. Everything was fair game, an object of contemplation and criticism and even ridicule. This was a moment of shared existence, where every voice counted, and none more than any other: left-wingers, conservatives, poor, rich. From the embers of liberation arose a new beast, a *public*, a true force to be reckoned with. The papers spoke of "public opinion," the council fretted over it, the assemblies debated its essence. It lay at the heart of senate debates, pulsed beneath the tens of thousands of comments on Facebook, animated the graffiti on city walls. Anyone who wished to rule the city would have to contend with this newly awakened public.

Abdul Hadi understood this transformation better than most. He knew that to undermine the latest Revolutionary Council, which was basking in newfound popularity, he would have to strike where it was most vulnerable: religion.

ON SECULARISM

Ten months of republican rule in Manbij raised more questions than it answered. What is the nature of freedom? What is the role of belief, duty, and solidarity in fashioning a government? As Assad's war machine continued to churn through towns and villages, and the rebel-controlled areas continued to suffer lawlessness, some activists said the very idea of freedom was insufficient if it was not paired with morality. But which morality? The ethical universe of the revolution, until now, could be described as "liberal morality." This doctrine goes something like this: Everyone has basic rights because they are human beings. People should not be unjustly imprisoned or tortured; they should be free to live life as they see fit, so long as they do not harm others; they should be free to speak their mind. Liberal morality says that our most important duty to others is to respect their rights. It is a series of don'ts—don't torture, don't falsely imprison, don't impede. It demands, at its essence, that we respect negative freedom.

In Manbij, after ten months of soaring inequality and rampant criminality, liberal morality came under criticism. After all, a society cannot be based solely on negative freedom, the freedom from interference. There remains the question of what *positive* duties we owe each other. Should we redistribute wealth, and if so, by how much? How should we educate our children? How should we organize society so that fellow citizens can live their best lives—that is, so that they can flourish? Two of the city's eighty rebel units were Islamist—the Levant Free Men and the tiny group called ISIS. And among the city's forty assemblies were a handful of new Islamic organizations. These groups argued that liberal morality was insufficient and possibly harmful—and that a better morality was on offer. Just as liberal morality provided a set of instructions for how we should behave toward each other, religion provided its own code—one that, its proponents argued, was richer and more supportive of human needs. Liberal morality tells us we should leave each other alone—but religion tells us we should actively care for each other.

Many revolutionaries saw no conflict between these two moral systems. To them, liberalism could coexist with religion. This is a core assumption of secularism—and the leadership of the revolution, from the senate to the Revolutionary Council to most assemblies, was secular. But what, exactly, is secularism? The *Path* offered the canonical definition:

> The secular state treats all the citizens of Syria equally, regardless of their religious affiliations. . . . This means separating *power* from religion. The English philosopher John Locke is the first to lay the foundations of a secular state; according to him, the state's purpose is to look after the worldly interests of its citizens, while religion seeks to save souls in the hereafter. The state, even with its laws and its weapons, cannot guarantee our survival in the hereafter, and therefore *it does not have the right to force its citizens to pray*. In fact, John Locke was himself religious, and he justified his preference for secularism in order to *preserve* religion from the manipulations of power.

So secularism is not atheism. Instead, the doctrine concerns the relationship between government and faith. Those revolutionaries arguing for a separation of mosque and state—who, incidentally, considered themselves devout Muslims—pointed to Syria's multiethnic, multi-confessional society. "The future Syria," declared the *Path*, "is a free and civil Syria, where everyone—*everyone*—lives in freedom and dignity, together in a beautiful mosaic."

What could be so terrible about that? In public lectures and on the written page, Islamist thinkers in Manbij offered three rebuttals. First, they pointed to the hypocrisy of Western secular powers, who refused to support the Syrian freedom struggle. What good was secularism if secular powers did nothing to prevent human rights atrocities?

Next, they lambasted the Baath regime's forty years of secular rule and pointed out that history's greatest crimes had come at the hands of secularists: "Have I told you about history's executioner, the secular communist from Russia, Stalin?" thundered one writer in the *Path*. "And who is Putin? He springs from Stalinism."

But the most profound critique offered by Islamists was that it is in fact impossible to be truly religious in a secular society. Their argument hinged on the difference between the laws laid down by governments and moral codes. Every society is governed by laws. Human institutions—courts and legislatures—create these laws. These laws can be whatever a state decides. But what justifies these laws? How do we know when a human-made law is unjust? Only by reference to some other standard—some moral code or higher law.

Senators and Revolutionary Council members believed it was possible to be Muslim and secular. This could be accomplished by making religion a purely private matter: It would be up to each citizen which faith they chose to adopt. Islamists pointed out, however, that this rarely works in practice. A citizen must follow the laws of the society in which she lives. When those laws are based on a higher law that is not Islam, she will be forced to either break the law or violate the precepts of her faith. For example, suppose the revolutionary government of Manbij outlawed discrimination on the basis of sexual orientation. Then the business owner who refused to serve a homosexual—citing his faith—would be unable to practice his religion fully.

Over time, because people are loath to break the law, they end up reinterpreting—and therefore changing—the tenets of their faith. Eventually, the principles of their religion are modified and no longer violate the state's foundational values. That raises the question: Why would anyone then bother adhering to their religion at all if it no longer offers distinctive moral guidance? This was the Islamists' fear—that secularism would force people to modify or even lose their faith. Secularists believe they are promoting pluralism, but in fact on key questions—adultery, abortion, punishment, and so on—only one set of values can form the basis of law, and all who disagree will be forced to abandon their beliefs or reshape them in profound ways, until their religion becomes so watered down as to be unrecognizable.

Religious liberals responded by arguing that personal faith, even when forced to accommodate the parameters stipulated by the secular state, could still exert a powerful force in an individual's life. Religion is much more, they argued, than following rules like those relating to abortion or homosexuality—it is also a metaphysical doctrine. They resented the Islamists' charge that their version of Islam was watered down, arguing instead that their faith merely evolved to accommodate changing times.

Regardless of which side of this debate is correct, what the liberals failed to appreciate was that Islamists were animated by a genuine concern: the loss of religion and, with it, religious identity. Islamists predicted that when religious values get subordinated to secular values, religion gradually disappears. Such a process, they argued, had already happened in the West: over centuries, many Orthodox Jews became reform Jews under pressure from the secular state and culture. Over time, many reform Jews no longer viewed Judaism as a matter of ritual and belief but merely as a cultural identity. And Islamists were keen to point out that church attendance has plummeted in the West in recent decades.

What's at stake in the secularism debate is not merely whether we should learn to live with diversity, but the prospect of losing religion itself.

"Those ignorant fools know nothing about Islam!" railed a writer in the Manbij weekly *Free Thought*. "They think Islam has nothing to do with politics and forget that Islam is a *complete* system." Islam, argued a writer in the *Sun*, is ultimately about how to live with others and ensure the moral health of everyone. "Islam is a way of life, and life is not *just* without all of us taking care of everyone's material needs and helping develop everyone's intellectual and psychological faculties."

For the past ten months, the city had adopted secularism, and to what end? The nihilistic slaughter of families, the exorbitant prices in the souk, the kidnappings—these were taking place in a context in which faith had receded, hidden behind closed doors and in the whispers of prayer. But faith was meant to be of this world, a tool to forge solidarity, to hold each other to account. "After the failure of socialism and communism, and after that of secular capitalism," declared a *Sun* writer, "they invented a new intellectual system under the title of 'religious liberalism.' But 'religious liberalism' is a mask for materialistic, soulless, capitalistic ideas. . . . Our society will not be satisfied except with the application of an Islamic system in its complete form."

| FIFTEEN |

June 2013

NEWS

The Free Aleppo Provincial Council created a political bureau, and Mr. Hasan al-Nefi was elected to head this office. —*Sun*

The staff of al-Shifa Hospital has gone on strike after one of the battalions assaulted a doctor and nurse at the hospital. —*Path*

After he had gone missing for two months, the ten-year-old child Mousab al-Alawi, from the village of Hasan Agha, which belongs to Manbij city, was found dead in a hole next to the house of one of his neighbors called Bassam. The killer—Bassam—lured the victim to his house and told him to enter the hole, which he had recently dug ... and closed the hole with the victim inside. In the meantime, the killer sent a message to the father of the victim demanding a ransom of [$25,000], but the father of the child ... did not pay the ransom because it was too large and he could not afford it. —*Path*

The judiciary system is the cornerstone of the modern state. The strength of the state is measured by the fairness of its judiciary system.... [Our] court should supply the revolution with justice, supervise the Free Syrian Army personnel, and become the nucleus of a new Syria, a Syria of justice and equality. —*Path*

People say: If the court executed just one kidnapper in Central Square, our situation would change! Because those who are unafraid of God's punishment need a swift punishment in this world to be deterred! —*Weekly Letters*

Statement No. 1 was issued by ISIS for the cities of Manbij and Jarablus. The statement asked that the smuggling taking place across the Turkish border be stopped, especially the smuggling of livestock and other goods, as it causes suffering for the people.
—*Panorama*

A GRIM DISCOVERY

Out in the country, not far from the main highway, among the olive trees, a shepherd chanced upon the body of a human male. Blood was streaked across his pale face. A section of his right temple was missing. Somehow, the man was still breathing. He was rushed to the public hospital, then transferred to Turkey, but doctors could not save him. According to his ID card, his name was Musa Jasim.

Musa Jasim did not advance beyond the sixth grade, according to a relative, "due to laziness in studies and a love of work." From age eleven he accompanied his father, a plumber, on the job. For years, Musa (Arabic for Moses) worked for the municipality unclogging drains, a tiring and thankless profession but one that allowed the family to build a nest egg, culminating in the purchase of a silver Saab. He started working as a taxi driver. At eighteen, he married, and within a few years he had three young children and a fourth on the way.

One evening, he was idling in his Saab at a roundabout when he accepted a few passengers and drove off.

He did not return home that night.

THE INVESTIGATION

The Revolutionary Police opened a murder investigation. Musa's silver Saab was nowhere to be found. The police issued an alert to the factions and assemblies and gas stations and mechanic garages and car washes, describing the make and model. Ten days later, a Saab was spotted at a car wash on the outskirts of town. The license plate was different, though, and so was the paint job. Still, investigators subjected the vehicle to scrutiny, noting its dents and the tears in its upholstered seats, and they noticed, on the rear window, a clean patch where the surrounding gossamer-thin layer of dirt vanished. Someone had removed a decal. Under proper lighting, it was possible to discern its palimpsest: English letters in a flowing script spelling *m-u-s-a*.

The driver was taken in for questioning, and he explained that he had recently purchased the vehicle from a certain Manhal Hammoudi for the rock-bottom price of 75,000 Syrian pounds—$750. Unsure what they would find at the Hammoudi residence—perhaps a kidnapping gang, armed to the hilt—the police passed the finding on to the Security Brigade. This outfit, recently formed by the senate to protect the city from external threat, was increasingly called upon for matters of law and order because it was better equipped than the police. When they raided the residence, they discovered it was no gang's lair but rather the home of a dirt-poor family. Manhal Hammoudi and a few relatives were arrested.

News of the arrest spread. Musa's murder had shaken the city; it was the third such gruesome act in the past two weeks—a young boy had been killed by his neighbor, and another man was killed in his own home. Crime had dropped after the Prince battle in early April, but was now once again out of control. Across the pages of newspapers and in assembly meetings, citizens debated the causes, but one thing was certain: The criminal justice system was woefully underfunded. The police lacked the equipment, prosecution lacked the personnel, and the judges took ages to bring cases to trial. Courthouse workers, paid starvation wages, were susceptible to bribes.

A circulating theory was that the courts, bogged down by rules and regulations and international conventions, were simply too ponderous to move at the pace needed to halt the crime epidemic. The courts operated according to the Unified Arab Code, which had been developed by Arab states—the same Arab states that now ignored Syria's plight. What good were these grand codes, what good were international human rights, when you were afraid to send your daughter to school because of kidnapping? What good, for that matter, is a republic that can't provide law and order?

THE INTERROGATION

After a couple of days, the chief suspect, Manhal Hammoudi, coughed up the truth. He and a few others had met the victim, Musa, at a car wash, and they became fast friends. They spent nights playing cards and smoking cigarettes, sometimes even staying overnight at each other's homes. One night, Musa was in his taxi at a roundabout when his friends approached. They asked for a ride to the countryside, where they had business, and insisted on paying the fare. Due to the crime wave, taxis were hesitant to accept customers at night, but these were Musa's friends, so he agreed.

It was dark when they neared the destination. The distant farmhouses were barely visible against the night sky. Manhal asked Musa to pull over because he needed to relieve himself. Musa steered onto the shoulder, shut off the engine, and stepped out. One of the men pressed the muzzle of a pistol against his head. "Guys, quit screwing around," Musa said. "This isn't funny!" He did not say anything further because the man pulled the trigger.

Under interrogation, Manhal claimed it was all a practical joke gone horribly awry—they had thought they'd loaded the gun with blanks.

They dumped the body in the bushes, stole the car, drove it through dusty backroads to a provincial town, repainted it, changed the license plate, and sold it for $750.

THE FAMILY DEMANDS JUSTICE

At the Security Brigade headquarters, a debate erupted over what to do with the prisoners. One fighter proposed executing them then and there, to show the public that the senate meant business when it came to crime. But for others, this was a line they could not cross. Not only did it violate every precept of justice, but what would the world think? Just imagine what Western capitals and human rights organizations would say if it emerged that the Free Syrian Army were executing unarmed civilians.

They handed the suspects over to the Revolutionary Police to await trial.

At RYM headquarters, Abdul Hadi was incensed. "Just watch," he told others. "Watch these killers walk free." In his eyes, a vast conspiracy had spun its web between the Revolutionary Council and the courts. One council member's brother worked as a judge at the court—an example of the nepotism that had spread through the revolutionary ranks. The court was hopeless. The only thing the council loved more than power, Abdul Hadi said, was hard currency. Money was their god, not freedom or equality or even the real God, and that's how it had always been. He predicted that the accused would slip judges a handsome bribe and walk free, like so many others.

Abdul Hadi's obsessive denunciations of the council and the Senate had begun to wear on the other RYM members. Even Oday, who was inclined to agree with his friend on most political matters, urged Abdul Hadi to move past earlier slights and recognize the positive steps the council had taken.

But Abdul Hadi felt vindicated when, one afternoon, relatives of Musa Jasim showed up at RYM headquarters. They'd heard rumors that the accused were arranging a bribe. RYM had a well-earned reputation for honesty, the visitors said, and they hoped for the group's intercession on their behalf. Abdul Hadi listened to the family's pleas, then said, "I have a better idea."

He walked the visitors to the Cultural Center. A banner reading THE ISLAMIC STATE OF IRAQ AND GREATER SYRIA hung out front. Inside, they found an ISIS commander who hailed from the Aleppo countryside and had recently joined the group. Abdul Hadi explained the family's ordeal; he related tales, confirmed and just overheard, of other prisoners who'd been released for the right sum. The commander listened patiently but replied that there was nothing ISIS could do. They could not interfere with the judicial process in the city, because they were just a faction, one among many. That is, unless the people themselves demanded it. He explained that if the public lost faith in the judicial institutions of the republic, then, and only then, could ISIS intervene. Before the relatives could utter a word, Abdul Hadi interjected to say that he *knew* this was what the people wanted—and he would prove it.

Back at RYM headquarters, he gave a rousing speech to fellow members, demanding justice for Musa and all other victims. He drew up banners and paid a visit to the Muslim Youth Assembly, a group he'd become close with in recent weeks. He also called on the Free Students Union, the vibrant assembly that had protested against divisions within the revolutionary ranks.

That Friday, June 13, under a blazing sun, with Musa's relatives in tow, the groups gathered in front of RYM headquarters. The crowd—some two hundred strong—began to chant: "The people want the execution of criminals!" They then proceeded to march toward the ISIS headquarters at the Cultural Center. "The people want real justice!" shouted the sweaty young men. From within, the ISIS guards watched the throngs. The door did not open. "The people want real justice!"

Abdul Hadi led the procession away from the Cultural Center, toward Main Street. They held banners decrying criminality, calling for law and order. Men and women stepped onto their balconies, watching the protesters stream past—not an unusual sight these days, except that there were no tri-star revolutionary flags, no banners calling for freedom. Instead, the word on the protesters' mouths, shouted at the top of their voices, carrying to the heights above, was "justice." The people wanted justice—the people wanted to be able to sleep soundly at night, to be able to send their children to school, to make a living, to simply live. Onlookers joined the procession. As the mass moved down Main Street, it grew, like an elongating organism. There were three hundred, then four hundred people. The crowd turned down avenues, looped around parks, circled roundabouts. It continued to grow. Five hundred, six hundred people. The procession passed the headquarters of Free Army factions, at whom they hurled bitter insults for failing to protect the city. By late afternoon, the crowd had reached the central courthouse. Protesters were pushing against the gates, hoping to break through. Policemen scrambled to the roof and trained their rifles on the crowds. Abdul Hadi was near the front; he knew little fear. Oday tried to pull him back. A police colonel appeared, voice hoarse, pleading for the crowd to disperse. But the protesters kept pushing against the gate. The policemen on the roof clutched their rifles; they had not signed up for this. A chant rose from the crowd: "The people want the execution of criminals!"

Three vehicles raced toward the crowd. Their black flags, emblazoned with the words, "There is no god but God, and Muhammad is His Prophet," whipped in the wind. Some ten ISIS members jumped out—perhaps the entire group in Manbij—and stationed themselves around the courthouse. The ISIS commander with whom Abdul Hadi had spoken strode up to the guards and demanded to be allowed in. The policemen refused and ordered him back. The commander opened his vest to reveal a bomb strapped to his chest. "I'll use it!" he shouted. "I have no fear!" The police backed away. "The people of Manbij and the relatives of the deceased have asked for justice," he said. "The people have asked us to deal with this case, and we're here to fulfill their wishes." The stunned policemen opened the gate.

ISIS members gathered the suspects—five in all—and stuffed them into their vehicles. As they drove off, a cheer went up from the crowd.

Back at RYM headquarters, the activists were astir. These people aren't afraid of anything, Oday exclaimed about ISIS. It was exactly what the city needed: Democracy cannot survive without security. Abdul Hadi hailed the commander's follow-through—he did exactly as he'd promised. But more than anything, his heart swelled with the knowledge that this was not just a victory for justice but a blow against the senate and the Revolutionary Council. Their time, he believed, was running out.

THE ACCUSED

Locked in a room in the Cultural Center, the five suspects tried to work out a plan. Only three of them had been present when Musa was murdered. One of the other two was Manhal's brother, Ayman. He was sixteen, and he had known nothing about the crime. Manhal was pacing the room, near tears, convinced that his captors would never allow any of them to see the light of day. Ayman, moved by his brother's plight, offered to confess to the crime. Because he was underage, he expected lenience.

ON THE LAW

When we hear the phrase "sharia law," we're likely to conjure images of sword-wielding fanatics with Old Testament sensibilities. Traditionally, though, less than 10 percent of sharia—which means "religious law" in Arabic—relates to criminal injury like murder, rape, or theft. The rest concerns prosaic matters of marital and family relations, commercial transactions, and ritual. The law was meant to be an all-encompassing guide for communal living in the absence of state institutions. In the early years of Islam, the "state" hardly existed, at least in the sense we understand it today. "People were not registered at birth, had no citizenship status, and could move to other lands and regions freely," explains the scholar Wael Hallaq, "there being no borders, no passports, no nationalities." Sharia became a way for communities to manage their own affairs, based on a set of guidelines stipulated in the Quran and on the sayings of the Prophet.

That meant that sharia placed a heavy emphasis on community stability and accord. In the case of murder, for example, the victim's next of kin had the power to decide remedial action: They could choose retaliation, or accept blood money, or grant a pardon. Judges often encouraged the payment of blood money, and in the early centuries of Islamic rule, capital punishment was applied far less than one might expect. Other penalties, like stoning in the case of adultery, were severe but almost impossible to implement in practice: There had to be four male witnesses to the act of penetration, and, according to Hallaq, "should any of the four testimonies contradict the other three in any fashion (e.g., with regard to the position of the two while having sex or where they were having it), the four witnesses will be charged with slander and whipped eighty lashes each."

In early Islam, the state had no role in either promulgating these laws or interpreting them; the laws themselves were fixed by Scripture, while interpretation fell to jurists who were beholden to the communities they served. By the nineteenth century, though, the relationship between law and community had morphed profoundly. When the British, for example, colonized India, they were perturbed by sharia's tendency to leave law in the hands of community members, who were inclined to promote reconciliation; Warren Hastings, the governor of Bengal, complained that sharia was "founded on the most lenient principles and on an abhorrence of bloodshed"—a poor tool for disciplining restive natives. Step by step, the European powers hacked away at sharia, especially its criminal and commercial provisions, until all that remained was the family law. One historian writes, of colonial rule in India,

> British justice turned out to be far more draconian—in practice as well as in principle—than Islamic justice had been,

> resorting much more frequently to capital punishment, and much less often to community-based methods of enforcement and reconciliation. . . . [The British in India were] far more concerned with public order, and with the specific use of the law to protect its own trade and commerce as well as authority, than was the old regime.

As Arab lands succumbed to foreign domination, natives confronted an unforgiving law that favored colonial interests. The secular laws imposed by the post-colonial Arab dictators were no better, as they favored the ruling clique. By the 1970s, some thinkers looked with nostalgia to the halcyon days of early Islam, where everyone, from the caliph to the lowliest peasant was—so they imagined—subject to the same law. In Syria, this remained a minority view. At the beginning of the revolution in Manbij, almost no one called for sharia law—the dream was for a new, *democratic* law that could replace the ossified legal regime of the Baath Party. But now, after eleven months of self-rule, which featured the dizzying highs of free expression and self-organization, but also the terrible lows of violent crime and yawning inequality, this nostalgia began to crop up in the pages of the press and in assembly lectures. It was in such an atmosphere that, when six foreigners raised the prospect of religious law, they were not laughed off. ISIS explained to members of RYM that their goal in Manbij was not simply to help defeat the Assad dictatorship. It was not merely to help the city govern itself; Abu Huzayfa the Egyptian, who'd visited RYM headquarters in April, told Abdul Hadi that his group harbored no interest in power. Instead their every waking breath was devoted to restoring sharia and, by doing so, heralding a new era of justice—true, impartial, blind justice. So as they held the suspects of Musa's murder in custody, they invited Musa's father to visit their headquarters. They presented him with an option, straight from sharia: As next of kin, how did he wish to right the spilling of blood?

Musa's father was a kindly old man, and immediately said that he was willing to pardon everyone in the car that day—or almost everyone. He was stuck deep in the recesses of shock and grief at the loss of the boy who'd labored by his side for so long, a boy who'd never harmed a fly and who sat behind the wheel of that silver Saab from sunrise to sundown for the family. He could not, try as he might, bring himself to forgive the young man named Karoom, who pulled the trigger. "Let the others go," he said, weeping. "Let them go, but for God's sake, I don't forgive Karoom."

THE JUDGMENT

It was Thursday evening, and at the headquarters of the Revolutionary Youth Movement, Abdul Hadi had lost the scowl he'd worn for weeks. He spoke to his comrades with a broad smile, his eyes shining. "Tomorrow," he promised, "the senate will learn what the word 'justice' means." When his friends asked him to explain, he demurred, and laughed instead.

The next morning, Friday, July 5, gunmen appeared on the roof of the Manbij Hotel. The structure had been vacant since last October's air strike, a gaping hole in the facade leaving it looking like it had suffered the blow of a wrecking ball. Flowing from the roof to the street was the massive flag Abel Os had hung on liberation day. Over the months, citizens had written on the fabric the names of men and women lost to air strikes. The flag had become a landmark, a giant adornment at the heart of downtown.

The gunmen removed the revolutionary flag and replaced it with the black banner of ISIS. The new flag was four stories long.

The city was humming with rumors, which drew people to Central Square, in front of the hotel. By late afternoon, dozens of people had stopped to gawk at the flag and the gunmen on the roof. Oday and other RYM members decided to see what the commotion was about, and by the time they arrived, ISIS members were conducting a soundcheck. More than a hundred people, including senators and members of the Revolutionary Council, were now milling about. Word flew from tongue to tongue that ISIS would announce their judgment against the murderers. Oday and some RYM comrades pushed through the crowd to the front, and received the shock of their lives: There at the entrance of the hotel, busy setting up tables and pasting ISIS flags onto the wall, was Abdul Hadi. With him were a few other RYM members.

A convoy of black 4×4s arrived and parked at each corner of the square. More ISIS fighters were stationed on the rooftops of nearby houses. For an hour, jihadi songs blared through the speakers, the crowd grew, and the people waited, though for what they were unsure. Finally a jeep with tinted windows appeared, and a man wearing a vest laced with explosives stepped out. Three men, hooded and shackled, were produced and herded toward the stage. The music ceased.

The man wearing the explosives took the microphone. He introduced himself—in an Egyptian accent—as the "prince" of a nearby ISIS branch. "I swear by God," he began, "we did not come here with the aspiration of ruling over you. We only want to implement God's law on earth." He spoke about the role of sharia throughout history, its application in the glory days of the early Islamic empires, its disappearance with colonialism and the secular dictatorships. He announced that the time had come to revive God's law. Because they themselves feared God, they wanted the people of Manbij to fear God as well. God prescribed in the Holy Quran, he said, the limits of human behavior, and those who feared His majesty should submit to His laws. No human community can survive, he continued, without justice. A community in which man is free to kill or rape is no community at all, it is the jungle. "Here, in Manbij, the people have suffered the rule of the jungle, and the God-fearing among you have beseeched us to apply God's law." He recounted the murder of Musa Jasim, the betrayal by those he believed to be friends, the stolen car, the confessions. Then he added that the criminals had been a gang that had raped and killed others—they had kidnapped a ten-year-old girl, raping her over the course of a week, and killed her.

A gasp went through the crowd. No one had heard these additional details.

"It has fallen to our judges to implement God's wishes, and because of these heinous crimes, these men—he read their names, which included Ayman, the sixteen-year-old who'd falsely confessed to save his brother—"are hereby sentenced to death." A cry rose from the masked ISIS members: "God is great!"

The crowd was silent. The ISIS members chiseled three indentations into the hotel facade. The three prisoners were dragged to the wall and made to kneel. They were on their knees, their backs to the crowd, their heads fitted into the indentations. An ISIS member in a balaclava read out a statement containing several verses of the Quran pertaining to the punishment of criminals, and stated that "these people were not wronged by anyone, but they wronged themselves by committing murder and theft." Oday, watching the man's every movement, could not believe his eyes. Two more men stepped forward, carrying rifles. He recognized one of them as the Tunisian who'd visited RYM headquarters a few months earlier.

Around Oday, people were whispering. Their bodies pressed close—grizzled men in red kaffiyehs and skinny boys in Adidas shirts. The gunmen took aim. The prisoners remained kneeling, perfectly still. No one in the crowd budged. Maybe they wanted to understand this new order, fill their hearts with it. Maybe they had simply had enough. Maybe some stayed for the sheer pornography of it all. The shots fired, the bodies jerked, and the cry rose again from the masked ISIS men: "God is great!"

For some time, no one knew what to do. The crowd lingered in a daze, silent. Oday turned to a friend. "My God," he said. "My God."

ISIS members loaded the bodies onto the back of one of the 4×4s and drove this grim exhibit slowly through the streets. The crowd did not disperse.

Suddenly, someone shouted, "Airplane!" A mad scramble—people running in every direction, some tumbling over others. Oday and a few RYM members fled through the side streets. Oday stopped after a few blocks, panting, and looked to the sky: as clear as heaven. He turned to his friends and realized that ISIS had shouted about an aircraft to trick people into dispersing. He was struck by the absurdity of it all, and he began laughing, bowled over, and only then did he realize that he was shaking.

THE AFTERMATH

That evening, a relative of Ayman, the slain sixteen-year-old, confronted the Egyptian ISIS leader. "How can you execute someone? Who gave you the right?" he demanded.

"We are only implementing God's law."

"But according to sharia, the next of kin has the choice, and he chose to pardon Ayman." He reiterated that Ayman had only confessed to save his brother.

The ISIS leader countered that Ayman was guilty of heinous crimes, including rape.

"Which girl is this that they raped? Show her to me."

He did not receive an answer, and was asked to leave. In fact, there had been no rape, no criminal gang—the trumped-up charges were ISIS's way of ensuring popular support for their deed. The group spread the fake news to the papers, which soon reported that the deceased had been guilty of rape.

Abdul Hadi had helped set the stage on execution day; he'd even arranged for the sewing of the black flag. But he had not expected an execution—he was certain that there would be a public trial, followed by imprisonment. He told his RYM comrades that he felt as if someone had plunged a knife into his own stomach. He could not sleep for days. He found the Tunisian, one of the executioners, and asked how he'd been able to sleep at night. The Tunisian replied, "It was the first time I've killed, and let me tell you, in my entire life I have not slept with such peace as I slept last night." Abdul Hadi found himself without words.

Later, he swore to his friends that he'd never go by the ISIS headquarters again. But Oday and the other RYM members could not hide their disgust. "What did you expect?" Oday demanded. "Do you know who you are dealing with here?"

The following day, the Revolutionary Council removed the ISIS flag from the hotel.

As RYM members went to their nightly meeting at headquarters, they noticed a freshly painted message written on the wall of the Cultural Center: "The Islamic State of Iraq and Greater Syria invites citizens to register any concerns about life in the city with us."

| SIXTEEN |

July 2013

NEWS

Three people died and many were injured due to an air strike on the city. . . . The first strike was near the Manbij Girls High School and the second one targeted a house next to the Recruitment Division. —*Path*

The Senate elections were held, and Munzer Salal won the presidency by majority vote. —*Path*

The Free Students Union established an office in the village of Umm al-Sateh, where they offered a sharia course. . . . The number of students exceeded 83, between five and thirteen years of age. The office also distributed food to poor families. —*Path*

A demonstration took place on Friday, July 19, 2013. . . . Protesters demanded holding monopolists accountable. They demanded price controls and also asked for the application of the laws of God. —*Panorama*

As the Revolutionary Council is responsible for supplying bread to all the people of Manbij at a price the poor can afford, we are going to raise the price of bread from 20 to 30 L[ira]s at the official Municipal Bakery, and from 25 to 35 Ls at the Reserve Municipal Bakery. —*Revolutionary Council Statement*

HOW THE EVENTS AFFECTED OLD FRIENDS

Oday could not bring himself to set foot in the headquarters of the Revolutionary Youth Movement. That squat structure of polished limestone and muntin windows, with the bouquets of flags along the roof and the messages of revolutionary hope scrawled across the facade, had been something greater than a meeting place—it had been home. He had never roused his prerevolutionary self out of bed early, but since liberation, he'd opened the cell phone shop at dawn so that he could plant himself in the corner of the RYM headquarters guest room by nine. He'd showed up day after day, as one does at an office. Oday had learned more here, from his comrades' arguments and wild opinions and practical jokes and searching monologues, than he'd ever learned at school. In fact, RYM *was* a school, a type of finishing school. He'd entered a wild-eyed boy and emerged, undeniably, a man.

All that in just one year. They'd marched against the regime, endured air raids, attended funerals. The real education came not in the face of death, though, but in the realization that politics was a struggle that never ended. They'd protested the transgressions of Free Army factions, staged walkouts from senate meetings, and marched in the cold for unity. Through it all, they were, irrefutably, the heart of this revolution.

Yet now, Oday knew the spirit had faded. His friend Abdul Hadi had grown so consumed by slights real and perceived that he wished for the Revolutionary Council and the senate to go up in flames. Oday understood his rage; he'd witnessed himself the arrogance of the city's merchants and men of property. When the Revolutionary Council staged the Turkey coup, he'd stood by Abdul Hadi's side. Just as he had when senators marched against ISIS, violating their promise to only protest the regime. But now, after witnessing three people's brains blown apart in the heart of downtown, he could stand by his friend no longer. He invited RYM members to his house—and they shared his concerns about Abdul Hadi's dangerous drift. Almost nightly, this group discussed the tensions in RYM and the city. They believed that the behavior of both sides—the Revolutionary Council and Abdul Hadi—was a black mark on the revolution.

In mid-July, Oday met privately with Abdul Hadi. It was Ramadan. The air was sluggish, the trees drooping. We don't know what words passed between these two, whose friendship had survived much, even the betrayal of prison. Oday was given to impulse, buffeted by flashes of anger or sadness, like a leaf in a raging current. The Revolutionary Youth Movement had consumed his attentions longer than any project in his life, longer than poetry or his courtship with Hala. And now he wanted out.

Oday's departure from RYM opened the floodgates: More than a dozen members announced their resignation soon after. Abdul Hadi visited their homes, imploring them to stay. He was more than willing, he said, to steer the group away from ISIS. In fact, he'd been just as shaken by the execution. He refused to drop his war with the council, but he was ready to turn RYM into a bulwark against the Islamists, a secular bastion. He'd show them a new path of resistance.

The others would not hear it. RYM shrank by a third, leaving Abdul Hadi and a group of mostly teenagers. At first, Abdul Hadi took the exodus as a profound insult, not just against him, but against the poor of the city. In his view, there was a two-front battle to be waged: against the regime *and* against the velvet elite. *The Pharaoh is dead. Long live the Pharaoh.*

After a while, he stopped visiting his old friends. He was as alone as he'd ever been. Perhaps the camaraderie of the early days was a mirage, and the talk of holding the wealthy and powerful accountable was just that—empty grandstanding. He redoubled his work with RYM, investing in those who were sticking by his side. The group launched a campaign to support displaced children, which included literacy workshops and a free haircut for orphans. A video of the endeavor shows Abdul Hadi sitting in front of rows of children singing the revolutionary anthem, the same one he used to sing with Oday and Abel Os:

> *Oh heaven, heaven*
> *Our country it is heaven*
> *Oh country with its dear soil*
> *Our country with its dear soil*
> *Even your fire is heaven.*

Abdul Hadi is swaying ever so slightly, in a trance. Occasionally his gray-eyed stare bores into the camera, as if to say, *I know the hidden truths.*

ISIS MAKES A PLAY

Why was the revolutionary elite so craven, so jealous of its privileges? That was what Abdul Hadi could not figure out. He began spending even more time with the Muslim Youth Assembly, one of the few groups opposing the new Revolutionary Council. When this organization had launched, the previous October, it focused on humanitarian endeavors. In recent months, though, they had raised the question of Islam in politics. According to Muslim Youth activists, the city's elite were craven by virtue of their secularism. They worshipped an abstract idea, freedom, which meant that real obligations to their fellow men and women—like feeding the hungry—went ignored. The Muslim Youth organized a ten-day Quran camp, which some RYM members attended, including one of Abdul Hadi's brothers. The RYM members returned transformed; one, Basil, notorious for his foul mouth and ribald sense of humor, was now stolid and introspective. Abdul Hadi's brother, a chain-smoker, had kicked the habit almost overnight. Abdul Hadi read the pamphlets they brought back, which offered practical advice on life and faith, and found their simple message of justice and communion profound. He was no religious man, but he could not deny the power of faith in ordering a community.

With the loss of his friends, Abdul Hadi began turning up now and then at ISIS headquarters, spending hours sipping tea and watching battle videos. He regaled younger RYM comrades with tales of ISIS valor on the front lines; they were in awe of the militant group, and impressed that Abdul Hadi had managed to befriend these wild-haired men from far-off lands. Abdul Hadi had spent much of his life feeling alone, always alone, against the world. His oldest friends had betrayed him and, worse, betrayed the city's poor. He wasn't sure what to make of the wild-haired men at the Cultural Center, or if he could even trust them, but with them, at least, he did not feel alone.

Those who encountered him that summer report that he was, in subtle ways, a changed man. He'd taken to addressing RYM comrades as "my brothers," an ISIS locution and a source of much amusement among his friends. "Next, you are going to show up in Afghan clothes and a long beard," one friend teased. Abdul Hadi laughed too, perhaps realizing how ridiculous he sounded. Yet most of the time he had a strange look on his face, as if he were perpetually puzzling out the deeper mysteries.

Under Abdul Hadi's editorship, *Panorama*, the RYM weekly, began carrying a column by ISIS that examined issues of the day in light of the sayings and deeds of the Prophet. The execution had sent shivers down the spines of many revolutionaries, but some—disturbed by the crime and disorder—saw it as a sign that there existed, finally, a group willing to take a stand. The Islamic State organization had grown to a dozen members, and began to make forays into the city's political life. ISIS launched the Fertile Crescent, an assembly that held Quran memorization competitions for children, conducted lectures on Islamic history, and distributed alms to the poor. More than a dozen people joined the assembly, none of whom belonged to ISIS proper. ISIS also founded a charity, which held lectures on sharia, Arabic, math, physics, and chemistry, to "raise awareness of science." With the start of Ramadan, they distributed dates and figs to displaced families, and contributed to citywide collection efforts for the *iftar* meal, to break the day's fast, for poor families. These activities, in the context of rising prices and insecurity, won the newcomers respect in some quarters. *Free Thought* ran an interview with a preacher who declared that ISIS fighters "truly serve God and care about Islam more than anyone else, but they can't do it alone and they'll need our help."

At the same time, the Fertile Crescent Assembly resolved to "clean up" the city by scrubbing the walls of slogans praising democracy—an act that infuriated the secular assemblies. The Revolutionary Council watched the events of the preceding weeks—the execution, the ISIS campaign for hearts and minds—with alarm. They vetted the imams of the city's forty-two mosques to ensure that they preached the local Sufi brand of Islam, which was not hostile to democracy. They resolved to clean up their own act—some Revolutionary Council members and senators enjoyed a glass of whisky now and then, and some offices and battalion bases were enveloped in the green haze of hashish.

The council cracked down on drug peddlers and shut the city's sole bar: they could not allow ISIS to paint the council as dissolute. But the most important task, in many council members' minds, was to limit Islamist iconography. At a senate session, they proposed banning black flags at demonstrations. They lost the vote—not because the majority favored the black banners, but because senators worried that the law would trample free speech rights. In fact, the proposal backfired, as those who harbored little interest in the black flag hoisted it as an assertion of their freedom of speech. Islamist assemblies organized rallies with a sea of black fabric waving in the wind. At RYM protests, black flags—including those with the ISIS logo—began to appear alongside the pro-democracy revolutionary flag.

Emboldened, ISIS decided to up the ante.

THE TIT FOR TAT OF A HOT SUMMER

The Great Mosque in downtown Manbij is the largest house of worship in the city. It was also the site of the first protest, back in April 2011. The mosque was crowded on Fridays, of course, but held services throughout the week, including lessons on Quranic interpretation. The instructor, Sheikh Abu Sayed al-Dibo, was one of the city's most respected men of the minbar. In his long and distinguished career, he'd penned books of poetry, a history of Manbij, and a treatise on Orientalism.

On July 9, 2013, he was delivering a lesson when an argument broke out between him and a young Tunisian member of ISIS. At issue was Sheikh Dibo's description of the prayer one says when visiting a grave; to the ISIS member, such prayers were sacrilege. The heart of the matter lay in when, or to whom, one might pray. Sheikh Dibo was schooled in Sufism, the religion of the land, which held at its center the strange, fantastical, miraculous figure of the saint, to whom one might worship, yearning for miracles.

To ISIS, which owes its theological roots to the austere Islam of Saudi Arabia, worshipping at the tombs of saints was nothing more than rank superstition. In fact, praying to the saints, or to ancestors, was a way of empowering them, elevating them above the status of mere mortals—which in effect meant denying the singular might of God. Sheikh Dibo's instructions on how to pray at the grave, as innocuous as they may have sounded to most in Manbij, struck the Tunisian ISIS member as a disavowal of monotheism itself.

As the argument grew heated, Sheikh Dibo could not believe the young man's insolence. The sheikh had studied religious law at Damascus University and earned a master's in Lebanon—whereas the Tunisian had not competed a day's worth of religious study in his life, relying instead on YouTube videos and stray sermons. "I have as many qualifications as you have years in age," Sheikh Dibo declared. To the Tunisian, though, that was precisely the problem: Islam was saddled with such men, who acted as gatekeepers to true knowledge. Saints, imams, and sheikhs stood between the individual and God. By rejecting such figures, ISIS was attempting something akin to the Protestant Reformation for Islam, where religion would be open to anyone who chose to believe, direct and unmediated. To Sheikh Dibo, this sounded like madness. "If you want to learn about your religion, I'll teach you!" he thundered.

That evening, ISIS summoned Sheikh Dibo to its headquarters. They debated doctrinal issues, and finally ISIS made a plea for pluralism: In a free city, the people should have the right to hear different views on the question of saints. Let the different ideas compete, let the people decide. To which the Sheikh responded, "I'll give you the pulpit over my dead body."

While Sheikh Dibo sparred with ISIS, a rumor shot through the city that he'd been detained, reaching the Revolutionary Council. Abel Os was head of the Office of the Revolutionary Movement, in charge of organizing demonstrations. He sprang to action. Working the phones, he managed to gather a few hundred people in front of council headquarters—which was across the street from the Cultural Center. It was late night. Under the glow of streetlamps, hundreds of people chanted, "Out, out out! The Islamic State get out!" A man shouted into a camera, "ISIS is just like the Syrian regime!"

When the news reached ISIS headquarters, they asked Sheikh Dibo to leave. This was the first time demonstrators had called for the expulsion of ISIS. The Islamic State had overplayed their hand.

The next day, two ISIS members visited Abel Os at home. "Why were you calling for our expulsion?" one demanded to know. But Abel Os countered that he had not chanted a word, and he pulled up a video clip that showed him standing quietly, surrounded by chanting protesters. "But you are the leader!" the ISIS member insisted. "You organized them!"

"I just organized a protest to release Sheikh Dibo," Abel Os said evenly. "I don't control what people chant."

"Do you want us to leave Manbij?"

Abel Os thought for a moment. "Everyone should have their say. It's a free city."

As they left, Abel Os cursed them in his heart.

The next day, Abel Os visited the headquarters of one Free Army battalion after the next. "ISIS is a cancer," he insisted. "You better kick them out of the city before they grow stronger!" It was the interlopers' imperiousness that bothered him. Who were they to dictate how people should pray? No faction, not even the Islamist Levant Free Men brigade, had interfered with local customs. "We've been praying here since our grandfathers and great-grandfathers' time," he said. "Now these foreigners are going to tell us how to worship God?" He exhorted the commanders to unite and arrest these men before it was too late. But the Free Army commanders could not understand Abel Os's urgency. There were only a dozen ISIS members, compared to a thousand Free Army fighters. Where was the fire? Sure, their ideas were beyond the pale, but they should be free to speak their mind.

The following evening, ISIS and its Fertile Crescent Assembly organized a lecture. The Revolutionary Youth Movement arranged chairs and tables and refreshments on the street in front of the Cultural Center. Abdul Hadi spread word through his networks, and the plaza filled with hundreds of people. An ISIS member stood at the dais, where he announced that the organization would be holding a religious trivia contest, followed by a lecture on life in the city. The festivities kicked off with songs blaring through the loudspeakers extolling jihad and self-sacrifice. The crowd grew to two hundred. A speaker began reciting Quranic verses.

Across the street, in the Revolutionary Council headquarters, his words reached Abel Os. He grabbed his phone. They would have to proceed carefully; they could not be seen to be protesting ISIS, who were, after all, merely offering religious opinions under conditions of freedom of speech. Abel Os hit on the idea of holding an anti-regime protest, loud and rambunctious enough to drown out the ISIS speakers. Within minutes, a few hundred protesters materialized and set off down Sundus Street, marching around Sheikh Aqeel mosque and circling back to the council headquarters—during which time the group doubled in size. Now, a mere fifty feet from the ISIS lecture, the crowd was waving revolutionary flags. A video clip shows the protesters chanting to the beat of a drum: "The Syrian raises his hand, the donkey's son we don't want!" And, "There is no god but God, and Assad is his enemy!"

Ignoring the protesters, ISIS proceeded with its trivia night, handing out rosaries, gilded Qurans, figs, and perfumes as prizes. They organized activities for children, including theater sketches and a game of hide-and-seek. The audience was laughing along. A comedian delivered bits about Assad, about how he'd been sired by donkeys, and the audience was in stitches. An ISIS member took to the dais and argued that Manbij should be ruled by religious law—not by drunkards and thieves—and that people should not be seduced by democracy, which promises the world but cannot even put food in bellies. He spoke of ISIS's battlefield exploits, about the need to join hands to fight the regime's tyranny. The drums from Abel Os's demonstration edged closer, drowning out the speaker. In response, the lecture attendees chanted: "Council of thieves!" They were furious; they wanted to listen to the lecture in peace. A new chant arose from their ranks, decrying the high price of bread: "A bag, a bag, a bag of bread for 100 liras!" They had turned their backs to the speaker and were inching toward the protesters. Violence was in the air.

But then the ISIS speaker called on the attendees to forget the disturbance. "Some people think that by shouting and screaming they can overthrow the regime. They think shouting will help us feed our children," he said. "Forget them! Assad will only fall with guns! Peace and prosperity will only come with sharia!" The crowd applauded. "You think that we are foreigners," the speaker said, "but I'm a Syrian, just like you. We're all brothers."

Unable to interrupt the event, the protesters dispersed.

To the lecture attendees, the council's efforts did not come across well. ISIS had not attacked any group in word or in deed; it had merely organized a religious festival to commemorate the holiest month of the year. By comparison, the Revolutionary Council's drum banging and chanting seemed boorish and out of touch. Now it appeared that the Revolutionary Council had overplayed its hand.

| SEVENTEEN |

August 2013

NEWS

A debate will be held next Saturday about democracy and Sharia, at the Great Mosque after the evening prayer, as part of the *Weekly Letters* debate series. —***Weekly Letters***

We are used to price increases every Ramadan, but this year seems to be different, because the prices are record highs. —***Path***

The dollar's price rose, and with it, prices increased. The dollar's price fell, but some prices remain high! Reason and logic say to those who exploit the people by imposing these prices: If you don't have mercy on your brothers, have mercy on yourselves and beware—the people will not remain silent forever! —***Weekly Letters***

A labor union was established in Manbij to secure the rights of workers who work on contract. The union will provide health insurance and more. —***Weekly Letters***

A WAR ON TERROR

They came bundled on the back of flat-bed trucks, packed into station wagons, and balanced on motorcycles. Two, three, four dozen families a day settled into abandoned schools. Tents were crowded together in playgrounds, clotheslines webbed between jungle gyms. Little armies of children fanned out onto the streets, begging for handouts or pilfering bread. Refugees who could afford it rented dirt-floored apartments in unfinished buildings, driving up rents for natives. At the vegetable market on Sundus Street, which Oday had surveyed from his balcony in his days of romance, refugees from Safira, a district beyond the southern Manbij countryside, erected stalls of cheap produce and fried pastries. Before long, the vegetable market was known as the Safira Market.

In July alone, ten thousand people arrived in Manbij.

They had fled Safira because of battles between the Free Army and the regime. The road to Safira skirts the great salt flats of southern Manbij, through miles of dun-colored land, past rolling hills dotted with cedars and old villages with names like Two Domes and Monk Farm. It was a stretch of wretched poverty where people eked out an existence as day laborers or on tiny plots that grew tomatoes, barley, and wheat. They lived in mud homes, domed at the top; from a distance, the villages gave the appearance of a herd of dromedaries. Throughout 2013, the regime and the rebels battled to control the area. Rebels seeded the main road with mines, tearing regime vehicles to shreds and killing nearly six hundred soldiers. It was such losses, perhaps, that provoked what came next.

The first glimmer of dawn had appeared in the village of Monk Farm when Umm Jumaa heard a loud banging at her door.

"Open up, you terrorists!"

Her brother-in-law Sheikho opened the door to see a dozen men in uniform—the uniform of the Syrian government's armed forces. A placard with the image of Bashar al-Assad was on their vehicle.

"Where are the terrorists?" a soldier demanded. Sheikho tried to answer that they were mere civilians. But the men barged in. The family's puppy yelped. The soldier shot it. They moved through the rooms, turning the house upside down. "Show us your weapons!" they shouted. Finding nothing, they proceeded next door.

By 10:30 a.m., the soldiers had combed the village and found neither terrorists nor weapons. As they left Monk Farm, a few white pickups rolled into the village. Out bounded ten soldiers. They arrived at Umm Jumaa's house. "They were tall, big guys with long beards, wearing different uniforms than the previous soldiers," Umm Jumaa recalled. They wore silver T-shirts bearing the image of Bashar al-Assad and a bearded man—possibly Iranian or Lebanese—whom she did not recognize. Their arms and neck were covered in tattoos. "Where are your weapons? Where is your gold?" a fighter called out. The men of her household, including her brother-in-law Sheikho, were marched off at gunpoint.

Umm Jumaa's house sits near the heart of the village, and from her window she watched the soldiers move door-to-door. They descended upon a neighbor's house. An old man emerged, arms outstretched. He'd recognized one of the soldiers as a distant relative, which appeared to enrage the soldier, who produced a knife and stabbed him multiple times. The soldier and his comrades dropped the old man's body into a well. Then they entered his house, and closed the door behind them. After some time they came out, carrying the bodies of the old man's family members, and threw them, one after the next, into the well.

The soldiers moved to the next house, and soon reappeared carrying more bodies, tossing them into the well.

In the next house, a man and a child were arrested. The man had fled the area when the Free Army took control, returning only recently. Such travel aroused the soldiers' suspicions. The man was blindfolded, stabbed, and thrown down the well. The child, a young boy named Haytham, was blindfolded and marched toward the well. With a slight push, he dropped into its depths.

Umm Jumaa continued to watch in terror from her window. Her cousin Barjas was produced from a house, stabbed, and tossed in the well. Same with her uncle Hameed.

The men of the household of Khadija Dukhan were arrested. When her children were detained, she threw herself in front of her youngest, Omar, who was ten. "Please leave him!" she begged. But Omar was stabbed and thrown in the well. Khadija's husband ran to the well; he was apprehended, knifed, and tossed in.

Around 2:00 p.m., Umm Jumaa heard the screams of a woman. A neighbor, Khawla Ibrahim, was being dragged on the ground by soldiers. She had just witnessed her husband's execution, and she was crying and writhing. She was beaten to stifle her screams, but this only induced a greater shrieking. She was covered in blankets and doused with gasoline. She went up in flames. The fire licked the edges of her door, banked up the mud walls, and consumed the roof. The column of smoke could be seen for miles.

The soldiers continued the house raids for hours. More children were thrown in the well, the youngest of them just seven months old.

Sheikho, Umm Jumaa's brother-in-law, was thrown in—but survived the fall. He lay in the darkness, on the bodies of his friends and neighbors. As he peered up at the narrow circle of sky, he cried out. Then he saw the circle of sky disappear—the soldiers were balancing something above him. They were about to release it. The well was shaped like a cone, narrow at the opening and wide at the bottom, which allowed Sheikho to roll away just in time as a terrifying crash sounded within the walls. They were dropping washing machines and refrigerators on the bodies. Then the soldiers fired hundreds of rounds into the well, as Sheikho lay along the edge, just out of the bullets' reach.

The soldiers returned to Umm Jumaa's house. With a pickaxe, they dug a crater near her front yard. One of the soldiers noticed her at the window and called out, pointing to the pit. Umm Jumaa could not understand him. He mouthed something and pointed again. She opened the window, and heard him say: "This is your grave."

She stood mute at the window. The soldiers continued to dig. Suddenly, they received a communication on a walkie-talkie and rushed to their vehicles. As the sun settled behind the hills, they drove off.

After some time, Umm Jumaa ventured outside. The village lay still, as if in the aftermath of a great storm. The doors to many houses were in pieces. The next morning, Umm Jumaa gathered the village's surviving children and women and set out on a dirt road. They needed to go somewhere far, but where, or how, no one knew. As the sun beat down, the procession neared a village and encountered a man fleeing in the opposite direction. "The regime is there!" he warned. The procession hurried on. They passed one village after the next, and in each, the regime's army was present, and columns of smoke hung in the air. They walked for hours, until reaching a distant village, far from the salt flats, and spotted Free Army flags hanging from the houses. They were safe.

Meanwhile, back in the hamlets along the main road, the regime continued to conduct its business. A few miles from Monk Farm, the Free Army had attempted to ambush a regime convoy. The clashes did not last long; the rebels fled for the mountains, and the regime troops headed for the village of Rasm al-Nafl. As the convoy, which bore flags with the likenesses of Bashar al-Assad and Iranian leaders, rolled toward the village, several families fled for the surrounding hills. A regime official, who had relatives in the village, caught up with them by motorcycle. He beseeched them to return, arguing that these soldiers hailed from the region and were here for the people's protection. Because the official was a son of the soil, the villagers believed him.

Once back in Rasm al-Nafl, the villagers gathered food and blankets to offer the troops. The soldiers went door-to-door. When they visited Abu Muhammad's house, he was pleased to host them—he'd abhorred the chaos of the last two years, craving the stability of the old days. He served dinner to the soldiers, praising their progress and discussing the movements of the "terrorists" in the hills. They left around 9:00 p.m. Two hours later, there was a knock on the door. It was one of the soldiers Abu Muhammad had hosted. "Leave the village with your family—now. We have orders to kill everyone."

Abu Muhammad could not believe it. But up and down the highway, hamlets were in flames. He decided not to risk it. He ran to a cousin's house to warn her, but she, too, found it incomprehensible. "The soldier is lying," she insisted.

Not long after, the air filled with gunfire and loud music and sectarian chants. A new unit had arrived and was conducting house searches. Six men from the al-Matar household were dragged outside. They were beheaded. The remainder were taken to the outskirts of the village for questioning. As they were beaten—one man so forcefully that he died—they were asked, again and again, if they knew any terrorists.

Soldiers arrived at the home of the Faraj family. Husband, wife, and three children, the youngest a five-year-old girl, were executed.

They burst into the residence of Abu Nawar, who owned a small grocery in the village. He also had three sons in the Free Army, a fact the family had kept well concealed. Still, he was executed. His body was drenched in gasoline and set ablaze.

Twenty people from the Mutayr family, who lived in a complex of three houses, were rounded up and executed. Their bodies were set alight, and their homes bulldozed.

Muhammad Abu Ibrahim was a tenant farmer who lived in a mud house. "I refused to leave the village because I didn't belong to any armed group," he recalled. "I'm a simple man who has nothing to do with politics." When the soldiers raided his home, they threatened to behead him in front of his wife and children if he didn't give up the hideouts of Free Army fighters. He and his wife begged them, swearing they knew nothing. He was taken to a house the soldiers had requisitioned. There, he and other captives were stripped naked. Sometime later, four of them were shot in the head. Muhammad was released the next morning, and upon returning home, he discovered that his house had been bulldozed with his wife inside.

The soldiers arrived at the home of Umm Adel. She was a mother of three; her husband belonged to the Free Army, but he'd quit months earlier because he couldn't make ends meet. He'd fled before regime forces arrived, and the soldiers demanded to know his whereabouts. When Umm Adel swore she did not know, she was thrown against the wall, kicked, punched, and struck with a pipe. "Then three soldiers raped me in front of my children," she recalled. "My children were screaming and crying."

The family was expelled from the house, which the soldiers proceeded to bulldoze. She fled with the children to her father's house—but her father and brothers were missing. Later, she learned that they had been beheaded and their corpses burned, dragged by tractors, and tossed in a well.

For weeks, the Syrian regime and its Iranian allies laid waste to the mud-and-stone houses in the hamlets up and down the road leading to Safira. Eventually the front lines shifted, and the regime forces turned their attention elsewhere, at which point the Free Army returned to the region. This allowed displaced locals, along with local reporters and investigators, to visit. The villages were empty, many houses in rubble. But the wells emitted a powerful stench of death. In the hamlet of Umm Amud, locals filmed themselves fishing bodies out of the well. On a wall was written "Assad or we burn the country"—signed by the National Defense Forces, a pro-regime militia. On another wall, they had left behind a second message: "This is the freedom you are asking for."

In Rasm al-Nafl, residents returned to find entire families wiped out: fifty-six members of the extended Fawaz household, including a two-day-old named Aweed; sixteen members of the Rawi household, ranging from an eighty-year-old grandfather to a toddler. One man returned to find his wife and seven children beheaded. Residents tallied 208 killed in the massacre.

In Monk Farm, residents returned a few days after the army departed. Two of them were walking by a well when they heard a noise—a human voice. It was Sheikho, the brother-in-law of Umm Jumaa, who'd survived without food or water. They lifted him to the surface. Umm Aziz, whose only child had been taken away, rushed to the scene. "Your son was down there," Sheikho said. In her agony, Umm Aziz embraced him, and was hit by the unmistakable smell of the dead. Sheikho proceeded to name those down below, some of whom had clung to life for a few days, but all of whom were now decaying.

A few months later, the regime returned and conquered the highway to Safira, along with the roadside hamlets, for good. A regime documentary television crew visited shortly thereafter. With the pulsing music of a film score in the background, the viewer is taken on a tour of the area and shown fire-blackened cars and pockmarked buildings—the work, we are told, of "mercenary terrorists." There are no residents anywhere.

ON POLITICS

No one knows how many people were killed in Syria during the war. Local human rights organizations estimate that, by mid-2013, more than one hundred thousand people died, a figure that is almost certainly a gross undercount. Most of the dead were likely civilians, the vast majority killed by the regime and its allies. The killing was targeted and systematic, a government policy designed to quell the rebellion.

This slaughter came in three forms. There was the house-to-house variety, the hulking men in bandoliers burning people alive, raping women—of which there exist many recorded instances, like Monk Farm, spanning multiple provinces. Such massacres require boots on the ground, though, which proved a challenge for the regime when swathes of the country fell under rebel control. So the second variety of killing came from bombers and helicopters; in some corners of the country, bombing raids became so commonplace that locals, upon overcoming the shock that their own government was dropping explosives on them, cobbled together an early-warning system for approaching aircraft by stationing spotters near air bases.

The third mode of death occurred in the dozens of detention centers strung across the country, some no larger than a few cells, others housed in sprawling military compounds. We know something of the inner workings of such repression due to regime defectors, who smuggled tens of thousands of government documents out of the country. These files, which include communiqués between branches of the security services, detail a government policy, drawn up in 2011, to crush the protests by targeting categories of people, such as demonstration organizers and those who "tarnish the image of Syria in the foreign media."

It's unclear how many people passed through this gulag archipelago, though some estimates suggest over one hundred thousand. In the early days, most detainees were released after confessing under torture, but as the rebellion spread, the torture grew more sadistic, and growing numbers of prisoners never returned home.

The regime catalogued these deaths, photographing the corpses, presumably so jailers could report their progress to superiors. In August 2013, an employee at Hospital 601, code-named Caesar, stuffed into his socks flash drives containing nearly fifty thousand images of bodies and fled the country. Caesar's photos provide the clearest evidence of the charnel house that was the Syrian prison system: naked corpses, faces battered beyond recognition, eyes gouged. The victims showed signs of severe malnutrition, their skin furrowed at the rib cage, limbs like twigs. They lay with an alien grimace, in the ghastly repose of the dead of a concentration camp.

For many Syrians, the scale of the horror unfolding in their country, orchestrated by such cold bureaucratic machinery, conjured one word: genocide. Yet according to the Genocide Convention of 1948, that word refers to the "intent to destroy, in whole or part, a national, ethnical, racial or religious group." Under these terms, the slaughter in Syria cannot be classed as a genocide; while many of the dead were Sunni Muslims, the government was clearly targeting anyone who opposed it, regardless of religion. To muddy things further, you could find Sunni Muslims in the regime's army and among Assad's supporters. But if the Syrian government's campaign of mass slaughter was not, legally speaking, a genocide, that may tell us more about our Western moral categories than it does about the devastation in Syria.

The concept of genocide arose following the horrors of World War II—it provides a moral compass of sorts, a standard against which we judge right and wrong. We see genocide as the "crime of crimes," the greatest possible injustice humans can inflict upon each other. Genocide is, for the secular West, the hallmark of "evil." What makes genocide evil? Industrial-scale slaughter is not enough; recent history is filled with grisly examples—such as General Suharto's mass killing of leftists in Indonesia—that do not rise to the conventional designation of genocide. Rather, what gives genocide its distinctive moral cast is that people are targeted merely for the ethnic or religious group to which they happen to belong. That is, people are targeted for something they did not *choose*, something they have no control over.

International law, then, does not consider the slaughter in Syria a genocide, because people were primarily targeted primarily for their political activity—something we normally understand as resulting from free choice. After all, no one forced Oday, Abdul Hadi, and others to launch the Revolutionary Youth Movement. But putting it this way seems to miss something important about the human condition. What if engaging in political activity is an essential exercise of our humanity, and to obtain the things we need to live a good life, we have no choice but to be political?

We tend to associate politics with the undertakings of political parties, which has made politics something of a dirty word: think of the hollow pageantry, the dissimulation, the greased palms, the horse-trading, the crass maneuvers of special interests. Politics, in this conception, happens behind closed doors; it involves scheming over the heads of ordinary people. It's no wonder that, given such a cynical kabuki, most of us want little to do with politics. The ancient Greeks, though, viewed the matter quite differently. Because we live in community with others, we can only obtain the things we desire through others. If we are powerful or wealthy, we can simply command others to do our bidding. But if we aren't, then we must coordinate, cooperate, cajole, and compromise with others. So politics, for the ancient Greeks, is the art of forming alliances to obtain the goods of collective life. It's what happens when neighbors organize a community garden, when parents band together to contest a school board election, when workers strike for better wages. Aristotle wrote, "The man who is isolated—who is unable to share in the benefits of political association, or has no need to share because he is already self-sufficient . . . must be either a beast or a god." From this, he concluded that the human "is by nature a political animal." He means that we cannot achieve our aims alone, that we must act collectively—and when we are inhibited from doing so, we have lost an essential part of our humanity.

There are many ways to stifle our political nature: dictatorial repression; legal and institutional barriers to political participation; poverty and precarity. And that—Syrians' political nature—is precisely what the Assad regime sought to eradicate. It was a campaign of extermination as total, as apocalyptic, as any genocide. Yassin al-Haj Saleh, an activist who was imprisoned with Hasan Nefi for many years, calls such slaughter "politicide." Whatever the term, the glaring truth is that the Syrian regime was indeed orchestrating the "crime of crimes."

Under dictatorship—what the Greeks called *tyranny*—laws and institutions make it impossible for ordinary people to form alliances to obtain collective goods. Manbij suffered forty years of dictatorship, during which time free associational activity was banned; there was no political party or professional association or labor union or religious institute or media organization or football team or chess club that was not controlled by the regime. Yet when the people of Manbij overthrew the government, independent councils and assemblies and newspapers and charities and unions appeared overnight. They did so because people felt compelled to secure the goods crucial to life, like free information and clean streets and fresh bread, and could only do so by allying with each other. In other words, the people of Manbij started doing politics. They felt they had no choice *but* to do politics, because that's what the situation demanded. No one taught them to be political. There were no international NGOs conducting trainings, no instruction manuals, no political theorists offering guidance. They engaged in politics simply because that is what people, given the opportunity, will do. What the revolution shows, in a striking confirmation of Aristotle's thesis, is that people are political animals—that when the fetters are removed, their political natures will flourish.

That an activity is natural, though, does not mean it comes easily. We naturally walk and talk, but it takes years to master these skills. Likewise, the people of Manbij were learning, in the most adverse of circumstances, how to be political: how to debate, how to listen, when to protest, when to abstain. The previous twelve months were a record of missteps and trials and tribulations; the leaders of the Revolutionary Council were learning to be more inclusive; the former members of RYM were grasping the art of compromise. And now, as the one-year anniversary of their experiment neared, the revolutionaries were about to face their biggest test yet.

| EIGHTEEN |

September 2013

NEWS

[A refugee] from Homs, who lives with his wife, daughter, and three disabled persons, was paying a monthly rent of 10,000 Syrian pounds. Then the price of the dollar increased, and the landlord came to him and said: I want 25,000 Syrian pounds for rent! The man from Homs pleaded, crying, 'Please fear God!' ... he fainted and was rushed to the hospital. His soul has since ascended to its Creator. May God have mercy on him. Who is there now for his wife and children? —**Weekly Letters**

The Free Syrian Youth Assembly announces a sit-in at Central Square ... to protest the high price of bread, fuel, and foodstuffs. —**Path**

WHAT HAPPENED WHEN THE CRISIS HIT

In August, the people of Manbij organized a festival, *A Year of Freedom*. Twelve months had passed since the regime's soldiers and Baath Party factotums had fled, twelve dizzying months in which residents held this city in their collective grip. For two days, life ground to a halt as crowds marveled at the explosion of artwork: on canvases along the sidewalks, on walls, on billboards—the portraits of young men who'd traded their lives for the city's security, the graffiti on ruined façades ("We Syrians ... are not sectarians or terrorists!"). The *Path* declared, "The human being is a mirror that reflects what he learns, sees, and feels from the arts." Short films were screened, dramas were staged. The production *How Does the Dervish Live?* received an ovation. The festivities took place amid the ruins of the house that had been destroyed in an air strike in February—which Mina had narrowly escaped—because even amid the revelry, the organizers said, they could not allow themselves to forget.

The senators spoke of a new beginning, of putting the previous year's acrimony behind them, and invited the city's assemblies and military factions—including their enemies, ISIS and RYM—to a luncheon. ISIS members sat beside democrats at long plastic tables piled with *lahmacun* pizzas, and for the moment, people believed that they were joined hand in hand in the face of a genocidal enemy.

Despite the crowds, such festivals prompted criticism. "I don't think it's right to hold parties," a man complained to the *Path*. "People of our beloved Syria are being killed while we drum and party." The trouble was that the regime was tightening the screws, with reports of fresh atrocities surfacing by the day, prompting even more families to seek refuge in Manbij—which now housed more than double its prewar population. Some refugees took apartments, but with zero tenant protections, many were fleeced by landlords, who hiked rents at will, "without care for values or customs," complained the *Path*. Soon, even native citizens were priced out of real estate, as rents tripled and quadrupled. To many Manbijis, this free market in housing seemed like the law of the jungle.

By mid-August, Manbij was teetering on economic collapse. The squeeze came from many directions and was not only due to migrants. Nationwide, fuel prices had jumped, in part due to the war and the breakdown of supply chains. The transportation crisis manifested everywhere: Bus operators took advantage of the fuel crisis to hike fares, with a trip from Manbij to Aleppo now costing 20 percent more than a few months prior; and with the border controls evaporated, cheap used cars flooded the market, though consumers complained that these jalopies broke down almost immediately.

Communication networks and financial infrastructure were similarly strained. The internet hardly existed except for the wealthy, because telecom companies were charging exorbitant rates. Public sector employees faced month after month of wage cuts. At the souk, the price of basic foodstuffs surged. The human cost of this collapse was visible across the city—the streets were crowded with legions of beggars, some as young as four or five years old. The middle class and the wealthy looked upon their mangy brethren with contempt; begging had become "a profession," a merchant complained to the *Path*. But the truth was, behind every bony outstretched hand was a tale of grief.

In the press, the mood turned decisively against the one freedom that many could no longer endure: the freedom of the market. The *Path*:

> Freedom is a sea sailed by travelers, fisherman, naturalists, explorers, pirates, and creatures which are known only to God, including fish—especially sharks. So, do we accept freedom for sharks? ... The sharks in our country exercise their freedom by raising prices, such as the price of medicine ... the merchants, the wholesalers, the shop owners in the grocery market are all sharks who do not care about values, ethics, or religion, and they are in a race against time to get rich at the expense of the health of the citizens.

"The greedy trader had never viewed his investment projects by any moral standard, or by any humanitarian standard," wrote a columnist in the *Sun*. "This type of economy is a form of terrorism and economic extremism."

What was to be done? The Revolutionary Council debated the issue but refused to consider what many saw as the only realistic step to managing the crisis: enacting price controls. Merchants would have balked and likely threatened to take flight with their riches—but the council could have responded by seizing their assets. Private bakeries and vacant apartment blocks could have come under council control, a nationalization that would have created a safety net for the city's most vulnerable. Revolutionary authorities could have seized the nearby Lafarge cement factory, which had made healthy profits for its French owners, to fund social services. But seizing property or imposing price controls was counter to the idea of liberal freedom, making it unthinkable to the elites who ran the city. Instead, the council resorted to plaintive appeals to the merchants' consciences. "We remind you that Ramadan is the month of mercy, and we, Muslim communities, should have mercy on each other so that God may have mercy on us. We should not exploit people and we should not raise prices or monopolize products as these behaviors are alien to Muslim morals." Yet to the merchants, the laws of supply and demand were more powerful than the dictates of Allah, so they paid little heed to the council's entreaties. The wealthy could not be morally persuaded to support their fellow citizens—they had to be coerced.

For Abdul Hadi and his fellow travelers, the economic crisis was an expression of a profound moral crisis plaguing their city. Implementing economic justice meant transforming people's understanding of what they owed each other. For four decades, the regime called itself "socialist" while subordinating every human need to the priorities of the Assad family. Then, for twelve months, a new order, calling itself "free" and "liberal," subordinated every human need to the priorities of the market. Now, the time had come to build a society ordered around the priorities of human need. Where socialism and liberalism had failed, religion—a system that put care and community first—could succeed. "The higher the price of the dollar gets, the stronger the shock of the poor," wrote a *Path* columnist. "These diseases have emerged as a result of the weakness of our souls, which have moved away from religion." The *Sun* ran a column describing how Caliph Omar, who ruled the Islamic community in the seventh century, reportedly enforced price controls. "This is a legitimate policy, in which the leader of a nation looks after the economic and existential interests of the citizens by protecting them from the avarice of merchants."

RYM held weekly demonstrations and called for a comprehensive program of reform: lower the price of bread and fuel, tax the wealthy, and nationalize bakeries. In the third week of August, with no response from the council, Abdul Hadi visited the ISIS headquarters at the Cultural Center. "People can't take any more," he told them. "The council must be stopped, now."

HANDS AROUND THE PEOPLE'S NECK

Everyone knew the city was about to explode. The anxieties and insecurities that kept people awake, that made them hunch over a calculator late at night, that made them visit the mosque on weekdays, coalesced into a single, abiding worry: bread. In November, the Revolutionary Council had raised the cost of a loaf at the public bakeries to 25 Syrian liras; then, in June, it hiked the price to 30 liras—double the price in just one year. And this was the subsidized bread, available only at two locations in the city. Those who could afford it visited the private bakeries, of which there were a dozen. But the private bakeries were charging exorbitant rates, some as high as 100 liras, causing further crowding at the public bakeries.

Such prices were caused by a variety of factors, but primarily by the bacchanalia of greed into which Manbij had descended when merchants and middlemen were liberated from government regulations. Private bakery owners had repeatedly staged lockouts, protesting this or that attempt by the council to manage prices. They bought wheat at council-subsidized prices and then took advantage of the grain shortage to make windfall profits. Middlemen appeared, linked to the private bakeries, who were able to obtain bread from the public bakeries for a fee. The council provided bread to Free Army factions at discount rates, but some fighters sold their provisions on the black market.

In late August, the council unveiled a bread distribution system it hoped would undermine the black market. After conducting a detailed census, they hired workers to distribute bread in each neighborhood, thereby eliminating the congestion at the bakeries and pulling the rug out from under the middlemen and private bakery proprietors.

But on the day of the program's rollout, people were shocked to discover that the council had raised the price of bread *again*—now to 50 liras. The council claimed this was necessary to cover the cost of workers and transport, but the poor were up in arms. Impromptu demonstrations broke out around the city. At the Great Souk, the crowd grew to a few hundred. They blocked the mouth of the market, chanting for price controls. Their voices carried down the corridors of the souk: "The people want fair prices!"

An ISIS member on a motorcycle pulled up to an activist and instructed him to shepherd the protest to the Cultural Center. The activist, a member of the Revolutionary Youth Movement, did as he was told. The crowd traversed a few city blocks and gathered in front of the ISIS headquarters. The crowd, now three hundred strong, chanted, "The people want to hold the Council of Thieves responsible!" A man named Abu Harith the Jordanian, now the leader of ISIS in Manbij, emerged and spoke to the protesters through the gate. He told them ISIS could solve the bread crisis if they controlled the grain supply—but the Revolutionary Council would have to relinquish it. "We listen to the will of the people," he said. "You must take your demands to the council."

The crowd, in a rage, left the Cultural Center and marched through the streets. When they passed open shops, their fury at a year of price gouging and greed boiled over. They smashed storefronts with sticks and threw rocks through windshields. The protest had become a full-blown riot. Some pedestrians saw the mob and fled, but others joined. The crowd set its sights on the Revolutionary Council headquarters. A video shows a frenzied horde. "The people want the downfall of the council!" they shout, trying to push their way inside council headquarters. Two council members are at the door, hands raised, pleading for calm. A young protester has pushed himself to the threshold. His eyes are wide, as if he'd never imagined he'd be able to breach this fortress of revolutionary power. He turns back and gestures for his friends to follow him. The crowd finally bursts into the headquarters.

Shampoo Sami, Mina's brother, was inside and managed to escape through a window. The protesters wrecked furniture. They photographed themselves sitting at the president's desk. They set fire to documents. A vehicle from the Security Brigade, the city's defense force, arrived. The mob left and headed back to the Great Souk. Along the way, they smashed storefronts and called for the execution of "monopolists." As the sky darkened, columns of smoke could be seen here and there around the city. Sirens wailed. Shopkeepers stood outside their properties with rifles to fend off looters.

Scattered protesters formed another procession. They called for the handover of the bread supply to the Islamic State. Among the demonstrators were RYM members, egging the crowd on. Senators and Revolutionary Council members were hiding in their homes. Oday was with his sister on the balcony, watching angry young men carrying black flags and pacing back and forth. His revolution was devouring itself. Abel Os was at home working the phones, trying to convince the senators to hold a counter-demonstration. They refused, fearing they'd be torn limb from limb. ISIS members remained in their compound, while people beyond their gates chanted for an "Islamic state."

Throughout, from the first protests in the afternoon to the rioting to the storming of council headquarters, the one person everyone looked for was nowhere in sight. Abdul Hadi did not venture outdoors that day. For months now, he had felt something twisting his insides. He could not at first put a name to the sensation, which he'd harbored while he sung revolutionary songs with his comrades, played practical jokes, and led demonstrations. It was only when the Revolutionary Council refused to acknowledge the results of the December election that he'd felt, in a strange way, relief. The twisting had acquired a name—rage, righteous rage—and finally, the slights that he and his family endured were no longer private, but a matter of public, collective concern. Now, as far as he was concerned, history had absolved him. The council's venality, its fixation on extreme ideas like freedom for the merchant, was plain for all to see. So as the masses internalized this lesson, as the streets turned inside out, leaving it unclear who was on the right side anymore, Abdul Hadi stayed home. He did not want it to be said, after all, that it was he who'd orchestrated this uprising. He had merely made manifest the truths that were hiding in plain sight. This was a new revolution, a people's revolution, against the usurpers. As smoke filled the night sky, and the angry men refused to leave the streets, Abdul Hadi finally, after so many months, felt understood.

Riots continued all week. On September 4, seven days after storming council headquarters, the masses were out in Central Square, again calling for the overthrow of the Revolutionary Council. The demonstrators included the city's poor—but also the bakery owners. These strange bedfellows had both invested hopes in RYM's message. For the poor, only an Islamic state could ensure price controls and curb the liberal elites' appetites. For the bakery owners, only the Islamic State could dismantle the council's new bread distribution system, which undermined the middlemen and the black market.

The next morning, three vehicles pulled up to the gate outside the Manbij Mills, the towering silos that housed the city's wheat supply. Out came nine ISIS fighters, led by Abu Harith the Jordanian. He had moved to the city in July to take over leadership of the Manbij branch of ISIS, which now was over two dozen strong. By all accounts a polite man who preferred persuasion to force, he strode into the mills and met with the director. He explained the situation: The Revolutionary Council had lost control of the streets, and people were clamoring for ISIS to take charge of bread distribution. ISIS was reluctant to do so, he said, but if they didn't act, he feared a full-blown revolution—which would only benefit the Assad regime. The director—a city employee—agreed to surrender the facility to ISIS, as long as he and the other employees could keep their jobs. Abu Harith the Jordanian agreed. The director explained the system to his guest: The city supplied a portion of its wheat to regime areas, in return for Assad's warplanes not bombing the facility. The remainder of the wheat was supplied to city bakeries, at a price set by the council—or now, by ISIS. The director phoned the council and informed them of the change in leadership.

The council was out of options. To storm the mills would risk a civil war. In the past, they had authorized outside factions to capture the Prince—ironically, the very action that had brought ISIS to Manbij. But the council enjoyed much more popular support then; now, it had lost all legitimacy. If it declared war on ISIS, would the population back them?

That evening, the members issued a statement:

> The Revolutionary Council . . . has done everything in its power in these exceptional circumstances to comfort the citizen and work to serve him and secure his needs. The Council is convinced that managing civil affairs is the concern of civilians, and that military factions belong on the front lines.
>
> And because some military factions have begun to interfere in civilian affairs—the latest is ISIS, which seized the mills, a civilian facility—the Revolutionary Council has decided to suspend its work until further notice.

The city of Manbij was now under the authority of the senate and the armed factions, which controlled the municipality, the judiciary, and the police force. But, crucially, the Mills were under ISIS control. "Whoever controls this facility," said a senator during a session, "puts their hands around the people's neck."

| NINETEEN |

September 2013

THE STRANGE, MARVELOUS CAREER OF 1ST LT. MAYMATI, PART 3

Around the country, ISIS was expanding its reach. In some liberated cities, especially those with more developed polities, they advanced their agenda through persuasion and political gamesmanship. But sometimes, they used sheer force—kidnappings, assassinations—to intimidate opponents. In Raqqa, a major liberated city southeast of Manbij, ISIS operatives even got into occasional street battles with Free Army factions. Still, ISIS presented itself as simply one among the thousand anti-regime armed factions, and there were many who believed them. But one rebel commander who saw in them something truly menacing was 1st Lt. Maymati.

Since leaving Manbij the previous July, Maymati had created his own rebel group and attacked regime outposts around the country. He took part in the battle to liberate Raqqa and many smaller towns and villages, and it could be said that no other man had single-handedly played such a pivotal role in overthrowing the regime in eastern Syria. His legend stretched far, and young men were eager to follow him into battle. So it was a terrible blow to the revolutionary forces when, one warm evening, he vanished.

He had been traveling between Raqqa and Manbij when armed men appeared on the road, shot at his vehicle, and detained him. A captured regime officer later claimed on video that his men had abducted Maymati, prompting rumors that he was now languishing in a regime prison. On the other hand, Maymati's men believe he was taken by ISIS, based on the fact that he'd received threats and had been warned to keep away from Raqqa.

Wherever the truth, Maymati was never seen again.

A DEBATE WITH ISIS

Wherever he went, Aimad Henezel took a pistol and a grenade. He'd begun carrying protection after he noticed a sedan parked near his house. Aimad had little taste for force, preferring long conversations over cups of tea to the life of the front lines. As a member of the original Revolutionary Council that had operated during the secret phase, he'd traveled to Idlib and Homs, slept in Bedouin tents and farmhouse storerooms, collected donations, then returned to his well-appointed home in the leafy quarter named for his family. A veterinarian by training, Aimad had an eye for detail; in May, he was elected to head the Revolutionary Council's bread distribution program. By September, if there was anyone who was the face of council policy—fairly or not—it was Aimad. After ISIS seized the mills, Aimad went to the press. The council had managed the bread supply as best they could, he said—prices were beyond their control. He told a *Path* reporter that the riots were manufactured—implying, but not naming, ISIS as the culprit. The current strife had nothing to do with bread, he insisted. Instead, it was a plot to overthrow the revolutionary government. And it was an attack on "the concept of freedom."

The *Path* sought comment from the other side. Like Aimad, Abu Harith the Jordanian, the leader of ISIS in Manbij, carried a pistol—but also wore a dynamite-strapped vest at all times. He denied that ISIS had a hand in the protests and claimed he'd even offered to collaborate with the senate and the Revolutionary Council, under certain conditions:

> I told them you have got to announce publicly that we will work together to fight the regime, corruption, secularism, democracy, and blasphemy. But they refused that, because they take orders from America, and they are scared of upsetting their masters. They even removed ISIS graffiti from the walls because they are cowards. If they were brave, they would meet us face-to-face.

Aimad knew what he had to do. He was a quiet man, prone to reverie, careful not to offend, the type who felt terrible interrupting someone. He did not accept his post as bread czar in order to sit with zealots wearing vests packed with explosives. But the democratic experiment, which he'd poured his life into, which had made him a wanted man by the regime, was teetering. If he didn't meet ISIS now, when some sort of agreement could still be hammered out, he feared it would soon be too late.

It was already dark when Aimad arrived one evening at the Cultural Center, accompanied by a couple of Free Army members. ISIS guards demanded that the visitors surrender their arms. Aimad said: "If you are afraid of meeting us face-to-face, I'll be sure to make that known." They were allowed to enter.

Inside, seated behind the desk, was Abu Harith. Next to him, in a soccer jersey and baseball cap, was Abdul Hadi. Aimad could not believe it—Abdul Hadi, revolutionary, son of the city, who'd suffered prison for democracy, *here*, in this vipers' nest. He knew RYM despised the council, but only now did he understand the full extent of their collaboration with ISIS.

Aimad collected himself, and began to explain the bread distribution process and efforts the council had made to address the problem of prices. As he spoke, Abdul Hadi repeatedly leaned over to whisper in Abu Harith's ear. The ISIS leader was a foreigner; he did not know the ins and outs of local politics. It was Abdul Hadi, Aimad realized, who was furnishing him with intelligence. Aimad was describing the process of bread production when suddenly the door flung open. Masked men filled the room. Before he knew it, a half-dozen gun barrels were pointing at him and his Free Army colleagues. One of the gunmen played a video clip for Abu Harith. It was taken at a senate session; Aimad was proposing a plan to establish checkpoints around the city and place imams under observation. "And finally," he said in the clip, "every military faction must submit to the authority of the Revolutionary Council, or we will fight them!" The roar of applause could be heard.

"You want to fight us?" Abu Harith snapped. "I will have you killed!" Aimad gripped his grenade. His heart was pounding through his chest. He was ready for anything. If he wasn't going to leave this room, neither would they. No one made a move. Someone tried to calm Abu Harith by explaining that the phrase "military factions" in Aimad's speech did not refer to ISIS—that ISIS was a "state," not a mere fighting unit. Aimad found himself nodding at this preposterous explanation. Abu Harith cooled slightly. He began to lecture Aimad on the need for Islamic law. Now Aimad was agreeing, desperate to extricate himself. But the gunmen were blocking the doorway. "We will make an example out of you," Abu Harith was saying, as Aimad continued to grip his grenade.

Abdul Hadi finally spoke up. "Oh sheikh, they have until now refused to hold a debate with the State. Why don't we have a public debate between the two sides, and let the people decide?" Aimad jumped on Abdul Hadi's proposal—and wondered if, under the carapace of hatred and envy, Abdul Hadi still recognized the council as fellow revolutionaries. Abu Harith agreed to the proposal, and everyone breathed easier. Aimad quickly left.

That Friday, Aimad approached the Great Mosque. The debate had been advertised all week, filling the prayer hall beyond capacity. He'd never spoken in front of so large an audience before. RYM members were organizing chairs, testing the microphones. As Aimad made his way through the crowd, he looked for friendly faces. He noticed a masked ISIS gunman, standing among the crowd. And another. Then more—at least a dozen. What kind of debate was this? He pictured himself at the lectern, a masked man rising, taking aim, the crowd scrambling. He began to curse himself—the sheer insanity of agreeing to a debate when one side was armed to the teeth! Without a word, he left the building.

The crowd waited. RYM tried to find another speaker to represent the council position, but could not get anyone on the phone. Abu Harith took the lectern, stating that he would proceed in presenting his case—and if the council refused to debate him, it would be further evidence that truth sided with the Islamic State. For the next thirty minutes, he delved into the details of bread distribution, throwing out statistics and anecdotes of waste, fraud, and mismanagement. No one could say where these figures came from; they were likely created out of whole cloth by Abdul Hadi. Nonetheless, Abu Harith succeeded in painting a picture: The Revolutionary Council were out-of-touch elites who had mishandled the city's most important commodity and cared little for the woes of everyday people, fixating instead on abstractions that rang sweetly in the air-conditioned hotels and plenary rooms of foreign capitals. It was a story laced with lies and exaggerations—there is no evidence that council members embezzled a single penny in fourteen months—but it held a kernel of deeper truth, a felt truth, which no objective observer could deny: The council represented the interests of the wealthy.

Abu Harith finished his remarks, and the crowd waited impatiently for a council representative's rebuttal. None came. The crowd began chanting, and the event morphed into an ISIS rally. The attendees poured onto the street. Black flags appeared.

The young men roved the streets, long into the night, demanding sharia.

WHEN THE RED LINE TURNED GREEN

Around this time, the Syrian regime fired nearly a dozen rockets into the Damascus suburb of Ghouta. Hospitals were soon inundated with convulsing patients, frothing at the mouth, fluid leaking from their eyes. They were dizzy, suffocating, spasming. Investigators later determined that the rockets contained sarin, a nerve agent, and that anywhere from four hundred to a thousand people had been killed. The tragedy shocked the war-hardened populace; in Manbij, activists organized a solidarity strike, shutting down the city. The regime had already carried out dozens of suspected small-scale chemical attacks. The Ghouta attacks were different, because they crossed Barack Obama's so-called red line—the limit beyond which, if the regime transgressed, the U.S. would intervene.

The U.S. Sixth Fleet was put on alert. A "forest of missiles," according to one press report, was stationed around Syria. No one knew when the U.S. attack would start, but on the ground there was a sense that the conflict was about to take an abrupt turn. Would U.S. cruise missiles decapitate the regime? Would American boots touch Syrian soil? Would the U.S. turn Syria into another Iraq? The Revolutionary Council of Aleppo formed twenty-eight situation rooms, comprising various revolutionary groups and rebels, to handle the potential crisis, from refugee flows to a free-for-all that might follow the killing of Assad. In Manbij, the *Sun* canvassed opinion on the question of whether the U.S. would intervene:

> Hussein M: Yes, because the regime has become a threat to Western interests, and because someone must stand against the tyranny of this regime and its president. The world can no longer remain silent.
>
> Free Student Union member: Yes, [the U.S.] will launch a military strike, but not to topple the regime, only to protect Western and Israeli interests—that is, to destroy the Syrian arsenal so that it is not controlled by the rebels.
>
> Ammar Haider: Yes, Western aircraft will bomb the regime, but not out of love for the Syrian people, but because the Syrian revolution has become a threat to American national security.
>
> "Kasser al-Samet": No, they will not launch a strike because... they fear Russia and Iran.

Around the city, a rumor spread that U.S. troops were en route. Various assemblies, from RYM to Girls of Tomorrow, organized demonstrations against foreign intervention. At the headquarters of one of the leading Free Army factions in the city, Anas Sheikh Weiss told the fighters under his command, "The American army is going to invade—and we will treat the American soldier as we treat the regime soldier!"

The suspicion stemmed, no doubt, from U.S. support of Israel and the disastrous Iraq invasion. But it was two years of false promises and hypocritical stances that truly turned the revolutionaries cynical. The revolution, which began in the spring of 2011, had mutated into an armed struggle by spring 2012. The U.S. and its allies had enforced an arms embargo against the rebels until early 2013; by that point, regional powers like Saudi Arabia, Qatar, and Turkey had begun supplying select groups with arms. It was not until the summer of 2013, after two years of bloodshed, that the U.S. authorized covert weapons shipments to the Free Army. By then it was too late. The resource-starved FSA fighters had turned to banditry, prompting the rise in popularity of Islamist brigades. Revolutionary governments like Manbij were under strain from internal and external enemies. Now, with the U.S. threatening direct intervention, it was difficult for revolutionaries to trust Obama's intentions. And when, ultimately, the U.S. decided against responding to the chemical attacks, the revolutionaries felt vindicated. Once the regime realized that it could slaughter its citizens without limit, Obama's red line became a green light for Damascus.

A writer in the *Path* declared:

> In short, the Western and Arab "friends" of the Syrian people are not actually friends—they are either enemies or they are neutral. They are looking after their own interests, and nothing more. Their actions, not their words, prove this. Our revolution only has God, and He is enough for us.

| TWENTY |

October 2013

NEWS

The brutal warplanes bombed the city of Manbij near the city center on Thursday morning, resulting in more than seven martyrs, including women and children, and more than ten wounded.
—*Free Thought Magazine*

Regime forces and the militia of Hezbollah . . . committed a massacre in Thiabiyya and al-Hussainiyah, killing about 130 people.
—*Path*

On Wednesday following the afternoon prayer, the Islamic State displayed its charitable deeds on a large screen in Central Square.
—*Weekly Letters*

THE SORDID TALE OF THE MAN THEY CALL THE PRINCE, PART 3

Not long after liberation, Shabaan Hasan, twenty-one, showed up at the offices of the *Path* asking for a job. Shabaan, son of a leftist, believed in speaking truth to power, and quickly worked his way up to the prized national beat. In May, he was sent to cover a case in the Aleppo revolutionary court. The front line was not far, and the court guards were frequently running onto the street to help direct traffic or deal with injuries. It was during one such commotion that Shabaan noticed the door to the prison was unguarded. He peered inside and saw a courtyard, where the sun was streaming onto potted plants, and prisoners were gathered for their daily dose of fresh air. Slipping inside, Shabaan observed that a few dozen prisoners grouped around one man. He was of slight bearing, wearing a polo shirt and jeans, and Shabaan realized that he was staring at the facility's most famous prisoner.

No one had heard a word from the Prince since April, when he'd been hauled away on a stretcher by the Aleppo brigades. For weeks, Manbij had witnessed protests, many organized by his wife, demanding his release. There were stories that the Prince had perished in prison, or that he'd been traded for regime-held prisoners. But here he was, standing before Shabaan, grinning and flashing a thumbs-up. Shabaan took out his recorder and interviewed the legendary commander. The Prince denied he'd been charged with a crime and swore he would return to Manbij, so that the poor would suffer no longer. "After I'm released, I'll punish anyone in Manbij who has wronged me or spread false rumors."

The next issue of the *Path* splashed Shabaan's photo of the Prince on the front page, together with the interview. This quickly became the best-selling issue in the *Path*'s history. News that the Prince was alive and vowing to return spread through the city, triggering demonstrations. Women led processions through downtown, calling for the Prince to save Manbij.

From the moment the Prince had found himself in the darkened cell, he began conspiring. One of his cellmates was released in May; in the short weeks they had spent together, the young man had grown enamored of the Prince and pledged to help. Swearing him to secrecy, the Prince dispatched him to bring news to his lieutenants back in Manbij. Slowly, over many weeks, the lieutenants drew up a plan. The Aleppo court was under the authority of the city's six main rebel factions. Each faction took turns guarding the facility. The Prince's followers met with the leader of one of the factions, a secular Free Army brigade. They regaled him with stories of the Prince's bravery, his devotion to the poor, and, most important, his hatred of Islamists. The Free Army faction, embroiled in its own struggle against Islamist brigades, agreed to a deal: If the Prince escaped, he would bring his loyal followers with him to join the rebel faction. Overnight, its numbers would triple, finally giving it the upper hand against the Islamists.

One afternoon in July, ten guards showed up for their regularly scheduled shift at the prison. As the outgoing shift piled into their vehicles, the replacements took their positions. What the outgoing shift did not realize, though, was that the replacements were not really guards—they were the Prince's followers, wearing guard uniforms given to them by the Free Army faction they were in league with. The incognito guards entered the cellblock, removed the Prince, and emerged onto the street in the powerful light of day. They were climbing onto pickups when another rebel faction, guarding a different section of the prison, noticed and opened fire. The pickups spun their wheels, reversed, and tried to speed away. Rebels in the guard towers began firing down. The Prince's men fired back, as the vehicles raced through the crowded streets of Aleppo. People fled indoors. The Prince demanded a weapon and, leaning out the cab window, fired rounds at his pursuers. Glass shattered. One of the Prince's men was struck. Blood was everywhere. But the Prince and his men managed to turn a corner, reached the highway, and were gone.

For the next two months, the Prince lay low in the villages north of Manbij. He converted a farmhouse into a new headquarters, where he spent his days surrounded by supporters. Then, one cool October morning, the city still in darkness, a convoy of a dozen trucks rolled through Manbij. The fighters took up residence in an abandoned government building. By sunrise, the news had shot across town: The Prince had returned. Crowds streamed through the streets in celebration. They carried revolutionary flags and held placards showing the Prince balancing on the busts of the two Assads. After so much strife and dissent, the mood was one of unity. The cold war between ISIS and the Revolutionary Council had strangled the city; ISIS had not even existed when the Prince had been here last—perhaps, in his return, people imagined a return to the sweet days after liberation, when the enemy was clear and comrades stood hand in hand. Or perhaps they imaged the Prince as a leviathan, the only force capable of settling the bitter disputes that had turned neighbor against neighbor. Whether he saw such a role for himself, we do not know, but when he stepped onto the rooftop of his new headquarters, he looked out over thousands of faces and raised his hand in salute, as if to say: *Reporting for duty*.

Of course, not everyone was rejoicing. The senate viewed his comeback with alarm.

But Abdul Hadi sensed an opportunity. He went to ISIS headquarters and explained the situation. As foreigners, most ISIS members had no clue what the Prince represented. Abdul Hadi said the Prince was a hero, here to uproot corruption and serve the poor. He regaled them with the Prince's battlefield exploits, his hatred of the Revolutionary Council. He was a gallant knight, a paragon of bygone values. Abdul Hadi neglected to mention that the Prince loathed Islamists and that he was fond of the bottle. All he chose to convey, or perhaps even believe himself, was that the Prince could be an ally in the war against the senate.

A few days later, the senate made its move. A convoy from the Levant Free Men, the Islamist brigade, surrounded the Prince's compound. On the loudspeaker, the Prince was ordered to exit the building, as he was wanted for "crimes against the revolution." The Prince's forces were outnumbered three to one. One of his men called RYM for support, and Abdul Hadi convinced ISIS to send a convoy of their own. Soon dozens of ISIS fighters were pointing their weapons at the Levant Free Men. An ISIS commander called out, "If you have any business with the Prince, you go through us!" Now it was the Levant Free Men who were surrounded, the Prince on one side, ISIS on the other.

What must have passed through Abdul Hadi's mind at this moment? For a long time, he'd been on the outside looking in, defined by stinging disappointments, a failed revolutionary. Now he'd become a mover of men, a kingmaker. The fighters of ISIS came from far and wide to this besieged city, and they did not solicit the advice of the merchants, the landlords, or even the imams. They sought *his* counsel. They mobilized to *his* suggestions. The Prince, that great knight, had commanded the adoration of thousands, yet his fate now rested, in an astonishing way, on *him*. There was not a person in Manbij who did not now know the name Abdul Hadi Bisher.

The ISIS fighters refused to budge. On the loudspeaker, their commander called out to the Levant Free Men: "You have five minutes to disperse!" A few senators, fearing a civil war, appeared on the scene.

"Three minutes!" the commander called out.

The senators were deep in discussion with the Levant Free Men fighters. Another minute passed. The fighters climbed into their vehicles. As the ISIS fighters cocked their weapons, the Levant Free Men pulled away, raising their hands in a show of surrender. ISIS allowed them to pass.

In the pages of the press and in the market stalls, word spread that a new alliance had formed—the Prince and ISIS. They were an odd couple indeed, but it served both sides well: ISIS was linked to the Hi-Lux Robin Hood, while the Prince gained much-needed muscle. The senate could not touch him while he enjoyed ISIS protection, but after a week basking in his newfound invincibility, he realized he was in a Faustian pact. ISIS was keen to stop him from resuming his old fundraising activities, and forbade him from erecting checkpoints in the city. They asked that he keep to his compound, eschewing the cavalcades through the city he'd used to show off his armory. "A man needs to breathe!" he complained to his charges. The plain reality was that the Manbij the Prince had returned to was a different city than the one he'd left. The question of whether Manbij should be a democracy or an Islamic state was on everyone's minds, and there was nothing the Prince found more reprehensible than religious law.

One morning in early November, he called his lieutenants into his office. He detailed the situation: a city hopelessly divided and succumbing to the siren song of religion. "Where are the old values, where is the old honor?" he asked. Hope was gone; everywhere he looked, there was only opportunism and scheming. The revolution should not belong to those who slept in soft beds—it was for those who slept on hay and woke with the warmth of the sun on their face. It was for the simple man, the plain woman. "Do you want to live under imams? Do you want to live under merchants?" he asked. "Or do you want to be free?"

The truth was, the Prince had been dreaming of freedom, true freedom, for many months now. From the moment he escaped prison, he felt his life had taken a terrible turn. Much of what he'd amassed was gone. His forces were a tenth their former size; he'd lost his vehicles and his arsenal. Sure, he still commanded the adoration of the street, but how could he protect his city from the merchants and the imams with hardly a lira to his name? Yes, he could remain in Manbij, under the protection of ISIS—but that is not who he was. As his stunned lieutenants listened, the Prince released them from their duties. He wished them the best of luck and gave them his blessings. Join ISIS, he said, or choose any other side, so long as it is honorable. "We are men! We live with honor, and we'll die by it!" Some of the lieutenants' eyes watered. "I love you," he concluded. "Each of you."

The next day, the Prince boarded a taxi alone and headed for the Turkish border. Not long after, he was on a fishing boat packed with hundreds of tired, dehydrated refugees, sailing across the Mediterranean, heading for the shores of Europe.

LIBERALS VERSUS POPULISTS

ISIS's seizure of the mills in early September seemed like a watershed in the group's struggle to build a popular base. All month, they managed bread distribution, even succeeding in cutting waste and lowering the price slightly. But ISIS did not control the city. They could not levy taxes, so they could not raise revenue to subsidize bread. By early October, the press was again complaining about the price of basic foodstuffs, and murmurs of a new protest movement could be heard. Eager to avoid falling into the conundrum the council had found themselves in, ISIS agreed to hand control of bread distribution to Free Army factions. Though ISIS's experiment was short lived, it signaled to the street that the group was competent enough to manage the city's institutions. But without full control of the levers of power—that is, without a state governed by religious law—they would be unable to address the economic crisis.

In October, ISIS went on the propaganda offensive, holding seminars detailing life under religious law. They culled examples from the history of early

Islam, when the differences between rich and poor were, they said, minimal, when leaders were bound by a moral code that superseded their earthly whims. They told stories of the leaders of the first Muslim community—caliphs—who kept greedy merchants at heel, enforcing price controls. They extolled zakat, the practice of giving alms to the poor, one of the five pillars of Islam. They produced videos and pamphlets describing life under a caliphate—universal public housing, free health care, a city so secure you could leave your doors open at night. No more kidnappings, no more checkpoints. No more families torn asunder, sons in far-flung lands, sweating under the hot sun in construction sites, returning home once a year. The picture was of an Islamic welfare state, a city not ruled by the wealthy or well connected, but by the just.

ISIS opened educational centers to teach basic science and history. They dispatched volunteers to visit the ill and the wounded in hospitals, distributing dates and milk. They gifted Qurans and perfume to patients. They took up collections at mosques for refugees. Wherever they went, they swore that under an Islamic state, the government would provide such services. The city had known fear and division for too long; under their rule, it would know brotherhood and sisterhood. The greatness of the city would be measured by the fates of the least among them.

The revolutionary leadership—the old council members, the senate—could not understand the allure of such a message. They had not risked their lives for free health care and price controls—they had braved bullets and prison for values greater and more noble than material goods. In a statement, the senate reminded the city: "We declare that this revolution is a revolution of dignity and not a revolution of the hungry! Because if we were hungry, we would have accepted the Assad regime, under which bread cost 15 Syrian liras!"

The vice president of the defunct Revolutionary Council said that the masses should have faith in the market, which "corrects itself": high prices would come down, according to the laws of supply and demand. To meddle in this process was tempting fate.

After a year of crisis upon crisis, these words felt tone-deaf to most people. Those who spoke loudest about "dignity" were those who did not have to worry about their next meal. They did not have to send their sons off to foreign lands to beg for work.

From the beginning, Abdul Hadi had warned everyone about these velvet elites, but people had not listened. Now, people sought him out, treating him like a prophet, someone who could peer into the tumult of the revolution and divine inner truths. But he was rarely at RYM headquarters anymore. Most days, he was at the Muslim Youth Assembly, discussing Islam. A year earlier, he'd mocked brigades that had taken Islamic names. Now, for the first time, he took a keen interest in the Quran and in the early history of his religion. In his youth, he'd taken male lovers; now, he condemned homosexuality as a Western perversion. He quit drinking. He understood himself as participating in a struggle much greater than a revolution against an autocrat, or even against a liberal elite. He was a foot soldier in a battle for justice, one that had been waged for thousands of years, and whose resolution was nigh.

Oday visited him now and then. Abdul Hadi tried to convince his old friend to rejoin RYM, but Oday would hear none of it. The stubbornness of the feuding sides weighed him down, sapping his old energies. Why couldn't the revolutionary leadership agree that wealth redistribution and law and order were necessary to save the democratic experiment? Why couldn't the opposition agree to give the council a chance? Most days, it was too much for him to contemplate, and he longed to leave the mess behind. His parents were searching for a bride, and though he resisted, for the first time he could understand the appeal of starting a family, of building castle walls around his brood and allowing the warring parties to sort it out without him. He implored Abdul Hadi to quit RYM, to find a wife of his own. But Abdul Hadi had discovered his métier. RYM had grown, and most of the recruits were under eighteen. In weekly demonstrations, he led the group like the pied piper. The demonstrations curled around city blocks, with not a single revolutionary flag in sight. Instead, one could only glimpse a sea of black banners.

Not long after, Abdul Hadi convened a meeting at RYM headquarters. Nearly the entire organization was present. There was Nabeel, RYM's putative leader; Nabeel's cousin Abboud, who had spent many childhood nights hiding in the closet as his father raged at the voices in his head, and who'd become the first in his family to attend university; Ahmed Dali, a soccer star; and many others. Also attending was an ISIS member, originally from Iraq. Abdul Hadi began by speaking about the early days of Islam, when equality and justice reigned, an age of splendor, when the Arab lands were the center of art, learning, and culture, when Europe was in a dark age of warlords and illiteracy. Something had gone terribly wrong, he explained, when the ways of those early generations of Muslims were abandoned. Society had forgotten the centrality of faith, turning to other political systems—communism, Baathism, liberalism—that failed to deliver social justice. And now, he said, look around—the rot in the city was because those failed doctrines continued to rule. Abdul Hadi delved into the sayings and deeds of the prophets, and how the city's religious establishment selectively interpreted these stories to uphold the status quo. He was wading into theology when one of the attendees interrupted. "I don't understand what you are talking about," he said. "Can you just get to the point?"

"The point," Abdul Hadi said, looking around the room, "is that to solve our problems, Manbij must become an Islamic state."

"And what's your suggestion?"

"I suggest," he said, pausing to find the right wording, "I suggest we take a vote, right now, on whether to join ISIS."

A couple of RYM members stood up. One said, "This is crazy, they are not with the revolution—they are just using it!"

"You're free to do as you please," Abdul Hadi said. "The revolution can only be saved through justice and equality."

The two RYM members gathered their belongings and left. The remainder—about two dozen, many only fifteen or sixteen—did not budge.

All those in favor, raise your hands, Abdul Hadi instructed. Almost two dozen hands went up.

From that day, ISIS was bankrolling RYM, allowing them to expand and attract more recruits. As word got around that Abdul Hadi had joined ISIS, his erstwhile comrades could not believe it: Abdul Hadi—goofy, immature, hardly a religious bone in his body. Oday took the news as an insult to their shared struggle and refused to see his friend. Another former RYM member accosted Abdul Hadi. "You are a dupe! These people hate the Free Army—how are they any different than the regime?" Abdul Hadi simply chortled. "This group is going to rule Syria in the future—you'll see." And for the son of a working-class family, condemned to the margins, attaching himself to such a force had a compelling logic. To dismiss him as a mere opportunist would be too simplistic. Like tens of thousands of Manbijis, he harbored a genuine disgust for the injustices on display in the revolution. After so much grief, betrayal, and poverty, liberalism's story—that affording everyone as much personal and economic freedom as possible brings happiness and success—rang hollow. So Abdul Hadi inscribed himself in a different narrative, one that, given the circumstances, had a reasonable claim to truth. In inhabiting this story, he believed it fully, as we all, in whatever story we inhabit, inevitably must.

Yet another ex-RYM member visited Abdul Hadi. "We made this revolution to overthrow the regime," he said. "That was our only goal. That's why we went out in demos. We risked everything for this. What are you doing?"

"ISIS will bring religious law," Abdul Hadi replied. "We rose up for justice, and that's what I want."

The ex-RYM member could hardly believe what he was hearing. He lit a cigarette. Abdul Hadi said, "Smoking is forbidden."

The ex-RYM member's eyes widened. "Who are *you* to tell me this? Would you like me to tell your new friends about *your* forbidden past?"

"Smoking is forbidden," he said again. "That's my last warning."

That week, Abdul Hadi devoted himself to recruitment. He was targeting even younger children—he'd just convinced a fourteen-year-old to join RYM. The assembly now counted over fifty members, all of whom were also members or supporters of ISIS. Meanwhile, membership of the ISIS military wing grew rapidly. The FSA faction Ammar bin Yasser joined ISIS en masse. Other Free Army fighters quit their brigades in the ones and twos, flocking to ISIS. The Islamic State was now the largest armed faction in the city. To show their gratitude, ISIS allowed Abdul Hadi unfettered access to their two headquarters, the Cultural Center and the Youth Center. He was given a set of keys to the Youth Center, which had been closed to the public for fear of air strikes. One Friday afternoon, he opened the equipment room. He assembled neighborhood boys and distributed jerseys: red to one side, white to the other. They erected goalposts in the cement lot behind the center, where Abdul Hadi had practiced barefoot so many years before. The children gathered, formed teams, and went at it. They screamed and laughed and tripped on the cold cement, and the commotion reached the street, so that passersby were drawn in, giving the teams spectators. It was the first soccer match since liberation, and Abdul Hadi watched the children play, a grin on his face.

| TWENTY-ONE |

November 2013

NEWS

In the past 10 days, Manbij governorate has been hit by three air strikes, the most recent of which targeted the garden of the National Hospital last Sunday. —**Weekly Letters**

The Students Without Borders Assembly distributed leaflets for their rent-control campaign, Bread or Housing, which aims . . . to pressure realtors and property owners to reduce rents. —**Path**

Is it possible to live a decent life under the revolution of dignity? Abu Ali, in his forties, a father of four girls and three boys, used to work as a traffic police officer. He has suffered a lot during his life and claims it's even worse now, as he lost his home and job. . . . Like Abu Ali, many people have lost faith in the revolution. —**Sun**

THE SUN SETS

Of Manbij's two dozen periodicals, which ranged from philosophical journals to tabloids to Islamist tracts to left-wing pamphlets, two commanded citywide readership, the *Path* and the *Sun*. In the beginning, the *Path* was opposed to the Revolutionary Council, devoting much ink to crime and poverty and exposés of rebel malfeasance. After the council election in May, though, the *Path* dropped its adversarial tone, assuming the posture of an outlet above the divisions rending the city. Columnists were given to abstract disquisitions on Islam; correspondents covered battles in other cities, perhaps not wanting to wade into Manbij's factional politics. Against this, its competitor, the *Sun*, made no airs about impartiality. From the beginning, it defended the Revolutionary Council, perhaps because if there was one thing Huzayfa Osman, its editor, loathed as much as the Assad regime, it was the Islamists. That gave the *Sun*'s reportage on ISIS a critical—some might even say unfair—cast. The paper claimed that the storming of council headquarters was pure political theater; that ISIS was in league with bakery owners; and that, beneath its populist veneer, the organization held working-class people in contempt. After weeks of such attacks, Osman was summoned to the Cultural Center to explain his paper's reporting.

He sat across the desk from an Egyptian. A pair of masked gunmen were at the door. Osman had considered ignoring their request, but wondered if he might use the opportunity to publish a column about ISIS headquarters. The Egyptian demanded to know why the *Sun* had slandered ISIS. Osman asked for evidence of their bias. The Egyptian: The *Sun* claimed that bakery owners, not the poor, were present during the bread riots. "Don't you verify facts before you publish them?" Osman said that he'd been present and even had a video. He played a clip of the rioters, and pointed out, here and there, a few bakery owners. The Egyptian retorted: "What about the others? There are thousands of people here."

The back-and-forth went on for some time, until finally the Egyptian said, "I learned that the *Sun* doesn't have any donors. We are willing to offer monthly donations, and pay 10,000 Syrian liras worth of salaries for each staff member. We'll offer you cameras, printers, and, most important, security—especially since the rebel factions don't like you for your nosy reporting."

"And what do we have to do in return?"

"Nothing, but your paper only reports on the exploits of the Free Army. You don't say a word about the Islamic State unless it is negative. You don't talk about our battles on the front lines, you don't mention our courts. You should do a story about how our courts function in other liberated cities, and how the public supports them."

"We tried reaching out to you many times for comment, but you don't cooperate. You are too secretive. We don't know who you are, what your goals are, who funds you. And whenever we publish anything, you get angry—and look, now you've summoned me here."

Suddenly, as if a switch had flipped, the Egyptian began to yell. "Who are you to ask me these questions? Who supports *you*? What are *your* goals? Do you get support from the infidel West or the Free Army?" He accused the *Sun* of pushing a secular leftist agenda, planted in Muslim brains by the West. He bellowed that the West and the *Sun* were trying to incite strife among Muslims. Eventually, he offered a resolution. "You are free to publish what you'd like. Our only request is that you submit each edition to us before it is printed, so that we can check for any mistakes, anything that violates religious law—God knows you've had many such errors in previous issues."

Osman had not said a word during this tirade but understood that he was not being offered a choice. The masked gunmen were blocking the exit. Osman tried to smile. "We'll meet with our editorial staff," he said, "and discuss it." The gunmen did not budge. "These are good suggestions," Osman said weakly.

"We'll wait for your answer," the Egyptian said.

Osman was allowed to leave. He was covered in sweat.

That evening, the editorial board discussed their predicament. If the *Sun* continued publishing, they would be acting in defiance of a group that was now the largest, most well-armed force in the city—and possibly the most popular. The freedoms that the *Sun* staff had enjoyed existed only because of an understanding, not spelled out anywhere but believed in by all sides with a fervor rivaling that reserved for God and His angels, that speech was sacred. Last year, when the *Path* accused a Free Army commander of corruption, his only conceivable recourse was a lawsuit. The revolutionary leadership and the opposition had not agreed on much, but on the question of free speech they were united. Something had turned in this city, though, so that freedom to speak one's mind had lost its shine—especially when families had mouths to feed. Such freedom seemed no longer a right but a luxury, an indulgence to be embraced only after life's essentials were met. If the *Sun* staff struck a defiant posture, exposing ISIS's demand in its pages, would the people raise their voices? A year ago, the RYM would have called a mass demonstration, and the *Sun* would have happily exposed ISIS. Now, Osman was unsure whom they could call on. It was only then, in this meeting, that the editors realized that the revolutionaries had lost the street altogether. A scrappy newspaper with a staff of a dozen operating on a shoestring budget, against a force armed to the teeth and able to turn out supporters in every neighborhood—this was no contest. The editorial staff agreed to suspend publication. The next issue announced:

> This statement is something people might not understand, but every word signifies many things we cannot say, things we have been unable to say until now. Why are newspapers shutting down? Why is genuine revolutionary work faced with accusations of bias? Journalism isn't about bias, it is about honesty and professionalism in delivering news that matters to the reader. Even though the *Sun of Freedom* newspaper was born from the womb of revolution, it never overlooked the

mistakes of revolutionaries, while also defending the principles for which we rose up. We reject subordinating the revolution to foreign agendas and alien political projects.

Sixteen months. Osman and his friends had begun by distributing mimeographed copies on street corners. They had no weapons, and yet they strode into the headquarters of rebel battalions, into the corridors of this council and that, armed with the faith that behind them stood a reserve army of their fellow citizens. They'd never taken a day of journalistic instruction in their lives, discovering how to write, how to work with lighting and arrange layout, on the job. They'd penned brilliant investigations, careful ruminations, absurd demands. They'd erred, publishing corrections, and so, with great effort, learned. Osman could not recognize the man he'd been sixteen months earlier. He now carried within him the knowledge that, when permitted to speak, he had much to say.

WESTERN IDEAS

By November, Manbij had become two cities, two warring tribes, so polarized that the precepts of truth itself were in question. Dispatches from the front were subject to allegations of "fake news." Writers found they could no longer publish poetry or a short story in literary journals without incurring an accusation of bias. No one was simply a "revolutionary" anymore—you were either an Islamist or a secularist. Some activists drifted from the assemblies; others tried to bury their heads in the sand. In this environment, Women of Freedom, the assembly Mina had helped launch, was floundering. The economic crisis pushed women to drop out, causing operating revenue to dry up. The assembly was forced to close *Peace Be Upon You*, the city's only women-run periodical.

To forestall collapse, Mina convinced the group to accept funding from an international nongovernmental organization—an unusual step in Manbij, where assemblies generally had no ties to outside parties. The NGO was founded by elite Syrians who lived abroad; they offered trainings in Turkey, and their sleek website touted phrases like "civil society" and "transitional justice," which were alien to the revolution in Manbij but en vogue among the cosmopolitan set. The NGO awarded Women of Freedom a grant to conduct training in "peace building" and "nonviolent resistance." Mina was brought to Turkey, where she was instructed on the role of civil disobedience in the American civil rights movement, the struggle against apartheid in South Africa, and the Indian anti-colonial campaign.

With the funds, Women of Freedom organized a workshop, where Mina lectured on Gandhi. She asked participants to offer examples of conflict from their own lives—a dispute with a neighbor, a rivalry with another assembly—and the group worked through how to solve the problem without violence. The workshop drew a poor turnout, so she visited the office of the Future Youth Assembly to invite them to collaborate. But the young men there looked exasperated. One of them said that by spreading this nonsense about "peace-building," Mina was ignoring the real issues—unemployment, crime, air strikes. He had always been a conscientious young man, participating in blood drives and soup kitchens organized by the Women of Freedom. He'd championed women's participation in the revolution, marched in support of the Revolutionary Council. Yet even he viewed Mina's prescriptions as delusional. "These are Western ideas," he said vehemently. "The only way to overthrow this regime is jihad. The only way to fix our city is religious law!"

Mina could not believe what she was hearing. She asked him to confer with his comrades and said she'd return the next day.

The next morning, she went to the office early. She wanted to read further about Mandela so she could develop better arguments. When she arrived, she noticed the lock had been smashed open. Inside, the room was in disarray: papers strewn about, furniture moved. She rushed to the corkboard, where she'd pinned her training posters—and found them torn to shreds.

Shaken, she stayed home for a few days. She called her supervisor at the NGO, who offered advice on how to deal with "extremists." She approached the Change and Development Assembly, a left-wing outfit, where she expected a better reception. Again, she went through the history of King and Gandhi, but once more the attendees resisted her message. "These are Western ideas," one of them repeated. "We are facing a genocide!" On the phone with her donor that evening, she was told if she couldn't convince others, it meant she herself was not convinced. She redoubled her efforts, poring through the training materials, scouring the web for historical examples of nonviolence that had worked against a regime of this nature.

Yet it wasn't merely the idea of civil disobedience that struck her comrades as so wrong-headed. After all, they themselves were civilian activists. Rather, the framing seemed utterly unconcerned about the real challenges plaguing the city. Mina was instructed by her donors to plan a series of trainings on subjects such as "international humanitarian law" and "transitional justice." Her training materials emphasized "freedom and dignity," but there was not a word about economic equality. The most pressing concerns of working-class Syrians were absent. In fact, the NGO—and many like it—were downright hostile to the demands of the poor. In her grant application, Mina was asked to what extent her organization agreed with the statement, "We dream of a Syria based on the principles of the free market."

Before long, she stopped showing up at the assembly's office.

A LONG RIDE HOME

One day, Sheikh Dibo, the religious scholar who'd criticized ISIS doctrines, was at the pulpit when two masked men approached and fired. The sheikh died instantly. Sometime later, a Free Army commander who'd threatened ISIS was abducted.

ISIS issued half-hearted denials of responsibility. But they hardly needed to say a word, because in cafes and market stalls, citizens were willing to denounce such rumors as fake news and to peddle the conspiracy theory that the old Revolutionary Council had authored the violence. Meanwhile, with more merit, people held the council and the Free Army responsible for the economy; the price of a bundle of bread was hovering at 50 Syrian liras. In the Great Souk, olive oil had quadrupled in price and butter tripled—in just two months. Middle-class families like Mina's had eaten through their savings. With inflation, Mina's husband had taken the equivalent of a 50 percent pay cut at the mills. She had been earning hard cash as a substitute teacher, but the city's education directorate had run out of money, and teachers had not been paid in months. The family's only hope was Mina's back pay, which she was owed from prerevolution days. But the cash was held at the regime's Ministry of Education, in government-controlled Aleppo. The family had tried everything to recover the money—calling friends in Aleppo, working contacts in the education ministry. When that failed, Mina's husband took a second job. When he was laid off, they borrowed from relatives.

None of it made a difference; Mina and her husband began skipping meals so that the children had enough. Mina awoke at night panting, reaching for her husband's warm body. She went to the window and studied the silos looming over the city. She prayed. She took sips of holy water from Mecca. The sense of impending calamity was still there when early morning cast the bedroom in a blue pallor. Many days passed like this, with wild scenes flashing through her mind—penned crowds, women throwing themselves at fencing, beating their breasts. Life had never flowed with abundance, but she had never tasted poverty before, either. She was not built for it, or if she were, her children were certainly not. That was what finally convinced her—the children. No matter what, they should be shielded. She told her husband one afternoon that they were left without a choice. She would have to collect her back salary in Aleppo.

Since Manbij had spun out of regime control eighteen months prior, it would have been a suicide mission for a man to cross lines. The regime maintained extensive lists; anyone remotely linked to the revolution was wanted for "terrorism." Even if you had nothing to do with politics, perhaps your son or cousin or friend did. But women faced less suspicion, unless their name was on a list. Mina set out early morning with a friend, a fellow teacher also hoping to collect back pay. Mina's name was almost certainly on a wanted list, so she brought her sister-in-law's ID.

They sat in the back of a shared taxi, and Mina pressed her face to the glass. The Manbij–Aleppo highway was lined with revolutionary flags. Soon they were in open country. Farmsteads, mud houses crowned with satellite dishes, cypress groves. The traffic thinned. Here and there, stone villages and golden fields of wheat. The taxi slowed. They passed a rebel checkpoint—the border of Manbij's revolutionary government. Burned-out vehicles lined the road. The driver rolled to a stop and told his passengers that from here they were on their own.

Mina walked a good mile, until she approached a crowd. They were in a scrum around a checkpoint. A Syrian regime flag was flying above. On the checkpoint booth were posters of Bashar al-Assad and his father. Mina was patted down. She pushed her way to the front and handed the guard the ID card. The guard was checking it against a computer. He hardly glanced at her. He was typing something.

The photo on the card looked nothing like her. She glanced at her friend. The recklessness of her plans now seemed like those of a stranger. This was not her—she was prudent, responsible. She should have convinced her husband to pack up the family and flee to Turkey. She pictured herself leading her son, Anwar, by the hand through sedge fields, crouching among the tall grasses, the Turkish gendarme post in sight, covering her daughter's mouth so she would not cry. Her husband was up ahead with the smuggler. The gendarme would not shoot at families. The Turkish people were good, they were kind. She was repeating this to herself like an incantation. The Turkish people were kind. She was risking her life here for nothing. She wanted nothing more than to see her husband one last time. A man was shouting, "Aisha!" She thought about backing away; no one would notice. She'd walk the mile back to the rebel checkpoint. She'd burst into tears and someone, a fellow revolutionary, would take pity, drive her back home. "Aisha!" a voice bellowed. Mina looked back at the stretch of no-man's-land. The horizon was mercilessly flat, as far as she could see. "Aisha!"

Mina came to her senses—Aisha was the name on the ID card. "That's me!"

"I was shouting your name!" the officer boomed. "Why didn't you answer?"

"I'm sorry sir," she said, her voice quivering. "I didn't hear you."

The officer was so angry he did not bother to look at the photo. He threw the ID card on the ground and shouted, "Go!"

When Mina picked up the ID card, she was standing in Syrian government territory. A few shared taxis were waiting. She realized that despite the cold, she was covered in sweat.

The taxi drove through the streets of west Aleppo. Mina had not allowed herself to imagine what this world, left behind upon liberation, looked like, and what she saw stunned her. Whereas the rebel-controlled parts of the city were in ruins due to air strikes, here the broad cedar-lined avenues were unblemished by war. It was as if she'd arrived in a different country.

The next morning, she and her friend visited the education directorate. Mina waited outside as her friend entered to collect both salaries. When she emerged, she looked concerned. "I'm really sorry," she said. "You were suspended."

Mina rushed in and was informed that her back pay had been seized and her pension canceled. Mina walked outside, in the biting air, and sat on the curb. She stared at the passing traffic, the vendors. She remained there, sobbing silently, for some time.

At the bus station, she found a shared taxi heading for the Manbij checkpoint. The main highway was closed, so the van rolled through the Safira District. The roadside markets were fire-blackened, the corrugated iron shutters mangled. Houses were split in half. There was not a human in sight. The shrubs were frosted with rime. They crossed the last regime checkpoint, and soon were in rebel territory, where the scenes of destruction continued. Rubble was heaped here and there as if in a junkyard. The word "Freedom" was spray-painted on the sides of cinderblock houses. Occasionally, she spotted children playing in the wreckage. Now and then, more signs of life appeared: clothes on the line, motorcyclists. The buildings were beginning to crowd together, and when she saw the sculpture of the open book, held aloft by two hands, she located the red-green-and-black tri star flag, the banner of her revolution, and felt a surge of hope. Somehow, she believed, they would survive.

There was a blackout in her neighborhood when she arrived. The muezzins were singing the call for the evening prayer. Many windows were candlelit. Her mother came to the doorway holding a gas lamp, her eyes red. "I thought your children lost you!"

Her husband appeared, and as they kissed, she could sense, though he would never admit it, that he had been crying.

| TWENTY-TWO |

December 2013

NEWS

Our brother Hasan Nefi was reelected to represent Manbij in the Aleppo Provincial Council. —*Weekly Letters*

On Thursday at noon, Manbij city was exposed to an air strike that killed five martyrs and wounded more than twenty-seven civilians. The aircraft targeted a residential building near the Sailboat Roundabout, causing great damage. —*Path*

RUMORS OF A WAR

When the flakes fell, the city gave the appearance of being trapped under a silver dome, the sky unbroken and featureless, while people remarked on the strange wind—unlike the winds of the Euphrates, the only gales they had ever known—which drove against breeze-block and Roman stone, against the wooden rafters of the Great Souk, against the balconies and portieres, with a force suggesting calamity, a doom more terrible than falling munitions. The snowflakes smothered the streets, the parked cars, the ogive windows, the copper cupolas, the sculpted roundabouts, and the many small, dark, one-room cinderblock dwellings. The sleet-filled wadi shone like steel. By nightfall the city lay in blackness, the homes lit with the sickly glow of candles, and people could hear the crackle of buckling wood, the rattle of windows, and the low walls of ambulances.

Winter storm Alexa was the first blizzard Manbij had witnessed in decades or, as some elders tell it, ever. This desert city was not built to sustain Alexa's wrath. By morning, the roads were coated in ice. The roofs of houses in working-class Sheikh Aqeel had caved in. The tent cities clinging to the city's outskirts were ruined; refugees had no winter coats or gloves. The chill wormed its way into every crevice of every house and apartment, every one-room shop. On the first night, the public hospital treated twenty-seven patients with frostbite, fractures, bruises, and slipped discs. Within two days, hundreds of such patients clogged the wards. "Syrians fell prey to this storm just as they have tasted death in all its forms," the *Path* lamented. "Either we die from Assad's shells or from the frost."

The city's coffers were nearly empty, so volunteers fanned out, hacking at the ice crystals, shoveling sidewalks. Everyone pitched in, from the assemblies to the senate, but the most pivotal assistance came from ISIS, which plowed roads and markets. ISIS members volunteered as traffic police. They distributed free bread in Central Square and the refugee camps. If one had conducted a poll, ISIS would easily have been the most popular entity in the city, armed or civilian. Eight months of painstaking political work—building coalitions, establishing front groups, circulating propaganda—and well-timed theater, like the execution and the storming of the council, had won them this following.

Still, the revolutionary leadership failed to learn the right lessons. In December, the senate drew up plans to revive the Revolutionary Council. As its first act, the body pledged not to tackle prices but to "restore the beauty and charm of our streets" by hiring street cleaners. The Revolutionary Council had lost its popular base, the ordinary men and women of the street, but it retained the allegiance of thousands of professional revolutionaries—the rebels and assembly members. The ISIS grandees knew that in their political battle with the council, they would need to attract the masses while putting pressure on these core supporters—which they did by arresting several activists on various charges, including spying.

One of the detained was Ahmed Tarboush, a member of the Manbij Human Rights Organization, an assembly that focused on violations committed by armed groups. He was thrown into the basement of the Cultural Center, which ISIS had converted into a prison. When an ISIS leader came to inspect the prisoners, Tarboush, who was also a journalist and had interviewed the man before, called out, "You know me! Why are you doing this?"—and received a stinging blow to the face. "Shut your damn mouth!" the ISIS leader shouted. "You son of a whore!"

Tarboush languished in the tiny cell for days. Once, the door to the main corridor swung open and Abdul Hadi entered. He was going to the bathroom. Tarboush banged on the bars. The two had marched side by side; Tarboush's assembly had once worked closely with RYM. "You have to help me!" he cried.

"Talk to them upstairs! Tell my family I'm here!" Abdul Hadi looked at his old friend but did not say a word. As Tarboush continued to bang on the bars, Abdul Hadi kept walking, as if no one were there.

Eventually, a senate delegation negotiated Tarboush's release. ISIS was now brazenly doing as it pleased, and the revolutionary authorities were left to plead and cajole. In liberated cities around the country, the balance of power had similarly shifted. Stories of kidnapped activists and assassinated rebel leaders were becoming impossible to ignore. In Aleppo, the leading association of religious scholars published a statement labeling ISIS criminal and enjoined its rank-and-file members to quit. Revolutionary councils in one city after the next issued decrees condemning the Islamic State. In the city of al-Bab, some thirty miles west of Manbij, protesters marched through the streets chanting against ISIS, "Do your jihad on the front lines and leave us alone!"

The plain truth was revealing itself: coexistence was impossible. The spark that led to the final confrontation came in late December, when ISIS and the Free Syrian Army clashed in a town near the Euphrates. A neutral party offered to mediate—but ISIS promptly arrested the negotiator, then tortured and executed him. Pictures of the man's bruised and mottled body made the rounds on social media, sparking furor among revolutionary ranks. Demonstrations rocked cities around the country. ISIS labeled those who participated in such protests "apostates," pledging to punish them under Islamic law. This fueled further anger, and Free Army units stormed ISIS strongholds in one town after the next. Within days, dozens of revolutionary towns and cities were free of ISIS, and the tri-star flag once again flew over the cupolas and farmhouses of western Syria.

WAR COMES TO MANBIJ

The Manbij branch of the Islamic State of Iraq and Greater Syria now had nearly two hundred members. All eyes were now on the revolutionaries of Manbij—would they move on ISIS, as their comrades in Idlib and Aleppo had done? A sense of foreboding took hold. The shops at the Great Souk closed early and the streets emptied. With the rolling brownouts, the apartment windows on Rabta Street were illuminated by candlelight. At round abouts, the Revolutionary Police shone flashlights in drivers' faces.

At the Cultural Center, ISIS leader Abu Harith the Jordanian held a meeting of top lieutenants. Abdul Hadi was in attendance. So were the members of the Jazeera soccer team, who were now leading figures in the organization. Abu Harith insisted there was no dispute in Manbij. He'd exchanged messages with the senate, who'd assured him that if ISIS refrained from interfering in local affairs, they would be left alone. No one wanted bloodshed.

Meanwhile, a few blocks away, at the Sheikh Aqeel mosque, senators and Free Syria Army commanders were meeting. After an hour of discussion, they agreed that the time had come. ISIS would never abide by the city's laws. Only one road remained. The operation would commence at dawn. Units were posted around the city. In the darkness, they took up positions in front of the Cultural Center and other ISIS facilities. Gunmen were perched on the roof of the hotel.

The senate understood that a brazen attack on ISIS, without the street's imprimatur, could backfire. So Abel Os organized a demonstration through the darkened avenues of Sarab, drawing residents onto their balconies. The procession crossed the wadi bridge, heading for downtown—though unlike RYM demonstrations, people did not join as it passed. The march reached Revolutionary Council headquarters. "The people demand the exit of the Islamic State!" the crowd chanted, and their voices could be heard at ISIS headquarters. Some ISIS members were eager to open fire on the demonstrators, but Abu Harith the Jordanian advised restraint. By midnight, the protesters dispersed.

Late that night, a convoy rolled through the backstreets laden with equipment donated by FSA groups in other cities: 14.5mm rounds, Soviet-made DShK heavy machine guns, RPG launchers.

Around 3:00 a.m., the lights finally went out in the Cultural Center, and its occupants settled into their cots. Abdul Hadi lay in the darkness. He tossed and turned all night, finally sitting up when he heard a voice repeating itself, a recitation filling the air: "In the name of God, the merciful and compassionate, all members of the Islamic State should surrender to the authorities. Do not shed your sacred blood for a criminal organization."

He jumped out of bed.

The message was blaring from mosque loudspeakers. The ISIS fighters scrambled for their weapons. They peered outside to discover that their facility was surrounded by the Free Army. Walkie-talkies started to crackle: ISIS strongholds around the city were encircled. All entrances to the city were closed.

Gunfire.

ISIS fighters fired desperately from behind the compound wall. For the first time in his life, Abdul Hadi grabbed a weapon and shot wildly into the dawn air. Shots rang back.

Nearby, Oday and other former RYM members braved the gunfire to meet at a friend's house. Was this civil war? They tried to formulate a plan to halt the violence, but the meeting devolved into accusations and counter-accusations. Some said RYM had brought ruin upon the city through their strident opposition. Others asked, What was this revolution for? *Who* was it for? Insecurity, poverty, favoritism—these had filled the cup of resentment to the brim, and when it overflowed, revolutionaries had no one to blame but themselves.

Meanwhile, over at the October Dam on the Euphrates River, Free Army ranks were thin because their comrades were assisting the fight in Manbij. ISIS seized the opportunity to overrun the Free Army base. They captured three Free Army members, marched them to the river, and executed them. An ISIS commander named Abu Muhammad the Egyptian declared himself ruler of the dam and threatened to cut off power to Manbij. ISIS sent a convoy with mounted 23mm machine guns to Manbij, where they burst through the southern cordon and were soon snaking through the city's streets to rescue their besieged comrades. But FSA units were ready, stationed near the Municipal Bakery. Heavy clashes ensued: bullets splintering windows, puncturing tires. A Red Crescent worker was gunned down by ISIS. But the group could not penetrate FSA defenses and withdrew.

A second ISIS cavalcade attempted to pierce the city's northern cordon, but the Free Army, occupying the roofs of apartment buildings, fired down. It was a rout. One ISIS truck escaped the scrum and wandered the streets like a lost animal, until Free Army rebels tracked it down, killed its two occupants, stripped them to their underwear, and left the bodies in the middle of Rabta Street. Abel Os heard about the desecration and shouted into the walkie-talkie, "Is this a jungle? Do we have no morality?" He commandeered a truck, recovered the bodies, and delivered them to the hospital.

At the Cultural Center, an ISIS sniper climbed to the roof, where he had a clean look at a Free Army unit stationed on the street below. When he fired, FSA fighters took cover behind parked cars and fired back. The ISIS sniper sprayed the street with bullets; one round struck Muhammad Ghaith Sheikh Weiss, a civilian, in his home. He was the family's only son.

On the first floor of the Cultural Center, Abdul Hadi aimed his weapon through a slit in the wall. The street was smoking, and he could not find the Free Army fighters. Suddenly, his thoughts turned to his RYM colleagues. They were mostly teenagers, and they had spent the night next door in the Youth Center, where they had been taking courses to enlist in the Cubs of the Caliphate, the ISIS youth group. They'd all joined RYM, and then ISIS, at his urging. He could not abandon them. After sending word up to the sniper, he stole out onto the street. Skulking along the compound wall, he stopped every few feet to listen. When he reached the edge of the wall, he sprinted across the alley to the next wall. Once inside the Youth Center, he found a few ashen-faced boys, and he hugged each one.

He remained with them as the sun rose. By noon, the gunfire petered out, and the exhausted voice of Abu Harith the Jordanian came over a walkie-talkie. He was instructing them to surrender.

Abdul Hadi stepped into the sunlight, his young RYM comrades in tow, with his hands up.

That evening, Nabeel went to collect bread at the Municipal Bakery. His arc was that of so many young, idealistic revolutionaries. After a rocky home life and stints as a migrant worker in Lebanon, he'd joined the protests and thrown himself into the world of RYM, marching alongside Oday and Abdul Hadi. When Abdul Hadi railed against the Revolutionary Council, Nabeel finally felt he'd found someone speaking the truth. And when Abel Os quit RYM, Nabeel was elected president—though in reality, he was Abdul Hadi's puppet. Only when RYM joined ISIS did Nabeel decide they'd gone too far, resigning and proclaiming a life of neutrality.

When he arrived at the bakery, he noticed the expressions of the guards—the same Free Army guards he'd said hello to every day—had changed. A dark look had come over their eyes. On his way home, Nabeel stopped at an internet cafe to visit friends. He hadn't been there long when a fleet of vehicles surrounded the cafe. Nabeel was ordered outside with his hands in the air, and he found himself staring at the muzzles of a dozen rifles. "Get down!" one Free Army fighter screamed. "Get down! You are under arrest!"

Nabeel, his face to the ground, called out, "What do you want from me?" He felt hands searching his body, then lifting him up. He was thrown into the back of an automobile. "What do you want?" Nabeel asked again.

A man in the front turned and barked, "Why did you demonstrate against us?" Nabeel recognized him as a senator. "You and your people caused this!" the man shouted.

Another Free Army fighter said, "Let him demonstrate against us—aren't we advocates of freedom?"

"Look what 'freedom' created," the first man shot back.

Senators and their allies came to inspect the prisoners in the lockup. One of them scolded the detainees, asking how they could have protested the council when they were all supposed to be on the same side. A man pointed his finger at Nabeel. "I considered you my comrade! *You* and your people helped pave the way for ISIS!"

That evening, the revolutionary security forces raided homes around the city. Having eliminated the core of ISIS in battle, they now viewed anyone linked to the organization, no matter how tenuously, as part of a fifth column. This meant, in practice, anyone who'd protested the Revolutionary Council in the past nineteen months. They mopped up hundreds of activists, arresting ISIS members who'd quit as well as those who'd flirted with joining but thought better of it. They threw entire assemblies—the Free Students Union, the Muslim Youth—behind bars. Some FSA figures took it upon themselves to detain anyone they suspected of harboring Islamist sympathies, even if they'd never uttered a word in favor of the Islamic State. Anyone with a beard could not be trusted.

Fighters surrounded Oday's house, but he sent a message to Abel Os, who told the senators to leave him alone. With this reprieve, Oday set to work trying to free his friends. He beseeched senators to control the rebels. Abel Os and Oday threatened to call a mass demonstration if the security forces did not ease off—and because Abel Os was himself a senator, this threat could not be ignored. The senate issued a directive forbidding security forces from arresting anyone who had not carried a weapon. Nabeel and other activists were released—but all ISIS members, including Abdul Hadi, remained in the lockup.

On January 7, 2014, three days after its forces routed ISIS, the senate convened. Senators broke into chants, praised God, and hugged and congratulated each other. The revolution in Manbij had faced its gravest threat and survived—and now comrades in other cities needed their aid. Once the Islamist menace was eradicated everywhere, and Assad was in a cage on trial, there would be time to settle differences. Now, the senators argued triumphantly, the opposition should understand their place. A senator announced, "We are finally the supreme word in the city!"

The assembly elected a new Revolutionary Council, with Aimad Henezel, who'd previously managed the bread portfolio, as revolutionary Manbij's third president. A law was passed reaffirming freedom of speech and assembly, with the senate inviting those "persecuted by ISIS to work in the city." The assembly passed a second ordinance criminalizing membership in ISIS.

Manbij, which had been a beacon of democracy in the region, was now the standard-bearer of anti-ISIS resistance as well. That Friday, nearly a week after the battle, crowds filtered out of the mosques, and here and there, cries went up: "Long live the Revolutionary Council!" Downtown, Abel Os led hundreds of young men through the street. They waved the tri-star flag, linked arms, and sang:

> *Free, free, freedom, we want freedom*
> *Despite you, oh Bashar, we will gain our freedom*

Once, they had sung those lines while neighbors leaned over balustrades and clapped, motorists honked, and the air was clean and the sun brilliant and hearts inflamed with purpose. But on this frigid Friday, they sang the same songs without conviction, as if the words were mere sounds, as if their steps followed a script. Their old joy was not evident; faces wan, legs trudging through the vacant streets, they felt smaller, more alone, than ever. No one rushed to the balustrades to watch the procession, and cars passed without their occupants stopping to comment. The city had exhausted itself, and people now hoped not for liberation but deliverance.

| TWENTY-THREE |

January 2014

IN DARKNESS SHINES A LIGHT

In the dank quarters, the men breathed noisome airs and huddled beside each other for warmth. A single high window was boarded up. When the lights were switched off, the cell was black as pitch. Eight of them lay here. None had known each other a year prior, but now they were more than comrades. Abdul Hadi looked upon his cellmates as spiritual brothers: vegetable peddlers and tire repairmen and roustabouts who had risen to the moral heights of this city, men whose existence made a kernel of sense in a world gone mad.

A week had passed since they were thrown into prison by the revolutionary leadership. They had had no contact with the outside; Abdul Hadi had been unable to get a message to his family. The rest, all RYM members, were convinced that one day the cell door would open and they would be marched to a field, made to kneel, and shot. But Abdul Hadi nourished some hope. Even here, in this makeshift prison in the basement of the city's finance directorate, he was convinced much work lay ahead of him.

Once a day, warders delivered stale olives, bread, and tea. Abdul Hadi took the opportunity to converse with the guards. They were his own age, and they seemed beaten down by the strife tearing apart their revolution. They had marched against the regime, then joined the rebels, spending weeks on the front lines, feeling the shudder of air strikes, watching comrades get torn limb from limb. Now, instead of protecting their city against the regime, they were logging thankless hours in this improvised dungeon. Abdul Hadi asked: Is this why you risked your lives? One guard said he was considering quitting the armed struggle and moving to Lebanon for work. Abdul Hadi pressed. Did you watch your friends die just to abandon your country?

The guards began spending afternoons with the prisoners, downing flagons of tea. Abdul Hadi held court, guards and prisoners alike drawn to his gifts as an orator. He was able to order the disparate strands of the previous years' chaos into a story they could understand: The city was embroiled not in a factional dispute, but a battle of cosmic proportions, one their ancestors too had waged, good against evil, just against unjust. As Abdul Hadi told it, in the near-total darkness of the cell, they all were facing a great test, the results of which were to be delivered not in this life but the next.

On the morning of January 8, the fifteenth of his detention, Abdul Hadi awoke to find a powerful glow illuminating the room. We can imagine a few moments of confusion as he slowly registered his cellmates, the filthy walls, the window—someone had unblocked the window. Perhaps tufts of weeds were visible, bobbing in the air—air that was flooding the cell. The window was open.

Abdul Hadi did not stop to ask questions. He pulled himself up, using the wall for leverage, and grasped the sill. He squeezed himself through, until he was lying on the gravel of the courtyard. It was just after dawn. He extended his arm back and pulled up a comrade. Within a few minutes, the cell had emptied. The group stole to the compound wall, hoisted themselves over, and tumbled onto the asphalt. The streets were deserted. The eight men decided to split up.

Abdul Hadi and a friend skirted alleyways until they came upon the great wadi, which separates the western quarters from downtown. A bridge spanning the wadi had a checkpoint manned by the Free Army. Units were stationed around town. Nowhere was safe—not within city limits, at least. They would have to find a way to reach the countryside. The quickest route was along the wadi itself, running south, emptying in a dirt field at the edge of town—which meant passing the Free Army checkpoint on the bridge.

Abdul Hadi and another prisoner lowered themselves into the wadi, which lay caked with glittering energy drink cans, drifts of plastic, and animal bones. They crawled in the filth, grasping the ridges in the cement basin. At the checkpoint were two soldiers. They were on the bridge, facing the street; Abdul Hadi crawled directly under them. He paused to listen. Carefully, he advanced.

It took an hour to crawl far enough to be out of sight. They climbed out of the wadi and found themselves on the southern edge of town, staring at brown fields. The grain silos lay east, the city behind. Perhaps Abdul Hadi glanced back to the stacked concrete blocks, tinged in morning blue, the only home he'd ever known. Or perhaps, understanding that there was no return, he did not look back at all.

Abdul Hadi walked the fields, through citrus groves and olive farms, and vanished.

ABU OMAR IS COMING

With the revolutionary flag flying above Manbij, ISIS was now eliminated west of the Euphrates, a stretch that included hundreds of autonomous towns and cities. Yet the danger had not subsided. In the nearby city of al-Bab, ISIS had sparked an uprising, leading to street battles between Islamic State sympathizers and the Free Syrian Army. The FSA was close to routing the insurgents when a video appeared online, shared tens of thousands of times. The clip inspired awe, even among the most battle-hardened Free Army fighters. It showed a procession of mud-spattered pickups driving through the desert east of the Euphrates. Some vehicles carried PK machine guns in their cabs. The final vehicle, a filthy white SUV sporting a black flag and an ISIS decal on the rear window, carried a man whose reputation had grown to legendary proportions. Few had seen him in person, fewer still had spoken with him, but everyone—rebel and regime soldier alike—knew his name: Abu Omar the Chechen.

Abu Omar, a twenty-eight-year-old from a desperately impoverished valley in the country of Georgia, was born Tarkhan Batirashvili to a Christian father and a Muslim mother. He grew up secular and enlisted in the Georgian military, joining the country's special forces, which were trained by the Americans. "In fact, the only reason he didn't go to Iraq to fight alongside America was that we needed his skills here in Georgia," a former Georgian defense official told McClatchy. When Vladimir Putin's Russian forces invaded Georgia in 2008, Batirashvili helped lead the defense in the mountains. Later, he was arrested for running weapons to Chechen rebels fighting against Russian forces. A prison stint, and his mother's death from cancer, led him to religion. In late 2012, he fled his homeland and, like thousands of young men soused with dreams of overthrowing tyranny, crossed into Syria. Once inside, he remade himself as Abu Omar the Chechen and built a formidable fighting unit, consisting of foreigners and Syrians, who quickly won acclaim for daring raids on Assad's military installations. Abu Omar became a household name, his pale visage and long red beard seen often in videos. The fact that no other rebel commander had received advanced military training—from the Americans, no less—added to his aura as the revolution's most dangerous fighter.

By late 2013, Abu Omar had pledged allegiance to ISIS, bringing along hundreds of battle-hardened veterans, many of them foreigners. The first videos of his convoy must have roused the vanquished ISIS elements. Then, a few hours after they appeared, a new batch was uploaded—now from the western bank of the Euphrates, showing an endless train of trucks loaded with men and guns.

Abu Omar was coming.

By late afternoon, the convoy reached a rebel checkpoint; north of here lay Manbij and neighboring cities, where the Free Army ruled without challenge. The checkpoint was manned by members of the Levant Free Men, the Islamist brigade, which fancied itself as neutral in the fight between ISIS and the revolutionaries. But in a shocking betrayal of revolutionary forces, the Levant Free Men unit allowed Abu Omar's convoy to pass. By sundown, Abu Omar's forces had arrived in a village two miles from al-Bab. The news spread quickly—no one had seen a column like this before. Some residents believed these were in fact regime soldiers, here to exploit the tensions between the Free Army and ISIS. Panic spread. The muezzins called for people to arm themselves—hunting rifles, knives, clubs, whatever they could find. But the Free Army was woefully outmanned and outgunned; Abu Omar's forces seized the grain silos and deployed snipers on rooftops. When the populace realized that it was ISIS, not the regime, that had surrounded the city, the resolve for resistance evaporated. Many returned home, saying they had no interest in defending the thieves of the Free Army.

Over the next few days, pockets of Free Army fighters held out against ISIS. On the dawn of the fourth day, calm prevailed and no gunfire could be heard. For the first time anyone could remember, the muezzins did not sing their morning song. The streets were covered in broken glass and shards of concrete. Downtown, some men ascended the art deco–style tower marking the central roundabout and planted the black flag of the Islamic State of Iraq and Greater Syria.

Meanwhile, Abu Omar awaited his next target.

THE SORDID TALE OF THE MAN THEY CALL THE PRINCE, PART 4

The fall of al-Bab was a profound blow to the revolutionaries of Manbij. The senate called an emergency meeting to plan for a defense of the city. The key to safeguarding it lay to the north: Jarablus. This collection of gritty apartment buildings and one-room shops straddled the Turkish border; it was the liberation of Jarablus, eighteen months earlier, that had paved the way for revolutionary takeover of Manbij. If ISIS seized this crossing—after already controlling al-Bab to the west and the October Dam to the east, Manbij would be surrounded on three sides.

ISIS supporters in Jarablus launched an uprising a day after the fall of al-Bab. Manbij fighters put out an emergency alert, calling on comrades far and wide to assist in putting down the insurrection. Word passed from person to person, then by walkie-talkie, and finally through the internet. The news eventually reached a young Syrian man in Greece. With hundreds of other refugees, he'd risked his life on the turbulent seas to reach Athens, and once on European soil, he'd put his days of revolution behind him. He slept on a park bench, hustling for change, and when he saved enough, he frequented the seedier clubs on Filis Street. Due to his implacable hatred of the Revolutionary Council, the Prince had allied with ISIS. Yet if there was one thing he despised more than the strait-laced bourgeois types of the council, it was the Janus-faced bearded ones. Al-Bab's fall hit him in the gut. The thought that the plague of ISIS could infect Manbij was unbearable—no matter how they had assisted him, no matter what side they were on. As reports of the coming fight in Jarablus flashed across the internet, he knew where he belonged.

Four days later, he was standing on Syrian soil. When news spread that the Prince had smuggled himself *back* to Syria, his old followers flocked to his side. Friends and supporters donated what they could for weapons. He linked with the Manbij rebels, and in mid-January, the Free Army rolled into Jarablus from three directions. ISIS put up heavy resistance, but were soon forced to barricade themselves in the Jarablus Cultural Center.

The next morning, the Free Army called on the ISIS partisans to surrender. There was no reply. The soldiers proceeded toward the Cultural Center a few feet at a time. At some point, a white Saab appeared. They crept toward the Cultural Center, and the vehicle crept alongside them. Suddenly, everything shook wildly and bodies were hurled in every direction and an enormous fireball rose above the city. The revolutionaries were in disbelief: a suicide bombing? The tragedy lit a primeval fuse in the remaining fighters, who rescinded the offer of surrender. They dynamited the Cultural Center, then pounded it with artillery until it was reduced to rubble. No one inside survived.

When word of the massacre at the Cultural Center reached Abu Omar the Chechen, he led a convoy toward Jarablus. His men quickly bore down on small checkpoints throughout the city. Free Army fighters dropped their weapons and fled. Only when the column reached the Prince's forces did it face resistance. The Prince was at the front, firing at the vehicles; his men were tossing grenades and launching RPGs. Though outnumbered, the Prince's forces advanced. Cars were shot up, concrete fell everywhere. Then the Prince took shrapnel to his leg. His fighters halted their advance, and he was rushed to a hospital in Turkey.

Abu Omar the Chechen's cavalcade pressed on to the center of Jarablus. The Manbij rebels came under extraordinary amounts of fire. The battle was turning into a rout. Free Army fighters broke ranks, fleeing through the streets. Some hid in alleys and stairwells. Most eventually escaped via the southern road, and by late evening they were back in Manbij. Others were captured by Abu Omar the Chechen's forces. They were decapitated, their heads impaled on the spikes of the Jarablus Cultural Center's railings.

The Prince's men fled east to a neighboring city. The next morning, a station wagon pulled up to their position, and as the soldiers inspected the vehicle, it exploded. Among the dead were the Prince's younger brother, who was only seventeen years old. From his hospital bed, the Prince moaned and writhed in anguish when he learned of the attack. He resolved to get up and return to the battle, though doctors had ordered complete rest. Within days, he was back on Syrian soil. His lieutenants advised him to establish a base in Manbij, where he enjoyed popular support, but the Prince insisted on staying near the Jarablus front line.

He roamed the hamlets along the border, plotting an assault on ISIS. Yet he was on alien turf, and his forces were scattered and attenuated. He woke one morning in his farmhouse headquarters to find himself surrounded by rebels from Aleppo—the same units that had arrested him earlier. This time, his captors took no chances. In a prison back room, the Prince, still seen by some as the revolution's great hope, brigand and hero all at once, was made to stand against a wall, and was executed in a hail of gunfire. He was thirty-two.

THE LONG MARCH

On January 12, 2014, the senate declared a state of emergency in Manbij. The nearest towns north and west were under ISIS control. All eyes were on Abu Omar the Chechen's convoy, stretched on the highway outside al-Bab like a giant snake, motionless under the desert sun.

Five days passed.

Manbij had become a city of ghosts. People remained indoors, the markets shut. School was canceled. Every morning, the senate met to discuss developments—but there were none. Abu Omar the Chechen's convoy had not stirred. News out of al-Bab and Jarablus was difficult to come by. Hasan Nefi, who'd returned to the city to help the senate, repeatedly requested reinforcements from other cities, but activists were wary of diluting their defenses and allowing ISIS to stage a rearguard attack.

By January 17, almost two weeks since ISIS had been expelled from Manbij, the mood lightened a bit. Jarablus and al-Bab were much smaller than Manbij; ISIS appeared to lack the forces to move on a city of this size. As the sun vanished, the city, without power, lay in darkness. For the first time in weeks, people emerged from their houses, carrying lanterns and torchlights. A few shops opened. Traffic returned to the streets.

Around 3:00 a.m., the earth shook. A fireball shot above the western edge of the city. Free Army units rushed toward the scene. There had been no sound of aircraft.

It took until early morning for authorities to realize that a car bomb had exploded. There were no injuries, but the city's animal-fodder warehouse had partially collapsed. Not long after, the Free Army received reports that Abu Omar the Chechen's convoy had lined up along the highway and looked ready to move. The city's units mustered near Manbij's western edge.

But the cavalcade did not budge. No movement was reported in Jarablus, either. Perhaps ISIS was testing the Free Army's state of readiness. The mood in the city relaxed again, and more shops opened. One could now see foot traffic downtown. For the first time in weeks, Abel Os felt comfortable opening the real estate office where he worked. He brought a walkie-talkie and listened to rumors and idle chatter between Free Army units.

Abel Os wondered if it was time to try to bridge the city's divides. He felt responsible, in a way, for the mess—he had founded RYM, bringing people like Abdul Hadi into the movement. Those youths had worshipped him. Should he have taken a firmer line, preventing them from protesting their own comrades? Then again, how could he, in good conscience, allow the Revolutionary Council to run roughshod over the principles of justice and equality? How could he defend the men he'd once appeared before with bowed head? There was rot in the soul of this revolution—in that he could not disagree with Abdul Hadi. But what was the solution? If the only choice was between the Islamic State and the kleptocracy, what was to be done? It was difficult for Abel Os, who'd grown accustomed to leading thousands through the streets, to admit he didn't have answers. He was pondering such mysteries when the walkie-talkie crackled in distress: reports of gunshots at the mills.

A Free Army unit arriving on the scene came under heavy fire. Taking cover behind parked cars, they realized that gunmen were occupying the roofs of the silos—the highest point in the city. FSA fighters there had been killed. But reports were that Abu Omar the Chechen's convoy stood rooted in position, forty miles to the east. Had a second ISIS unit infiltrated the city?

The FSA unit retreated. The loss of the mills from under their noses was a catastrophic blow. The Free Army leadership declared another emergency, calling on every able-bodied man to defend the city. Around 2:00 a.m., a station wagon pulled up to the Municipal Bakery. Masked gunmen jumped out, detained the guards, and entered the facility, which operated around the clock. The leader of the group, a tall, thin man wearing a ski mask, demanded to speak to the supervisor. The masked man ordered him to keep his workers on the job. "Everything continues as normal," he said. "We want no disruptions."

"Who are you?" the supervisor asked.

"We are your new authorities."

The masked man spoke with a nasal whine. It was a voice the supervisor had heard before. He tried to place it. The man's eyes were achingly familiar—winter-gray, self-assured. He'd seen those eyes many times, on the streets in the sweltering days of summer, in front of thousands of young men. He knew those eyes—he knew exactly who he was speaking with.

"You are Abdul Hadi!"

The man laughed. "Go home, Ali," he said. "We'll take it from here."

By morning, the city was in a panic. With ISIS seizing the bread facilities, no one knew what might come next. Mina and her family had been staying downtown at her parents' house. When she heard that ISIS was occupying the mills, she rushed to check on her apartment. She arrived to find a checkpoint marked by an ISIS flag. She asked to be allowed to see her home, but no one was allowed to pass.

The Free Army leaders had been so focused on Abu Omar the Chechen's convoy that the thought of a second ISIS unit had never occurred to them. They debated whether to muster an immediate assault—thereby threatening the mills, the population's lifeline—or to secure the perimeter to repel an attack from Abu Omar's side. In the end, they chose the latter course, keeping vigil throughout the day. Abu Omar the Chechen's convoy did not budge. There was no movement from the north or south, either. That evening, walkie-talkies squawked with intel: The convoy would depart in the morning for Raqqa, bypassing Manbij.

Early the next morning, as predicted, the convoy roused to life, creeping along the highway. But at the roundabout, instead of turning south for the Raqqa road, the cavalcade powered ahead.

Abu Omar the Chechen was coming for Manbij.

A Free Army unit sped toward the enemy. The two sides met at a university campus west of the city. ISIS unleashed a barrage of artillery, the mortars crashing down around Free Army locations. PK machine guns sprayed the campus with lead. Students fled on foot, by the hundreds, along the highway. Within hours, Abu Omar the Chechen had secured the university. The Free Army regrouped downtown. That evening, the city was still.

The next morning, the first videos from the university surfaced on social media, and what the Free Army fighters saw was more gutting, more traumatic, than all the battlefield deaths they'd witnessed: Hundreds of people—Manbij residents, their friends and neighbors—had turned up to welcome the Islamic State fighters. The soldiers watched the clips over and over, speechless. A sense of profound shock spread to units across the city, a shock so deep that now, for the first time, some fighters wondered if the battle was already lost.

The following day, a four-wheel drive stopped near a Free Army position. When Manbij fighters approached, the vehicle exploded in a ball of fire. The facade of a nearby carpet factory was blown clean off. The suicide bomber had killed an FSA commander and wounded twenty-five others. Abel Os sat at home, walkie-talkie on his lap, head buried in his hands, trying to process the fact that such a scourge, known to him only in news reports of faraway places like Iraq and Afghanistan, was visiting his homeland. Around town, the bombing induced a terror unlike that brought by Assad's warplanes: People saw in parked vehicles and slow-moving traffic the potential of a ticking bomb.

By afternoon, an ISIS contingent was marching through the western neighborhoods. FSA units met them here and there, firing, using automobiles for cover. The invaders did not know the streets, which the Free Army exploited to stage ambushes. When some ISIS fighters were pinned down near the Sailboat Roundabout, the asphalt a few blocks away began to explode in bursts of dusts. ISIS was shelling the city. One mortar landed near a cluster of houses, wounding a young woman. When the sons of Abu Hammoud, a teacher, rushed out to aid her, another mortar slammed into the earth nearby. Both were killed.

Abel Os was listening to the mayhem on his walkie-talkie. Someone was screaming for help. A man shouted, "Back, back, get back!" A voice pleaded for ammunition. "We have three down!" Suddenly, a voice crackled: "We killed your hero! We killed Haseeb Sutto"—a Free Army commander. The voice belonged to an ISIS fighter. "He's now under my boots!"

On the afternoon of January 22, after three days of battle, members of the Revolutionary Council met at the Manbij Hotel. Outside, the air popped with gunfire. In the dim generator-powered light, the men reproached each other bitterly. They cursed comrades from other cities, who, reluctant to leave their areas undermanned, did not send reinforcements. They denounced the merchants and weapons dealers, who were profiting in the revolutionaries' hour of greatest need. Most of all, they inveighed against friends and neighbors, men and women they'd grown up with, who were now quitting this grand project.

Sitting in his living room, Abel Os refused to accept the reality. The trouble, he believed, was manpower—and what could he do better than rouse his neighbors? It was he who'd inspired the youths of Sarab to raise their voices, he who'd sparked the formation of the secret citywide body of protesters. He ran to Rabta Street, where he saw a gathering of Free Army fighters and offered to raise volunteers from the neighborhood. One of the fighters responded respectfully, "But, uncle, they won't come."

The sun was setting, and the sky glowed orange. Abel Os reached another group of fighters on the north side, led by his old karate friend Anas Sheikh Weiss. "I bet I can raise about twenty men," Abel Os said. But he was told, "There's nothing they can do." The revolutionaries had lost popular support, sapping their will to fight. To wage a battle now would risk plunging the city into civil war—which they could not accept, because this was their home.

Abel Os returned to the real estate office. He sat behind his desk, staring through the decal-covered window at Rabta Street. A few fighters ran past, carrying large sacks of bedding. The walkie-talkie squawked with reports of clashes by the mills, gunfire near the public park, a pro-ISIS rally in Sheikh Aqeel. By 11:00 p.m., Abel Os could not stand to be in the office any longer. He closed the shop and left to walk home. The lights were out on Rabta Street. Not a star could be seen above. It was then that he noticed that, for the first time in three days, the city had fallen quiet. No gunfire, no shelling. It was as if the world had stopped turning on its axis, as if the city sat frozen, liberating itself from the constraints of time and space, even from the weight of human bodies, and there was no one left, neither ally nor enemy, save Abel Os himself.

He arrived home to find his neighbor sitting near his gate. He was a fellow senator, a man with whom Abel Os had been at odds in many a vote. His face was ridged with pain.

"There's no one left except us," he said.

Abel Os bid farewell to his wife and children and climbed in his neighbor's vehicle. They drove through the dark streets to the easternmost roundabout and saw a few dozen revolutionary leaders standing together, illuminated by the headlights of parked cars. He saw senators, leaders of Free Army factions, members of the Revolutionary Council, leaders of various assemblies. He saw *Path* reporters, ex-RYM activists. A discussion was underway. Abel Os stood silently; he had nothing to offer. The men embraced and shook hands—some had been political rivals, others close friends, but now, by dint of popular will, all had been cast out together. They climbed into their vehicles and abandoned the city of their birth.

THE ISLAMIC STATE OF MANBIJ

The next morning, January 23, 2014, one year, six months, and four days after Manbij inaugurated its democratic experiment, a prodigious convoy of SUVs, carrying heavy machine guns and black flags, rolled down the city streets. Phalanxes of armed men were marching along Main Street. They trooped through the side streets, and people stepped out onto their balconies to greet them. There was a palpable sense that the time of chaos and inequality was over; some women ululated, some men cheered. A few vehicles proceeded toward the Great Souk, blaring songs of jihad and heroism through loudspeakers. It was a majestic sight: the gritty, long-haired men emerging from months on the front lines, the cornucopia of muzzles and flags, the machine guns, the up-armored Humvees—pilfered from the U.S.-backed Iraqi army—the young boys scampering alongside, hoping to catch a glimpse of these warriors.

The fighters assembled in Central Square. A crowd gathered. Men in ski masks grinned and raised their index finger to the sky, symbolizing the return of monotheism to the land. Everything hitherto—democracy, freedom—had been false idols, luring people away from the only font of justice and equality: the Lord of all worlds. Giant speakers were wheeled in. The gathering continued to swell. There was now an energy to the crowd, as people jostled to move to the stage, stretching their necks this way and that. The speakers blasted religious music, and journalists working for ISIS pointed their cameras and held up boom mics. A small motorcade of tinted SUVs appeared. Out stepped white-skinned men in black jumpers, among them a broad-shouldered fighter with a beard the color of scarlet—Abu Omar the Chechen.

The great commander did not speak but surveyed the crowd. Everyone pressed closer for a look—almost no one had seen a Chechen before. Other fighters were heard speaking English, and people surmised they were British.

A masked man spoke of his vanquished foes: "Do these people support our religion? By God, they are all hypocrites! By God, Bashar al-Assad did not do what these people did! . . . Why did they do this? For money! They get thousands of dollars from John Kerry! . . . Glory be to God! God's law will rise in spite of their noses, in spite of the noses of these infidels!"

The crowd cheered. The contempt with which ordinary Manbijis viewed the revolutionaries—the same people they'd marched behind eighteen months prior—was something to behold. Around town, impromptu rallies broke out, especially in poorer neighborhoods. Now, finally, peace and security would settle on the land. Now, finally, their children's stomachs would be full.

In the afternoon, ISIS dissolved the senate, the Revolutionary Council, all Manbij's forty or so assemblies, and the newspapers. Then the arrests began—anyone who'd taken up arms against the Islamic State was rounded up. As ISIS leaders were not from the area, they relied on the intelligence of local groups, such as Ammar bin Yasser, the Free Army unit comprised almost entirely of working-class kids from the Jazeera soccer team, who had pledged allegiance to the Islamic State a few months earlier. People were hooded and marched to waiting automobiles.

In the evening, the shops opened for the first time in days. The *mushabbak* sellers sold their treacly pastries and the muezzins crooned. When people went to bed, the city was nestled in a comfortable silence, the sky crowded with stars. In the morning, they awoke to a tinny voice, projecting through speakers driven by sedans, singing a song entitled "Our State Is Victorious."

That morning, Mina decided to return home from her parents' place. She hired a taxi, which brought her and the children to a checkpoint outside the silos. She approached the ISIS guards and begged to be allowed home, as it contained her photographs, her jewelry, her diary. She was told that the area was seeded with mines, that Free Army snipers were hiding among the grain elevators. Still, she pleaded—she needed to see her apartment, stand among the children's toys, smell the upholstery. Finally, the guard said, "You may retrieve your possessions, but we are not responsible for what happens to you."

She told her children to wait in the taxi, and allowed herself to be blindfolded and bundled into a vehicle. She felt it lurch right and left. A voice asked for her apartment number. The blindfold was removed and Mina saw the door of her apartment, undamaged. Inside, she buried her face in her clothes. She collected what she could in a bag and allowed herself to be blindfolded again. The car lurched left and right again, then came to a halt. The door opened, and someone else got in. A new voice asked about the Free Army. Did she know anyone in the FSA? When was her last contact with revolutionaries? Fear drove through her. She lied and said she knew no one, that she was uninvolved in the events of the past few years. The car was on the move again.

"Where are we going?" she asked.

"We need to know the names of everyone you know in the Free Army," the voice commanded.

She swore she knew nothing. The car bounced along an unpaved road. She understood they were heading out of the city, into the desert somewhere. She was going to be marched into the scrub. They were going to seize her belongings. The image of her husband flashed through her mind; he'd been holed up in despair in his room after the collapse. Her mind was a jumble of images, sounds, sensations—she felt the powerful urge to sleep, to lie down on the bare earth. Suddenly, she said, "I'll give you money."

"What?"

"We have gold. I'll give you money." She was crying.

The voice did not answer. The car was turning, lurching here and there.

After a few minutes, it stopped. The blindfold was removed. They were back where they'd started—the taxi, the beautiful gold taxi, still waiting. Her children were sitting up front. Her youngest was on the driver's lap, peeking through the windshield. Mina felt she'd lost her legs—she could not move.

"Well," the man said. "What are you waiting for? Go home. If you want to donate money to the State, please see the Office of Endowments."

At the taxi, Mina hugged her children and took a long, languorous drag on a cigarette.

On the final night of democratic rule, Hasan Nefi had chosen not to abandon the city. He hid in a friend's house, where he kept awake the whole night, waiting for news over the walkie-talkie. It was silent. At eight in the morning, he opened the door to see masked fighters roaming the streets. Family members called and warned him not to return home—ISIS fighters had come by looking for him. He sent for his family, who squeezed into a taxi and met him in a different neighborhood. Together, they took the backroads through the northern countryside, avoiding checkpoints. By late afternoon, they had crossed into Turkey. But Hasan did not consider himself a refugee; he was certain the Free Army would recover his city.

That evening, ISIS fighters seized Hasan's house and his possessions.

Someone was banging on the front door. It was evening, and the streets were quiet. During the final battle, as the air echoed with gunfire, Ibrahim had refused to follow the news. Sunk in bitterness, he blamed the rebels for this disaster. But now, after the smoke had cleared, he understood his anguish not as bitterness but as rage—he hated the revolution as much as he hated Assad.

The banging grew louder.

Ibrahim opened it to find three masked men with Kalashnikovs.

"Are you Ibrahim Kasem?"

He said he was.

"We have information that you belonged to the Free Army. We'd like to ask you a few questions."

Before Ibrahim could reply, one of the masked men spoke in a familiar voice.

"Tell them everything you know," he said. "Just tell the truth, and everything will be fine."

Ibrahim could not utter a sound. That voice—buttery, eloquent—contained within it an essence so intimate, so much a part of Ibrahim, that he froze.

"Adam?" was all Ibrahim could muster. The masked man said nothing, but Ibrahim knew at once. His baby brother, for whom he'd braved the floodwaters to save his schoolbooks, the light of the family, the star pupil at Aleppo University, the aficionado of T. S. Eliot—had joined ISIS. Ibrahim knew his brother had grown disillusioned with the rebels, abandoned by the so-called international community, spurned by his society's elites. But was this the answer?

Haltingly, his throat dry, Ibrahim recounted his experiences in the Free Army: fighting under the Prince, witnessing the banditry. The men listened without saying a word. Ibrahim said he wanted nothing to do with politics anymore, that he wished only to find steady work and provide for his children. Finally, one of the men spoke: Ibrahim was to report within forty-eight hours to a newly established "repentance" center, where he would formally confess his involvement with the rebels and undertake a course in sharia.

Before Ibrahim could ask anything, the men were gone.

In a mud hut in the nearby town of Kobani, Abel Os sat with his friends. For long hours, he hardly spoke. He did not own a smartphone, and was glad of it. When people began reading aloud news from his city, he stood up and strode out.

After a while, he could hardly endure the people around him. They were obsessed with troop movements, rumors, snippets of news of ISIS misdeeds. He wanted to shout, with all his might, "It's over!" But he said nothing.

On the twelfth day of exile, he decided he'd had enough. He yearned to be as far away from his erstwhile comrades as possible. His only desire was peace; he cared little for assemblies and speeches and horse-trading. There had been a time when everything was ordered, when right and wrong stood opposed and an honest man could find his bearings. But no more. Now, he decided, he wanted nothing more than to open a shop in Sarab, have a pot of *juz muz* ready, and be among his people. Perhaps he was wanted by ISIS. Perhaps he would be arrested the moment he set foot in Manbij. He thought again about *Oss*, the interjection, the command, the way of life. *Oss* had carried him when he fled his creditors, when he sat on the crowded beaches of Beirut. It had driven him back home to face his enemies, and he had shown them what he was truly capable of. Maybe ISIS was waiting for him, but he realized he no longer cared.

He was going home.

Sunrise to sunset, Oday sat on the balcony above Sundus Street, waiting for the visitors. He watched the crowds at the vegetable market haggling in loud, confident voices. The mouth of the Great Souk yawned before him; perhaps women streamed through, carrying bags of almonds and dates, and young boys sold cups of steaming tea. Each of them, Oday believed, had been abandoned. He wrote on Facebook:

> They betrayed you, they destroyed you, they made you an arena for spoils. They did not care about the slaughtered children and the demolished homes, they did not care about the widow in her tent. Those who truly sacrificed for your sake are now under the dust and above the clouds—and those who remain have sold you for dollars.

But even as he cursed the revolutionaries, he did not mince words about the new rulers, who were conducting arrest campaigns around the city:

> Oh ISIS—is this how your Islam will be? Doesn't God say it's better to demolish the Kaaba stone of Mecca than to target an innocent person?

Oday would not allow himself to believe that the revolution was finished. Two years earlier, Hala had told him that politics was ephemeral but love was forever. In his bones, he knew she was wrong. If forced again to choose between love and rage, he'd choose rage, he'd choose revolution, a thousand times. He would pick himself up, dust himself off, forget the terrible missteps of the past eighteen months. He would reconnect with old friends and make new ones, cobble together networks, build coalitions. Yes, there would be sacrifices. They would be detained again, perhaps beaten. They would live in fear, running through alleyways. But they would be wiser, more practical, more attuned to the needs of their neighbors. And this time, because they would do it right, they would win. So let ISIS come get him, he must have told himself—he'd seen it all, and survived it all, before.

He left the balcony, went downstairs, and awaited the knock at the front door.

On the roof of one of the Manbij grain silos stood Abdul Hadi Bisher. He, too, had been faced with the demands of love and rage—solidarity with his revolutionary brethren, or indignation at the revolution's iniquities—and chose the latter. But where did indignation end and obsession begin? Had he battled the Revolutionary Council, or had he battled his shadow self, which was born from a lifetime of slights—or both? It hardly mattered. If he paused to reflect on his journey at all, he would have seen a story of improbable triumph. Without his help, ISIS would probably not have grown much larger than the six members they'd arrived with back in April. He'd been the éminence grise behind every pivotal moment in the previous six months: the July execution, the summertime debates, the August storming of the Revolutionary Council headquarters. So when Abdul Hadi ran his eyes over the vista below, he must have felt exalted above the concrete blocks and exhaust-smelling warrens. He would inhabit a new city, one different than he'd ever known, which spread for miles around, and was built of the sleekest marble and the clearest glass, the towers climbing to the heavens, the streets without squalor, streets busy with purpose, peopled by men and women joined in common struggle. It was a city of workshops and warehouses, simple mosques and well-kept cemeteries, but there were no gates or lines, no *wasta*, no rich or poor, so that he could face every citizen like a fellow human being. This was Abdul Hadi's city of justice.

BOOK FOUR

The State
2014–2016

Prologue

Over the course of the revolution, some towns in Syria never developed democratic institutions, in large part due to the ferocity of Assad's bombers and snipers. Others did, but were besieged, and their inhabitants, reduced to starvation, surrendered *en masse* to the regime. Some towns never succumbed to ISIS. While the events in Manbij say something about the possible trajectories of the Syrian war, they also speak to a greater historical truth.

The word "democracy" combines the ancient Greek *demos* and *kratos*. The latter refers to "power," or "rule." *Demos*, it is often said, means the "people"—but in ancient times it usually referred to non-elites: the masses, the poor, those of low status and little means. So for the ancient Greeks, democracy meant the rule of the non-elites.

This fact underlies two important trends in the history of democracy. First, in the usual telling, democracy springs forth from the minds of great men, political geniuses like Locke and Madison. In fact, the historical record shows that democracy usually emerges through struggle from below, by the anonymous and mostly forgotten, often at the price of considerable bloodshed. Ancient Athens was dominated by chieftains and tyrants until 508 BC, when ordinary citizens rose in what the scholar Josiah Ober calls the "Athenian Revolution," ushering in a new form of government in which the *demos* held power in their own hands. Ancient Rome was governed by patricians, a class of landowning aristocrats who dominated all political institutions. Beginning in 500 BC, and lasting nearly two hundred years, the working-class plebeians waged a series of struggles for political equality. This period, called the Conflict of the Orders, resulted in non-elites winning a share of political representation.

Likewise, at its founding, the United States was an oligarchy of white property-owning men. It took two hundred years of struggle—strikes, riots, sit-ins, protests, and a civil war—to evolve into a system in which non-elites enjoyed a genuine political share.

According to detractors, elites opposed democracy in order to protect their privileges. The elites themselves, though, offer a more nuanced defense of restricting the democratic participation of non-elites. For example, the American founding fathers proposed a "representative democracy"—that is, one in which the masses would not have direct say, but elect representatives in their stead—because it could curtail the capricious impulses of direct democracy. Madison argued that a polity should guard against both the unaccountable power of a minority and the tyranny of the majority. Suppose the masses vote to strip the rights of a minority, or for a demagogue? Members of the Revolutionary Council in Manbij made a strikingly similar argument in restricting the participation of assemblies in governance.

In light of what happened, the council members' concerns seem vindicated. Yet that would miss a second important historical trend: Persistent economic inequality usually sounds democracy's death knell. In the latter years of the Roman Republic, landowners amassed unprecedented riches while plebeians floundered, spawning resentment that infected many corners of society. In the context of this soaring inequality—that is, of ordinary people's loss of power—there appeared, for the first time, populist politicians like Julius Caesar, who promised reforms while accruing dangerous degrees of power themselves. Other elites fiercely resisted the populist surge but refused to make meaningful concessions to address the citizenry's core grievances. Ultimately, civil war led to the fall of the republic and the rise of dictatorship.

In 1848 France, a popular uprising overthrew the monarchy, demanding universal manhood suffrage and wealth redistribution. The revolution established government-owned workshops that employed the poor, but were bitterly opposed by the wealthy. A conservative government shut them down, prompting bloody riots. Eventually, the masses voted for Louis Napoleon Bonaparte, nephew of the famed emperor, in a landslide. He styled himself as all things to all people—a paragon of order to the right, a champion of the poor to the left. As soon as he was elected, he cracked down on freedoms of press and assembly, and dissolved parliament. Before long, he declared himself emperor.

So when the *demos* have power wrested away, tyranny becomes attractive. Tyrants promise security, food on the table, and a spark of self-worth—a self-worth that the old elites had so thoroughly trampled. The masses, demeaned and starved, see in tyranny a tantalizing elixir of equality and self-respect, which will liberate them from elite domination and deliver them from wants and anxieties. As countries around the world slide from democracy into oligarchy—rule of the few—by wrenching power from ordinary people and vesting it in judges and corporations and billionaires and other unaccountable actors—authoritarian populism has spread. Of course, it may be that while all happy democracies are alike, every unhappy tyranny is tyrannical in its own way. The Islamic State's tyranny draws on the cultural resources of the Middle East—Islam—while Assad's tyranny drew upon a different but also uniquely Middle Eastern heritage, Arab nationalism. Yet the tyrannical *impulse* of authoritarian populists is the same everywhere. In one context the authoritarian is railing against non-Muslims, in another context it is immigrants. No matter the cultural tropes, the forms of mobilization are identical: Those who feel powerless and hopeless, who are embittered by the rapacious greed of elites controlling their democracy, will begin to question the very idea of democracy itself. If tyranny is where democracies go to die, inequality is the cause of death.

| ONE |

As Mina approached her parents' home, dread crawled up her chest. Her parents had fled to Turkey, while her brothers, who were in the Free Army, had regrouped in another town. The neighborhood around her lay empty. She moved through the street with hollow footsteps, passing vacant houses with doors hanging from hinges. The door to her parents' house had been smashed, as if with an axe, and a red ribbon was strung across the jambs. She looked around. Smoke rose in the distance. The sun was gray, the air frigid. She peered inside, but it was a cave. The wind picked up, rattling the ribbon, then screeching through the alleyways, and as it screeched, she could hear a human voice.

An elderly woman was calling from across the street. She shuffled over. "Don't be afraid!" she said. She had brought a thermos of tea, and the pair sat on the sidewalk in front of the house. "Tell your family to come back," she said. "This militia is like the other militias!"

The next day, Mina's parents and sisters stood in front of the axed door. She'd arranged for a smuggler to bring them back from Turkey. "What are we waiting for," her younger sister said. "This is our house!" She cut the ribbon. Soon they were exploring the unlit corridors. The couches had been ripped to shreds. Her brother Sami's oud and accordion had been smashed. Everything smelled of gasoline—the intruders had apparently planned to set the house ablaze, then changed their minds.

There was a knock at the door. Mina quickly wrapped her face in a scarf. Three Islamic State members wearing bandoliers and carrying rifles entered the hallway. "Where are your apostate brothers?" one asked. Mina said she did not know. Another produced a piece of paper that stated that her brothers' possessions were to be confiscated because they had fought against the Islamic State. The officials rifled through closets, overturning mattresses, even opening jars of lentils and bottles of olive oil. They carted off everything her brothers owned, leaving only her parents' belongings.

That evening, by candlelight, Mina and her sisters scrubbed the house clean. Mina bedded down in the living room, exhausted, bathed in the stench of gasoline.

―+·+―

For many days, Mina refused to leave the house. She felt a tension in her shoulders. Steeped in darkness, she wrapped herself in blankets. Her father made trips to the grocer and the baker, while she helped her sisters and mother in the kitchen. She avoided the front door, which remained smashed—a gateway to a world of brambles, icy winds, and gunmen.

One day, the lights came on. Mina turned on the radio. A voice said, on repeat:

> To the honorable people of Manbij, we, your children in the Islamic State in Iraq and Greater Syria, command ourselves and you to follow what God Almighty has commanded us to do, and we forbid ourselves and you to do what God and His Messenger, may God bless Him and grant Him peace, have forbidden. Therefore, the following matters are strictly and permanently prohibited:
>
> First: It is forbidden for women and girls to go out with makeup, and we bind ourselves and you to the legal dress code that God Almighty and His Messenger, may God bless Him and grant Him peace, have commanded us to wear.
>
> Second: The sale of cigarettes is strictly prohibited.
>
> Third: It is forbidden to smoke cigarettes in public.
>
> Fourth: It is prohibited to display nude or scantily clad pictures on the facades of shops and cars. Please remove these pictures.
>
> Fifth: Barbers are prohibited from shaving Muslims' beards, otherwise the barber will be held accountable.
>
> Sixth: During the call to prayer it is forbidden to open shops, and in general for Muslims to be on the streets and neighborhoods.
>
> Seventh: Regarding any insult committed by any of our sons in the Islamic State in Iraq and Greater Syria, please file a complaint against this member. We are your sons, and your

blood will be preserved before our blood, your honor upheld before our honor, and your necks protected before our necks.

To our dear people in the city of Manbij: For any person who exceeds these limits, the offender or their guardian will be subject to accountability.

The next day, Mina heard shouting in the street. When she pressed her ear to the gap in the door, she realized it was a recorded voice, repeating these injunctions over and over.

The radio announced additional edicts. Speaking in favor of the defunct Revolutionary Council or the senate was tantamount to apostasy—which was punishable by death. Attempting to form an assembly was now a capital offense. So too was any hint of criticism of Islamic State policies, whether on the lips or online. The Revolutionary Court was disbanded, and the police force dispersed. An internal security force would keep the city safe from "secularists" and "apostates" and "enemies of the peace." Rules on prayer and dress would be enforced by the Hisba, or accountability police.

When Mina peered through a chink in the front gate, she could see black vans of the Hisba crawling along the street. Black was now the hue of her city. All the revolutionary murals had been smeared over in black. Billboards were plastered in black tape. The Book Roundabout was coated in black paint. The central police station and the schools and bakeries were all black too.

Mina's father returned from fetching bread. He reported that a wooden stall on the street corner was playing ISIS battles on a loop on a large screen. The production quality of these clips was impressive, with pulsing scores and dazzling special effects. Teenagers gathered around, downloading the clips onto their phones and laptops. Carts rolled down Mina's street blasting ISIS fight songs and Quranic verses.

In early February, a week after seizing power, the Islamic State issued a law of repentance. Anyone who had stood against ISIS before it seized power—in word or deed—was to present themselves to the Repentance Office and provide a full accounting of their crimes. If the penitent disavowed his past activities, pledging to never oppose the State again, he would be free to live in Manbij in peace. Those who failed to do so would be rendered outlaws and put to death.

People soon learned just what this meant. A former Free Army fighter named Alaa confessed to participating in the final battle against ISIS back in January. After receiving a signed and stamped letter of repentance, he was able to live unmolested in Manbij for a few weeks. He'd neglected to mention, however, that during that final battle he'd briefly served as a guard for the prison housing ISIS captives. When this information was discovered, Alaa was promptly arrested. He swore he'd merely forgotten to mention this stint, which had only lasted a couple of days, but the interrogators would not hear it. He was told, "You had your chance," and was executed.

In the mornings, Mina's husband left to work at the mills, which were back up and running. Until he returned, Mina sat with her children—Anwar and two girls—in the dusky confines of her parents' house. Now and then, she could hear the voice on a loudspeaker through the walls. *It is forbidden to open shops during*—the snippets came as she helped her mother chop parsley for tabouleh—*will be held accountable.*

Anwar asked why he couldn't play outdoors. "It's really boring outside," Mina insisted. "There's no one there."

When her husband returned in the late afternoon, he would bring stories. There was the case of Abu Ali, who ran a car dealership with his neighbor, a woman named Zahra. They were turning a tidy profit, and before long, a romance developed—though both were married. Eventually, they quarreled over finances, ending the affair and the business venture. Abu Ali owed Zahra a large sum, and when he didn't pay, she went to the police. Abu Ali was arrested. Under interrogation, he defended himself by impugning Zahra's character. She was hauled in for questioning, leading investigators to discover an illicit clip of her with Abu Ali. Both were charged with adultery, then tried and sentenced.

Not long after, a crowd gathered on the lip of the main wadi running through town. ISIS members drove up in convoys. A few had brought their own stones, but most fished them out of the wadi. They piled the stones, some as large as a fist, into a mound. The two convicts were produced and made to sit in the basin of the wadi. They were bound and gagged. An officer from the religious police spoke about how adultery can tear apart a community.

A shout of "God is great!" went up among the ISIS members. Someone hurled a stone, which hit Abu Ali in the throat. He doubled over. More shouts, more stones. The projectiles struck with dull thuds. Abu Ali and Zahra's moans could be heard by the crowd. The stones rained down, the cheering growing louder. After a while, no one could hear them moan any longer. The bodies were returned to the families for burial.

As she listened to these stories, Mina felt a force gathering in her chest. Her husband wanted to move back to their apartment at the mills, but she refused. She pictured an Islamic State checkpoint, its masked men with long hair. Some days, she could hardly rouse herself from bed, let alone move across town.

Through the walls came the voice: *We bind ourselves and you to the legal dress code.*

Mina sometimes found herself drifting back to the days of revolution. She'd raced from one building to the next, assembly to assembly, as if every minute had a purpose. So many new faces, fresh ideas. In the intermittent light of her parents' living room, she wondered if she'd foolishly allowed herself to concoct a fable, if she'd given herself so wholly to what now could only be considered a delusion. They'd batted around grand ideas about justice and freedom as if the fate of the world depended on it. But were those words genuine? Were people simply hoisting the banner of freedom to advance their own causes? She could no longer trust her own memories.

One evening, winds battered the windows and heavy rains lashed the awning. The power was out. By candlelight, she cut pieces of chicken for her daughter, while her husband ate silently. A surprising calm washed over her, and she was struck by the sensation that somehow, everything would work out, that providence would provide, and her own fears quieted. After dinner, she carried the candle to the bedroom and fit herself into a niqab, just to see how it would feel. She studied herself in the mirror, draped in black, hands in black gloves.

She returned to the living room. Her husband was playing with the children. Her father was dozing. The rain drummed the windowpanes—and suddenly she realized the source of her calm: She could not hear the voice.

The next day, after her husband left for work, and after she'd fixed lunch for her father, she grabbed Anwar by the hand. Where are you going, her mother asked, concerned. Just a stroll, Mina answered. Before her mother could reply, Mina had stepped into the front yard. The sky was leaden, the wind blowing. She opened the gate, navigating through the eye slits of her niqab, and turned toward the Coffeepot Roundabout.

. . . the offender or their guardian will be subject to accountability . . .

The voice was back. She stopped in her tracks. Anwar was tugging at her hand, but she held back. *This is not a foreign land,* she told herself. *These are not foreign streets.* She tried to conjure the image of herself marching, with a dozen other women, in the stillness of that August day three years ago, which now felt like three decades—it was on this very street. *If I stood then,* she told herself, *I can walk now.*

She put one foot in front of her, then another. The voice swelled. Mina concentrated on the ground as she walked. Anwar was pulling her along, thrilled to be outdoors.

The voice intensified: . . . *may God bless him and grant Him peace, has commanded us to wear* . . . It was so loud that Mina had to marshal every ounce of strength not to look up.

She kept walking, and the voice began to recede. Soon she came upon the Coffeepot Roundabout. The plaza looked very different from the days of revolution, when it had been filled with bumper-to-bumper traffic, colorful bunting, impromptu demonstrations. Now, a few children led their cocooned mothers by the hand. A handful of men in scraggly beards sat here and there. She could see the lights of the Manbij Hotel. According to her husband, it had been repurposed into an ISIS prison.

As she turned and walked back home, the voice was again right in her ear. *We bind ourselves and you to the legal dress code* . . . She looked up. There was a wooden cart, piled with *mushabbak* pastries. On one corner sat a small speaker, broadcasting the Islamic State's injunctions. The man behind the cart was very old. As she passed, he did not even glance at her.

The voice receded and she reached her front door. Inside, she took off her niqab and collapsed onto a floor cushion.

—⁘—

Mina approached the al-Aqsa mosque in downtown Manbij. She saw women in niqabs standing guard, holding Kalashnikovs. She entered to find hundreds of women seated on the floor. Many were holding infants. Every individual who'd worked for the Assad regime—including teachers, who were in the employ of the Ministry of Education—was required to attend a reeducation class.

A woman carrying a rifle approached the dais. She introduced herself as Umm Shuhada—the mother of martyrs—and said that she was a Kuwaiti and had already married three ISIS fighters, the first two of whom had died. She lifted her veil to reveal keen eyes and smooth skin, and Mina found her striking. She began to lecture about Islam, explaining that the women gathered here, as former and perhaps future teachers, were responsible for raising the next generation of Muslims. "Throw out the filth of secularism and democracy," she said. "Tear it from the pages!" She wished the government would simply collect the old textbooks and burn them on a pyre. "You've lived under a regime of lies," she said. "Now, you will begin your journey to the truth."

An infant began crying. "Leave your child at home next time!" she bellowed.

She proceeded to discuss the Quran, offering an exegesis on a passage dealing with the question of women's clothing. Women were to dress modestly, which she said meant they should not reveal an inch of their bodies, even their hands. As if for the first time, Mina considered the question of the niqab. She'd donned one almost without thinking—that old dictate, *be honorable*, had slipped past her defenses. She had been too mired in fear and grief, in what she now recognized as a broken heart, to obsess about clothing. Yet now, listening to a sermon about modesty, something hardened within her.

The speaker continued analyzing a passage about the Prophet's wives—distorting those holy and exalted words, Mina was now certain. Suddenly, Mina found herself turning to a neighbor. "This is insane," she whispered. "That's not what the verse means."

Her neighbor elbowed her. "Shut up!" she hissed. "Are you crazy?"

Mina kept quiet and listened. She realized she was sweating. The speaker perorated on the need for a male guardian when leaving the house, for which she pointed to Quranic passages. Mina recognized she'd submitted to this stricture as easily as the next woman—but why? It was one thing to nurse a broken heart, quite another to watch the victors gloat. "She's filling people's heads with lies," Mina snapped to her neighbor.

The woman squeezed Mina's knee. "Shut up, for the love of God!"

Mina shook herself free. She wondered if she should raise her hand. She knew the verse in question by heart:

> O Prophet! Ask your wives, daughters, and believing women to draw their cloaks over their bodies. In this way it is more likely that they will be recognized as virtuous and not be harassed. And God is All-Forgiving, Most Merciful.

It was clearly directed at the Prophet's wives, she believed—not a commandment for all women, in all times and places. Mina shifted, getting ready to stand. Just then her neighbor grabbed her leg, pulling her down with all her might. "You're going to get beheaded!" she whispered.

Mina's heart was hammering. She wanted to say something, make a grand gesture, shout to the heavens. She wanted to run at the lectern, smash it to pieces the way they had smashed her furniture, the way they had smashed her revolution.

Her revolution—the phrase struck her with incredible force. For nearly her entire life, she'd lived under the heavy shadow of honor, never thinking to question it. Then, for eighteen brief months, the world glimmered. What she saw in those eighteen months, she knew then, she could never unsee.

The woman continued her speech, now pounding her fist, now shouting, now pacing. A long time passed before Mina realized she'd stopped listening. By then, she knew she would not submit.

Mina peered through her lace curtain, into the alley. It had been a week since she'd left her parents' house and moved back to her apartment. The religious police's black van had been on the prowl all morning. It had rolled down her alley, past her window, then circled back. In its presence, the alley was transformed into some alien locale, as if the dirt road, the rainbow-colored puddles, and the overhanging electric cables no longer belonged to her city.

But Mina had become convinced there was a way to recover what was lost. Quietly, over weeks, she'd reached out to her former comrades in Women of Freedom, her defunct assembly. Now, on this sweltering afternoon, they were arriving at her house. She watched as they approached, walking past the idling van. Once inside, they shed their niqabs.

Almost everyone had refused to participate at first. "You're asking for a death sentence," said one. Mina replied: You marched against the regime—wasn't that also a death sentence? All she was asking for was a meeting. But this time it's different, she was told again and again. Mina recruited her sisters, who fanned out to the houses of old comrades, taking Mina's son as cover. They floated the idea that they would meet and talk—not as Women of Freedom, but simply as a group of friends. After all, was it illegal for friends to meet indoors? Finally Rima, a onetime Women of Freedom activist, agreed. She was losing her mind being homebound and was desperate for company. Once Rima buckled, others followed. In the end, about a dozen women showed. Some had worked on *Peace Be Upon You*, the assembly's newspaper. A few women were from Girls of Tomorrow, also defunct. Now, as Mina served hummus and falafel, she proposed they hold informal gatherings. Let's steer clear of politics, Mina said, and focus on family life.

One afternoon, they gathered in her living room, which they had reconfigured as a stage set. All week, the women had been scripting a play. At stage right was a woman with a fake beard, playing the father, and to her left was a woman in the role of his daughter. A few other women, including Mina, played her brothers. Another woman, as the mother, was hunched over, sweeping the floor. A camera recorded the scene:

FATHER: What are you doing?

DAUGHTER: I got exams tomorrow.

BROTHER: Come on, get up and make us lunch. You don't need to study.

MOTHER: Get up and cook for your brother.

DAUGHTER: Mom, I have an exam tomorrow!

MOTHER: Your brother works hard and comes home tired, and you sit home every day!

The women stifled their laughter. They continued with other scenes: a father cursing his daughter while doting on his son, a mother who orders her daughter to clean the floors while encouraging her son to go out and play.

SON: *(Lights cigarette in exaggerated fashion.)* I'm a man.

FATHER, *speaking to daughter.* Go make tea! And get him an ashtray!

MOTHER, *to daughter*. Get him an ashtray, you idiot! Don't stand there like an idiot. Do some work. Go watch after your little brothers.

SON: Alright, I'm going out to look for some chicks.

FATHER: Yes, go and have fun, son.

The women burst into laughter. In another scene, the daughter begs to go out to see her friends, while the father insists she take a guardian. She refuses, saying she'd rather not have friends at all. The father—whose fake beard is falling off at this point—prepares to launch a tirade, but the women again dissolve into laughter.

The plays were only for their own eyes—the content would have gotten them hauled into black vans. But Mina and her comrades felt a familiar rush, like the old days. Each of them carried the burdens of their children, their parents, even their neighbors, often with little thought to themselves. Without the backdrop of revolution, where every form of authority was in question, they could not stand up to the domineering father or overbearing brother. But here they could inhabit a different mode, take part in a different narrative, to remind them what had once been, and therefore, might be possible once more.

The next week, the group agreed to educate themselves, learn more about revolutionary victories and defeats in other countries. Each week, someone was assigned to research a subject—apartheid in South Africa, the Taliban in Afghanistan—and present it to the group. Emboldened, Mina raised the question of ISIS directly. Its message was poisoning the minds of the youth, she argued; in fact, the Islamic State was an extension of the chauvinism baked into the dictates of honor. The meanness at the heart of the Islamic State could not be unraveled from the dominion of husbands, brothers, and fathers, she asserted. She was in the midst of this speech when the front door shook with a forceful knocking.

The women froze.

The banging grew louder. Mina slunk over to the sill and peered through the lace curtain. Outside, idling in a low groan, was a black van. She turned and put a finger to her lips.

More knocking.

Mina called out, "Who is it?"

No answer. Mina's daughter, age two, said loudly, "Mama?" She grabbed the child and covered her mouth. Mind racing, Mina rehearsed excuses. They were planning a wedding. No, it was an engagement party. A Quran study circle—but where was her Quran? She tried to remember where she'd stored it. But what if they asked to speak to each woman individually?

Banging.

Mina blurted out, "There are no men here! I can't talk to you."

The banging stopped. The silence was absolute. Her daughter was squirming in her grip. Eventually, she heard a car door slamming. She peeked through the window, and felt like a log had rolled off her shoulders: The van was driving away.

That evening, the women did not leave. They debated, conjectured, tossed off plans. They discussed the imperative *be honorable*—what did it truly mean? The revolution had taught them a different notion of honor: to stand for your family, your community, with conviction, even if it meant paying the ultimate sacrifice. The brush with the religious police had somehow charged the women with the light of the old days. They spoke of what they'd done in the stillness of that August afternoon three years prior, when they'd single-handedly revived the city's protest movement. They saw the world once more through those old eyes, and they conjured up a boldness that could no longer be repressed.

In the dark, with the power failing yet again, they held a vote, agreeing to revive the revolution in the city of Manbij.

| TWO |

"Who said death comes only once? If you live in Syria, you'd see how many times you die."

Oday clicked Send on the post. He was spending hours on his balcony, in the bitter cold, looking out over the shadowed cupolas. Once the traffic died, and the apartment windows succumbed to gloom, there was only the soughing wind through the trees, the impenetrably overcast sky. His face was lit by the phone screen, as he posted dark thoughts on Facebook.

The calamity was not something that had suddenly befallen his own people. They had been living a tragedy for more than forty years. What pained him was that *his* friends had been responsible—this he could not comprehend. The young men in the Free Army, those heroes in whose name he'd chanted and marched, had abandoned their hometown. His friends in RYM marched alongside him but then destroyed the very democracy they'd built. As Oday sat on the balcony, after a long day at the shop, he understood he was not merely despondent at the political turn but in the throes of merciless grief.

One afternoon, he posted on Facebook:

> What will become of Syria? Is it going to end up like Afghanistan? Will the U.S. and the West allow ISIS to expand even further? On the other hand, isn't this all our fault? We brought this on ourselves.
>
> *Comment from ISIS member*: My brother, the State will expand whether you want it to or not, as this great religion will reach all corners of the earth, from east to west.
>
> *Oday*: Is it logical to build a state on the skulls of the poor? I'm with Islam, but the poor are only getting poorer.

Friends visited his shop, imploring him to keep his mouth shut. But Oday had never been one for prudence. A few days later, he wrote on Facebook, "I will continue to speak up about anyone who offends our helpless people, and I will not care about blame and reproach."

He went to see his old friend Abdul Hadi, who also advised him to keep quiet. Oday replied that if everyone had done so, there'd have been no revolution in the first place. "This is different," Abdul Hadi advised. "This government has brought peace. People are tired of chaos."

As the air warmed and the peach trees broke into blossom, a curious trend overtook the city: Doors were left open. Cars were parked in alleyways without concern, and parents sent their children on errands after dark. A year prior, doctors were held at gunpoint, taxi drivers murdered. Now, crime had truly vanished. As promised, the Islamic State achieved what the Revolutionary Council had not.

Still, Oday could not accept that people would be willing to trade freedom for security, just as they had done under Assad—it felt as if the entire city was in the grip of a collective delusion. Families strolled through the Great Souk, and fathers brought home grease-soaked *mushabbak* for their daughters, as if the carts blaring jihadi songs and the black facades were small but necessary sacrifices for inner calm. Oday posted:

> There is the type of human who adores getting whipped and can only live on this earth by acting like a sheep. Those humans create tyranny—and then complain about the injustice of tyranny.
>
> There are people who adore slavery, and if it rains freedom, they will take out an umbrella.

But ultimately, it wasn't the people's fault, he reasoned. Who could be blamed for wanting to protect their children? No, he placed this disaster at the feet of the revolutionaries—his friends and comrades. He wrote: "There are people who act just like frogs: if you try to seat them on a golden chair, they jump right back to the swamp."

Oday spent those early spring days in a circumscribed world, drifting between his shop, his balcony, and his bed. He did not step foot in Abu Hajjal's, the billiards hall, where young Islamic State members would gather around the PlayStation. He did not climb the rooftops, nor did the green haze of hashish, illegal but still available, call to him. He'd abandoned those pleasures long ago for the revolution. But Oday could not stick to his balcony routine. So he took long walks—around the track on the Municipal Stadium, where Abdul Hadi used to train; in and out of the dead-end street where he'd been arrested after the sit-in; by the old Baath Party headquarters, where the Revolutionary Youth Movement had held their meetings; past the alley of Roman stone. He walked the upscale Rabta Street, where Hala lived with her husband, a gold merchant. Then he would return home, barricading himself in his bedroom against this city of the undead.

Only after discussion with Bushra, his sister, did Oday decide this could not go on. The road ahead would have to look different from the rough-hewn path behind him, marred by so many false turns. The choice, again, was between modes of life: Out in the political world, in a city so cruel and capricious that it chewed up simple and honest souls; or behind fortress walls, devoted to family. He told Bushra he'd given up on freedom, democracy, equality—false and ruinous idols. He could not read another word or watch another clip about "revolution."

Instead, Oday decided to get married.

Once, Oday had seen his father as a tyrant, chained to dogma. Now, on reflection, it seemed to Oday that at every step, his father might have been right. The old man had insisted he keep away from Abdul Hadi and other truculent youths. He'd entreated his son to steer clear of the protests. He'd demanded he put his mind to books, which Oday had scoffed at, only to come to realize that it was his college-educated friends who'd managed to escape to Europe. What other paths had Oday denied himself because of the desultory days of youth?

If his father had known about Hala, he would have exploded in anger. Oday would've fought back, even if it had meant getting cast out of the family. But now it seemed to him that what people called love was nothing but flowers for a year, then boredom and bitterness for thirty. Had Oday truly even loved Hala? She'd been "neutral" in the face of barbarity. She did not see herself living for her city, her country. True love, Oday realized, was built on shared values. It was forged through the anchor of obligation, grounded in the traditions of his elders. So Oday began to look for a bride and imposed only two conditions: that her family be close in temperament and outlook to his own, and that she support the revolution. Before long, a friend suggested his own sister, Rima. His family had long been friendly with Oday's, and her brothers had taken part in protests. Oday hadn't seen Rima in years, not since she was a teenager, so he asked around. The reviews came back glowing. She'd excelled in school and was a fervent revolutionary. Oday announced to his parents that he wished to ask for Rima's hand.

Not long after, he was seated in Rima's living room, where both families had assembled. As everyone watched, sweat poured down Oday's forehead, and he fumbled his words. An uncle slapped him on the back, laughing. "Relax! You aren't breaking the law!" Rima's father spoke to him loudly, enunciating as if he were speaking to a child. Sitting there in his starched three-piece suit, Oday could only reply, "Yes, sir" and "No, sir." His mother described how he worked the shop till late, how he'd mastered cell phone repair. His father said, "My son survived prison twice, he's a true man."

Trays of sweets were placed before him. Rima's aunt observed, "He doesn't eat."

Then the door opened, and a few young girls led in, by the hand, a young woman with a soft face, eyes trained on the ground. She was carrying a tray with coffee. She served Oday's parents and then her own, and finally, lowering herself slightly, as if balancing a jug on her head, wordlessly offered a cup to Oday. As he clasped the cup, he stole a glance, just as her gaze raked across his face, and they both looked away.

The next week, Oday's family visited with the ring. Oday was allowed to sit next to Rima, but under the watchful eyes of her aunts and sisters. He managed a few meaningless words, while she sat red-faced. An aunt asked about wedding preparations. He remembered when neighbors threw lavish wedding celebrations while regime bombs were slamming into apartment buildings, while people could hardly afford bread. Now, in a soft voice, he requested an austere wedding—no dancing, no henna party—and when Rima spoke for the first time, saying that such austerity was a way to honor the revolution's martyrs, Oday must have felt pride, or perhaps the first pangs of what he later understood as love.

A few days later, Oday obtained her phone number. The silences on the first call were painful, but Oday blamed himself. In the dark folds of the alley of Roman stone, he and Hala had built a private universe, far from prying eyes. Now, though, it felt as if he carried the weight of his family's name on his shoulders. It was Rima who first broke the ice, by reminiscing about the revolution. Only then did Oday unburden himself, telling her about the imprisonments, the fracturing of the Revolutionary Youth Movement, his wayward brother in arms Abdul Hadi. In due course, they were speaking every night. Rima confessed that when Oday used to visit her brother during the protest days, she would watch him enter from her bedroom window. "You were shy even then," she laughed.

Oday began to work like a man possessed. He'd purchased a tiny plot opposite his house, then built a cinderblock house. After hours at the shop, he was busy cladding and painting it himself. He poured his savings into furniture and kitchen supplies. Every third or fourth day, the couple sat together under the scrutiny of the family. Soon, though, the attention was relaxed, and the couple were able to wander the front yard. He placed her hand in his, traced its contours.

The wedding party was so small it fit into a single room. Under ISIS, dancing the *dabke* was forbidden, so the guests sat in a circle as children scampered here and there. Oday placed a baklava in Rima's mouth, and the room broke out in applause. He was patted on the back, asked to eat more. He was teased about the forthcoming morning, when he'd wake up a man. When he sat beside Rima, his hair must have stood on end.

That night, Oday and Rima crossed the street and entered the half-finished one-story house that would be their new home. They entered the bedroom, alone together for the first time, but Oday was too embarrassed to touch her. He slept beside his wife as if he were an intruder, terrified of moving, of waking her.

One afternoon, friends gathered at Oday's new house to congratulate the groom. There was Ahmed, who'd attended the city's first protest in 2011; Fawaz, who'd sung Oday's poetry at marches; Nabeel, whom Oday had sprung from detention when he was wrongly accused of ISIS membership by the revolutionaries. All of them had belonged to the Revolutionary Youth Movement, and the conversation turned to the past, to the days before rancor and division. They sang their anthem:

> *Oh heaven, heaven*
> *Our country it is heaven*
> *Oh country with its dear soil*
> *Our country with its dear soil*
> *Even your fire is heaven.*

They told tales of old protests, when Abel Os and Abdul Hadi marched with a common purpose. They laughed until their sides hurt about the time Abel Os blew a whistle, causing mayhem. Oday chided friends for their bachelorhood. I'm married to the revolution, Nabeel replied. I'll get married when the regime falls! Which regime, someone asked. Both of them, Assad and ISIS, he retorted. Oday replied that he used to say the same—but now, he laughed, he understood what marriage really was.

Not long after, though, Oday visited Ahmed, with whom he'd founded RYM, and confessed that marriage wasn't so simple. To the world, Rima was the very image of the demure daughter, but when they were alone, she filled the room with her seemingly effortless charm, as if she were inviting him into a powerful secret. But it was another powerful secret that weighed on him: When he entered the bedroom and saw her available body, he froze. She must have whispered that it was okay, that she loved him, but he lay awake at night, gripped by unknown phantoms. Weeks had passed in this fashion. He wondered if somehow the revolution, with its betrayals and losses, had sapped his manhood, if perhaps the regime had destroyed it when they'd hung him like a shank of meat in the damp cell. Ahmed assured him this happened to many young men, that the problem was purely between his ears. Oday was not consoled. He spent his days at the shop in an obsessive stupor. Then came the terrible discovery that when he was by himself, everything was in working order. The problem, he feared, was Rima.

The thought struck a new chord of fear, and to compensate he showered her with affection. He worked even later at the shop, saving to refurbish the house: damask wallpaper, crystal sconces in the guest room—nothing was too good for her.

On Facebook, he wrote:

> *My heart aches with yearning*
> *With you I cannot be*
> *For you alone I am burning*

Yet such prostrations failed. Each night, he was seized by terror at the sight of her naked body.

So consumed was Oday by the woes of his marital bed that he hardly noticed the changes around town—the ever-multiplying edicts issued by the Islamic State government, the new checkpoints, and the subtle, surprising hints of revolutionary life.

In early April, graffiti appeared on a wall on the city's west side: DOWN WITH ISIS! DEATH TO TRAITORS!

Almost overnight, the number of black vans multiplied on the streets. A video surfaced of the culprit, who is seen spray-painting the illegal words. But the camera, which shook wildly, did not capture the artist's identity. ISIS announced a state of emergency, offering a reward for information leading to the arrest.

No one came forward.

Authorities responded by ramping up arrests for moral offenses: men dragged to court for smoking or short beards, women hauled in front of a judge for not covering properly. Then, in early May, news spread that something awful had taken place at Central Square. Huzayfa Osman, the founder of *The Sun of Freedom*, who had been unemployed since its shutdown, later recalled:

> As soon as I heard the news, I rushed to Central Square, and I saw a crowd of people around a child, and I tried to get close to see what had happened... and when I did, I saw something I'll never forget.
>
> He was just an adolescent, tied by his hands to the top of a tree, and blood was flowing from his slaughtered head, forming a small pool under his feet. His mother was sitting at his feet, embracing him, trying to lift him up, thinking he was still alive. Her screams filled the air. Her tears mixed with the child's blood, and it threw me into a dizziness, into nausea, and then, for the first time in my life, I had a great desire to scream: Where is God? Where is He?

People had averted their eyes during the earlier executions of adulterers out of sheer exhaustion, or because they were willing to accept the warm embrace of law and order after years of chaos. But the sight of a child tied to a tree aroused something in people's hearts. It was the talk of dinner tables and workrooms, and people began to look at the authorities with new eyes. And then, when the backstory emerged, the city erupted in rage.

Yusef, sixteen, had worked with his father selling vegetables in the souk. He had broken into his neighbor's house to steal. When the neighbor discovered him, she screamed for help as he escaped. She then reported the break-in to the police, adding that the boy had attempted to rape her. Authorities arrested, tried, and executed Yusef in just three days—after which, in remorse, the woman admitted she'd fabricated the rape accusation to compel the police to action.

People were stunned that the caliphate, the so-called guardians of justice and fairness, could run so unjust and unfair an investigation. If these charges were false, what other decisions had the authorities rushed? Who else in the lockup was in fact innocent? To make matters worse, the investigator in the case had little training, having been a drug-runner before joining ISIS. A post appeared on the main Manbij Facebook forum likening the murder to the killing of Hamza al-Khateeb, the child from Daraa whose penis was severed under torture by the Assad regime.

ISIS agents began patrolling internet cafes, demanding cafe owners turn over browser data. But with the internet now on phones, such restrictions weren't enough. So at checkpoints people were made to show their devices, which led them to hide their smartphones at home and carry a simple Nokia when venturing out. This aroused further suspicion, leading people with Nokias to sometimes get arrested merely on the suspicion that they had a second phone.

Still, the critical posts mounted. New graffiti appeared on the central courthouse walls: O ISIS, YOUR JIHAD IS CUTTING HEADS AND PERSECUTING WOMEN. How was someone able to graffiti a core ISIS facility, in one of the most heavily policed sections of town? A second message: ISIS, YOUR WEAPONS ARE EVIDENCE OF YOUR WEEKNESS. And then: ISIS, WHY DO YOU ENSLAVE US WHO WERE BORN FREE?

One day, a new Facebook account appeared, called the Free Islamic Movement:

> As the Prophet, peace be upon him, said: "The best jihad is to speak truth in the presence of tyranny." Our struggle is against the so-called Islamic State, which has no connection to actual Islam, and which knows nothing of Islam except its outward appearance. We initiate our struggle against this transgressive group using the power of truth. We ask the people of Manbij, and the people of Syria, to support us in our struggle against these oppressors and to fulfill their duty, not for our sake but for the sake of our great religion and our beloved country.

The account began spreading news of arrests—authorities shutting down barbers, threatening shopkeepers who allowed women to enter their establishments without the legal attire. The page became one of the heaviest trafficked in the city, offering something like an independent news source for the first time since the collapse of the revolutionary republic.

One afternoon, the site published a video. It shows a woman clad in black, with only her eyes and fingers visible. It's broad daylight, and the rumble of traffic can be heard. Behind her is a black gate, its bars crossing the facade like a fortress. Above is a black signboard of the Islamic State. The woman's eyes are dark, and nail polish is visible on her fingers. In her outstretched hands, in front of this ISIS courthouse, she holds a revolutionary flag. It appears homemade, the three stars poorly aligned. Possession of this flag, the standard of democracy, was punishable by death. The woman speaks, and she is just audible above the traffic:

> Shame on you men of the city! Your women are raising the flag while you are sitting at home. We are filming in front of the headquarters of the so-called Islamic State, at the Islamic court in Manbij. We raise our flag on this day in occupied Manbij.

Within hours, the video was downloaded—then quickly deleted—on phones across the city. At a secret meeting of the Women of Freedom, Mina kept asking, in astonishment, who *is* this? The stunned women fought the urge to save the clip, to soak up its dangerous, alluring energy. In his two-room hovel, Ibrahim studied the clip, then made sure to delete it before his brother visited. Abel Os didn't have a smartphone, but when a friend showed him the video, he watched it only once, and then left immediately for home.

The clip spread beyond city limits, reaching towns still under revolutionary control, and even towns and villages in the heart of the caliphate. It hopscotched from refugee phone to refugee phone. In his apartment in the quiet Turkish city of Gaziantep, Hasan Nefi watched the video carefully, as if to memorize her voice, the stitching on the flag. It reached even the Syrian diaspora in Europe, and beyond.

And on his balcony, sitting with a friend, Oday played the clip over and over, as if sheer repetition would reveal its secrets. The video forced him to contend with the possibility that he'd been wandering the mists of self-pity, that what had seemed like defeat was merely a phase in a longer, grander struggle than he'd first imagined. He saw the city's roadside propaganda stalls and ubiquitous black walls as temporary edifices built by confused, impotent men.

The revolution was alive. In fact, it had never died.

All week, Oday was in a frenzy, roving from house to house, sitting for tea, feeling people out. He had resolved to meet every single former member of the Revolutionary Youth Movement, except those who now belonged to ISIS, to see where there might be a flicker of the former enthusiasm. One night, he gathered a few in his home, showing off a post on the Free Islamic Movement's page: "History repeats itself. Here we are, the youth of Manbij, just as we once wrote on the houses of Assad, today writing on the houses of ISIS."

In this fresh spring, with the cedars thick in the park, he moved with raw energy. It was an energy that blasted away fear and even the instinct for self-preservation.

One day an ISIS member, a Kuwaiti, entered Oday's shop. As the man browsed phones, Oday quipped: Even al-Qaeda thinks your Islam is crazy. The man took great offense, appalled at Oday's impudence.

Later, Oday visited old friends in RYM who'd joined ISIS. They were younger, open-faced and naive, in thrall to Abdul Hadi. Oday excoriated the caliphate, imploring the young men to quit with dignity intact.

It was that same raw energy that must have impelled him to publish a poem on Facebook:

> *Turn away from the ignorant and the foolish*
> *For everything they said is boorish*
> *It has never harmed the waters of the Euphrates*
> *If into it some dogs waded*

A member of the ISIS secret police appeared at Oday's shop. Oday knew him well: He was a former RYM member and a friend of Abdul Hadi's. "Who do you mean by 'dogs'?" he demanded.

Oday laughed and asked if it was now illegal to write poetry about animals.

"We know exactly what you mean," the ISIS official said.

Oday pleaded ignorance. That evening, he shared the story with friends, laughing, and they saw in his eyes a glint like the early days of revolution.

A month later, Rima told Oday that she was pregnant. When he announced the news to his family, his father distributed sweets in the neighborhood.

Oday began leaving the shop during working hours, without explanation, returning home later and later. When he was at the shop, and even at home, he was texting furiously—on a burner phone.

One evening, he stayed out all night, reappearing only at the predawn prayer. Rima pressed, but he would not say a word.

The morning light hit the city, revealing leaflets everywhere: across the entrance to the Great Souk, pinned to windshields. Workers arriving at workshops in the industrial belt in the northern neighborhoods found leaflets stuffed into shutter handles. Each contained a single word: *STRIKE!* The date, May 18, 2014, was the following day.

That afternoon, the Free Islamic Movement published a statement hailing the general strike. Members of the defunct Revolutionary Council, who had been expelled to various Syrian and Turkish towns, echoed the call. Free Syrian Army groups, also scattered to the four winds, posted in support from hideouts and refugee shanties.

On the radio, the Islamic State announced that anyone participating in the strike would be deemed in league with democracy—tantamount to apostasy.

At Oday's shop that evening, Hussein, an old RYM friend, paid a visit. Oday refused to admit to having a hand in the proposed strike. Still, Hussein tried to reason with him. If caught, Oday would not be sent to Aleppo, tortured, and return a hero. "You will be executed. This isn't a joke," he told Oday. "You are going to be a father."

Later in the evening, as Oday and his coworker closed the shop, conversation turned to the strike. They agreed to show up at nine the next morning. If workers around the city stayed home, they would not open the shop. But if fear proved the victor and the city opened as usual, they would too. They embraced.

At home, Oday had dinner with Rima. They discussed her appetite, as Oday worried she wasn't eating enough. Through the window came a tinny voice recording, demanding that people report to work in the morning. Oday paid it no mind. The young couple discussed plans to visit Rima's parents that weekend and spoke of the guest room renovations. Oday reeled off ideas; now he was talking about constructing a second floor. There was a levity about him Rima hadn't noticed before. In their three months together, months in which she had fallen hard, she'd detected beneath his aura of solicitude a kind of melancholy. But this evening, as they sat together in the stillness of their house, with the tinny voice leaking through the windows, she realized that Oday finally seemed unburdened, even happy.

In the morning, the entrance to the Great Souk was as dark as a vault. At the vegetable market, there was not a cart in sight. Oday was standing near the shop. He wore a mad grin, his eyes red, unslept. "I'm not opening the shop," he told his coworker. "I want to see what they will do."

A pickup truck rolled through downtown. Packed into the bed were a group of ISIS members. One was shouting into a loudspeaker: Do not let yourself be swayed by the apostates and the infidel West! Open your businesses! Report to work! Do your duty!

Here and there, more patrols called out similar threats. But Manbij was a ghost town. Incredibly, workers were staying home. Shopkeepers were refusing to open. The city was on strike.

On the radio, ISIS claimed the strike was a ploy by the infidels. People were not showing up to work due to Free Army threats. The Islamic State promised to "protect" anyone who wanted to work.

The streets remained deserted.

By 10:00 a.m., the Great Souk was still shuttered. The industrial belt was silent.

11:00. An ISIS member began spray-painting each shuttered storefront with a green stripe, so that authorities could track who had struck.

By noon, the city was still shut down, and ISIS was in a panic. Authorities ordered all civil service employees who could handle a weapon to report to the police station to help respond to "sedition." ISIS tactical radio networks were crackling with alarm. A member radioed his superior, "Oh sheikh! We have apostates everywhere! Let's seek God's help and cut their heads off after the noon prayer, to terrify people and end the problem!" His commander tried to defuse the situation, insisting everything was under control. "There's no problem, none at all!" he replied. "Photograph the closed shops. Photograph them all, take a hammer with you, break the locks!"

Some merchants, hearing that their shops had been opened, rushed to the scene. Drawn by the commotion, hundreds of people gathered at the covered souk. The ISIS chief barked to his charges, many of whom were from out of town, "Everyone who hears me now on the radio, ask the brothers where the covered market is and go there. I want you to surround the crowd!"

At that moment, on Facebook, Free Army groups addressed the people of Manbij: "We hear ISIS calling out through the minarets that it will punish you—from here we call on you to become one hand in the face of injustice, oppression, and this killing machine! Stand in your strike just as you did against the Assad regime!"

The crowd at the souk pressed up to the shops, trying to roll the shutters down again. ISIS members were screaming at the knotted mass, ordering them away. The crowd was angry—the kind of anger that overpowers self-regard and is blind to past and future. The faces of the ISIS members, on the other hand, showed disbelief, which then morphed into its own variety of anger. Between these two furies lay the awful possibility of violence—and suddenly someone shouted, "God is great!" It was from the crowd. More voices joined in, until it was no longer a shout but many voices in the rhythm and cadence of the old days: a chant. It was the same chant they'd shouted in the face of Assad's tyranny, a reminder that God is greater than all things, even those who claim to speak in His name.

The chanting broke at the sound of gunfire. The crowd fled in all directions. On the walkie-talkie, the ISIS chief demanded to know, "Who opened fire, for God's sake?" A voice came back from one of his lieutenants: "That was me—I shot one of the dogs!"

Protesters were beaten, thrown to the ground. The person who led the chants was pinned down. His name was Abdo Juneid, a carpenter in his twenties. He was hauled away and never seen again.

The crowd dispersed.

ISIS pickups crawled through the streets, loudspeakers demanding of citizens, "Report to work! It's your duty!" But the streets remained without traffic, without a pedestrian at all, and as the late-afternoon sun blazed over the city, the Islamic State operatives were at a loss.

A new post appeared on the Free Islamic Movement page:

> Let it be known to the Islamic State of Iraq and Greater Syria, and recorded in the history of the revolution, that this was the first peaceful mass movement against what is called ISIS.

> You have shaken the ground beneath these tyrants, oh people of Manbij!

An ISIS Hi-Lux rolled up to Oday's shop. Oday stood in front, watching the truck idle. Someone from the back called out, "Why isn't this shop open?" Oday recognized the fighter—Abu Obeida the Iraqi. He was a squat, round-faced member of the security team, who despite his nom de guerre was a son of Manbij. He'd previously been a member of the Jazeera soccer team and had been active in the RYM orbit.

"I'm free to keep the shop closed if I want," Oday replied.

"That's illegal," came the shout.

"You can't force me to work—I'm not a slave."

The impudence must have stunned Abu Obeida. He climbed down. Suddenly, he was face-to-face with Oday. "What did you say?"

Oday did not budge.

Before he knew it, Oday was staring at a revolver. "Open!"

With his voice steady, he said, "Every shop is closed. I'm not going to open."

The revolver was thrust into his temple. For what must have felt like minutes, no one moved. Then Oday pushed the gun away.

Events transpired at great speed. Oday felt himself thrown to the ground. As he struggled, more hands and feet were accosting him. His friend Maraar, who'd been nearby, tried to intervene, but he too was struck down.

Oday and Maraar were hauled to the back of the truck. Oday tried to break free but felt the weight of three or four men on him. The truck began to move.

Back in 2011, Maraar and Oday had been arrested together after the sit-in. Maraar had cried as they were taken to Aleppo, with Abdul Hadi assuring him, "You are a hero, you've done this for your city." Now, as the truck bounced along, Maraar did not make a sound. Oday tried to shout, but with the men sitting on him, he could hardly breathe.

As the sky darkened, minarets blared a message to the mostly empty streets: curfew. No one was allowed out after 8:00, and no motorcycles at any hour. ISIS was blocking all exits from the city. Buses and taxis were turned back.

Escape was impossible.

| THREE |

At the Cultural Center, which had been transformed into an operations room, ISIS grandees were in crisis. Their caliphate, their utopia, had suffered its first serious blow. Fortunately, the Islamic State had recovered control, but the men in the room now understood the honeymoon was over. Six months earlier, the masses had marched through the streets waving black flags in support of the cause. Now, for their own good, they could no longer be trusted to help build this kingdom of justice.

The man in charge of the emergency response to restore stability was short and broad-shouldered, with an ample belly and coal-black eyes—Abu Zubair, who hailed from the Aleppo countryside. He had joined the revolution for democracy and then, like so many others disillusioned by the corruption and inequality, gravitated toward the Islamic State. Some ISIS officials wanted to execute anyone who took part in the strike, but Abu Zubair felt this was madness, or at least practically impossible. Instead, he wanted to find the ringleaders—cut off the head, the body dies.

In the room, listening carefully, was Abdul Hadi. He'd seen the flyers calling for the strike, and he knew his old comrades were behind it. But he never expected the population to go along. After years in which he, more than anyone, had kept an ear to the street, he was shaken by the possibility that the city was spinning out of his grasp. He agreed the only answer was to find the organizers, show them no mercy. The life of his city depended on it.

Late in the evening, members of an ISIS security patrol entered, hardly able to contain themselves. They had caught the leader. "The infidel tried to hide his role," one said, "but we searched his premises." The contraband was damning: leaflets calling for the strike; notebooks in which phone numbers were jotted down; even—and this was the most incriminating—a revolutionary flag. Like the flag raised by the mysterious woman on the viral video. There was an underground resistance in Manbij, and they had just uncovered its puppet master.

"Who is it?" Abu Zubair asked.

"His name is Oday al-Hema," came the reply.

Abdul Hadi felt as if a thunderbolt had passed through him. His mouth went dry. As Abu Zubair asked his lieutenants to find out everything they could about this Oday, Abdul Hadi was as silent as a stone. Papers were brought in, phone calls made. Abu Zubair was listening, slowly realizing that the culprit's best and oldest friend was right here, in this room. He turned and stared at Abdul Hadi.

"You've been very quiet," he said.

Abdul Hadi said nothing.

"Speak to what you know about Oday."

Friedrich Nietzsche said that resentment is an emotion of the weak, of those who lack power. The propensity of the resentful to see knives everywhere, even the desire to hurt others, stems from this fundamental lack. People hurt others to *imagine* their own power. "One hurts those whom one wants to feel one's power, for pain is a much more efficient means to that end than pleasure," Nietzsche wrote. "Pain always raises the question about its origin while pleasure is inclined to stop with itself without looking back."

But Abdul Hadi was no longer among the weak. The thousand tiny dramas and colossal tragedies of history had ripped him from the ranks of the weak and hoisted him into the ranks of the best and greatest. He was liberated from the prison of resentment, and now, in the seat of power, believed he had discovered the truest freedom. The inverse of resentment, in the Nietzschean mold, is magnanimity: The powerful embody the virtues of grace and beneficence, supporting the weak not out of pity or sympathy but as an exercise, or even celebration, of power itself. Call it noblesse oblige—this was the task Abdul Hadi placed before himself.

After ISIS seized control, he was appointed director of municipal services. His brother Muhammad, once the close friend of fellow engineer Ahmed Rahmo, president of the first Revolutionary Council, was appointed mayor of the city. When Muhammad had won the city's first genuine election, he had pledged to support human rights and democracy. Now, he and his brother, loyal servants of the caliphate, took to wearing Afghan clothes and grew long beards.

Abdul Hadi oversaw relief aid for refugees and the poor. When he wasn't behind his desk, he was visiting widows and the homeless to document their needs, organizing livelihood surveys, or negotiating with Islamic State offices in other cities to acquire aid. He could be spotted around town, driving a gray van, windows down, Kalashnikov slung over his shoulder. Once a month, he'd travel to the front lines, a requirement for all Islamic State employees.

When he ran into old revolutionary friends, he was terse, as if idle chatter were a luxury, and swift to rebuke. Once, he noticed an old RYM comrade lighting a cigarette: "Don't ever let me see that again," he warned.

He chanced upon another former comrade wearing a tight sweater, showing off his bulging muscles. "That's obscene," Abdul Hadi snapped.

His friend couldn't believe this was coming from Abdul Hadi, of all people, who at one time smoked hash on rooftops and fell head over heels for other boys. "What's gotten into you," the friend laughed. But Abdul Hadi was not laughing.

Sometimes, he beseeched his old friends to join the organization. One close confidant from the RYM days replied that ISIS were no different than the Assad regime—the dictator in a suit and tie replaced by a dictator with a beard and gown. The Islamic State's goal, he insisted, was "to destroy the revolution." Abdul Hadi replied, "There is no revolution anymore. That was all a lie. I only care about the caliphate."

Only with Oday did he unfasten the armor of power, allowing, for a moment, his old self to emerge. Not long after the takeover, he'd bumped into Oday at the market. Oday burst into laughter at the sight of Abdul Hadi's Afghan clothes—"You can't be serious!" he said. Abdul Hadi replied, "Come on, you're being too harsh! Give us time." Oday stopped laughing. He put his arm around his friend and said he loved him, but he could never accept what had happened. Oday said he did not blame Abdul Hadi, but he had chosen his own path. Abdul Hadi returned his old friend's hug and said they would meet soon.

That had been four months prior—a simpler, more crystalline era. Now, in the ill-lit operations room, facing security chief Abu Zubair, Abdul Hadi narrated Oday's story: how he'd organized the city's first demonstration, his two imprisonments by the regime, the birth of the Revolutionary Youth Movement. "He's not like the other revolutionaries. He cares about justice," Abdul Hadi said. "He hated the Revolutionary Council from day one."

"Well, now he's dealing with them," Abu Zubair replied.

An abyss was forming in Abdul Hadi's stomach. "Do we have evidence?" he asked.

"We'll get evidence," Abu Zubair said.

That week, Abdul Hadi visited the operations room every day, acting as if he were keen to keep abreast of security developments, whereas in truth he simply longed to hear snippets about Oday. Once, he worked up the nerve to ask about the investigation. Abu Zubair sighed, saying it would be a lengthier process than he'd anticipated. "Your friend isn't confessing."

One afternoon, Abdul Hadi showed up at the prison with falafel sandwiches for Oday. He spoke to the warden, an old friend from the democracy days, who allowed him to enter the dank, winding corridor that led to the cells. He was about to arrive at Oday's cell when he found himself face-to-face with Abu Zubair.

"What are you doing here?" Abu Zubair asked.

"I brought us lunch," he stammered. They went to Abu Zubair's office, where, over the meal, they discussed the problem of apostates in the city.

Another afternoon, Abdul Hadi was at the security office when Abu Zubair suddenly said, "Let's go see your friend." Abdul Hadi followed him underground and was soon overwhelmed by the stench of human waste. With hardly any light, he felt his way along the walls. A murmur could be heard, which resolved into moaning, then screaming, terrible screaming, and Abdul Hadi recognized the voice, which in simpler times always carried a touch of goofiness, but now had an alien quality, so that he knew immediately it both was and was not Oday. He entered a windowless room and saw four young men dangling from the ceiling, the walls splattered with blood.

When he spotted Oday, blindfolded, hanging in the center of this abattoir, a dark gauze seemed to pass over Abdul Hadi's eyes. His knees buckled, the room spun, and he reached out to Abu Zubair for support. Oday was bone thin—he must have lost forty pounds in a month of imprisonment. Abu Zubair raised a cable and began whacking Oday, who cried out, "O God! O God, you oppressors!"

Abdul Hadi fled the room. He stood in the hallway, struggling to catch his breath. Tears were streaming down his cheeks.

Abu Zubair asked, "What's gotten into you?"

Abdul Hadi struggled to compose himself. "I was hoping he'd join us, and not side with the apostates," he offered.

"Ah yes," Abu Zubair said. "It is a tragedy."

Abdul Hadi began pleading Oday's case. "Why don't you forgive him and offer him a chance to join us?"

Abu Zubair replied that repentance was impossible for someone who'd tried to overthrow the caliphate.

A shudder of courage shot through Abdul Hadi, and he countered: "You will never break him." He related a story from their days imprisoned together in Aleppo. Oday had been subjected to electric shocks, waterboarding, the wheel—and each time, with every ounce of strength he could muster, he fired back at the regime adjutants, "Down with the dictatorship!" This induced more ferocious torture. When he was brought back to the cell, clinging to life, the cellmates told him to keep his mouth shut or he'd get himself killed. "There are worse ways to die," Oday said, "than to be a martyr for freedom." The broken, emaciated men began to cry, and even Abdul Hadi, though he was angry with his friend, found his eyes wet. Oday had become a cell leader, and the other inmates consulted him about how to handle the interrogations, how to ration food, how to keep the nightmares at bay. When he was released, Oday gave a few hundred liras as a tip to the guard, and said, "I'll give you the rest once we've overthrown the regime."

Abu Zubair broke into laughter, shaking his head. "What kind of guy is this?" Then he gripped Abdul Hadi's shoulders and told him to be strong. Oday was a great man, he allowed, but he was also an apostate. "There's only one remedy for the apostate."

Every day, after being returned from the torture session, Oday crawled into the cell corner. The windowless room, measuring fifteen feet to a side, housed some twenty prisoners. In the cell was Maraar, who'd been arrested with him, and who was also accused of organizing the strike. There was Sheikh Ismail, an imam who was detained after denouncing ISIS in his sermons, and Hussein, who was accused of maintaining contact with the Free Army, and whose arms were broken from the torture, leaving the other prisoners to feed and bathe him. There was also an uncle of the Prince, who was in for hawking cigarettes, and an American, who'd apparently traveled to Syria to join one of the rebel factions. After months of torture, the American began shouting in strange tongues, practicing karate moves, and banging his head against the cement walls.

Abu Jude, a falafel vendor, was in on false charges. When interrogation sessions produced nothing, he was transferred to a cell the size of a broom closet, which was standing room only. When he banged on the door pleading to go to the bathroom, he was ordered to relieve himself where he stood. He remained on his feet for twenty days.

A teenage inmate named Firas was forced into the tire and thrashed across his bare feet. After some time, he cried out, "I'll tell you everything!" He claimed he knew the ringleaders of the strike. He was driven through the streets, where he pointed to pedestrians at random. In all, 114 people he picked out were arrested and tortured. Firas was then executed.

One day, Abu Zubair entered the cell and motioned to a middle-aged inmate named Hashim. A schoolteacher before the revolution, he'd been elected to the second revolutionary council, which was enough to land him in the lockup.

Abu Zubair asked Oday, "What do you think of Mr. Hashim here?"

"He was my science teacher in seventh grade. My God, I hated him!"

The cell burst into laughter.

"That's because he was so lazy!" Hashim countered, to more laughter.

"Hashim was against the elites, and he fought for the poor," Oday said. "He's a good and honest man."

Most days, Oday could hardly stand, though it seemed he'd lost all fear of his captors. He'd still not confessed, but had surrendered his email password under torture. The interrogators then read his verses, his veiled denunciations of the caliphate, and tortured him further. Yet in a cell of bruised and bleeding men, it was Oday who kept spirits up. He recited poetry and led political discussions. The prisoners reminisced about the days of revolution and freedom, now so distant, and debated their mistakes. After weeks of abuse, in which they wet themselves, in which blood and snot streaked the floors, the body lost its special valence. The men no longer knew shame, and this induced a new, perverse type of freedom. They no longer cared what the others thought.

Still, the idea of obligation clung to them. They wrapped each other's bandages, dressed each other, held each other's penises so they could urinate. This was a new form of camaraderie, even as not a single soul beyond their friends and neighbors—not their fellow revolutionaries around the country, not the news-watching public around the world, not the human rights organizations or world leaders—remembered their existence.

Oday was on the watch for depression, which would slip into the cell suddenly, afflicting one man or another, until everyone was in its grip. He would hobble through the narrow confines, asking each inmate to share a memory or two, asking what they'd do when they were released, what they would eat. He insisted to everyone he'd be released soon, because he had not cracked. They'd found evidence he was behind the strike, but it was circumstantial. "When I'm out," he said, "I'm going to start a campaign for all of you."

✣ ✣

One day, Oday asked for a notebook and a pen, and Abu Zubair, perhaps moved by Abdul Hadi's stories, or maybe because he was curious what Oday was thinking, agreed. At once, Oday crouched in the corner, scribbling away by the faintest light. Though ISIS's methods were indistinguishable from the regime's, it was this notebook, and the freedom to write, that brought Oday back to his prison cell in Aleppo. There, he'd kept a notebook, and spent hours crafting a poem that contained the lines: "We raised our index fingers at him and his malice / soon we will raise our flag above his palace." That seemingly political composition had also carried themes of regret, loss, and friendship—his attempt to offer an olive branch to Abdul Hadi. His new verses also hovered on the themes of friendship and loss, but Oday had long since cast aside regret. It might simply have been that he could no longer conceive of himself independently of his trials. If destiny placed him here, in this clammy cell with these battered men, it was for a purpose.

A few weeks later, Oday was taken for investigation. Abu Zubair used the opportunity to enter the cell and read Oday's notebook. He found dozens of poems extolling the revolution, along with diary entries detailing his torture. There was a letter to his wife, Rima, in which he wrote that he was ready to die for the revolution and promised that Manbij would one day be liberated from ISIS.

As a former revolutionary, Abu Zubair grudgingly admired Oday's spirit, but felt he had no choice but to burn the notebook. When Oday returned and saw his month's labors reduced to cinders, he stared at Abu Zubair and his body stiffened, as if it were about to take a blow. A wild look passed over his eyes, the look of a man with nothing left to lose. He rocked slightly, then was overcome by tremors. No one in the cell said a word. Abu Zubair watched intently.

Suddenly Oday burst into tears and slammed his own head against the wall. "Oh, you oppressors!" he cried. He continued slamming his head against the wall, over and over, until blood poured down his cheeks.

As the days passed, Oday adopted a position of full defiance. When the prisoners were ordered to attend sharia reeducation courses, he refused. The wardens were flabbergasted: No one within prison walls—or beyond them—had dared disobey a direct order. The next morning, he rebuffed the breakfast of olives and bread. "Your State will not win!" he shouted. "You will be trampled!"

The insubordination transcended that which could be disciplined through the body. Run-of-the-mill torture would not suffice. Oday was transferred to another wing of the prison, where he was kept in a broom closet. Solitary confinement had been the only method of torture not yet applied.

Maraar, Oday's diffident friend, who had been arrested with him, and who had withstood the tire and waterboarding, was also placed in solitary. Their cells were adjacent, the walls thin enough to communicate through. Oday carried on long conversations with Maraar, which morphed into a plot for rebellion: Oday would pretend to lose consciousness, and when the guard entered, he would overpower him, then open the other cells. What Oday and Maraar did not realize was that ISIS had posted a sentry outside their cells. He reported the plot to superiors.

One afternoon, seven guards rushed in. Oday was thrown into the hallway, where he was caned viciously. With every blow, Oday cried out, "Down with the State!" He was pinned down. "Down with the State!" A guard clutched Oday's jaw, as if to break it off its hinge. "Down with the State!" A lit match appeared. "Down with the—"

Oday let out an unearthly scream, which must have filled every dank corridor and permeated the narrow cells, even the ceiling, so that it could be heard in the investigators' quarters above. The guards were trying to burn his mouth. His lips were on fire. He struggled with what seemed the strength of three men, but six men were atop him. The hallway filled with the leathery smell of roasting flesh.

When he was finally back in his cell, Oday could hardly open his mouth. His chin was covered in burns. But he'd kept the pen, which he now used to scrawl anti-ISIS slogans on the walls. The words "Down with the State!" appeared over and over, in different sizes.

Once this writing was discovered, Oday was tied to the wall and only allowed down once a day for mealtime.

"Your friend is still refusing to confess," Abu Zubair told Abdul Hadi. ISIS was certain Oday was in cahoots with a broad network of resistance—the enshrouded woman raising the flag, the graffiti campaigns—but they couldn't make him crack.

For a month now, Abdul Hadi had been in Abu Zubair's ear, encouraging him to offer Oday repentance. But Oday was making it difficult, and Abu Zubair wanted Abdul Hadi to see what this intransigence was costing. He led Abdul Hadi back downstairs to the interrogation room. There, chained to the wall, head hanging, blindfolded, was Oday. His lips were savagely discolored. His right arm appeared to be hanging off its socket. His left foot was twisted. At the sound of visitors, his head raised slightly.

A guard began whacking the broken arm at the socket. "Who is the woman!" the abuser demanded. "What's her name?"

Then, in a voice that lashed Abdul Hadi to the core—a voice thick with phlegm, feral, almost not of this world—Oday bellowed, "I don't know what you are talking about!"

Again, it was as if a dark gauze came over Abdul Hadi's vision. The room spun. He steadied himself, then rushed out of the cell. In the hallway, he grasped the walls, those walls of bile and blood, and everything went black.

At home, Abdul Hadi's mother tried to force him to eat, but he refused. He slammed the door to his room. Inside, on his bed, he studied a spot on the wall. The traffic outside rose and fell. He was one of the most important men in Manbij, he told himself. He focused intensely on the spot, as if it would surrender secrets, spill the mysteries of his city, his people. Outside, the air cooled and the streetlights switched on. He was one of the most important men in Manbij—of this, he was certain. A man to be seen with, a man who'd delivered justice to his people.

He closed his eyes. There was a faraway knocking. Abdul Hadi thought back to when he'd addressed RYM rallies, how the faces on the city's benighted people had looked up at him, ready to follow him to hell and back, if only he could deliver a better life for their children. *Hell.* Here was an idea Abdul Hadi, even in his newfound piety, had not much considered. He could not, try as he might, picture hell, and this fact caused him some alarm. What if he could not because, in fact, he already lived in the worst of all possible worlds? He laughed at the idea, and its absurdity placed him in a better mood. He went for a walk in the thick July night. For some reason, the streetlights were now dead. The storefronts were shuttered. Was there another strike? He slowly registered the absence of traffic—no taxis, no pedestrians. It was as if everyone had abandoned the city. But then, at the far end of the street, he saw a shadow, a slender figure, moving toward him. Only when he got within handshake distance did he realize it was Oday. Oday! He was free! Abdul Hadi's heart leapt, and he moved to embrace his old friend. But Oday pushed him away. "Help me escape," Oday said. "Escape where? You are already free," Abdul Hadi cried. "Help me escape, I can't bear the pain." Abdul Hadi tried again to embrace his friend, but in that moment, when he was pushed away again, he saw Oday's white, fleshless arms.

Abdul Hadi snapped awake. Now, in his bed, the streetlights casting soft shadows in his room, the traffic gently rising and falling, he found he could not stop crying. As he sobbed, the mantle of his imperial self, as one of the most important men in Manbij, was shed. So too was that of Abdul Hadi the daring revolutionary, Abdul Hadi the martyr in an Aleppo prison, Abdul Hadi the soccer star. Once again he was that shy, solicitous boy who could not make friends at school because everyone already had their circle, until another skinny boy named Oday found him. He must have been sobbing loudly, because there was a knock at the door again, and then it swung open. His older brother Muhammad clasped him and shouted his name. Abdul Hadi did not know what to say—Muhammad, the mayor of Manbij, servant of the caliphate. He, like Abdul Hadi, was one of the most important men in the city, but they were also, in the grand scheme of the State, cogs in a vast, terrible machine. Suddenly, Abdul Hadi buried himself in his brother's arms. "This is bigger than me!" he wept. In the early days of the revolution, when Abel Os had returned from prison, he, Oday, and others had gathered around him as if he were a hero from another age. But Abel Os had been withering: This is bigger than all of you, he'd warned. Don't sacrifice your lives—you are too small, too insignificant, to make a difference when the powers that be are so immense.

Only now, after so much loss, did Abdul Hadi understand. "I didn't ask for this! This is bigger than me!" he said, over and over, deep in his brother's chest, nearly choking on his sobs. He thought he could use his newfound power to quell his demons, to right the wrongs of the world. Transforming himself into an ISIS grandee, he had liberated himself from resentment, but at what cost? What seemed like freedom was only a mask for power, and he realized, with horror, that he could never be free. True freedom belongs to the dead. His mother entered the room, and he sensed her stroking his back, as he drowned in Muhammad's arms. He identified within him a profound sense of remorse, a sensation that was entirely new to him. How he wished he could have found another path! *He* had brought ISIS to the city, *he* had brought this on Oday. But what could be done? The old world was dead; every decision, no matter how tiny, was set in stone. Nothing could be undone. His sights had been so foolishly set on Bashar al-Assad. But time, he now realized, was the greatest dictator. Its tyrannical rule could never be overthrown.

His brother was shaking him. "Don't let anyone see you like this!" he said. "Or it will be our necks!"

The promises had seemed pure, the city of justice gleaming, but Abdul Hadi finally understood he had been caught in a fever dream.

| FOUR |

Abel Os sat in the back seat of a taxi as it passed the low-slung factories of the industrial belt, the giant silo of the city's reserve bakery, and finally, the Cardamom Market, where, so many years ago, he'd begged for loans from the motorcycle men. It was early February 2014, a week after ISIS seized power, when Abel Os had decided to tempt fate and end his exile. In his youth, he had roamed the reaches of his country, working under the blazing sun, waiting at muster zones, under construction girders. He'd seen the glistening beaches of Beirut, the winding souks of Damascus. Through these travels he knew he could never stay far from home long. And what was home? That craggy street in Sarab where his father had once erected a bubble gum stand, where he'd learned the principle of *perpetual motion*, which now sounded so remote and farcical it felt like a fairy tale. Yet he believed his father was still there, somehow, in the crevices of that road, in the cinderblock houses. It was this archaeology of loss that brought Abel Os back to Manbij.

When he spotted black flags here and there, he felt a flash of anger. "They've turned this place into Afghanistan," he said to the driver.

The driver said nothing.

Abel Os had forty-seven dollars. He'd bargained the driver down to twenty, and wondered what was left in the key box in his bedroom closet. When they reached his house, he asked the driver to wait.

He hugged his wife and kissed his children—he'd not been away for as long as a week since they'd been born. He showered, shaved, and returned to the taxi. He wanted to see about his old job at the real estate office.

In the back seat, he hunched over his Nokia phone, making sure it was swiped clean of the numbers of revolutionaries. When he realized the car was not moving, he looked up and saw men in black masks, rifles cocked, climbing out of a pickup that flew the flag of the Islamic State.

―✦ ✦―

Abel Os was hauled to the Repentance Office. For a few hours, sitting in a wicker chair, speaking to a man in a mask, he recounted in detail his activities: the protests against the regime, the founding of RYM, the mobilizations against ISIS.

In the end, the ISIS official said, "Our prince has ordered that if even one of you has killed a thousand of us, if you repent, we will accept it."

"I want nothing to do with all this," Abel Os said. "I only got involved to overthrow Assad."

"The revolutionaries were all apostates. They worshipped democracy."

"I understand you feel this way," Abel Os said, rising from his seat. He extended his hand. "Have a good day."

On the way home, he realized that he'd not responded as his old self would have: *Yes, my lord*, or even *Yes, my sheikh*.

―✦ ✦―

As the months went by and the dark fog of ISIS rule descended, Abel Os kept quiet. When the executions began, he refused to discuss them with friends. They mistook his reticence for self-preservation, but in truth, it was not the Islamic State that had consumed his thoughts—it was the old days of freedom. How green and simpleminded he had been! He'd had the heart of a child, running through the streets shouting about freedom. Now, he burned with shame.

The world was ordered precisely and always had been. The fools who'd ignored this were now either rich and powerful or dead. He was haunted by the vision of those eighteen months of democracy: the colorful gonfalons, the sweat-glistened crowds, the late-night meetings, the powerful, visionary eyes of Abdul Hadi, eyes that seemed to bore into him even now. He caught himself in the depths of profound remorse. It was *he* who'd encouraged Abdul Hadi and the others to form the Revolutionary Youth Movement. *He'd* allowed his resentments to overwhelm his good sense, providing fodder for the usurpers.

In the spring, when the anti-ISIS graffiti began appearing on walls and facades, Abel Os felt some combination of concern and derision, like a father watching his son repeat his own mistakes. When the city filled with talk of the posts from the mysterious Free Islamic Movement, Abel Os thought: The internet is the realm of fantasy. Here, on the asphalt streets, among the concrete warrens, hope had been outlawed. When the city went on strike, Abel Os stayed home, viewing the action not as heroism but as folly, as perverse self-sacrifice. When news reached him that Oday had been arrested, though, Abel Os could bear the silence no longer.

One by one, he met former RYM members now in ISIS. These young men, clinging to the hardened, pious affect of their adopted movement, still could not help but revere the old karate master. They promised to help.

Abel Os sought out Abdul Hadi. When they met, he ignored the ridiculous Afghan clothes and embraced him. "Uncle," Abdul Hadi said respectfully, "I am doing my best, but please know this is bigger than me."

The summer passed. One afternoon, Abel Os was visiting the blacksmith Mustafa Haddad, an old RYM stalwart, when conversation turned to Oday. Neither had heard a hint about his condition, and they had been barred from bringing him food. Oday's father could still be seen at the cell phone shop, but his eyes betrayed a broken spirit. Oday's wife was now four months pregnant.

Abel Os told Mustafa he could not believe the men holding Oday were once his comrades who'd risked their lives for freedom. Anger gripped him and he could feel his chest tightening. He felt Mustafa's hand on him. The injustice, the *betrayal*—this was the word. Mustafa was shouting something. Abel Os turned to look, but couldn't find his friend.

His head was spinning. Slowly, the world reappeared.

The stress was getting to him. It was probably high blood pressure, Mustafa surmised, convincing Abel Os to come for a ride on his motorcycle. They reached Aleppo Road, the hot air blasting their faces. He treated Abel Os to ice cream, and finally the karate man calmed himself.

"Please see a doctor," Mustafa advised.

Three days later, in early September, Abel Os rode his motorcycle to the Cardamom Market. He crossed Central Square, the buses waiting for passengers, the cedar trees on the corner. A knot of people stood around one of the trees. Abel Os stopped. Someone was slumped beneath a bough. Pressing forward, he saw it was a body—a headless body—and a wave of nausea hit him. The head was a few feet away. He recognized the victim as a revolutionary, a member of the Free Army. The condemned man's mother was wailing, wiping blood from the forehead of her beheaded son. Abel Os raced away, heart throbbing, sweat pouring down his face.

After a while, he realized he'd been driving at random. The buildings were leaning, now close to toppling. The asphalt was near his face. But he could no longer see the asphalt or the buildings. They were a blur behind a waterfall, mere shapes.

He was brought home sometime later, and the world once again righted itself. Standing around him were his family, his wife fanning him. He was taken to the doctor, who peered into his eyes. Abel Os rested his chin in a stirrup and pressed his eyes into a whirring machine, just as his mother had done years before. One eye had been badly injured a while back during a blow he'd received playing soccer. Now his other eye was in peril. The doctor explained that nothing could be done here in the caliphate. The only recourse was the same eye hospital in Damascus where he'd taken his mother. But that was regime land, where he'd be arrested in a heartbeat.

So Abel Os scraped together his savings and headed for Turkey. There, for the first time in his life, he checked into a hotel. The doctor injected his eye, and instructed him to return in fifteen days. But Abel Os could not afford to stay fifteen days in Turkey, as he'd spent everything on a single night's hotel. He chose to head back to the caliphate, then return for his appointment.

It was a decision he'd regret for the rest of his life.

The May strike had rattled ISIS officials, convincing them to enact sweeping reforms. Until then, Manbij had been known among Islamic State partisans as "mini-London," due to the preponderance of foreign fighters, including Europeans and Americans, who called the city home. After the strike, though, the authorities transferred them to other cities. They dismantled the city's operations room, which had directed attacks abroad, and relocated senior ISIS leaders. But the strike's most important outcome, from the point of view of the city's residents, was the growth of welfare services—and it was Abdul Hadi's job to carry out this program.

He oversaw an expansion of provisions for the poor, and for refugees living in schools and tents. The authorities reintroduced the fuel subsidy, which had been cut by Bashar al-Assad's reforms in the 2000s. They solved the bread distribution crisis by building public bread dispensaries around the city. Families began sending their children to wait in line for bread, no longer afraid of the skies—since the ISIS takeover, Assad's warplanes had stopped targeting the city, because for the time being the regime was focused on crushing democratic rebels elsewhere.

By September 2014, the Islamic State stretched from Manbij, its westernmost city, to Fallujah, in Iraq, more than five hundred miles away—an area the size of the United Kingdom. The border between Iraq and Syria no longer existed. Some ten million people now called the caliphate home. This breadth allowed for economies of scale. In Manbij, authorities were able to attract investment—Mosul traders, Raqqa industrialists, even Lefarge, the French cement company. It was not only the poor but the merchants who applauded the new policies. The government subsidized the construction of a new market downtown, granting merchants low-rent storefronts. Up went new apartment buildings in the rococo Gulf style.

Manbij's mayor, Muhammad—Abdul Hadi's older brother—solved the city's electricity woes by confiscating generators and transistors from merchants and putting them to public use. The government enforced the payment of electricity bills—they had gone unpaid during the revolution—which allowed the city to recoup expenses. For the first time since the regime days, Manbij had uninterrupted power. During the revolution, one could sometimes turn on the faucet to find it dry; the new authorities imposed regulations around water usage on car washes and farms. People marveled at the new ordinances, some of which they had not even seen during the Assad years. An army of food safety inspectors graded restaurant cleanliness and tested the meat at shawarma stands. The health directorate cracked down on the sale of expired and knockoff medications. ISIS was making the proverbial trains run on time.

The strike, therefore, had been both an astounding success and a spectacular failure. The action had improved the quality of life—but ISIS had survived stronger than ever. Authorities painted over the anti-ISIS slogans on the walls. They monitored internet cafes, so that posting political messages became next to impossible. The resistance was extinguished.

In June, the Free Islamic Movement published its final statement:

> In my country, a group has usurped the name of Islam. . . . In my country, they kill and plunder in the name of Islam. In my country, after someone is killed, they are hung with a sign around their neck listing fabricated charges. . . .
>
> In my country, there are those who are offended because a woman has inadvertently lifted her scarf slightly, while they feel no pain for the child made an orphan by the barrels of death. . . .
>
> What country is this? This is the so-called Islamic State of Iraq and Greater Syria.

This plaintive last gasp fell on deaf ears. For people who wished to put food on the table, send their children to school, dance at their daughter's wedding, the bargain they'd struck was at least better than the alternative—freedom without security. A new mood settled on the city, and people trained themselves to look the other way when someone was strung up on a pole. Their silence was purchased at the prospect, they believed, of filling their children's bellies.

In this new calm, many citizens flocked to join the Islamic State. There was Zain, a democratic revolutionary who'd fled to Turkey after the ISIS takeover. His passion was humanitarianism, but he could not find a job in that sector, so friends back home convinced him to return. He was hired by the Islamic State to do charity work. The Jessi brothers followed a different path. Before the revolution, they'd lived on the streets in Greece, working as pimps and drug pushers. They joined the security wing of ISIS—once under society's boot, now they inspired fear and respect. There was Ahmed, a huge fan of the theater, "especially dark comedies," he recalled later. "It had been my only wish to become a theatrical actor. I used to dream of studying at the Higher Institute of Dramatic Arts, but it only accepted people from wealthy and well-connected families." He wound up as an electrician, eventually under the employ of the Revolutionary Council during the democratic years. When ISIS took over, he was hired to oversee power-line maintenance for the caliphate. A young man named Yasser had devoted years to the bottle. "My life was empty," he later recalled. "I had no goals, no plans for the future." Joining ISIS helped him get sober, convincing him of a life devoted to something greater than himself.

It seemed to Abel Os as if half his neighbors had signed up to work for the caliphate. The fact sunk him further into depression, and he missed his follow-up appointment in Turkey. He had hardly a lira to his name—certainly not enough to make the arduous journey across the border and pay for a hotel. A week passed, and his wife, in desperation, reached out to friends and relatives without his knowledge. So many people came forward with donations that Abel Os received enough funds to stay in Turkey for three days and see the sights.

He planned out every detail. Technically, subjects of the caliphate were not permitted to leave, but a few intrepid taxi drivers were willing to brave the backroads and circumvent checkpoints for the right price. Abel Os found a driver through his old revolutionary friends and visited him at his house one night, explaining he wanted to depart at five the next morning. After a handshake, he headed for his brother's shop. It was early evening, and the muezzins were wailing.

At the shop, a white pickup pulled to a stop. Three ISIS members emerged. "Are you Abel Os?" one asked.

In times past, Abel Os would have fled. He could easily have outrun them. They were not locals and did not know the backstreets. But something within him had perished the day the first black flags went up around town. He felt old, his bones ached, his soul was battered.

"Yes," he said, and followed them wordlessly into the truck.

"I'm supposed to torture you," Abu Zubair, the ISIS official, told him. Abel Os was sitting in the interrogation room, but without a blindfold. "But that will cause a riot. We know how the people praise you. So tell me, why are you so beloved?"

"I only fought for the revolution. I never stood against you."

Abu Zubair produced a video, taken over a year earlier, during the height of the democratic period, when Abel Os was leading a demonstration against ISIS. He hadn't mentioned this during his repentance hearing. Such an omission was punishable by death.

"There are laws here," the official explained. "Without the rule of law, a society cannot function."

Abel Os said nothing.

"I want to help you," Abu Zubair continued. "But rules are rules."

News of Abel Os's arrest galvanized old RYM activists. They approached their former comrades, now ISIS members, demanding an end to the insanity. They spoke as if they were friends of the ISIS cause: It was one thing to detain members of the Free Army, and even arresting Oday, who'd helped incite an uprising against the caliphate, had its logic. But imprisoning Abel Os, who'd not uttered a word against the new authorities? What could this accomplish? It would turn the street against Islamic rule.

Indeed, many ISIS members appeared genuinely embarrassed. So many of them had come to political awakening through street protest, an art everyone associated with Abel Os. He was poor and without political ambition, qualities even the most hardened ISIS members admired. "I'll find a way to get him out," one leading ISIS commander said.

A week passed, then two weeks. Abel Os needed to travel to Turkey for treatment, otherwise risking permanent damage to his eyes.

"I'll see what I can do," Abdul Hadi said. Another week passed. Friends and comrades were showing up at ISIS offices every day. They were making house calls with ISIS members, drinking many cups of tea, listening to numbing lectures about Islamic law.

Another week passed.

At night, as he lay among the sleeping inmates, Abel Os tried to focus on the frame of light bleeding through the cell door. The light seemed to be fading. He caught himself again with remorse—did *he* build these walls, by turning the working-class youth against the Revolutionary Council? But what was a democracy that only catered to the wealthy? He tried to revive memories of simpler, purer times. He regaled other inmates with stories of the uprising, the daring nighttime protests, the Friday afternoons fleeing through the alleyways. But it was difficult for others to hear these tales. Those were days of hope, and hope, the men now believed, was folly.

When Abel Os was ordered to interrogation, he tripped in the hallway. Gathering himself, taking a few paces, he tripped again. "Walk, you fool! Or did you forget how?" He felt a sharp pain in his ribs. They were elbowing him.

The interrogation room was dimly lit, and Abel Os could not make out the man asking questions. He went through everything again. They did not lay a hand on him and returned him to the cell.

At the caliphate's information office, Abel Os's wife threw herself at the feet of the official. "Please!" she cried. "He's missed his operation!" She begged for a furlough, swearing she would return him to the lockup herself after the operation. She offered to have herself imprisoned in his place. She wailed, banging on the desk. The official ordered her removed.

A few days later, his son tried. He too offered to stay in his father's place while he received treatment, like human collateral. He was told to keep out of adult business.

The commotion had drawn attention to Abel Os's plight, and soon the entire city knew he was languishing in prison.

Abel Os wondered if he could work out where in the building Oday was being kept. But no one in his cell had a clue. When the guard brought food, he tried to raise the question. "Worry about yourself!" the guard snapped.

In the evenings, as the inmates slept beside him, remorse again crept up his chest. Somewhere beyond these walls, he thought, Abdul Hadi is behind a desk, working. Or out for a stroll, or on the pitch, in his absurd clothing. He was like an errant son, and Abel Os, like any good father, could not help blaming himself.

He was called again for interrogation. He fumbled his way along the cement walls. By now, even the guards had taken pity. They led him patiently, as if bringing a horse to water. The interrogations had by now become conversations. Abu Zubair was fascinated by Abel Os, who'd not graduated the ninth grade yet had won the adoration of thousands. He asked him to narrate stories of the revolution, especially of the early days, listening with unconcealed interest. Abel Os could not make out Abu Zubair in the dim light, but he'd grown accustomed to his gravelly voice, floating above him somewhere.

Back in the cell, inmates helped Abel Os feed himself. He was at a basin, feeling the enormous power of a waterfall before him, the spray rising off the rocks. Peering through, he could see the blurry forms of other prisoners, as if they belonged to another world.

One morning in November, there was a banging on the cell door, and Abel Os heard his name. He groped along the wall, then was guided by prisoners' hands to the door. He felt the damp draft of air. A voice greeted him with warmth. "Gather your belongings, uncle."

He felt himself being ushered through the hallway. "Stairs," a voice said. "One leg in front of the other. Slowly, slowly." He labored up the flight, pausing now and then to be sure he wasn't on a landing. He entered another hallway. He could hear conversations, the opening and closing of doors. His hand was grabbed. Someone was shaking it. "You have many friends in this city," said the voice, which he recognized as that of Abu Zubair. He was led through another hallway, then suddenly he found himself outside, in the cold November air. He could hear the rumble of traffic.

He inched toward the street corner. Voices floated by. He craned his neck back and forth, trying to gauge a pause in the traffic. The vehicles were racing past. The shouts of children, vendors calling out prices. The traffic was unrelenting. But even if it slowed, even if he could cross the street, he did not know how to get home.

At length, a voice reached him. "Abel Os!" He turned. "Congratulations! Are you free?" Abel Os could not place the voice, but quickly realized he was unpracticed in such an art. "Well, they released me from prison," he joked, "but are any of us free?"

"That's the truth."

"With whom am I speaking?"

The man said his name, and clarified that they'd never spoken before—he was simply one of Abel Os's many admirers. "You always stood for the revolution, and you always stood for the poor," he exclaimed.

"Well, that's ancient history," Abel Os replied.

"But we'll never forget it." The man clasped his hand, and Abel Os felt himself being led home, through the streets of his city.

| FIVE |

In August 2014, three years after U.S. forces withdrew from Iraq, President Obama announced a new Iraq war, this time to halt the Islamic State's expansion. The next month, ISIS attacked Kobani, a predominantly Kurdish city thirty-five miles north of Manbij. In response, the United States launched an aerial offensive. For the first time, U.S. forces were on Syrian soil, backing a group of Kurdish fighters, and U.S. bombs struck Syrian targets. The American mission quickly morphed into a grander gambit: to destroy the caliphate.

In Manbij, checkpoints sprang up. Kurds were immediately under suspicion. Many were thrown into prison on the slightest pretext. Three hundred Kurdish students were arrested, along with their teachers.

With the appearance of checkpoints, Mina stopped leaving the house. In the four months since the strike, she'd tried to cleanse herself of old ties, dissolving Women of Freedom, avoiding the souk or anywhere else she might run into her comrades. After Oday's arrest, she was convinced she carried a scent of guilt, and though she couldn't say how, she knew they could smell it on her. Pray to God, keep indoors, build a private sanctum, she told herself. Whenever a black van passed her window, she was seized by dread. She found relief only late at night, as the lights of the mill blinked through her window, and she cocooned herself in her blanket, her husband snoring beside her.

A month later, her sister Maya was arrested. Miraculously, she was released after a few weeks. She described to Mina how she'd been suspended from the ceiling, then moved cell to cell while blindfolded. They were still searching for the flag-bearing woman. The interrogator presented dozens of photographs of women, including a few she recognized from Women of Freedom, but she feigned ignorance. They showed a picture of Mina, whom she admitted was her sister. She was left for days in a cell the size of a small pantry. They brought other women into the cell, including a couple of her comrades from Women of Freedom. With guards watching, they pretended not to know each other. Eventually, without explanation, she and a few other inmates were released.

That same evening, the family decided they could no longer stay in Manbij. Mina's husband found a taxi driver who offered to smuggle them out for thousands of dollars. It would deplete their savings, but after what had happened to Abel Os, he wouldn't risk cutting corners on the escape. So he forked over everything, then returned home and told the family to get ready. There was no time to pack. Mina gathered her identification papers and gold jewelry. Only much later would she pause to reflect on all she was leaving behind: her lace wedding dress; a mug emblazoned with her and her husband's name; a tole flower vase gifted by her mother; an ewer of Zamzam water from Mecca; a box of photo albums in three-ring binders; her diary; and her laptop, containing thousands of pages of revolutionary poetry, photographs, minutes from meetings, and other mementos of a time she now understood as a journey through a dreamscape.

It was past midnight when the family piled into the taxi. The lights of the mills burned in the night. They rolled onto an uneven country road. "Are we saying bye-bye?" her four-year-old daughter asked.

"No, we are just going for a trip," Mina said. "We'll be home soon."

The sun had not yet risen when the family arrived in Turkey.

Ibrahim Kasem never truly recovered from the shock of seeing his baby brother Adam morph into a feared ISIS commander. When Adam came to visit, guards waited outside. He doffed his bandolier and sipped tea with Ibrahim, and it was just like the old days, before the madness had taken hold of so many minds. Adam spoke of order, justice, piety, but to Ibrahim his words belied a deeper irrationality, an absurdity he couldn't quite grasp. Under the caliphate, Ibrahim steered clear of the authorities, focusing on construction work and his growing family, which now numbered four children. After the strike, he carefully raised the question of the arrests to his brother, but Adam professed ignorance. He said he had no interest in the life of the city—his calling was on the front lines, leading the mujahideen, the holy warriors, to battle. The university boy who once spouted T. S. Eliot was readying himself for a battle between the caliphate and the infidel West to determine the future of humanity.

Not long after, Adam led a unit on a raid near the desert to attack an American position. He and four comrades were in a civilian vehicle. The driver pulled up to a rest stop, where he got out to fetch water. At that moment, the car exploded from a drone strike. Adam died instantly.

Ibrahim did not allow himself to grieve. Instead, he was furious—at his brother for throwing away his life, and at himself for not trying to stop him. His sacrifices, his long hours under construction rafters, were for Adam. If he'd thrived, landing a job after university, so would they all. But somewhere along the journey, they were blown off course.

With Adam gone, Ibrahim, a former member of the Free Army, felt he'd lost his guardian angel. With every execution, with every fresh body hanging from the boughs at Central Square, Ibrahim worried he might be next. He stopped going to work and sent his children out to run errands. Whenever he heard the groan of an idling car in front of his house, he panicked. One night, he woke up in a sweat, convinced he heard a scraping noise coming from the front yard.

Before long, the truth struck him with painful clarity: He must get out. To remain in the caliphate was suicidal. He paid a smuggler nearly all his remaining life savings. His wife and children would stay behind and join him when it was safer to travel. Early one morning, he was taken by motorcycle through country roads, cutting across olive groves and between tracts of farmland. The smuggler dropped him off at a location north of the city and pointed to a distant hill— the border between the caliphate and Free Army territory.

Ibrahim set off and within an hour reached the hill. At the summit stood a tiny village—the edge of the caliphate. Beyond it, a dirt road stretched toward the horizon. He slipped behind the shrubbery at the village's edge and waited. A family emerged from a house and sprinted down the road. Tires screeched and a pickup truck materialized. Islamic State members bundled out, arrested the family, and, as the women wailed, threw them into the back of the truck.

Ibrahim waited. Just as the truck pulled away, he crept forward. Ahead of him, on a berm, an ISIS guard sat on a chair. He crawled on all fours around the berm, keeping out of sight until he reached a small dirt path, rutted with footprints. For an hour, as sweat streamed down his face, he crept along.

A burst of gunfire—he wasn't sure where from. He sprinted into an orchard. After some time, he came upon a farmer plowing his fields. Ibrahim waved his hands, but the farmer did not say a word, simply pointing to a water tank in the distance. Ibrahim looked around and realized he was utterly lost. The farmer continued to plow. Ibrahim studied him—was he pointing him toward an Islamic State position? Somewhere, a DShK machine gun hammered the air. The thuds grew louder, but the farmer did not turn around.

Ibrahim took a deep breath, then ran with all his might toward the water tank. The machine gun started firing wildly. Voices were shouting. Suddenly, two soldiers appeared.

"Take off your jacket! Hands in the air!"

Ibrahim walked toward the men, holding up his jacket, his eyes locked on the muzzles pointed at his chest. As he got closer, he saw what might have been the most beautiful sight to grace his eyes in years: the tri-star flag of the Free Army.

"You're safe now," the soldier told him.

Ibrahim collapsed onto the soil. The fighters gave him water and cigarettes.

That evening, after interrogation by the Free Army, Ibrahim arrived at the base of a massif. Led by another smuggler, he and a few families traversed the scree slopes until they located a trench that ran around the foothills and up to the border. One by one, the party descended into the trench—women carrying babies on their hips, fathers holding two children at once.

Ahead, Ibrahim could see a furrow in the earth. The border. A guard tower loomed in the distance. The smuggler advised the party to wait for the all-clear—Turkish gendarmes were patrolling in the vicinity. An hour passed.

Images flooded back to Ibrahim of the long days spent in trenches with the Free Army, when the world would suddenly exploded into flames and his comrades' shouts would fill the air. He pictured himself pounced upon, handcuffed, thrown into the back of a truck. Sitting, stewing, he felt the tension up and down his body. He could bear it no longer. Without even a glance around him, he pulled himself out of the trench, lowered his head, and ran straight toward the furrow. The smuggler was shouting behind him.

When he reached the furrow, he leaped into the air. The air crackled with gunfire. His left foot slammed into the rocks on the far side, while his right foot dangled in the ditch. With all his strength, he pulled himself up. Bullets continued to whiz past. A voice was blaring over the loudspeaker in Turkish. Keeping his head down, he ran with a limp. In an instant, he made it past the border crossing and into an olive grove. He hobbled along through the olive trees, until he finally reached a gravel road on the other side and dropped to his knees. When he opened his eyes, he saw, in the distance, gleaming office towers and cars speeding down a highway. Above a gas station, rippling against its pole, was the crimson flag of the Republic of Turkey.

—•—•—

In the cool autumn days, Abdul Hadi was showing up less and less at his office in the Directorate of Public Services. Since that night months earlier when he'd seen the ghastly sight of Oday, he was adrift. Crushing remorse and self-reproach filled his hours. Bitterness was the order of the land, and he, the bitterest of the lot, saw a hopelessness in the eyes of passersby, in the verses on city walls, in the vans with tinted windows. Yet bitterness was not enough. What could he do? He toyed with quitting the Islamic State and absconding to Turkey. Yet what would be said then of the man who had led the masses, standing for justice and equality, only to escape like a thief? So instead, he merely stayed home, sometimes not even rolling out of bed. ISIS officials turned up and importuned him to report for work. When they asked what the problem was, he replied he'd been battling illness. But the officials must have sensed his flagging enthusiasm, because one day he found his name on a conscription order—he was to report for jihad. Shirking the call-up was a punishable offense, especially now that the caliphate was at war.

After dawn prayer, Abdul Hadi and other conscripts left Manbij in a van. They sang songs extolling holy war and listened to sermons urging it. They arrived at a village near Kobani, and the next morning, Abdul Hadi led a squadron of seven fighters in an assault on a post of Kurdish anti-ISIS rebels. When the battle ended, Abdul Hadi stepped over the bodies of fighters, climbed up an iron railing, and pulled down the enemy flag. Below, his comrades cheered: "Abdul Hadi, Abdul Hadi, the strong and brave!" As the words reached his ears, his chest must have warmed in self-pity. After all, he'd always tried to do the right thing. The conspiracies of power were bigger than him; he could not be faulted for being a cog.

The next day, he was invited to picnic with his comrades, but he declined. Maybe now he could walk away from the caliphate, head held high. He'd tried to serve his city by standing up to Assad's tyranny, then by standing up to the Revolutionary Council's inequity. Now, with the Islamic State having outlived its utility to the people, he could walk away, hands clean, heart pure. Who could blame him?

That evening, his commander called and said: You've been a loyal soldier; without you, we would not have achieved these great heights. He was instructed to visit a nearby farm, where a surprise was waiting. Abdul Hadi was driven over and found himself before a heavily guarded building. Several European ISIS guards were milling about. He was led up the stairs and told his surprise lay behind the second door to the right.

Because of the previous day's battle, Abdul Hadi had hardly slept in twenty-four hours. He imagined sinking into a cloud-soft bed, closing his eyes, sleeping for eternity. When he entered, he saw a bed with a duvet—and his heart stopped, because next to the bed stood a woman wearing nothing but a bodice and underwear. He froze. She laughed and said hello.

"I'm Abdul Hadi," he said in a dry voice. "Who are you?"

"My name doesn't matter."

Abdul Hadi looked around. The door behind him was closed.

"I'm not going to talk to you until you tell me your name." She did and, heart pounding, he sat beside her. "I'm not like the others," he said. "I'm not going to touch you."

She smiled and said, "You men are all the same. Take your clothes off."

"This is wrong," he stammered. "I don't agree with all the policies here."

She took his hand. "I'll get paid either way. It's your decision."

Abdul Hadi told her he was a committed revolutionary, a stalwart champion of justice. He remembered when he'd stood in front of an ocean of damp faces one August afternoon a year prior, accusing the Revolutionary Council of allowing prostitution to flourish. He must have known the charge was unfair, maybe even a total fabrication, but he was drunk with righteous anger, thrusting him into a great responsibility that sometimes called for expedience in the face of truth. He told her again that he couldn't do this, that it was against his religion and the laws of the land. Suddenly, she sat on his lap and kissed his neck and Abdul Hadi felt himself in the grip of a force that overpowered every atom of thought. He was pulled into bed. It was as if he could see himself from above, as if the events were happening to some third party, and the time passed without logical structure, without coherence, like a dream.

When it was over, he threw his clothes on and rushed out the door. Outside, soldiers asked if he'd enjoyed himself and would come for jihad again, but Abdul Hadi couldn't answer them. He asked to be directed to the bathroom to take a shower. Later, he sat in the garden drinking tea, thinking about how he'd finally traversed an outermost boundary. He was not a soldier of righteousness, he realized with horror, he was a putrid, stinking animal. An animal that should not show its face to his brothers, to his mother—his mother! What would she say? He was driven back to the battlefield, where he holed himself up in a shack, refusing visitors. Eventually, he joined his unit and, while storming a village, was shot in the leg. He was evacuated to Manbij.

At home, his secret weighed on him. He called his commander and asked to see her again. "You like your reward, eh?" the commander said with a laugh. Within a few days, he was back at the heavily guarded building. When he entered the room, she said with a smile, "I knew you'd be back!" The room was now warmly furnished, with red flowers, dim lights projecting stars on the ceiling, a hanging paper moon. He confessed he wanted to spend the night with her—but he'd promised himself he would not touch her. He only wanted to get to know her. She agreed. He was drinking up the sight of her body when a knock came at the door, and someone brought in a tray of dried fruit and nuts. Abdul Hadi left to call his family—telling them he was on a mission—and returned to find her undressed, stretched out on the bed. Again they kissed, and with his promise shattered, time once more lost its coherence. In the morning, she ran warm water over his body in the shower and gently washed him with soap.

On the way home, Abdul Hadi stopped at the mosque to pray. Before long, he was back behind the desk at the Directorate of Public Services of the Islamic State of Iraq and Greater Syria, Manbij branch.

In early 2015, U.S.-backed forces captured Kobani. The caliphate was shrinking. Meanwhile, the U.S.–Iran nuclear deal—signed a year earlier, marking a significant détente between the rival powers—unleashed a series of unforeseen consequences. Saudi Arabia, Iran's arch-nemesis, viewed the deal with such alarm that it began backing hard-line rebels in Syria to counter Iranian influence. With an overflowing arsenal, these militias threatened the Syrian coast, home to Alawites, the Assad family's core base of support. The regime appealed to Russia, whose forces began bombing rebel targets in September 2015. There were now three distinct air forces—those of Assad, the U.S., and Russia—crowding the skies above Syria. Moscow claimed to be targeting ISIS and Islamist brigades like the Levant Free Men, but in fact it was the democratic rebels who bore the brunt of the attacks.

People in Manbij woke to rattling bed frames as jets thundered overhead. Some evenings, they climbed the rooftops to watch the sky flash white and orange as Russian bombs slammed into rebel positions outside Aleppo. It was terrible and beautiful, and they watched as if these were fireworks at the edge of the world.

Abel Os could not see the show, but he'd learned to distinguish the aircraft by sound: Assad's warplanes came in a rumble, low and close to the ground, while Putin's were a swoosh somewhere higher up, and Obama's like a distant zap, way up in the stratosphere. Since his release from prison, he'd gradually acquainted himself with a life in darkness. He could now recognize rooms of the house and navigate stairs on his own. Still, Hammoudi, his ten-year-old son, would not leave his side. "Wherever he wanted to go," Hammoudi later recalled, "I was the eyes through which he saw. I could not play with other kids in the neighborhood because I didn't want to leave him." Abel Os's other children had to learn to adjust their language, avoiding phrases like, "look at that," so that he wouldn't sink into despair.

"When I saw his condition," a friend later recalled, "I cried quietly and said to myself, 'How could this mountain who used to lead thousands now be led by my hand?'" Abel Os put on a brave face, cracking jokes and twirling nunchucks, but when he stumbled down the stairs, he felt hot shame.

His brother Shukri took over most financial duties, running a tiny bread stall at which Abel Os nominally worked. Most days, they sat discussing the war. It was early 2016, and U.S.-backed forces had just seized villages near the Euphrates. Meanwhile, regime forces recaptured eastern Aleppo, killing thousands. That meant Manbij was cut off on all sides, an island of theocracy.

Every week, the U.S.-backed forces crept closer to Manbij. Occasionally air raids struck the city itself. Ordnance hit the Manbij Hotel, still an ISIS prison, which had been bombed by the regime during the republican period. A few prisoners escaped, but ISIS quickly reasserted control.

One afternoon not long after, Shukri was on his bicycle running an errand when a terrific blast struck the neighborhood. Abel Os's other brothers rushed to the hospital, unzipping body bags, to confirm their worst fears: Shukri had taken shrapnel to the neck. Eight people had died.

At the funeral, Abel Os was helped to the dais. Three years had passed since he'd addressed a crowd. He led a prayer, his words barely audible. Then he exploded: "Down with Bashar! Down with Russia! Down with America!" The mourners repeated in chorus. He shouted it again. People came in off the street. The chorus intensified. Abel Os was sobbing. "Down with Bashar! Down with Russia! Down with America!"

That spring, the U.S.-led coalition announced an offensive to capture the city of Manbij.

| **SIX** |

At night, while his family slept, the earth trembled ever so slightly. No one else picked up on it, but Abel Os could sense such things. He fumbled up the stairwell, emerging into the cool currents. He could feel the spray of sands from the suburbs, the breeze fingering his hair. *Thud*. There it was again. Far, far in the distance, to the east, near the river.

The next morning, Abel Os heard on the radio that the American-backed forces were fifteen miles from the city. Listening to the news, he tried to parse the truly arcane network of alliances descending upon his hometown. The fighting force was called the Syrian Democratic Forces, an American invention that cobbled together a mélange of brigades, the most important of which was the Kurdistan Workers Party, a left-wing guerrilla outfit. Since the 1970s, the PKK, as it was known in Kurdish, had waged an insurgent campaign aimed at liberating the Kurds, a stateless people split among Turkey, Syria, Iraq, and Iran, using car bombs, assassinations, and even suicide attacks.

During Manbij's republican period, the PKK established an assembly, called the People's House, and sought to recruit among the city's Kurdish population. They'd tried to enlist their fellow Kurd Abel Os, and to bankroll the Revolutionary Youth Movement, but failed on both counts. So it came as something of a shock when, after years of the revolutionaries' pleas for Western support, the U.S. chose a front group of the PKK as its ally in the fight against ISIS. But unlike the ragtag Free Army, which Obama disparaged as "former doctors, farmers, pharmacists and so forth," the PKK was a disciplined organization. Recruits trained for years in the mountains and submitted to iron-fisted authority. Men and women fighters undertook a vow of celibacy. Whereas most Free Army units had ties only to their hometown, the PKK ran chapters across northern

Syria. They may have made for a curious pairing with the U.S. military, but in Washington's eyes, they were the most capable fighting force in Syria.

Alongside the PKK front groups, the Syrian Democratic Forces included several Free Army rebel units. Most of the revolutionaries who'd been expelled from Manbij two years prior refused to take part in the offensive, denouncing the PKK as secretive and authoritarian; but others, including Jund al-Haramain, the rebel faction that had been founded by 1st Lt. Maymati, joined the SDF. Abel Os marveled at the strange turn of events: Bricklayers and blacksmiths and grocers he'd grown up with were now working with Kurdish leftists and the U.S. military, the greatest power on earth.

The next day, the first of June, the radio announced that the SDF had captured Star Castle, which overlooks the banks of the Euphrates. Abel Os used to picnic at the old fort as a child. He tried to imagine American special forces soldiers sitting in its shade alongside his old Free Army comrades.

Later that week came news that the SDF had captured dozens of villages in the suburbs. At night, the tremors were now loud enough to wake the whole family. Abels Os could pick out the American aircraft zipping high overhead. "The cost of just one of those planes could feed our entire city for the rest of our lives!" he proclaimed to Hammoudi. It became impossible to sleep through the night. His four-year-old daughter shrieked when the house rattled, so she was brought in to sleep with her parents. The mornings delivered a strange dread, as the invading forces inched closer. Abel Os loathed the caliphate with all his heart, but the tragedies of the revolution had taught him to hold hope in abeyance. When he thought of the Free Army, scenes of the republic flashed before him, and bitterness welled up in his chest. When he thought of the Americans and the PKK, on the other hand, he saw an abyss, an unknown.

Suburban villages were collapsing rapidly. ISIS dispatched volleys of suicide bombers whose trucks careened into enemy positions. The SDF line broke, then easily reformed. More villages fell. Panic swept Manbij. Friends phoned Abel Os. "They won't enter the city," one insisted. "There are hundreds of thousands of civilians!" But Abel Os expected little from either side, least of all decency.

The SDF was blocking nearly all roads out. Authorities in Manbij spread the alarm; loudspeakers called on citizens to store food, especially wheat. Not long after, Abdul Hadi visited Abel Os. Since Abel Os's release from prison, Abdul Hadi made it a point to visit every few weeks. "Hello uncle," he would say. "How are you feeling?" Perhaps he was gnawed by guilt, but Abel Os could not trust him. Now, Abdul Hadi told his old mentor that ISIS members were sending their families out of Manbij.

On the morning of June 9, the news tore through town that the SDF had captured the remaining road out. The city was surrounded. On loudspeakers, the authorities announced that anyone attempting to flee would be guilty of abandoning the caliphate—and turning their back on God. Private hospitals and clinics shut down for lack of staff, leaving only the public hospital open at reduced capacity. The internet was disconnected.

For two weeks, Abel Os followed the confused reports on the radio. The shelling on the suburbs was intense. Then, one evening, the city went dark. Abel Os was led by Hammoudi up the stairs. They sat on the rooftop. Hammoudi described to his father how the American bombs were turning night into day, casting the cupolas and high-rises in a strange light. He described the arc of mortar shells, the fires. A few shells hit the neighborhood with an ear-splitting crash, cratering the street in front of their apartment. After a whining shriek came another tremendous blast—a shell slamming into something across the street. There was a momentary silence, then the sounds of women screaming. The shell had just missed Abel Os's house.

No one ventured outdoors anymore unless absolutely necessary. With the power gone, the radio went silent. For a few days, it was impossible to know what was happening. Families with generators purchased a few liters of petrol and were able to work radios and televisions. The city was now under siege: neither food nor medicine could enter, and no one could leave. Bread could no longer be found anywhere. The faucets went dry. By day fifteen, food and water had almost entirely run out.

Abel Os and his wife stopped eating, saving what they had—old crackers, cans of tuna—for the children. The booms felt closer and closer, until it seemed as if the warplanes were right on top of them. On July 7, the fighting reached the Book Roundabout. ISIS broke into houses, dragging men away on accusations of passing information to the enemy. Kurds, in particular, fell under suspicion. One morning, Abdul Hadi came to Abel Os's house. As the sky thundered, he asked Abel Os to rally the neighborhood to defend the city. "There's no neutrality anymore!" Abdul Hadi said. "It's either us or them. The Americans and the PKK are going to kill everyone they find." Abel Os listened politely, nodding now and then, then thanked his former protégé. But he had no intention of lifting a finger, and they both knew it.

A few days later, Abel Os was in front of his house when a burst of gunfire hit the neighborhood. He called to Hammoudi to take him inside. He was being led to the door when he heard a man's voice. "Come with me," the man ordered. Abel Os could feel a steel muzzle biting into his side. "Go inside, Hammoudi," Abel Os said calmly. Abel Os was shoved into an ISIS patrol car and driven away.

Within an hour it was impossible to leave the neighborhood. Smoke rose from multiple fires. At night, the world seemed to lurch, the very fabric of the air somehow warped, and massive fireballs could be seen. The city's main water pipe burst. The towering grain silos were bombed. The police station and the public hospital were in flames. "The truth of the coalition warplanes is that there is no mercy in the hearts of those who flew them," one resident recalled.

By the second week of July, SDF forces had fought their way to the outskirts of Sarab. Ismail Hamash, one of Abel Os's neighbors, was home at the time. As clashes erupted in Bilal Mosque across the street, Ismail's adult son pleaded with his father to leave—but the old man was afraid ISIS would seize their property. His son squeezed out a back window, crawling along canopies. He took refuge in a relative's home, leaving his parents and a sister behind. A few hours later, a pair of ISIS members forced their way into Ismail's house, climbed the roof, and fired on SDF positions across the street. The family fled to the kitchen, hiding under the dining table. U.S. Special Operations soldiers, among the most well-trained and equipped personnel in the world, could have braved incoming fire, inched closer, and attempted to storm the enemy's position. Instead, they called in air support that dropped a laser-guided bomb, weighing 500 pounds or more, which slammed into Ismail's house, killing the ISIS members and driving the ceiling into the basement—so precisely that the front and back walls were still standing. Ismail and his daughter were killed instantly.

The blast pulverized a wall of a neighboring house, killing his brother, sister-in-law, and mother. Somehow, Ismail's wife managed to survive, and she crawled through the rubble to get help. Darkness had set in by the time her sons could return to the scene of the attack to search for their loved ones. But as they approached the house, they were fired upon by SDF. They hid in a neighboring house, but every time they tried to move, they received a volley of RPG rounds. They left without laying eyes on the bodies of their father and sister.

Meanwhile, the battle was raging in the suburbs. American forces raided the village of Oj Qana, targeting its mosque, which ISIS was using as a headquarters—but wound up killing twenty-two civilians, half of them children. For days, villagers found tiny feet, torsos, and scalps. Residents in Tokhar, a riverside hamlet in the northern suburbs, gathered nightly in four houses on the village outskirts, hoping to evade gunfire and bombs. Every evening, an American drone hovered overhead, filming the villagers' procession from their scattered homes to these makeshift bunkers. The basements grew crowded with farmers, mothers, schoolgirls, and small children. Early one morning, around 3:00 a.m., the houses exploded. Thick smoke covered the sky. Limbs were strewn across the rubble. Children were buried under collapsed walls. People from surrounding villages spent two weeks digging out bodies. The coalition announced that it had destroyed "nine ISIL [ISIS] fighting positions, an ISIL command and control node, and 12 ISIL vehicles." Investigators later documented at least 120 dead civilians and no evidence of ISIS in the area.

On July 21, SDF issued ISIS an ultimatum to leave the city within forty-eight hours. In six weeks of fighting, the American alliance had wrested control of nearly all the suburbs and was occupying a few city districts. Their forces were within sight of downtown and had Sarab surrounded. But the Islamic State responded with a ferocious assault, deploying suicide bombers and truck bombs on multiple front-line positions simultaneously. They captured a half-dozen villages overnight. ISIS fighters doused streets with petrol and set them ablaze, hoping the billowing smoke would provide cover from aircraft. When this failed, they draped bedsheets over alleyways, but drones shot these to tatters. ISIS members booby-trapped empty houses, and many SDF fighters were torn to shreds. A U.S. military spokesman admitted, "This is a fight like we haven't seen before."

The Islamic State's ranks were still thousands of fighters strong. They comprised Manbij natives, of course, as well as members from around Syria and Iraq. But the fiercest fighting was waged by the Islamic State's foreign legions—made up of Russians, French, Brits, even Americans. Arrayed against them was an equally diverse U.S-led coalition: American, French, and British special forces, the PKK (which included Turkish and Iranian members), a smattering of Free Army groups, and a bizarre medley of leftist groups from around the globe whose members had, like ISIS, journeyed to Manbij: the Armed Forces of the Poor and Oppressed, who were followers of the old Albanian dictator Enver Hoxha; the International Freedom Battalion, a collection of European and American volunteers, some of them anarchists, others ex-military; the Liberation Army of the Workers and Peasants of Turkey, a Maoist formation; and communists from Greece, Spain, and Latin America. The PKK–controlled People's Protection Units included an all-female section, whose members were noted for their courage.

By late July, the two sides were battling street by street. With snipers nesting on rooftops, every step outdoors was a dance with disaster. Families began cramming together in a single house—thirty or forty people in a basement—in the desperate hope of staying safe. These were fetid cellars of encrusted dishware, hillocks of dirty diapers, open cans of tuna, candy wrappers, propane camping stoves, the unending screeching of babies, the sulfurous stench of clogged toilets, jealousy, nerves that boiled over into argument, teenage embarrassment, and lots of prayer.

In one house, a young man volunteered to venture out to find bread. As he neared a services office, he was shot in the stomach by an SDF sniper. Nearby, a woman and her children stole through an alleyway, looking for a house to take them in. An SDF sniper's bullet struck her in the head, leaving her children to wander the battle zone alone. A man named Shahoud al-Khalouf was considered the neighborhood's Romeo, having fallen madly in love with a girl at first sight. They married, and when the siege began, he forked over his life savings to smuggle his wife and children out of the city. He was out looking for clothes to send his children when he was shot dead by an ISIS sniper. "He was a day laborer living for his wife and children," his brother said, "but fate chose death for him."

The fighting reached Rabta Street, with SDF controlling one side and the Islamic State the other. One night, as air strikes were pounding houses on the Islamic State side, a resident named Hajj Muhammad chose to make a break for the SDF side and take his family with him. They crept along the street until SDF soldiers were in sight. Hajj Muhammad held his toddlers in his arms and raced across. Suddenly, the air exploded in gunfire. He made it across, but two SDF soldiers were hit. As their comrades returned fire, more family members sprinted across—but his seventeen-year-old daughter was struck. She lay on the asphalt, bleeding. With the snipers, it was impossible to reach the hospital. All night, Hajj Muhammad and his wife sat by her side, sobbing. Finally, the girl took their hands and tried to console them, promising they would all be reunited in paradise. She asked to be buried with her bangles and her favorite peach-cream ball gown, because she knew they made her look beautiful.

Death, death, and more death. The air over the city was lava red. Bodies were strewn in the street, in gardens and culverts; amid the heat, a miasma of death overtook the neighborhoods. People stepped outdoors and were enveloped in the stench but could not always find the source. The fabric of society was torn asunder: neighbor against neighbor, friend against friend. Men were forced to choose between rescuing a wounded wife or a wounded daughter. Even the conversations of the secular-minded took on eschatological tones. If the world was ending, was this divine judgment? How could a peaceful protest of some one hundred people through sleepy, rain-slicked streets, have mutated into this—into fire and fury from the sky, death squads, land mines, armies of men and women from dozens of nationalities fighting for a city none of them had even heard of a few years earlier? The landmarks of the revolution were scarred from gunfire or had gone up in flames: the Cultural Center, the hotel, the old RYM headquarters, the old Revolutionary Council offices, City Hall, the central courthouse, the senate. It was as if the revolution were an excrescence to be burned off the face of the earth.

By late July, the U.S.-led coalition held more than half the city. In the ISIS-controlled enclaves, predominately around the city center, the caliphate's soldiers were prepared to resist to the end. But in government facilities, workers were fleeing. All afternoon, Abel Os heard shouts from the corridor outside his cell. In the past month, he and his cellmates—mostly Kurds—had felt the earth vibrate, tasted the cakes of dust falling from the ceiling, heard the whistle of rockets. But whenever he inquired, his jailers would only say, "The infidels are losing!" Now, he heard a key working the cell lock, and felt hands grabbing his biceps. "Out! Out!" A waft of smoke hit his nostrils. Footsteps, people running. He grasped the walls, then negotiated the stairs. He believed he was now on the ground floor. He stood helplessly, ears pricked to the slightest movement.

"Uncle," a voice suddenly said. "Don't be afraid, I'll take you."

"And who is this?"

The man introduced himself as an ISIS guard. "We'll never forget your service to the revolution," the voice said, as he was led outdoors. The clamor of gunfire grew louder.

After a while, Abel Os said, "And what about your service to the revolution? What did the Islamic State achieve?"

The man did not answer.

Abel Os was led by hand down a street. Every few paces, his guide instructed him to crouch. A jet shrieked overhead. The booms were close enough that Abel Os could feel the shock wave. The smell of cordite was powerful.

"I don't know what's right and what's wrong anymore, uncle."

At length, Abel Os asked, "My son, how old are you?"

"Seventeen."

Abel Os was eased up a step, and he gathered he was on a traffic island of some sort. His guide said nothing. The cacophony was in all directions, as if they were at the absolute center of the maelstrom. Long minutes passed.

"Baba!" shouted a voice. It was Hammoudi. He felt himself squeezed, and Abel Os tousled his boy's hair. He turned to thank the guard. "Get out of this while you can. Everything they told you was a lie."

"Baba?" Hammoudi said. "There's no one there."

Back home, Abel Os sequestered himself indoors as shells exploded around the neighborhood. All around, apartment buildings had collapsed, trapping men and women and their children. With every thud, the family braced themselves. After a few days, with the last cans of mortadella finished, the family decided they should try to make for Milk Street, which marked the beginning of SDF territory. But escape looked impossible: A neighbor reported that folks from around Sarab were stuck at the Bucket Roundabout, where a pair of ISIS fighters were brandishing rifles, threatening to shoot anyone trying to leave. A surge of anger shot through Abel Os: He imagined himself striding up to these thugs, wrenching the weapons from their hands, and pounding them to a pulp, as if he were ten years younger. He knew he wouldn't be able to stop. They would beg for mercy, but he would keep pounding. People would try to pull him off, but he wouldn't quit until they were meat. He was pacing his living room, bumping into the coffee table, knocking over photographs. "Baba!" He saw himself with blood on his fists. He would step over their bodies and lead his people to the wadi. "Baba!" Finally, he realized that Hammoudi was grabbing him. "Baba, stop! You are scaring me."

It rained that evening. Hammoudi scaled the roof to collect rainwater in plastic bottles. In the living room, the family shared a single bag of tea.

All week, Abdul Hadi could not get out of bed. A squad of fighters visited, demanding that he, like all employees, pick up a weapon and defend the caliphate. But he could not; his world had become a dark cell, as dark as the one holding Oday, and the slightest disturbance—the morning light, the screech of falling bombs—sent spasms of pain through his skull and down his spine. He had the vague awareness of a doctor shining a light in his eyes, and he heard pronouncements of "migraines" and "shell shock." There was a suggestion of a cranial bleed. But the public hospital was overflowing, and the road there blocked by SDF forces.

Even if he could, though, Abdul Hadi did not want to budge. Six weeks earlier, he'd rushed to join the defense of the city. He took perverse comfort in concluding that the whirlwind around him was too big for him—the world's first true Islamic caliphate in eight hundred years was fighting against the greatest military force in history. Just a cog, he'd carry out his duty, allowing providence to decide the outcome. He organized food distribution for fighters. He helped round up citizens suspected of leaking information to the enemy. He told his family to remain strong because the city depended on them.

But after witnessing air strike upon air strike, with apartment buildings all around him leveled and entire families—toddlers, grandmothers, neighbors who hated ISIS—crushed, after watching a woman shrieking that her son was under the rubble, then watching her fight off relatives who tried to pull her away, something in Abdul Hadi broke. He took to bed and drew the shutters. He could no longer be sure what was real. The caliphate was crumbling, maybe the world itself was ending. Who was he if not an august official responsible for the city's poor? Without the caliphate, he was simply someone who'd betrayed his friends, his city. The thought was monstrous, and it felt as if even a sliver of light would expose his tragedy. So he kept himself in the dark.

The idea occurred to surrender himself to the invading forces. But would they show mercy? What could they, who comfortably obliterated families, know of mercy? Could he reach out to his old revolutionary comrades? He had connections with Jund al-Haramain, the Free Army group now part of the attacking coalition. But then the image of himself in American custody, in an orange jumpsuit trooping around in the heat of some tropical island, became impossible to shake. So as the battle raged in the surrounding apartment blocks, he remained in bed, obsessing over his fate.

Around town, thousands of ISIS soldiers were doing the same. By early August, fighters were surrendering to SDF in droves. An ISIS leader in Raqqa sent a letter to the leader of the forces defending Manbij: "Inform all our besieged brothers that we will never accept withdrawal and that they must endure even if only one of them remains; and that we have deemed licit the blood of any who withdraws without permission." Deserters were shot. Their homes were set ablaze by caliphate officers. Meanwhile, their soldiers continued to commandeer civilian homes. One afternoon, a caliphate platoon showed up at Abel Os's residence. "Out, out! We need this location!" Abel Os felt himself being dragged by Hammoudi, while pots and pans clanged and his wife sobbed. There was time only to gather identification documents. They crept down the street to Abel Os's sister-in-law's home.

Finally, in mid-August, ten weeks after the start of the war, ISIS cut a deal with the U.S.-backed forces: Islamic State members and their families would be allowed to withdraw to Jarablus, the town twenty miles to the north, which still belonged to the caliphate, in return for surrendering the city. The morning of the announcement, terror swept the neighborhood. The Islamic State soldiers were going house to house, ordering people at gunpoint to join their exit convoy as human shields—insurance that the coalition would not renege on the deal and bomb the convoy, which had already happened in Iraq. Abel Os's neighbor went out on reconnaissance; the news came back that ISIS would be at their door in under a half hour. Abel Os jumped to his feet and announced that they would have to make a dash for the SDF position.

Outside, he directed the family through the alleys between the houses. Even blind, he knew these streets better than anyone: It was here that he'd practiced karate as a boy, here he'd hid from the motorcycle men. As they skulked along the passageways, people leaned out of their windows. "O Abel Os, where are you going?"

"ISIS is going to take us all. Follow me!"

Few needed convincing. The alleyways filled with men wheeling bicycles, women balancing crying babies on their hips, teenage girls swaddled in black niqabs, old men being led by young boys. Despite the deal, the air was filled with the furious racket of gunfire and the buzz of drones and the piercing whine of rockets and the deafening crash of mortars. They came upon a three-way intersection. ISIS snipers were stationed at the far end of both sides of the street. Ahead was a bombed-out building. The safest route was across the street and through the Swiss-cheese-like holes of the building. One by one, people sprinted across. Rippling cracks of machine-gun fire hit the asphalt. Abel Os took a deep breath and, with Hammoudi slightly in front of him, ran hard. He tumbled and could hear the macadam burst around him. Back on his feet, he ran with all his might.

Neighbors were hit and lay on the street bleeding. No one could go back for them. Hammoudi and Abel Os's wife were in tears. "Don't be afraid," he said, scooping up his daughter. "I won't ever leave you." They picked their way through rubble. Abel Os fell over, slicing his shin, scraping the skin off his forearm. They stepped through a gaping hole in the facade of a house and found themselves in someone's living room, or what had once been a living room. Hammoudi led them through a darkened hallway, through gaps in a wall and into a ruined kitchen and through another wall opening. The mephitic stink of rotting meat drifted toward them. Through another apartment, a disaster zone, where it was impossible to believe a family had once lived. Finally, they came to a gap in the back wall, and felt the humid outside air.

It was 30th Street—under control of SDF. "There's a yellow flag," Hammoudi whispered. Abel Os refused to allow anyone else to step through first. He placed both hands through the gap and called out, "We're civilians!"

Before he knew it, hands were on him, forcing him down. Voices were shouting. As his family emerged from the outlet, they were pinned down one by one. In the end, dozens were seated on the sidewalk, facing the muzzles of SDF soldiers. An hour passed. The SDF soldiers appeared to be conferring on how to handle this crowd. Now and then, gunshot rang out on the street behind them.

Another hour passed. Only now, with a chance to breathe, did Hammoudi take in the surrounding scene—a panorama of destruction so vast and terrible that he did not know how to even begin describing it to his father. Every second or third building cratered and skeletal. Burned-out vehicles. Part of the public hospital looked like it had been demolished. Mountains of rubble everywhere. There were no cats or dogs in sight. There was not even birdsong. "It's like a nuclear strike," someone said. In a garbage dump, legs and arms were sticking out. A body of an ISIS fighter lay on the road. An elderly woman walked over and spat on it. An obese man was decomposing some twenty meters away. Whenever the wind blew, death washed over the crowd.

The SDF soldiers finally reached Abel Os. He spoke to them in Kurdish. "Why didn't you say you were Kurdish?" one exclaimed. "We wouldn't have made you sit here." The family's documents were registered. As the soldiers went through the crowd, they removed many men for questioning. Some were never seen again.

That afternoon, a convoy of Islamic State fighters and their families, along with civilian hostages—some two thousand people, all from Sarab—drove north, past the reserve bakery and the Cardamom Market, and left the city. Not long after, the yellow flag of the SDF flew in Security Square, where previously the black flag of ISIS had flown, and before that the tri-star banner of the democratic revolution, and before that the red-and-black standard of Bashar al-Assad.

In the ISIS convoy, eyes closed, was Abdul Hadi Bisher.

—•—•—

They walked in a daze, as if they had spent months in the recesses of a cave and emerged into the harsh glare of the sun. The survivors of this cataclysm weren't preoccupied with the new order, at least not yet. Nor were they accustomed to wrapping their minds around the idea of American might. Instead, they were asking a more elementary question, one that posed itself to thousands of minds in thousands of different ways: Who are we? Who am I? They had been subjects of a dictator, citizens of a republic, believers in a caliphate—all now exposed as cruel fabrications. Amid the rubble, the lies were legion: There was no such thing as an "international community," only blocs of states that selfishly guarded their interests. There was no such thing as "human rights," except in faraway plenaries and conference rooms, in the fantasies of men and women with printed name tags and advanced degrees. Who, then, were they? The war seemed to strip man and woman and child to their barest essentials, as the niceties and flourishes of civilization appeared to fall away: The grandfather hoarding canned food while telling his neighbors he had nothing, the woman watching through her window as a man writhed in pain. Lives solitary, poor, nasty, brutish, and short. Yet even now, in their darkest moments, they realized this was not quite right. When Hamid al-Osman, seventy-four, returned to his bullet-scarred home, opened the door, and suffered a blast that threw him onto the asphalt and severed his left hand, people raced forward, braving land mines, and rushed him to the hospital. When orphaned boys and girls were discovered in the shells of bombed-out houses, they were taken in by neighbors who raised them as their own. In Sarab, folks took up a collection for Abel Os, who could no longer work to feed his family. In the old days of Assad, when fear had set people's hearts against one another, meanness and pettiness were in abundance. Now fear could not be dislodged, but neither could the experience of those eighteen months of self-rule. So while the answer to the question still eluded them, the contours of one were in sight: No matter how ordinary, how defeated, they believed they were still people who could make the world.

But for now, people occupied themselves with the most immediate concerns: There were houses to rebuild, loved ones to recover. On that first evening—which the new authorities were calling liberation day—SDF and U.S. soldiers picked through the rubble of the prison under the Manbij Hotel. Some prisoners had escaped, but many others remained chained to the walls. The authorities shined flashlights on the begrimed faces, interrogated them, jotted down their information. Oday's father rushed to the hotel. At first, the guards would not allow him to enter. But he was ready to fight them, to be shot dead. Finally, he was allowed inside. He descended the stairwell into complete darkness. Struck by a pestilential odor, he nearly fell over. He was led to a hallway where prisoners crouched along the wall. Many were eating.

"Oday!" he cried. "My son! I'm here!"

There was no answer. He grabbed a flashlight from a guard. They were living skeletons, cheekbones sharp enough to cut with, eyes hollow. Gray whiskers growing in patches.

"Where is Oday?" he shouted.

One prisoner said he did not know anyone by that name. A few others nodded.

His father demanded to speak to the commander. The officer went through their interrogation logs and confirmed there was no Oday here.

In subsequent days, Oday's father visited other SDF offices and was told the same thing.

There was no trace of Oday anywhere.

**BOOK
FIVE**

Between
Things Ended
and Things
Begun
2017–2024

| ONE |

MARCH 2017

In the dark, we groped along the cement walls. The smell of mildew rose from the damp floorboards. The stairwell was narrow, creaking underfoot. Hammoudi led Abel Os by the hand. "Slowly, slowly," he whispered. I followed. On the first landing—one's eyes must become accustomed to the dark—piles of bricks were scattered about. We turned up a second flight. There, on the second landing, was a dark stain. The body of an ISIS fighter had been found here, I was told. The world consisted only of our breathing and our footfalls. We huffed up a third flight, a fourth. The stench of rotting trash was overpowering. Heading up to the fifth landing, the walls were faintly illuminated. A thin frame of light came into view, and with it, the unmistakable sound of birdsong.

We stepped out onto the roof, into the brilliant winter sun that revealed an eviscerated cityscape. I was in Manbij, in a country people still called Syria. Below spread a panorama of spectacular ruin: half-standing buildings, soot-stained cupolas, crumbling minarets, exploded bridges, hillocks of rubble. Skeletal apartment blocks, pitted by air strikes, rose over the onion-domed masjids. The Manbij Hotel stood darkened above the vista, a chunk of its facade missing.

But Abel Os could not see any of this. He stood near the ledge, as he did every dusk, allowing the breeze to caress his skin. Hammoudi grabbed him and said, "Baba, they are back."

I peered over the ledge and saw, under a pink sky, the birds of Manbij alighting on the crown of the Cultural Center. It wasn't clear what attracted the flocks: perhaps it was the nearby wadi, or maybe someone had dusted the rooftop with feed.

Eight months had passed since the great battle, three years since the republic. Abel Os, who was now forty-four, gripped the railing as the breeze lifted his wisps of hair. In a ripple, a flock of pigeons flushed from the Cultural Center and pitched onto the roof of the Youth Center, where, as a child, Abdul Hadi played soccer barefoot, and where Abel Os once gave karate lessons. Hammoudi described their flight, and the pink sunlight falling on the cupolas, the knot of traffic outside Security Square—which was once more, like the regime days, closed to traffic. Abel Os leaned over the balustrade as if to get a better look. He had come here almost every day for six months, a timeless stretch where the country felt frozen, bringing his mind again and again to the old scenes: the adjutant shouting "unity or freedom?," the bullets zipping overhead, the crowds pouring into the square, his climb up the flights of the Manbij Hotel to unfurl the flag, the senate meetings, the applause and pats on the back, the jealousy and intrigue and mad hope of a world briefly turned upside down.

It was nearly dark now, the air still. Hammoudi told his father lights were coming on. A jet raced overhead. On the far hills, I could see little fires from war, or civilization, or both.

Abel Os groped toward the door to go home.

The protagonists of Manbij's revolution were scattered far and wide. The dictator still sat safe inside his palace in Damascus, while the rest of the country burned, riven into warring fiefdoms.

Was it all worth it? I came to Manbij because I wanted to know: Would it have been better for people never to have stepped onto the rain-slicked streets that April afternoon in 2011 and demanded freedom? Should they have kept quiet, choosing a desolate peace over the horrors that followed? Certainly, tens of thousands would still be alive. Families would be unbroken, cities intact. So many people risked their futures, only to find their world gone to ashes. Looking at everything that's been lost, was it not now perfectly reasonable to give in to despair? And if not, how was one supposed to resist that temptation?

This isn't merely a question for Syrians. In an epoch of crumbling institutions and rising oceans, it's one we all confront. To persist in the shadow of great loss demands a certain kind of hopefulness—and that, ultimately, is why I'd come: to investigate the limits and possibilities of hope in a damaged world.

In the weeks after the collapse of ISIS, Abel Os received a small grant from the new authorities, the Syrian Democratic Forces. He established a kiosk near the Coffeepot Roundabout, where he sold cigarettes and bubble gum. It was about the same size and in roughly the same location as the roadside stall his father had run. Hammoudi, now twelve, served as his eyes. Together, they worked from sunrise until midnight, neighbors dropping by to say hello and exchange rumors. But now, the sense of permanence, the notion of building a life here, was gone. People spoke to Abel Os in affected, nostalgic tones, as if each meeting might be the last. He felt it too, because he knew his city was in limbo—that something had to give. The Syria he once knew had fractured into four mutually antagonistic blocs: the regime-controlled southwest, propped up by Russian airpower and Iranian militias; the rebel-held northwest, under Turkish protection; the SDF-governed northeast, where Manbij now sat under American watch; and the southeast, where the caliphate still clung to power.

His biggest worry was Turkey, whose main enemy was the SDF, because it was run by Kurdish guerrillas who'd been waging a decades-long insurgency on Turkish soil. Turkey was arming and funding some of the old Manbij Free Army units, urging them to storm the city to reclaim their homes. At night, Hammoudi described for his father the flashes of the northern sky, as Free Army artillery struck the suburbs. People expected an invasion from the north at any moment.

Meanwhile, Assad and his Iranian allies saw a golden opportunity in the instability. The regime controlled the southern suburbs, inching ever closer to the city itself. Now and then, regime agents snuck into the city to raise Assad's red-and-black flag, photograph themselves, and then upload the pictures to social media. Every time they did, it spawned panic on Manbij's streets.

Wedged between these dual threats, life in the city seemed frozen. Traffic at the souk was down. No one was willing to start a business or save money for an apartment. Abel Os wanted to put money away for his daughter, who'd look to get married in a few years, but the kiosk was often in the red.

When I visited, he and Hammoudi offered to show me around the neighborhood. At the wadi, entire apartment blocks lay in ruins. Pillars rose from the earth like plinths of an ancient forum. Inside the remains of a housing complex, there were tattered couches, sneakers, a quilted mattress with the batting spilling out, torn notebooks, half a coffee table. The facades of some of the apartment buildings had been blown clear off, exposing the rooms like a dollhouse.

Hammoudi spotted a clothesline strung up between beams. "Baba," he said, tugging his sleeve. "A family still lives there."

JANUARY 2018

One morning, two men showed up at Abel Os's door. They shook his hand and congratulated him, explaining that as a Kurd, and as one of the most beloved figures in the city, he had been awarded a seat on the legislative council. This body, comprised of people from all walks of life, was to draw up laws for the city.

A week later, Abel Os attended the council's opening ceremony. He shook hands and posed for photographs. Soon, he was sitting through daily legislative sessions, listening as fellow lawmakers debated regulations on street cleaning and taxi medallions. At home, he received visits from his constituents, who complained about the economy. The authorities were providing bread and fuel subsidies but allowed a black market in staple goods to flourish—and officials were profiting handsomely. In session, he raised the issue of corruption but was shut down by the chair—with Turkey and the regime eyeing Manbij, this was not the time.

Then families began visiting his home to ask after loved ones who'd been whisked off the street and thrown into prison. Some had been arrested for Facebook posts criticizing SDF corruption, others for denouncing the new government's efforts to ban the niqab. When Abel Os highlighted these cases in session, he heard crickets. Then, when the SDF launched a conscription campaign, carrying off young men and, even more controversially, young women to fight on the front line against Turkey, complaints started flooding his home. He broached the issue in session, but again met with an awkward silence. By now, a few months into his service, the truth was clear: The Syrian Democratic Forces were democratic in name only. There was no freedom of speech or assembly, no free and fair elections. The government in Manbij was a dictatorship.

One afternoon, he was visited by a pair of men from the PKK, the Kurdish guerrilla group behind the Syrian Democratic Forces. They tried to appeal to him as a fellow Kurd, asking him to temper his criticisms so that the "people" would support the new authorities. The Turks are ready to invade, one agent warned. Did Abel Os really want to weaken the city's resolve with his comments? He countered that if the new system was so precarious that it couldn't accommodate dissent, it wasn't worth protecting. One of the operatives then told him, sharply, to keep out of politics. "These issues are bigger than you."

A few weeks later, Abel Os was in bed when his windows rattled with a boom. Hammoudi led him outside, toward a fire at Coffeepot Roundabout. They found his kiosk in flames. The entire stock was ruined. Hammoudi wanted to call the police, but Abel Os told him to forget it. The authorities blamed the attack on "Turkish mercenaries," but he knew better. The next morning, neighbors crowded into his guest room, and the question of whether he should leave town arose.

Abel Os's entire life had been marked by his smallness—by the motorcycle men who'd helped themselves to merchandise at Tear of Roses, by his meek supplication at the police station ("Yes, my lord"), by his comrades in the Revolutionary Council, who saw him as nothing more than a vegetable peddler. It was a smallness that churned within him. Now, too, he must have felt the same impulse, through sheer force of habit, to lower his head and mutter, "Yes, my lord." Instead, the next morning at session, he found himself rising to speak. In a firm voice, he decried the legislative council as a shell, denounced the abuses taking place on the streets of his city, and resigned. As the stunned council members watched, he strode out the door.

At home, he sat waiting for the knock at the door, the fleet of police vehicles waiting outside—it was his ritual, his lot in life. But none came.

A few days later, neighbors took up a collection, and Abel Os opened a new kiosk at the Coffeepot Roundabout.

JUNE 2018

In Manbij's gritty southern district, I sat with Ibrahim on a balcony in the sluggish heat, under the stars. Around us were the accoutrements of his cladding trade: a chalk box, a rivet gun, a wheelbarrow. The house was overflowing with children, including Ibrahim's six and three belonging to his brother, with whom he lived. His brother's house was destroyed by the Americans during the war.

Unable to cope with refugee life, Ibrahim returned a month after ISIS was expelled. Coming back to Manbij must have been like walking through an old home after a divorce. He passed by the council buildings, the barracks where he served in the Free Army, the square where he witnessed all those speeches. The burned-out husks of vehicles still lined the roads. When he reached home, before he could even knock, the door burst open and Kawthar, his daughter, ran into his arms. He'd spent six months away from them—"the hardest months of my life," he said—and only then, in his presence, did his wife confess that they'd suffered hardships far greater than they had been willing to let on. In the final days of the battle, as they were fleeing the neighborhood, a land mine ripped open the street, killing a little girl. Everyone ran in a mad panic. His son Mustafa was injured by shrapnel, blood pouring down his face.

Now, his relatives were advising him to flee again, to avoid possible arrest. Ibrahim's brother had been in ISIS, and Ibrahim himself served in the Free Army. Around town, former Free Army members and revolutionaries had been picked up on vague charges. Some had never been seen again. Even those who'd never spent a day in ISIS were sometimes arrested for the sins of their husbands, brothers, or fathers.

Mustafa appeared on the balcony as we spoke. His father eased him into his lap. "I'll never leave my city again, even if they come for me."

One afternoon, Ibrahim was on the phone with a childhood friend from Little Hyena, who said there was someone who wished to speak with him.

"Hello?" A female voice. "Ibrahim, is that you?"

The voice pierced Ibrahim's chest; he could hardly breathe. He knew the voice intimately—even if twenty years had passed.

"Samira?" he asked. Suddenly, he was thrust back into the dirt lanes of Little Hyena, and there he was descending the Crossing. He was in the old barn, sitting on hay, Samira on his lap.

"I've been wanting to talk to you for a long time," she said.

The two exchanged numbers. They began texting nonstop, trading stories like in the old days. Samira brought him up to speed on her life: The marriage to her neighbor had been a disaster. He was cruel and mercurial, and there was little spark between them. Many nights, she cried herself to sleep. After a dozen years, she gathered the courage to divorce him. Then came the revolution. She lost brothers to regime bombs, a house to American bombs. Through it all, she clung to the idea of human decency, of warmth in a cold world, which she would find if she just looked hard enough. And so her mind returned, again and again, to the most decent man she'd ever known, the person who was truly and unambiguously the love of her life. One day, she told Ibrahim as much: She'd never stopped loving him, and if her life had any shape now, any future, it was by his side.

Stunned, Ibrahim said he needed time to think. His marriage had been arranged by his mother. There was less passion in its thousand fiercest nights than in a single hour spent holding Samira by the silver waters of the Euphrates. He remembered, with a shiver of excitement, the taste of Samira's chapped lips, the scent of her earthy *oud*.

He cared for his wife deeply. But to call what he felt for her and what he felt for Samira by the same name would be to render the word "love" meaningless. Over the years, when he drew up the idea of love from his most hidden reservoirs, his desires always took the form of Samira. She was burned into his psyche; in that sense she'd always been by his side. And so he realized that he, Ibrahim Kasem, husband, father of six, had never stopped loving another woman.

Over the next few weeks, Ibrahim was feverish with activity. He was working construction sites, coming home, eating dinner with his wife and children, then retreating to the rooftop to call Samira. With her, the hours slipped away. As a seventeen-year-old, he'd found her impossibly equanimous; now, as he neared forty, he was astonished that she hadn't changed. She spoke with unswerving belief in the future, as if the terrible war years had never happened. It was at the end of one of these conversations that she asked him to leave his wife.

For a few days, Ibrahim thought long and hard about the nature of desire—how it seems to strike you like an illness, or like madness, through no doing of your own. How desire chooses you, like a hand reaching down from heaven—or up from hell. But as he tried to reason through his affliction, he found he could not act as if the preceding years had never happened. He could not unsee what he'd seen. He remembered his comrade's limp body flying through the air, and the moment he'd received the phone call about his brother. He recalled the young men he'd known, the followers of the Prince, the hashish-addled eighteen-year-olds in Hi-Luxes who tore apart their homeland in their lust for freedom—only to create new and unimaginable monsters. Ibrahim realized that freedom was too hollow a principle to build a life around, at least on its own. Against the unbridled freedom to pursue his desires, he saw the power of duty and obligation and solidarity. The sense that he had an obligation to his wife, and to his children, was too powerful to shake. Some things in life were more important than freedom.

It was a dark evening, and he sat with the lights off as he dialed Samira's number. She remained quiet as he told her he could not leave his wife, and that they should never speak again. He hung up and deleted her number from his phone.

OCTOBER 2018

In the beginning, Ibrahim, Abel Os, and all the other Manbij revolutionaries took for granted that the purpose of a political community was to ensure personal freedom for its members. But the failed experiment in democracy convinced some of them of the dangers of anointing any single value or human good above all others. The Assad dictatorship exalted equality above all else, while the Islamic State venerated piety. The Syrian revolution—and the Western world, whence its ideas came—extolled personal freedom above all. Personal freedom is important, but when obsession with this one value justifies allowing people to go hungry or live on the streets, it mutates into a type of tyranny: the tyranny of the market. Revolutionaries like Ibrahim now understood that they'd been wrong about freedom's privileged place in the pantheon of human desires. There is, in fact, a set of goods or values that all humans strive for, including fellowship, health, esteem, and material security. Each is as vital to human flourishing as the next, and only citizens living in a polity that recognizes this truth have any chance of thriving.

For Abel Os and Ibrahim, the city was teeming with such lessons. They could walk the arched bridge over the wadi, which traverses a trash heap in which bodies were still being discovered. To enroll their children in school or renew their IDs, they had to visit Security Square, once the heart of their democracy, where they were made to endure searches and answer questions. They would stand in line at the bakery and notice, a few spots ahead, a man who was formerly a judge in an Islamic State courthouse, now shorn of his beard and clad in T-shirt and jeans, like their other neighbors.

Revolutionaries in exile—like Mina Saba and Hasan Nefi—may be relieved of these torments, but they face indignities of a different order. In 2018, I traveled to southeast Turkey to visit Mina in Nizip, a gloomy town with low-slung industrial buildings, crumbling forts, old minarets, and streets filled with many, many Syrian refugees. Mina lived with her family in an ill-lit second-floor apartment. On the street below roamed packs of children orphaned by the war. The Turks acted as if their guests had worn out their welcome, and Mina could feel their glares when she ventured out. She'd begun taking Turkish lessons and made her children do the same, though she knew that still wouldn't make this home.

She was desperate to return to Syria, but not because it felt like home, either. Two years earlier, her brother Shampoo Sami had been riding with the Free Army, who were battling ISIS in the town of Jarablus, when a roadside bomb tore through his vehicle and killed him instantly. In her grief, she cursed the land of her birth—the land of her greatest loss. Somewhere in the clutter of her home was the letter Sami had written her years before, which he'd asked her to open only if he died. She wanted to find a way back to Syria simply to hold that letter, to read it, to speak to Sami one last time. When I asked her if it was all worth it, she told me that was like asking if one should regret a long marriage that produced children, and for several years a loving home, before descending into acrimony and divorce. Her lived history had so thoroughly configured the present that an alternative way of being seemed impossible.

Not long ago, she visited a cafe with one of her sisters. As the two women sipped Turkish coffee, marveling at the country's modernity—the glass towers, the concrete cubes, the electric trams—a man leaned over, snarling, and shouted at them in Turkish: "If you come here, speak our language!" Once, Mina would have been so rattled as to flee. As that old dictate *be honorable* stirred within her, she would have barricaded herself indoors. The image of police officers bursting into her home and dragging away her family, all undocumented refugees, would have suggested itself. That old dictate is still there, of course, in the way she walks and dresses, in where she allows her eyes to rest. But where she once saw a supernatural essence ruling over mortal affairs, she now perceives an artifice erected by ordinary men and women, people just like herself. A once terrible and brilliant force has lost its sheen of power. She ignored the man, finished her coffee, and, after a while, paid her bill.

From his exile in the nearby town of Gaziantep, Hasan Nefi, too, endured whispers and stares from his Turkish neighbors. He enrolled his daughter in a Turkish school and encouraged them to learn the language, but from the beginning Hasan was certain his exile was temporary. At first, he was convinced the Free Army would return. Then he was sure the caliphate would crumble, and revolutionaries would need to be ready to fill the vacuum. He became active in the National Democratic Progressive Party, the first time he'd belonged to a political party since his student days. He attended party conferences, penned statements, and helped draw up a platform. He argued with his comrades that freedom had little value if people's basic needs were not met, and that the party should articulate a vision for what a genuine democracy would look like. For Hasan, the revolution never really ended.

When we met in a cramped party office in Gaziantep strewn with manifestos and mailers, he acknowledged that the situation was more complicated than he'd initially believed. The revolution now faced not one tyrant, but two—Assad and the U.S.-backed SDF, which ruled eastern Syria with an iron fist. Since the fall of the caliphate, he'd been writing columns and appearing on television denouncing Manbij's new rulers. In response, the SDF expropriated his house in Manbij. They'd seized the houses of almost all the leading revolutionary activists. But while the others kept quiet, hoping to quietly negotiate to get their property back, Hasan took to the airwaves. Within a few days, the authorities returned his home, embarrassed by the criticisms from the city's oldest and most celebrated political prisoner. The house now stood vacant, but Hasan was convinced, even if hardly anyone believed it, that one day he'd return.

DECEMBER 2018

In October 2017, SDF forces captured Raqqa, the capital of the caliphate. Thousands of surviving Islamic State fighters, along with their families and captives, fled east. In the months following, American, Russian, and Syrian bombs crashed down daily upon houses, schools, hospitals, farms, and orchards in the eastern province of Deir al-Zour. Whole families were killed, entire generations wiped out. Nowhere in the caliphate was safe. Some Islamic State members quit their posts and fled for their lives. Abdul Hadi was among them, and he ended up paying a smuggler to help him escape. He braved a trek through the desert, slipped through SDF-controlled cities, and wound up in northwest Syria, in the sliver of soil still under the control of anti-Assad rebels.

There, in hiding, he tried to imagine himself walking the streets of his hometown, organizing soccer matches at the Municipal Stadium. But he couldn't avoid the fact that he was one of the losers, that history had chewed him up and spat him out. The sensation of a drill boring into his skull, which he'd first felt in the waning days of the caliphate, came often now. There were good days and bad, but mostly bad, when rousing himself from bed seemed impossible, and even the light of the outside world was painful. He didn't work, relying instead on his brothers' incomes. He avoided the news, deleted his Facebook account, and kept to himself.

On good days, when he rose from the abyss, he was awash in feelings of profound remorse and longing. He replayed to himself minor encounters from years past, moments he made his comrades laugh, speeches he gave, and he would briefly feel liberated from the old ressentiment, as if defeat helped him finally understand its toxicity to the soul. On such days, he was struck by an overwhelming desire to make amends, rebuild bridges. One afternoon, he sent a message to his chief antagonist during the democratic years, Munzer Salal, the erstwhile senator who represented, for Abdul Hadi, the embodiment of gilded privilege. "We were all caught up in the great upheaval," Abdul Hadi wrote, acknowledging that there were regrets all around. For his part, Abdul Hadi was deeply sorry for whipping up anti-council hysteria and dividing the city. "We may not agree on everything, and certainly not on policy," he wrote, "but my approach was not the answer." He asked if Munzer might spread word through his networks of his contrition, so that he might see his old friends again, so that he might emerge from hiding and live a normal and decent life.

Munzer wrote back, telling Abdul Hadi, in so many words, to go to hell.

I had been visiting Manbij and Turkey to better understand how the revolutionaries were contending with their defeat, and there was one last person I needed to see. I'd interviewed Oday al-Hema's friends, family members, and lovers, watched his videos and listened to his poems, sifted through his diary entries and Facebook posts. I'd been able to reconstruct his movements in the revolution by the day, sometimes the hour. But we had never spoken. Of course, I wanted to meet the person I felt I knew so intimately, hear his experiences in his own words. I wanted to ask him, like the others, whether it was worth it. More importantly, I wanted to understand how, in the pits of agony, he found the will to resist. How he could refuse the idea that hope was lost, when the world around him seemed to insist otherwise.

The trouble was, Oday had vanished. I set out to find him.

| TWO |

JANUARY 2019

A gravel driveway led past stands of orange trees. The branches leaned over a low white fence. I was on the outskirts of Manbij, the grain silos looming in the distance. At the end of the driveway sat a small stone house. This was Oday's family farm.

I knocked on the door, but there was no answer. A trio of cats appeared from the hedges, watching me with interest. I continued to knock, then peered through the window. As dark as a tomb. Sills worn, cracks spreading along the facade, roof sagging—it wasn't right to call this a farmhouse. It was a hut, a countryside hut. I was about to leave when the door opened and there appeared a remarkably short man with a broad, lined face and tufts of white hair. I recognized him as Oday's father.

We'd only spoken on the phone, and he was happy to receive me. Before long, we were sitting in plastic chairs on the porch, sipping coffee. He told me that after Oday was arrested, ISIS operatives raided his house, looting his cash and hunting rifles. He was thrown in prison, presumably in a cell not far from Oday, and accused of aiding his son's activities. "They told me, 'Your son is the mastermind against us—that's your fault.' I denied this, and they cursed at me. I told them, 'I'm your elder, you must respect me! I'd rather you shoot me than disrespect me.' But then they began to beat me, calling me the father of whores."

He had been released after a couple of days. As we were speaking the door opened, and an ample woman appeared carrying fruit. Oday's mother. She walked as if she'd just trekked a mile, fanning herself despite the frigid air, and sank noisily into a chair. After her husband's release, she told me, she'd ventured to the security office to ask after her son. An official studied a file on a computer screen, then said, "These are grave accusations." She asked to visit him but was rebuffed. The family appealed to Abdul Hadi, who assured them that he was doing all he could.

In those difficult early days, she dropped by Oday's house every afternoon to sit with his wife. Rima could not stand sleeping alone, so she moved in with Oday's parents, into Oday's old bedroom. There, the two women washed and folded his clothes and, when the clothes got musty, washed them again. Winter arrived, and with it, a baby boy. Rima believed that the adults, lusting after power and wealth, had steered her city into a terrible storm, but he was innocent of their sins, and it was that innocence, she insisted, that would be her rescue. She named the child Baraa, innocent. When Oday returned home, she knew he would rejoice at the name.

But spring arrived, and Oday did not return home. When she or her mother-in-law tried the security office, they were refused entry. Abdul Hadi was not returning calls. Then, in the summer, more than a year after Oday's arrest, came a flicker of hope. A man just released from prison said he'd shared a cell with Oday. Their son was in good spirits, he said, and the authorities had been unable to break him.

Nearly a year passed when another prisoner emerged. He relayed that Oday had found religion, that he'd been given a Quran, which he studied day and night. In the depths of that abattoir, the book gave him strength. Oday's mother tried again to visit, but the authorities wouldn't hear of it. They would not even accept a bribe.

Then the war came. As U.S.-backed forces approached the city, ISIS took revenge on the families of democratic revolutionaries. Oday's family was forced by ISIS fighters at gunpoint from their home. Their house was set ablaze. The windows of the cell phone shop were smashed and the drawers cleaned out. The family relocated to this farmhouse, which Oday's father had hoped would be a retirement home. But as the front lines crept toward the city, the area around the farm became a battle zone. While the family hunkered indoors, ISIS fighters skulked through the orange groves. Missiles rained down. When the fighters retreated, they chopped down the trees. They also torched the farm, but Oday's father managed to quench the flames.

After Oday didn't turn up in the prisons, Oday's father began to suspect he'd been taken in the ISIS convoy that had fled the city. Multiple reports claimed that the convoy contained prisoners. Through friends, he was able to track it: snaking north to the town of Jarablus, then east to the Euphrates, followed by a turn south, then running alongside the river for maybe fifty miles. The convoy dispersed somewhere near Raqqa, and the trail went cold.

One afternoon, a young man showed up at the farmhouse. He was ghostly thin, and his hands trembled as he held a coffee cup. He spoke timorously, as if he could be snatched away at any moment, and he had difficulty looking Oday's parents in the eye. Introducing himself as Marwan, from Raqqa, he spoke of fifteen days in detention under ISIS in Dibsi Afnan, a mud-brick farming town in the Raqqa countryside. Imprisoned on false charges of caching weapons, he was electrocuted and caned, then tossed into a windowless cell that held six other men. As the days passed, he befriended his cellmates, one of whom was a young man who introduced himself as Oday, from Manbij. The men shared poetry and discussed religion, but Oday did not say much else about his past life. Then, Marwan recalled, not more than a week after his arrival, gunfire sounded through the walls. When a guard opened the cell door, the prisoners overpowered him. They fled through the corridors into the blinding afternoon light and saw ISIS guards in a panic and helicopters buzzing overhead. Hundreds of prisoners made a run for the gates—but Marwan held back. He watched as a crowd squeezed through an embrasure to find themselves face-to-face with soldiers from the Syrian regime—Assad's forces were racing to capture the town. Meanwhile, a convoy of ISIS guards rounded up some prisoners and carried them off as they fled out the back gate. Marwan and a few prisoners also managed to escape through the rear, into the open desert. He ran, without looking back. Oday was not with him, which meant he was either captured by the regime or taken away with retreating ISIS fighters.

The possibility that Oday was in regime custody had not occurred to his parents. Now, a dark vista opened up: Oday banished to the desert prison in Palmyra for fifteen, twenty years. The thought of decades without touching her son's arms, stroking his hair, overwhelmed his mother. For three years, she had strung clothes on the line and swept the porch with an eye to the surrounding sedge fields, as if her son might emerge at any moment.

One afternoon, Oday's father received a phone call from a man connected to the Syrian regime's intelligence services. He said that a certain Oday from Manbij was in government custody, and that he could verify that this was their son. Yes, the old man nearly shouted, to which the caller explained that such inquiries were highly irregular, outside standard operating procedure. He was willing to help because he wanted to ease families' suffering, but it would not be easy. Palms would need to be greased, officials made to look the other way, while he worked to access prison rolls. Oday's father said that he was ready to do anything. They arranged to wire the caller the equivalent of a few thousand dollars, half due then and half upon completion of the job. After the transfer, though, Oday's father called to find the line disconnected. Months passed without a trace of the caller. Finally, Oday's uncle made contact with a regime officer, bribed him, and learned there was no one by the name of Oday al-Hema in the regime's detention logs.

MARCH 2019

In the spring, U.S. forces surrounded Baghouz, a town in the southeasternmost corner of Syria, the last scrap of soil belonging to the caliphate. Some fifty thousand people—ISIS fighters, their families, and an assortment of civilians with nowhere to flee—were living in ditches as munitions rained down. Thousands of people likely died, though the real count is unknown. It was probably one of the deadliest acts of military violence in a generation. After five years, and immeasurable destruction, the caliphate was no more.

The survivors—which, local news reported, included ISIS captives—were herded to U.S.-supported holding facilities, which ran the gamut from cargo decks to open-air camps. SDF was treating every adult male as an ISIS member, even if they claimed to be a prisoner *of* ISIS. I tried to imagine Oday in a brightly lit airplane hangar, with hundreds of other prisoners of war, garbed in an orange jumpsuit.

I returned to Oday's farm. "If they want to keep him until they sort things out, that's fine," Oday's father said desperately. "We just want a sign." His eyes were watering. The wind was picking up, and I wrapped myself tighter in my scarf. Sweat streamed down Oday's mother's forehead. She was looking off into the sedge fields. The old man was crying now. "I tried my best to protect him," he said. "We forbade him from getting involved in the protests. We screamed, we threatened him. But we failed." A helicopter was flying low across the sky. In the distance, in the gray air, the city lights twinkled. He buried his face in his hands. "It's my fault. It's all my fault!"

The next afternoon, Oday's father gave me a sheet of paper on which he scribbled the names and numbers of people who had seen his son in prison. As he clasped my hands, I repeated that I could make no guarantees. That evening, I met a barber who took me into the closet in the back of his salon—away from the prowling secret police—to tell me about the three days he'd spent in a cell with Oday. A few mornings later, I located a man who had been in the convoy of prisoners that ISIS carried off. He did not see Oday—the prisoners were dispersed among the ISIS fighters—but described to me the harrowing journey.

The meetings piled up. Oday was a ghost: He was seen among a crowd of prisoners, his name was on the lips of guards—but I could not pin him down.

Wherever I turned, I encountered people searching for loved ones. I met an old man whose daughter, I discovered, had been the masked woman who'd raised the revolutionary flag in front of the ISIS courthouse, sparking the uprising against the caliphate. This was Huda Muhammad, the founder of the Girls of Tomorrow Assembly; she was eventually caught by ISIS, never to be seen again.

When we spoke, his eyes were swimming, his face contorted in agony. "I used to believe in justice," he told me. "I used to believe in this great principle, because I thought this principle would save us. But now"—he looked at me, tears streaming—"I'm against this word. I am against this concept. I hate the idea of justice, because there is no justice, it is not real, it was told to us to deceive us. I realize there is something more important, more real, than justice. It is charity. Charity in the Quran is the highest value, it is a type of tolerance. It means to forgive those who treat you badly."

His voice suddenly rose. "But now, I can't find charity! I cannot find it in my heart! I can't forgive them. I cannot do what the Prophet recommended. I cannot find it!" He buried his head in his hands, weeping uncontrollably. "I couldn't help her! I couldn't keep my baby safe!"

Some of the missing were surely dead, buried under mounds of rubble, or blown to bits and unrecognizable. But there were flickers of evidence that some had survived. I met a woman who had been sifting through published photos of an SDF detention camp, with ISIS members in prison jumpsuits and buzzcuts, when she spotted her son, who in fact did not belong to ISIS but had been their captive. News of such miracles spread, leaving families in thrall to the words of the mercurial authorities, who would neither confirm nor deny anything.

The missing were a legion. Their presence, in their ceaseless absence, loomed over daily life, like a huge army encampment outside town, just past the hills, beyond the reach of ordinary mortals. Your sons and daughters lived there, beyond the hills, unable to find adulthood. Husbands were waiting, asking you to raise the children well. You could not mourn, you could not move on. Your loved ones shared the same sky, the same sun and stars, but the world beneath was hopelessly fractured. They were undead, somewhere between heaven and hell, their existence a condemnation of a global order that allowed this calamity. An uprising for democracy was mostly ignored, and the terrible reaction—Assad's bombs—simply allowed. Even the U.S. war against ISIS, brutal as it was, offered a chance for redemption. But Washington had not moved a muscle to sort out the dead and missing. The U.S. could force the SDF, which it funded and armed, to open its prison rolls—or if there were no such rolls, to create them. It could interrogate the many ISIS leaders in custody. But it chose to do nothing.

For what felt like hours, Oday's mother stared into the sedge field behind the farm. Why he'd emerge from these reeds she couldn't explain, but she felt it in her bones. When she cooked *kibbe* for Baraa, she wondered what they were feeding Oday. She sat in front of the television watching soaps, allowing herself to be carried away—but then Oday's shining face would break in, and in her guilt, she'd switch off the television. There was no respite. For those left behind, the search was an obsession, a fact all the more wrenching because there didn't seem to be anything to actually do.

My SDF contact was a bookish young man with large eyes; his favorite author was Noam Chomsky, and he liked to lecture me on American imperialism. "There's nothing you can do about the missing," he warned. "It's a dangerous file."

"Why is it dangerous?"

"There are big powers in this game. Big, big powers."

I told him I didn't know what that meant.

"It's a tragedy, but nothing can be done. Look—even my own father is missing. We don't know where the old prisoners are. My strong advice to you: Forget it."

But I couldn't, so I began researching SDF prisons, slowly developing contacts among the authorities and the families of prisoners. There was no trace of anyone named Oday al-Hema. But there was one place I had yet to look, a massive detention camp in eastern Syria where ISIS captives were locked up—alongside ISIS members and their families. I met people who had been recently released, and two mentioned having once come across a man from Manbij named Oday.

DECEMBER 2019

The crowd was thick. The guards were shouting, but they were drowned out by the wind. The wind flogged the blue and white flags of Kurdish security. There were workers in soiled overalls, children squirming here and there. I was made to spread, as hands groped my body, searched my pockets. Sand was in my hair, burning my eyes. Guard towers looked down on me. I made my way to a set of prefab trailers that functioned as the camp administration headquarters.

I was in a giant detention camp that occupied a few square miles of desert near the Iraqi border, called al-Hol. Some seventy thousand people—the last survivors of the caliphate—were interned here. They hailed from more than fifty countries—Brits and Swedes and Russians and Algerians and Uyghurs and Trinidadians who had joined ISIS, alongside Syrians and Iraqis. Many inmates were civilians with ISIS family members, while others had nothing to do with ISIS at all. Yazidis enslaved by ISIS commanders, teenage girls married off by their families, and couples simply looking to escape the American bombing campaign have landed in al-Hol. More than half the prison population were children, the majority of whom were younger than twelve. All the residents were under indefinite detention—as if Guantánamo were the size of a city, and its inmates were mostly women and children. Properly speaking, al-Hol might be the world's largest concentration camp.

The SDF ran the camp, bankrolled by U.S. dollars. "Do you have any idea how many people come here begging us, crying in front of us?" the man behind the desk in the administration office asked me, throwing his hands up. "Everyone is missing someone! This crisis is the burden of us Syrians. Everyone comes here, but what can we do?"

"These are terrorists here," offered another man, seated on a leather couch.

They claimed, amazingly, that they kept no records of who entered the camp. So many inmates gave false names and lacked identification that the camp authorities apparently gave up and threw everyone—ISIS, anti-ISIS, captive—in together.

Near the prefab trailer complex, a dirt road branched in various directions. Tens of thousands of yellow and beige United Nations–issued tents spread to the horizon. Red water drums rose above this nylon metropolis. I reached a crowded thoroughfare lined with one-room shops that sold tea, energy drinks, Mars bars, cotton candy, soft serve, bras, and eyeliner. A mass of women in black drifted through the stalls. Children darted between them. Every woman covered her face; some also covered their eyes. A boy of about nine ran up to me. He looked East Asian.

"Mister!" he said.

I asked where he was from, and he said again, "Mister!" I switched to Arabic, and he replied, haltingly, that he was Uyghur. I showed one of the shopkeepers, who was a camp inmate, photos of Oday. He shrugged. Al-Hol was a teeming city, an entire ecosystem, with throngs of black-clad women in every direction, and when I scanned their forms, some tall and birdlike, some round and stubby, some being led by children, some walking alone, I sensed above all else the sheer futility of my quest. I walked down a dirt lane between rows of tents. In one tent, from a slit in the nylon, a pair of eyes watched me. From a second tent, a boy emerged, cocked his hands in the shape of a pistol, pointed it at my head, and fired. I turned into another lane. Each looked identical to the last. I was attuned to the shifting air, broken now by a stray shout, now by the thrum of a chopper. A clutch of women approached. They were engaged in conversation but fell silent as they passed me. I lost all sense of direction as I headed deeper into the tent neighborhoods. A terrible wind was picking up, bringing a great swell of sand in from the desert, and I turned to find my way out.

FEBRUARY 2020

I returned with a humanitarian agency that was distributing vitamins and milk formula. The camp was divided into nine sectors, each housing some eight thousand inmates. Aid groups provided basic services, while the U.S.-backed Kurdish forces patrolled the perimeters and occupied the guard towers. Within the sectors, though, the inmates were left to rule themselves. As a result, ISIS reestablished its caliphate inside camp walls. In each sector, a band of all-women ISIS religious police patrolled for dress-code infractions. Men and women were dragged from their tents to appear before a makeshift sharia court. Inmates were accused of spying for the U.S., or of being in cahoots with the old revolutionaries. Each day, bodies turned up: a pregnant Indonesian woman tortured to death; a fifty-year-old Pakistani woman stoned and tossed in a cesspit; a young man with sixteen knife wounds.

In every tent I visited, I showed photos of Oday. I collected hearsay: There was a man named Oday, from "Manbij or Aleppo," living in sector six; there was a former ISIS captive who lived in sector four, but he was dragged from his tent one night and shot in the head. But facts were impossible to pin down. I was a visitor from beyond the barbed wire fence, a strange god, a possible source of succor, whom people want to please. And they were often mired in their own search—everyone was missing a husband or wife or children.

In some tents, women appeared to be captives of other inmates. There was a woman in sector five who seemed to be in thrall to another, older woman in her tent. She hesitated to speak and looked to the older woman before every answer. Later, through a neighbor, she passed me a poem:

> *The arrival of my message winged*
> *Is proof that my struggle*
> *Reached you with the caress of the breeze*
> *And the rest with the blowing wind*

My dream is to bolt
But the doors of reality are bolted

Some claimed they knew an Oday from Manbij, others that they regularly saw someone resembling Oday walking with children in sector seven. But the more I poked around, the more walls went up. People were tense, alert to betrayal. The camp was teeming with spies belonging to ISIS, the SDF, and perhaps other parties. An inmate named Sarah told of waking up one dawn to voices. She stepped outside to see two masked men carrying guns with silencers. One of them "pointed a light to my face, without saying a word," she said, "and put a finger to his lips." He went inside. "Please don't," she heard her husband say. "May God point you to the light—" She heard gunshots. When the men left, she found her husband dead. She still remembers seeing his teeth strewn across the blanket.

There was at least one murder seemingly every night. In the mornings, bodies were found clogging the sewage ditches. When I walked the dirt lanes, hemmed on both sides by tents, I felt watched. No one wanted to talk, no one invited me in. When the sky grew dark, I noticed there was not a soul about. The floodlights turned on, casting the camp in an alien glow, as if we were colonists on a distant, barren planet.

JANUARY 2021

The truth must lie with ISIS themselves, I thought, and on one of my visits I found just the man to help penetrate the Islamic State network. I sat with him one winter afternoon in his tent, which he'd outfitted with floor cushions and hanging bulbs, an homage to the bungalow he'd once had on the outside. Abu Ahmed, who possessed the regal bearing of a man accustomed to addressing tribal gatherings, had a well-grooved Bedouin face and wore a checkered *shemagh* scarf twirled around his gray hair. He and his family arrived in al-Hol after fleeing ISIS and American bombs. It was a displacement that might have reduced someone less resourceful to despair, but Abu Ahmed threw himself into camp life, befriending neighbors and smoothing over daily calamities. He roved from tent to tent, ensuring that detainees received their allotment of bread and cooking gas. In short order, he was serving as a representative of the camp's tens of thousands of Syrians to the authorities, a role that filled him with pride.

Through him, I gained an audience with a leading ISIS commander. I knew to not immediately raise the question of missing people, so I asked him to tell me about his life. He was eager to describe the savagery visited upon civilians by American warplanes, the houses flattened by laser-guided bombs, the nights he dug through rubble with his own hands to save children. He spoke of Baghouz, the slice of territory near the Iraq border that was the Islamic State's last stand. Thousands of people—fighters, their families, their captives, and random civilians—were forced to live in foxholes as hellfire rained down. Every morning, they emerged to find hundreds or even thousands of bodies.

Most of our discussions continued in this fashion, as he detailed American crimes but said not a word of his own. I let him talk. Over months, I gained his trust. Finally, one afternoon I raised the question of missing people, and he put me in touch with an ISIS operative in the field who was "conducting operations." That individual connected me to a second operative, based in Idlib Province. We communicated by leaving voicemail messages. He told me that he knew all about Oday, and that he could lead me to him.

But first, he said, he needed something in return. He had a nephew, eight years old, imprisoned in al-Hol. He asked me to find a way to release him.

For a few days, I didn't reply. No child should be imprisoned, and if there was a way I could help release him and the tens of thousands of other interned children, I'd have done so in a heartbeat. But I could not trade favors for information. Of the countless people I'd interviewed, very few had asked for a quid pro quo. I began to consider the dark possibility that I was the victim of an elaborate scam—as when callers sprung out of the woodwork to prey on Oday's parents. But my source provided details about Oday's time in prison that I'd verified from other sources. It was clear he knew Oday—or knew a lot about him.

I told him I could not help. He should connect me to Oday for the sake of his parents, not in the hope of anything in return.

He blocked my number.

The next day, I was seated in front of Abu Ahmed. Five murders took place not far from his tent the night before. He believed all sides—SDF, the Assad regime, ISIS, criminals—were preying on the families of the missing. "Don't answer unknown numbers," he warned me. "Don't meet anyone unless it's in a public place. Don't tell anyone anything about yourself."

Two mornings later, Abu Ahmed and his adult sons were walking home from the mosque tent when a man approached. He was wearing Adidas running shoes and track pants, as if out for a jog, and he'd covered his face in a *shemagh*. Abu Ahmed turned to greet the man, who raised his arm and fired a pistol. The bullet tore through Abu Ahmed's neck. One of his sons ran at the attacker and was shot in the face. Another son raced forward, and the man fired wildly. Amid the screams, Abu Ahmed lay in the dirt, dying.

His surviving son insisted my search had nothing to do with this—Abu

Ahmed had been liaising with authorities, and everyone who did so was getting gunned down. Still, I was surprised to find within myself a rising anger. For years, I'd listened to stories of unfathomable suffering, but I offered nothing. I listened and transcribed. A miserable, even execrable, response to tragedy—people here needed doctors and nurses and therapists and imams and maybe even poets, but certainly not me. Now, it seemed obvious that piecing together the truth of Oday's fate was an impossible task. We gather truth "limb by limb," the poet John Milton writes, but "we have not yet found them all . . . nor ever shall do."

I was coming to terms with the cold reality that some things may never be known, because I could not trust the people who claimed to have answers, and because every side had an interest in burying the issue. Then, one afternoon in the depths of winter, I stumbled upon a breakthrough.

| THREE |

MARCH 2021

One day at al-Hol, a former revolutionary from Manbij spotted Abu Obeida the Iraqi, the Islamic State enforcer who'd arrested Oday on the day of the strike. I'd known about him for a long time: despite his *nom de guerre*, he was born and bred in Manbij. Abu Obeida was a notorious member of the caliphate's feared secret police and had personally disappeared hundreds of revolutionaries. When the caliphate crumbled, he vanished; some said he was killed in an air strike, others that he was on the run in Turkey. I'd put out word to my networks across Turkey and Syria, sending photos and suggestions of how he might look in disguise—and here he was.

By now, I was well sourced inside the camp, and eventually I was able to find someone who lived in a tent near Abu Obeida. It was a long shot. I kept things vague, explaining I was researching the revolution in Manbij and its aftermath. The message was delivered. A month passed, and then, to my great surprise, I received a note back: he wanted to meet.

In the months I'd been away, al-Hol seemed to have gotten even more crowded; in the misery of proximity, armies of children were roving through dusty lots, hurling stones at each other, getting into fights. As I walked among the tents, that old sensation of being watched returned. I entered my contact's tent and sat myself on a floor cushion. Many minutes passed. Why was he willing to meet me? He was an active member of ISIS, working closely with fighters on the outside. He would dangle the prospect of meeting Oday in exchange for some favor. He would seek to use me, mold me to his ends. But I sensed Abu Obeida was different—because here, finally, I had an advantage. He was not some anonymous voice gurgling through my phone speaker. I was not at the mercy of his self presentation—because I knew all about him. I even knew his real name. His backstory, which I had researched extensively, exemplified a classic archetype in this revolution: pro-democracy activist turned religious zealot. I decided to tell him what I knew, putting him on the defensive.

But perhaps he lured me here to take me hostage, as part of a desperate escape plan. In nearby prisons, ISIS inmates had rioted, attempting to break out. The murders in al-Hol continued; here, in sector five, six bodies were discovered that week. ISIS gunmen pulled people from their tents and marched them to the "courthouse"—a tent not far from here—where judgment was rendered. Gunfire was heard at all hours of the day. Children were told to keep away from the sewage ditches because of the bodies.

The flap opened and the tent filled with light. A large silhouette filled the entrance and moved along the wall. When it was dark again, I could see a sizable man wearing a jellabiya, a khaki army jacket, and a checkered *shemagh*. He had a flat nose to fit his broad, unlined face, which was rimmed with a salt-and-pepper beard. His eyes were thoughtful, even mischievous. He placed his hand over his heart, introducing himself with a false name.

"I'm glad you are here," he began. "You can see the situation we live in, the filth, the desperation. Our children are dying, our widows are hungry. Where is the international community? We need your help." He was a humanitarian, he told me, then proceeded to describe his fundraising efforts. This man, who was responsible for the horrors endured by so many, was making a rapid sales pitch, as if he were afraid I'd slip out of the tent at any moment.

"I heard about the murders," I said.

"You see—this is what we're living through. It's the administration, they are killing people."

"People say it is ISIS cells."

"I don't know anything about all that—I just want peace. We want to go home."

"Do you miss home?"

"Of course, who doesn't?"

"What do you miss?"

"What's not to miss? The trees, the streets. It would look shabby to you, I'm sure. Where are you from?"

"New York."

"So it would definitely look shabby to you. But the dust, the trees, the soil, that's where we grew up, that's our blood."

"Where are you from?"

"I'm from Syria, western Syria."

"Well, to be frank, I heard you are from Manbij."

He watched me carefully. The tent was dusky and frigid, and through the nylon came the distant chop of rotary blades. A girl in a niqab entered, bearing an enameled tray with tea. I told him about my research, dropping names—the names of RYM activists, Free Army commanders, ISIS officials. If he was surprised I knew so much, he didn't show it. I asked him if he knew Abel Os.

"A great man. Everyone in the city loves him."

"He went blind in an ISIS prison."

"That was a tragedy. It was a chaotic time. So much chaos. We did our best." The "we" had slipped into the tent, an admission that he knew I knew who he was.

"What do you think of Abdul Hadi?"

"A weasel. He and his brother only wanted power."

"What was your job in the Islamic State?"

"I was working for God."

"And what did God want you to do?"

"It was a chaotic time. I was helping with security." There was a pause. "If they know I'm talking to you, they will kill me and kill you, too."

"Who?"

"The Hisba." The religious police.

"Why are you talking to me, then?"

"It's the humanitarian issue—but why are you here? What do you want from us?" We were feeling each other out. I described my book, the years of interviews. I noticed, for the first time, a bulge in his hip, and now I couldn't take my eyes off it. Watching me, he adjusted his position so that I could see it clearly, so that the frame of the pistol was unmistakable.

"The Islamic State has been defeated," I said, "and is now confined to this camp. Did you make any mistakes? Do you have regrets?"

"We made mistakes, like anyone else—we're human, after all." Things were out in the open at last. "We started a multifront war—against the Kurds, the Free Army, the Americans, the Iraqis." He described the tradition of ceasefires and armistices in the Prophet's time.

I asked him to tell me about his life. "My life was not good before the war. I was spending my time on the streets with my friends. I began working in Lebanon—this was before the war—as a painter, and this work was very tough, very, very tough, because I was painting the sides of buildings. Most of us were simple workers." He and his friends from the Jazeera soccer club joined the protests from the beginning. "We wanted two things: freedom and democracy."

I pictured him marching alongside Abel Os and Abdul Hadi and Oday—whose name I had not yet broached—waving the flag of freedom.

"We saw the bombing and the dead people and the injustice of the regime," he continued. "The regime didn't care whether you were civilian or armed—everyone was targeted. We were forced to carry weapons to preserve our dignity. Because when someone tries to destroy your family and your neighbors, if you have dignity, you'll try to defend your community."

He sided with RYM in its opposition to the Revolutionary Council. When ISIS appeared, he was enthralled by its message of equality and justice. He and his friends—nearly the entire Jazeera squad—joined en masse.

"You were a revolutionary," I finally said, "but once in ISIS, you arrested many revolutionaries—many of your former friends." The tent was darker than ever. "Do you regret it?"

There was a moment of silence. I could see the whites of his eyes.

"To be clear," he said, "the Islamic State didn't arrest those revolutionaries because they were for or against ISIS—they were arrested because they were against God's rule on earth. I joined ISIS because it was the right thing to do, not because of this or that leader, not for any earthly reward. Just for the sake of God. My duty was to deal with anyone who was against the rule of God."

I said nothing. He continued, "For example, you are from America. If someone in the U.S. commits a heinous crime, they are given the death penalty. You have the death penalty, yes?" I nodded. "So when that person violates American law, he receives the punishment according to your law. In the same way, we have our law. We have rule of law. We don't do anything randomly."

"So you don't regret it?"

"How could I, when I was doing the right thing?" A faraway, shrill shout reached my ears. It was the shout of a woman, just audible through the nylon. Abu Obeida looked unperturbed. There was a long pause. Shadows filled the tent, the whites of his eyes shining. The strip of light around the tent flap was fading; I had to leave before dark, because that was when the murders began.

"What do you remember of the strike?"

"It was never going to affect the State," he answered, as if expecting this line of inquiry. "The issue for the State was purely religious—we had no fear of being harmed politically or militarily by the strike. As for the Free Army, it was fighting under the blind banner of secularism—of democracy. Whoever does not believe the word of God is supreme—but believes the word of the people is supreme—is a polytheist. God Almighty said, 'And fight them until persecution is no more, and religion is for God. But if they desist, then let there be no hostility except against the wrongdoers.'"

The woman was still screaming outside. I moved to rise to see if we should help, but he raised his hand, motioning me to remain seated. "Don't get involved," he warned. "It's bigger than you."

"On the day of the strike," he continued, "we went out on patrols." He described "advising people and reminding them that the matter involved apostasy and blasphemy. We told them to not take this matter lightly. At the same time, we did not attack the owners of closed shops." The screaming had ceased; there was no sound but the desert wind lashing the nylon.

"There were some closed shops, but not more than ten," he said.

This, I knew, was a bald lie. But I did not press the matter.

"How many were arrested?" I asked.

"Not many. They were all supporters of the Revolutionary Council and of America."

"Did you arrest Oday al-Hema?"

He screwed up his eyes at the name. "Oday al-Hema?" There was a long pause, as if he were scouring his memory. "Yes, we arrested him."

"What happened to him?"

"Oday was living in the caliphate and he was safe, no one touched a hair on his head. But he was opposed to God's rule in the city. During the strike, he was taking videos and sending these videos to secular people outside the city. We caught him red-handed."

"I mean, what happened to him after his arrest?"

"He went to prison."

"And then?"

"We killed him."

It felt as if I'd taken a blow to my midsection. "When?"

"Maybe a year or so after his arrest." He said it as if he were speaking of an errand, of taking out the trash.

"That's not true," I countered. "He was spotted in an Islamic State prison after the fall of Manbij."

"Did you confirm it was him?"

"No, just someone by that name."

"There are ten thousand Odays! The one you are asking about is dead."

I began to tell him about the various sightings, the Islamic State operatives claiming he was at large, the clues he was in regime or American custody—but he waved his hand.

"Oday is dead," he said with terrible finality. "We killed him."

MAY 2021

In the subsequent months, I kept in touch with Abu Obeida, and through him, I was able to find other Islamic State operatives. Armed with the truth, I was impervious to their schemes, so the pieces quickly fell into place. Not long before the U.S. invasion, Oday had been transferred to the neighboring city of al-Bab, and housed in a prison. Early one morning, he was ordered into the back of a dump truck with a few other prisoners. He would not have been told where he was headed—he must have believed that he was being transferred yet again. He was driven to a field on the outskirts of town. He was told to march to a trench. At this point, he would have understood the moment had come—but he did not run. He shouted something that the Islamic State witness could not understand, or chose to forget, and bullets ripped his body apart.

I told members of Oday's family what I'd learned. Still, in the teeth of all the evidence, they were unimpressed. Oday's uncle told me he had obtained fresh information that his nephew was in American detention. The ghosts of Oday and all the missing still haunt families who refuse to accept what's done is done, that the simplest explanation is, after all, the best explanation.

In the early evenings, as the sun fell on her face through the windows, through the dirt-spattered glass, Oday's mother waited. Because here, Oday was not dead. On the contrary, he was expected at any moment, emerging from the sedge fields, picking leaves from his hair, panting and parched, because he had traveled far, farther than she could imagine, and she wanted to be ready. She knew it was absurd to expect him to have walked; she knew in her heart he would be delivered in a taxi, or a military vehicle of some sort, because that was how those who have been lost over the years, and then found, returned. When I spoke to her, she did not hear my words. When I met his father, he peered into my eyes as if searching my depths, because he wanted the real truth, not my suppositions. He allowed me to depart without showing me to the door. He hardly left the farmhouse anymore, and expressed no desire to visit the city: What if he were gone one day and that was the day Oday came home? It was possible. His boy would walk through the rooms of a house stripped of people and memories. He wished to be present when Oday returned, because he wished to say—and this he had never said to anyone, for any reason—that he was sorry. He knew he'd been hard on the boy, demanding the best of him, maybe even too much, but if he, a father, a man, couldn't protect and guide him, who could? When Oday returned, this would all be sorted out.

He told me all this, but I couldn't see Oday here. I see Oday in a farmhouse much deeper in the country, far from prying eyes. He is wearing a T-shirt and jeans, perhaps "Tome Hilfiger" knockoff jeans, and has spread before him flags and sheets of paper with lists of names. He is with two or three friends. They discuss the recent transformations—the increasingly dictatorial presence of SDF, the cruel indifference of the Americans, and, that ever-present fact of life, like the sun and the moon, the alpha and the omega: the regime of Bashar al-Assad. He will not see the tempest that briefly swept up everyone he knows as a failure, because failures require endings, and there can be no ending while he continues to plot, while he still has hope.

JUNE 2021

Inside his rebuilt kiosk at the Coffeepot Roundabout, Abel Os sat behind stacks of cigarette cartons, while Hammoudi handled the transactions with customers. He listened to the radio obsessively, waiting for any nugget of news to confirm his conviction that the revolution was still alive: a scuffle between Free Army rebels and regime soldiers resulting in a captured checkpoint in Idlib; an Iranian leader killed by an American drone. But the news of Oday's death seemed to extinguish the last vestiges of this irrational hope, so that he could no longer ignore the truth: Assad had won. Even American-imposed sanctions, which caused the lira's value to plunge and immiserated the country, could not touch the Leader in his palace, or his relatives and business associates.

Abel Os became afflicted with harrowing dreams, in which he was walking amid a field of corpses, and when he looked right and left, he saw his mother and father walking alongside him. He would tell friends he was not long for this earth, that his body, with its growing aches and pains, yearned for peace. One evening, he sat Hammoudi down and told him he'd soon become the man of the family. He should work with diligence and honesty, Abel Os said, and he must never, ever take a loan. On Fridays, when his friends gathered in his living room, he no longer brought up the days of revolution. Instead, he spoke only of where he wished to be buried—behind Sheikh Aqeel mosque, where the senate used to meet. His friends, who sensed the dark shadow of depression, sought to raise his spirits. They told him he would live to see Hammoudi married and starting a family of his own. He would see Hammoudi's children live free—because the dictator, omnipotent though he may be, was not immortal. He would die, the people would rise again, and change would come. But Abel Os laughed it off. "Not before I die," he said.

One day, a revolutionary in exile asked me to pass along a small cash donation to Abel Os. When I visited Manbij, I offered it, but Abel Os refused. "I can work with these hands," he said, holding them up. We talked for a while about the news—both Turkey and the regime were again threatening to invade Manbij—and then I said goodbye. I left the donation on the kiosk counter, under a carton of knockoff Marlboro Reds. A few weeks later, Abel Os returned home from the kiosk and keeled over from a heart attack. He was rushed to the hospital, and died at dawn. He was forty-eight.

The SDF does not allow people to raise the revolutionary flag, or even discuss the revolution in public, so his funeral made no mention of the events that turned a roadside vendor into a household name in this small city. But later, after neighbors and relatives had gone home, his closest friends gathered in a guest room in Sarab. They were former members of RYM, erstwhile supporters of the Revolutionary Council, and those who took no sides except to stand against the dictator, and they sang old revolutionary songs late into the night.

| FOUR |

MAY 2023

From his new home in northeastern France, a town of spires and red sandstone facades called Saint-Dié-des-Vosges, Hasan read the news as grief rose within him: Syria was getting readmitted to the Arab League, the coalition of Arab states that had expelled it in 2011. Bashar al-Assad visited Saudi Arabia, which had previously opposed his rule, and basked in a warm reception. The besuited dictator was all smiles, delivering a triumphant speech calling for "peace in our region."

After half a million dead and thirteen million displaced, Bashar al-Assad had won. The road to his rehabilitation on the world stage beckoned. Consulates and embassies reopened. Several European countries called for rapprochement with Damascus. The Biden administration floated loosening or even canceling sanctions.

For Hasan, the final blow came when Turkey proposed reconciliation. One of the first powers to condemn Assad's massacres in 2011, Turkey provided a haven for millions of Syrian refugees and backed the rebel movement. But by 2020, with the revolution defeated, the remaining rebels were clinging to a slice of territory in northwest Syria that had come under Turkish occupation. Turkey effectively prohibited the rebels from attacking the regime, so most fighters simply quit and went home. As Turkish leaders made overtures to Assad, the mood in Turkey toward Syrian refugees hardened. Anti-Syrian riots broke out in multiple cities. Schoolchildren were bullied, and Syrians were afraid to speak Arabic in public. Hasan could not stomach the stares of his Turkish neighbors, and eventually managed to win resettlement through the United Nations. He took very little with him, but made sure to pack a few revolutionary flags.

He felt the cold stares in France too, though unlike in Turkey, migrants here were protected by the law. His daughters enrolled in school and quickly learned French. But Hasan, consumed with caring for his son, who has autism, struggled to master the language. France did not recognize his diplomas, nor those of his wife, who was an engineer. At sixty, he would need to find work as a driver or a cook.

Meanwhile, he devoted his free time to what he did best: agitation. In print and on-air, he denounced the normalization of Bashar al-Assad. This drew the ire of certain other exiled Syrian revolutionaries, who accused him of clinging to old fantasies, of burying his head amid the terrible truth of Assad's victory. These former revolutionaries, like the officials of powerful states everywhere, voiced one abiding principle: *Be realistic*. Once Assad was brought back into the fold, they argued, he would recognize the comity of nations, he would issue reforms. These "realists" claimed the hard truths of logic and history were on their side, because revolution had accomplished nothing—nothing except unremitting misery. Diplomacy was the only solution.

For a long time, Hasan had believed history was a river, sometimes narrowing, sometimes widening, as it flowed to its final destination, where humans would live in the light of reason. But it was hard to deny that the previous years seemed to make a mockery of Hegel's teleology. In fact, it made a mockery of any theory that saw a logic in history, that predicted that humanity's ups and downs happened for a purpose. Now, it was the "realists" who'd claimed the mantle of reason, and who called on Syrians to accept the fait accompli.

So Hasan returned to his first and oldest love: poetry. In an article entitled "Don't Reconcile!," he took inspiration from the Egyptian poet Amal Dunqul:

> *Do not reconcile*
> *Even if they give you gold*
> *I wonder*
> *If I were to gouge out your eyes*
> *and replace them with two gems*
> *would you see?*
> *These things are priceless*

Against the "narrow utilitarian political framework" of realpolitik, Hasan wrote, stood the poetic register, the language of morality. Even if the entire world embraced Assad, and even if this were the only option, the true revolutionary should never allow anyone to forget the moral consequences. Week after week, he penned a version of the same message, which felt like something between a mournful exhortation and a catechism: The revolution must continue.

DECEMBER 2024

Despite Hasan's convictions, even he was surprised when, in the summer of 2023, protests flared in regime-controlled southern Syria against the government's decision to cut fuel subsidies. For the first time in a decade, demonstrators set Assad posters ablaze and stormed Baath Party offices. By the next summer, protests had spread to northern areas under Turkish domination. Thousands of people participated in a "Dignity Sit-in" in a dozen northern towns, demanding Turkey cease its rapprochement with the regime and insisting that rebel groups—who'd hardly fired a shot in years—launch a new offensive against Assad.

From his home in France, Hasan threw himself into organizing. He reconnected with old friends from Manbij who were now living in Turkish-controlled areas. He met new activists, young men and women who'd never raised their voices before, but who'd drunk up their parents' stories of revolution. Before he knew it, Hasan was thrust into that seemingly long-gone world: conducting straw polls, debating strategy, arguing until dawn. When protesters were arrested by Turkish-backed armed groups, he helped organize campaigns for their release. Activists formed coordinating committees, as in the early days. Hasan cautioned his new comrades about what he'd learned from past mistakes, advocating for a movement that was inclusive and populist, one that put the everyday concerns of working-class people first. The activists drew up a list of demands, including a call for a Syria-wide democratically elected revolutionary leadership. After so much loss, after the depths of defeat, Hasan and his comrades were still refusing extinction.

The regime's greatest fear was that the northern and southern movements would link, so they began massacring people with increasing frequency. On November 26, 2024, regime artillery shelled villages in the Turkish zone, killing at least fifteen civilians, including six children. Usually, the rebels offered little response to such atrocities. But the next morning, four rebels dressed in Syrian army fatigues approached a checkpoint belonging to the government's 47th Regiment, at a hillock marking the boundary between the Turkish zone and regime territory, and asked for water. Then they opened fire, killing all the soldiers present. In the ensuing hours, guerrillas overran nearby outposts. The offensive was the first serious rebel military activity in years. Hasan, who was in touch with the rebels, learned that the aim was to protect civilians by pushing regime forces beyond artillery range. Within a few hours, rebels seized more than a dozen villages. The wild thought occurred to Hasan that some of the families displaced from those villages, who'd been living in tents for years, would finally be able to return home.

The next morning, Hasan had to read the headline three or four times to believe it: The entire 47th Regiment had collapsed. He hit the phones, discussing with comrades how best to take advantage. The immediate challenge was to activate mutual aid networks: The Russians would surely assault the front line, and regime warplanes would target markets and schools. His phone lit up with messages from the field. Soon, he was on television, demanding that the world direct its attention to the looming massacre.

But the Russians did nothing. Even the regime's warplanes remained grounded.

By evening, news arrived that the 102nd Regiment had also collapsed. In mere hours, a thousand soldiers had abandoned their posts. Now the road to Aleppo was astonishingly clear. On the morning of the twenty-ninth, rebels drove through the streets of downtown Aleppo, raising the revolutionary flag. After a decade of retreat, the rebels managed to capture Syria's largest city in just two days.

Everyone waited for the counteroffensive. Most expected that the regime forces would raze the city, a bloodbath unlike anything seen before. But Hasan wasn't so sure. He began to grasp the inner contradictions of the regime: rehabilitated on the world's stage yet rotten to its core, unable to pay even its most loyal fighters. He believed regime soldiers would regroup in the Syrian heartland, ceding Aleppo to the revolutionaries. That meant time was on the rebels' side. They should build strong ties with the community, Hasan argued, turning Aleppo into a beacon of revolutionary governance—even if it took years. He urged his comrades to establish political bodies, to look after bread distribution and trash collection.

But the rebels pushed ahead.

They reached the outskirts of Hama, where this time the regime forces put up a spirited fight. Hasan was following the battle blow-by-blow on his phone when, late one evening, he was stunned by a revelation: The Russians had abandoned their ally. So too had the Iranians. Without these foreign powers behind them, regime soldiers were no longer willing to die for their leader—not when they were on the edge of starvation themselves. *He is alone*, he kept repeating, as if trying out the words, testing reality. *The tyrant is alone.*

Hama fell, and Hasan saw images of highways choked with fleeing cars. They were carrying regime officials and supporters. By December 7, only eleven days after the start of the offensive, but thirteen long years since children spray-painted "It's your turn, oh doctor" on a schoolyard wall, rebels reached the Damascus suburbs.

Rumors were flying: unmarked helicopters alighting on rooftops, regime soldiers shedding their uniforms curbside. But Hasan tried to ignore it all. The counterattack was coming. For many days, he'd not slept more than an hour at a stretch. He appeared on television eyes red, voice raspy. He found himself questioning the certainties of life, maybe even his very conception of history.

In the early hours of December 8, in the Tadamon neighborhood of Damascus, an elderly man opened his front door and stepped into the alley. He wasn't sure what drew him out. Under a moonless sky, he walked along mounds of rubble, past steel girders rising like alien totems. He walked down the main street, which had been razed to the ground by his government. When he reached the neighborhood's entrance, he saw that, for the first time in his life, the guard box was vacant. Downtown, a young man bicycled to Umayyad Square, under the saucer-like streetlamps, and it dawned on him that there were no police anywhere. A woman stepped onto her balcony near the old city, feeling the cool air on her skin, studying the empty street below. Nearby, a voice could be heard. Someone was shouting. "Wake up! Bashar has fallen!" He was screaming as if possessed, as if his life depended on it, his voice breaking. "Bashar has fallen! Syria is free!" His voice caromed through the empty street, echoing as he screamed again and again. There was a swell of shrieking women. More voices were shouting, "Bashar has fallen!" People were shouting from their balconies, their kitchens, their bedrooms—but none of them really believed it.

Hasan, too, could not accept it. His thoughts were no longer ordered. Reason, his guide for so long, abandoned him. More rumors flashed onto his phone: Assad had fled in a Russian transport jet; rebels were opening the prisons. He messaged comrades, but nothing was certain. There was no solid ground beneath him. The sunlight filtered through the windows. It was a cold French morning, the streets of Saint-Dié-des-Vosges subdued, the people heading to church. But in his living room, Hasan's family was huddled together, obsessively refreshing their feeds. Around 10:00 a.m., Syrian state TV, which just the previous day had denied all reports of troop withdrawals, displayed the following words:

> The revolution is victorious. The criminal Assad regime has fallen.

A howl went up in the room. Hasan stared, motionless, at the message. Across Syria, a country that had until recently ceased to exist, people flooded town squares and city parks. Revolutionary flags, contraband for so long, hidden under mattresses, in vintage trunks, lit up the streets. They waved banderoles, their faces bright in the sun. They burst into dance, they held each other and sobbed, and no one could say what was real. This was impossible, Hasan told himself. Against the hard facts of life, the iron truths of history. Hasan excused himself. In his bedroom, the door closed, he began to sob. He lost himself, sobbing harder than he'd ever sobbed before, and he wasn't sure if these were tears of joy or heartbreak or shock—or if, on this impossible day, it was all one and the same. He choked on his sobs, asking if this could be real, asking how fate had somehow picked *him* among the legions lost and forgotten to be alive at this moment. He found himself back in the desert fortress, the tiny skylight above, the sixteen years stolen, the friends who never made it home. Now he understood that he wept tears of relief, because it had all been for this day. Yet the *reasons* those things happened somehow did not culminate in something sensible, something logical. He knew that in the coming days he'd appear on television, offering a sober analysis: The Russians had been embroiled in Ukraine and could not come to the tyrant's aid; the Iranians had been hammered by Israel; the regime army, staffed by conscripts who'd not been paid in months, had reached a breaking point. He knew that, when looking back, he would mold history to the arc of reason. But in that moment, he had no real explanation for what had just happened. He could find no resolution of inner contradictions, no march toward absolute understanding. No, what happened was absurd, and in embracing absurdity, he found a new kind of freedom, a freedom that can only be grasped by the light of faith. With this knowledge, he wept again, for a long time.

I walk through the streets I've walked so many times before, but now the city is resplendent. The balconies are festooned with streamers and pennants; Main Street teems with vendors, girls walking in twos and threes to school, men heaped onto motorcycles, as revolutionary songs blare through open windows. From the rooftop of the Manbij Hotel hangs the green-and-black tri-star flag, smaller than the one Abel Os hung on the first liberation day, some twelve years earlier. People speak of this second, more total liberation gingerly, as if reality might change its mind at any moment and snatch it all away again. On the cement wall near the soccer stadium, a young man is painting a mural of a sun rising over green and black fields.

The rebels expelled SDF from Manbij shortly after Assad fled. In a second-floor office in City Hall, I find a few men seated behind a desk, with a crowd gathered to meet them. They are Hasan's old comrades, and they have just reestablished the Revolutionary Council. It's still early days, but there's talk of reviving the senate as well. The former editors of *The Sun of Freedom* are proposing its relaunch. Meanwhile, exiled revolutionaries are pouring back, tossing off grand ambitions—political parties, a national parliament, a new constitution. I want to ask about the old mistakes, about the price of bread, but I can't bring myself to do so. For now, the activists are holding the past at a safe remove, and I find myself doing the same.

But outside the old prisons, fathers and mothers linger by the gates. You can sometimes recognize them by their clouded glass stares. They pass out flyers showing a photo of their son or daughter, along with a phone number.

One morning, I head for the desert. Families, curious citizens, and journalists are now exploring the dungeons pried opened on liberation day, from which emerged skeletal men and women. But I'm interested in an even deeper slice of the past. Palmyra prison, where Hasan was immured for so many years, was considered too brutal even for Bashar al-Assad, who shut it down when he assumed power in 2000. During the civil war, ISIS captured the facility and claimed to have blown it up, but I want to see what's left.

I find that much of the grounds are indeed in ruins, but in a few hours I manage to locate Hasan's cell, mostly intact. The walls are covered in words scrawled by inmates. There are poems, verses from the Quran, a drawing of someone's girlfriend. The sun trickles through the skylight. I video-call Hasan, and his pixelated face appears on my phone. I show him his cell, which he has not seen in twenty-five years, but which he has never truly left. He is quiet for a while. "The victory is bittersweet," he says. "Maybe any victory worth having is bittersweet."

I'm responding, but his eyes are distant, and I know he is with those who were with him here, those who never imagined such a day and those who imagined it a thousand times.

Victory is bittersweet for Abdul Hadi, too. After liberation, he visited Manbij for the first time in years. He saw his old house, the soccer field where his star briefly ascended. He did not try to see the old RYM headquarters, though, and left the city the same evening. Back home, in his self-imposed exile in northwestern Syria, his mind turns obsessively on the bygone days, on fleeting encounters and festering slights, but most of all on those he'd hurt. Some days, he takes to his bed, afflicted by mysterious ailments, even as his doctor declares him sound of body, even as his brother grabs him by the shoulders. When he hears a car out front, he goes to the window, but it's never for him.

For very different reasons, Mina, too, is severed from this new Syria. On liberation day, she shed her tears, sang into hoarseness, wondered what Sami, looking down, would be thinking. But she also remembered her first liberation day, twelve years prior, when they'd driven through the dimming twilight, singing revolutionary songs. That old hurt, that betrayal of a world briefly illuminated and then engulfed in darkness, was still inside her. Until the lineaments of freedom become clear—until the revolutionaries propose a sound economic policy, until she and her husband can work in dignity—she will bide her time in Turkey, she will watch, and she will hope.

Ibrahim, however, has no such qualms. On liberation day, he immediately took off from his cement-mixing job, mounted a motorcycle, and toured his city. His body thrummed with excitement. With new eyes, he saw the park benches, the chipped fountains, the signs blistered in rust. He congratulated strangers. A wave of ambition has passed through him: He will save up, treat his wife to a trip to Damascus, a city she has never seen. He will buy a motorcycle for his son and maybe build another floor for his house. Still, he knows there's much cause for concern. The new revolutionary authorities seem to be struggling to enforce law and order; there's talk of scrapping the bread subsidy; and many former regime officials, with so much blood on their hands, have disappeared without a trace. But he does not dwell on all that, because he has an inexplicable feeling that somehow, things will work out in the end.

A former inmate of al-Bab prison tells me that until the final moments, Oday was attempting to organize fellow detainees.

Among his many pages of poetry, one line strikes me as something of a philosophy: "I am open to the world, even if it closes in on me, even if it kills me." Faced with a damaged and failing world, what might we legitimately hope for? Hope might seem like a feeling, an emotional register—yet during the dictatorship and repression, when Oday and so many others experienced the pits of despair, they did not lose hope. They had no delusions about their prospects, yet somehow, their despair and hope lived together, strange bedfellows. While it's certainly possible to hold contradictory feelings at once, Oday's hope does not seem the obverse of despair. In fact, to place them both in the category *emotion* seems to miss something important. There was a persistence to Oday's hope, and that of his comrades, through the ups and downs, that we don't normally associate with emotion. Hope, for him, was not simply a feeling, like love or rage or any other passion, but a disposition, a trait of character.

Most character traits reveal themselves through action—a courageous person takes worthwhile risks, a distrustful person shuns friendships and romances. What action does hope express? I keep returning to Oday's line "I am open to the world," because I have seen this sentiment, expressed in many ways, in so many diaries and columns and videos, in the pages of the *Sun* and the *Path*, from the fingertips of a member of Women of Freedom when, at the height of the caliphate, she exhorts her fellow revolutionaries in exile, "Come back to Syria, even if death is the price." To be open to the world, even as it closes in and feels like an eminently hostile place, is to be appropriately vulnerable. An abiding fact of life is how little power we wield over reality. Anything worth doing—falling in love, having children, joining a political movement, standing against oppression—puts us at the mercy of forces outside our control, at the mercy of risk.

Being hopeful, Oday's life seems to suggest, is being the type of person who can live comfortably with a certain level of risk, someone who is appropriately vulnerable. But what level of risk? When faced with the uncertainties of human life, there are at least two ways we can go wrong, two extremes. On the one hand, we might seek to master our vulnerability, eliminating all possibility of risk. We become Panglossian, clinging to foolish hope, bent on taming reality, shaping it to our will. The drive to master reality, to eliminate risk, was precisely the affliction of the Assad dictatorship—and every other government that spies on its population, controls thought and expression, or justifies oppression in the name of public safety. Yet it is also the affliction of technocratic liberals, who believe politics happens above the heads of ordinary people—because it is too great a risk to trust the fickle masses—and of Silicon Valley titans, who seek to eliminate vulnerability altogether through technology.

On the other hand, we can succumb to our vulnerability, wallow in it, allow it to rule us. Such submission is at the root of the politics of fear—the program of those who prey on our vulnerabilities by scapegoating others, by heightening anxieties, even when those anxieties might have a legitimate source. The politics of fear was the Islamic State's program, but many political cultures have their own versions.

Abdul Hadi could not live with his vulnerability. He was enslaved by it, and it led him, in ways he could have never imagined, to moral disaster. But Oday, I am certain, did not surrender to his anxieties—nor did he fall into the other extreme of unbridled hopefulness. He understood full well that the possibility of reviving the revolution was dim and, at times, was appropriately depressed by this hard truth. Yet he saw in the world around him the glimmer of possibility, and indeed, the revolution's astonishing success years later vindicated his view. To the very end, he was not overwhelmed by his vulnerability, nor did he seek to overpower it. There, between these extremes, lies the virtue of hope.

There are no formulas or algorithms for what counts as appropriate hope, but there are lives that are lived, stories that are told. Oday's hope, I now understand, was a radical hope: that no matter the disaster in front of him, goodness is possible, even if it is impossible to know how and when it might arrive. Such a hope believes there are fates worse than death. It acts as if another world is possible, while accepting that the world may "close in on you" first. It is a hope that, when transmitted to children, or left behind in books and songs and institutions, can grow and multiply. This is sometimes called a "revolutionary tradition."

Those in the revolutionary tradition, like Hasan, like Oday's friends, still meet in living rooms to talk politics, to dissect their comrades' successes and missteps. They know the liberation will not end Syria's problems. There will be new woes, unforeseen inequities, fresh abuses. But they also know they stand in a tradition, and they hear in the world's upheavals echoes of their own.

They see their story in the French Revolution of 1789, which smashed the old aristocratic order and briefly birthed a democracy, before devolving into Napoleon's dictatorship. Yet the French tradition survived, leading to further revolutions in 1830, 1848, and 1871. It was only after nearly one hundred years of upheaval, in which ordinary people rose time and again, that modern French democracy took shape. Likewise, they believe the great upheaval of 2011 is but the first of many, and those future struggles will be waged by their children and their children's children.

Not long after I left Syria for the last time, the new government in Manbij appointed officials who'd been tainted by corruption allegations during the revolution. Overnight, flyers materialized on the streets, denouncing the decision. The next day, people stepped into Central Square in threes and fours and fives. The rebel authorities, many of whom had never faced a protest, watched in silence, holding their rifles. Hundreds marched down Main Street, past the Manbij Hotel, past City Hall, waving the tri-star flag and raising their fists. Maybe some of them knew Oday and the first generation of revolutionaries. But most did not. They came out for love and rage, singing songs they knew by heart, chanting slogans that came naturally, and they were not crossing a threshold into a great unknown. They came out simply because it is who they are, because of what has been awakened, because of the fire that cannot be put out.

ON METHODOLOGY

When I began this project in 2017, I quickly realized that I would face a host of difficulties. In a highly polarized context of revolution and civil war, where fear and anger prevail, how to avoid the obvious fact that narrators will present their stories in the best possible light, or try to minimize or elide important but embarrassing truths? And even when they strive to be truthful, how to contend with the fragility of memory? Finally, perhaps most important of all, how might I, an outsider, win the trust of those who lived through extraordinary, and extraordinarily painful, events? In a normal context, such hurdles might have been enough to ward me off this undertaking. But I began to understand this was no normal context, because revolution is precisely one of those extraordinary events that can render impractical ideas workable and unthinkable ideas thinkable.

Early on, I was interviewing Huzayfa al-Osman, a founding editor of the *Sun of Freedom*, when he mentioned the names of several individuals I was looking to track down. He offered to help, and I hired him as a research assistant. He conducted interviews on my behalf, which I occasionally followed with interviews of my own. Before long, I'd assembled a research team half a dozen strong—all protagonists of the revolution in Manbij. They fanned out across Syria, Turkey, and Europe, tracking down nearly everyone who had an important role in the events. They proceeded to interview their own friends and comrades, and I sometimes conducted follow-up interviews. People did not always trust me, but they trusted their fellow Syrians, with whom they had marched down Main Street and stood shoulder to shoulder in Central Square. You might call this approach "collective journalism."

I also took advantage of a valuable resource the uprising made available: the social media record. The Syrian revolution was perhaps the first major global event to unfold on social media, as activists uploaded videos of nearly every collective event described in these pages. My colleagues archived every relevant YouTube video, Facebook post, and tweet they could find. We also amassed a collection of newspapers published during the revolution. Others generously donated private collections of cell phone videos. Together, these sources formed an unprecedented archive of revolutionary experience.

With collective journalism and social media, I was able to overcome some of the traditional obstacles to crafting empirically grounded, truthful narrative nonfiction. First, we were able to collect an extraordinary amount of data, far beyond what I could have done on my own. Together, we carried out nearly two thousand interviews for this book. Second, we were able to address the challenges of self-interested narration and faulty memories by interviewing dozens of sources for nearly every event and personality depicted herein. For example, to construct the scenes in Chapter 3 of Book 3, which detail the day the city overthrew the regime in 2012, my team and I interviewed nearly two dozen sources. The resulting narrative illustrated a strong consensus on key events and scenes on that day, as well as a *Rashomon*-style divergence now and then, as people inevitably differed in memory and emphasis. I then triangulated this source material with other elements of the historical record—in this case, hundreds of YouTube clips, private phone videos, and social media posts from that day, as well as news articles and diaries. After adjusting the narrative to accommodate these facts, we conducted follow-up interviews with several of the original sources. In this manner, we iteratively refined the narrative until we ironed out inconsistencies and settled on a reasonably accurate final product. Of course, differences of interpretation or recollection sometimes persisted; I flag such cases in the endnotes.

We applied a similar approach to the personalities who appear in this text. For example, over several years, I conducted nearly thirty interviews with Abel Os, and my colleagues conducted an additional ten interviews. This provided the backbone of Abel Os's life and thoughts. Additionally, we interviewed thirty-four other sources, including his friends, coworkers, relatives, comrades, and rivals. I triangulated these with the videographic record, then moved iteratively between sources and Abel Os until we were confident of the veracity of the narrative. This method ensured that almost every single incident portrayed in this book—from closed-door meetings to public rallies—was drawn from multiple sources.

In the notes below, every personality and key event is organized into a corpus, consisting of dozens of interview sources as well as relevant social media and other material. Our team made clear to the interview subjects that their responses would help inform this book. Everyone was given a choice of whether to be included under their real name or a pseudonym. In the case of Oday, whom I never met, I was aided by a detailed diary he kept and several Facebook pages belonging to him—but otherwise, we used the same method of interviewing dozens of people who knew him well.

It's ironic that interiority and subjective experience can only be reliably reproduced in nonfiction through collective effort. Through the process of collective journalism, I found that people were eager to talk. The cataclysm of the previous fifteen years left terrible wounds—during most of the research period, people were speaking to us under the assumption that their revolution had failed. They sometimes spoke to us for catharsis, sometimes for glory, sometimes out of bitterness. People wanted their sacrifices commemorated, their losses grieved. They clung to an idea, perhaps outmoded, that putting their experiences to paper was an act on a continuum with the revolution itself. This despite the fact that dredging up old memories, and looking truth in the face, demands courage. Nietzsche writes that "the strength of a person's spirit [is] measured by how much 'truth' he could tolerate, to what extent he needs to have it diluted, disguised, sweetened, muted, falsified." What he perhaps misses is that such strength of spirit rarely, if ever, springs autonomously from the single great-souled man or woman. Instead, strength arises through shared struggle, through collective experience, through belonging. It was in acknowledgment of this truth, therefore, that researching this book was a collective act.

PRINCIPAL SOURCES

Ibrahim Kasem: I first met Ibrahim in Manbij, Syria, in 2017. Between 2017 and 2025, I conducted several in-depth interviews with him in person and over the phone, and my research assistants conducted multiple follow-up interviews. In total, our team interviewed Ibrahim over thirty times. We also interviewed several of Ibrahim's family members, including one of his brothers, to corroborate details of his life story. Finally, I traveled with Ibrahim three times to the Euphrates riverbank, where the ruins of Little Hyena lie submerged. Ibrahim was able to point out various landmarks of his childhood, which proved invaluable in providing details for this chapter. Ibrahim requested that I change his family name to protect his identity and security.

Hasan Nefi: We first met in Gaziantep, Turkey, in the spring of 2017. Between 2017 and 2025, I conducted several in-depth interviews with him, mostly over the phone, and my research assistants conducted several follow-ups. In total, our team interviewed Hasan nearly two dozen times. We also made use of Hasan's voluminous writings and political analyses, most of which appeared for Syrian opposition outlets after 2011. We also interviewed twenty-one of

Hasan's comrades in the protest movement. These interviews are all contained in the Manbij Protesters corpus and the MRC corpus.

Abel Os: I first met Abel Os in Manbij, Syria, in late 2017. Between 2017 and 2021, I conducted in-depth interviews with him in person and over the phone, and my research assistants conducted multiple follow-up interviews. In total, Abel Os was interviewed over forty times by our team.

In addition, we interviewed thirty-four other sources who knew Abel Os at different stages of his life. These constitute the Abel Os corpus. These sources are: Abu Ahmed Ibo, Abu Khalid (coworker), Abu Nasser al-Nazbo (friend), Abu Shadi (nephew), Abu Shadi Farghali, Ahmed al-Faraj (friend and RYM member), Ali Abu Saddam, Ali al-Jaadan (coworker, Lebanon), Ali al-Suwadi (Lebanon), Ali Darwish, Anas Sheikh Weiss (karate partner), Anas Taljabini, Bakir Abu Muhammad, Fahd al-Oseb (nephew), Hajj Hussein al-Ghalazi, Hajji Gulay (friend), Hasan al-Issa (neighbor), Hasan Gulay (friend), Hassan al-Essa, Hussein Abu Raed (RYM member), Hussein al-Daher, Hussein al-Khalazi (neighbor), Hussein al-Qallathi (neighbor), Jassim al-Nabzo (karate trainee), Khaled (Ras al-Ain), Maher Abu Muhannad (karate partner), Mahmoud Oseb (brother), Mana (wife), Muhammad Oseb (son), Muhammad Osman (karate trainee), Muhannad Oseb (nephew), Mustafa Haddad (RYM member), Nasser al-Nabzo, and Saleh Oseb (brother).

The Abel Os corpus also includes hundreds of photographs and home videos from various points in Abel Os's life, including his time on muster zones, his wedding, and his karate training.

Oday al-Hema: I first began researching Oday's story in 2017. We built a roster of Oday's friends, relatives, and acquaintances, whom we interviewed in Syria, Turkey, and Europe between 2017 and 2025. These interviews belong to the Oday corpus: Abboud Salo, Abdul Aziz Abu Saleh, Abdul Hadi al-Bisher, Abdul Salam Bakkar, Abel Os, Aboud Solou, Abu Hasan, Ahmed al-Faraj, Akrema al-Hema (brother), Alawi Khaleef al-Maraar, A. K. (mother of Ibrahim Maraar), Ali al-Khaled, Ammar al-Kaoud, Bushra al-Hema (sister, pseudonym), Mina Saba, Fawaz al-Hussein, Hajji Gulay, Hala al-Muhammad (pseudonym), Hamada al-Hussein, Hasan Gulay, Jameel al-Akla, K. A., Maher al-Hema (father), Mahmoud Abu Ali (relative), Mustafa al-Hamza (uncle), Nidal S., O. M., Reem al-Hussein (wife), and Saleh Abu Nayyaf.

The corpus also includes Oday's diary and his Facebook posts, which opened up his inner world, as well as hundreds of photographs and videos.

Mina Saba: I first met Mina in 2017 in Nizip, Turkey. Between 2017 and 2025, I conducted several in-depth interviews with her in person and over the phone, and my research assistants conducted multiple follow-up interviews. In total, Mina was interviewed nearly twenty-four times by our team. In addition, we interviewed ten of her friends and family: A.H. Muhammad, A. H., A. S. (relative), A. Saba (brother), H. Saba (sister), Israa Sheikh Weiss (friend), J. Saba (father), M. Saba (sister), S. Saba (brother), and Y. K. (husband). These interviews are gathered in the Mina Saba corpus.

Finally, I was able to make use of Mina's diary, which she kept intermittently over the years, and a voluminous archive of videos and documents from the Women of Freedom assembly.

Abdul Hadi al-Bisher: When I began researching this book, Abdul Hadi was in hiding. We conducted seventy-one interviews with his friends and family between 2017 and 2024. Between 2023 and 2025, my research team and I spoke to Abdul Hadi directly over the phone, and the team visited him at his home, to corroborate our portrayal and to fill in missing details. Beyond Abdul Hadi himself, the principal sources for Abdul Hadi's life were: Abel Os, Abdul Aziz al-Bisher (brother), Abdul Basit al-Shiyukhi, Abu Abdo, Abu Ayhem, Ahmed al-Faraj, Akrama al-Hema, Ammar al-Hussein, Aqeel Abo, Basil Abu Saeed, Basil al-Daroubi, Hasan al-Askar, Jamil al-Okla, Kamal Abu Warda, Khaled al-Saleh, Khalil Matar, Muhammad Abu Nadeem, Muhammad Ali al-Faraj, Muhammad Osman, Mustafa Sheikh Ibrahim, Naser al-Nabzo, Nidal S., Obada, Omar al-Faraj, Qutaiba al-Khalaf, Saleh Nayyaf, Shadi al-Munla, S. Q., S. R., and Suleiman Suleiman. These constitute the Abdul Hadi corpus.

DATASETS

Two thousand interviews were conducted for this book. For ease of reference, I've arranged the interviews into corpora, themed around a central topic. The endnotes refer to these datasets to give the reader a clear understanding of the source of any given material. For example, in Book 2, Chapter 5, the sentence "As Manbij's foremost political prisoner, his [Hasan Nefi's] opinion was much sought after," the source listed in the endnotes is the MRC corpus. This refers to the dataset that holds the interviews supporting this assertion.

Abdul Hadi corpus: Consists of interviews with thirty sources who knew Abdul Hadi.

Abel Os corpus: Consists of interviews with thirty-four sources who knew Abel Os.

Al-Hol corpus: Between 2021 and 2024, we conducted interviews with 105 individuals who were living in al-Hol camp: A. F. M., Abu Abdullah, Abu Firas, Abu Hussein, Abu Mahmoud, Abu Natheer, Ahmed al-Hussein, Aisha Um Abdul Rahman, Alaa, Ameena, Areej, Asmaa Jamil Hammoud, Ayat, Ayna'a, Basmah, Bint Tunisiyeh, Daad Umm Fatima, Deya Taleb, Enas Abdul Salam al-Jasim, F. M. A., Fadia Um Salman, Fateh Muhammad Haj Muhammad, Fateh Um Mahmoud, Fatima M. R., Fatima Mohammad Abdulkader, Fatima Muhammad al-Zein, Fatima Um Khalid, Foutaim Mohammad al-Mohammad, Hala, Halima Issa Musaitef, Hassan Muhammad Tahan, Um Khalid, Hazar, Heba, Howaida al-Jassem, Huda, Iman Ismail Abdo, Iman Khader Sweid, Israa Ahmed, Istabraq, Jawaher, Johaynah Um Hussein, Juhaina Abdel Kafi Jumaa, Kawthar, Khadija Hamed, Khalil al-Ibrahim Majid, Khawla Qasim al-Wali, Khitam Shibli Abdel Razzaq, Layla Umm Ali, M. K. Q., Maha, Mahmoud Jumaa Sayed Abdel Rahman, Manal, Manar, Marwa Hassan al-Omar, Maryam Ibrahim Jumaa, Maymouna, Mohammad Ahmad al-Wakaa, Mona, Nagham, Nawader, Nisreen, Nour al-Ali, Nour al-Huda, Nour Hassan al-Husain, Qasim Khaled Ahmed, Raeefa Mohammed Masto, Raghad, Rama, Rama Taha al-Jazzar, Rasha, Rawiya Sultan Hammada, Reham Ahmed al-Abdullah, Roula Mohammed Masto, Sahbaa Ibrahim Qasoom, Sa'id al-Faraj, Salwa Ali al-Hamoud, Samaher, Samar, Sanaa, Sarah, Sarah Muhammad Ali, Sawsan, Shahad, Shaimaa Ismail Saleh, Soumaya Ahmed al-Amer, Umm Abdo, Umm Abdul Aziz, Umm Abdullah, Umm Ala'a, Umm Ali, Umm Hamid, Umm Hamza, Umm Hussein, Umm Ismael, Umm Khaled, Umm Omar, Umm Reham, Umm Roa'a, Umm Saeed, Umm Thair, Umm Zaid, Yassin Ahmed al-Faraj, Zahraa Mahmoud Kola, and Zainab Ali al-Daban.

Bread Survey corpus: In 2022, I commissioned a study of Manbij's bread and bakery system. We interviewed key individuals in the Manbij Revolutionary Council who oversaw the bread portfolio, along with employees in Manbij's Central Bakery Furnace, the Manbij Mills, and private bakery owners. We investigated bread prices over two decades through interviews and by examining technical reports. Finally, we conducted a survey in the Sheikh Aqeel neighborhood of households to determine affordability concerns and consumption habits. Key interviews in this corpus included Aimad al-Din al-Henezel, who oversaw the bread program; Amer K., who oversaw the Grinding Department at the Manbij Mills; and Mahmoud al-Ali, who had extensive experience in the bread sector.

Caliphate corpus: Between 2017 and 2024, we interviewed sixty-nine current and former members of the Islamic State: Abboud al-Daroubi, Abboud al-Shami, Abu Ahmed 1, Abu Ahmed 2, Abu Hadeel, Abu Hussein, Abu Obeida al-Iraqi, Abu Waheeb, Ameera al-Shawakh, Fatima 1, Fatima 2, Fawzeya Hussein al-Ali, Hajar Um Ismail, Hammouma Qasem Wali, Hanin, Hassana Um Khalid, Hasoun, Jamila Muhammad al-Muhammad, Johaynah Um Hussein, Khalid al-Saleh, Khalil al-Ibrahim Majid, Khawla Qasim al-Wali, Mahasen Sheikh Ali, Maryam, Qutaiba al-Khalaf, Raeefa Mohammed Masto, Raneem Jasem Hamad, Roula Mohammed Masto, Sahar, Sa'id al-Faraj, Sarah, Suzan, Um Abdul Aziz, Um Aisha, Um Alloush, Um Fatima, Um Ibrahim, Um Issa, Um Jamil, Um Khaled, Um Namr, Um Omar, Um Qasem, Um Rashed, Um Raymesa, Umm Ayoub, Umm Hajar, Umm Hassan, Umm Moaz, Umm Qasoura, Umm Saif, Yassin Ahmed al-Faraj, Zainab, Zainab Issa Shawakh Muhammad, and fifteen individuals who declined to be named.

We also interviewed several civilians who were not linked to ISIS but who were able to provide useful information about the subject: Abu al-Jude, Abu Daoud, Abu Muhannad, Abu Omar, Abu Sayed, Hussein Omar Samawi, and Mahmud al-Tayy. This dataset also includes thousands of ISIS statements, flyers, and pamphlets that we collected from the internet and from Manbij.

Caliphate Prison corpus: To better understand Oday's circumstances in ISIS prison, we interviewed the following individuals who spent time in Caliphate prisons: Abu al-Jude, Abu Hasan, Akrama al-Hema, Hassan Hamdo, Hussein al-Hashem, Ismail Abu Suhaib, and Muhammad al-Binshi.

Caliphate Video corpus: This dataset consists of a voluminous archive of ISIS videos, including propaganda clips and filmed executions, which a source made available to us. It also includes thousands of photographs and videos taken in Manbij during the Caliphate, some by ISIS supporters and some by civilians or ISIS opponents.

Central Square corpus: Between 2017 and 2021, we interviewed fourteen people involved in the pivotal sit-in at the Central Square on December 23, 2011: Abel Os, Abdul Hadi al-Bisher, Abdul Karim Mustafa, Ahmed al-Faraj, Jasim al-Sayed, Mohsen Kinaan, Muataz Abu Riyadh, Muhammad Abdi,

Muhammad Osman, Munzer Salal, Mustafa al-Hamza, Nidal S., Riadh Abdul Salam, and Zakaria Qarisli.

Mina Saba corpus: Consists of several interviews with ten of Mina's friends and family.

Final Battle corpus: We interviewed dozens of people about their experiences during the battle between the U.S.-backed forces and ISIS. The most important of these sources were: Abdul Latif al-Khalouf, Abdul Latif al-Sheikh, Abdul Somaa, Ahmed al-Khattaf, Ahmed Shaddad, Fatima Fuad al-Jabari, Hussein al-Hammash, Hussein Omar Samawi, Imad Askar, Khalil al-Askari, Mohammed al-Barho, Mohammed Ali al-Hilal al-Jabari, Mohammed Haidar, Muhammed Awsab, Sami Bahjat al-Hilal, and Yasser al-Khalouf.

First Protesters corpus: We interviewed twelve individuals who took part in or witnessed the first two protests in Manbij, on April 15 and April 22, 2011. The interviewees were: Abdul Karim Mustafa, Abu Jalal, Abu Muhammad, Ahmed al-Faraj, Hamada al-Hussein, Hasan al-Weiss, Hasan Hamdo, Mahmoud al-Ali, Munzer Salal, Mustafa al-Hamza, Subeib al-Alawat, and Zakaria Qarisli.

Flood Interview corpus: To further corroborate details of Ibrahim Kassam's life story, as well as to fill in details about village life, my research team and I conducted interviews with seventy-one people who'd lived in Little Hyena and surrounding villages on both sides of the Euphrates. Forty-five of the people we interviewed were from Little Hyena. Interviews were conducted in Syria, Turkey, and the United Arab Emirates, in person and over the phone.

The corpus also includes nearly a dozen home videos of village life from before the flood, as well as photographs and maps.

The interviewees were: Abd al-Hadi al-Hasan, Abed al-Ahmed, Abu Abed, Abu Alaa Abu al-Abed, Abu Ali, Abu Ammar, Abu Haleema, Abu Khalaf, Abu Khaled, Abu Luwai, Abu Maher, Abu Mahmoud, Abu Nayef, Abu Omar, Abu Othman, Abu Saleem, Abu Saleh, Abu Shadi, Abu Shaheen, Abu Taleb, Abu Yahyha, Adnan Selmo, Ahmad Jasem Ben Mahmoud, Ahmed Abu Ibrahim, al-Haj Hussein, Ali Mustafa Muhammad, Ali Yusef al-Dishu, Faysal al-Hassan, Faysal al-Najem, Faysal Hassan Hassan, H. Hussein, Hamud Humaydi al-Awad, Hassoon Jassim al-Ali, Hussein al-Dandan, Hussein al-Hussein, I. A., Ibrahim Abu al-Muhammad, Ibrahim Ahmad Sheikh Ali, Ibrahim al-Hamad, Ibrahim Jabil al-Moh, Ibrahim Jassim Bin Hassan, Ishmael Shuhada, Ismael al-Nayef, Jassim Abu Ibrahim, Juma'a Hamad, Karkur al-Hamda, Khalid al-Hajji, Khalid al-Hussein,

Mamu Ahmed, Mohammed al-Ibrahim, Muhammad al-Ameer, Muhammad al-Badush, Muhammad al-Jassim aka Abu Hisham, Muhammad al-Shawakh, Muhammad Hajj Mahmoud al-Tah, Muhammad Husso, Muhammad Jasim bin Ibrahim, Muhammad Muhammad bin Ibrahim, Mustafa Ahmed al-Hassan, Mustafa al-Ali, Mustafa Dishu, Nur al-Din al-Ahmed Abu Ahmed, S.A., Umm Abed, Umm Ahmed 1, Umm Ahmed 2, Umm Omar, Yasseen Weiss Ben Ali, and Yunis Abu Muatassim.

Huda al-Muhammad corpus: We interviewed the following individuals regarding Huda al-Muhammad, the Girls of Tomorrow Assembly, and feminist politics in Manbij: Abdul Hadi al-Muhammad, Abdul Hamid al-Mansur, Abdul Hekawati, Abu Ali Samou, Ali Hindi, Ali Shlash, Ammar Hazweni, Asad Idris, Dhiyab al-Muhammad, Mina Saba, Firas al-Ali, Hussein Abu Jana, Hussein al-Daroubi, Huzayfa al-Osman, Israa Sheikh Weiss, Muhammad Kullal, Omar al-Muhammad, Qusay Nihad, and Watan Daroubi.

Liberation corpus: Between 2017 and 2022 we interviewed the following individuals about liberation day (July 19, 2012) and the days leading up to it: Abel Os, Abdul Aziz al-Saleh, Abdul Hadi al-Bisher, Abu Hasan, Abu Muhammad, Abu Muhannad al-Khudr, Abu Omar, Ahmed al-Faraj, Ahmed Rahmo, Ali Saleh al-Jasim, Anas Sheikh Weiss, Hasan al-Khalaf, Hasan Nefi, Hussein al-Akeedi, Hussein Omar Samawi, Jassim al-Sayed, Latouf Hajj Muhammad, M.A., Muhammad al-Ali, Muhammad Bashir al-Khalaf, Saleh Muhammad, Saleh Ibrahim al-Hasan, Suheib al-Alawat, and T. K. (a former police officer).

In addition, we collected hundreds of photographs and videos of the events.

Manbij Flood corpus: In 2019, I commissioned a survey of forty-one flood survivors living in Manbij to better understand the flooding and aftermath. Of these, twenty-one participants were selected for further in-depth interviews, which were carried out by Muhammad Osman. All interviews were conducted in Manbij. Seven of the interviewees were from Little Hyena. These interviews were anonymous.

While the Flood Interview corpus focused on everyday village life and village history, the Manbij Flood corpus interviews focused on the flood itself, the government's compensation scheme, and survivors' post flood experiences.

Manbij Protesters corpus: Through interviews, we compiled a list of eighty-four individuals who were active during the Manbij civil protest phase (April to December 2011) or the republican phase (July 2012 to January 2014) in one of the assemblies. We managed to interview fifty-nine of these, often multiple times. The interviewees were: Abel Os, Abboud al-Daroubi, Abdul Aziz al-Mashi, Abdul Hadi al-Bisher, Abdul Hamid al-Mansur, Abdul Karim Mustafa, Abdul Satif al-Hadad, Abu al-Fadl, Abu Ammar, Abu Ayhem, Ahmed al-Beru, Ahmed Humeidi, Ahmed Mahmoud, Ahmed Mohamed, Ahmed Tarboush, Aimad al-Din Henezel, Ali Abdullah al-Hamo, Ali Saleh al-Jasim, Amin al-Haji, Amin al-Khalaf, Ammar Hazweni, Anas Hassou, Anas Muhammad, Anas Sheikh Weiss, Basil Abu Sayed, Fayez Ramdan, Firas al-Ali, Ghanem Ahmed, Hanif Abu Yasser, Hanni Salal, Hasan al-Khalaf, Hasan Hamdo, Hussein al-Dahir, Huzayfa al-Osman, I. K., Iman al-Jassim, Ismail Abu Suheib, Jasim al-Sayyed, Kamel Suleiman, Latouf al-Hajj Hasan, Mohammad al-Assi, Muataz Abu Riyadh, Muhammad Abdi, Muhammad al-Manbiji, Muhammad Khatib, Muhammad Osman, Munzer Salal, Musab Hassou, Nazeer K., Salah Ibrahim al-Hasan, Sayed S., Shabaan al-Hasan, Shadi Abu Muhammad, Suheib al-Alawat, Sultan Baggari, Turki al-Jassim, Watan al-Daroubi, Yasser al-Moh, and Zakaria Qarisli.

Manbij Revolutionary Council (MRC) corpus: Through interviews and analyzing media reports, we were able to determine the identities of every member of Manbij's various self-governing bodies and formal protest bodies, including the Local Coordinating Committee; the first Constitutive Revolutionary Council, which operated in secret from November 2011 until July 2012; the First Manbij Revolutionary Council, which operated from July 2012 to April 2013; and the Second Manbij Revolutionary Council, which operated from April 2013 until September 2013. In total, this amounts to forty-two individuals in cabinet-level or leadership positions. Of these, we interviewed twenty-six: Abdul Basit al-Shayukhi, Abdul Karim Mustafa, Abdul Raouf Shayko, Abel Os, Abu Abdullah, Abu Faisal, Ahmed Rahmo, Aimad al-Din Henezel, Ali Saleh al-Jasim, Anas Sheikh Weiss, Fayez Ramadan, Ghanem Abu Dhiyab, Hajj Latouf Muhammad, Hani Salal, Hasan Nefi, Ibrahim al-Binshi, Majed al-Jumaa, Muataz Abu Riyadh, Muhammad al-Jasim, Munzer Salal, Mustafa al-Abdullah, Riyadh Hajj Muhammad, Saadedine Soma, Saleh Ibrahim al-Hasan, Turki al-Jasim, and Zakaria Qarasli. We also interviewed seventeen individuals who worked for these bodies at various times, and other associated individuals.

Maymati corpus: In 2020 and 2021 we interviewed ten people with direct experience with Maymati: Abu Ahmed (former Free Army colleague), Abu Haroun (cofounder of Jund al-Haramein), Abu Hussein (former police colleague), Ahmed al-Faraj, Ahmed Rahmo, Ali Silo, Huzayfa al-Osman, Jasim

Atroush Abu Muhammad (father-in-law), Muhammad al-Khatib, and Salah Muhammad.

Missing Persons corpus: Between 2021 and 2025, we conducted fifty-four interviews with individuals whose loved ones are missing, either at the hands of the Syrian regime or ISIS: Abdul Aziz Sheikh Mahmoud, Abdul Hannan al-Kaoud, Abdul Karim Barakat, Abdul Latif Najjar, Abu Rabea, Ahlam al-Saud, Ahmad al-Araj, Ahmad al-Hassoun, Ahmad Kaywan, Ahmed al-Hassan, Ahmed Hammouche, Aida Baku, Alam Fatimah al-Thaher, Ali Hamoush, Ali Jatila, Amal Bousho, Fatima Muhammad, Firas Najib, H.K., Hana Hamidi, Hassan al-Abbasi, Hebat Allah Barakat, Hussain al-Hussain, Hussein Zalkha, Imad Wehbe, J.A.D., Jamila Khalil, Khaled al-Hassan, Khalid al-Thaher, Maher al-Saleh, Maher Hajj Hassan, Mahmoud al-Shihabi, Mahmoud Mosto al-Rajab, Mahmoud Saqqar, Manal Nasser, Manar Fares, Mohammed Saleh, Mohammed Sheiha's wife, Muhammad Bakri, Muhannad Hajj Hassan, Mustafa al-Bayour, Om Mahmoud, Omar Haj Omar, Omar Najjar, Osman Haj Ahmed, Serageldin al-Omar, Turki al-Jassem, Um Mahmoud, Um Mahmoud Adel, Umm Mahmoud, Umm Ziyad, Yahya Hafez, Yahya Mayo, and Zakariya al-Zaed.

Oday al-Hema corpus: Consists of interviews with twenty-seven sources who knew Oday.

Poverty corpus: To better understand the effects of Syria's economic transformations between 2000 and 2011, our team conducted seven interviews with individuals from Manbij who suffered financial hardship. These interviews were conducted between the fall and winter of 2020. The individuals included day laborers, housewives, and unemployed people: Assayil, Aymen al-Jasim, Khalil al-Hussein, M. A., Mahmoud al-Bakkar, Mahmoud al-Musaitif, and Yusef al-Ali.

Rebel corpus: Between 2018 and 2021 we interviewed thirty-two individuals about the armed struggle: Abel Os, Abu Hasan, Abu Haroun al-Banawi, Abu Maan, Abu Muhammad, Abu Shakir, Ahmed al-Akl, Ahmed Nuri al-Ghathwan al-Ghanayemi, Alaa M., Anas Sheikh Weiss, Ali Silo, Azzedine Soma, Bassam Abu al-Abed, Bilal Assaf, Ghanem Abu Dhiyab, Hasan al-Awni, Hasan Nefi, Hussien al-Daher, Ibrahim Bannawi, Ibrahim Kassem, Issa al-Jaber, Jouma al-Daroubi, M. A., Muhammad Ali Issawi, Musab Husso, Mustafa Abu Suleiman, Nidal S., Omar Abu Fahid, Qahtan al-Sharqi, Saadedine Soma, Saleh Muhammad, and Yasser Abu Obaida al-Dumlakhi.

In addition, Jeremy Hodge carried out social media and open-source analysis to augment these interviews.

Republic Battle corpus: The following individuals were key sources on the battle between ISIS and the Free Army in December 2013 to January 2014: Abel Os, Abu al-Mughirah al-Manbiji (FSA), Abu Ma'an (Security Brigade), Abu Muhammad (FSA), Abu Rudeyna (ISIS), Abu Shilouh (Security Brigade, RYM), Abu Zaki (FSA), Adnan Abu Faisal (FSA), Aimad al-Din Henezel (MRC), Anas Sheikh Weiss (FSA), Ghanem Abu Dhiyab (FSA), Hamada al-Hussein (Ahrar Syria brigade, RYM), Hasan al-Khalaf, Hasan Nefi, Hussein Ibo (Ahrar al-Sham), Hussein Omar Samawi (civilian), I.S. (FSA), Mustafa Haddad (RYM), Mustafa Sheikh Ibrahim (RYM), Qasim Taljabini (FSA), Salah Abu Ismail (Security Brigade), and Zakaria Qarisli (FSA).

Republic Video corpus: We collected nearly 3,000 videos covering the republican period between July 2012 and January 2014. These videos were primarily drawn from the fifty-six YouTube channels identified and archived in the Social Media corpus, along with four large private collections. The most important of these private collections belonged to Muataz Abu Riyadh, who generously made his archive available for research purposes. The Republic Video corpus consists of multiple videos depicting nearly every event described in Book 3, except for private meetings.

RYM corpus: Between 2019 and 2022 we interviewed twenty leading members or close associates and observers of RYM, in Europe, Syria, and Turkey: Abdul Hadi al-Bisher, Abdullah Abu Raneem, Abel Os, Abu Ayhem, Abu Tayyeb, Ahmed al-Faraj, Fawwaz Abu al-Walid, Fayez al-Ramadan, Fayez K., Hatim al-Daroubi, Hussein Abu Raed, Hussein al-Hashem, M. K., Muhammad Abu Nadeem, Muhammad al-Khatib, Muhammad Junaid, Mustafa Hadad, Mustafa Sheikh Ibrahim, Nabeel D., and Yasser al-Shuweikh.

The corpus also includes nearly one hundred videos of RYM protests and meetings. Some were found on YouTube, but most were from private collections.

Safira corpus: We conducted interviews with several eyewitnesses to the massacres that took place in Safira district in the summer of 2013 (covered in Book 3, Chapter 17).

From Rasm al-Nafl: Abu Aziz, Abu Ghasan, Abu Ismael, Abu Muhammad Said, Abu Nawar, Abu Yasin, Muhammad Abu Abdo, Muhammad Abu Ibrahim, Um Adel, and Um Aziz.

From Mazra'a [Monk Farms]: Aida, Fadel al-Faraj, Hasan al-Ibrahim, O.W., Um Aziz, Um Jamal, and Um Juma'a.

Other witnesses: Abdul Nasser (human rights activist), Ammar al-Salmo (civil defense responder), Hussein Khattab (Shahba Press Agency), Saeed Eido (Syrian Institute for Justice and Accountability), and Yussef Hussein (lawyer).

SDF corpus: Between 2017 and 2024, we interviewed thirty-six individuals linked to the Syrian Democratic Forces and/or the Kurdistan Workers Party: A. N., A. R., A. S., Abu Ali Barad, Anas al-Ahmed, B., D., Farouk al-Mashi, Fatima Oussi, Firas al-Irani, Ghalia Nemat, H. K., Haval H., Haval J., Haval M., Haval Sa., Haval Sh., Ibrahim Al-Bannawi, J. A., J. A. 2, J. A. 3, J. B., J. H., J. M., K. Q., Maher al-Aouni, Maher K., Mohammed Adel, Mohammed Ali al-Abou, Mohammed Sheikho, Nazefa Khalou, Omar Ismail, S., S. D., and Z. A.

Note: "Haval" means comrade in Kurdish.

Soccer corpus: To better understand the culture of soccer in Manbij, we interviewed thirty-six individuals involved in sports in the city. These were: Abdo Hussein, Abdullah Askar, Abu Hashem, Abu Hasan, Ahmed al-Hajj Hussein, Ammar Tahan, Anwar al-Saeedi, Basel Abu Saeed, Basil al-Droubi, Faraj Muhammad Ali, Farouk al-Hasan, Firas al-Ahmad, Ghasan al-Farari, Hamoudi Basrawi, Hussein Mahmoud, Ibrahim Weiss Ben Ali, Ismail Abu Muhammad, Kamal Al-Hasan, Kamal Uthman, Khalil Kousa, Louai Ajlan, Mahmoud Hajj Qasim, Mahmoud Ibrahim, Mahmoud Maamo, Mousa al-Obeid, Muhammad al-Dabek, Muhammad al-Issa, Muhammad Ghazali, Mustafa Rummo, Omar Dada, Rami Daoud, Shadi Ghazali, Yahya al-Abboud, Yahya Hatto, Yasser al-Jasem Abu Awsh, and Zico.

Many of these individuals provided details about Abdul Hadi's life.

Social Media corpus: The number of social media sources we used is perhaps too extensive to list, but the key YouTube channels were: #Manbij Syrian Democratic Forces Abu Layla, #4Manbij, Abd al Karim Layla, Abduljalil Alsaeid, Abdullah al-Sheikh, Abdullah Ghanem, Abdulmohsen Saadeddin, ABN LYA, Abo allaith, Aboalhasen aleppo, Abu Emir, Abu Khaled Fursan Furat, Abu Qusal, ADAR press, Adnan al-Hussein, AEN Network?, Ahmad Ibrahim, Ahmed al-Hajj, Ahrar Suriya Free Army, AJ+, Al Etihad Press, al Adi'at al-Islamiyya Brigades, Al-Murhana al-Ahmed, Albu Azizi al-Halabi, Aleppo and Idlib, Aleppo Media Center, Alhart yaseen, Almanbegeeal, Alser ax, Arta FM, ASO, Atareb glory, Azad Minbic, Baran misko, Basma Suriya, Bisher al-bisher, Center for Documenting the Syrian Revolution, DEMOCRACY 4

SYR, Destaya Hunder, Documents Syria, Duru'a' al-Thowra, Ehmed Dadelî, Freedom aleppo, Furat FM, Furat Press, Hareth Abu al-Haq, Hassan Abu Mousab, Homs Never Die, Ishak adiga, Jabhat al-Akrad l'Nusrat Sha'abni al-Suri, Katibat Salah al-Din al-Ayyoubi, Leuaaltawheed1, Liwa al-Islam in Aleppo and its countryside, Liwa al-Islam in Aleppo and the Surrounding Countryside, Local Coordinating Committees for Manbij and the Surrounding Countryside, Mahmud Abo Baker, Ma'jizat al-Thowra, Manbej1, Manbejnews1, Manbij al-Fayha'a, Manbij al-Hadat, Manbij military council, Manbij News, Manbij Syria, Marea0city, Maskana inf, Maskana inf m, Mazlum Fendi, Military Council for Manbij and its Countryside, Minbij TV, Moataz Abu-Rayad, Moetaz AboRyad, Mohammad Dhib Bakar, Mr aldale, Muhammad Jalal, Mustafa al-Na'imi, Nezar Frah, Nour Media Center, PMM, Qasioun, RUMAFS, Saleh al-Dandn, SDF press channel, Shaam Network S.N.N., Shahba Media, Shahba Press Agency, Sowt al-Haq, Squriesh, St. Baseil, Syria Dreams, Syria32011, Syriafree2011, SYRIAN AFAK, Syrian Dreams, Syrian Media Center, Syrian Revolution LLC Union in Aleppo, SyriaOne Hand, Talib Ahmed, Tall Refaat City, Tel Refaat 1, Ugarit News—Aleppo and its Countryside, Ugarit News—Syria, Union of Free Students of Syria, Union of Syrian Revolution Coordinating Committees in Aleppo, Yasin Abu Ra'id, Yelizar Benyavskiy, Yousef al-Za'im, YTS, Zajil News Network, and Zouhayr Hnidel.

Many of these no longer exist, but some are still available online.

WORKS CITED

YOUTUBE VIDEOS

AbabilBird8. (2011, December 20). مجزرة كفرعويد في جبل الزاوية (إدلب) الجزء الأول [Massacre of Kafr Aweid in Jabal Al-Zawiya (Idlib)—Part One] [Video]. YouTube. https://www.youtube.com/watch?v=b67r-phyZI8

Abu Shadi al-Safirani. (2013, March 22). السفيرة-حرق بيوت قرية الجنيد من قبل ميليشيا الاسد [Al-Safira: Burning of houses in the village of Al-Junaid by Assad's militia] [Video]. YouTube. https://www.youtube.com/watch?v=kHYPg18wrd4

ahmad alakhtareeny. (2015, March 10). داعشي يفضل بشار الأسد على الجيش الحر [An ISIS member prefers Bashar al-Assad over the Free Syrian Army] [Video]. YouTube. https://www.youtube.com/watch?v=jOgl_mYyJ3Y

Al Aan TV. (2012a, September 1). مظاهرات مستمرة في منبج ومعاناة ما انفكت تزداد اشتدادا [Ongoing demonstrations in Manbij and ever-increasing suffering] [Video]. YouTube. https://www.youtube.com/watch?v=ae6rgWjpEMw

Al Aan TV. (2012b, December 19). أهالي منبج ينتخبون مجلساً ثورياً لمدة سنة في ريف حلب [The people of Manbij elect a revolutionary council for one year in rural Aleppo] [Video]. YouTube. https://www.youtube.com/watch?v=SdTlQbZGvSk

Al Aan TV. (2013a, August 10). "فتيات الغد الحر" هيئة نسائية في ريف حلب من أجل تفعيل دور المرأة ["Free Tomorrow's Girls": A women's organization in rural Aleppo to activate the role of women] [Video]. YouTube. https://www.youtube.com/watch?v=3NtrLTja9Ug

Al Aan TV. (2013b, February 7). شباب سوريون في منبج بحلب ينظمون معرضا للأعمال الفنية [Syrian youth in Manbij, Aleppo organize an art exhibition] [Video]. YouTube. https://www.youtube.com/watch?v=zgq6REPxSws

Al Aan TV. (2013c, January 18). معرض كاريكاتور في منبج يستنشق الحرية [A caricature exhibition in Manbij breathes freedom] [Video]. YouTube. https://www.youtube.com/watch?v=emCAV9cyblA

Al-Safira News. (2013a, May 21). السفيرة: استمرار انتشال جثث من آبار قرية ام عامود [Al-Safira: Continued recovery of bodies from the wells of Umm Amoud village] [Video]. YouTube. https://www.youtube.com/watch?v=74K1bPkgPlY

Al-Safira News. (2013b, May 24). السفيرة: قوات النظام تحاول اقتحام قرية القبيتين 24-5-2013 [Safira: Regime forces attempt to storm the village of Qubatein, 24-5-2013] [Video]. YouTube. https://www.youtube.com/watch?v=fvkXX5n8Jmo

Ali hasan. (2013, August 24). مجازر ارتكبتها عصابات الاسد بقرية الجنيد في بلدة السفيرة +18 24 أغسطس 2013 [Massacres committed by Assad's gangs in the village of Al Junaid in the town of Al-Safira +18, August 24, 2013] [Video]. YouTube. https://www.youtube.com/watch?v=uOXZx2hL8ml

aljazeeramubasher. (2024, December 17). ليلة سقوط بشار الأسد [The night of Bashar al Assad's fall: Footage published for the first time of a Syrian waking his neighborhood with news of the regime's collapse] [Short video]. YouTube. https://www.youtube.com/shorts/1mI1cBCnnPE

WORKS CITED

almanbegee. (2011, April 23). مظاهرة مدينة منبج في ريف حلب في يوم الجمعة العظيمة [Demonstration in the city of Manbij, Aleppo countryside, on Great Friday] [Video]. YouTube. https://www.youtube.com/watch?v=mukC1OkE9oc

Alzakout, R. (Director). (2015). *Home* [Film]. Heinrich Böll Foundation Beirut–Middle East. https://www.youtube.com/watch?v=cUnUtBFGXCA

Amri Mubasher Syria. (2012a, July 16). ريف حلب الشرقي - منبج - إعلان تشكيل كتيبة جند الحرمين | . [Eastern Aleppo countryside—Manbij—Announcement of the formation of the Jund al-Haramain Battalion] [Video]. YouTube. https://www.youtube.com/watch?v=6FsqC6VvSjM

Amri Mubasher Syria. (2012b, July 21). حلب - منبج الجيش الحر وسط متظاهري المدينة 20-7-2012م [Aleppo—Manbij: Free Syrian Army among city demonstrators, 20-7-2012] [Video]. YouTube. https://www.youtube.com/watch?v=h5nEvCGOwh8

Basma Syria. (2012, November 3). تقرير عن مجلس امناء الثورة في مدينة منبج [Report on the Revolutionary Trustees Council in the city of Manbij] [Video]. YouTube. https://www.youtube.com/watch?v=Szk9CwTiC7E

Basma Syria. (2013, December 16). فتيات الغد الحرفي منبج [Girls of Tomorrow, Manbij] [Video]. YouTube. https://www.youtube.com/watch?v=hL2hzQ0_muo

Bisher albisher. (2013a, August 12). الحراك الثوري في منبج ضمن فعاليات حملة ايثار في مدارس الضيوف شباب [The Revolutionary Youth Movement in Manbij as part of the Ithar campaign activities in guest schools] [Video]. YouTube. https://www.youtube.com/watch?v=karks30lj2c

Bisher albisher. (2013b, August 28). ريف حلب-منبج: مظاهرة حاشدة ضد المجلس الثوري في منبج [Rural Aleppo—Manbij: Mass demonstration against the Revolutionary Council in Manbij] [Video]. YouTube. https://www.youtube.com/watch?v=GUu8ORhC9dM

Documentation Center of the Syrian Revolution. (2012, July 19). تحرير سوريا: فرحة الأهالي بتحرير مدينة منبج 19-7-2012 [Liberation of Syria: Residents' joy at the liberation of Manbij city, 19-7-2012] [Video]. YouTube. https://www.youtube.com/watch?v=P0dJAiUVWtE

Documentation Center for the Syrian Revolution. (2012a, August 13). حلب | الباب - الطيار المجرم النقيب روني ابراهيم راشد [Aleppo | Al-Bab: The criminal pilot Captain Roni Ibrahim Rashid] [Video]. YouTube. https://www.youtube.com/watch?v=GrI5t4vITRU

Documentation Center for the Syrian Revolution. (2012b, August 13). حلب | الباب - الطيار المجرم النقيب روني ابراهيم راشد [Aleppo | Al-Bab: The criminal pilot Captain Roni Ibrahim Rashid] [Video]. YouTube. https://www.youtube.com/watch?v=zpCPlUMIAfg

Ebraheem Arabo. (2013, September 5). شهادة مفصلة لاحد الناجيين من مجزرة البئر في مزرعة الراهب [Detailed testimony of a survivor of the Bir massacre at Mazraat al-Raheb] [Video]. YouTube. https://www.youtube.com/watch?v=ympb71FzRc0

Halab News Network H.N.N. (2013, June 24). ريبورتاج مؤثر عن قرية أم عاموند في ريف حلب HD [Important: Emotional report about the village of Umm Amoud in rural Aleppo HD] [Video]. YouTube. https://www.youtube.com/watch?v=mjF6vjQsbyY

Hussam Al3raqi. (2017, April 25). اقوى 5 مشاهد ل ميماتي باش في وادي الذناب الجزء الثالث [The 5 strongest scenes of Memati Baş in Valley of the Wolves, season 3] [Video]. YouTube. https://www.youtube.com/watch?v=RQIBMqoW750

Ibn al-Ghouta. (2020, June 1). يا يما ولالا هي حمص شو صار بحالا يا يما ولالا [Oh mother, oh Lala, this is Homs—what has happened to it, oh mother, oh Lala] [Video]. YouTube. https://www.youtube.com/watch?v=2b3i3MySfbc

Jurohak bqalbi tadag. (2014, January 5). رتل أسود الشرقية بإتجاه حلب لدك الصحوات بقيادة عمر الشيشاني 5-1-2014 [Eastern Lions convoy toward Aleppo to strike the Sahwat, led by Omar al-Shishani, 5-1-2014], [Video]. YouTube. https://www.youtube.com/watch?v=Mne5Kko0pas

lewa alislam. (2013, July 13). مظاهرة في مدينة منبج تقرع الطبول لتشويه على الدولة الاسلامية بكمرة أعلامي لواء الاسلام [Demonstration in Manbij beating drums to disrupt the Islamic State, filmed by Liwa al-Islam media] [Video]. YouTube. https://www.youtube.com/watch?v=iPBYhlXJyv0

M. al Hamoud. (2012, September 22). الرقة بيان اقتحام بوابة تل أبيض وأسر عدة ضباط وصف ضباط [Raqqa: Statement on the storming of Tal Abyad gate and capture of several officers and non-commissioned officers] [Video]. YouTube. https://www.youtube.com/watch?v=4N95du_quhU

Maktab Ma'adan. (2013, March 3). بدء عملية غارة الجبار في محافظة الرقة [The start of the Ghara al-Jabbar operation in Raqqa Governorate] [Video]. YouTube. https://www.youtube.com/watch?v=qiKIkTxD_6k

WORKS CITED

manbej1. (2014, May 20). محادثة بين أبو لقمان أمير داعش في منبج وعناصره يوم الإضراب في المدينة 2014/5/18 [Conversation between Abu Luqman, ISIS emir in Manbij, and his fighters on the day of the city strike, 18/5/2014] [Video]. YouTube. https://www.youtube.com/watch?v=y98dyeeX36Q

Manbij and Its Countryside Coordination Committee—Local Coordination Committees. (2014, July 1). فلم وثائقي عن مدينة منبج بريف حلب الجزء الاول [Documentary film about the city of Manbij in the Aleppo countryside, part one] [Video]. YouTube. https://www.youtube.com/watch?v=JTYrpa8XuuA

Masasit Matti. (2013, May 15). مصاصة متة: انا بحب التمثيل [I love acting] [Video]. YouTube. https://www.youtube.com/watch?v=K8KXcotIOEM

Moetaz AboRyad. (2013a, January 22). ريف حلب - منبج || تشكيل كتلة رابطة حرائر منبج وريفها لتفعيل دور [Aleppo countryside—Manbij: Formation of the Free Women of Manbij bloc to activate the role of women in the revolution and build Syria's bright future] [Video]. YouTube. https://www.youtube.com/watch?v=XCtwlGgw6Xs

Moetaz AboRyad. (2013b, January 26). منبج || مجزرة نتيجة القصف بصاروخ فراغي [Manbij: Massacre as a result of vacuum missile bombing 1/26/2013] [Video]. YouTube. https://www.youtube.com/watch?v=STISQkAI8vU

Mohammad Dheeb Bakkar. (2014, January 6). اقتحام عناصر الكتيبة الأمنية مع ثوار منبج لمبنى الخدمات الفنية وتحريره من داعش [Storming of the Technical Services building in Manbij by Security Battalion members and revolutionaries, liberating it from ISIS] [Video]. YouTube. https://www.youtube.com/watch?v=m6fePT1K7bU

Orient News. (2013a, June 22). مجزرة في منبج بحلب [Massacre in Manbij, Aleppo] [Video]. YouTube. https://www.youtube.com/watch?v=Ox9EMTQGFjw

Orient News. (2013b, September 6). ريف الرقة: معاناة أهالي بلدة حلبية بسبب القصف والنزوح [Raqqa countryside: Suffering of Halabiya residents due to shelling and displacement] [Video]. YouTube. https://www.youtube.com/watch?v=0kvKTSjDVFQ

Radio AlKul. (2016, August 24). "Radio Alkul" يكشف عن تفاصيل جريمة قتل أب لولديه في ريف حلب [Radio Alkul" reveals details of a father killing his two children in Aleppo countryside] [Video]. YouTube. https://www.youtube.com/watch?v=9NRK-5JEw-Y

Raqqa News Network. (2012, November 3). الرقة منح الأمان للعساكر اثناء تحرير معبر تل ابيض [Raqqa: Granting safety to soldiers during the liberation of the Tal Abyad crossing] [Video]. YouTube. https://www.youtube.com/watch?v=qyBx4N5nNtg

Resala Post. (2019, June 11). لحظة إعلان موت حافظ الأسد [The moment of announcing the death of Hafez al-Assad] [Video]. YouTube. https://www.youtube.com/watch?v=cUlBw7aqdDE

SHAAMSNN. (2014, January 17). ريف حلب منبج آثار الدمار جراء انفجار سيارة مفخخة يوم أمس 17 1 2014 [Rural Aleppo, Manbij: Effects of destruction from a car bomb explosion yesterday, 17-1-2014] [Video]. YouTube. https://www.youtube.com/watch?v=YVFVTuCmHqQ

ShaamNetwork S.N.N. (2011a, April 22). شام - حلب - منبج و مظاهرة الجمعة العظيمة 22-4 [Aleppo—Manbij and the Great Friday demonstration 22-4] [Video]. YouTube. https://www.youtube.com/watch?v=l37zkakFj3I

ShaamNetwork S.N.N. (2011b, April 22). شام - منبج - مظاهرات الجمعة العظيمة 22-4 ج1 [Manbij—Great Friday demonstrations 22-4, Part 1] [Video]. YouTube. https://www.youtube.com/watch?v=TRAtZJfo7B0

ShaamNetwork S.N.N. (2011c, April 23). شام - منبج - مظاهرات الجمعة العظيمة 22-4 [Manbij—Great Friday demonstrations 22-4] [Video]. YouTube. https://www.youtube.com/watch?v=SsHkvvihWzU

ShaamNetwork S.N.N. (2011d, July 15). منبج || مظاهرة جمعة أسرى الحرية 15 7 2011 [Manbij || Demonstration of "Prisoners of Freedom Friday" 15-7-2011] [Video]. YouTube. https://www.youtube.com/watch?v=oxr16nnNlcwA

Shahba Press Agency. (2013, August 30). رسم النفل|| جولة ومقابلات في القرية التي شهدت مجزرة راح ضحيتها 208 أشخاص [Rasm al-Nafl: Tour and interviews in the village that witnessed a massacre claiming 208 lives] [Video]. YouTube. https://www.youtube.com/watch?v=PQTZoK7T6U0

Sky News Arabia. (2013, September 5). بلدة حلبية شبه فارغة بعد نزوح سكانها [Halahiya town nearly empty after residents flee] [Video]. YouTube. https://www.youtube.com/watch?v=R6kw8cnYkf0

syria32011yt. (2011a, May 13). مظاهرة سوريا حرية سلمية [Syria demonstration: Freedom, peaceful] [Video]. YouTube. https://www.youtube.com/watch?v=hOHiwGpuk54

syria32011yt. (2011b, June 29). منبج 29-6-2011 - بركان حلب يبدأ من منبج [Manbij 29-6-2011—The Aleppo volcano begins from Manbij] [Video]. YouTube. https://www.youtube.com/watch?v=jtHVIdj3fqg

SYRIAN AFAK. (2012a, November 23). سهرة لثوار مدينة منبج المحررة [An evening for the revolutionaries of liberated Manbij city] [Video]. YouTube. https://www.youtube.com/watch?v=ww6k2xEvo1c

SYRIAN AFAK. (2012b, December 4). مظاهرة ضد المجلس الثوري في مدينة منبج 4/12/2012 [Demonstration against the Revolutionary Council in the city of Manbij, 4/12/2012] [Video]. YouTube. https://www.youtube.com/watch?v=E7LNQZ0HnIY

Tall Refaat City. (2013, May 24). ريف حلب _"السفيرة"_ عودة شباب قرية القبتين الى بيوتهم بعد خروج عصابات الأسد منها 24-05-2013م [Aleppo countryside ("al-Safira"): Youth return to Qubatein village after Assad forces leave, 24-05-2013] [Video]. YouTube. https://www.youtube.com/watch?v=nDou0XZwk6o

The Permanent Page of President Bashar al-Assad. (2013, October 12). وثائقي من الميدان الطريق الى خناصر بطولات الجيش العربي السوري 12 10 2013 [Documentary from the field: The road to Khanasser, heroics of the Syrian Arab Army, 12-10-2013] [Video]. YouTube. https://www.youtube.com/watch?v=GoC3V9tpDyA

UgaritNews—Syria. (2011, September 3). منبج حلب , اعتصام للشباب أمام فرع الأمن العسكري للمطالبة بالمعتقلين ج1 [Manbij, Aleppo: Youth sit-in in front of the Military Security Branch demanding the release of detainees, Part 1] [Video]. YouTube. https://www.youtube.com/watch?v=JIJ4Ko8Bm8k

Ugarit News. (2012a, March 16). أوغاريت منبج حلب , انشقاق الملازم عبد الوهاب 16 3 Manbej Aleppo الخلف [Manbij, Aleppo: Ugarit—Defection of Lieutenant Abdul Wahab al-Khalaf] [Video]. YouTube. https://www.youtube.com/watch?v=JdsdWxl9BAw

Ugarit News. (2012b, December 30). أوغاريت منبج حلب , معرض كاريكتر ثوري [Ugarit Manbij Aleppo, revolutionary caricature exhibition] [Video]. YouTube. https://www.youtube.com/watch?v=BYnRl47iRGU

Umayyad Live Syria. (2012, September 26). اقتحام الطابق الثالث في المعبر الحدودي في تل ابيض [Storming the third floor at the border crossing in Tal Abyad] [Video]. YouTube. https://www.youtube.com/watch?v=DhHLscR_ncM

Walat TV. (2013, January 17). تقرير عن مدينة منبج [Report on the city of Manbij] [Video]. YouTube. https://www.youtube.com/watch?v=OGWdedz0EvY

WaSsOoM1. (2011, March 26). مظاهرة سوريا ريف حلب منطقة منبج 26-3-2011 (15).3 [Syria demonstration, Aleppo countryside, Manbij area 26-3-2011 (15)] [Video]. YouTube. https://www.youtube.com/watch?v=0Hsb9DrpBrA

Yasmin al-Safira. (2013, October 15). ريف حلب - السفيرة - جولة في قرية حقلة - 2013/9/20 [Aleppo countryside—al-Safira—Tour of Haqla village—20/9/2013] [Video]. YouTube. https://www.youtube.com/watch?v=lNuvdvi8l4k

Zajil Network. (2012, December 19). ريف حلب -منبج- 18-12-2012- تشكيل المجلس المحلي [Aleppo countryside—Manbij—18-12-2012—Formation of the local council] [Video]. YouTube. https://www.youtube.com/watch?v=DWvjIrKxqko

ALL OTHER WORKS

Ababsa, M. (2015). Agrarian counter-reform in Syria (2000–2010). In R. Hinnebusch & T. Zintl (Eds.), *Syria from reform to revolt: Vol. 1. Political economy and international relations* (pp. 83–107). Syracuse University Press.
Abboud, S. (2015). Locating the "social" in the social market economy. In R. Hinnebusch & T. Zintl (Eds.), *Syria from reform to revolt* (pp. 97–113). Syracuse University Press.
Abou Dehn, A. (2012). عائد من جهنم [Returning from hell] (5th ed.). Dar Jadid.
Aboud, S. (2008). On the brief "Damascus Spring." In J. Azarva, D. Pletka, & M. Rubin (Eds.), *Dissent and reform in the Arab world: Empowering democrats*. American Enterprise Institute.
Abu al-Kheir, S. (2011). *Al-tariq ila Tadmur: Kahf fi al-sahra' (al-dakhil mafqud, wa-l-kharij mawlud, 1981–1986.* الطريق الى تدمر: كهف في الصحراء [The road to Tadmur: A cave in the desert (Who enters is lost, and who leaves is reborn), 1981–1986]. Dar al-Aalam.
Abu-'Uksa, W. (2016). *Freedom in the Arab world: Concepts and ideologies in Arabic thought in the nineteenth century*. Cambridge University Press.
Akkad, Nour. (2010, May 6). Asma Al Assad: Syria's first lady and all-natural beauty (slideshow). HuffPost. https://www.huffpost.com/entry/asma-al-assad-syrias-firs_n_226714
Al Abdeh, M. (2013, November 21). Rebels, Inc. *Foreign Policy*. https://foreignpolicy.com/2013/11/21/rebels-inc
Al Arabiya English. (2011, November 26). Syria's Aleppo Central Prison: A microcosm of Assad's regime. *Al Arabiya English*. https://english.alarabiya.net/articles/2011/11/26/179354
Al-Faraj, A. (2021a, May 2). *Manbij protest history* [Unpublished report].
Al-Faraj, A. (2021b, May 21). *The sit-in at the Manbij public square* [Unpublished].
Al-Faraj, A. (2022a, July 6). *The people of Manbij discuss 1st Lt. Maymati* [Unpublished].
Al-Faraj, A. (2022b, August 31). *The Revolutionary Council elections* [Unpublished report].
Al-Faraj, A. (2023, June 6). *The battle between the Free Army and ISIS* [Unpublished].
Al-Haj Saleh, Y. (2012). *Bil-khalas, ya shabab! 16 'aman fi al-sujun al-suriyya* [At last, young men! Sixteen years in Syrian prisons]. Dar al-Saqi.
Al-Jaba'i, G. (1994). أصابع الموز [*Banana fingers*]. Wizarat al-Thaqafeh Suriye.
Al Jazeera. (2011a, March 20). Syria protests: At least one killed in Daraa. *Al Jazeera*. https://www.aljazeera.com/news/2011/3/20/syria-protests-at-least-one-killed-in-daraa
Al Jazeera. (2011b, December 23). Syria group urges UN action over "massacre." *Al Jazeera*. https://www.aljazeera.com/news/2011/12/23/syria-group-urges-un-action-over-massacre/6
Al Jazeera. (2023, May 19). Assad gets warm welcome as Syria welcomed back into Arab League. *Al Jazeera*. https://www.aljazeera.com/news/2023/5/19/assad-gets-warm-welcome-as-syria-welcomed-back-into-arab-league
Al-Kawakibi, A. R. (2022). *The nature of tyranny: And the devastating results of oppression* (A. Chaikhouni, Trans.; L. T. Goldsmith, Foreword). Oxford University Press.
Al-Khalaf, Q. (2023, July 10). *Profiles of the caliphate in Manbij* [Unpublished].
Al-Khalaf, Q. (2024, January 5). *The Islamic State in Manbij* [Unpublished].
Al-Khalidi, S., & Barrington, L. (2016, August 12). U.S.-backed forces give Islamic State fighters 48 hours to leave Syria's Manbij. Reuters. https://www.reuters.com/article/us-mideast-crisis-syria-islamic-state-idUSKCN10N178/
Al-Khatieb, M. (2014, January 10). Syria's second revolt, against ISIS. *Syria Deeply*. https://deeply.thenewhumanitarian.org/syria/articles/2014/01/10/syrias-second-revolt-against-isis
al-Majlis wa al-Nas (2013, June 1 and June 15). Issues 1 and 3.
al-Masar al-Horr. (2012–2013). Individual issues are cited in the endnotes.
Al-Naji, 'A. (1999). حمامات الدم في سجن تدمر [Bloodbaths in Tadmur prison]. Syrian Human Rights Committee. https://www.shrc.org/wp-content/uploads/2008/07/tadmurbloodbaths.pdf
al-Rai al-Horr. (2013). Individual issues are cited in the endnotes.
Al-Roumi, M. (Director). (2005). *Black iris* [Film].
Al-Sabouni, M. (2016). *The battle for home: The vision of a young architect in Syria*. Thames & Hudson.
Al-Sarraj, M. (2007). كما ينبغي لنهر [As the river should]. Dar al-Arabiya lil-Uloom.

al-Suri al-Horr. (2013, June 28–July 18). Issues 2–4.

Al-Zarier, B., Rateb, A., & Adely, T. (2017, May 18). *Idlib's rebel court system in disarray, says former judge.* Syria Direct. https://syriadirect.org/idlibs-rebel-court-system-in-disarray-says-former-judge/

Alderman, L., Peltier, E., & Saad, H. (2018, March 10). ISIS is coming: How a French company pushed the limits in war-torn Syria. *New York Times.* https://www.nytimes.com/2018/03/10/business/isis-is-coming-how-a-french-company-pushed-the-limits-in-war-torn-syria.html

Ali, A. S. (2016). Manbij: Washington punishes the first city to rebel against ISIS. *Al-Safeer* [Article no longer available online].

Ali, F. (2015). *On the Forgotten Banks of the War.* The Syrian Network for Print Media.

Aljaml. (2012, October 31). ملازم أول عائد إلى الخدمة: السلطات التركية تسهل تهريب الأسلحة إلى سورية [First lieutenant returning to service: Turkish authorities facilitate arms smuggling into Syria]. *Aljaml.* https://www.aljaml.com/node/101022

Almohamad, A., Al-Nabo, A., & Houri, H. (2023). ISIS's impact on Syrian intangible cultural heritage: Marriage customs and rituals in the region of Manbij. *Contemporary Levant*, 8(2), 123–141.

Amiralay, O. (Director). (1974). *Everyday life in a Syrian village* [Film]. General Organization for Cinema.

Amiralay, O. (Director). (2003). *A flood in Baath country* [Film]. Audiovisual Multimedia International Production.

Amnesty International. (1987, December). *Syria: Torture by the security forces* (AI Index: MDE 24/09/87). https://www.amnesty.org/ar/wp-content/uploads/2021/06/mde240091987en.pdf

Amnesty International. (2000, December). *Syria: Health concerns/prisoners in Tadmur prison* (AI Index: MDE 24/24/00). https://www.amnesty.org/fr/wp-content/uploads/2021/06/mde240242000en.pdf

Amnesty International. (2001, September). *Syria: Torture, despair and dehumanization in Tadmur Military Prison* (AI Index: MDE 24/014/2001). https://www.amnesty.org/en/documents/mde24/014/2001/en/

Amnesty International. (2011a, April 8). *Death toll rises amid fresh Syrian protests.* https://www.amnesty.org/en/latest/press-release/2011/04/death-toll-rises-amid-fresh-syrian-protests/

Amnesty International. (2011b, August 23). *Syria's surge of deaths in detention revealed.* https://www.amnesty.org/en/latest/press-release/2011/08/syriae28099s-surge-deaths-detention-revealed/

Amnesty International. (2011c, December 22). *Syria imposes death penalty for arming "terrorists" as civilian massacres continue.* https://www.amnesty.org/en/latest/news/2011/12/syria-imposes-death-penalty-terrorism-civilian-massacres-continue/

Amnesty International. (2012, March). *'I wanted to die': Syria's torture survivors speak out* (Index: MDE 24/016/2012). https://www.amnesty.org.pl/wp-content/uploads/2012/03/2012-03-12_Torture_report_final_with_pictures_and_track_changes.pdf

ANA New Media Association. (2012, December 28). Bloody Bread Friday [Facebook status update]. Facebook [Post no longer available].

ARA News. (2016a, June 4). *US-backed Syrian Democratic Forces advance against ISIS near Manbij, liberate eight villages.* http://aranews.net/2016/06/us-backed-syrian-democratic-forces-advance-isis-near-manbij-liberate-eight-villages/

ARA News. (2016b, June 5). *SDF-led Manbij Military Council cuts off ISIS supply route between Raqqa and Manbij.* http://aranews.net/2016/06/sdf-led-manbij-military-council-cuts-off-isis-supply-route-raqqa-manbij/

Arab Center Washington DC. (2025, February 6). *Liberation from the "human slaughterhouse": A dark history of imprisonment in Syria.* https://arabcenterdc.org/resource/liberation-from-the-human-slaughterhouse-a-dark-history-of-imprisonment-in-syria/

Arendt, H. (1993). *Between past and future: Eight exercises in political thought.* Penguin Books.

Asad, T. (2003). *Formations of the secular: Christianity, Islam, modernity.* Stanford University Press.

Asher-Schapiro, A. (2016, March 15). *The young men who started Syria's revolution speak about Daraa, where it all began.* VICE. https://www.vice.com/en/article/the-young-men-who-started-syrias-revolution-speak-about-daraa-where-it-all-began/

WORKS CITED

Associated Press. (2011, December 1). *UN: Syria now in a civil war.* CBS News. https://www.cbsnews.com/news/un-syria-now-in-a-civil-war/

Association of Detainees and the Missing in Sednaya Prison. (2019, November). *Detention in Sednaya.* https://www.admsp.org/wp-content/uploads/2021/07/sydnaia-en-final-November-s-11-07-2019.pdf

Attum, A. (2012). يسمعون حسيسها [They hear her faint sound]. Al-Moussasa al-Arabia lil-Dirasaat wal Nashr.

Avrahami, Z. (2024, June 24). *EU countries call for renewed ties with Assad regime to stem Syrian refugee tide.* Ynetnews. https://www.ynetnews.com/article/bks2yqcur

Azmeh, S. (2014). The uprising of the marginalised: A socio-economic perspective of the Syrian uprising (LSE Middle East Centre Paper Series No. 06). LSE Middle East Centre.

Baker, A. (2024, December 11). How many people have died in Syria's civil war? *New York Times.* https://www.nytimes.com/2024/12/11/world/middleeast/syria-civil-war-death-toll.html

Bantman, C. (2013). The era of propaganda by the deed. In D. Berry, A. Crossley, & C. Bantman (Eds.), *New perspectives on anarchism, labour and syndicalism: The individual, the national and the transnational* (pp. 93–112). Cambridge Scholars Publishing.

Barnard, A. (2011, May 23). Syria's Rami Makhlouf: The president's cousin and economic powerhouse. *New York Times.* https://www.nytimes.com/2011/05/24/world/middleeast/24makhlouf.html

Batatu, H. (2012). *Syria's peasantry, the descendants of its lesser rural notables, and their politics.* Princeton University Press.

Bayraqdar, F. (2006). خيانات اللغة والصمت [The betrayals of language and silence]. Dar Jadid.

BBC News. (2011a, June 4). *Syria: 'Dozens Killed' as thousands protest in Hama.* https://www.bbc.com/news/world-middle-east-13642917

BBC News. (2011b, June 5). *Syria unrest: 'Deadly clashes' in Jisr al-Shughour.* https://www.bbc.com/news/world-middle-east-13662296

BBC News. (2011c, December 23). *Syria unrest: 'Dozens of bodies found dumped' in Homs.* https://www.bbc.com/news/world-middle-east-16044458

BBC News. (2012a, January 19). *Syria unrest: Jabal al-Zawiya 'massacres.'* https://www.bbc.com/news/world-middle-east-16287450

BBC News. (2012b, June 8). *Houla: How a massacre unfolded.* https://www.bbc.com/news/world-middle-east-18233934

Berlin, I. (1969). *Four essays on liberty.* Oxford University Press.

Blanford, N. (2013, August). The battle for Qusayr: How the Syrian regime and Hizb Allah tipped the balance. *CTC Sentinel, 6*(8). https://ctc.westpoint.edu/the-battle-for-qusayr-how-the-syrian-regime-and-hizb-allah-tipped-the-balance/

Bogardus, K. (2011, August 3). *PR firm worked with Syria on controversial photo shoot.* The Hill. https://thehill.com/business-a-lobbying/98252-pr-firm-worked-with-syria-on-controversial-photo-shoot/

Buck, J. J. (2011, March). Asma al-Assad: A rose in the desert. *Vogue.* https://archive.org/details/a-rose-in-the-desert

C-SPAN. (2011, March 30). *Syria President Bashar al-Assad speech to parliament* [Video]. https://www.c-span.org/program/international-telecasts/syria-president-bashar-al-assad-speech-to-parliament/248525

Calhoun, C., Gaonkar, D. P., & Taylor, C. (2022). *Degenerations of democracy.* Harvard University Press.

Central Intelligence Agency. (1984). *The Ba'th Party of Syria.* https://www.cia.gov/readingroom/docs/CIA-RDP88T00096R000300330001-3.pdf

Clezadlo, A. (2015, December 18). The most unconventional weapon in Syria: Who ar *Washington Post.* https://www.washingtonpost.com/opinions/the-most-unconventional-weapon-in-syria-wheat/2015/12/18/81a0ae0-9cf4-11e5-bce4-708fc33c3200_story.html

CNN Wire Staff. (2012, September 20). *Deaths mounting in Syrian towns; children being tortured, U.N. official says.* CNN. https://www.cnn.com/2012/09/19/world/meast/syria-civil-war

WORKS CITED

Cook, B. I., Anchukaitis, K. J., Touchan, R., Meko, D. M., & Cook, E. R. (2016). Spatiotemporal drought variability in the Mediterranean over the last 900 years. *Journal of Geophysical Research: Atmospheres, 121*(5), 2060–2074.

Coquio, C., Hubrecht, J., Mansour, N., & Mardam-Bey, F. (Eds.). (2021). *Syrie, le pays brûlé: Le livre noir des Assad (1970–2021)* [Syria, the scorched country: The black book of the Assads (1970–2021)]. Actes Sud.

Cowell, A. (2013, June 26). War deaths in Syria said to top 100,000. *New York Times*. https://www.nytimes.com/2013/06/27/world/middleeast/syria.html

Krylov, A. S. (2013). The middle class concept in François Guizot's memoirs (Basic Research Program: Working Papers, National Research University Higher School of Economics). https://www.hse.ru/data/2013/10/31/1283245859/36HUM2013.pdf.

Dabbagh, H. (2007). *Just five minutes: Nine years in the prisons of Syria*. Bayan Khatib.

Dagher, L. (2024, December 12). Origin of the Syrian Revolution flag. *L'Orient Today*. https://today.lorientlejour.com/article/1439477/origin-of-the-syrian-revolution-flag.html

Daher, J. (2017, October 17). *Pluralism lost in Syria's uprising*. Century Foundation. https://tcf.org/content/report/pluralism-lost-syrias-uprising/

Daoudy, M. (2009). The Syrian gender curriculum: Between the lines of the Nationalist Project. In S. Joseph (Ed.), *Gender and Citizenship in the Middle East* (pp. 183–204). Syracuse University Press.

Davison, J., & King, L. (2016, July 7). *U.S.-backed forces drive into Islamic State-held city, monitors say*. Reuters. https://www.reuters.com/article/idUSKCN0ZN1ZZ/

De Elvira, L. R., & Zintl, T. (2014). The end of the Ba'thist social contract in Bashar Al-Asad's Syria: Reading sociopolitical transformations through charities and broader benevolent activism. *International Journal of Middle East Studies, 46*(2), 329–349. https://dx.doi.org/10.1017/S0020743814000130

Deniz, E. (2024, July 3). *Syrian immigrants in Turkey fearful to leave homes after flurry of racist attacks*. Duvar English. https://www.duvarenglish.com/syrian-immigrants-in-turkey-fearful-to-leave-homes-after-flurry-of-racist-attacks-news-63511

Deutsche Welle. (2016, July 23). *Fierce clashes with IS militants in Syria*. https://www.dw.com/en/fighting-in-syrias-town-of-manbij-as-us-backed-forces-battle-is-militants/a-19423432

Dirks, N.B. (2006). *The Scandal of Empire: India and the Creation of Imperial Britain*. Cambridge, MA: Belknap Press.

Drevon, J. (2024). *From jihad to politics: How Syrian jihadis embraced politics*. Oxford University Press.

Dukhan, H. (2022). From shame to pride: The politics of Shawi identity in contemporary Syria. *Middle East Journal of Culture and Communication, 15*(4), 377–384.

Dunqul, A. (1976). لا تصالح [Do not reconcile] (Shimaa Eid, Trans.). Polarabicpoetry. Tumblr. https://www.tumblr.com/polarabicpoetry/91953926521/%D9%84%D8%A7-%D8%AA%D8%B5%D8%A7%D9%84%D8%AD-do-not-reconcile-by-amal-dunqul

European Commission. (n.d.). *Syria: EU trade relations with Syria*. Retrieved June 8, 2025, from https://policy.trade.ec.europa.eu/eu-trade-relationships-country-and-region/countries-and-regions/syria_en

Fadil, K. (1985). في القاع: سنتان في سجن تدمر الصحراوي [In the abyss: Two years in Tadmur desert prison]. Syrian Human Rights Committee. Archived at https://web.archive.org/web/20240422022547/https://www.shrc.org/?p=7502

George, A. (2003). *Syria: Neither bread nor freedom*. Zed Books.

Ghazul, S. (2018, March 2). "ميماتي" الثورة السورية ["Memati" of the Syrian Revolution]. Ayn al-Medina [Article no longer available online].

Global Centre for the Responsibility to Protect. (2012, May 30). *Statement on Houla Massacre, May 2012*. https://www.globalr2p.org/publications/statement-on-houla-massacre-may-2012/1

Gluckstein, D. (2011). *The Paris Commune: A revolution in democracy*. Haymarket Books.

Goha's Nail (2014, Aug. 27). Guest post: Manbij and the Islamic State's Public Administration. Jihadology [Article no longer available online].

Gopal, A. (2020a). The Arab Thermidor. *Catalyst, 4*(2), 85–137. https://catalyst-journal.com/2020/09/the-arab-thermidor

Gopal, A. (2020b, December 21). Clean hands. *New Yorker*. https://www.newyorker.com/magazine/2020/12/21/clean-hands

Gopal, A. (2024, March 18). Invisible city. *New Yorker*. https://www.newyorker.com/magazine/2024/03/18/invisible-city

Gopal, A., & Hodge, J. (2022). Social networks, class, and the Syrian proxy war. In P. Bergen, C. Rondeaux, D. Rothenberg, & D. Sterman (Eds.), *Understanding the new proxy wars: Battlegrounds and strategies reshaping the Greater Middle East*. Hurst Publishers.

Goulden, R. (2011). Housing, inequality, and economic change in Syria. *British Journal of Middle Eastern Studies*, 38(2), 187–202.

Hale, S., Poulson, C., Winslow, E., Mahrousa, M. B., & Alhayes, M. (2023, December). *Creating hope in conflict: A humanitarian grand challenge*. Grand Challenges Canada. https://humanitariangrandchallenge.org/wp-content/uploads/2023/12/Hala-Systems-Outcome-Case-Study.pdf

Hallaq, W. B. (2009a). *An introduction to Islamic law*. Cambridge University Press.

Hallaq, W. B. (2009b). *Sharī'a: Theory, practice, transformations*. Cambridge University Press.

Hammad, M. S. (n.d.). تدمر: شاهد ومشهود [Tadmur: Witness and witnessed]. Syrian Human Rights Committee. https://www.shrc.org/?p=15321

Hilton, D., & al-Aswad, O. (2024, December 16). *Hamza al-Khatib was a symbol of Syria's revolution. His family paid the price*. Middle East Eye. https://www.middleeasteye.net/news/hamza-al-khatib-was-symbol-syrias-revolution-his-family-paid-price

Hinnebusch, R. (1989). *Peasant and bureaucracy in Ba'thist Syria: The political economy of rural development*. Westview.

Hinnebusch, R. (2004). *Syria: Revolution from above*. Routledge.

Hinnebusch, R. (2021). *Authoritarian power and state formation in Bathist Syria: Army, party, and peasant*. Routledge.

Hokayem, E. (2023, May 23). Assad comes in from the cold. *Foreign Affairs*. https://www.foreignaffairs.com/syria/assad-comes-cold

Holes, C. (2004). *Modern Arabic: Structures, functions, and varieties*. Georgetown University Press.

Hornblower, S., & Spawforth, A. (Eds.). (2005). *The Oxford classical dictionary* (3rd ed.). Oxford University Press.

Human Rights Watch. (n.d.). *World prison massacres*. https://www.hrw.org/legacy/advocacy/prisons/killings.htm

Human Rights Watch. (1995, July 1). *Syria: The price of dissent*. https://www.hrw.org/report/1995/07/01/price-dissent

Human Rights Watch. (1996, April 1). *Syria's Tadmor Prison: Dissent still hostage to a legacy of terror*. https://www.hrw.org/report/1996/04/01/syrias-tadmor-prison/dissent-still-hostage-legacy-terror

Human Rights Watch. (1999). *World report 1999: Syria: Human rights developments*. https://www.hrw.org/legacy/worldreport99/mideast/syria.html

Human Rights Watch. (2007, October). *No room to breathe: State repression of human rights activism in Syria*. https://www.hrw.org/reports/2007/syria1007/3.htm

Human Rights Watch. (2011a, March 21). *Syria: Government crackdown leads to protester deaths*. https://www.hrw.org/news/2011/03/21/syria-government-crackdown-leads-to-protester-deaths

Human Rights Watch. (2011b, March 24). *Syria: Security forces kill dozens of protesters*. https://www.hrw.org/news/2011/03/24/syria-security-forces-kill-dozens-protesters

Human Rights Watch. (2011c, June 1). *"We've never seen such horror": Crimes against humanity by Syrian security forces*. https://www.hrw.org/report/2011/06/01/weve-never-seen-such-horror/crimes-against-humanity-syrian-security-forces

Human Rights Watch. (2011d, August 3). *Syria: New assault on Hama*. https://www.hrw.org/news/2011/08/03/syria-new-assault-hama

Human Rights Watch. (2012a, April 9). *In cold blood: Summary executions by Syrian security forces and pro-government militias*. https://www.hrw.org/report/2012/04/09/cold-blood/summary-executions-syrian-security-forces-and-pro-government-militias

Human Rights Watch. (2012b, May 27). *Syria: UN inquiry should investigate Houla killings*. https://www.hrw.org/news/2012/05/27/syria-un-inquiry-should-investigate-houla-killings

Human Rights Watch. (2012c, December 13). *Delivered into enemy hands: US-led abuse and rendition of opponents to Gaddafi's Libya*. https://www.hrw.org/report/2012/09/05/delivered-enemy-hands/us-led-abuse-and-rendition-opponents-gaddafis-libya

Human Rights Watch. (2013, September 10). *Attacks on Ghouta: Analysis of alleged use of chemical weapons in Syria*. https://www.hrw.org/report/2013/09/10/attacks-ghouta/analysis-alleged-use-chemical-weapons-syria

Human Rights Watch. (2015, December 16). *Syria: Stories behind photos of killed detainees*. https://www.hrw.org/news/2015/12/16/syria-stories-behind-photos-killed-detainees

Institute of Medicine. (2010). *Mitigating the nutritional impacts of the global food price crisis*. National Academies Press. https://doi.org/10.17226/12698

International, Impartial and Independent Mechanism (IIIM). (2024, December). *The Syrian government detention system as a tool of violent repression* [Public redacted version]. United Nations. https://iiim.un.org/wp-content/uploads/2024/12/IIIM_DetentionReport_Public.pdf

IRIN News. (2008). Syria: Wealth gap widening as inflation hits poor. *New Humanitarian*. https://www.thenewhumanitarian.org/report/76607/syria-wealth-gap-widening-inflation-hits-poor

Jadaliyya (2011, May 31). *Funeral of tortured Syrian child Hamza al-Khatib (video)*. https://www.jadaliyya.com/Details/24045

al-Tamimi, A. J. (2021, February). Hafez al-Assad's speech on the seventeenth anniversary of the Ba'athist revolution (1980). *Aymenn Jawad Al-Tamimi's Blog*. https://aymennjawad.org/2021/02/hafez-al-assad-speech-on-the-seventeenth

Johnston, P. B., Shapiro, J. N., Shatz, H. J., Bahney, B., Jung, D. F., Ryan, P. K., & Wallace, J. (2016). *Foundations of the Islamic State: Management, money, and terror in Iraq, 2005–2010*. RAND Corporation.

Kelley, C. P., Mohtadi, S., Cane, M. A., Seager, R., & Kushnir, Y. (2015). Climate change in the Fertile Crescent and implications of the recent Syrian drought. *Proceedings of the National Academy of Sciences, 112*(11), 3241–3246.

Khaddour, K., & Mazur, K. (2017, February). *Eastern expectations: The changing dynamics in Syria's tribal regions*. Carnegie Middle East Center. https://carnegieendowment.org/research/2017/02/eastern-expectations-the-changing-dynamics-in-syrias-tribal-regions?lang=en

Khalifa, K. (2014). *In praise of hatred* (L. Price, Trans.). St. Martin's Press.

Khalifa, M. (2023). *The Shell*. (P. Starkey, Trans.). Interlink Books.

Khatib, L. (2011). *Islamic revivalism in Syria: The rise and fall of Ba'thist secularism*. Routledge.

Kilcullen, D., & Rosenblatt, N. (2014). The rise of Syria's urban poor: Why the war for Syria's future will be fought over the country's new urban villages. *PRISM, 4*, 33–45.

Koelbl, S. (2005, February 21). Syria: A 101 course in Mideast dictatorships. *Der Spiegel International*. https://www.spiegel.de/international/spiegel/syria-a-101-course-in-mideast-dictatorships-a-343242.html

Landis, J. (2011, March 31). Speech to the Syrian Parliament by President Bashar al-Assad: Wednesday, March 30, 2011. *Syria Comment*. https://joshualandis.com/blog/speech-to-the-syrian-parliament-by-president-bashar-al-assad-wednesday-march-30-2011/

Lear, J. (2006). *Radical hope: Ethics in the face of cultural devastation*. Harvard University Press.

Lewis, N. N. (1987). *Nomads and settlers in Syria and Jordan, 1800–1980*. Cambridge University Press.

Loveluck, L., & Mekhennet, S. (2019, September 3). Tension, fear and violence in Syria's al-Hol displacement camp. *Washington Post*. https://www.washingtonpost.com/world/at-a-sprawling-tent-camp-in-syria-isis-women-impose-a-brutal-rule/2019/09/03/3fcdfd14-c4ea-11e9-8bf7-cde2d9e09055_story.html

Lutsky, V. B. (1969). *Modern history of the Arab countries* (L. Nasser, Trans.). Progress Publishers.

MacFarquhar, N. (2011, March 20). Officers fire on crowd as Syrian protests grow. *New York Times*. https://www.nytimes.com/2011/03/21/world/middleeast/21syria.html

MacFarquhar, N. (2012, July 18). Syrian rebels land deadly blow to Assad's inner circle. *New York Times*. https://www.nytimes.com/2012/07/19/world/middleeast/syrian-rebels-land-deadly-blow-to-assads-inner-circle.html

MacIntyre, A. (2007). *After virtue: A study in moral theory* (3rd ed.). University of Notre Dame Press.

Maias, M. (Director). (1998). فوق الرمل، تحت الشمس [*Over the sand, under the sun*] [Film].

WORKS CITED

Mapping MENA. (2024a). *Aleppo Central Prison.* https://mappingmena.org/map/syria/aleppo-central-prison

Mapping MENA. (2024b). *Mezzeh Prison.* https://mappingmena.org/map/syria/mezzeh-prison

Mark, J. J. (2011, March 6). The Atrahasis epic: The great flood & the meaning of suffering. World History Encyclopedia. https://www.worldhistory.org/article/227/the-atrahasis-epic-the-great-flood--the-meaning-of/

Martínez, J. C., & Eng, B. (2015, February 4). Syria feature: The Assad regime's bread crisis. EA WorldView. https://eaworldview.com/2015/02/syria-feature-assad-regimes-bread-crisis/

Marx, K. (2020). *The eighteenth Brumaire of Louis Bonaparte* (S. K. Padover, Trans.). Verso. (Original work published 1852)

McAdam, D. (1988). *Freedom summer.* Oxford University Press.

Mohammad, H. (Director). (2006). Rihla ila al-dhakira [*A journey into memory*] [Film].

Moore, J., & Netjes, R. (2016, October 15). Exclusive: Private ISIS letter outlines group's merciless tactics ahead of Mosul battle. *Newsweek.* https://www.newsweek.com/2016/10/28/exclusive-isis-letter-merciless-mosul-tactics-battle-iraq-508719.html

Mu'as'as, R. (2012). [حمام زنوبيا] [Zenoubia's bath]. Dar al-Janoub.

Munif, Y. (2020). *The Syrian Revolution: Between the politics of life and the geopolitics of death.* Pluto Press.

Munif, Y. (2021, October 27). *The Syrian revolt and the politics of bread.* Transnational Institute. https://www.tni.org/en/article/the-syrian-revolt-and-the-politics-of-bread

Naddaff, A. J. (2017, September 5). Pixels of war: Photographing the house of Assad. *Syria Deeply.* https://deeply.thenewhumanitarian.org/syria/community/2017/09/05/photographing-the-house-of-assad

NBC News. (2011, April 19). *Syria to lift decades-old emergency laws.* https://www.nbcnews.com/id/wbna42660660

Nefi, H. (2023, January 14). لا تصالح [Don't reconcile]. Syria TV. https://www.syria.tv/%D9%84%D8%A7-%D8%AA%D8%B5%D8%A7%D9%84%D8%AD-0

New Arab. (2016, August 13). *Thousands of victims of Tel al-Zaatar massacre still missing.* https://www.newarab.com/features/thousands-victims-tel-al-zaatar-massacre-still-missing

Niazi, T. (2025, January 9). *The drought that felled Assad.* Foreign Policy in Focus. https://fpif.org/the-drought-that-fell-assad/

Nietzsche, F. (2006). *On the genealogy of morals* (W. Kaufmann & R. J. Hollingdale, Trans.). Vintage Books. (Original work published 1887)

Obama, B., & Friedman, T. L. (2014, August 8). President Obama talks to Thomas L. Friedman about Iraq and world affairs. *New York Times.* https://www.nytimes.com/2014/08/09/opinion/president-obama-thomas-l-friedman-iraq-and-world-affairs.html

Ober, J. (1996). *The Athenian revolution: Essays on ancient Greek democracy and political theory.* Princeton University Press.

Office of the United Nations High Commissioner for Human Rights. (2011, August 16). *Report of the United Nations High Commissioner for Human Rights on the situation of human rights in the Syrian Arab Republic* (A/HRC/18/53). https://www.ohchr.org/Documents/countries/SY/Syria_Report_2011-08-17.pdf

O'Gorman, N. (2020). *Politics for everybody: Reading Hannah Arendt in uncertain times.* University of Chicago Press.

Olson, M. (1974). *The logic of collective action: Public goods and the theory of groups* (2nd ed.). Harvard University Press.

Orient News. (2013, August 17). مؤسسة المسار الحر تقيم مهرجان "عام على الحرية" بمدينة منبج [Al-Masar Al-Horr Foundation organizes "A Year of Freedom" festival in Manbij]. https://orient-news.net/ar/news_show/4903

Oweis, K. Y. (2011, March 10). *In Syria's parched farmlands, echoes of Egyptian woes.* Reuters. https://www.reuters.com/article/world/in-syrias-parched-farmlands-echoes-of-egyptian-woes-idUSTRE72910H/

Panorama. (2013). Individual issues are cited in the endnotes.

Pettit, P. (1997). *Republicanism: A theory of freedom and government.* Oxford University Press.

Podsiadlo, E. (1966). Iraq's vital rivers of antiquity. *Arab World,* 12(7), 12–15.

Prothero, M. (2015, September 16). U.S. training helped mold top Islamic State's top military commander. *Miami Herald.* https://www.miamiherald.com/news/nation-world/world/article35327940.html

Qabbani, N. (n.d.). *The impossible love* [Arabic poem]. Arabic.fi. https://arabic.fi/poems/38

Qatar Shares (2010, May 20). *A father in the countryside of Aleppo kills his four children.* https://www.qatarshares.com/vb/showthread.php?366944-%C3%C8-%DD%ED-%D1%ED%DD-%CD%E1%C8-%ED%DE%CA%E1-%C3%E6%E1%C7%CF%E5-%C7%E1%C3%D1%C8%DA%C9-%D5%E6%D1-%E3%C4%E1%E3%E5

Qena, N. (2012, September 20). *Syrian rebels seize border crossing with Turkey: Strategic boost allows fighters to ferry supplies into the country.* Associated Press. https://www.timesofisrael.com/syrian-rebels-seize-border-crossing-with-turkey/

Rammal, S. (2019). Education in Syrian state schools before 2011 (Jenine Abboushi, Trans.). *Syria and its people* (Research paper series). Tarikhi. https://tarikhi.org/wp-content/uploads/2019/08/Education-English.pdf

Reed, S. (1984, February 19). Syria's Assad: His power and his plan. *New York Times.* https://www.nytimes.com/1984/02/19/magazine/syria-s-assad-his-power-and-his-plan.html

Reuters. (2016, July 23). *Islamic State shuns withdrawal offer in surrounded Syrian city.* https://www.reuters.com/article/world/islamic-state-shuns-withdrawal-offer-in-surrounded-syrian-city-idUSKCN1030BO/

Robinson, E., Johnston, P. B., Mann, S., Egel, D., Rothenberg, A. D., & Stebbins, D. (2017). *When the Islamic State comes to town: The economic impact of Islamic State governance in Iraq and Syria.* RAND Corporation.

Rogin, J. (2021, October 7). Biden is tacitly endorsing Assad's normalization. *Washington Post.* https://www.washingtonpost.com/opinions/2021/10/07/biden-is-tacitly-endorsing-assads-normalization/

Rudaw. (2016, August 8). *SDF offer ISIS passage out of Manbij if they release civilians.* https://www.rudaw.net/english/middleeast/syria/080820162

Salem, M. (2024, November 28). *Syria's rebels, government and Iran: What's behind the new escalation?* CNN. https://edition.cnn.com/2024/11/28/europe/syria-rebels-government-iran-analysis-intl/index.html

Samawi, H. (2024, May 5). *A testimony of the final battle between SDF and ISIS* [Unpublished].

Sarraj, B. (2016). من تدمر إلى هارفارد [From Tadmur to Harvard]. CreateSpace Independent Publisher.

Saul, J. (2021). *Collective trauma, collective healing.* Routledge Mental Health Classic Editions. Taylor & Francis.

Schmitt, E. (2012, June 21). C.I.A. said to aid in steering arms to Syrian opposition. *New York Times.* https://www.nytimes.com/2012/06/21/world/middleeast/cia-said-to-aid-in-steering-arms-to-syrian-rebels.html

Selby, J., Dahi, O. S., Fröhlich, C., & Hulme, M. (2017). Climate change and the Syrian civil war revisited. *Political Geography, 60,* 232–244.

Sells, M. (Trans.). (2011). *Abundance from the desert: Classical Arabic poetry.* Syracuse University Press.

Sen, K., & al Faisal, W. (2012). Syria neoliberal reforms in health sector financing: Embedding unequal access? *Social Medicine, 6*(3), 171–182.

Shahin, K. (2024, June 27). The disintegration of Assad's army. *New Lines Magazine.* https://newlinesmag.com/reportage/the-disintegration-of-assads-army/

Shams al-Horreya. (2012–2013). Individual issues are cited in the endnotes.

Stace, W. T. (1955). *The philosophy of Hegel.* Dover Publications.

Stockman, F. (2011, July 3). Syrian regime enlisted local firm for activism training. *Boston Globe.* http://archive.boston.com/news/nation/washington/articles/2011/07/03/syrian_regime_enlisted_local_firm_for_activism_training/

Syrian Arab News Agency (2011, June 20). *Speech of H.E. President Bashar al-Assad at Damascus University on the situation in Syria* [Article no longer available online].

Syrian Center for Policy Research. (2013, January 30). *Socioeconomic roots and impact of the Syrian crisis.* https://scpr-syria.org/wp-content/uploads/2024/08/SCPR_Syria_Crisis_Report_2013_EN.pdf

Syrian Human Rights Committee. (2007, June 27). *The Tadmur (Palmyra) prison massacre on its 27th anniversary.* https://www.shrc.org/en/?p=20458

Syrian Network for Human Rights. (2013, July 8). *Prisoners and the events of Aleppo Central Prison.* https://snhr.org/blog/2013/07/08/prisoners-and-the-events-of-aleppo-central-prison/

Syrian Observatory for Human Rights. (2016, June 10). *The Syria Democratic Forces control 75 villages and farms and get closer to Manbej city and more casualties in Coalition's airstrikes.* https://www.syriahr.com/en/46880/

Syrian Revolution. (2014, May 18). [Twenty-six martyrs were killed in Aleppo and its countryside on Wednesday . . .]. Facebook. https://www.facebook.com/Syrian.Revolution/photos/a.10150397575815727.619133.420796315726/10152544145845727

Taleghani, R. S. (2021). *Readings in Syrian prison literature: The poetics of human rights.* Syracuse University Press.

Taub, B. (2016, April 18). The Assad files. *New Yorker.* https://www.newyorker.com/magazine/2016/04/18/bashar-al-assads-war-crimes-exposed

Terc, A. P. (2011). *Syria's new neoliberal elite: English usage, linguistic practices and group boundaries* [Doctoral dissertation, University of Michigan].

Triebert, C. (2016, July 6). An open source analysis of the Fallujah "convoy massacre"(s). Bellingcat. https://www.bellingcat.com/news/mena/2016/07/06/an-open-source-analysis-of-the-fallujah-convoy-massacres/

Turkish Minute. (2024, September 21). *Pro-Turkish forces detain 18 in Syria for protesting Ankara's possible rapprochement with Damascus.* https://turkishminute.com/2024/09/21/pro-turkish-forces-detained-18-syria-for-protest-ankara-possible-rapprochement-with-damascus/

United Nations General Assembly. (1948). *Convention on the prevention and punishment of the crime of genocide.* United Nations Treaty Series, 78, 277.

United Nations Human Rights Council. (2014). *Report of the independent international commission of inquiry on the Syrian Arab Republic.* https://www.ohchr.org/en/hr-bodies/hrc/iici-syria/report-independent-international-commission-inquiry-syrian-arab-republic

United Nations Security Council. (2017). *Letter dated 13 January 2017 from the Chair of the Security Council Committee pursuant to resolutions 1267 (1999), 1989 (2011) and 2253 (2015) concerning Islamic State in Iraq and the Levant (Da'esh), Al-Qaida and associated individuals, groups, undertakings and entities addressed to the President of the Security Council* (S/2017/35). United Nations. https://undocs.org/S/2017/35

U.S. Embassy Damascus. (2008, November 26). *2008 UN drought appeal for Syria* (ID 08DAMASCUS847_a) [Diplomatic cable]. WikiLeaks. https://wikileaks.org/plusd/cables/08DAMASCUS847_a.html

Walsh, D. (2011, August 11). Exclusive: A visit to Hama, the rebel Syrian city that refused to die. *TIME Magazine.* https://time.com/archive/6952700/exclusive-a-visit-to-hama-the-rebel-syrian-city-that-refused-to-die/

Wedeen, L. (2019). *Authoritarian apprehensions: Ideology, judgment, and mourning in Syria.* University of Chicago Press.

Weekly Letters. (2013). Individual issues are cited in the endnotes.

Weismann, I. (2015). *Abd al-Rahman al-Kawakibi: Islamic reform and Arab revival.* Oneworld Publications.

Wilkinson, T., & Peltenburg, E. (2009). Long-term landscape and settlement studies. *Bulletin of the Council for British Research in the Levant,* 4(1), 33–49.

Winters, P. (Director). (2001). *Damming the Euphrates* [Film]. Ajans 21; Kinomad Productions. https://www.archaeologychannel.org/en/video-guide-summary/229-damming-the-euphrates

World Vision. (2025, July 1). *Syrian refugee crisis: Facts, FAQs, and how to help.* https://www.worldvision.org/refugees-news-stories/syrian-refugee-crisis-facts

Worth, R. F. (2012, October 6). Citing U.S. fears, Arab allies limit Syrian rebel aid. *New York Times.* https://www.nytimes.com/2012/10/07/world/middleeast/citing-us-fears-arab-allies-limit-aid-to-syrian-rebels.html

Young, M. (2017, August 21). The triumph of politicide. *Diwan* [blog]. Carnegie Middle East Center. https://carnegieendowment.org/middle-east/diwan/2017/08/the-triumph-of-politicide?lang=en

Yovitchitch, C. (2010). Qal'at Najm: A fortress and a castle on the shores of the Euphrates. *Chronos,* (23), 69–87.

Zenko, M., & Wolf, A. M. (2014, April 1). *Syria civil war total fatalities.* Council on Foreign Relations. https://www.cfr.org/blog/syria-civil-war-total-fatalities

NOTES

PREFACE

vii **These men and women:** I'm grateful to Christopher Hill's book on the English civil war, *The World Turned Upside Down*, for this phrase.

BOOK 1: ONE

Note: In 2019, I commissioned A. H. H., who is from Little Hyena, to produce an in-depth ethnographic report on his village. Below, I refer to it as the Little Hyena Report. He drew from his own recollections and interviews he conducted with friends and relatives. The final report contained demographic data, maps, photographs, and details of various aspects of village life, including courtship, marriage, food preparation, fishing and farming practices, schooling, and leisure.

3 **Every afternoon:** The village's official name is Dabaa Saghireh (ضبعة صغيرة), which I've translated as Little Hyena.

3 **It was an undulating country:** This description is based on my visits.

3 **Just up the river:** This description is based on my visit. See also Yovitchitch (2010).

4 **Here and there one could:** See, for example, Wilkinson & Peltenburg (2009).

4 **A trace of that memory:** See Mark (2011).

4 **In the beginning:** This translation is from Mark (2011).

5 **The tax-hungry Ottomans:** This history is drawn from the Flood Interview corpus; Podsiadlo (1966); Lewis (1987); and Batatu (2012).

5 **The schoolhouse Ibrahim went to:** "Mr. Weiss" is a pseudonym.

5 **Mr. Faraj, who lectured:** A pseudonym.

5 **Mr. Jalal could read:** A pseudonym.

6 **They doted on Adam:** A pseudonym.

6 **From there, he could:** Ibrahim's recollection; corroborated more generally by Flood Interview corpus home videos.

7 **A house was going up:** These details are from the Little Hyena Report and the Flood Interview corpus.

8 **The Crossing had always:** Flood Interview corpus.

8 **They sat on donkeys:** Little Hyena Report, village map.

8 **Under the brilliant noonday sun:** Flood Interview corpus (interview with Samira's friend).

8 **listening to the cicadas:** This description is based on my visit and Ibrahim's description of a typical summer night, as well as his recollections of that night.

9 **He saw salmon, mullet, catfish:** Ibrahim's recollection. The Flood Interview corpus confirms the presence of these fish more generally.

9 **Marwan, the tailor:** A pseudonym.

9 **Illuminated by the pale glow:** Flood Interview corpus (interview with wedding participant).

10 **The *taama* was dialect:** Little Hyena Report.

11 **Manbij named Muhandas:** A pseudonym. Information on the family and its feudal relations is from the Flood Interview corpus.

11 **Overseers meted out beatings:** Flood Interview corpus; Manbij Flood corpus.

11 **The intellectuals, on the other hand:** Details on the Baath Party and the area's transition from feudalism are drawn from the Flood Interview corpus; Manbij Flood corpus; and Hinnebusch (1989, 2004, and 2021).

NOTES

12 **One day in the 1960s:** Flood Interview corpus; Manbij Flood corpus.
12 **The government now provided:** See also Hinnebusch (1989).
12 **Workers completed the Euphrates Dam:** *Tishreen* (Feb 3, 1985) "Euphrates Dam a Big Achievement for al-Asad Leadership. President Hafiz al-Asad: 'We wanted the Euphrates dam as a way of supporting our economy and a means to a basic change in the life of our society.'"
13 **She'd loop around the Luqman house:** "Luqman" is a pseudonym. Flood Interview corpus.
13 **Ibrahim set off:** I was able to see this (now submerged) dirt path from a boat.
14 **One day that winter, Abu Talib:** This scene is based on an interview with Abu Talib's son from the Flood Interview corpus.
14 **Ibrahim's grandfather told him:** Detail from an interview with Ibrahim and from the Flood Interview corpus.
14 **His friend Muaz's grandfather:** Manbij Flood corpus.
14 **One day, Mayor Rahman:** This scene is from an interview with Ibrahim, corroborated by the Flood Interview corpus.
15 **Soon, a pair of villagers:** Flood Interview corpus.
15 **A theory developed:** Flood Interview corpus.
15 **They established camp at:** Interview with Hajji Ahmed in the Manbij Flood corpus.
15 **The air of intrigue:** Flood Interview corpus.
17 **Hamad household:** A pseudonym. Manbij Flood corpus.
17 **Citing the coming dam:** Manbij Flood corpus.
17 **Once, Ibrahim's father:** This scene is from Ibrahim's recollection, and could not be independently corroborated. But interviews in the Abel Os corpus (see chapter 3 notes) contain very similar stories.
18 **When he arrived at:** Ibrahim's recollection, corroborated by the Flood Interview corpus.
18 **The Hasans had decamped:** Manbij Flood corpus.
18 **His friend Muaz:** Manbij Flood corpus.
18 **But many families:** Manbij Flood corpus.
18 **The sun had set, the massifs:** Ibrahim pointed it out to me as we stood on a nearby spot.
18 **Not long after, a flatbed:** Manbij Flood corpus.
18 **At night, the only sounds:** "The village became a ghost town where only the sounds of tree branches and leaves shaken by the wind were heard at night," from the Manbij Flood corpus.
19 **Abu Talib had rigged:** This scene is based on an interview with Abu Talib's son, in the Flood Interview corpus.
19 **Ibrahim was in the orchard:** For further context on the flood, I drew from several films: Amiralay (1974, 2003), Winters (2001), and al-Roumi (2005).
19 **In the early-morning:** Manbij Flood corpus.
19 **Now it was lapping:** Manbij Flood corpus; Flood Interview corpus.
20 **Everywhere, villagers were escaping:** Manbij Flood corpus; Flood Interview corpus.
20 **In the afternoon, serpents appeared:** Manbij Flood corpus. For example, an interviewee said, "These snakes used to live on the banks of the river, they were not water snakes. When the water rose, these snakes escaped from the water and they came toward the village. There were hundreds of them."
20 **An ox stood rooted:** Manbij Flood corpus. An interviewee said, "[It was] almost completely immersed in the mud and [we] tried to get it out, it was submissive to its fate and completely exhausted."
20 **Up and down the road:** This scene is from multiple interviews in the Manbij Flood corpus.
20 **Some families were gathered at the graveyard:** Manbij Flood corpus. Another interviewee said, "Others didn't move their dead, so the dead stayed under the debris and water."
20 **Abdul Rauf, who lived near the grocer:** From Ibrahim's recollection. Abdul Rauf could not be located, but the Manbij Flood corpus tells of similar scenes.
21 **His friend Rami decided to swim:** This scene is from an interview with Rami (a pseudonym), contained in the Manbij Flood corpus and corroborated by others in the corpus.
21 **Ibrahim sat with his mother:** Ibrahim's recollections; Manbij Flood corpus.
21 **The main road was strewn with snakes:** Manbij Flood corpus. An interviewee said, "The snakes were numb or dead because of the intense power of the water waves."

NOTES

21 **The mayor of a nearby town:** Manbij Flood corpus.
22 **Soon the main road:** Manbij Flood corpus.
22 **For ten days after:** Ibrahim's recollection; Manbij Flood corpus.
22 **Some fifty villages now lay:** Through the Manbij Flood corpus and the Flood Interview corpus, my research team was able to confirm fifty-four flooded villages.
23 **The people of Little Hyena:** Manbij Flood corpus.

BOOK 1: TWO

24 **Hasan Nefi's greatest fear:** Unless otherwise noted, the primary source for all material in this chapter is Hasan Nefi. His experiences were corroborated by several key sources, including, in childhood, two friends who asked to remain anonymous: M. J. and N. O. Additional corroboration was provided by Huzayfa al-Osman (Manbij Protesters corpus).
25 **If I'm ever mistreated:** See Sells (2011).
25 **Hasan's father would:** Hasan said: "His hands were like sandpaper."
25 **Whereas traditional English poetry:** See Holes (2004).
26 **One hot March morning in 1980:** The account of the early 1980s regime incursions into Manbij is supported by Faruq Sheikh Weiss (MRC corpus), who was linked to the Muslim Brotherhood and experienced those events, and by Abu Tayyeb, another witness (RYM corpus).
27 **He discovered that the army:** See, for example, New Arab (2016).
27 **In exchange for this beneficence:** For more on this social compact, see Gopal (2020).
28 **On the right were:** See Batatu (2012).
29 **On the grounds of the University of Aleppo:** This description is based on photographs and my visit.
32 **"Name":** There are no available corroborating witnesses to these interrogations, but they echo numerous contemporaneous reports from human rights investigations and interviews with other prisoners. See, for example, Amnesty International (1987).
34 **They had a comrade:** A pseudonym.
34 **He recognized that his life:** Hasan said, "I saw no future, only an endless tunnel."

34 **Five years passed in a cell:** Important corroborating information for these years in Aleppo Central Prison is drawn from al-Haj Saleh (2012). Al-Haj Saleh shared a cell with Hasan. Additional corroboration is also from Coquio, et al (2021). The descriptions of the cell and the prison are based on my visit and Hasan's recollections.
34 **There were communists:** al-Haj Saleh (2012).
35 **He was living:** The shape of the building is visible in Mapping MENA (2024a).
36 **"Why do you think ruling":** Quoted in Reed (1984).
36 **Syria's prison archipelago:** For details on Mezzeh Prison, see Mapping MENA (2024b).
36 **A stay at the two-story:** On Hafez al-Assad's reported imprisonment in Mezzeh, see George (2003).
36 **The Baathist government added:** Association of Detainees and the Missing in Sednaya Prison (2019). On CIA renditions, see Human Rights Watch (2012c). On the Palmyra massacre, see Syrian Human Rights Committee (2007).
37 **These imaginative wanderings:** I am grateful to Stace (1955) for informing my understanding of Hegel.
39 **Hasan awoke to shouting:** I've drawn on dozens of sources to corroborate and amplify Hasan's account of his time in Palmyra (Tadmur Prison, in Arabic). Key sources included memoirs of ex-prisoners: Hammad, M. S. (n.d.), Fadil (1985), al-Naji (1992), Bayraqdar (2006), Dabbagh (2007), Abu al-Kheir (2011), Abou Dehn (2012), and Sarraj (2016); and novels or other fiction written by former prisoners: al-Jaba'i (1994), al-Sarraj (2007), Attum (2012), Mu'as'as (2012), Khalifa (2014), and Khalifa (2023). I also benefited from two films about Tadmur prison: Maias (1998) and Mohammad (2006).

Human rights organizations have also documented many of the forms of torture that Hasan experienced. Key sources include Amnesty International (1987, 2000, and 2001) and Human Rights Watch (n.d., 1995, 1996, 1999). I am grateful to the Syrian Human Rights Committee (https://www.shrc.org/), which has curated some of these sources, as well as Taleghani (2021), from whom I found a number of these sources.

I also made use of the Facebook group "Diaries of Sednaya Prison" (https://www.facebook.com/groups/alhwarr) and the "Network of Survivors of Tadmur Prison" (https://www.facebook.com/groups/999282009021747), both of which contain testimonies of those who were interned in Palmyra prison. Finally, I visited the prison itself, from which I drew several descriptions.

39 **They pulled up to:** This description is based on Hasan's recollection. It was still pastel-colored when I visited.

39 **On one wall was painted:** This description is based on my visit.

39 **"You missed the Welcome Party":** On the Welcome Party, see the International, Impartial and Independent Mechanism (2024).

40 **His group was led:** This description is based on my visit.

41 **After breakfast came recess:** On Breathing Time, see, for example, Bayraqdar (2006).

42 **On occasion, a prisoner:** On the German Chair, see Amnesty International (2012).

44 **Prison authorities erected nooses:** See, for example, Sarraj (2016).

47 **My features are the deserts of Manbij:** I'm grateful to Lylla Younes for this translation.

49 **That evening, they found themselves:** I visited what I believe to be Hasan's cell in Sednaya, which I used to corroborate the descriptions.

50 **He spotted the Book Roundabout:** These descriptions are corroborated by my own trips along this same route.

BOOK 1: THREE

52 **The size of a trash bin:** This description is based on a photograph.

52 **Dirt paths wended around the cottages:** Abel Os corpus.

53 **Authorities soon noticed:** Abel Os corpus.

53 **Then, when he was thirteen:** Details of this cinema house were provided by Ahmed al-Faraj (Abel Os corpus).

53 **Eventually, Abdul Qader located:** Abel Os corpus.

53 **One frigid, rainy night:** Anecdote from Hassan Issa (Abel Os corpus).

53 **Down the street was:** This description is based on my visits.

54 **There was no new:** Abel Os's recollection.

54 **Once, a group of workers were relaxing:** This anecdote is from Abu Khalid (Abel Os corpus).

55 **His hands could swallow:** This description is from photographs and the Abel Os corpus.

56 **Tear of Roses was no mere stall:** Abel Os corpus.

56 **When a brawl broke out:** This anecdote is from Ali al-Jadaan (Abel Os corpus).

56 **When city toughs catcalled:** Abel Os corpus.

57 **"Today, oh brothers!":** Resala Post (2019).

57 **Billboards were covered in black tarp:** Naddaff (2017); Abel Os corpus.

57 **Millions of peasants became teachers and civil servants:** See, for example, Hinnebusch (1989). See also Gopal (2020a). On Syrian public-sector employment, see Abboud (2015).

57 **It provided free health care to the poor:** Sen & al Faisal (2012); Hinnebusch (1989).

57 **Motorists filled their vehicles:** Khatib (2011).

57 **Housewives purchased cooking gas:** Syrian Center for Policy Research (2013).

58 **A man at the desk kept a bodkin:** Abel Os corpus.

58 **"With our blood, with our souls":** Abel Os corpus.

58 **"The threshing floors":** Al Tamimi (2021).

58 **Bashar, on the other hand:** This and other related details are from Buck (2011).

58 **Longtime dissidents:** Aboud (2008).

59 **To fund its social programs:** Azmeh (2014).

59 **When the USSR collapsed:** Azmeh (2014).

59 **In Syria, the most important subsidy:** Khatib (2011), IRIN News (2008).

59 **This new way of life:** For more on the new ethos, see De Elvira & Zintl (2014) and Khatib (2011).

59 **DECREE NO. 83:** Ababsa (2015).

59 **LAW NO. 28:** This and the subsequent three decrees are from Abboud (2015).

60 **In all, the government:** Daher (2017).

60 **It inked an agreement:** Abboud (2015). On the EU deals, see European Commission (n.d.).

60 **Turkey:** Abboud (2015).

60 **In short order, supermarket shelves:** Azmeh (2014); Abel Os corpus.

60 **For some, life was now:** Terc (2011).

60 **Eager to attract:** Stockman (2011).

60 **Asma al-Assad enlisted:** Bogardus (2011).

60 **"Asma al-Assad is glamorous":** Buck (2011).
60 **"We couldn't help but notice":** Akkad (2010).
60 **The empty lot announcing:** The description of Sarab in this paragraph is from Abel Os's recollections, the Abel Os corpus, and photographs and videos of the neighborhood from that time.
61 **One afternoon, he stood:** Bank details are corroborated in the Abel Os corpus.
61 **Abel Os placed his brother:** Details of Abel Os's activities in Heroes Dojo are from the Abel Os corpus.
62 **His co-trainer was:** Anas Sheikh Weiss (Abel Os corpus).
62 **He lived in a large house:** Abel Os corpus.
62 **There were professional singers:** This description is from Abel Os's recollections, the Abel Os corpus, and photographs.
62 **As the government privatized:** On soaring rents, see IRIN News (2008).
62 **On the northwest edge:** This description is based on photographs and my visits.
63 **He sat face-to-face with a man in a leather jacket:** The scene is based on Abel Os's recollections, corroborated with the Abel Os corpus. Details on the motorcycle moneylending system were additionally drawn from the Poverty corpus.
63 **Paper cups were put out:** Description is based on Abel Os's recollections, the Abel Os corpus, and photographs.
64 **Sometimes he would rise and retreat:** Abel Os corpus.
64 **Long after 16th of October Street:** This description is from a photograph.
65 **"Today, or we'll make you":** "We'll make you disappear behind the sun" is a common Syrian saying.
65 **"We're from the Shiyuki family":** Additional details on this exchange and this family are from the Abel Os corpus.
65 **He visited Gulay:** Additional details on this scene are from the Hasan Gulay interview (Abel Os corpus).
65 **The next day, Abel Os stood:** Abel Os corpus.
65 **Abel Os stepped outside:** Abel Os recollection.
65 **Main Street would have been thronged:** This description is based on my visits.
66 **Policemen were dozing in plastic chairs:** From Abel Os's recollection and the Abel Os corpus.
66 **Sometime after the dawn prayer:** From Abel Os's recollection and photographs.
67 **Soon the wheat stalks out east:** On the drought, see Oweis (2011).
67 **Scientists determined:** Cook et al. (2016).
67 **The desiccated carcasses of livestock:** Abel Os corpus; Poverty corpus.
67 **Many farms fell into foreclosure:** See, for example, Niazi (2025).
67 **more than a million people fled:** Kelley et al. (2015). For an alternative analysis that questions this level of migration, see Selby et al. (2017).
67 **Ghost villages were swept through:** This description is based on home videos sourced from the Poverty corpus.
67 **New Syria was in bloom:** This description of Homs is from my visit, photographs, and al-Sabouni (2016).
68 **He awoke to the saucer-shaped streetlights:** This description is based on photographs from 2009.
68 **Since his previous visit:** Goulden (2011).
68 **Billboards promised:** This description is based on a photograph from 2009.
68 **They approached the crowded:** This description of the hospital is based on a photograph from 2009.
69 **Some days later, a few:** This scene is drawn from Abel Os's recollections and the Abel Os corpus.
70 **Between 2006 and 2008:** Institute of Medicine (2010).
70 **The cost of wheat and rice:** Kelley (2015).
70 **New shantytowns sprang up:** Kilcullen & Rosenblatt (2014).
70 **In the Sabra neighborhood of southern Beirut:** This description is based on my visit.
70 **There was Khalil, who worked in a grocery:** Interview with Khalil al-Hussein (Poverty corpus).
71 **There was Ibrahim:** Interview with Ibrahim al-Jassim.
71 **"Women in their underwear":** Interview with Ibrahim al-Jassim.

BOOK 2: PROLOGUE

75 **In Manbij, there were:** These scenes are from videos in the Republic Video corpus. See also Daher (2017).
75 **In 2010, a debt-addled Manbij native:** Zakaria's story was originally reported in the regime-linked *al-Watan* newspaper

in 2010. The issue is no longer available online, but the article is summarized in Qatar Shares (2010). Additional information about this incident can also be found at Radio Alkul (2016). The story was also written about in Manbij's revolutionary press.

75 **Around the same time:** U.S. Embassy Damascus (2008).

BOOK 2: ONE

Note: In addition to the First Protesters corpus, the Oday corpus, and other interviews with people identified here, this chapter drew upon a diary entry from Mustafa al-Hamza (Oday's uncle).

77 **Oday was never one to pay much mind:** Oday corpus.
77 **The affairs of world:** Bushra al-Hema.
77 **The grim propriety:** Mustafa al-Hamza.
77 **He fancied himself a poet:** Ali al-Khaled.
77 **He was intrigued by Arab history:** Mustafa al-Hamza, Jamil al-Okla ("he loved history a lot . . . [but] he failed his ninth-grade exams").
77 **He and his friends scaled the rooftops:** Abel Os.
77 **Instead, it was through:** The scene of Oday's encounter with Hala is drawn from interviews with Hala and Abboud Salo. The description of the alley of Roman stone is from my visit.
78 **In the vegetable market:** The description of the market is from my visits. Reference to the price ("forty lira") is based on Bushra's recollections of the price at that time.
78 **Oday studied the market:** Bushra al-Hema.
78 **Hala—that was her name:** A pseudonym.
78 **He'd confided in Bushra:** A pseudonym.
78 **The trouble was:** Abboud is a pseudonym.
78 **He'd joined Oday and his friends:** Oday corpus.
78 **On Oday's own street:** Abel Os.
79 **They studied Hala's routine:** The description of Oday's plotting and encounter with Hala is from Bushra al-Hema and Abboud Salo.
79 **A routine developed:** Hala al-Muhammad.
79 **Oday would return home:** Bushra al-Hema.
79 **He drove out to the country:** Jamil al-Okla.
79 **Bushra took matters:** This scene is drawn from interviews with Hala and Bushra.
79 **His father had dropped out of the sixth grade:** This description of Oday's father's life is from an interview with his father, Maher al-Hema. Descriptions of his father's strictness are drawn from the Oday corpus. For example, Abdul Salam Bakkar said: "Oday was watched by his father due to his strictness, as he was forbidden from wearing jeans or styling his hair with gel."
80 **He rebelled:** Oday corpus.
80 **The house shook:** Bushra al-Hema.
80 **Oday would retreat with friends:** Jamil al-Okla.
80 **But if the world saw him as** *that kind of guy*: Bushra al-Hema, Abboud Salo.
80 **For the first time, Oday paid:** Oday corpus.
80 **As he watched the scenes:** Oday's views in this paragraph are from Mustafa al-Hamza and Bushra al-Hema.
81 **And to do all this:** Ali al-Khaled ("he felt incredible pressure on his shoulders").
81 **A friend in whom he'd confided:** Details of the poem episode are from Ali al-Khaled.
81 *And I know I'm living in exile*: Qabbani (n.d.), translation mine.
81 **The next afternoon, Oday made:** Ali al-Khaled.
81 **That week, Oday kept to his house:** Details of Oday's week are from Bushra al-Hema.
81 **The encounter only lasted a few moments:** Bushra al-Hema, Hala al-Muhammad.
81 **That night, he burned through packs of cigarettes:** Bushra al-Hema.
82 **When the next afternoon finally arrived:** Oday later related his wait to Ali al-Khaled.
82 **But then suddenly he found himself:** Hala al-Muhammad, Ali al-Khaled.
82 **The city was resplendent:** This description is from Bushra al-Hema, my visit to that balcony, and Abboud Salo ("the whole world could not contain his joy when he looked at our city").
82 **Here, in the pure air above Sundus Street:** Bushra al-Hema.
82 **On March 18, 2011:** Human Rights Watch (2011a).
82 **In clashes, four young men were killed:** Human Rights Watch (2011a).

NOTES

82 **At a funeral procession:** Human Rights Watch (2011a).

82 **State TV aired images:** Human Rights Watch (2011a); the government's claim of American and Israeli provenance is from the Oday corpus, from interviewees who recall watching this on television.

82 **He watched his friend's satellite TV:** Abdul Salaam Bakkar.

82 **The channels showed images:** Oday corpus; see also MacFarquhar (2011).

82 **Crowds torched:** Al Jazeera (2011a).

82 **Makhlouf, who was said to control:** Barnard (2011).

83 **Oday adopted a bearing of propriety:** Mustafa al-Hamza.

83 **He'd recently come to understand:** The description of Oday's thoughts and daily rendezvous are from Hala al-Muhammad.

83 **The alley was unlit:** The description is based on my visit.

83 **There was much Oday:** Ali al-Khaled.

83 **Oday had not thought this way before:** Oday corpus.

83 **He disciplined himself:** The description of Oday's plans are from Hala al-Muhammad and Mustafa al-Hamza, along with Oday's diary.

83 **The old man scoffed:** Oday's diary.

84 **The one-room shop:** The description of the shop is from Abdul Salam Bakkar and photographs.

84 **He quit the whiskey-pickled nights:** Bushra al-Hema.

84 **After hours, in the dark folds:** Hala al-Muhammad.

84 **He imagined leading her by the hand:** Oday's diary.

84 **Sometimes he'd wonder:** Oday's diary.

84 **In fact, the image:** Bushra al-Hema.

84 **He would become a lawyer:** Hala al-Muhammad.

84 **He would be chauffeured:** Hala al-Muhammad.

84 **"Our president is a good man":** Abdul Hadi al-Bisher.

84 **The chaos produced wild rumors:** Oday corpus.

84 **In Manbij, prices at the market crept upward:** Abel Os.

84 **One day, to allay fears, a crowd:** This scene is drawn from fourteen YouTube videos from the WaSsOoM1 channel. The first is available at WaSsOoM1 (2011).

84 **When Oday and Hala saw these scenes:** Hala al-Muhammad.

85 **Meanwhile, satellite channels:** Oday corpus. Amnesty International (2011a) reports that 171 people were killed after 23 days.

85 **In the privacy:** This scene is from Abdul Salam Bakkar.

85 **Even Oday's father:** Bushra al-Hema.

85 **The president was standing:** Descriptions and quotations are from C-SPAN (2011).

85 **"Look how humble he is":** Bushra al-Hema.

85 **Oday was deeply impressed:** Oday's diary.

85 **In the afternoons, Oday:** Abdul Salam Bakkar.

85 **He recognized the desperation:** The description is from photographs of Manbij in March 2011.

86 **Oday felt he alone was immune:** Bushra al-Hema.

86 **He was to become a military lawyer:** Hala al-Muhammad.

86 **And then he called one evening:** This scene is from Abboud Salo.

86 **Finally, Bushra went to investigate:** Bushra al-Hema.

86 **He was gripped by a terrible fear:** Bushra al-Hema.

87 **But he was stalking her every move:** Hala al-Muhammad.

87 **Oday returned to the shop. He sold:** Scenes in this paragraph are from Bushra al-Hema.

87 **Oday could not bring himself to step:** Bushra al-Hema.

87 **At some point he recalled:** Yasser is a pseudonym.

87 **Mysteriously, Yasser had told him:** The confrontation scene is from Abboud Salo and Hala al-Muhammad.

87 **He finally reached Hala by landline:** Abboud Salo ("Oday said when he spoke to her finally, her voice sounded very small and faraway").

87 **Late into the night:** The description is from a photograph of Maher Communications.

87 **Standing in front of the decal-covered storefront:** Abdul Salam Bakkar.

87 **He saw the meanness of the human heart:** Bushra al-Hema.

87 **A friend prevailed on him to leave town:** Jamil al-Okla.

88 **He rested in the shadow of the great castle:** The description of the Aleppo trip is from Abdul Salam Bakkar.

88 **He had long, lustrous:** Oday's diary.
88 **He lived in an apartment:** Mina Saba.
88 **Shampoo Sami drew him aside conspiratorially:** Abdul Salam Bakkar, who was present for this exchange.
88 **He loved his president:** Abdul Salam Bakkar.
88 **Over the next days:** Bushra al-Hema ("Oday began to hate everyone and said the Syrians deserved what was happening").
88 **The rains came:** Photographs from the week of April 15, 2022, belonging to Abel Os.
88 **"It's your turn, oh doctor":** For background on this story, see Asher-Schapiro (2016).
88 **Oday was disgusted:** Bushra al-Hema.
88 **He appeared pained:** The scene of Oday's motorcycle trip is from Mustafa al-Hamza. The scene's descriptions draw on a trip I took retracing Oday's steps that day.
89 **Mustafa was the most intelligent person:** Bushra al-Hema.
89 **After bidding farewell:** Abdul Salam Bakkar, who was present at the cafe.
89 **And then he paced his dark balcony:** Abdul Salam Bakkar.
89 **The next morning, sedans:** Abdul Salam Bakkar.
89 **But the morning:** Mustafa al-Hamza.
90 **He felt as if he were locked in a closet:** Oday's diary.
90 **A force of this magnitude:** Bushra al-Hema.
90 **Oday found Shampoo Sami:** Abel Os.
90 **Later, in Shampoo Sami's apartment:** This meeting scene is from Hasan Hamdo.
90 **According to Syria's so-called Emergency Law:** NBC News (2011). A week later, the regime lifted the Emergency Law, but with no effect: protesters were still gunned down or arrested. See Human Rights Watch (2011c).
90 **If you wished to hold a formal meeting:** Human Rights Watch (2007).
90 **The five young men were university graduates:** First Protesters corpus.
90 **That Friday, April 15:** Maher al-Hema.
91 **Oday entered the Great Mosque:** This scene is from the First Protesters corpus, primarily Hasan Hamdo.
92 **The next afternoon:** Landis (2011).
92 **The unrest had spread to Homs:** Amnesty International (2011a).
92 **In Manbij, Peugeots:** Ahmed al-Faraj.
92 **Oday was convinced he carried a message:** Ahmed al-Faraj.
92 **He met with Shampoo Sami and the others:** Hasan Hamdo.
92 **On Thursday, Sami was summoned:** This police incident was recounted by Hasan Hamdo.
93 **The next afternoon, Friday, April 22:** This protest scene is drawn from the First Protesters corpus, six photographs, and six cell phone videos taken by participants. Five of these videos were also available on YouTube at the time of publication: ShaamNetwork S.N.N. (2011a), ShaamNetwork S.N.N. (2011b), ShaamNetwork S.N.N. (2011c), almanbegee (2011), and syria32011yt (2011a).
93 **Despite the somber mood, Oday was grateful:** Oday's sentiments and movements throughout this scene are from Hamada al-Hussein, who was by his side during the protest.
94 **No one could later remember:** Some sources claimed it was Omar al-Qarisli, others that it was Oday, but most said they did not know for sure.
95 **In one video, Oday appears:** This video is no longer on YouTube, but Oday can be seen in a gray-and-red sweatshirt in almanbegee (2011).
96 **His only wish:** Oday's diary.
97 **Oday was seated in front of his father:** This scene is from Maher al-Hema.
97 **That evening, for the first time:** This scene is from Hamada al-Hussein and Mustafa al-Hamza.

BOOK 2: TWO

99 **The men stood in rows, heads bowed:** This protest scene is from Ahmed al-Faraj and Anas Muhammad (Manbij Protesters corpus).
99 **A week had passed:** Hamada al-Hussein (Oday corpus).
99 **Oday was carried along:** Ahmed al-Faraj (Oday corpus).
99 **But he'd lived a thousand lives:** Hala al-Muhammad (Oday corpus).
100 **There were shouts of "Get back, get back!":** This description is based on cell phone video and Anas Hassou (Manbij Protesters corpus).

100 **He proceeded down Qambur Street:** This description of Oday's escape is from Ahmed al-Faraj, who was not far behind.

100 **"I'd like this one," 1st Lt. Maymati said:** This prison scene description is from Anas Muhammad (Manbij Protesters corpus).

101 **The next morning, in the officers' lounge:** This scene is from Saleh al-Hussein, a police officer who was present.

101 **Roz was round-faced:** Abu Roz descriptions are based on his photographs.

102 **"My God," Hala said:** This scene is from Hala al-Muhammad.

102 **Now he spent his days alone:** Bushra al-Hema.

102 **He'd come to possess:** Bushra al-Hema; Oday's diary.

102 **When afternoon services concluded:** This scene is from Abel Os; Ahmed al-Faraj; and al-Faraj (2021a), an unpublished article on Manbij's protest history.

103 **The glass storefront was:** Based on a photograph.

103 **The congregants emerged from Saladin Street:** al-Faraj (2021a).

104 **In Daraa, protests continued:** On suppression and Hamza al-Khateeb, see Amnesty International (2011b).

104 **Circulated on social media:** Jadaliyya (2011).

104 **On June 3, fifty thousand protesters gathered:** BBC News (2011a).

104 **In a remote northwest region:** BBC News (2011b).

104 **As the protests spread:** BBC News (2011a).

104 **In Daraa, the population was under siege:** Hilton & al-Aswad (2024).

104 **On June 20:** Syrian Arab News Agency (2011).

105 **That evening, a friend:** This scene is from Abel Os and Muhammad Abdi (Manbij Protesters corpus).

106 **Under the floodlights:** This scene is from Abel Os and Muhammad Abdi (Abel Os corpus).

106 **Abu Shakir:** This is a pseudonym. His real name is Zakaria Qarisli, of the First Protesters corpus.

107 **Mostly, the man-made gully:** This description is based on my visits.

107 **Inside, eight men were seated:** This meeting scene is drawn from Abel Os and the Manbij Revolutionary Council corpus, especially Abdul Karim Mustafa and Ahmed Rahmo.

107 **Leather couches were tucked into the corners:** This description is from Abel Os.

108 **There was Abu Salah:** This is a pseudonym. His real name is Abdul Karim Mustafa, of the First Protesters corpus. This description is based on my meetings with him.

108 **With delicate features:** This description is based on my meeting with him.

110 **The video shows an empty street:** syria32011yt (2011b). See also ShaamNetwork S.N.N. (2011d).

110 **For his screen name:** Ahmed al-Faraj, Saleh Abu Nayyaf (Oday corpus).

110 **Oday stopped by:** Abel Os.

110 **Two evenings later, at his real estate office:** This scene is primarily from Abel Os, with additions and corroborations from Ahmed al-Faraj and Abdul Hadi al-Bisher.

111 **Oday kept shouting, "It's Abel Os!":** Ahmed al-Faraj.

111 **By then the protesters:** The detail about residents watching is from Abel Os, who learned of it from residents on Rabta Street after his release.

111 **Back at the station:** This was told to Abel Os by Maymati after the liberation.

112 **When Abel Os appeared:** This protest scene is from Abel Os, with additions and corroborations from the First Protesters corpus.

112 **Images of muster zones in Beirut:** Abel Os said: "I started imagining the good days back in Lebanon. I can't believe I thought they were good, but this was my condition at the time. I remembered even the beaches we went to and the nights with my friends and with the workers."

113 **Abel Os's blindfold was removed:** This prison scene is from Abel Os. There were no other witnesses available to corroborate it, but it tracks closely with the experiences of many other detainees, as well as published investigations.

113 **He was loaded into the van:** The registration detail is according to Abel Os and corroborated by the First Protesters corpus.

BOOK 2: THREE

114 **This was the way of the *shawi*:** See Dukhan (2022).

114 **There was the story of Mariam:** This is a pseudonym. The anecdote is from Hussein Omar Samawi and corroborated by the research team.

114 **Mina's neighbor, Mona:** This is a pseudonym. The anecdote is from Muhammad Osman and corroborated by the research team.

114 *Honor* **was the reason:** The additional detail about Sami's life is from Ali Shlash and Ahmed Humeidi (Manbij Protesters corpus).

114 **No one had to spell this out:** The "legs akimbo" description is based on a photograph.

115 **She rose every morning:** This description is based on my visits.

115 **The school stood in front of a midden:** This description is based on my visits.

115 **"It's all lies":** Abu Ammar, Mina's husband.

115 **When her colleagues:** This anecdote was corroborated by the research team.

116 **Art had been his calling since high school:** Abdullah al-Hussein (Mina Saba corpus).

116 **He envisioned a mural populated:** Ahmed al-Faraj.

116 **His apartment was increasingly:** This detail is from the Oday and First Protesters corpora.

117 **She saw his life as a path:** Mina Saba: "I always thought in that time that he was lost. Our whole family always worried about him since he was young, especially my father. We wanted to help him find his way from the forest to a good job and family. I even imagined he would have a studio."

117 **Born in a mud house:** These details are from Mina's father.

118 **Local Coordinating Committee members:** Manbij Protesters corpus.

118 **The Syrian flag features:** See Dagher (2024).

118 **The city had fallen:** This description is from Mina's recollection.

119 **In a low voice:** This protest, which took place in July 2011 near the village of Kejli in the southern Manbij countryside, is well documented in the Manbij Protesters, First Protesters, and Manbij Revolutionary Council corpora.

119 **Ahmed Rahmo of the LCC:** As recounted by Ahmed Rahmo (Manbij Revolutionary Council corpus).

119 **The story was the same:** As recounted by Zakaria Qarisli (First Protesters corpus).

120 **"I'm really sorry":** As recounted by Mina's father.

120 **She owned a book that detailed:** These details are from Mina's diary.

120 **Before, the nationalism textbook:** See Daoudy (2009) and Wedeen (2019).

120 **As soon as she graduated:** For more on these camps, see Central Intelligence Agency (1984) and Rammal (2019).

121 **She imagined Sami:** Mina Saba: "I wondered if Sami was in there like a box of worms."

121 **A small crowd gathered:** This scene is from Abel Os and the Abel Os corpus.

121 **One young man said:** This exchange is from Abu Ayhem, quoted in al-Faraj (2021a).

121 **Finally, after much cajoling:** Abel Os's prison ordeal could not be independently verified, but it closely tracks the testimonies of several other prisoners, as well as human rights investigations. See Amnesty International (2011b).

124 **"The next time we send":** Abel Os.

125 **Sami tried sitting again in front of a canvas:** Abdullah al-Hussein (Mina Saba corpus).

125 **Yet he viewed the opprobrium:** Abdullah al-Hussein (Mina Saba corpus).

126 **Gripping Sami's brown arm:** This description is based on photographs.

126 **Her husband did not share:** Mina's husband (Mina Saba corpus).

126 **Six years younger:** This description of Hanan Soma's college life is from interviews with her (in the Mina Saba corpus).

127 **On a regular Thursday afternoon:** This protest scene is drawn primarily from Mina Saba, with corroboration from Hanan Saba, Abdul Hadi al-Bisher, and Ahmed al-Faraj, and an unpublished cell phone video.

127 **The women stood:** This is the Coffeepot Roundabout of the Hazowno neighborhood. I retraced the protesters' route in this area to provide some of the descriptions in this scene.

128 **One said, "They are peaceful protesters!":** This can be heard in an unpublished video.

BOOK 2: FOUR

130 **On a rooftop overlooking the Coffeepot:** Nidal S.

130 **Oday was getting worked up:** Abdul Hadi.

NOTES

130 **One afternoon when Abdul Hadi was five years old:** This scene is from Muhammad Ali al-Faraj (Abdul Hadi corpus).

130 **They walked down a broad avenue:** This description is based on my walk and photographs.

131 **Hafez al-Assad stared down from giant posters:** This description is based on photographs.

131 **In the middle:** This description is based on my visit.

131 **That evening, Abdul Hadi:** Abdul Hadi corpus.

131 **She understood what Abdul Hadi did not:** Muhammad Ali al-Faraj.

131 **One day, Abdul Hadi was led by his mother:** Khaled al-Saleh.

131 **On Fridays, he'd tell:** Ahmed al-Faraj.

131 **He was lightning quick and nimble:** Soccer corpus.

131 **He played barefoot:** Shadi al-Munla.

131 **When this was spotted:** Ahmed al-Faraj.

131 **Older players at the Youth Center:** Soccer corpus.

131 **When the coach visited Abdul Hadi's parents:** Soccer corpus.

132 **He'd pass the clothes to a friend:** Ahmed al-Faraj.

132 **Abdul Hadi was playing in Aleppo:** This scene is from several sources in both the Soccer and Abdul Hadi corpora.

132 **He couldn't afford to attend road games:** Naser al-Nabzo.

133 **Getting benched was for Abdul Hadi a great calamity:** Shadi al-Munla.

133 **his father insisted it was a providential sign:** This description of Abdul Hadi's father's beliefs is from Abdul Hadi and Muhammad Ali al-Faraj.

133 **When tryouts for Manbij City's adult squad:** Mahmoud Hajj Qasim (Soccer corpus).

133 **Weeks later:** Shadi Munla.

133 **except now one could detect a distinct chip:** The chip-on-the-shoulder detail is from the Abdul Hadi corpus.

133 **His dream was not for himself:** In addition to Abdul Hadi's recollections, details of his youth coach days are from Muhammad Ali al-Faraj, Khaled al-Saleh, Ammar al-Hussein, and Omar al-Faraj of the Abdul Hadi corpus.

133 **Sometimes he bent the rules:** Muhammad Ali al-Faraj.

133 **Unlike other coaches:** Ammar al-Hussein.

133 **Sure, it was a far cry:** Shadi al-Munla.

133 **He signed up for the *shaabi* league:** Soccer corpus.

133 **In truth, he felt:** The anecdote about Oday not understanding is from Ahmed al-Faraj.

134 **In August, the regime's forces:** Human Rights Watch (2011d).

134 **When the siege concluded:** Office of the United Nations High Commissioner for Human Rights (2011).

134 **The army had left graffiti on the walls:** Walsh (2011).

135 **Oday . . . could no longer contain himself:** Nidal S. This is a pseudonym.

135 **The city's quiescence, he believed:** Nidal S.

135 **It was late Thursday night:** The description of this meeting is from Nidal S. and Abdul Hadi, who were present, and Abdul Aziz, who was not present.

135 **There was Maraar:** Ibrahim al-Maraar. He was later killed by ISIS, but I interviewed his parents, Alawi Khaleef al-Maraar and A. K. (Oday corpus).

135 **Earlier that day:** Muhammad al-Kinj, from Jarablus. His story is from al-Faraj (2021a).

136 **His eyes gleamed:** Nidal's description.

136 **All summer, Hala and Oday:** This scene is from Hala al-Muhammad.

136 **Now, in the early-evening light:** In addition to Abdul Hadi's recollections, this protest scene is from interviews with Ahmed al-Faraj and Shadi al-Munla, who were participants, along with several cell phone videos. One of the videos is still available on YouTube at the time of writing: Ugarit News - Syria (2011). In addition, I visited the area and Ahmed al-Faraj guided me through the route by which Oday and Abdul Hadi fled, which I drew upon for descriptions.

137 **What Abu Roz didn't know:** al-Faraj (2021a).

139 **At the directorate he was conducted:** Additional details to corroborate and add to Abdul Hadi's recollections of the prison scene are from Nidal and Shadi al-Munla.

139 **Oday, in a blindfold, sat behind a desk:** This scene is from Jamil al-Okla, who was picked up separately while home from university. He was brought to the interrogation room where Oday was being questioned while blindfolded.

141 **The cell in Aleppo Central Prison had no windows:** In addition to Abdul Hadi's recollections, this scene draws substantially from Nidal. The events the two men describe about Aleppo Central Prison match those found by human rights investigators. See Syrian Network for Human Rights (2013).
141 **We raised our index fingers:** Abdul Hadi memorized this poem and repeated it to us many years later.
142 **It was sky blue:** This description is based on my visit.

BOOK 2: FIVE

143 **At the heart of every protest lies a paradox:** For more on the issue of collective action, see Olson (1974) and McAdam (1988).
144 **In the ten days after the sit-in:** al-Faraj (2021a) and Manbij Protesters corpus.
144 **1st Lt. Maymati employed a tactic:** Maymati later told this to Ahmed al-Faraj (First Protesters corpus).
144 **LCC members and fellow travelers:** Hasan Nefi, Ali Saleh al-Jasim (MRC corpus).
144 **One school, which might be called:** The stonecutter image is from a quote widely attributed to Jacob Riis.
144 **The competing view:** For more information, see Bantman (2013).
145 **As Manbij's foremost:** MRC corpus.
147 **They came in the dark, in batches:** The revolutionary council meeting scene is from the MRC corpus, with Abel Os, Hasan Nefi, Ahmed Rahmo, and Abdul Karim Mustafa as the principal sources.
147 **A solitary bulb burned in the farmhouse:** Abel Os's description.
147 **Inside, a woodstove:** These descriptions are from Abel Os.
148 **Unlike other engineers:** This appraisal is from a number of sources in the MRC corpus.
148 **With powerful arms and:** This description is based on photographs and my meeting with him.
149 **Abu Salah:** Pseudonym of Abdul Karim Mustafa.
149 **Aimad Henezel:** This description is based on my visits with him.
150 **A half-dozen others:** The full list is as follows: Ahmed Rahmo (president); Mustafa al-Abdullah (secretary); Hasan Nefi (Political Office); Abel Os and Abdul Karim Mustafa, "Abu Saleh" (Office of the Revolutionary Movement); Anas Sheikh Weiss (Aid Office); Abdul Jalil Aliyan (Education Office); Abdul Rauf Shayko and Mustafa al-Abdullah (Legal Office); Muhammad al-Jasim (Medical Office); Munzer Salal (Office of Religious Affairs); Sameh al-Hamad (Office of Security); Ahmed al-Taan (Office of Foreign Relations); Ahmed Rahmo (Office of Social Services); and Aimad al-Din Henezel (Office of Media). The Office of Military Affairs was initially unfilled; then, after a few months, Saadedine Soma and Yusef Ajjan al-Hadid were appointed.
151 **After today, the entire council:** This pledge was not kept, as the council was forced to meet at various points in the next few months.
151 **They drafted:** Social Media corpus.
151 **Some one-third of Syrians:** See also Khaddour & Mazur (2017).
152 *Change is coming*: Social Media corpus.
152 **Some of the leaflets promised:** Social media corpus. "Sleeping lion" was a pun, as "Assad" means "lion" in Arabic.
152 **Checkpoints materialized around the city:** Social Media corpus; Abel Os.
152 **A young man in possession:** Social Media corpus; MRC corpus.
152 **Leaflets appeared accusing:** MRC corpus.
152 **That night, the Revolutionary Council:** MRC corpus; on not taking revenge, the Social Media corpus.
152 **In the Idlib countryside:** Al Arabiya English (2011).
152 **In early December:** Associated Press (2011).
152 **The regime drafted a law:** Amnesty International (2011c).

BOOK 2: SIX

153 **Abdul Hadi froze:** The prison and release scenes are primarily from Abdul Hadi and Nidal S., with amplifications from the Abdul Hadi corpus.
153 **Nidal Kinjawi:** A pseudonym.
153 **They were herded through a long corridor:** The primary source for the prison description is Nidal. The description matches the prisons I visited after the fall of the regime.

NOTES

155 **For a young man unable:** Abdul Hadi: "I finally began to see the hand of God."
155 **Oday reached his father:** Maher al-Hema (Oday corpus).
155 **When Hala saw him:** Hala al-Muhammad.
156 **There, he saw the city:** Oday's diary.
156 **But at home, his parents:** Oday corpus.
156 **Whenever he left:** Oday's mother.
156 **During his confinement:** Oday's mother.
156 **When the old man asked Oday:** Maher al-Hema.
156 **He'd become impulsive, walking across town:** Hala al-Muhammad.
156 **They held each other:** Hala al-Muhammad; the "stars burning" description is based on my visits to the alley.
156 **On December 18, the villages of Mount Zawiya:** See BBC News (2011c); Al Jazeera (2011b).
156 **The imam was bayonetted:** BBC News (2012a).
156 **Some seventy-five people were killed:** Estimates range from seventy to two hundred. Human Rights Watch (2012a) puts the figure as at least seventy-four.
156 **The next day, a clip:** AbabilBird8 (2011).
156 **The citizens of Manbij awoke:** Social Media corpus.
157 **In teachers' lounges:** Mina Saba; Abboud al-Daroubi (Manbij Protesters corpus).
157 **It was only after:** Ibrahim's life recap and his brother's actions are from Ibrahim al-Jassim and the Manbij Protesters corpus.
157 **He confided in his:** Additional descriptions of Muhammad are from Ibrahim's second brother, Mustafa al-Jassim.
157 **Now, though, with this mysterious:** Manbij Protesters corpus.
158 **On Friday, December 23:** This description is based on photographs and videos from the Central Square corpus.
158 **Among them were several:** "Mohsen" refers to Mohsen Kinaan (Central Square corpus).
158 **Rahim:** Central Square corpus.
158 **Tariq and Alaa:** Central Square corpus.
158 **The police appeared astonished:** Videos in the Central Square corpus.
158 **Meanwhile, a few blocks away:** al-Faraj (2021b).
158 **The crowd grew mirthful:** al-Faraj (2021b).
158 **Placing arms on shoulders:** Videos in the Central Square corpus.
159 **The vehicles had sealed:** Descriptions of the area are drawn from the videos in the Central Square corpus and my visit to the area with Ahmed al-Faraj.
159 **Some time passed:** Central Square corpus.
159 **For a brief moment:** Central Square corpus.
159 **The policemen inched forward:** Videos in the Central Square corpus.
159 **One of the patrol car doors:** Central Square corpus.
159 **It was at that moment:** Ahmed al-Faraj (Central Square corpus).
159 **A few protesters managed to slip:** Central Square corpus.
160 **Revolutionary Council members took to:** Munzer Salal (Central Square corpus).
160 **The sky was overcast:** This detail is from the video "Sit-in of Manbij revolutionaries after the arrest of 30 sons of Manbij 12/23/11," which has been removed from YouTube (Central Square corpus). According to the National Centers for Environmental Information, the average temperature in Aleppo on that day was 49 degrees Fahrenheit; Manbij is typically cooler than Aleppo in winter.
160 **A Syrian flag flapped:** "Sit-in of Manbij revolutionaries..." video.
160 **"Prayer is not illegal":** Central Square corpus.
160 **The father of one of the arrested:** The father of Majed al-Ibrahim, a medical student who belonged to the Albu Banna tribe, from al-Faraj (2021b).
160 **Political intelligence headquarters:** This detail was related to Ibrahim.
160 **Hala answered the phone:** This telephone exchange is drawn from two sources, Hala al-Muhammad and Abboud Salo.
161 **When he'd described:** Hala's phrase: "My heart shattered into a thousand pieces."
161 **As a former detainee:** Hala: "There will be a black star next to your name!"
162 **For how long:** This detail is based on Hala's estimation of the time, and the "Sit-in of Manbij revolutionaries" video (Central Square corpus).
162 **Abel Os ignored the first message:** This protest scene is based on the Central Square corpus, especially Abel Os and Abdul Hadi, and al-Faraj (2021b).
163 **When news reached them:** The council member who littered the highway with nails was Munzer Salal (Central Square corpus).

163 **The effect was of:** This image is based on videos from the Central Square corpus.

163 **Abdul Hadi's eyes were wet:** Abel Os witnessed this encounter.

164 **Bodies were pushed:** This image is based on videos from the Central Square corpus.

164 **Then, out of the thousand:** This is attested to by several sources in the Central Square corpus.

164 **The throngs swayed and clapped:** "Sit-in of Manbij revolutionaries" video (Central Square corpus).

164 **"He who doesn't participate has no honor!":** "Sit-in of Manbij revolutionaries" video (Central Square corpus).

164 **"We don't want you!":** al-Faraj (2021b).

165 **The air was filled with scattered chants:** This image is based on videos from the Central Square corpus.

165 **"The people want the downfall of the regime!":** This image is based on videos from the Central Square corpus.

166 **But truth stands:** This sentiment is from Arendt (1993).

166 **Now, in the darkness:** This description is based on my visit retracing the route of the march.

BOOK 3: ONE

171 **Oday Receives a Visitor:** This scene is from Ahmed al-Faraj, who was present. It was corroborated by the Manbij Protesters corpus.

172 **The Strange, Marvelous Career:** This section drawn from the Maymati corpus, in particular from interviews with his father-in-law, Jasim Atroush Abu Muhammad, and Abu Hussein, a former colleague.

172 **When Abdul Wahab Khalaf:** Father-in-law (Maymati corpus); al-Faraj (2022a).

172 **Perhaps it was his:** This description is based on a photograph and from Abu Hussein's description (Maymati corpus).

172 **As one Manbij native:** Ahmed al-Faraj (Maymati corpus).

172 **A colleague later recalled:** Abu Hussein.

172 **One summer,** *Valley of the Wolves***:** Abu Hussein. See Hussam Al3raqi (2017) for a clip of the eponymous Maymati. This was also discussed in Ghazul (2018), but the article is no longer available.

172 **1st Lt. Abdul Wahab was transfixed:** Maymati corpus.

172 **It was not lost on people:** Maymati corpus.

173 **Sitting in Oday's living room:** This scene is from Ahmed al-Faraj. Maymati's claims are corroborated by al-Faraj (2022a).

173 **Oday wasn't sure what to say:** Ahmed al-Faraj's impression.

174 **On March 15:** Manbij Protesters corpus; al-Faraj (2021a).

174 **"What do you expect us to do?":** This detail is from Ahmed al-Faraj, who was present.

174 **He said, "Listen to me!":** Maymati corpus.

174 **"God is great!":** This scene is captured in Ugarit News (2012a).

174 **The crowd chanted: "May-mat-i!":** Ahmed al-Faraj.

174 **Stones and batons flew:** Maymati corpus.

174 **Someone had uploaded:** This video is part of the Maymati corpus, but has been removed from YouTube.

174 **A few days later, 1st Lt. Maymati appeared:** This description is based on a video in the Maymati corpus that has been removed from YouTube.

BOOK 3: TWO

175 **In recent weeks, relations:** The details about Saladin's defection and his father's response are from Mina Saba (Mina Saba corpus).

175 **They gathered in an old, weather-stained barn:** This description is based on my visit.

175 **The mood was tense:** This scene is drawn from interviews in the MRC corpus, in particular Abel Os, Abdul Karim Mustafa, and Hasan Nefi.

175 **Under the pale glow of fluorescent tubes:** This description is based on my visit.

176 **Back in 2005, Mustafa Tlass:** Koelbl (2005).

176 **Those advocating the peaceful:** Hussein Omar Samawi.

176 **The sky above the old farmhouse paled:** Based on Abel Os's estimation of the time; MRC and Rebel corpora.

177 **A Kalashnikov:** Abu Maan (Rebel corpus).

177 **he took the back roads:** Oday corpus.

177 **He returned each time:** Abdul Hadi al-Bisher (Oday corpus).

177 **In the end, the council:** Rebel corpus.

NOTES

177 **One afternoon, a prominent:** This scene is from Nidal S., who witnessed it (Rebel corpus).

177 **In an emergency:** Abel Os (MRC corpus) and Nidal S. (Rebel corpus).

178 **On Friday, May 25:** Al-Faraj (2021a).

178 **That Friday, for the first time:** al-Faraj (2021a).

178 **At night, Oday:** Abdul Hadi al-Bisher (Oday corpus).

178 **They stole through:** This detail is from photographs of the strike.

178 **On the morning of May 30:** Manbij Protesters corpus; unpublished cell phone video.

178 **Abu Roz had called for backup:** Maymati told this to Abel Os after liberation.

178 **The following week:** al-Faraj (2021a).

178 **Four masked men drove:** This scene is from multiple sources in the Rebel corpus.

BOOK 3: THREE

179 **On May 25, 2012:** Human Rights Watch (2012b).

179 **That evening, regime forces:** BBC News (2012b).

179 **The United Nations confirmed:** Global Centre for the Responsibility to Protect (2012).

179 **In Manbij, the Revolutionary Council:** MRC corpus.

179 **In Manbij, the doyen:** Details on Abu Habib's life are from interviews in the Rebel corpus.

180 **What he needed, though, was funds:** Details on funding and arms are from Ibrahim Bannawi, who worked closely with Abu Habib (Rebel corpus).

180 **On July 11, a video:** Amri Mubasher Syria (2012a).

180 **When the Revolutionary Council learned:** MRC corpus.

180 **A few days later, security forces:** Details of the Jarablus battles are from Abu Muhannad al-Khudr, Abdul Aziz al-Saleh, Abu Hasan, and Saleh Muhammad, from the Liberation corpus. They all participated in or witnessed the events.

180 **Abu Habib placed his weapons:** This scene is from Abu Hasan.

181 **Flying high above the squat houses:** This description is based on a photograph in the Liberation corpus.

181 **The following day, Abu Habib's fighters:** This scene is from Saleh Muhammad and Issa al-Jaber of the rebel corpus, and corroborated by other sources in the Liberation corpus.

181 **The windshield was blown out:** This description is based on a photograph in the Liberation corpus.

182 **Lt. Maymati drove his bullet-riddled:** This description is based on a video in the Liberation corpus.

182 **The next day, July 18:** MacFarquhar (2012).

182 **In the morning, residents:** Unless otherwise noted, all details in this section are from the Liberation corpus.

182 **Government forces had retreated:** This description is based on photographs.

182 **Under a brilliant sun:** This description is based on videos. Dozens of videos from liberation day are still available on YouTube. See, for example, Amri Mubasher Syria (2012b) and Documentation Center of the Syrian Revolution (2012).

182 **He called Manbij authorities:** Abu Hasan (Maymati corpus); Abel Os.

182 **He called Aleppo for instructions:** T. K., former police officer (Maymati corpus).

183 **In the police station:** T. K., former police officer.

183 **Posters of Assad:** This description is based on my visit.

183 **Pedestrians stopped:** This description is based on videos (Liberation corpus).

183 **Council members, wearing ski masks:** This scene is from Hasan Nefi and Anas Sheikh Weiss (MRC corpus).

183 **They looked as people did:** This description is based on videos (Liberation corpus).

183 **When the convoy:** This scene is from T. K., Abu Hasan, and others in the Maymati corpus, with additional details from my visit to the area, where I interviewed eyewitnesses.

184 **Muhammad Bayram:** These details are based on my interview with his father, Yaqub Bayram, and other members of his family in Manbij in 2018.

184 **People emerged from their houses:** This description is based on videos (Liberation corpus).

184 **He ran back to the protest:** Abel Os estimated there were three thousand people.

184 **The crowd was frenzied:** This description is based on videos (Liberation corpus).

184 **Women leaned over the balustrades:** This description is based on videos (Liberation corpus).
184 **A procession of dirt-spattered:** This scene is based on videos (Liberation corpus).
185 **They checked on an army post:** This scene is from Saladin Saba.
185 **And what songs!:** These descriptions are based on videos (Liberation corpus).
185 **They made for the stairs:** Abel Os took me on this same journey, which provided additional details for this scene.
185 **From the rooftop:** This description is based on photographs (Liberation corpus).
186 **From the street:** This scene is from Ahmed al-Faraj, who witnessed it.
186 **The roar of the crowd:** This description is based on photographs (Liberation corpus).
186 **The multitudes gathered:** This scene is based on videos (Liberation corpus).
187 **The crowd was chanting:** This description is based on videos (Liberation corpus).
187 **The city of Manbij:** Social Media corpus.
188 **In a packed room:** This scene is drawn from several sources, mostly from the MRC corpus, as well as Muhammad Bashir al-Khalaf.
189 *Free, free, freedom*: See, for example, Ibn al-Ghouta (2020).

BOOK 3: FOUR

190 **For many hours, Oday stood:** The scene of Oday standing on the balcony is from Bushra al-Hema: "When we sat there, the city and the market looked like it always did." The description of the city is from my visits to that market, and videos of the market from July 2012.
190 **From the balcony, Oday:** This description is based on my visit to the balcony and what is visible from that vantage point.
190 **Pedestrians ambled freely up:** This description is based on videos (Liberation corpus).
190 **But his friend Abdul Hadi:** These descriptions of Abdul Hadi's activities in July 2012 are from the Abdul Hadi corpus.
190 **These days, Abdul Hadi:** Shadi al-Munla (Abdul Hadi corpus).
191 **He and his friends began making prank calls:** This was corroborated by a recording of one of these calls (Abdul Hadi corpus).
191 **After asking around:** The key rebel brigades operating in those early months after liberation were: Jund al-Haramein, Shuhada Manbij, Thuwwar Manbij, al-Karama, Ahrar Suriya, the PKK, Fursan al-Furat, Ammar bin Yasser, al-Adiat, Numan, Abu Ayub al-Ansari, and al-Qaqa.
191 **"What's with these":** Abu Ayhem (RYM corpus).
192 **In late July, Ahmed Rahmo:** This scene is drawn from multiple sources in the MRC and Liberation corpora. The prime sources are Ahmed Rahmo, Saleh Muhammad, Hussein al-Akeedi, and Hasan Nefi.
192 **"First Lieutenant Abdul Wahab Maymati":** Social Media corpus.
192 **Not long after, the council convened:** This scene is drawn from multiple sources in the MRC and Rebel corpora. Ahmed Rahmo and Ibrahim Bannawi (who were on opposing sides in this dispute) were the prime sources. Bannawi is in the SDF corpus.
193 **The Revolutionary Youth Movement:** The principal sources for this section are the RYM and MRC corpora.
193 **One evening:** This story is from multiple sources in the RYM corpus.
193 **"Is that what a government":** Ahmed al-Faraj.
193 **As his voice rang out:** Video from the Social Media corpus.
193 **Abdul Hadi, Oday, and their friends:** This scene is drawn from the MRC and RYM corpora. MRC and RYM sources did not agree on the tenor of the debate: The MRC believed it to be respectful, and the RYM rejected this interpretation. I've used my judgment to represent the RYM interpretation, because I feel it better explains subsequent events.
194 **"Don't stick your nose":** Anas Sheikh Weiss doesn't recall saying this, but multiple RYM members attest to it.
194 **Oday, who could not believe the tone:** He explained this later to his comrades (RYM corpus).
194 **But then a young man in the crowd:** Hussein Abu Raed (RYM corpus).
195 **The gathering consisted:** This scene is drawn from multiple sources in the RYM corpus.
196 **"Look at Abel Os, he's the secretary general":** Ahmed al-Faraj.

NOTES

197 **"Dear Fellow Citizens!":** Social Media corpus.
197 **Some people walked up:** This description of RYM's activities is from the RYM corpus.
197 **Each morning presented:** RYM and Manbij Protesters corpora.
197 **"We felt responsible":** Ahmed al-Faraj.
197 **The group mediated:** Hussein Abu Raed.
198 **When a Free Army faction:** Also captured in the Republic Video corpus.
198 **On Fridays, the square:** Republic Video corpus. On the general sentiment at this time, and for images of RYM protests, see Al Aan TV (2012a).
198 **Soon others sought to replicate:** In the republican period, the following were the most important assemblies: Change and Construction, Civil Tendency, Fertile Crescent, Free Doctors Organization, Free Engineers, Free Ladies of Manbij, Free Lawyers, Free Patriots, Free Students Union, Free Syrian Youth, Free Teachers, Free Tribes, Future Current, Future Doctors Organization, Future Youth Authority, Girls of Tomorrow, Home, Islamic Action Front, Islamic Levant, Kurdish Local Council, Liberal Teachers, Manbij Human Rights, Muslim Youth, Peasants Collective, People for Justice, People's House, Revolutionary Youth Movement, Students of Faith, Students Without Borders, Women of Freedom.
198 **Future Youth Assembly:** Nazeer K., a founding member (Manbij Protesters corpus); *Shams al-Horreya* (2012, October 7), Issue 5.
198 **While the Civil Tendency:** *al-Masar al-Horr* (2012, November 27), Issue 11.
198 **The assembly launched a health insurance:** Social Media corpus.
198 **The Free Patriots Assembly:** Manbij Protesters and Social Media corpora.
198 **Some assemblies were based:** Manbij Protesters and Social Media corpora.
199 **The Free Ladies Assembly:** Mina Saba; Social Media corpus.
199 **mini-parliaments of the people:** I'm grateful to Gluckstein (2011) for this phrase, which he used in a different context.
199 **It was the day before Eid:** This scene is drawn from Sayed S. (Manbij protesters corpus), who was an eyewitness,

and Mu. K. (RYM corpus), also an eyewitness, who lost his mother in the attack. Additional sources include *Shams al-Horreya* (2012, November 8), Issue 8; Ali (2015); and dozens of videos (Social Media corpus).
199 **Old men in *shemagh*:** All scenes in this passage are from the Manbij Video roster.
199 **The sun slipped:** This description is from a video from shortly before impact.
200 **Firas al-Ali, an activist:** This passage is from Ali (2015).
200 **In that day's massacre:** This count is according to the Revolutionary Council (Social Media corpus).
201 **Among the dead:** Mu. K. (RYM corpus).
201 **Real estate prices crashed:** From Abel Os, who was working at a real estate office at this time.

BOOK 3: FIVE

202 **According to *October*:** The name in Arabic is *Tishreen*; this detail is from the RYM corpus.
202 **Huzayfa Osman:** These details are from Huzayfa al-Osman (Manbij Protesters corpus).
203 **"We didn't have much money":** I. K. (Manbij Protesters corpus).
203 **The lead editorial:** *Shams al-Horreya* (2012, August 22), Issue 1.
203 **"I came across two":** *Shams al-Horreya* (2012, November 11), Issue 9.
203 **But decades of sclerotic:** *Shams al-Horreya* (2012, September 29), Issue 4.
204 **Hasan answered that:** *Shams al-Horreya* (2012, October 7), Issue 5.
204 **"If the right to speak":** *al-Masar al-Horr* (2012, September 3), Issue 1.
204 **"The prisoners are kept":** *al-Masar al-Horr* (2012, October 15), Issue 6.
204 **"It has been more than two months":** *al-Masar al-Horr* (2012, October 8), Issue 5.
205 **One contributor wrote that freedom means:** *al-Masar al-Horr* (2012, November 5), Issue 8.
205 **Two weeks later, the *Path*:** *al-Masar al-Horr* (2013, May 20), Issue 36.
205 **The British philosopher:** Berlin (1969).
205 **Two weeks later:** *al-Masar al-Horr* (2012, November 20), Issue 10.

BOOK 3: SIX

207 **"Many villages in the Manbij suburbs"**: *al-Masar al-Horr* (2012, October 8), Issue 5.

207 **"Last Thursday morning, the city of Manbij suffered"**: *al-Masar al-Horr* (2012, October 22), Issue 7.

207 **"There was a low turnout"**: *Shams al-Horreya* (2012, September 29), Issue 4.

207 **"The city of Manbij witnessed"**: *Shams al-Horreya* (2012, September 22), Issue 3.

207 **"The former deputy"**: *Shams al-Horreya* (2012, September 15), Issue 2.

208 **"The free students of Manbij"**: *al-Masar al-Horr* (2012, October 8), Issue 5.

208 **"We received many complaints"**: *al-Masar al-Horr* (2012, September 10), Issue 2.

208 **The sky was overcast**: RYM corpus.

208 **The streets trilled**: Republic Video corpus.

208 **It was Abdul Hadi who spearheaded**: Abdul Hadi corpus.

208 **The school where he was employed**: Hussein Abu Raed (RYM corpus).

208 **"You have one chance"**: RYM corpus.

208 **A surviving video shows**: A similar video is still available on YouTube at the time of publication: SYRIAN AFAK (2012a). The actual video has been removed, but it is in the Republic Videos corpus.

209 **But Abdul Hadi was increasingly**: RYM corpus.

209 **The council was offering salaries**: MRC corpus.

209 **In late September, RYM**: This scene is drawn from the RYM corpus, especially Mustafa Hadad, Hatim al-Daroubi, Abel Os, and Ahmed al-Faraj; and Muhammad al-Ali (Liberation corpus).

209 **The old squeaking chairs**: Abel Os.

209 **Now there was only the groan**: Ahmed al-Faraj.

210 **The force of the blast**: Scenes of the devastation are visible at 8:27 of Manbij and Its Countryside Coordination Committee—Local Coordinating Committees (2014), a documentary about regime bombings in Manbij.

210 **It missed its mark**: Scenes of the destroyed house are visible at 10:40 of Manbij and Its Countryside Coordination Committee—Local Coordinating Committees (2014).

210 **The caption read**: *Shams al-Horreya* (2012, September 22), Issue 3.

210 **Oday and the others went to bed**: Ahmed al-Faraj.

BOOK 3: SEVEN

Note: Descriptions of the Senate were informed by a series of recordings of Senate sessions by Yaser Munif, which he generously made available for this research.

211 **"The Free Syrian Lawyers"**: *al-Masar al-Horr* (2012, November 20), Issue 10.

211 **"Despite torrential rains"**: *al-Masar al-Horr* (2012, November 27), Issue 11.

211 **"In an operation"**: *al-Masar al-Horr* (2012, November 27), Issue 11.

211 **"The School of Agriculture"**: *Shams al-Horreya* (2012, November 25), Issue 11.

211 **"The *Sun of Freedom*"**: *Shams al-Horreya* (2012, November 11), Issue 9.

211 **In early November**: Republic Video corpus.

212 **Lights were hung from the rafters**: Republic Video corpus.

212 **Oday visited the stockyard**: Abdul Salam Bakkar (Oday corpus).

212 **It was nearly a year**: Abboud Salo (Oday corpus).

212 **Abdul Hadi was worried**: Ahmed al-Faraj (Abdul Hadi corpus).

212 **Manbij's refugee population**: For example, *al-Masar al-Horr* (2012, October 6), Issue 6.

212 **Meanwhile, the regime**: The aircraft and aftermath of the bombing is visible in Manbij and Its Countryside Coordination Committee—Local Coordinating Committees (2014).

212 **The pilot crashed**: Documentary Center for the Syrian Revolution (2012a, 2012b).

212 **"What Eid"**: *Shams al-Horreya* (2012, November 4), Issue 8.

212 **Lines of boys and girls**: Republic Video corpus.

213 **In the Arab world**: For more on the politics of bread, see Munif (2020), Munif (2021), and Martínez & Eng (2015).

213 **In Manbij, this wheat**: Details of the bread distribution system are from the Bread Survey corpus.

214 **When Bashar al-Assad inherited**: Bread Survey corpus.

NOTES

214 **By 2011, free-market reforms:** Bread Survey corpus.
214 **Upon liberation:** Bread Survey corpus.
214 **But then, one morning:** Bread Survey corpus.
214 **An impromptu protest:** *al-Masar al-Horr* (2012, November 20), Issue 10; *Shams al-Horreya* (2012, November 25), Issue 11; Abboud al-Daroubi (Manbij Protesters corpus).
214 **Later, the Revolutionary Council apologized:** Social Media corpus; Abboud al-Daroubi.
214 **This latest price increase stemmed:** See, for example, *Shams al-Horreya* (2012, December 9), Issue 13.
214 **The shockingly high prices:** *Shams al-Horreya* (2012, December 30), Issue 16; Al Abdeh (2013).
214 **Here and there at roadside stands:** Republic Video corpus.
214 **Private bakeries used the excuse:** *al-Masar al-Horr* (2012, October 1), Issue 4; *al-Masar al-Horr* (2013, January 28), Issue 20.
214 **A woman complained:** *Shams al-Horreya* (2012, December 30), Issue 16.
214 **The council formed:** *al-Masar al-Horr* (2012, October 1), Issue 4.
215 **By November, even middle-class:** Republic Video corpus.
215 **"Whoever raises prices":** *Shams al-Horreya* (2012, December 9), Issue 13.
215 **The *Path* went further:** See, for example, *al-Masar al-Horr* (2012, December 10), Issue 13; *al-Masar al-Horr* (2012, December 17), Issue 14.
215 **Yet there was a growing sense:** MRC corpus.
215 **The group, together with allied assemblies:** *Shams al-Horreya* (2012, November 11), Issue 9.
215 **As ever, it was Abdul Hadi:** Obada (Abdul Hadi corpus).
215 **The Senate Convenes:** The Senate (Umana' al-Thawra) formation and meeting scene are drawn from the MRC and RYM corpora. The principal sources were Abel Os, Ahmed al-Faraj, Huzayfa al Osman, Munzer Salal, and Mustafa Sheikh Ibrahim. In addition, details are drawn from the Senate founding documents, *Shams al-Horreya* (2012, November 25), Issue 11, and Basmat Syria (2012).

215 **The November night was unusually balmy:** Republic Video corpus.
215 **The lampposts outside were switched off:** Republic Video corpus.
216 **This new council would address:** The quoted phrase is from the Senate's founding charter.
216 **The Council of Trustees:** The details in this paragraph are from the Senate's founding charter. See also Basmat Syria (2012).
216 **Yet when the speaker:** The objections raised in this paragraph are captured on video, in the Republic Video corpus.
216 **Others took issue:** The quoted phrase is from the Senate's founding charter.
217 **Oday stood to speak:** Abel Os is the source of this exchange.
217 **They rolled their eyes:** This is according to the RYM corpus. Those in the MRC corpus allege that some RYM activists were being childish, an allegation supported by an anecdote by the RYM activist Mustafa Sheikh Ibrahim in the RYM corpus.
218 **For a few moments, the hall was quiet:** MRC corpus.

BOOK 3: EIGHT

219 **"Last Wednesday":** *al-Masar al-Horr* (2012, December 3), Issue 12.
219 **"The city's hospitals":** *al-Masar al-Horr* (2012, December 31), Issue 16.
219 **"Water was cut off":** *Shams al-Horreya* (2012, December 9), Issue 13.
219 **"When winter began":** *al-Masar al-Horr* (2012, December 17), Issue 14.
219 **"On Thursday, December 6":** *al-Masar al-Horr* (2012, December 10), Issue 13.
219 **In the bitter cold:** SYRIAN AFAK (2012b); RYM corpus.
219 **The crowd marched around:** Republic Video corpus.
220 **Leading the procession:** RYM corpus.
220 **He watched the work of the assemblies:** RYM member Abu Ayhem said about Abdul Hadi: "The Revolutionary Council was made of the rich people, and though at first the situation was not bad, soon we started to question: why's the price of bread going from 15 to 35 liras? And if you are wealthy and in control, why don't you make better streets? . . . Abdul Hadi

220 **The awkward goofiness:** RYM corpus, Abdul Hadi corpus.

221 **In this proposed system:** Details of this system are from the elections bylaws documents.

221 **President Ahmed Rahmo:** Ahmed Rahmo (MRC corpus). Council member Ali Saleh al-Jasim gives more insight into the Council's thinking: "One of its most important conditions [for elections] is stability. Therefore, the elections of the People's Council were illegitimate, unlike the Revolutionary Council, which was legitimized by the revolution, where the Revolutionary Council led the revolutionary movement against the regime until its withdrawal." (MRC corpus)

221 **"Every day we hear":** *Shams al-Horreya* (2012, December 30), Issue 16.

221 **RYM launched festivities:** All descriptions in this scene are from Al Aan TV (2012b), al-Faraj (2022b), the RYM corpus, and my subsequent visit to the site.

221 **Over the preceding week:** al-Faraj (2022b).

222 **Facing pressure from the old council:** Abel Os.

222 **"If you don't stand with us":** Abel Os.

222 **As voting was underway:** al-Faraj (2022b). The election, which took place on December 6, 2012, was covered by *al-Masar al-Horr* (2012, December 10), Issue 13, and *Shams al-Horreya* (2012, December 9), Issue 13.

222 **Posts were filled:** *al-Masar al-Horr* (2012, December 10), Issue 13; Zajil Network (2012).

222 **The *Path* crowed:** *al-Masar al-Horr* (2012, December 10), Issue 13.

222 **New president Muhammad Bisher pledged:** *al-Masar al-Horr* (2012, December 10), Issue 13.

222 **Oday spoke at a gathering:** Abel Os, Ahmed al-Faraj.

222 **The *Path* carried:** *al-Masar al-Horr* (2012, December 3), Issue 12.

223 **The famed nineteenth-century French statesman:** See Krylov (2013).

223 **The senate mooted changing:** MRC corpus.

223 **Every word has a history:** The material in this paragraph is drawn from Abu-'Uksa (2016) and Lutsky (1969).

223 **This might seem surprising:** Hornblower & Spawforth (2005).

223 **A trenchant critic of Ottoman colonialism:** See Weismann (2015) for Kawakibi's biography.

223 **Shortly before his death:** al-Kawakibi (2022). The original title uses the word استعباد, which literally means *enslavement*, though translators often opt for the broader term *oppression*.

224 **Interference and domination are different:** The distinction between interference and domination explored here, which Kawakibi anticipated, is drawn from Pettit (1997).

224 **The Romans called a system:** Pettit (1997).

225 **After a few days conducting media interviews:** A surviving documentary film from that period, Walat TV (2013), features an interview with Muhammad al-Bisher. Abel Os, Abdul Hadi, and Oday are visible at 1:08.

225 **They decided to reverse the recent:** RYM corpus.

225 **However, the Free Army faction:** *Shams al-Horreya* (2012, December 30), Issue 16; Kamel Suleiman (Manbij Protesters corpus); Ahmed Rahmo (MRC corpus).

225 **The new council accused the old:** *Shams al-Horreya* (2012, December 30), Issue 16; *al-Masar al-Horr* (2012, December 31), Issue 16.

225 **Friday, December 28:** See, for example, ANA New Media Association (2012).

225 **The next day, RYM activists gathered:** This scene is from multiple sources in the RYM corpus, and from al-Faraj (2022b).

225 **Oday believed that the price decrease:** Oday corpus.

225 **"Let the two councils unite!":** Republic Video corpus. *al-Masar al-Horr* echoed this sentiment: "The two councils could unite, with a left wing and a right wing . . ." *al-Masar al-Horr* (2012, December 12), Issue 13.

226 **The *Path* noted sardonically:** *al-Masar al-Horr* (2012, December 10), Issue 13.

226 **One afternoon, Abdul Hadi and his brother Muhammad:** This scene is drawn from Abdul Hadi, Hasan Nefi, and Hussein al-Hashem (RYM corpus), who was present. According to Hasan Nefi, Muhammad al-Bisher struck first, but multiple witnesses said the opposite.

226 **That evening, Muhammad Bisher:** This scene is recounted in al-Faraj (2022b), who witnessed it.
227 **The new council's inaugural statement:** Zajil Network (2012).
227 **That was the real usurpation:** Muhammad al-Bisher's words and reaction are based on Ahmed al-Faraj's testimony, and corroborated with Abdul Hadi al-Bisher.

BOOK 3: NINE

228 **"The [revolutionary authorities] arrested":** *Shams al-Horreya* (2013, January 20), Issue 19.
228 **"*The Free Path* visited":** *al-Masar al-Horr* (2013, January 7), Issue 17.
228 **"A number of people":** *al-Masar al-Horr* (2013, January 14), Issue 18.
228 **"Qadri Jamil, deputy":** *al-Masar al-Horr* (2013, January 28), Issue 20.
228 **As winter mists settled over Manbij:** Republic Video corpus.
228 **In the evenings, Mina walked:** The principal sources in this chapter are Mina Saba, Mina's diary, and Israa Sheikh Weiss (Mina Saba corpus). Corroborating details were drawn from the Social Media corpus, the Republic Video corpus, *al-Masar al-Horr* issues 17–21, and *Shams al-Horreya* issues 17–23.
229 **Fragments of verse:** The poem is briefly visible at the start of Ugarit News (2012b). The translation is my own. The verses are by Syrian poet Sulaiman al-Issa.
229 **Streets had become open-air art exhibits:** Ugarit News (2012b). Further information about these exhibits comes from the artist Ahmed Humeidi (Manbij Protesters corpus).
230 **Not long after, Mina was in a basement:** This scene is from Mina Saba and Israa Sheikh Weiss.
230 **Two dozen women sat in a circle:** The video announcing the formation of this group is available at Moetaz AboRyad (2013a).
231 **"He who doesn't have":** *Shams al-Horreya* (2012, November 25), Issue 11.
232 **"For a long time, we have been screaming":** *Shams al-Horreya* (2012, December 9), Issue 13.
233 **The council headquarters felt:** Additional details from this scene are from the Republic Video corpus, which contains stock footage of the Revolutionary Council in action.
233 **But when Mina raised her proposal:** According to interviewees in the MRC corpus, they felt their rule was too weak to embolden tribal conservatives by including women on the council.
234 **"You gaze upon me":** *Shams al-Horreya* (2012, December 9), Issue 13.
234 **"Now we have our freedom":** *Shams al-Horreya* (2012, December 9), Issue 13.
235 **Waking up under Manbij's gray skies:** The details in this paragraph are from the Republic Video corpus and drawn from several interviews across different corpora.
235 **A Neutral Committee had formed:** *al-Masar al-Horr* (2013, January 14), Issue 18.
237 **The leader of this wing:** Information about Huda is from the Huda al-Muhammad corpus.
237 **"She was not the type of person":** Muhammad Kullal (Huda al-Muhammad corpus).
237 **Before long, Huda and her sister:** Additional details about the activities of the Girls of Tomorrow are from the Girls of Tomorrow Facebook page (Social Media corpus) and several videos (Republic Video corpus). Examples include Al Aan TV (2013a) and Basma Syria (2013).
237 **"The motto of our assembly":** *al-Masar al-Horr* (2013, May 20), Issue 36.
237 **Huda took part in revolutionary theater:** Details on theater are from Mina Saba. On the column, see, for example, *Shams al-Horreya* (2013, April 7), Issue 30 and *Shams al-Horreya* (2013, April 28), Issue 33.
237 **"People are displaced from time":** *al-Masar al-Horr* (2013, May 20), Issue 36.
238 **The *Sun* began running:** *Shams al-Horreya* (2012, December 9), Issue 13.
238 **"Some predicted that we would not last":** *al-Masar al-*Horr (2013, May 20), Issue 36.

BOOK 3: TEN

239 **"RYM announced an open peaceful":** *al-Masar al-Horr* (2013, February 25), Issue 24.
239 **"On January 15, 2013":** *Shams al-Horreya* (2013, January 20), Issue 19.

239 **"A large number of Manbij's battalions":** *al-Masar al-Horr* (2013, January 14), Issue 18.
239 **"There has been a slight improvement":** *al-Masar al-Horr* (2013, February 11), Issue 22.
239 **"Fuel prices decreased":** *Shams al-Horreya* (2013, January 6), Issue 17.
239 **Despite the dull skies of January:** Descriptions in this paragraph are from the Republic Video corpus.
240 **Once, they sued the editors:** *al-Masar al-Horr* (2013, January 14), Issue 18.
240 **Muhammad Bisher's council imposed:** *al-Masar al-Horr* (2013, February 25), Issue 24.
240 **Home, a revolutionary artists' assembly:** Ahmed Humeidi (Manbij Protester corpus).
240 **Manbij had never held such a festival:** Details on the Syria Mosaic festival are from Mina Saba; Ahmed Humeidi; Al Aan TV (2013b); *al-Masar al-Horr* (2013, January 21), Issue 19; *al-Masar al-Horr* (2013, March 18), Issue 27; the documentary *Home* by Rafat Alzakout (2015); and a documentary by the marionette troupe Masasit Matti (2013).
240 **A documentary crew captured:** Masasit Matti (2013).
240 **A film crew captures:** Beginning at 8:52 in Alzakout (2015).
241 **Surprisingly, the power was steady:** Mina Saba.
241 **In the boxlike apartments:** Republic Video corpus.
241 **Not everyone saw the sparkle:** Details of the strike are from the Republic Video corpus; *al-Masar al-Horr* (2013, January 28), Issue 20; *Shams al-Horreya* (2013, January 20), Issue 19; Syrian Revolution (2014); and Mina Saba.
241 **Activists visited the hospital:** Republic Video corpus.
242 **One told a documentary crew:** Masasit Matti (2013).
242 **On Narrative:** This section was informed by research on the therapeutic effects of narrative, including Saul (2021). I am grateful for discussions with Jack Saul for helping shape my views here.
242 **People filed through the pergola:** Descriptions of the performance are from the Republic Video corpus.
242 **The exhibition hall displayed:** These works can be seen in Al Aan TV (2013c) and Ugarit News (2012b).
243 **When someone complains:** MacIntyre (2007).
244 **They issued a new call:** Social Media corpus.
244 **RYM led a long procession:** Republic Video corpus.
244 **As they drove through the streets:** The aftermath of the blast can be seen at Moetaz AboRyad (2013b) and Orient News (2013).
245 **But then, those arbitrary lives:** The story of Taha Radwan is from *al-Masar al-Horr* (2013, February 18), Issue 23 and an interview with one of his relatives.

BOOK 3: ELEVEN

246 **"Thirteen prisoners":** *al-Masar al-Horr* (2013, February 18), Issue 23.
246 **"Approximately":** *al-Masar al-Horr* (2013, February 18), Issue 23.
246 **"On Thursday evening":** *Shams al-Horreya* (2013, February 17), Issue 23.
246 **How Ibrahim Decided:** Ibrahim is the primary source of the details of his rebel exploits, with several sources in the Rebel corpus providing corroboration.
246 **In the early-morning glow:** Details are from a video taken by Ibrahim (Republic Video corpus).
247 **It was steady work:** Additional details are from the Poverty corpus.
248 **His unit occupied:** Details are from a video taken by Ibrahim (Republic Video corpus).
248 **The cement walls:** Ibrahim: "The walls were bursting around us in many small places."
249 **Most had joined the Free Army:** Many stories in the Rebel corpus mirror Ibrahim's.
249 **There was, for example, Hasan Sex:** Hasan Sex's story is from interviews with Hasan al-Awni (his real name) and others in the Rebel corpus, which includes his close friends.
249 **"Fear and tension":** Bassam Abu al-Abed, the brother of the Prince (Rebel corpus).
250 **Hasan was able to get close:** Ahmed Nuri al-Ghathwan al-Ghanayemi (Rebel corpus).
250 **Bilal Assaf:** This story was related by Bilal Assaf (Rebel corpus) and corroborated by others in the corpus.

253 **a Kalashnikov:** Abu Maan (Rebel corpus).
253 **It was the heyday:** Abu Maan; *al-Masar al-Horr* (2013, March 18), Issue 27.
253 **"The only way":** *al-Masar al-Horr* (2013, February 25), Issue 24.
253 **The *Path* pleaded:** *al-Masar al-Horr* (2013, February 25), Issue 24.
253 **The Gulf regimes:** For more on foreign attitudes to the Syrian conflict, see Gopal & Hodge (2022).
254 **Middlemen appeared:** Abu Maan; Gopal & Hodge (2022).
254 **The United States was reluctant:** See, for example, Worth (2012).
254 **In 2012, the CIA launched:** Schmitt (2012).
254 **"If they really wanted":** *al-Masar al-Horr* (2013, January 28), Issue 20.
254 **"Only Russia's position":** *al-Masar al-Horr* (2013, February 18), Issue 23.
254 **"Anyone who hears":** *al-Masar al-Horr* (2012, December 10), Issue 13.
255 **The Sordid Tale:** Principal sources for the Prince's exploits are Bassam Abu al-Abed (his brother) and Hasan al-Awni, from the Rebel corpus; Nazeer K. and Hussein al-Dahir, from the Manbij Protesters corpus; Fayez K. from the RYM corpus; and Ibrahim.
255 **Alone, forgotten, embittered:** The description of the mood and atmospherics of FSA units is based on my visits to such units in 2012.
255 **Days passed:** Details of the Battle of Tel Abyad are sourced from participants including Hasan al-Awni and Ibrahim, as well as dozens of videos in the Republic Video corpus.
255 **Over a meal:** See, for example, M. al-Hamoud (2012), where Maymati and the Prince are standing side by side after the Tel Abyad battle.
256 **Turkish authorities canceled:** Rebel corpus.
256 **Amid this tumult:** The Prince's movements here are related by Bassam Abu al-Abed.
257 **A camera captured the final moments:** These scenes are from Ummayad Live Syria (2012), Raqqa News Network (2012), and several videos from the Republic Video corpus.
258 **Maymati and a comrade:** This scene is related by several people in the Rebel corpus.

258 **Rebels tore down:** CNN Wire Staff (2012).
258 **"I'm a free Syrian!":** Qena (2012).
258 **The fighters gathered atop:** This scene is from several videos in the Republic Video corpus, including one shot by Ibrahim.
259 **So he approached a cousin:** RYM corpus.
259 **The Prince gathered a group of friends:** Abel Os.
259 **One day, the Prince appeared:** Abel Os, Republic Video corpus.
259 **But where did he obtain the weapons?:** Details of the Prince's corruption are from the MRC and RYM corpora. Bassam Abu al-Abed acknowledges these incidents but justifies them on the grounds of needing matériel to fight the regime.
260 **He was collecting tens of thousands:** Prince supporters claim the amount they collected was an order of magnitude less, but given the price of weapons and ammunition, this seems unlikely.
260 **One was Jund al-Haramain:** Saleh Muhammad (Rebels corpus), Al Abdeh (2013), Gopal & Hodge (2022). Ibrahim Bannawi, a leader of Jund al-Haramein, denies these allegations, but they are widely attested.
260 **Jund seized one:** The so-called Reserve Furnace. Ibrahim Bannawi acknowledges this seizure and justifies it on the grounds of needing to fund the fight against the regime.
260 **These "bread brigades":** *al-Masar al-Horr* (2013, January 14), Issue 18, *al-Masar al-Horr* (2013, February 4), Issue 21.
260 **East of the city:** Al Abdeh (2013).
260 **"I was told by people":** *al-Masar al-Horr* (2013, February 25), Issue 24.
260 **The road in front of him:** This description is based on my visit to the area.
262 **Blood as dark as:** Ibrahim: "It looked like 'Coca-Cola was pouring from his thigh."
262 **"There's something new":** Ibrahim: "I saw something new in his eyes."

BOOK 3: TWELVE

263 **"Three consecutive":** *al-Masar al-Horr* (2013, March 4), Issue 25.
263 **"RYM organized":** *al-Masar al-Horr* (2013, March 4), Issue 25.
263 **"A considerable":** *Weekly Letters* (2013, April 4), Issue 5.

263 **"During the past":** *al-Masar al-Horr* (2013, March 11), Issue 26.
264 **"In a quick visit":** *al-Masar al-Horr* (2013, March 4), Issue 25.
264 **"Two whole years":** *al-Masar al-Horr* (2013, March 18), Issue 27.
264 **"Just as under":** *Shams al-Horreya* (2013, April 7), Issue 30.
265 **"We might not fret":** *al-Masar al-Horr* (2012, December 17), Issue 14.
265 **"The demand":** *al-Masar al-Horr* (2012, December 17), Issue 14.
265 **The largest of these groups:** For more on Ahrar al-Sham, see Drevon (2024).
265 **The Levant Free Men appeared first in western Syria:** Their entry into Manbij, and their founding statement, is covered in *Shams al-Horreya* (2012, December 30), Issue 16.
265 **Most of the fighters:** Details about Ahrar al-Sham's membership are from Hussein Ibo, former member (Republic Battle corpus).
265 **Many activists worried:** See, for example, *al-Masar al-Horr* (2012, December 17), Issue 14.
265 **"We ought to live":** *al-Masar al-Horr* (2013, January 28), Issue 20.
265 **But Muhammad Bisher's new council:** RYM corpus.
265 **The Levant Free Men responded:** *Shams al-Horreya* (2012, December 30), Issue 16.
266 **But the police themselves:** Bassam Abu al-Abed (Rebel corpus).
266 **The Sordid Tale:** Testimony of the battle between the Prince and Ahrar al-Sham is drawn from Bassam Abu al-Abed and Hasan al-Awni (Rebel corpus); Ali Saleh al-Jasim (MRC corpus); Fayez K. and Shabaan al-Hasan (RYM corpus); Hussein Omar Samawi; and Ahmed al-Faraj, Abel Os, Hussein Abu Raed, and several others from the RYM corpus. Additional sources include *al-Masar al-Horr* (2013, April 8), Issue 30 and *Shams al-Horreya* (2013, April 7), Issue 30.
266 **One evening, representatives:** This scene is drawn from Bassam Abu al-Abed and Hasan al-Awni from the Prince's side, several figures from the MRC corpus, and *al-Masar al-Horr* (2013, February 25), Issue 24.
266 **Later that same night:** *al-Masar al-Horr* (2013, April 1), Issue 29.

267 **The Prince invited the *Path*:** *al-Masar al-Horr* (2013, March 25), Issue 28.
267 **The old council saw the raid:** Ahmed Rahmo (MRC corpus).
267 **RYM pledged to remain independent:** RYM corpus.
268 **The senate held an:** MRC corpus, RYM corpus.
268 **When the words hit Oday's ears:** Abel Os.
269 **News spread that the senators:** MRC corpus.
269 **At 10:00 p.m., he positioned armed lookouts:** Republic Video corpus.
269 **Most of his faction:** Including Ibrahim, who was stationed at the front.
269 **There must have been at least a hundred vehicles:** Hussein Omar Samawi, who photographed the convoy.
269 **From his second-floor windows:** According to Bassam Abu al-Abed and Hasan al-Awni.
269 **Families gathered in kitchens:** Ahmed al-Faraj.
270 **Those living nearby:** Republic Video corpus.
270 **"Get back," a young fighter screamed:** Republic Video corpus.
270 **Chunks of concrete:** Republic Video corpus.
271 **Another senator shouted:** This is according to Ahmed al-Faraj, who witnessed the scene.
271 **Some came to gawk:** Republic Video corpus.
271 **Some milled near the scene:** Ahmed al-Faraj.
271 **The procession of 4×4s:** Republic Video corpus.
271 **None of them were even Syrian:** The six men belonged to rebel faction Liwa' al-Muhajireen wa al-Ansar, which consisted entirely of foreigners.

BOOK 3: THIRTEEN

272 **"Mr. Zakaria Al-Khalaf":** *al-Masar al-Horr* (2013, April 22), Issue 32.
272 **"A Revolutionary Police officer":** *Shams al-Horreya* (2013, April 21), Issue 32.
272 **"Two demonstrations":** *Weekly Letters* (2013, April 4), Issue 5.
272 **Abdul Hadi thought of:** Abdul Hadi's thoughts and actions in this chapter are primarily from Abdul Hadi, Ahmed al-Faraj, and Abel Os, with supporting details from others in the RYM corpus.

NOTES

273 **They even spoke a different tongue:** For more on such urban–rural distinctions, see Dukhan (2022).

273 **Matters came to a head:** Details on the Aleppo Provincial Council elections in Turkey are from Hasan Nefi and Abel Os; Ahmed al-Rahmo (MRC corpus); Ahmed al-Faraj and Yasser al-Shuweikh (RYM corpus); Saleh Muhammad (Rebel corpus); *al-Masar al-Horr* (2013, March 4), Issue 25; *al-Masar al-Horr* (2013, March 11), Issue 26; *al-Masar al-Horr* (2013, March 25), Issue 28; and *al-Masar al-Horr* (2013, April 8), Issue 30.

274 **But when the delegation:** Old Council supporters claim this was done on a technicality (MRC corpus).

274 **Back in Manbij:** Ahmed al-Faraj.

274 **RYM took to the streets:** *al-Masar al-Horr* (2013, February 25), Issue 24; *al-Masar al-Horr* (2013, March 11), Issue 26.

274 **"Where is our":** *al-Masar al-Horr* (2013, March 25), Issue 28.

274 **"The people who have rebelled":** *al-Masar al-Horr* (2013, April 8), Issue 30.

275 **For the *Sun*, he wrote:** *Shams al-Horreya* (2013, January 6), Issue 17.

275 **"This is the deep state":** Yasser al-Shuweikh (RYM corpus).

277 **A Meeting of Worlds:** This scene is from several interviewees in the RYM corpus, primarily Abdul Hadi and Ahmed al-Faraj. Much of the dialogue is from Ahmed al-Faraj's meeting notes.

277 **Abdul Hadi left home:** Details from this walk are taken from my own walk retracing Abdul Hadi's steps. Descriptions of the murals are from the Republic Video corpus.

277 **As on most nights:** I confirmed the presence of mulberry trees during my visit to the Youth Center.

278 **He was squat:** Social Media corpus.

278 **He introduced his "brothers":** These descriptions are from the RYM corpus and Social Media corpus.

278 **Oday asked:** Ahmed al-Faraj.

278 **Oday explained:** Ahmed al-Faraj.

279 **"Assad corrupted the minds":** *al-Masar al-Horr* (2013, March 11), Issue 26.

280 **Three days earlier:** Technically, the group's name is the Islamic State of Iraq and the Levant (al-Sham).

280 **Oday said he'd welcome:** Ahmed al-Faraj.

280 **A black flag hung:** This scene is from Abdul Hadi and Ahmed al-Faraj, who were present.

280 **Printed on it:** Social Media corpus.

281 **But Abel Os had seen enough:** The official statement read: "As a result of developments on the scene in Manbij, the Executive Office of the Revolutionary Youth Movement has decided, after deliberation and discussion, [to] accept the resignation of brother Abdul Qader Oseb, AKA 'Abel Os' from the presidency of the RYM. The Executive Office of RYM … thanks the brother Abel Os for his efforts in the revolutionary movement."

282 **RYM elected as its new leader:** Nabeel is a pseudonym.

282 **In mid-April:** The Battle of Qusayr. See Blanford (2013).

282 **The efforts culminated:** Details of the summit are from the MRC and RYM corpora.

283 **He handed the megaphone:** Details of Munzer Salal's speech are from Munzer Salal, interviewees in the RYM corpus, and the Republic Video corpus.

284 **"The Cultural Center does not belong to any faction":** Republic Video corpus.

284 **Security Square filled with:** This scene is drawn from the MRC, RYM, and Republic Video corpora.

284 **An ISIS commander emerged:** RYM corpus.

284 **Munzer asked him:** Details of this scene are from Munzer Salal and Abdul Hadi.

BOOK 3: FOURTEEN

288 **"Dr. Ahmed Taan":** *al-Masar al-Horr* (2013, April 15), Issue 31.

288 **"On Monday":** *Weekly Letters* (2013, May 9), Issue 10.

288 **"The Girls of Tomorrow":** *Shams al-Horreya* (2013, April 28), Issue 33.

288 **"Guests from":** *Weekly Letters* (2013, May 9), Issue 10.

288 **"At approximately":** *Weekly Letters* (2013, May 23), Issue 12.

289 **The walls were adorned:** *Shams al-Horreya* (2013, May 12), Issue 35.

289 **When the nominees:** RYM corpus.

289 **Oday, too, boycotted:** Ahmed al-Faraj.

289 **So the majority of RYM:** Details on the election are from the MRC corpus, especially Ali Saleh al-Jasim and Mustafa

al-Abdullah; the RYM corpus; Abel Os; *al-Masar al-Horr* (2013), Issues 33, 34, 35, and 44; *Shams al-Horreya* (2013, May 6), Issue 34; and *al-Suri al-Horr* (2013, July 18), Issue 4.

289 **In his victory speech:** *Shams al-Horreya* (2013, April 28), Issue 33.

290 **The final cabinet:** Details of the list are from *al-Masar al-Horr* (2013, May 13), Issue 35.

290 **"To the esteemed owners":** Social Media corpus.

290 **This was just the beginning:** *al-Masar al-Horr* (2013, June 3), Issue 38; *al-Masar al-Horr* (2013, July 31), Issue 46.

291 **The *Path* wrote:** *al-Masar al-Horr* (2013, May 6), Issue 34.

291 **These publications:** I've translated the name al-Bayan as "The Declaration."

292 **On Secularism:** I've drawn some of the key ideas of this section from Asad (2003).

293 **"The secular state":** *al-Masar al-Horr* (2012, November 27), Issue 11.

293 **"The future Syria":** *al-Masar al-Horr* (2012, December 24), Issue 15.

293 **"Have I told you":** *al-Masar al-Horr* (2013, March 4), Issue 25.

295 **"Those ignorant fools":** *al-Rai al-Horr* (2013, September 1), Issue 36.

295 **"Islam is a way of life":** *Shams al-Horreya* (2013, May 12), Issue 35.

295 **"After the failure":** *Shams al-Horreya* (2013, May 12), Issue 35.

BOOK 3: FIFTEEN

296 **"The Free Aleppo":** *Shams al-Horreya* (2013, June 23), Issue 41.

296 **"The staff of":** *al-Masar al-Horr* (2013, June 17), Issue 40.

296 **"After he had":** *al-Masar al-Horr* (2013, June 24), Issue 41.

296 **"The judiciary":** *al-Masar al-Horr* (2013, February 4), Issue 21.

296 **"People say":** *Weekly Letters* (2013, March 28), Issue 4.

297 **"Statement No. 1":** *Panorama* (2013, May 22), Issue 1.

297 **A Grim Discovery:** This chapter is drawn from the following sources: interviews with A. A. and A. K., who are linked to the victim's and perpetrator's families, respectively (both spoke on the condition of anonymity); Huzayfa al-Osman (Manbij Protesters corpus), who was an eyewitness to the execution; Ahmed al-Faraj, Abel Os, Nabeel D., and Hatim al-Daroubi (RYM corpus), all of whom witnessed the execution and Abdul Hadi's machinations; Abu Maan, commander of the Security Brigade; *Shams al-Horreya* (June and July 2013), Issues 40, 43, and 46; the Revolutionary Council's newspaper, *al-Majlis wa al-Nas* (2013, June 15), Issue 3; and *al-Suri al-Horr* (2013, July 4), Issue 3.

297 **Out in the country:** This description is based on my visit to the area, as well as descriptions from Musa al-Jasim's father, Abdul Aziz al-Jasim.

297 **Blood was streaked:** This description is based on a photograph from the Social Media corpus.

297 **Musa Jasim did not advance:** These details are from Musa al-Jasim's father, Abdul Aziz al-Jasim.

297 **The Revolutionary Police:** Details on the police investigation are from Musa al-Jasim's father, Abdul Aziz al-Jasim, and *Shams al-Horreya* (2013, June 16), Issue 40.

297 **The driver was taken in for questioning:** Abdul Aziz al-Jasim.

298 **This outfit:** Details of the Security Brigade investigation are from interviews with Abu Maan, a brigade commander.

298 **Musa's murder had shaken:** *al-Suri al-Horr* (2013, June 28), Issue 2.

298 **The courts operated:** See, for example, al-Zarier et al. (2017).

298 **After a couple of days:** Abdul Aziz al-Jasim, A. K.

298 **It was dark when:** This scene is drawn from the testimony of M. S. H. to Musa's father after the execution. M. S. H. was in the car.

299 **At the Security Brigade headquarters:** Abu Maan: "Then the discussion of what to do with him began. That discussion reached a dead end. Everyone was saying execute him and [I was] saying hell fucking no."

299 **At RYM headquarters:** RYM corpus.

299 **A banner reading:** Social Media corpus.

299 **Inside, they found:** This conversation is based on interviews with Abdul Hadi and A. A.

300 **The crowd—some two hundred strong:** Republic Video corpus.

300 **Abdul Hadi led the procession:** Details of this march and the encounter at the al-Ghassania Courthouse are from Abdul Hadi, A. A., and Ahmed al-Faraj.
300 **As the mass moved down:** Republic Video corpus.
300 **Protestors were pushing against:** Republic Video corpus.
300 **Oday tried to pull him back:** Ahmed al-Faraj.
301 **Three vehicles raced toward the crowd:** Republic Video corpus.
301 **These people aren't afraid:** Ahmed al-Faraj.
301 **Locked in a room:** These details are from Abdul Aziz al-Jasim.
302 **"People were not registered":** Hallaq (2009a).
302 **Sharia became a way:** I drew the ideas in this section from Hallaq (2009a and 2009b).
302 **Other penalties:** Hallaq (2009a).
302 **When the British:** This example is in Hallaq (2009a).
302 **One historian writes:** Dirks (2006).
303 **In Syria, this remained a minority view:** Khatib (2011).
303 **Musa's father was a kindly old man:** This scene is from Abdul Aziz al-Jasim.
304 **It was Thursday evening:** Abdul Hadi descriptions are from Ahmed al-Faraj.
304 **The next morning, Friday, July 5:** The execution scene is from the eyewitness testimony of Huzayfa Osman, Ahmed al-Faraj, and Abel Os.
304 **The new flag was four stories long:** This description is based on photographs from the Social Media corpus.
304 **The man wearing the explosives:** This speech is partially captured in the Republic Video corpus.
305 **Oday, watching the man's every movement:** He related this to Ahmed al-Faraj afterward.
305 **Their bodies pressed close:** Republic Video corpus.
306 **Oday and a few RYM members:** Oday's movements and feelings here are from Ahmed al-Faraj, who was by his side.
306 **That evening:** As related by Abdul Aziz al-Jasim.
306 **But Oday and the other RYM members:** Ahmed al-Faraj.
307 **As RYM members went:** The message is visible in a photograph in the Social Media corpus.

BOOK 3: SIXTEEN

308 **"Three people":** *al-Masar al-Horr* (2013, June 24), Issue 41.
308 **"The Senate elections":** *al-Masar al-Horr* (2013, July 10), Issue 43.
308 **"The Free Students Union":** *al-Masar al-Horr* (2013, July 10), Issue 43.
308 **"A demonstration":** *Panorama* (2013, July 24), Issue 10.
308 **"As the Revolutionary Council is responsible":** *Shams al-Horreya* (2013, June 16), Issue 40; Social Media corpus.
309 **Oday could not bring himself:** As related to Ahmed al-Faraj, Abel Os, and Abdul Hadi.
309 **That squat structure:** The description is based on my visit and photographs.
309 **He invited RYM members:** RYM corpus.
309 **The air was sluggish:** RYM corpus and Republic Video corpus.
310 **He was more than willing:** RYM corpus.
310 **A video of the endeavor:** Bisher albisher (2013a).
310 **When this organization had launched:** Details on the Muslim Youth Assembly are from Abu Tayyeb, one of its founders.
311 **The RYM members returned:** These anecdotes are from Ahmed al-Faraj.
311 **Those who encountered:** These details are from interviews in the Abdul Hadi corpus.
311 **ISIS launched the Fertile Crescent:** *Panorama* (2013, May 22), Issue 1.
312 **ISIS also founded a charity:** *Panorama* (2013, May 22), Issue 1.
312 **Free Thought ran an:** *al-Rai al-Horr* (2013, September 1), Issue 36.
312 **At the same time:** *Panorama* (2013, May 22), Issue 1; Munzer Salal (MRC corpus).
312 **The Revolutionary Council watched:** MRC corpus.
312 **They vetted the imams:** Munzer Salal.
312 **At a senate session:** Abdul Karim Mustafa (MRC corpus).
312 **Islamist assemblies organized rallies:** *Shams al-Horreya* (2013, July 4), Issue 30.
313 **The instructor, Sheikh Abu Sayed al-Dibo:** Sheikh Dibo's story is based on interviews with his son Aqil al-Dibo, his cousin Ibrahim al-Dibo, and Abel Os.
313 **On July 9, 2013:** This scene is based on Aqil al-Dibo, Ibrahim al-Dibo, and Abel Os.
314 **Under the glow:** See, for example, lewa alislam (2013).

314 **The following evening:** This scene is drawn from Munzer Salal and Abel Os, who were eyewitnesses, along with several videos in the Republic Video corpus.

315 **Within minutes, a few:** Republic Video corpus.

315 **A video clip shows:** Republic Video corpus.

315 **The drums from Abel Os's demonstration:** Republic Video corpus.

315 **"Some people think":** Republic Video corpus.

BOOK 3: SEVENTEEN

317 **"A debate":** *Weekly Letters* (2013, July 11), Issue 19.

317 **"We are used":** *al-Masar al-Horr* (2013, July 17), Issue 44.

317 **"The dollar's price":** *Weekly Letters* (2013, July 18), Issue 20.

317 **"A labor union":** *Weekly Letters* (2013, July 4), Issue 18.

317 **A War on Terror:** This chapter is based on the Safira corpus, augmented with several open-source reports and videos. Key videos include Shahba Press Agency (2013), Orient News (2013b), and Sky News Arabia (2013).

317 **They came bundled:** This description is drawn from the Republic Video corpus.

318 **In July alone, ten thousand people:** Social Media corpus.

318 **The road to Safira skirts:** This description is drawn from my visit.

318 **The first glimmer of dawn:** "Monk Farm" is a translation of Mazra'at al-Raheb. The details from this massacre are drawn from seven eyewitness testimonies and several testimonies of those who visited the area after the regime forces withdrew (Safira corpus). See also Ebraheem Arabo (2013), which details the testimony of a survivor of the wells massacre.

320 **Meanwhile, back in the hamlets:** Videos of the aftermath of this assault along the highway include Tall Refaat City (2013), al-Safira News (2013b), and Yasmin al-Safira (2013).

320 **The clashes did not last long:** The details of the massacre of Rasm al-Nafl are drawn from ten eyewitness testimonies and several testimonies of those who visited the area after the regime forces withdrew (Safira corpus).

322 **For weeks, the Syrian regime:** Abu Shadi al-Safirani (2013); Ali Hasan (2013).

322 **In the hamlet of Umm Amud:** al-Safira News (2013a).

322 **On a wall was written:** Halab News Network H.N.N. (2013).

322 **On another wall:** Halab News Network H.N.N. (2013).

322 **A regime documentary television crew:** The Permanent Page of President Bashar al-Assad (2013).

323 **On Politics:** In this section I have drawn from Aristotle's *Politics* and O'Gorman (2020).

323 **Local human rights organizations:** Cowell (2013).

323 **Most of the dead were likely civilians:** This is my assessment. The Syrian Observatory for Human Rights finds that one-third of the fatalities were civilians, but very few of the civilian deaths in the massacres of this chapter, or those in Manbij that I have documented, have been documented by SOHR. Given that rebel and regime fatalities are much easier to track due to Facebook postings, this suggests that the SOHR grossly underestimates the number of dead civilians, and that civilians in fact comprise the majority of the dead. See Zenko & Wolf (2014).

323 **So the second variety of killing:** On early warning systems, see Hale et al. (2023).

323 **We know something of the inner workings:** Taub (2016).

323 **It's unclear how many:** Arab Center Washington DC (2025).

323 **The regime catalogued these deaths:** These details are from Taub (2016).

323 **The victims showed signs:** These images are available online. See for example Human Rights Watch (2015).

324 **Yet according to the Genocide Convention:** United Nations General Assembly (1948).

325 **Yassin al-Haj Saleh, an activist:** Young (2017).

BOOK 3: EIGHTEEN

327 **"[A refugee] from Homs":** *Weekly Letters* (2013, July 18), Issue 20.

327 **"The Free Syrian":** *al-Masar al-Horr* (2013, July 10), Issue 43.

327 **In August:** *al-Masar al-Horr* (2013, July and August), Issues 45 and 47; Orient News (2013).

NOTES

327 **For two days:** Republic Video corpus.
327 **The *Path* declared:** *al-Masar al-Horr* (2013, August 21), Issue 48.
327 **The production:** *al-Masar al-Horr* (2013, July 24), Issue 45.
328 **The senators spoke of a new beginning:** This description is from Munzer Salal (MRC corpus).
328 **"I don't think it's right":** *al-Masar al-Horr* (2013, April 29), Issue 33.
328 **prompting even more families:** On migration from Safira, see *Shams al-Horreya* (2013, June 23), Issue 41.
328 **Manbij—which now housed more than double its prewar population:** This population estimate is mine, based on several interviews across the corpora.
328 **Some refugees:** *al-Masar al-Horr* (2013, July 17), Issue 44.
328 **The human cost of this collapse:** Republic Video corpus.
328 **The middle class:** *al-Masar al-Horr* (2013, August 21), Issue 48.
329 **"Freedom is a sea":** *al-Masar al-Horr* (2013, July 17), Issue 44.
329 **"The greedy trader":** *Shams al-Horreya* (2013, July 8), Issue 43.
329 **Revolutionary authorities:** See Alderman et al. (2018).
329 **"We remind you that Ramadan":** Revolutionary Council statement on July 7, 2013 (Social Media corpus).
330 **"The higher the price":** *al-Masar al-Horr* (2013, June 10), Issue 39.
330 **The *Sun* ran:** *Shams al-Horreya* (2013, June 23), Issue 41.
330 **In November, the Revolutionary Council:** On the June hike, see *Shams al-Horreya* (2013, June 16), Issue 40, and *al-Majlis wa al-Nas* (2013, June 15), Issue 3.
330 **But the private bakeries:** On overcrowding, see *Shams al-Horreya* (2013, June 23), Issue 41.
330 **Such prices were caused:** The details in this paragraph are from several sources, primarily Aimad al-Din al-Henezel and Mahmoud al-Ali (Bread Survey corpus), as well as *Shams al-Horreya* and *al-Masar al-Horr* issues from the summer of 2013.
331 **In late August:** The Council described its vision in its newsletter, *al-Majlis wa al-Nas* (2013, June 1), Issue 1. The rollout is described in *al-Masar al-Horr* (2013, July 17), Issue 44.

331 **The council claimed:** Aimad al-Din al-Henezel (Bread Survey corpus).
331 **Impromptu demonstrations broke out:** Descriptions of these demonstrations are from several videos in the Republic Videos corpus, along with interviews with Ali Saleh al-Jasim and Mustafa al-Abdullah (MRC corpus); Huzayfa al-Osman (Manbij Protesters corpus); Ahmed al-Faraj; Abel Os; Muhammad Abu Nadeem (Abdul Hadi corpus); Abu Maan (Rebel corpus); and Mustafa Haddad and Muhammad Junaid (RYM corpus).
331 **Their voices carried:** Republic Video corpus.
331 **An ISIS member on a motorcycle:** This is according to Muhammad Abu Nadeem, the RYM activist who was approached by ISIS.
331 **The crowd, now three hundred strong:** Republic Video corpus.
331 **The leader of ISIS in Manbij:** This scene is related by Ahmed al-Faraj and Muhammad Abu Nadeem, who was present.
331 **They smashed storefronts with sticks:** Republic Video corpus; *al-Masar al-Horr* (2013, September 7), Issue 51.
331 **A video shows a frenzied horde:** Bisher albisher (2013b).
332 **A vehicle from the Security Brigade:** This is according to Abu Maan.
332 **Along the way:** Republic Video corpus.
332 **Oday was with his sister:** Bushra al-Hema (Oday corpus).
332 **He did not want it to be said:** Abdul Hadi's thoughts here are according to Muhammad Abu Nadeem, with whom he discussed his views at the time.
332 **Riots continued all week:** *Shams al-Horreya* (2013, September 1), Issues 50–51; *Shams al-Horreya* (2013, September 9), Issue 52.
333 **The next morning:** This scene is from Amer K., a Manbij Mills employee (Bread Survey corpus) and Ali Saleh al-Jasim (MRC corpus).
333 **By all accounts a polite man:** Details on Abu Harith's background are from Abboud al Shami, who was an ISIS member.
333 **That evening:** Revolutionary Council statement on September 5, 2013 (Social Media corpus).
334 **"Whoever controls this facility":** This was uttered by Ali Saleh al-Jasim during

a Senate session in June. This session was recorded by Yaser Munif.

BOOK 3: NINETEEN

335 **He took part in the battle:** See, for example, Maktab Ma'adan (2013).

335 **He had been traveling:** These details are from his father-in-law, Jasim Atroush Abu Muhammad, and his fellow rebel Abu Ahmed. They disagree on his fate; Abu Muhammad believes Maymati was captured by the regime and imprisoned, while Abu Ahmed believes he was kidnapped and executed by ISIS. The fact that no word of Maymati has emerged following the overthrow of the regime lends some credence to Abu Ahmed's version.

336 **Wherever he went:** Details of this debate are from Aimad al-Din Henezel and Ali Saleh al-Jasim (MRC corpus), and Ahmed al-Faraj.

336 **Instead, it was:** *al-Masar al-Horr* (2013, September 7), Issue 51.

336 **"I told them you have":** *al-Masar al-Horr* (2013, September 7), Issue 51.

336 **He was a quiet man:** This description is based on my meetings with him.

337 **Inside, seated behind:** This scene is from Aimad al-Din Henezel. Ahmed al-Faraj, who visited shortly after, confirmed Abdul Hadi's presence.

337 **That Friday, Aimad approached:** This scene is from Aimad al-Din Henezel; *al-Masar al-Horr* (2013, September 21), Issue 53; and *Shams al-Horreya* (2013, September 9), Issue 52.

338 **He pictured himself:** Aimad al-Din Henezel: "I told myself that this isn't a debate but a planned assassination—perhaps in the midst of the conversation someone would shoot me under the pretext of anger and excitement."

338 **The attendees poured onto the street:** Republic Video corpus.

338 **Around this time:** For details on the attack, see Human Rights Watch (2013) and United Nations Human Rights Council (2014).

339 **A "forest of missiles":** *Shams al-Horreya* (2013, September 1), Issues 50–51.

339 **The Revolutionary Council of Aleppo:** *al-Masar al-Horr* (2013, September 14), Issue 52.

339 **In Manbij, the *Sun*:** *Shams Horreya* (2013, September 1), Issues 50–51.

339 **Various assemblies:** RYM and Manbij Protesters corpora.

339 **At the headquarters:** This scene was witnessed by Abu Maan (Rebel corpus).

340 **"In short, the Western":** *al-Masar al-Horr* (2013, July 3), Issue 42.

BOOK 3: TWENTY

341 **"The brutal warplanes":** *al-Rai al-Horr* (2013, October 14), Issue 42.

341 **"Regime forces":** *al-Masar al-Horr* (2013, October 19), Issue 57.

341 **"On Wednesday":** *Weekly Letters* (2013, October 10), Issue 32.

341 **Not long after liberation:** Details in this section are from Shabaan al-Hasan and Huzayfa al-Osman (Manbij Protesters corpus); the Prince's brother, Bassam Abu al-Abed (Rebel corpus); Fayez K. (RYM corpus); and Ahmed al-Akl, a rebel who helped smuggle the Prince out of prison.

341 **He peered inside and saw a courtyard:** This description is based on a photograph he took.

342 **For weeks, Manbij had witnessed:** Hussein Omar Samawi.

342 **"After I'm released":** *al-Masar al-Horr* (2013, May 20), Issue 36.

342 **The next issue of the *Path*:** *al-Masar al-Horr* (2013, May 20), Issue 36.

342 **From the moment the Prince:** Details of the Prince's escape are from Ahmed al-Akl, who helped arrange it, as well as Hussein Ibo of Ahrar al-Sham and Bassam Abu al-Abed, the Prince's brother.

343 **Whether he saw such a role for himself:** This scene is from the Republic Video corpus.

343 **He went to ISIS headquarters:** Abdul Hadi's movements here are from Ahmed al-Faraj and several sources in the Abdul Hadi corpus, chiefly Muhammad Abu Nadeem.

343 **On the loudspeaker:** Republic Video corpus.

344 **An ISIS commander called out:** Republic Video corpus.

344 **The ISIS fighters refused to budge:** Republic Video corpus.

344 **"A man needs to breathe!":** Hasan al-Awni (Rebel corpus).

NOTES

344 **One morning in early November:** This scene is from Bassam Abu al-Abed and Hasan al-Awni.
345 **Eager to avoid falling:** *al-Masar al-Horr* (2013, September 21), Issue 53.
345 **In October:** These details are from *Panorama* (2013, September), Issues 15 and 16, and the RYM corpus.
346 **The revolutionary leadership:** *al-Rai al-Horr* (2013, September 1), Issue 36.
346 **In a statement:** Statement from the General Committee of the Custodians of the Revolution, October 13, 2013.
346 **The vice president:** *al-Masar al-Horr* (2013, October 19), Issue 57.
346 **From the beginning:** These details are from multiple sources in the Abdul Hadi corpus. Key details were provided by Muhammad Abu Nadeem and Nabeel K.
347 **Oday visited him now and then:** Akrama al-Hema (Oday corpus), Muhammad Abu Nadeem, Ahmed al-Faraj.
347 **His parents were searching for a bride:** Oday's diary.
347 **The demonstrations curled:** Republic Video corpus.
347 **Not long after:** This scene is from attendees Suleiman Suleiman and Nabeel D. (RYM corpus), and Abboud al-Daroubi (Caliphate corpus).
347 **There was Nabeel:** These details about Abboud's childhood are from interviews with him.
348 **Oday took the news:** Ahmed al-Faraj.
348 **Another former RYM member:** Suleiman Suleiman.
348 **Yet another ex-RYM member:** Abu Abdo (Abdul Hadi corpus).
349 **Ammar bin Yasser:** Abu Hasan (Caliphate corpus), Mustafa Hamza (Oday corpus).
349 **They screamed and laughed:** Republic Video corpus.

BOOK 3: TWENTY-ONE

350 **"In the past 10 days":** *Weekly Letters* (2013, October 31), Issue 35.
350 **"The Students Without Borders":** *al-Masar al-Horr* (2013, November 16), Issue 61.
350 **"Is it possible":** *Shams al-Horreya* (2013, September 23), Issue 54.
351 **He sat across the desk:** This scene is from interviews with Huzayfa Osman and his unpublished report on the same subject. Corroborating material was drawn from the RYM corpus.
352 **"This statement":** *Shams al-Horreya* (2013, October 9), Issue 56.
353 **Some activists drifted:** This detail is according to several sources in the Manbij Protesters corpus.
353 **The assembly was forced:** Israa Sheikh Weiss (Mina Saba corpus).
353 **The NGO was founded:** This description is based on the organization's website, as well as the application documents Mina signed and made available to me.
354 **With the funds:** The principal sources in this section are Mina, Israa Sheikh Weiss, Watan al-Daroubi, Ammar Hazweni, and others in the Manbij Protesters and Huda al-Muhammad corpora.
354 **But the young men:** They belonged to the Union of Free Students assembly.
354 **When she arrived:** This description is based on a photograph Mina took.
355 **One day, Sheikh Dibo:** *Shams al-Horreya* (2013, September 1), Issues 50–51.
355 **Sometime later:** Muhammad Kinj, of the Ashab al-Yamin brigade; *al-Masar al-Horr* (2013, November 2), Issue 59.
355 **Meanwhile, with more merit:** Bread Survey corpus.
355 **In the Great Souk:** Bread Survey corpus.
356 **They sat in the back of a shared taxi:** The sources for this journey are Mina and the fellow teacher.
356 **Soon they were in open country:** The description of the trip and the return draws on details I gathered when making the same trip, and from Mina's photographs.

BOOK 3: TWENTY-TWO

359 **"Our brother":** *Weekly Letters* (2013, December 12), Issue 41.
359 **"On Thursday":** *al-Masar al-Horr* (2013, December 21), Issue 66.
359 **When the flakes fell:** This description is based on the Republic Video corpus.
359 **Winter storm Alexa:** *al-Masar al-Horr* (2013, December 21), Issue 66.
359 **The roofs of houses:** Republic Video corpus.
360 **On the first night:** *al-Masar al-Horr* (2013, December 21), Issue 66.

360 **"Syrians fell prey":** *al-Masar al-Horr* (2013, December 21), Issue 66.
360 **Everyone pitched in:** *al-Masar al-Horr* (2013, December 21), Issue 66.
360 **As its first act:** Manbij Revolutionary Council statement, December 11, 2013 (Social Media corpus).
360 **One of the detained:** These scenes are from Ahmed Tarboush, corroborated by two others also arrested at that time (Manbij Protesters corpus).
361 **In Aleppo:** "Aleppo Scholars Association Issues Fatwa Ordering Fighters to Quit ISIS," November 14, 2013 (Social Media corpus).
361 **In the city of al-Bab:** al-Faraj (2023).
361 **The spark that led:** The neutral party was headed by Abu Rayyan. See al-Khatieb (2014) and the ISIS statement "The Truth About the Murdered Doctor, Abu Rayyan," January 4, 2014.
361 **War Comes to Manbij:** Sources in this section are from the Republic Battle corpus, which includes figures from both sides.
361 **With the rolling brownouts:** Republic Video corpus.
361 **Abu Harith insisted there was no dispute:** This is according to Abu Rudeyna, ISIS member (Republic Battle corpus).
362 **Meanwhile, a few blocks away:** This is according to Hasan Nefi (Republic Battle corpus).
362 **Gunmen were perched:** Republic Video corpus.
362 **So Abel Os organized a demonstration:** Abu Ayhem.
362 **"The people demand the exit":** Republic Video corpus.
362 **Some ISIS members:** This detail is according to Abu Rudeyna.
362 **Late that night:** Republic Video corpus.
362 **"In the name of God":** Republic Video corpus.
362 **For the first time in his life:** Nabeel K.
363 **Nearby, Oday and other:** RYM corpus.
363 **They captured three:** al-Faraj (2023).
363 **A Red Crescent worker:** Abel Os.
363 **One ISIS truck escaped:** This anecdote is from Abel Os.
363 **At the Cultural Center:** This scene is from Hussein Omar Samawi.
363 **Suddenly, his thoughts turned:** This is according to Mustafa Sheikh Ibrahim (Republic Battle corpus).
364 **Once inside the Youth Center:** Mustafa Sheikh Ibrahim.
364 **Abdul Hadi stepped:** al-Faraj (2023).
364 **That evening, Nabeel went:** This story is from Nabeel and is also mentioned in al-Faraj (2023).
365 **That evening, the revolutionary security:** Salah Abu Ismail (Republic Battle corpus).
365 **They threw entire assemblies:** al-Faraj (2023).
365 **Fighters surrounded Oday's house:** Abel Os.
365 **With this reprieve:** Ahmed al-Faraj.
365 **The senate issued a directive:** Al Haya' al-Sharia of Manbij statement, January 5, 2014 (Social Media corpus).
365 **On January 7, 2014:** Ali Saleh al-Jasim.
365 **The assembly elected a new:** Revolutionary Council and General Council of the Custodians of the Revolution Statement, January 7, 2014 (Social Media corpus).
366 **That Friday:** Republic Video corpus.
366 **Downtown, Abel Os led:** Republic Video corpus.

BOOK 3: TWENTY-THREE

367 **In Darkness Shines a Light:** This scene is from Abdul Hadi al-Bisher, Abdul Aziz al-Bisher (his brother), Nabeel D. (RYM corpus), and Abu Shilouh of the Security Brigade (Republic Battle corpus). I also drew some details from my visit to the makeshift prison.
368 **On the morning of January 8:** This escape scene is from Abdul Hadi and Abdul Aziz.
368 **Abdul Hadi and another prisoner:** I retraced his steps, which informed my descriptions here.
369 **In the nearby city of al-Bab:** al-Faraj (2023); Anas Sheikh Weiss (Republic Battle corpus).
369 **The FSA was close to routing:** Jurohak bqalbi tadag (2014).
369 **Abu Omar, a twenty-eight-year-old:** Biographical details are from Prothero (2015).
369 **Once inside, he remade himself:** He was a leader of Liwa' al-Muhajireen wa al-Ansar, to which the six foreigners who arrived in Manbij in April 2013 belonged.
369 **Then, a few hours after:** Republic Video corpus.

370 **But in a shocking betrayal:** I obtained a copy of the letter detailing the negotiations between the two sides. Abu Omar posed as an ally to Ahrar al-Sham.

370 **The news spread quickly:** Details of al-Bab's mood are from al-Faraj (2023).

370 **Over the next few days:** Details of these days are from Anas Sheikh Weiss, who participated in the battle.

370 **The streets were covered:** Republic Video corpus.

370 **Downtown, some men ascended:** Republic Video corpus.

370 **The Sordid Tale of the Man:** Details of the Prince's denouement are from his brother Bassam Abu al-Abed, Hasan al-Awni, Fayez K., and others in the RYM corpus.

370 **This collection of gritty apartment buildings:** This description is based on my visit.

371 **Four days later:** al-Faraj (2023).

371 **At some point, a white Saab:** al-Faraj (2023).

371 **They dynamited the Cultural Center:** Republic Video corpus.

371 **Abu Omar the Chechen:** Details of this rout are from Anas Sheikh Weiss and al-Faraj (2023).

372 **They were decapitated:** Republic Video corpus.

372 **The Prince's men:** Republic Battle corpus.

372 **Among the dead:** Shadi al-Jasim, the Prince's half brother.

372 **He woke one morning:** Details of the Prince's death are from his brother Bassam Abu al-Abed and Fayez K.

372 **In a prison back room:** The Prince's execution took place in the autumn of 2015.

372 **On January 12, 2014:** MRC corpus, Social Media corpus.

373 **For the first time in weeks:** Republic Video corpus.

373 **There were no injuries:** Abel Os visited the scene that morning.

373 **A Free Army unit arriving:** al-Faraj (2023), Republic Battle corpus.

374 **Around 2:00 a.m.:** This scene is from Aqeel Abu, who spoke to the bakery director that evening, as well as several sources in the Bread Survey corpus.

374 **The two sides met at a university campus:** Republic Video corpus.

375 **Students fled on foot:** Republic Video corpus.

375 **The next morning:** Security Brigade commander Abu Maan was in the operations room when the videos appeared, and he "lost all resolve," he later recalled (Rebel corpus).

375 **The facade of a nearby carpet factory:** The aftermath is visible at SHAAM SNN (2014).

375 **FSA units met them:** Such engagements can be seen, for example, in Mohammad Dheeb Bakkar (2014).

375 **When some ISIS fighters:** Republic Battle corpus.

375 **One mortar landed near:** al-Faraj (2023).

375 **A man shouted:** Based on a recording made by Abel Os.

375 **On the afternoon of:** MRC corpus.

376 **The sun was setting:** Republic Video corpus.

376 **Not a star could be seen above:** This is per Abel Os's recollection.

376 **His face was ridged with pain:** "He looked in anguish," according to Abel Os.

377 **The next morning, January:** Republic Video corpus.

377 **There was a palpable sense:** Republic Video corpus.

377 **It was a majestic sight:** Republic Video corpus.

377 **The fighters assembled in Central Square:** This scene is based on several videos from the Republic Video corpus.

377 **A masked man spoke:** Ahmad Alakhtareeny (2015).

377 **The crowd cheered:** Republic Video corpus.

378 **As ISIS leaders were not:** Abu Hasan (Caliphate corpus).

378 **When people went to bed:** Republic Video corpus.

378 **In the morning, they awoke:** al-Faraj (2023).

378 **That morning, Mina:** This section is from Mina Saba, and several sources in the Mina Saba corpus.

379 **On the final night:** This section is from Hasan Nefi.

379 **Someone was banging:** This section is from Ibrahim.

380 **In a mud hut:** This section is from Abel Os and Ahmed al-Faraj.

381 **Sunrise to sunset:** This section is drawn from Oday's Facebook page, his diary, and Bushra al-Hema.

381 **The mouth of the Great Souk:** This description is based on my visits to the balcony.
382 **On the roof of one:** Aqeel Abo saw Abdul Hadi on the silo roof that day.

BOOK 4: PROLOGUE

385 **So for the ancient Greeks:** Calhoun et al. (2022).
385 **Ancient Athens was dominated:** Ober (1996).
386 **He styled himself as all things:** Marx (1852/2020).

BOOK 4: ONE

Note: Book 4 makes use of two detailed reports on the Caliphate's history in Manbij, written by an Islamic State leader: al-Khalaf (2023, 2024). We obtained these in 2024.

389 **As Mina approached:** Unless otherwise specified, Mina is the primary source for all material in this chapter. Her interviews were augmented and amplified by several sources in the Mina Saba corpus.
389 **The door to her parents' house:** I drew some descriptions here from my later visit to the house.
389 **The sun was gray:** Mina's recollection.
390 **A voice said, on:** "First Declaration" of the Islamic State, January 26, 2014 (Social Media corpus).
391 **The radio announced additional edicts:** I have gathered hundreds of these edicts, most of them circulated online (Social Media corpus). Important edicts include: Ordinances on Municipal Regulations, Ruling on Alcohol, Decree on Women, Decree on Curriculum, and Decree on Amputating the Hands of Thieves.
391 **Black was now the hue of her city:** ISIS video corpus.
391 **The production quality:** Many of these clips are part of the Caliphate Video corpus.
391 **In early February:** Confirmed by several ISIS sources in the Caliphate corpus, as well as those who took part in the repentance procedures, such as Abu al-Jude.
391 **A former Free Army fighter:** This story is from al-Khalaf (2023).
392 **There was the case of Abu Ali:** Corroborating interviews on this case were held with Abu Ali's cousin, also named Abu Ali Shiyuki.
392 **Not long after, a crowd gathered:** Caliphate Video corpus.
394 **Now, a few children led:** Caliphate Video corpus.
395 **Every individual:** "A Call for Teachers to Join the Sharia Course in Aleppo Province," ISIS statement, July 5, 2014.
395 **She introduced herself:** Several sources in the Caliphate corpus mention Umm Shuhada.
396 **Mina peered through her lace curtain:** Additional details about these subterranean meetings are from the Women of Freedom archive of documents, which included hundreds of videos, written statements, audio files, and more.
396 **It had rolled down her alley:** This description is based on my subsequent visit to the area.
397 **Finally Rima:** A pseudonym.
397 **All week, the women:** The video clips of these plays are part of the Women of Freedom archive.

BOOK 4: TWO

400 **"Who said death comes":** These posts are taken from Oday's Facebook pages. He maintained two, one of which was predominantly poetry (Oday corpus).
400 **He was spending hours:** Bushra al-Hema (Oday corpus).
400 **Once the traffic died:** This description is based on my subsequent visits to the area.
400 **His face was lit:** There were no lights on his balcony.
400 **As Oday sat on the balcony:** Oday's diary (Oday corpus).
401 **Oday spent those early:** Bushra al-Hema.
401 **So he took long walks:** Bushra al-Hema, Maher al-Hema (Oday corpus).
402 **Once, Oday had seen:** Oday corpus.
402 **But now it seemed to him:** Oday corpus.
402 **Before long, a friend suggested:** Her official name is Reem al-Hussein (Oday corpus).
403 **Not long after:** This scene is from Bushra al-Hema, Reem al-Hussein, and Ahmed al-Faraj (who was not present, but heard its details from Oday).
403 **Oday was allowed:** Bushra al-Hema and Reem al-Hussein.

NOTES

403 **The silences:** Reem al-Hussein.
404 **He placed her hand:** This detail is from Ahmed al-Faraj, who witnessed it.
404 **Under ISIS:** For more on wedding customs in Manbij under ISIS, see Almohamad et al. (2023).
404 **Oday placed a baklava:** Bushra.
404 **They entered the bedroom:** This detail is from Ahmed al-Faraj, who heard it from Oday.
404 **One afternoon:** RYM corpus.
404 **There was Ahmed:** Ahmed al-Faraj, Fawaz al-Hussein (Oday corpus), and Nabeel D. (RYM corpus).
405 **Not long after:** The source of this information on Oday's marital woes is Ahmed al-Faraj.
405 **In early April:** Photographs of this and almost all other graffiti in Manbij in that period are part of the Caliphate corpus.
405 **A video surfaced:** Caliphate Video corpus.
406 **Huzayfa Osman:** This is from Huzayfa's testimonial (Manbij Protesters corpus).
406 **Yusef, sixteen, had worked:** This story is from Huzayfa Osman; Abu Sayed, a friend of Yusef's family; Abu Omar, who owned a shop near the execution site; and al-Khalaf (2023), which contains a profile of the judge.
406 **A post appeared:** Social Media corpus.
407 **ISIS agents began:** Muhammad Kullal (Huda al-Muhammad corpus).
407 **New graffiti appeared:** Caliphate corpus.
407 **One day, a new Facebook account:** Social Media corpus. At the time of publication, the page was still online: https://www.facebook.com/profile.php?id=100071928452323
407 **One afternoon, the site published:** At the time of publication, the video is still available at https://www.facebook.com/share/v/1AcY5o9fka/
409 **And on his balcony:** Bushra al-Hema.
409 **The video forced him:** Oday's diary.
409 **All week, Oday was in a frenzy:** Ahmed al-Faraj and Hasan Gulay, brother of Ahmed Gulay, who planned the strike with Oday.
409 **One night, he gathered:** Ahmed al-Faraj.
409 **One day an ISIS member:** Aboud Solou and Ammar al-Kaoud (Oday corpus).
409 **Later, Oday visited old friends:** RYM corpus.

410 **A member of the ISIS secret police:** This anecdote is from the RYM corpus and confirmed by Abu Rudeyna, the ISIS member in question.
410 **That evening, he shared:** RYM corpus.
410 **When he announced the news:** Fawaz al-Hussein (Oday corpus).
410 **Oday began leaving:** Mahmoud Abu Ali (Oday corpus).
410 **Rima pressed:** Reem al-Hussein (Oday corpus).
410 **Members of the defunct:** Social Media corpus, MRC corpus.
410 **Free Syrian Army groups:** Social Media corpus, Rebel corpus.
410 **On the radio:** RYM corpus, Caliphate corpus.
410 **At Oday's shop that evening:** Abdul Aziz Abu Saleh (Oday corpus).
410 **At home, Oday had dinner with Rima:** This scene is from Reem al-Hussein.
411 **In the morning, the entrance:** This description is based on videos of early mornings at the souk and vegetable market in previous strikes.
411 **Oday was standing near the shop:** Abdul Aziz Abu Saleh.
411 **A pickup truck rolled:** Caliphate Video corpus. This scene is also from Abu Obeida al-Iraqi, the ISIS member who was leading this group of fighters in the truck (Caliphate corpus).
411 **Here and there:** Caliphate Video corpus.
411 **The city was on strike:** Several videos in the Caliphate Video corpus capture the strike.
411 **An ISIS member began spray-painting:** Hussein Omar Samawi (Caliphate corpus).
411 **Authorities ordered all:** Bread Survey corpus.
411 **A member radioed:** As of publication, this conversation could still be heard online at manbej1 (2014).
412 **At that moment, on Facebook:** Social Media corpus.
412 **The crowd was angry:** This scene is from the Caliphate Video corpus and Naser al-Nabzo (Abdul Hadi corpus).
413 **An ISIS Hi-Lux rolled up to Oday's shop:** This scene is from Abdul Aziz Abu Saleh, Akrama al-Hema (Oday's brother), and Abu Obeida al-Iraqi, who arrested him.

BOOK 4: THREE

414 **At the Cultural Center:** This scene is from various sources in the Caliphate corpus, along with Abdul Hadi.

414 **The man in charge:** Details on Abu Zubair are from Abdul Hadi, Abu Obeida al-Iraqi, and Qutaiba al-Khalaf, a leading ISIS member (Caliphate corpus), and Muhammad al-Binshi (Caliphate Prison corpus).

414 **Late in the evening:** This group was led by Abu Obeida al-Iraqi, who recounted this event in an interview.

415 **Friedrich Nietzsche said:** Nietzsche (1887/2006).

415 **After ISIS seized control:** Details of Abdul Hadi's activities in the Caliphate come from several sources in the Abdul Hadi corpus, as well as from Qutaiba al-Khalaf, his supervisor in the Caliphate (Caliphate corpus). Qutaiba al-Khalaf is a pseudonym.

416 **Once, he noticed:** Mustafa Sheikh Ibrahim (Abdul Hadi corpus).

416 **He chanced upon:** Ammar al-Hussein (Abdul Hadi corpus).

416 **The Islamic State's goal:** Suleiman Suleiman (Abdul Hadi corpus).

416 **Oday burst into laughter:** Oday related this anecdote to Ahmed al-Faraj.

417 **That week, Abdul Hadi:** Unless otherwise noted, Abdul Hadi is the primary source in this section.

417 **When he spotted Oday:** This scene is from Abdul Hadi, but interviewees in the Caliphate Prison corpus conveyed similar scenes.

418 **Every day, after being returned:** These scenes are from the Caliphate Prison corpus, and especially Hussein al-Hashem, who shared a cell with Oday.

418 **There was Sheikh Ismail:** Ismail Abu Suhaib and Hussein al-Binshi, cousin of Muhammad al-Binshi (Caliphate Prison corpus).

418 **Abu Jude, a falafel vendor:** Abu al-Jude (Caliphate Prison corpus).

418 **A teenage inmate named Firas:** This anecdote, from several sources in the Caliphate Prison corpus, was confirmed by Abu Obeida al-Iraqi.

419 **One day, Abu Zubair entered:** This scene is from Hussein al-Hashem.

420 **One day, Oday asked:** This story is from Abdul Hadi, corroborated by Abu Obeida al-Iraqi.

420 **There, he'd kept a notebook:** All these years later, Abdul Hadi still had this poem memorized.

420 **A few weeks later:** This story is from Abdul Hadi, corroborated by Abu Obeida al-Iraqi.

420 **Oday was transferred:** The story of Oday's transfer and attempted rebellion is from Abdul Hadi, with additional details from Abu Obeida al-Iraqi and several other sources in the Caliphate Prison corpus.

421 **The hallway filled:** This detail is from Abu Obeida al-Iraqi, who was present at the time.

422 **At home, Abdul Hadi's mother:** This scene is from Abdul Hadi, with additional details from his brother Abdul Aziz.

BOOK 4: FOUR

424 **Abel Os sat in the back seat:** Unless otherwise noted, Abel Os is the primary source for all events in this chapter.

425 **Abel Os was hauled:** Abel Os's experience in the Repentance Office is mirrored by several sources in the Caliphate corpus.

426 **One by one, he met:** RYM corpus.

426 **One afternoon:** Mustafa Hadad (RYM corpus).

426 **He crossed Central Square:** Images of this execution are in the Caliphate Video corpus.

427 **Until then, Manbij:** Ali (2016). Note that Abdul Hadi is also mentioned in this article, which appears in a Lebanese publication. See also United Nations Security Council Report (2017), page 9, which highlights Manbij's role as providing a "physical operations base" for internationally directed ISIS attacks.

427 **After the strike, though:** Ali (2016).

427 **He oversaw an expansion:** Abdul Hadi and Qutaiba al-Khalaf (Caliphate corpus); Suleiman Suleiman (Abdul Hadi corpus).

427 **The authorities reintroduced:** Bread Survey corpus.

427 **They solved the bread:** I documented these dispensaries during my visits to Manbij after the fall of ISIS.

NOTES

428 **This breadth allowed for economies:** For more on Islamic State finances, see Johnston et al. (2016) and Robinson et al. (2017).

428 **In Manbij, authorities:** This is according to several civilian sources in the Caliphate corpus.

428 **Manbij's mayor, Muhammad:** Qutaiba al-Khalaf.

428 **People marveled at the new ordinances:** Several such ordinances are in the Caliphate corpus.

429 **There was Zain:** A pseudonym. His story was collected as an oral history as part of the Caliphate corpus.

429 **The Jessi brothers:** Their story was featured in al-Khalaf (2023), and two of their wives were interviewed as part of the Caliphate corpus.

429 **There was Ahmed:** A pseudonym. His story was collected as an oral history as part of the Caliphate corpus.

429 **A young man named Yasser:** A pseudonym. His story was collected as an oral history as part of the Caliphate corpus.

429 **A week passed, and his wife:** According to Mana, his wife (Abel Os corpus).

430 **Abu Zubair produced a video:** This video appears to be the same as one in the Republic Video corpus.

430 **News of Abel Os's arrest spread:** RYM corpus.

430 **"I'll find a way":** According to a relative of the commander Khudr al-Khudr.

430 **"I'll see what I can do":** Ahmed al-Faraj.

431 **At night, as he lay:** Additional information about Abel Os's imprisonment is from Ali Abu Saddam, who shared a cell with him (Abel Os corpus).

431 **At the caliphate's information office:** According to Mana and Hammoudi, his son.

432 **He felt the damp draft of air:** Abel Os: "The air felt different and a little wet, so I knew I was out of the main part of the prison."

432 **He inched toward the street corner:** I later stood on the exact same street corner with Abel Os as he recalled his sensations in that moment.

BOOK 4: FIVE

434 **Many were thrown into prison:** The Caliphate corpus records numerous instances of arbitrary arrests of Kurds, such as Dr. Azad Wali, who had been part of the Revolutionary Council headed by Muhammad al-Bisher.

434 **Three hundred Kurdish students:** Caliphate corpus.

434 **With the appearance of checkpoints:** Unless otherwise noted, Mina is the primary source for the material in this section.

435 **Only much later:** The diary and laptop were later recovered and form a key part of the Mina Saba corpus.

435 **Ibrahim Kasem never:** Unless otherwise noted, Ibrahim is the primary source for the material in this section.

436 **Early one morning, he was taken:** I later retraced part of this journey with Ibrahim, which I used to amplify the descriptions.

437 **Above a gas station:** Ibrahim: "The flag was flying and twisting in the wind."

437 **In the cool autumn days:** Abdul Hadi is the primary source in this paragraph, with additional information from several sources in the Abdul Hadi corpus.

438 **Shirking the call-up:** Abdul Aziz, Abdul Hadi's brother, provided additional details in this paragraph.

438 **Below, his comrades cheered:** Caliphate Video corpus.

438 **That evening, his commander:** The primary source of this section is Qutaiba al-Khalaf, Abdul Hadi's superior. At first, Abdul Hadi denied the scene, but after repeated inquiries he confirmed it and added further details, including his thoughts and feelings about the encounters.

439 **Suddenly, she sat on his lap:** Abdul Hadi: "I lost my sense at this point. I could not think anymore."

440 **Meanwhile, the U.S.–Iran nuclear deal:** For more on how this affected Syria, see Gopal & Hodge (2022).

440 **People in Manbij woke:** This is according to several civilian sources in the Caliphate corpus.

440 **Since his release from prison:** Abel Os.

440 **Abel Os's other children:** Muhammad Oseb, his son Hammoudi.

440 **"When I saw his condition":** Bakir Abu Muhammad (Abel Os corpus).

441 **Abel Os put on a brave face:** Mana, his wife (Abel Os corpus).

441 **His brother Shukri took over:** This is according to Mahmoud Oseb, his brother (Abel Os corpus).
441 **Ordnance hit the Manbij Hotel:** Caliphate Video corpus.
441 **A few prisoners escaped:** Caliphate corpus.
441 **One afternoon not long after:** This scene is from Mahmoud Oseb and Abel Os, along with clips from the Caliphate Video corpus.
441 **At the funeral, Abel Os:** Abel Os and Mahmoud Oseb.

BOOK 4: SIX

442 **At night, while his:** Abel Os is the primary source for the scenes involving him, with additional details from his son Muhammad Oseb, wife Mana, and brother Mahmoud Oseb (Abel Os corpus).
442 **But unlike the ragtag:** Obama & Friedman (2014).
443 **Suburban villages were collapsing:** ARA News (2016a).
443 **The SDF was blocking:** ARA News (2016b).
443 **Not long after, Abdul Hadi:** Abdul Hadi and Muhammad Oseb.
444 **On the morning of June 9:** Syrian Observatory for Human Rights (2016).
444 **On loudspeakers:** Final Battle corpus.
444 **The internet was disconnected:** Final Battle corpus.
444 **There was a momentary:** The victims of this airstrike were interviewed as part of the Final Battle corpus.
444 **The city was now under siege:** Many details of life under siege were provided by Hussein Omar Samawi, who wrote an extended testimony as part of the Final Battle corpus. See Samawi (2024).
444 **On July 7:** Davison & King (2016).
444 **ISIS broke into houses:** Final Battle corpus.
444 **One morning, Abdul Hadi came:** This story is from Muhammad Oseb and Abel Os.
445 **Smoke rose:** Caliphate Video corpus.
445 **At night, the world:** Samawi (2024).
445 **"The truth of the coalition":** Samawi (2024).
445 **By the second week of July:** Mana and Muhammad Oseb.
445 **Ismail Hamash:** This is based on an interview with his nephew Hussein Hamash, along with several eyewitnesses and photographs (Final Battle corpus).

445 **Instead, they called:** That the strike was a JDAM is based on analysis of the blast pattern and the precision, which suggests laser guidance.
445 **American forces raided:** Details of this massacre are based on several interviews and site visits to Oj Qana village. Interviewees include Muhammad al-Barho, Sami Hilal, Muhammad al-Hilal, and Fatima al-Jabri, all of whom lost close relatives in the bombing. The massacre took place in June 2016, while the Tokhar massacre took place in July.
445 **Residents in Tokhar:** Details of this massacre are based on nearly a dozen interviews and a site visit (Final Battle corpus). See also Gopal (2020b).
446 **On July 21:** Reuters (2016).
446 **ISIS fighters doused streets:** These descriptions of ISIS activities are from several civilian sources in the Final Battle corpus.
446 **A U.S. military spokesman admitted:** Deutsche Welle (2016).
446 **Islamic State's ranks were:** According to Islamic State sources in the Caliphate corpus.
447 **These were fetid cellars:** This description is drawn from several sources in the Final Battle corpus.
447 **In one house:** This story is recorded in Samawi (2024).
447 **An SDF sniper's bullet:** Samawi (2024).
447 **A man named Shahoud al-Khalouf:** From an interview with his brother, Yasser Khalouf Ali al-Radis, and other eyewitnesses (Final Battle corpus).
447 **One night, as air strikes:** This story is from al-Khalaf (2023) and corroborated by eyewitness accounts in the Final Battle corpus.
447 **The air over the city:** This image and subsequent descriptions are from the Caliphate Video corpus.
448 **By late July:** Final Battle corpus.
449 **All around, apartment buildings:** Final Battle corpus.
449 **He was pacing:** This scene is from Abel Os and Muhammad Oseb.
449 **All week, Abdul Hadi:** The primary source of Abdul Hadi's thoughts and actions is Qutaiba al-Khalaf, his commander. Abdul Hadi subsequently confirmed and expanded upon the account.
450 **But after witnessing:** These descriptions are from Abdul Hadi.

NOTES

450 **"Inform all our besieged":** Letter dated August 7, 2016, from the Islamic State Delegated Committee. The letter is first cited in Moore & Netjes (2016).

450 **Deserters were shot:** al-Khalaf (2023).

450 **Finally, in mid-August:** On this deal, see Rudaw (2016) and al-Khalidi & Barrington (2016). This was corroborated by several sources from the Islamic State in the Final Battle corpus. The deal was reportedly negotiated by Muhammad Ali al-Jasim.

450 **The Islamic State soldiers:** On the Fallujah convoy, see Triebert (2016).

451 **Abel Os jumped to his feet:** The main sources of the story of this escape are Abel Os, Mana, Muhammad Oseb, and two neighbors (Final Battle corpus).

451 **Despite the deal:** Caliphate Video corpus.

452 **Every second or third building:** This description is based on a video from that same location taken a few days later (Caliphate Video corpus).

452 **There were no cats:** According to Muhammad Oseb.

452 **In a garbage dump:** These scenes are from Muhammad Oseb.

452 **That afternoon, a convoy:** This description is from Khalil al-Askari, who was in the convoy (Final Battle corpus).

452 **In the ISIS convoy:** According to Qutaiba al-Khalaf.

453 **The grandfather hoarding:** These stories are from Samawi (2024).

453 **When Hamid al-Osman:** Samawi (2024).

453 **On that first evening:** This scene is from Maher al-Hema (Oday corpus).

453 **The authorities shined flashlights:** There are several videos showing these moments (Caliphate Video corpus).

BOOK 5: ONE

459 **People spoke to Abel Os:** Based on my observations.

459 **One morning, two men:** This account is from Abel Os, his son Muhammad Oseb, his brother Suleh Oseb (Abel Os corpus), and several sources in the SDF corpus.

460 **One afternoon, he was visited by:** I received several similar visits from PKK officials who attempted to pressure me into representing the group's interests, as did a number of my sources.

461 **In a firm voice:** This was corroborated by an SDF source in that meeting (SDF corpus).

461 **Unable to cope:** Ibrahim is the primary source for this account. His family members corroborated and amplified the account.

462 **One afternoon, Ibrahim was on the phone:** Ibrahim is the primary source of this account.

464 **Two years earlier, her brother:** Sami's death is documented in the Social Media corpus.

464 **Not long ago, she visited:** Mina is the primary source of this account.

465 **From his exile:** Hasan Nefi is the primary source of these accounts, with corroboration and amplification from the MRC corpus.

465 **Whole families were killed:** See, for example, Gopal (2024).

466 **Some Islamic State members quit:** Caliphate corpus.

466 **Abdul Hadi was among them:** The primary source of these details is Qutaiba al-Khalaf, his supervisor, who tried to help him escape.

466 **There, in hiding:** Abdul Hadi is the primary source of these reflections.

466 **One afternoon, he sent:** Munzer Salal is the primary source of this anecdote, with confirmation from Abdul Hadi.

BOOK 5: TWO

469 **In those difficult early days:** The account of Oday's family's ordeal after his disappearance was corroborated and amplified through interviews with several sources in the Oday and the Missing Persons corpora.

471 **Some fifty thousand people:** The details of life in Baghouz during the siege were drawn from several interviews with survivors (al-Hol corpus) and by my visit to the scene.

471 **SDF was treating:** This is based on several sources in the al-Hol corpus and the fact that I witnessed this phenomenon many times during the final battles.

471 **That evening, I met a barber:** Abu Rabea (Missing Persons corpus).

471 **A few mornings later, I located a man:** Khalil al-Askari (Final Battle corpus).

472 **I met an old man:** Abdul Hadi al-Muhammad.

472 **I met a woman:** H. K. (Missing Persons corpus).
473 **My SDF contact:** Anas al-Ahmed (SDF corpus).
474 **I was in a giant detention camp:** Much of the language in this paragraph is from Gopal (2024).
475 **I returned with a humanitarian agency:** The Centre for Humanitarian Dialogue.
475 **Each day, bodies turned up:** Lovelace & Mekhennet (2019); al-Hol corpus.
476 **An inmate named Sarah:** Oral history from Sarah, al-Hol corpus.
477 **Five murders took place:** According to Abu Ahmed and camp authorities.
477 **Two mornings later:** This scene is from one of Abu Ahmed's surviving sons, Ahmed al-Shummari, and confirmed by multiple eyewitnesses.

BOOK 5: THREE

479 **I was not at the mercy:** In addition to several sources in the Caliphate and MRC corpora, the following individuals were key to providing information about Abu Obeida: Mahmud al-Tayy, his relative; Abu Muhannad, his neighbor; Abu Daoud, his friend; Abu al-Jude, a former prisoner of ISIS; Mustafa al-Hamza, who fought in the same Free Army unit; and Akrama al-Hema, Oday's brother. The first four names are civilians in the Caliphate corpus.
483 **In the subsequent months:** This information about Oday's end is from several sources in the Caliphate corpus, chief among them Qutaiba al-Khalaf.
485 **Abel Os became afflicted:** The principal sources for Abel Os's final days are Muhammad Oseb and Ahmed al-Faraj.
486 **But later, after neighbors:** Muhammad Oseb and Ahmed al-Faraj.

BOOK 5: FOUR

487 **Syria was getting readmitted:** Hokayem (2023).
487 **The besuited dictator:** Al Jazeera (2023).
487 **After half a million dead:** Baker (2024), World Vision (2025).
487 **Several European countries:** Avrahami (2024).
487 **The Biden administration:** Rogin (2021).
487 **Anti-Syrian riots broke out:** Deniz (2024).
488 **In an article entitled:** Nefi (2023). The full poem is available at Dunqul (1976), translated by Shimaa Eid.
489 **For the first time in a decade:** This can be seen on Facebook here: https://www.facebook.com/watch/?v=980577926388902
489 **When protesters were arrested:** Turkish Minute (2024).
489 **On November 26, 2024:** Salem (2024).
489 **But the next morning, four rebels:** Several details in this paragraph are from Shahin (2024), corroborated by my own visit to the front line shortly after.
490 **The next morning, Hasan:** Shahin (2024).
490 **By evening, news arrived:** Shahin (2024).
491 **Rumors were flying:** This is based on my analysis of Twitter in real time during these events.
491 **In the early hours of December 8:** The story of the man from Tadamoun (named A. K.) is based on my interview with him in that neighborhood shortly after the liberation. We took the same walk described here.
491 **Downtown, a young man:** This is based on an interview I conducted in Damascus shortly after the liberation.
491 **A woman stepped onto:** This is based on an interview I conducted in Damascus shortly after the liberation.
491 **Nearby, a voice could be heard:** This scene is captured on video at aljazeera mubasher (2024).
491 **"The revolution is victorious":** I saw this message myself on Syrian State TV.
493 **He saw his old house:** Abdul Hadi corpus.
493 **Back home:** Abdul Hadi's behaviors are based on descriptions from Muhammad Osman and Qutaiba al-Khalaf, who visited him.
494 **A former inmate of al-Bab:** K. A. (Oday corpus).
494 **Among his many pages:** Oday's diary.
494 **Most character traits:** For the material in this section, I am indebted to insights from Lear (2006), as well as the works of Alasdair MacIntyre and Aristotle.

ACKNOWLEDGMENTS

This book would have been impossible, even inconceivable, without Muhammad Osman and Hussein Samawi. They led a research team that traversed Syria, Turkey, and Europe to find stories from Manbij, their hometown. In Osman and Samawi, I not only found valuable guides to modern revolution; I also gained lifelong friends. The team they directed grew at times to nearly a dozen researchers, only some of whom I'm at liberty to name here: Ahmed al-Faraj, Ahmed Muhammad, Ahmed al-Wawi, Ali Saleh al-Jassem, Fayez Haidar, Huzayfa al-Osman, Khaled al-Kamla, Murhaf Sheikh Weiss, and Omar al-Hajj.

The research behind this book would not have been possible without the support of colleagues at the Zomia Center. I'm grateful to Nick McDonell and Anita Sreedhar for their vision in establishing the organization; in particular, it was Anita's ability to connect with people in the most diverse and extreme of circumstances that made an organization like Zomia possible. I also owe my gratitude to Tom Peter for his efforts in helping establish Zomia on the ground, for conducting key interviews related to the flood in Chapter 1, and for interviews with former members of the Islamic State; Hussein Akoush for his hundreds of hours of meticulous and empathetic interviewing of participants in the revolution, and in particular for his research into the massacres near Safira described in Book 3; and Jeremy Hodge, a talented researcher from whom I learned much.

As we dug up sources, we realized that the vast amounts of printed matter produced in the revolution should be preserved for future generations. I am indebted to Hussein Omar Samawi, Murhaf Sheikh Weiss, Sari al-Attasi, Shireen Akram Boshar, and Sumaya Awad for translating Manbij's revolutionary newspapers as part of this preservation project. I'm also grateful to Sumaya for helping me conduct background interviews with Israa Sheikh Weiss, a member of Women of Freedom. I wish to thank Lylla Younes for her translation of Hasan Nefi's poem "Embrace."

I consider myself fortunate to have received support from several institutions throughout the research and writing of this book. I am grateful to the

Lannan Foundation for its generous support during the early years of this project, and special thanks goes to Sarah Knopp. I wish to thank my colleagues past and present at the Center for Humanitarian Dialogue, who supported many of my trips to Syria, especially Christine Sandström, Clancy Rudeforth, David Harland, Ouseph Tharakan, Tom Gregg, and Zubin Malhotra. I am indebted to Peter Bergen and New America for supporting my research efforts. At Arizona State University's Future Security Initiative, I wish to thank Daniel Rothenberg for his generous support, and more important, for his friendship. Many thanks to the Center for the Study of Religion and Conflict for providing me with an intellectual home. I wish to thank my colleagues there: Matt Correa, John Marc Sianghio, Tracy Fessenden, and especially John Carlson for his steadfast support over the years.

I am grateful to my colleagues at the *New Yorker*, including David Remnick and the rest of the editorial staff. Special thanks go to Daniel Zalewski for his profound editorial wisdom over the years. At Simon & Schuster, I am deeply indebted to Jonathan Jao for believing in this project, and for his unflagging commitment to the manuscript. Under his editorial guidance, the book was vastly improved. I also wish to thank Mindy Marques for her support, as well as Janet Byrne and Julie Hersh for their punctilious copyediting, and Jennie Miller for her editorial support. I am grateful to Sam Nicholson, whose assistance was essential in helping me bring the manuscript into its final shape, and to Vrinda Condillac for her valuable suggestions. And many thanks to Alice Whitwham, my indefatigable agent, who believed in this project even before I did.

I wish to express my gratitude to friends who took the time to read the manuscript and offer valuable feedback: Peter Bearman, Nick McDonell, Victor Blue, and Xita Rubert.

Finally, I am deeply indebted to the countless Syrians who welcomed me into their homes over the years, even as the world outside seemed to be falling apart, and shared their most intimate memories. They taught me much about mourning, resilience, and power—lessons for which I will be eternally grateful.

End

INDEX

NOTE: Page references in *italics* refer to figures and photos.

abayas, 127
Abbasid Caliphate, 4, 118
Abboud (Hala's brother), 78–79, 81, 86–87, 90, 98, 102, 136, 161
Abboud (Nabeel's cousin), 347
Abdul Hadi. *see* al-Bisher, Abdul Hadi
Abdul Karim, 272
Abdullah, Mustafa Hajj, 289–92
Abdul Nasser, Jamal, 34
Abel Os. *see* Oseb, Abdul Qader (Abel Os)
Abu Ahmed, 476–78
Abu Aido, 252
Abu Ali (executed adulterer), 392
Abu Ali (newspaper interviewee), 350
Abu Azzam the Egyptian, 284–86
Abu Habib, 179–81, 188, 192
Abu Hammoud, 375
Abu Harith the Jordanian, 331, 333, 336–38, 361–62, 364
Abu Huzayfa the Egyptian, 278–81, 287, 303
Abu Ibrahim, Muhammad (massacre survivor), 321
Abu Jude, 418
Abu Muhammad (massacre victim), 320–21
Abu Muhammad the Egyptian (ISIS commander), 363
Abu Nawar (massacre victim), 321
Abu Noah, 278
Abu Nour (FSA rebel), 252
Abu Obeida the Iraqi, 413, 479–83
Abu Omar the Chechen (Tarkhan Batirashvili), 369–75, 377
Abu Qatada the Tunisian, 278, 281, 305–6
Abu Risha, Omar, 25, 283
Abu Roz (Hadi Ali Ibrahim), 101, 111, 113, 137, 174, 178, 182–83, 207, 281
Abu Salah (schoolteacher and protester), 108, 110, 149–50

Abu Shakir (protester), 106–7, 109, 111, 119–20, 149
Abu Yahya (FSA rebel), 250–53
Abu Zubair, 414–21, 430, 432
"Adam's Dream" (play), 240
Adra prison, 36–37
adultery, 391–92
Agricultural Projects Committee, 15
Ahmed (FSA rebel), 248–49
Ahmed (ISIS recruit), 429
Ahmed (Oday's friend), 404–5
Alaa (executed adulterer), 391–92
Alaa (protester), 158
al-Alawi, Mousab, 296
Alawite sect
  Assads and, 28
  shabiha (government supporters) as, 97
  U.S.–Iran nuclear deal (2014) and, 440
  wasta girls of Baath Party, 120–21
Al-Baath (newspaper), 59–60
al-Bab, fall to ISIS, 369–70
alcohol, 312
Aleppo Central Prison, 120, 122–23, 140–42
Aleppo Freedom (soccer team), 123, 132, 147
Aleppo revolutionary government. *see also* Free Syrian Army (FSA, Free Army); Republic battle
  condemnation of ISIS, 361
  Free Aleppo Provincial Council (Assad opposition/rebels), 274, 275, 282, 296
  Ministry of Education, 355–58, 395
  Revolutionary Council of Aleppo, 339
  revolutionary court of, 341, 342
Aleppo Unity (soccer team), 123, 132, 147
Alexa (winter storm), 359–60
Al-Hol detention camp, 473–78, 479–83, 502
al-Hussainiyah massacre, 341
al-Ali, Firas, 200
Ali (FSA rebel), 260–62

INDEX

Al-Jalaa (soccer team), 132
Ammar bin Yasser (militia), 191, 349, 378
Anwar (Mina's son), 117, 125, 234, 356, 392–94
Arabs
  Arab League states, 487
  Arab nationalism and Syrian flag, 118
  Baath Party, rise of, 11–13
  classical poetry of, 25, 29
  culture of (*see* clothing; gender roles)
  on *jumhuriya* (to assemble), 224
  Syrian independence won by, 11
  World War I conscription of, 24
Arab Spring slogan, 169. *see also* Manbij protesters, civil protest phase (April to December 2011)
Armed Forces of the Poor and Oppressed, 446
Army of the Two Sacred Places (Jund al-Haramain), 180–81, 191–93, 260, 450
"The arrival of my message winged" (Al-Hol inmate's poem), 475–76
al-Asleh, Riad, 177
al-Assad, Asma, 58, 60
al-Assad, Bashar and regime
  air strikes on Manbij by, 199–201, 207–10, 211–12, 239–45
  Arab nationalism and tyranny of, 387
  in Damascus, following SDF conquest of Manbij, 463
  economy under, 214
  fall from power, 490–92
  family members killed/wounded in Damascus (July 2012), 182
  al-Hema's early loyalty to, 80–81, 83–85, 88, 89, 92
  Hezbollah's defense of, 272
  Manbij avoided by, under Islamic State rule, 427
  Manbij military strikes by, 239–45, 341, 350
  Manbij Mills and bread supply to, 333
  massacres of Syrian villages by, 317–26, 338–40, 489–90
  mocking of, by ISIS, 315
  mocking of, by secular protesters, 208, 229, 242
  New Syria economy transition under, 57–62, 70
  normalization attempts (2023), 487–88
  October portrayal of, 202
  ophthalmology background of, 58, 88
  public addresses in response to early uprisings, 85, 92, 104–5
  regime members' departure from Manbij (2012), 182–87
  Russian weapons supplied to, 228, 289
  as "traitor," 164
  "Unity, Freedom, Socialism" (slogan), 196
al-Assad, Hafez
  as Alawite, 28
  death of, 57–58
  economy under, 57, 59, 90, 126, 131, 213–14
  "Our Country Is Precious" (song) and, 126
  prison system and, 35, 36
Assaf, Bilal (FSA rebel), 250–52
atheism, secularism vs., 293
Atrahasis (Babylonian epic), 4
authoritarianism, tyranny of, 385–87. *see also* Islamic State (2014-16)
Ayman (alleged murderer), 301, 305, 306

Baath Party. *see also* al-Assad, Bashar and regime; al-Assad, Hafez; Manbij protesters, civil protest phase (April to December 2011); prisons of Syria
  corruption of, 27–28, 58, 64, 66–67, 69
  Islamists on secular rule of, 293
  leadership camp of, 120–21
  Muslim Brotherhood origin and, 176
  National Current Party outlawed by, 27
  New Syria transition under Bashar al-Assad, 57–62, 70
  portrayal of uprisings (2011) by, 82–84
  rise of, 11–13
  RYM's use of Manbij headquarters, 196
  Sami's father's appeal to, 120
Baghouz conquest (2019), 471
Barjas (massacre victim), 319
Basil (RYM member), 311
Bassam (alleged murderer), 296
battle for Manbij (United States vs. ISIS). *see* Syrian Democratic Forces (SDF) and capture of Manbij
Bayram, Muhammad, 184, *184*
Ben Ali, 126
Berlin, Isaiah, 205–6
Biden, Joseph, 487
al-Bisher, Abdul Hadi, 130–42
  Abu Obeida on, 481
  arrest and imprisonment, 138–42, 153–56
  author's methodology and, 501
  battle of the Prince and, 269–70
  early life and soccer career of, 130–34, *134*
  early protests and, 130, 134–38, 158, 244
  ISIS, and Oday's arrest, 414–23, 469
  ISIS, and the Prince's return to Manbij, 343–44
  ISIS, as jihad hero, 437–40
  ISIS, director of municipal services, 415

INDEX

569

ISIS authority enabled by, in Manbij, 299–307, 309–11, 314, 329–30, 332, 337, 382, 422–23, 495
ISIS introduction and, 259, 272–82, 284, 286–87
ISIS recruitment by, 346–49, 363–64
ISIS role, Abel Os on, 425–27, 430, 432
LCC organization and, 107
marriage plans shunned by, 212, 215
MRC control of Manbij, 186–87
MRC (new) council and, 220, 222, 225–26
MRC (second) council election and, 289, 291–92
Nefi and, 190–91
Oday's friendship with, at time of caliphate, 401–4, 409, 413, 416
in Republic battle, 360–65, 367–68, 382
Revolutionary Council and protest turning point, 158, 163, 165
RYM inception, 193–98
RYM opposition to Council of Revolutionary Trustees, 215–18
RYM's role on MRC, 208
SDF siege of Manbij, 443–44, 449–50, 452
self-imposed exile of, 466, 493
al-Bisher, Muhammad (Abdul Hadi's brother), 240
battle of the Prince, 265
ISIS role of, 415, 423, 428
MRC and, 107, 149, 198, 199, 222, 226–27, 272–74
Rahmo's early work relationship with, 149–50, 273, 415
RYM and, 217
Women of Freedom's approach of, 235
Bonaparte, Louis Napoleon, 386
bread and bakery system of Manbij
author's methodology and, 502–3
bakery owners at bread riots, 333, 351
bread brigades, 260
bread prices under MRC, 213, 213–15, 225, 308, 315, 317
Day of Bloodied Bread (December 28, 2012), 225
ISIS, Abdul Hadi's capture of bread facilities, 373–74
ISIS, distribution under, 427
ISIS and takeover of bread supply, 327–30, 332, 333, 336–38
ISIS relinquished control to Free Army factions, 345
Manbij Mills, importance of, 115, 213–14, 333–34, 374
MRC (old council) distribution of, 266

as MRC (second administration) priority, 290–91
Municipal Bakery, 191, 193, 214, 225, 308, 363, 364, 374
"Breathing Time" (Palmyra prison), 41–42, 44, 46–47
Britain, India colonized by, 302–3
Buhturi (poet), 25

Caesar (hospital employee), 323
caliphate. *see* Islamic State (in Manbij, 2014–16); Islamic State of Iraq and Greater Syria (ISIS)
Cardamom Market, 62–63
cell phones, early Manbij use of, 83–84, 86. *see also* social media
Central Intelligence Agency (CIA), 36, 254
Central Square sit-in, 135–42, 144, 149, 159, 163, 190, 503–4
Change and Development Assembly, 198, 354
Cities of Salt (Munif), 37
City Hall (Manbij), 183, 193
civil protest phase. *see* Manbij protesters, civil protest phase (April to December 2011)
Civil Tendency Assembly, 198, 199
class and economic issues. *see also* bread and bakery system of Manbij
Abdul Hadi's resentment toward MRC, 309–11, 314
author's methodology, 507
Consumer Protection Department (MRC), 214–15
despair of Manbij, man who drowned his children, 75, 222
fuel prices, 213–15, 239, 328, 489
inequality among protesters, 135–36
MRC, old vs. new councils, 272–77
MRC and senate structure, 215–18
MRC and taxation debate, 215
MRC (First) on economy, 204–5, 208
representation debated during republican period, 219–27
revolution as equalizer for, 151
sharia law demands in response to, 308
soccer culture and, 133
tyranny from inequality, 386–87
wasta (connections) and, 58, 120–21, 131, 135, 148, 154, 193, 287, 382
clothing
abayas, 127
jellabiyas, 6, 8, 10, 18, 21, 85, 94, 139, 255, 261, 480
niqabs, 230–31, 393–95, *394*
Coffeepot Roundabout, women's protest at, 127–29, 130, 135, 393–94

Conflict of the Orders, 385
Consumer Protection Department (MRC), 214–15
Corrie, Rachel, 237
Council and the People (MRC second council publication), 291
Council of Revolutionary Trustees (Manbij senate), 215–18, 334, 345
crime
  corruption of officials (*see individual names of regimes*)
  ISIS and public executions for, 297–307, 391–92, 401, 405–7, *408*, 426
  during republican phase, 193, 195, 197, 207, 239, 264–65, 296
  weapons purchased with kidnapping ransom, 259–62
Critique of Practical Reason (Kant), 26
Cubs of the Caliphate (ISIS youth group), 363–64
Cultural Center (Manbij), 24–26, 66, 229, *283*, 283–84, 299, 307, 371

Dali, Ahmed, 347
Damascus National Security headquarters bombing, 182
Daraa, violence in, 82–86, 88–92, 101, 104, 106, 108, 115, 126, 140, 407
Day of Bloodied Bread (December 28, 2012), 225
Declaration (weekly newspaper), 291
al-Dibo, Sheikh Abu Sayed, 313–14, 355
Dignity Brigade, 191
Dignity (soccer team), 133
domination, freedom and, 222–25
"Do not reconcile" poem (Dunqul), 488
"Don't Reconcile!" article (Nefi), 488
Dukhan, Khadija (massacre victim), 319
Dunqul, Amal, 488

economic issues. *see* bread and bakery system of Manbij; class and economic issues
Egypt
  France's invasion of (1798), 223
  Nasser and, 34
  uprisings in (2010–11), 80, 84, 86
Eid celebrations, 199, 211–13
Emergency Law (Syria, 1963), 90
Euphrates Dam, 12
Euphrates farm communities. *see* Little Hyena (village)

Facebook. *see* social media
Fahim (imprisoned debtor), 64
falaka (torture tactic), 66–67, 69
Faraj family (massacre victims), 321

Fawaz family (massacre victims), 322
Fawaz (Oday's friend), 404
final battle (United States vs. ISIS). *see* Syrian Democratic Forces (SDF) and capture of Manbij
Firas (ISIS prisoner), 418–19
flag-bearing woman, 407–9, 434–35, 472, 505
"Flying Carpet" (torture tactic), 32–34, 122
"For Manbij" (journalist), 290
France
  Egypt invaded by (1798), 223
  French Revolution, 199, 386, 496
  Syrian migrants in, modern-day, 487–88
  Syrian rule by, 11, 24, 36
Free Doctors of Manbij, 220
freedom
  domination and, 222–25
  "Free, free, freedom, we want freedom" (revolutionaries' song), 189, 366
  Khalaf on, 272
  as "negative" vs. "positive," 205–6, 223, 292
  Shampoo Sami on sweetness of, 241
Free Islamic Movement, 407, 409–10, 412–13, 425, 428
Free Ladies Assembly, 199, 230
Free Lawyers of Manbij, 220
Free Men of Syria Brigade, 191
Free Path (newspaper)
  departure from Manbij, 376
  editorial stance, 350
  free speech and, 352
  inception of, 204–6
  as secular, 265
  stories and headlines of, 207–8, 211, 215, 219, 222, 226, 228, 235, 237, 239, 240, 245, 246, 253, 254–55, 260–61, 263–65, 267, 272, 274, 279, 288, 291, 293, 296, 308, 317, 327–30, 336, 340, 341, 342, 350, 359, 360
Free Patriots Assembly, 198
Free Students Union, 234, 274, 300, 308, 339, 365
Free Syrian Army (FSA, Free Army), 246–62. *see also* Jund al-Haramain; Republic battle
  Assad regime civilian massacres and, 318–22
  battle of White Hill (Tel Abyad), 255–60
  crime and corruption, 260–62, 264–65
  free speech prohibition by ISIS, 352, 353
  at Henezel's meeting with ISIS, 337
  Houla region massacre (May 2012) and, 179, 184–85
  inception of, 178
  international community's role in, 253–55
  on ISIS in Manbij, 314
  ISIS street battles with, 335

Jund al-Haramain (Army of the Two Sacred Places), 180–81, 191–93, 260
  liberation day (Manbij, July 19, 2012) and, 184, 186
  Manbij Hotel as prison of, 204
  Military Council (Council of Revolutionary Trustees), 216, 239
  militia factions of, Jund al-Haramain, 180–81, 191–93
  MRC on factions and militias of, in Manbij, 191–93, 197–98
  October Dam liberated from Assad regime by, 211
  Office of Military Affairs (First MRC) and, 226–27
  the Prince and, 342–45
  recruits to, 246–53
  as secular, 265
  on strike by businesses (May 18, 2014), 412
  Syrian Democratic Forces and rebel units of, 443, 446
  Syrian refugees in Turkey and, 436–37
  weapons of, 203, 340
  Weiss and, 339
  woman fighter in, 211
Free Syrian Lawyers Assembly, 211
Free Syrian (MRC second council publication), 291
Free Syrian Youth Assembly, 327
Free Thought Magazine, 295, 312, 341
Fuaz, Mr. (karate instructor), 53, 71–72
fuel prices, 213–15, 239, 328, 489
Future Youth Assembly, 198, 202, 234, 354

gender roles, 228–38. *see also* Girls of Tomorrow; Women of Freedom
  arranged marriage, 78
  courtship practices and, 6–10, 13–18, 20–21
  flag-bearing woman protester on social media, 407–9, 434–35, 472, 505
  Free Ladies Assembly, 199, 230–32
  Girls of Tomorrow, 237–38
  honor and expectations of women, 86–87, 114–16, 398–99
  honor killings, 75, 78–79
  ISIS edicts and, 389–93
  Islamic State's arrest/imprisonment of women, 434–35
  Manbij protests, women's roles in, 114–19, 125–29
  prostitutes used by Islamic State, 438–40
  women as torture victims, 266
  women's Coffeepot Roundabout march, 127–29, 130, 135, 393–94
  women soldiers, 211, 446

genocide, concept of, 324–26
Genocide Convention of 1948, 324
Georgia, Russia invasion of, 369
"German Chair" (torture tactic), 42
Ghouta, chemical attacks on, 338–40
Girls of Tomorrow, 237–38, 288, 339, 397, 472
global financial crisis (2008), 70, 75
Goethe, Johann Wolfgang von, 35
Gopal, Anand
  in Manbij and Turkey, 457–59, 465, 466–67
  methodology of, 497–510
  search for Oday by (*see* al-Hema, Oday, ISIS imprisonment of)
government supporters. *see shabiha*
Greater Arab Free Trade Area, 60
Great Mosque (Manbij), 91–93, 312–13
Greece (ancient), political philosophy of, 324–25
Guizot, François, 223
Gulay (pushcart vendor), 65, 69

Haddad, Mustafa, 426
Haider, Ammar, 339
al-Haj Saleh, Yassin, 34, 325
Hala (Oday's girlfriend), 78–87, 90–91, 93, 96, 98–99, 102, 136, 155–56, 160–62, 212, 402–3
Hallaq, Wael, 302
Hamash, Ismail, 445
Hama (Syria) massacre (1982), 89, 108
Hameed (massacre victim), 319
Hammoudi, Ayman, 301, 306
Hammoudi, Manhal, 297–99, 301
al-Hariri, Salim, 181
Hasan, Shabaan, 341–42
Hasan (revolutionary). *see* Nefi, Hasan
Hashim (teacher/prisoner), 419
hashish, 260, 312
Hastings, Warren, 302
Haytham (massacre victim), 319
Hegel, Georg Wilhelm Friedrich, 37–38, 47, 146, 488
al-Hema, Baraa (son of Oday), 469, 473
al-Hema, Bushra (sister of Oday), 78–81, 86–87, 90, 97, 402
al-Hema, Mr. (father of Oday), 426, 468–73, 484
al-Hema, Mrs. (mother of Oday), 468–73, 484
al-Hema, Oday, 77–98
  Abdul Hadi's friendship with, 130, 133–34, 163
  on Abdul Hadi's ISIS membership, 299–301, 304–6, 347–48
  air strikes by Assad (October 2012), 210
  author's methodology and, 498–99, 500

INDEX

al-Hema, Oday (*cont.*)
  Daraa (Syria) uprisings, interest in, 82–86, 88–92
  early loyalty to Assad, 80–81, 83–85, 88, 89, 92
  early protest activity, 90–98, 99–100, 102, 110–12, 121, 125, 177–78, 244
  legacy of, 494–96
  on Maymati, 171–74
  MRC and, 186–87, 209, 222, 225, 289
  MRC tension and ISIS takeover, 275, 277–80, 282, 284, 287
  Nefi's inspiration during imprisonment of, 190
  Prince, battle of, 267–68
  Prince as cousin of, 259
  in Republic battle, 363–65, 381–82
  Revolutionary Council and protest turning point, 153–56, 158, 160–65
  RYM and, 193–98, 209, 217–18
  RYM and, resignation of, 309–10
  search for, following SDF's conquest of Manbij (*see* al-Hema, Oday, ISIS imprisonment of)
  sit-in at Central Square and, 135–42, 158
  "Turn away from the ignorant and the foolish" (poem), 409–11, 413
  youthful romance of (*see* Hala)
al-Hema, Oday, ISIS imprisonment of, 468–78, 479–86
  Abu Obeida on, 479–83
  Al-Hol detention camp interviews, 473–78
  arrest and torture by ISIS, 413, 414–23, 426, 430–31, 453–54
  author's methodology and, 503
  marriage of, 402–5, 410–11
  parents' vigil for, 468–73, 484
  prisoners' disappearance after SDF's conquest of Manbij, 453–54, 466–67, 471–73
  RYM friends' gathering with Oday, 404–5, 409–10
  scam involving, 470–71
  social media posts by, criticizing ISIS, 400–401, 406–7, 409–10
  strike by businesses and, 410–13
al-Hema Rima (wife of Oday), 397, 402–5, 410–11, 420, 426, 469
Henezel, Aimad, 149, 336–38, 365
Hezbollah, 254, 259, 272, 282, 289, 341
Hisba (accountability police), 391, 396, 398, 481
Home (revolutionary artists' assembly), 240–43
homosexuality, 141, 347
Homs, violence in, 92, 102, 118, 127, 150, 152

Hosni, Hasan, 263
Houla region massacre (May 2012), 179
Hoxha, Enver, 446
Huffington Post, 60
Humeidi, Ahmed, 219
Hussein (Oday's friend), 410, 418

Ibn Arabi (mystic poet), 35
Ibrahim, Khawla (massacre victim), 319
Ibrahim (from Little Hyena). *see* Kasem, Ibrahim
Idlib province massacre, 156–58
Idlib province protests, 150, 152, 175
"If I'm ever mistreated, I'm apt" (Buhturi), 25
"And I know I'm living in exile" (Qabbani), 81
India, British colonization of, 302–3
international community, 176. *see also* Syrian Democratic Forces (SDF) and capture of Manbij; United Nations; United States
  appeal to Western powers for weapons, 203
  Assad regime supported by Russia, Iran, and Lebanese militias, 289
  concept of, 453
  FSA and role of, 253–55
  Islamists on secularism of West, 294–95
  Obama's "red line" and, 338–40
International Freedom Battalion, 446
Iran, 253, 254, 259, 264, 289, 440, 490, 492
Islam
  Alawites and, 28, 97, 120–21, 440
  early, and the "state," 301–3
  early Islam and concept of the "state," 301–3
  Eid celebrations, 199, 211–13
  FSA factions and Islamic names, 191
  Great Mosque (Manbij), 91–93
  on interest-bearing loans, 63
  ISIS ideology and, 282–87
  Islamic State's tyranny and, 387
  MRC's wariness of "bearded men," 259, 265–66
  Muhammad (Prophet), 191, 287, 395–96
  Quran, 302, 305
  Ramadan, 312, 314–16, 329
  substance use banned by, 312
  Sufism of Manbij, 150, 312–13
  Sunni population as regime victims and supporters, 97, 324
Islamic State (in Manbij, 2014–16), 383–454. *see also* social media
  author's methodology, 503
  edicts of, 390–91
  end of (*see* Syrian Democratic Forces (SDF) and capture of Manbij)
  geographic reach of (September 2014), 427–28

INDEX

Hisba (accountability police), 391, 396, 398
  Manbij as isolated territory of (2016), 441
  prostitutes used by, 438–40
  public executions by, 297–307, 391–92, 401, 405–7, *408*, 426
  reeducation by, 395–96
  strike by businesses against (May 18, 2014), 410–13, 414–23, 482
  tyranny of, 385–87
  United States and offensive in Syria (2014–15), 434, 435, 438, 440–41
Islamic State of Iraq and Greater Syria (ISIS), 272–87
  Abdul Hadi's recruitment for, 346–49, 363–64
  Al-Hol detention camp presence of, 473–78, 479–83, 502
  author's methodology, 503
  Baghouz conquest (2019) and end of caliphate, 471
  bread distribution relinquished by, 345
  charity as propaganda of, 346, 359–60, 415–16, 427–28
  employees' frontline requirement, 416
  expansion of, throughout Syria, 434 (*see also* Islamic State (2014-16); Islamic State (in Manbij, 2014-16); Republic battle (December 2013-January 2014))
  Fertile Crescent assembly of, 311–12, 314
  foreign legions of, 446
  Henezel's meeting with, 336–38
  jihad extolled by, 304, 315
  Manbij residents' growing interest in (July 2013), 308–16
  Manbij's economic strain and free speech prohibition, 350–58
  MRC new/old council tension and, 272–77, 282–87
  "my brothers" locution of, 311
  the Prince and, 343–45
  public executions by, 297–307
  RYM and, 277–87, 309–11, 314–16, 328, 330, 332, 333, 347–49, 363–64
  secularism debate in Manbij (June 2013), 292–95
  on sharia law, 301–7, 308, 350–55
  on smuggling, 297
Islamists. *see* Islamic State (in Manbij, 2014–16); Islamic State of Iraq and Greater Syria; Levant Free Men
Ismail, Sheikh, 418
Israa (activist), 230–38, 240–41
Israel, 14, 27, 82, 84
al-Issa, Ahmed, 164

Jahiliyyah (Age of Ignorance), 29, 287
Jamil, Qadri, 228
Jarablus battle (July 2012), 180–81, 192, 370
Jasim, Musa, 297–301, 303, 305
al-Jasim, Nawras. *see* the Prince
Jazeera (soccer team), 133, 191, 361, 378, 481–82
jellabiyas, 6, 8, 10, 18, 21, 85, 94, 139, 255, 261, 480
Jessi brothers (ISIS recruits), 429
Jisr al-Shughur (region), 104
Jonah (Prophet), 263
Jordan, 17–18, 23, 254
Julius Caesar, 386
jumhuriya (to assemble), 224
Jund al-Haramain (Army of the Two Sacred Places), 180–81, 191–93, 260, 443, 450
Juneid, Abdo, 412

Kant, Immanuel, 26
karate, Abel Os and, 52, 53–55, 71
Karim, Abdul, 272
Karoom (alleged murderer), 303
Kasem, Adam (brother of Ibrahim), 157–58, 160, 247, 262, 379–80, 435–36
Kasem, Ibrahim
  on Assad regime's fall, 494
  author's methodology and, 499
  in Beirut, 71, 247
  early romance of, 6–11, 13–18, 20–21, 462–63
  escape to Turkey, 435–37
  family's farming lifestyle, 3–13, 14–23, *22*, 71
  in FSA, 246–49, 255, 258, 260–62
  Manbij return, following SDF conquest, 461–64
  marriage and children of, 247, 260, 262, 462–63
  Republic battle and arrest of, 379–80
  Revolutionary Council and protest turning point, 157, 166
  social media criticism of ISIS watched by, 408
Kasem, Kawthar (daughter of Ibrahim), 461
Kasem, Mustafa (son of Ibrahim), 461
al-Kawakibi, Abd al-Rahman, 223
al-Khalaf, Zakaria, 272
Khalil (grocery worker), 70–71
al-Khalouf, Shahoud, 447
al-Khateeb, Hamza Ali, 104, 140, 407
al-Khatib, Ahmed Moaz, 264
kidnapping ransom, for weapons, 259–62
al-Kinj, Muhammad, 135, 137
Kinjawi, Nidal, 135–36, 139–41, 153–55

INDEX

Knights of the Euphrates, 191
Kurds
   Free Men of Syria Brigade, 191
   in FSA, 256
   Kurdistan Workers Party (PKK) and, 191, 442–44, 446
   Manbij population of, 115
   Manbij population of, Abel Os as, 52–53, 209
   Manbij population of, during SDF invasion, 444–45, 448–52
   United States and backing of, 434, 435, 438, 440–41

Lebanon
   Hezbollah, 254, 259, 272, 289, 341
   Israel war (1982), 27
   Syrians working in Beirut, 70–72, 247
   Tel al-Zaatar (refugee camp) massacre, 27
legal system. *see also* crime
   Aleppo revolutionary court, 341, 342
   Emergency Law (Syria, 1963), 90
   international law on genocide, 324–26
   judiciary system and, 296
   sharia law, 301–7, 308, 350–55
   Supreme State Security Court, 37
Levant Free Men (Ahrar al-Sham/Free Men of the Levant), 265–71, 292, 314, 343–45, 370, 440
liberalism, liberal vs. religious, 292–95
Liberal Teachers Assembly, 198
liberation day (Manbij, July 19, 2012), 229, 247, 273, 277, 283, 291, 453, 493–94, 505
Little Hyena (village), 3–23
   author's methodology and, 504–5
   Baath Party, rise of, 11–13
   farming and lifestyle in (1980s), 3–13
   farming and October Dam construction, 14–23, *22*
   flood refugees of, 157
   historic background of, 3–5, 11
   Kasem's visits to flooded remains of, 247
Local Coordinating Committee, 107–12, 118–25, 135, 146–47
Locke, John, 293
al-Loz, Mustafa, 103

M., Hussein, 339
al-Maamo, Muhammad, 201
al-Maamo, Sabah, 201
MacIntyre, Alasdair, 243
Madison, James, 385, 386
Maher Communications, 83–84, 86
Maimonides (Jewish philosopher), 4

Makhlouf, Rami, 82, 196
Manbij (2017–2024), 455–96. *see also* al-Hema, Oday, ISIS imprisonment of
   Abel Os's return to, 457–61, 463–64, 481, 485–86
   Hasan's exile from, 464, 465
   Ibrahim's return to, 461–64
   Mina's exile from, 464–65
   SDF's capture of Raqqa (caliphate capital), 465–66
   Syria and events of 2023–25, 487–96
Manbij, city description
   Cultural Center of, 24–26, 229, *283*, 283–84, 299, 307, 371
   Directorate of Political Security, 138, 163, 190
   FSA units of, 254
   Great Mosque of, 91–93
   Hazowno neighborhood of, 244
   Kawakibi Street, name of, 223
   Manbij Hotel, different iterations of, 95, 185–86, 188, 204, 212, 304–7, 394, 441, 492
   one-year anniversary of liberation, 291
   population size of, 143
   proximity to farming communities, 5–6, 11, 12, 15, 23
   Sarab neighborhood, 52–56, 58, 61–71, 424, 446–46, 449, 452
   Sheikh Aqeel mosque, 158–59, 174
   Syria Mosaic festival, 240–43
   wadi (man-made gully) of, 107, 211
   Youth Center, 66, 209–10, 277, 280, 283, 349
Manbij, governance of. *see* Islamic State (in Manbij, 2014–16); Manbij (2017-2024); Manbij, republican phase (July 2012 to January 2014); Manbij protesters, civil protest phase (April to December 2011); Syrian Democratic Forces (SDF) and capture of Manbij; *individual entries for Manbij Revolutionary Councils*
Manbij, republican phase (July 2012 to January 2014), 167–382. *see also* class and economic issues; Council of Revolutionary Trustees (Manbij senate); Republic battle (December 2013-January 2014); *individual entries for Manbij Revolutionary Councils*
   air strikes by Assad regime, 207–10, 211–12, 239–45
   author's methodology and, 505–6, 508
   battle of the Prince and Aleppo fighters, 266–71, *267*
   bread distribution program (*see* bread)

INDEX

Council of Revolutionary Trustees (senate) inception, 215–18
elections, air strike fears about, 216, 221, 274, 275, 282, 290
ISIS and (*see* Islamic State of Iraq and Greater Syria)
ISIS and takeover of bread supply, 327–34
ISIS early presence in Manbij, 272–87
Levant Free Men and, 265–71
liberation day (Manbij, July 19, 2012), 229, 247, 273, 277, 283, 291, 453, 493–94, 505
Maymati's role in, 171–74, 177–78, 179–89
military members' defection to rebellion, 175–78
newspapers started under, 202–6
People's House (PKK assembly) and, 442
refugee population of Manbij, 212, 317–18, 328
republicanism, defined, 224
Revolutionary Police, inception, 209
travel by Manbij residents, 355–58
Manbij City Juniors (soccer team), 132
Manbij Human Rights Organization, 360
Manbij Mills, 115, 213–14, 333–34, 374
Manbij protesters, civil protest phase (April to December 2011), 73–166. *see also* class and economic issues; Manbij Revolutionary Council (Constitutive Revolutionary Council, November 2011 to July 2012)
Abel Os's arrest, 112–13
Arab Spring slogan, 169
Ariha uprisings and, 104
author's methodology and, 505–6
Bashar al-Assad's public addresses, 85, 92, 104–5
"breaking the wall of silence" metaphor for, 93
Daraa violence and, 82–86, 88–92, 101, 104, 106, 108, 115, 126, 140, 407
Deir al-Zour violence and, 104
Douma violence and, 118
Egypt uprisings and, 80, 84, 86
events leading to, 75
freedom as goal of protesters, 82, 94, 117–18, 123–24, 128–29, 169
global financial crisis (2008) events and, 75
Great Mosque (April 22, 2011), 92–98, 134
Hama violence and, 134
as historical transformation, 146
Homs violence and, 92, 102, 118, 127, 150, 152, 175
Idlib violence and, 150, 152, 156–58, 175
al-Kinj's arrest and death, 135, 137
Libya revolution and, 146
Manbij, Cardamom Market (June 2011), 106–7
Manbij Local Coordinating Committee planning and (June 2011), 107–12
problem of collective action in, 143–45
protesters' arrests and release, 119–25
Revolutionary Council inception, 145–52
second Manbij protest (May 2011), 99–104
sit-in at Central Square, 135–42, 144, 149, 158, 163, 190, 503–4
social media strategy of, 108–12
thwarted uprising attempt (April 15, 2011), 90–92
Tunisia uprisings and, 77, 80, 84–86
women's protest at Coffeepot Roundabout, 127–29, 130, 135, 393–94
women's role in, 114–19, 125–29
Manbij Revolutionaries Brigade, 191
Manbij Revolutionary Council, re-established (2025), 492–94, 496
Manbij Revolutionary Council (Constitutive Revolutionary Council, November 2011 to July 2012)
author's methodology and, 506
government employees as targets of, 151
Idlib Province massacre response by, 156–58
inception of, 145–52
manifesto and first leaflets distributed by, 151–52
military members' defection to, 175–78
ministerial positions of, 149–51
problem of collective action phenomena and, 143–45
sit-in at Central Square, 144, 153–56, 159, 503–4
turning point in protests, 158–66, 169
Manbij Revolutionary Council (First, July 2012 to April 2013). *see also* class and economic issues
Assad regime's air strike during Eid (2012), 199–201
Assad's portrayal of, as terrorists, 202
author's methodology and, 506
battle of the Prince and Aleppo fighters, 266–71
cabinet expanded by, 208
Council of Revolutionary Trustees (senate) of, 215–18
countryside constituents of, 233
early self-governance of, 187–89
economy under, 204–5, 208
freedom debated during republic period of, 205–6
on FSA factions and militias, 191–93

Manbij Revolutionary Council (First, July 2012 to April 2013) (*cont.*)
  independent assemblies, inception of, 193–98, 201
  legal system under, 211, 214, 215, 240
  Maymati fired by, 192
  Maymati's role in inception of, 171–74, 177–78, 179–89
  Nefi's inspiration for, 145–52, 190–91
  Neutral Committee, 235
  new council and assemblies, 219–25, 235–38 (*see also individual names of assemblies*)
  new council's confrontation of old council, 225–27, 239
  old council approached by Women of Freedom, 233–34
  republic's newspapers on, 203–4
  RYM inception, 193–98
Manbij Revolutionary Council (Second, April 2013 to September 2013). *see also* class and economic issues
  Abdullah administration elected, 289–92
  author's methodology and, 506
  election of, 289–92
  Fertile Crescent (ISIS assembly) in, 311–12, 314
  ISIS and takeover of bread supply, 327–30
  ISIS expulsion called for, in demonstrations, 313–16
  Jasim's murder, handling by, 297–99
  Jasim's murder and ISIS authority as challenge to, 299–307
  secularism debate in Manbij and, 292–95
  Security Brigade of, 298, 299
Manbij war of ISIS and revolutionaries. *see* Republic battle (December 2013-January 2014)
Maraar (Ibrahim al-Maraar, protester), 135–36, 139–41, 153–55, 413, 418, 421
Mariam (divorced woman), 114
Marwan (man from Raqqa), 470
al-Matar family (massacre victims), 321
Maymati, 1st Lt. (Abdul Wahab Khalaf)
  disappearance of, 335
  FSA role of, 255–58
  illustration of, *173*
  Jund al-Haramain's creation and, 181, 450
  Manbij protesters' arrests by, 66–67, 69, 100–103, 111, 113, 124, 139
  MRC's firing of, 192
  MRC's inception and role of, 144, 152, 171–74, 177–78, 179–89
  nickname of, 172–73, 275

  as protester, 84, 178–79
  as revolutionary, 171–74
  Revolutionary Council and protest turning point, 159
Mezzeh Prison, 36–38
Military Council (Council of Revolutionary Trustees), 216, 239
Milton, John, 478
Mina. *see* Saba, Mina
missing persons, author's methodology, 507. *see also* al-Hema, Oday, ISIS imprisonment of; prisons of Syria
Mohsen (student and protester), 158
Mona (woman threatened with honor killing), 114
money lenders ("motorcycle men"), Abel Os's use of, 61–70
Monitor Group, 60
Monk Farm village (massacre site), 318–23
MRC. *see individual names of Manbij Revolutionary Councils*
Muhammad, Hajj, 447
Muhammad, Rachel, 237
al-Muhammad, Huda, 237, 472, 505
Muhammad (Abdul Hadi's brother). *see* al-Bisher, Muhammad
Muhammad (Prophet), 191, 287, 395–96
"mukhtar" (problem solver), 56, 64, 71, 105
Municipal Bakery, 191, 193, 214, 225, 308, 363, 364, 374
Munif, Abdelrahman, 37
Muslim Brotherhood, 28–30, 43, 176, 288
Muslim Youth, 220
Muslim Youth Assembly, 300, 310–11, 346–47, 365
Mustafa (Ibrahim's uncle), 83, 88–89, 97
Mutayr family (massacre victims), 321
"My features are the deserts of Manbij" (Nefi), 47

Nabeel (RYM president), 282, 347, 364–65, 404
Najib, Atef, 88
Najjar, Muhammad Ali, 241
National Current Party, 27–30, 33–34
National Defense Forces (pro-Assad regime militia), 318–23
National Democratic Progressive Party, 465
The Nature of Tyranny and the Struggle of Enslavement (Kawakibi), 223
Nefi, Hasan, 24–51
  arrest and confession of, 31–34
  on Assad normalization and fall from power, 487–93
  author's methodology and, 499–500

INDEX

on collapse of communism and nationalism, 203, 237
conditions of freedom offered to, 38–39
"Don't Reconcile!" (article), 488
early Manbij life of, 24–31
exile from Manbij, 409, 464–65
Free Aleppo Provincial Council role of, 296
imprisonment of, 31–34, 35–42, *41*, 45–51, *48*, 101
Manbij seized by MRC, 183, 186–88
MRC as inspiration of, 145–52, 190–91
"My features are the deserts of Manbij" (poem), 47
National Current Party activism of, 27–30, 33–34
new MRC council and, 221, 224, 226–27
Obsessions and Longings (poetry), 29–30, 34, 48
prison release of, 49–51
Provincial Council election and, 274
in Republic battle, 359, 372, 379
second MRC election and, 291
Sun articles on MRC's vision, 203–4
trial and sentencing of, 37
on weapons use, 176–77
Women of Freedom and, 233
Nefi, Mr. (father of Hasan), 24–26, 29, 31–32
Nefi, Mrs. (mother of Hasan), 34, 36, 51
"negative" freedom, 205–6, 223, 292
Neutral Committee (MRC), 235
newspapers and publications of republican period. *see also* Free Path; Sun of Freedom; Weekly Letters
    Council and the People (MRC second council), 291
    Declaration (weekly newspaper), 291
    Free Syrian (MRC second council, magazine), 291
    Free Thought Magazine, 295, 312, 341
    Panorama (periodical), 291, 297, 308, 311
    Peace Be Upon You, 236, 353
    Spaces (Nefi, journal), 291
    Weekly Letters (periodical on Islam as religion of peace), 291
Nidal (protester), 135–36, 139–41, 153–55
Nietzsche, Friedrich, 415, 499
niqabs, 230–31, 393–95, *394*
Noah's Ark (Quran), 4

Obama, Barack
    on Assad's chemical weapons, 254
    on Free Army, 442
    "red line" of, 338–40
    Syria offensive by (2014–16), 434, 435, 438, 440–41
    U.S.–Iran nuclear deal, 440
Ober, Josiah, 385
Obsessions and Longings (Nefi), 29–30, 34, 48
October (Assad regime newspaper), 202
October Dam, 14–23, *22*, 75, 211, 222, 290–91, 363
October (newspaper), 59–60
Oday. *see* al-Hema, Oday
"Oh heaven, heaven" (revolutionary anthem), 209, 310, 404
Omar (Caliph), 330
Omar (massacre victim), 319
Oseb, Abdul Qader (Abel Os), 52–72
    Abel Os name of, 54
    Abu Obeida on, 481
    arrest by Assad regime, 66–67, 69, 112–13, 118, 120–24, 423
    arrest by ISIS, 430–33, 434
    Assad's air strike (October 2012), 209–10
    author's methodology and, 498, 500, 502
    battle of the Prince, 267–70, 276–77
    Beirut work of, 70–72, 247
    brother's eulogy by, 441
    death of, 486
    early life in Manbij, 52–56
    on economic issues, 57–61, 213, 332
    eyesight of, 427, 429, 430, 440–41
    ISIS expulsion called for, in demonstrations, 313–16
    karate and, 52, 53–55, 71, 72, *72*
    as Kurd, 52–53, 209
    Manbij residents' reverence for, 430–33, 448–49
    Manbij return, following SDF conquest, 457–61, 463–64, 485–86
    Manbij return by (2014), 424
    Manbij uprisings (May–June 2011) and role of, 103–12
    marriage and children of, 63–64, 67, 424, 431 (*see also individual names of family members*)
    MRC and role of, 176–78, 182, 184–85, 187–89, 222, 225, 290
    as "mukhtar" (problem solver), 56, 64, 71, 105
    real estate work of, 110, 112, 121
    release from, 423
    remorse about revolution, 425–26, 431–32
    repentance hearing, 425, 430
    in Republic battle, 362–63, 365–66, 373, 375–76, 380–81
    Revolutionary Council and protest turning point, 162–65
    RYM and role of, 147–52, 194–98, 217–18
    RYM resignation of, 276–77, 281

Oseb, Abdul Qader (Abel Os) (*cont.*)
   during SDF invasion of Manbij, 442–45, 448–52
   sit-in at Central Square, 134–35, 140
   social media criticism of ISIS watched by, 408
   Tear of Roses business of, 55–58, 61–70, 195, 277
   whistle incident, 110–11, 404
Oseb, Hammoudi (Abel Os's son), 440, 444–45, 449–52, 457–60, 485
Oseb, Mana (wife of Abel Os), 63–64, 67, 69, 71
Oseb, Mr. (father of Abel Os), 52–55
Oseb, Mrs. (mother of Abel Os), 67–68
Oseb, Shukri (brother of Abel Os), 61, 63, 67, 69, 441
al-Osman, Hamid, 453
al-Osman, Huzayfa, 202, 350–53, 406, 497. *see also Sun of Freedom* (newspaper)
Ottoman Empire, Syria rule by, 4–5, 11, 24, 223
"Our Country Is Precious" (song), 126

Palestine Branch (prison), 36, 115
Palestinians, 27, 30, 70, 237
Palmyra prison, 36, 39–49, *48,* 493
Panorama (newspaper), 291, 297, 308, 311
Peace Be Upon You (newspaper), 236, 353
Peasants' Collective Assembly, 198–99
People's General Assembly (MRC), 219–25, 235–38
People's House (PKK assembly), 442
People's Protection Units (PKK), 446
Phenomenology of Spirit (Hegel), 37–38, 47, 146
PKK (Kurdistan Workers Party), 191, 442–44, 446, 460. *see also* Syrian Democratic Forces (SDF)
political philosophy. *see also* freedom; legal system
   Assad regime as "socialist," 330
   civil disobedience and nonviolence, 353–55
   democracy, history of, 385–86
   democracy as goal of protesters, 303
   democracy slogans, erased by ISIS, 312
   democracy vs. sharia law debates, 317
   early Islam and concept of the "state," 301–3
   freedom debated during republican period, 205–6, 222–25
   Girls of Tomorrow on use of weapons, 237–38
   Greece (ancient) on, 324–25
   individual dignity and, 204
   international law on genocide, 324–26
   justice and sharia law, 300–307
   justice/injustice vs. misfortune, 125–27
   Manbij as de facto city-state, 216
   morality, Nefi's study of, 26
   morality and revolutions, 146, 265
   Nefi on collapse of communism and nationalism, 203, 237
   "politicide," 325
   republicanism, 224
   secularism debate in Manbij, 292–95
   tyranny of authoritarianism, 385–87
   Women of Freedom on nonviolence, 236–37
"positive" freedom, 205–6, 223, 292
poverty. *see* class and economic issues
the Prince (Nawras al-Jasim), 255–61, 266–71, *267,* 276–77, 298, 342–45, 370–72, 418
prisoners, of ISIS. *see* al-Hema, Oday, ISIS imprisonment of
prisons of Syria
   Adra prison, 36–37
   Aleppo Central Prison, 120, 122–23, 140–42
   death of inmates in, 43–44
   detention centers and civilians, 323–24
   jailers' behavior in, 44–45
   Mezzeh Prison, 36–38
   Palestine Branch, 36, 115
   Palmyra prison, 36, 39–49, *48*
   political prisoners released from (1991), 35–36
   rules imposed on prisoners, 40, 42
   Sednaya prison, 36, 49
   soup/urine incident, 43
   torture used in, 32–34, 40–49, *41,* 122–23
problem of collective action, 143–45
"propaganda of the deed," 144
prostitution, 438–40
Provincial Council (Aleppo Province), 274

Qabbani, Nizar, 81, 264–65
Qatar, 253, 254, 265, 340
Quran, on Noah's Ark, 4
Quran, study of. *see* Islam
Qusayr battle, 289

R. H. High School, 187, 188
Radio Monte Carlo, 26
Radwan, Taha, 245
Rahim (student and protester), 158
Rahmo, Ahmed
   arrest and imprisonment of, 119, 120, 135
   battle of the Prince, 265
   Muhammad al-Bisher's early work relationship with, 149–50, 273, 415
   MRC and role of, 107–9, 111–12, 148–52, 188, 192–94, 221, 227

INDEX

Ramadan, 312, 314–16, 329
Raqqa (caliphate capital)
    Maymati's disappearance from, 335
    SDF's capture of, 465–66
Rasm al-Nafl village (massacre site), 320, 322
Rawi family (massacre victims), 322
The Red and the Black (Stendhal), 37
Red Crescent, 236, 363
referendum day (2000), 58
Repentance Office (ISIS), 391, 425, 430
republicanism, defined, 224. *see also* Manbij, republican phase (July 2012 to January 2014); political philosophy
Republic battle (December 2013-January 2014), 359–82
    Abdul Hadi's and RYM arrested, 364–65, 367–68
    Abdul Hadi's capture of bread facilities, 373–74
    Abdul Hadi's enabling of ISIS and, 382
    Abu Omar the Chechen's role in, 369–77
    al-Bab's fall to ISIS, 369–70
    author's methodology, 508
    Ibrahim Kasem's arrest, 379–80
    Manbij's fall to ISIS, 377–78
    Manbij's third Revolutionary Council elected, 365–66
    October Dam, fall to ISIS, 363
    the Prince's role in, 370–72
    revolutionary leaders' departure, 376–77, 379, 380–81
    revolution as choice between love and rage, 381–82
    rumors leading to war, 359–62
    Mina Saba's return home during, 374, 378–79
Revolutionary Council of Aleppo, 339
Revolutionary Councils of Manbij. *see* Manbij Revolutionary Council (Constitutive Revolutionary Council); Manbij Revolutionary Council (First); Manbij Revolutionary Council (Second)
Revolutionary Court (MRC), 215, 240, 391
Revolutionary Police, 209, 215, 228, 266, 271, 272, 297–99, 361
Revolutionary Youth Movement (RYM)
    Abel Os's resignation from, 276–77, 281
    arrests during Republic battle, 364–65, 367–68
    arts festival and, 244
    author's methodology and, 508
    battle of the Prince, 267–70, 276–77
    against foreign intervention, 339
    freedom as interpreted by, 205
    inception, 193–98, 201

ISIS and, 272–87, 309–11, 314–16, 328, 330, 332, 333, 347–49, 363–64
    MRC support solicited by, 208–9
    Nabeel as leader of, 272
    new (MRC) council and, 219–27
    Oday's reuniting with, at time of caliphate, 404–5, 409–10
    "Oh heaven, heaven" (anthem), 209, 310, 404
    opposition to senate by, 215–18
    second MRC as "unity" government, 289–92
Revolution (Assad regime newspaper), 202
Rome (ancient), 385, 386
Russia
    Assad regime and, 228, 253, 254, 264, 289, 490–92
    Georgia invaded by, 369
    U.S.–Iran nuclear deal and, 440
RYM. *see* Revolutionary Youth Movement (RYM)

Saba, Hanan (sister of Mina and Sami), 126–28
Saba, Maya (sister of Mina and Sami), 127
    family's escape to Turkey, 434–35
Saba, Mina
    arts festival, 240
    on Assad regime's fall, 493–94
    author's methodology and, 501, 504
    on brother's protest activities, 114–21, 124–29
    Coffeepot Roundabout march by, 127–29, 130, 393–94
    edicts under ISIS rule, 389–93
    exile from Manbij, following SDF's conquest, 464–65
    on identity of social media protester, 408
    on injustice, 125–26
    Manbij seized by MRC, 185, 189
    military strikes, 244–45
    Republic battle and return home by, 374, 378–79
    revolutionary activism outlet sought by, 228–32
    Revolutionary Council and protest turning point, 166
    travel to Aleppo by, 355–58
    Women of Freedom inception, 232–38
    Women of Freedom work prohibited by ISIS, 333–35
    women's meetings, under ISIS rule, 396–99, 434–35
Saba, Mr. (father of Mina and Sami), 117, 119–20, 124, 126, 175, 234, 244, 391

Saba, Mrs. (mother of Mina and Sami), 115, 118, 119–20
Saba, Saladin Soma (brother of Mina and Sami), 125, 127, 175, 180, 185
Saba, Sami (Shampoo Sami)
  arrest and release of, 119–25
  art of, 114, 125, 240–41, 244
  death of, 464
  economic crisis riots and, 331
  Manbij seized by MRC, 185
  nickname of, 100, 241
  protests by, 88, 90–92, 100, 111, 114–19, 125–29
  Saladin Saba's defection, 175
  second MRC election and, 290
Sabra camp (Beirut), 70
Safira village (massacre site), 318, 322, 508–9
Salal, Munzer, 108, 148, 150–51, 176–77, 230, 273, 282–87, 308, 466
Saleh, Yassin al-Haj, 325
al-Samet, Kasser, 339
Samira (Little Hyena resident), 6–10, 13–18, 20–21, 462–63
Sarah (Al-Hol inmate), 476
Saudi Arabia, 180, 253–54, 340, 440, 487
al-Sayyab, Badr Shakir, 25
secularism, debate on, 292–95. *see also* political philosophy
Security Brigade (second MRC), 298, 299
Sednaya prison, 36, 49
Sex, Hasan, 249–50, 269–70
shabiha (government supporters), 97, 99–100, 102–4, 119, 130, 138, 177
Shami, Abdul Baser, 210
Shami, Yamen, 210
sharia law, 301–7, 308, 350–55
Sheikh Aqeel mosque, 158–60, 174
Sheikho (massacre survivor), 318–19, 322
Shiyuki family, 65
sit-in at Central Square, 135–42, 144, 149, 159, 163, 190, 503–4
16th of October Street (Manbij), 58, 61
soccer and soccer teams
  Abdul Hadi's early life and soccer career, 130–34, *134*
  Aleppo Freedom, 123, 132, 147
  Aleppo Unity, 123, 132, 147
  Al-Jalaa, 132
  author's methodology, 509
  class and culture of, 133
  Dignity, 133
  Jazeera, 133, 191, 361, 378, 481–82
  Manbij City Juniors, 132
  relegation system of, 132

shaabi league, 133
  Syrian Premier League, 132
social media
  author's methodology and, 497–98, 509–10
  Facebook forums about Manbij, republican period, 291–92
  flag-bearing woman on, 407–9, 434–35, 472, 505
  ISIS criticism on, at time of caliphate, 400–401, 406–10, 412–13
  ISIS welcomed to Manbij on, 375
  Maymati's appeal to protesters videotaped, 174
The Sorrows of Young Werther (Goethe), 35
soup/urine incident, 43
Soviet Union, Syrian aid from, 59. *see also* Russia
A Space for Forgetting (exhibition), 219, 242, 244
Spaces (Nefi, journal), 291
Star Castle, 3–4, 443
State Security Directorate, 180
Stendhal, 37
"stonecutter approach," 144
storytelling, purpose of, 243
Students Without Borders Assembly, 350
Sufism, 150, 312–13
Sun of Freedom (newspaper)
  "I Am a Woman" section of, 238
  inception of, 202–4
  ISIS threats and closure of, 350–53
  Mina's poem in, 234
  Nefi's articles in, 203–4
  relaunch plans (2025), 493
  stories and headlines in, 207, 208, 210, 212, 214, 215, 219, 228, 235, 239, 246, 264–65, 272, 275, 288, 295, 296, 329, 330, 339, 350
Supreme State Security Court, 37
Sutto, Haseeb, 375
Syria. *see also* al-Assad, Hafez; Islam; Manbij protesters, civil protest phase (April to December 2011); prisons of Syria; soccer and soccer teams; *individual place names*
  drought (2006), 67, 70, 75
  Emergency Law (1963), 90
  feudalism in, 11–12, 16, 21
  flags of, 118, 169
  French colonization of, 11, 24, 36
  global financial crisis (2008), 70, 75
  Hama massacre (1982), 89, 108
  health care in, 68
  historic background, 3–5, 11
  military service requirement, 16, 55
  Ottoman rule of, 4–5, 11, 24

INDEX

referendum day (2000), 58
Supreme State Security Court, 37
war with Israel (1973), 14
Syria (2023–25), 487–96
  Assad and normalization attempts during, 487–88
  Assad's fall from power, 490–92
  Assad's massacres and fighting during, 489–90
  legacy of Oday and revolutionaries, 494–96
  Revolutionary Council re-established, 492–94, 496
  SDF expulsion from, 492
Syria, civil war. *see also* weapons; *individual names of factions*
  bombing raids against civilians, 323
  civilian massacre statistics, 323
  Damascus National Security headquarters bombing, 182
  Day of Bloodied Bread (December 28, 2012), 225
  detention centers and civilians, 323–24
  Hezbollah and, 254, 259, 272, 289, 341
  Houla region massacre (May 2012), 179
  ISIS spread during (*see* Islamic State of Iraq and Greater Syria)
  Jarablus battle (July 2012), 180–81, 192, 370
  massacres by Assad regime, 317–26
  Obama's "red line" and, 338–40
  Qusayr battle, 289
  Shuyukh massacre (July 2012), 181
  third year of, 264
Syria, economy of. *see* class and economic issues
Syria Mosaic (arts festival), 240, 242, 244
Syrian Arab Army (Assad regime), 202, 228
Syrian Democratic Forces (SDF) and capture of Manbij, 442–54
  Al-Hol detention camp, 473–78, 479–83
  author's methodology, 509
  freedom of speech under, 486
  ISIS defection/desertion during, 449–50
  ISIS families' escape from Manbij, 444
  ISIS surrender, 450–52
  Manbij governance and lifestyle of residents following, 457–63
  Manbij residents in exile following, 464–65
  Manbij residents under fire during, 444–49, 451–52
  Manbij survivors of, 452–54
  PKK's role in, 442–44, 446, 460
  Raqqa (capital of caliphate) conquest (October 2017), 465–66
  SDF as U.S.-led coalition, 441, 442–43
  SDF's expulsion from Manbij, 492

Syrian Premier League (soccer), 132
Syriatel, 82

Taan, Ahmed, 288
Tarboush, Ahmed, 360–61
Tariq (student and protester), 158
Tear of Roses (shop), 55–58, 61–70, 195, 277
Tel al-Zaatar (Palestinian refugee camp), 27
Thiabiyya massacre, 341
Tlass, Mustafa, 176
torture and beatings. *see* Islamic State of Iraq and Greater Syria (ISIS); prisons of Syria
Tunisia, 77, 80, 84–86, 126
Turkey
  arms supplied by, 340
  battle of White Hill (Tel Abyad) and, 255–60
  FSA support and international community, 254
  Greater Arab Free Trade Area and, 60
  Manbij residents' exile in, 464–65
  Provincial Council (Assad opposition/rebels) held in, 274, 275, 282
  as SDF enemy, 459, 460
  Syria and hostilities of (2024), 489
  Syria and proposed reconciliation by (2023), 487–88
"Turn away from the ignorant and the foolish" (Oday's poem), 409–10
tyranny of authoritarianism, 385–87. *see also* Islamic State (2014–16)

Umm Adel (massacre survivor), 321–22
Umm Amud hamlet (massacre site), 322
Umm Aziz (massacre survivor), 322
Umm Jumaa (massacre survivor), 318–20
Umm Shuhada (mother of martyrs), 395
United Nations, 109, 152, 179, 474, 487
United States
  Baghouz conquered by, 471
  Biden presidency, 487
  CIA, 36, 149
  democracy and history of, 385–86
  FSA support and international community, 254
  Obama presidency (*see* Obama, Barack)
  prisoners of ISIS and accounting by, 472–73
  Syrian blame of, for uprisings (2011), 82, 84
  Syrian humanitarian funding request denied (2010), 75
  Syria offensive by (2014–16), 434, 435, 438, 440–41
  U.S. Special Operations, 445
"Unity, Freedom, Socialism" (Assad regime slogan), 196
University of Aleppo, 29–30

Valley of the Wolves (Turkish soap opera), 172–73, 275
Vanguard (National Current Party publication), 30
Vogue (magazine), 60

wasta (connections), 58, 120–21, 131, 135, 148, 154, 193, 287, 382
waterboarding, 32–34
weapons
  chemical weapons used by Bashar Assad, 338–40
  chemical weapons used by Assad regime, 254–55
  cost of airplanes, 443
  FSA supply of, 253–55
  Girls of Tomorrow on use of, 237–38
  ISIS members' dynamite vests, 280–81, 284, 301
  kidnapping ransom for, 259–62
  Qatar's supply to Levant Free Men, 265
  supplied to Free Army by United States, 340
Weekly Letters (publication)
  inception of, 291
  stories and headlines, 263, 272, 288, 291, 296, 317, 327, 341, 350, 359

Weiss, Anas Sheikh, 62–64, 69, 148, 150, 176, 193–95, 230, 236, 339, 376
Weiss, Muhammad Ghaith Sheikh, 363
"Welcome Party" (Palmyra prison torture), 39–40
"We raised our index fingers at him and his gang" (Oday), 141
"What is Secularism?" (Taan), 288
whistle incident, 110–11, 404
White Hill (Tel Abyad), battle of, 255–60
Women of Freedom, 232–38, 240, 244, 353–55, 408, 434

Yasser (ISIS recruit), 429
Yasser (nurse), 87
A Year of Freedom (festival), 327–28
"You gaze upon me, wonder in your eyes. Why?" poem (Mina Saba), 234
Youth Center (Manbij), 66, 209–10, 277, 280, 283, 349
Yusef (executed youth), 406

Zahra (car dealer), 392
Zahra (Palestinian teacher), 115
Zain (ISIS recruit), 429
Zakaria (man who drowned his children), 75, 222
Ziad (Nefi's comrade), 34